Modern African Drama: Critical and Theoretical Approaches

DAMLÈGUE LARE

Modern African Drama: Critical and Theoretical Approaches

GALDA VERLAG 2019

Bibliografische Information der Deutschen Nationalbibliothek
Die Deutsche Nationalbibliothek verzeichnet diese Publikation in der Deutschen Nationalbibliografie; detaillierte bibliografische Daten sind im Internet über http://dnb.ddb.de abrufbar.

© 2019 Galda Verlag, Glienicke
Neither this book nor any part may be reproduced or transmitted in any form or by any means electronic or mechanical, including photocopying, micro-filming, and recording, or by any information storage or retrieval system, without prior permission in writing from the publisher. Direct all inquiries to Galda Verlag, Franz-Schubert-Str. 61, 16548 Glienicke, Germany

ISBN 978-3-96203-027-8 (Print)
ISBN 978-3-96203-028-5 (Ebook)

DEDICATION

To my Readers
To the Literary Studies World
To the African Literature Lovers
And to Contributors of African Critical Studies

ACKNOWLEDGEMENTS

I am grateful to my beloved wife Yendouboa Lamboni Epouse Lare, my sons Djieyendou and Pagyendou for the great contribution they brought in the materialization of this book.

I thank Galda publishing company for editing my first two books *Diction and Postcolonial Vision in the Plays of Wole Soyinka* (2016), *African Feminism, Gender and Sexuality* (2017). I remain indebted to them for this edition too.

Although most of the articles in this volume were written within the past ten years of my teaching modern African drama at the universities in Togo, this volume has been given a complete shape with materials found in US libraries. So I would like to express my sincere gratitudes to the Fulbright Programme Managers for granting me a year fellowship which enabled me to find consistant materials in the USA to complete this research work.

I express my sincere gratitudes to Professor Kwame Dawes at the University of Nebraska-Lincoln for his expertise in African literary criticism.

I also thank Professor Ekotto Frieda from the University of Michgan Ann Abbor for her great contribution.

To my mentor, Professor Komla Messan Nubukpo, honorary Dean of the Faculty of Arts and Humanities, University of Lome, Togo I say big thanks.

CONTENTS

Dedication v
Acknowledgements vii

PART ONE 1

The Contour of Critical Theories 1

Nativism and the Quest for Indigenous Aesthetics 1

Defining Drama in African Context 1

Aspects of Narratology 1

Postcolonial Theatre in Search of a Referential Frame of Theory 1

1 INTRODUCTION: SITUATING CRITICAL THEORY AND LITERARY CRITICISM IN AFRICAN DRAMA 3

1.1. The Focus of Critical Theory of African Drama 4
    1.1.1. Theoretical Schools and Movements 6
        1.1.1.1. Structuralism, Poststructuralism and the Afrocentric Schools of Thought 6
        1.2.1.1. Structuralism and Panafricanist Critical Theory 6

1.2.1.2. Nativism and the Quest of Indigenous Aesthetics 11
1.2.1.3. Marxism in Africa 12
1.2.1.4. Contextualizing Cultural Materialism in
African Arts 15
1.2.1.5. Towards the Decolonization of African Drama and
Theatre: The Bolekaja Criticism 17
1.2.1.6. Postmodernism in African Context 20
1.2.1.7. Afropolitans 22

References 29

2   NATIVISM AND THE QUEST OF INDIGENOUS AESTHETICS: STRUCTURALIST AND POSTSTRUCTURALIST READINGS   31

2.1. Ferdinand de Saussure in Africa: Structuralist Understanding of
African Drama 32

2.1.1. What Structuralist Critics Do 34
2.1.2. Poststructuralism 35

2.2. The Elements of Domestication 38

2.2.1. Setting 38
2.2.2. Characters and characterization 41
2.2.3. Themes as Structurally Based 44
2.2.4. Dramatic Material as Structurally Grounded 45
2.2.5. Language 47

References 72

3   DEFINING DRAMA IN AFRICAN CONTEXT: A NEW HISTORICIST APPROACH   75

3.1. Designation and Function of Ritual, Festival and Drama in
Traditional African Context 79

3.1.1. Ritual: Designation and Function 79

3.1.2. Festival: Designation and Function..82
3.1.1. Arguments in Favour of the Existence of Drama in
 Traditional Africa: the Example of Nigeria............................84

3.2. Parallelism between Greek Theatre and African Theatre.............86
3.2.1. Advocates of Divorcing Drama from Ritual.........................89
3.2.2. Personal Critical Stance..90
3.2.3. Transition from Oral to Written Drama in Greek Theatre
 Context..90

References..95

4 ASPECTS OF NARRATOLOGY: AFRICAN ORAL NARRATIVES AS DRAMA 99

4.1.1. From Theoretical Groundings to The Basic Narrative Modes:
 'Mimetic' or 'Diegetic'?...99
4.1.2. Narrative focalization: Oral Narratives and their Theatrically
 Implied Meanings..104
4.1.3. Who is Telling the Story: Narrative Realism.......................106
4.1.4. The Handling of Time in the Story.......................................109
4.1.5. Speech and Thought Representations..................................111
4.1.6. The Packaging of Stories...113
4.1.7. Epic Performance...119

References..123

5 POSTCOLONIAL THEATRE IN SEARCH OF A REFERENTIAL FRAME OF THEORY 125

5.1. An Outline of Postcolonial Theory in African theatre Studies..125
5.1.1. Hybridity..127
5.1.2. Ambivalence...128
5.1.3. Cultural Difference, Enunciation, and Stereotype..............129
5.1.4. Mimicry...130
5.1.5. Third Space...131

5.6. Western Modernity 133
   5.1.7. Knowledge 134
   5.1.8. Universalism 134
   5.1.9. Postcolonial Theory in African theatre Studies 136

5.10. Criticisms 141

5.11. Postcolonial Critical Configurations 156
   5.11.1. The Phase of Cultural Nationalism 1850 - 1950 156
   5.11.2. The Consolidation of the Canon: Postcolonial
        Theory from 1951-1970 165
   5.11.3. Postcolonial Theory from 1972 to the Present Day 170
   5.11.4. Towards a Redefinition of Postcolonialism:
        The Theory of Afropositivism 175

Notes: 178

References: 178

PART TWO 181

Symbolism, Cultural Materialism, Political Morality,
Marxism, Feminism, Resistance Theories 181

6 SYMBOLIST AND NATURALIST READINGS OF AFRICAN DRAMA 183

6.1. Symbolism, Naturalism and Realism 183
   6.1.1. An African Variant of Symbolism: Theory and Reading
       Strategy 186
   6.1.2. Naturalism and Realism in the Context of
       African Drama 196

References 204

7 AFRICAN PERSPECTIVES ON CULTURAL MATERIALISM AND POLITICAL MORALITY 207

7.1. Understanding Cultural Materialism 207

7.2. Applying Cultural Materialism to African Drama 209

 7.2.3. Cultural Materialism in African Drama Context 211
 7.2.3. Theatre for Liberation in Africa... 215

References.. 227

8 MARXIST PERSPECTIVES ON NGUGI WA THIONG'O'S & MICERE GITHAE MUGO'S *THE TRIAL OF DEDAN KIMATHI* AND *WOLE SOYINKA'S KING BAABU* 231

8.1. Background to Marxism.. 231

 8.1.1. The Birth of Political Consciousness and the Imperatives of Freedom in *The Trial of Dedan Kimathi and King Baabu* ... 234
  8.1.1.1. Reading History for Socio-political Reconstruction in *The Trial of Dedan Kimathi*.. 234
  8.1.1.2. The Birth of Political Consciousness and the Imperatives of Development in *King Baabu* 238
 8.1.2. Marxist Dramatic Symbols Expressive of Political Consciousness **242**

References.. 251

Webliography 252

9 FEMINIST PERSPECTIVES OF AFRICAN FEMALE DRAMATISTS 253

9.1. Conceptualising Feminism 253

9.2. The first Wave of African Feminism: Adverting Radicalism...... 259

9.2.1. Nawal El Saadawi (Egypt) 260
9.2.2. Zulu Sofola (Nigeria) 263
9.2.3. Flora Nwapa (Nigeria) 268
9.2.4. Tess Osonye Onwueme (Nigeria) 271
9.2.5. Efua T. Sutherland (Ghana) 273
    9.2.5.1. Feminist Inclinations in Foriwa 274
    9.2.5.2. Women's Images in Edufa 276
9.2.6. Ama Ata Aidoo (Ghana) 277

9.3. Second Wave Feminism: Chinyere Grace Okafor's
The New Toy Toy and Irene Isoken Oronsaye-Salami's
Sweet Revenge 278

9.4. Third Wave African Feminists 284

References: 286

10 POSTCOLONIAL RESISTANCE IN FEMI OSOFISAN'S *NO MORE THE WASTED BREED* AND LEKE OGUNFEYIMI'S *SACRIFICE THE KING* 289

Resistance Theory 289

10.1. The Aesthetics of Resistance of Femi Osofisan and
Leke Ogunfeyimi 291

  10.1.2. *Sacrifice the King*: Leke Ogunfeyimi's
    Poetics of Resistance 294

10.2. The Language of Resistance in *No More the Wasted Breed and
Sacrifice the King* **296**

  10.2.1. Diction 296
  10.2. 2. Dramatic Symbolism Fostering Resistance 304

References 307

PART THREE 309

Psychoanalytic Criticism 309

Ethnicity and Conflicts Postmodernism 309

Intertextuality... 309

Black Consciousness Aesthetics 309

11 A PSYCHOANALYTIC APPROACH TO OLA ROTIMI'S THE GODS ARE NOT TO BLAME 311

11.1. The Tenets of Psychoanalitic Theory 311
   11.1.1. What Freudian Psychoanalytic Critics Do 312
   11.1.2. Lacanian Psychoanalysis... 313

11.2. Psychoanalytic Discourse Analysis in Ola Rotimi.................... 316

11.3. Metaphors of Alienation: Africa' Neocolonial Predicament .. 323
   11.3.2. An Interaction View of Metaphors 330
      11.3.2.1. Man Against Man: a Metaphor of Colonization 331

References... 332

12 ETHNICITY, CONFLICTS AND PEACE STRATEGIES IN FEMI OSOFISAN'S WOMEN OF OWU 335

12.1. Ethnic Studies and School of Thought in Africa........................ 335
   12.1.1. Ethnic Diversity: The Informing Rationales of Tribal Conflicts in Nigeria 337
   12.1.2. A Literary Spectrum of War Trauma 343
   12.1.3. Self-Indexation /Criticism: A Step toward Appeasement 345
   12.1.4. Conflict Resolution, A Means for Pacific Coexistence...... 348

References... 351

13 THE AESTHETICS OF MARXISM AND POSTMODERNISM IN OSOFISAN'S *ONCE UPON FOUR ROBBERS* AND SOYINKA'S *JERO'S METAMORPHOSIS* 353

13.1. Theory in Context: The Vanguards of Postmodernism 353
    13.1.1. What Postmodernist Critics Do 356
    12.1.2. Postmodern Inflections in Femi Osofisan.......................... 358
    13.1.3. A Way to Controlling Armed Robbery 367
    13.1.4. From Text to Context: Exploring Osofisan' s and Soyinka's Postmodern Languages 369

References... 374

14 AN INTERTEXTUAL READING OF TIME, SPACE AND NARRATIVE POETICS IN ADE SOLANKE'S *PANDORA'S BOX* AND NGUGI WA THIONG'O'S *WIZARD OF THE CROW* 377

14.1. Dramatic Texts and Novelistic Texts: Showing versus Telling . 380
    14.1.1. The Narrative Voice or the Mediating Narrator: Where Intertextuality Matters 385
    14.1.2. Time, Space and Narrative Poetics...................................... 388
        14.1.2.1. Time 388
        14.1.2.2. Space 392

13.2. Symbolic Representation of Space 395

References... 397

15 BLACK CONSCIOUSNESS AESTHETICS IN MAISHE MAPONYA'S *THE HUNGRY EARTH* AND JANE TAYLOR'S *UBU AND THE TRUTH COMMISSION* 399

15.1. Conceptualizing South African Conflicts in Maishe Maponya's Dramatic Aesthetics 400

15.2. The Symbolism of Mediation Fostering Black Consciousness: Jane Taylor's Model 407

References 417

PART FOUR   419

Sociocriticism 419

Cultural Studies 419

Afropolitanism 419

Ecocriticism 419

16   A SOCIOCRITICAL APPROACH TO FRANCOPHONE DRAMA AND THEATER   421

16.1. Historical Survey: The William-Ponty Formula 422

16.2. The Dominant Genres: Village Drama, Urban Drama, and Historical and Political Drama 424

16.3. New Perspectives 428
  16.3.1. Institutions 428
    16.3.1.2. New Experiments 430

References 433

17 ASPECTS OF TOGOLESE THEATRE: FROM CULTURAL PARLANCE TO POLITICAL INFLECTIONS   437

17.1. The Aesthetics of Indigenous Popular Theatre and Its Contribution to Cultural Development 439

17.1.1. Festivals... 439
17.1.2. Theatrical Folktales 441
17.1.2. Political Inflections: Senouvo Agbota Zinsou and Kangni Alemdjrodo Speculating on Political Morality in Togo 446

References.. 459

18   AFROPOLITANISM IN ADE SOLANKE'S *PANDORA'S BOX*   461

18.1. The Roots of Afropolitanism in the postcolonial Space: The Search for Survival... 462

18.1.3. Negotiating Identity in Diasporic Space: Afropolitanism and the Metaphor of Migration 466
18.1.4. Cultural Ambivalence 468
18.1.5. Afropolitan View of Multiculturalism: A New Model of Identity.. 471
18.1.6. African Global Citizen: a Quest for New Identity and Self-redefinition 473
18.1.7 Cultural Homecoming: Ade Solanke's Perspective 475

References.. 480

19   INTERROGATING POST-APARTHEID LEGACY FROM HUMAN RIGHTS PERSPECTIVE: A READING OF ATHOL FUGARD'S SELECTED PLAYS   483

19.1. Discourse Against Marginality: Athol Fugard's Advocacy of Human Rights in *No Good Friday and My Children! My Africa!*............................ 484

19.2. From Interrogating to Foreseeing Resilience: Reconstruction of Human Rights 494

References.. 502

20 ECOCRITICISM AND ENVIRONMENTAL ETHICS IN WOLE SOYINKA'S *THE BEATIFICATION OF AREA BOY* 503

20.1. Man as the Pathogenic Agent of Climate Change 504
   20.1.1. Human Activities on the Ecosystem 504
   20.1.2. The Spectrum of Pollution 509
      20.1.2.1. Water pollution 509
      20.1.2.2. Noise and Air Pollution 510
      20.1.2.3. Solid Waste 512
      20.1.2.4. Grassroots Effects of Pollution on Environment 512
      20.1.2.5. Literary Perception of Soyinka's Bioethical Pragmatism 515

References 520

Web sites 521

Conclusion 523

Index 531

PART ONE

THE CONTOUR OF CRITICAL THEORIES IN AFRICAN DRAMA AND THEATRE STUDIES

NATIVISM AND THE QUEST OF INDIGENOUS AESTHETICS

THE NARRATOLOGY OF ORAL NARRATIVES

DEFINITIONAL APPROACHES TO DRAMA

POSTCOLONIAL THEORY

1

INTRODUCTION: SITUATING CRITICAL THEORY AND LITERARY CRITICISM IN AFRICAN DRAMA

This book means to offer critical and theoretical approaches to modern African drama and plays, by looking at texts from the perspectives of different literary theories.

African drama and theatre studies have been objects of controversial debates by African and non-African scholars. Eurocentric critics have denied the existence of indigenous African drama and implicitly denied the existence of a correlation between critical theory and dramatic literature as a body of knowledge. Scholarship on the field has claimed that theatre and/or drama were not African artistic forms and must have been imported from Europe. This claim threw a fierce intellectual debate on the question whether African theatre disciplines can be object of serious critical theory study and whether one needs to define a contextual theoretical framework for this field. They also wondered if the existent literary theories of literature in general can be used to interpret and understand scientifically the functional modes of drama and theatre in Africa. Pondering over the question, Chinyere Nwahunanya in his book *Literary Criticism, Critical Theory and Postcolonial African Literature* (2012) has offered a number of theoretical insights worth considering. His definition of critical theory, literary criticism and their scope of analysis in the context of African literature are very helpful. I will summarize his ideas before investigating on the trajectory made by critical theory of African drama.

The study of African drama is the study of literary artifacts, which are, the imaginative verbal constructs that emerge from the creative consciousness of drama artists. One major problem theatre scholars have been confronted to is how to engage in literary studies with these verbal constructs. There exists an epistemological skepticism about African dramatic literature, and it arises from the arguments that if the study of anything is meant to confer any type of knowledge on the reader, drama as literature by its nature is not studiable, because, the argument holds, it has no separate, independent existence. Part of this argument rests on the assumption that we can only read, enjoy and appreciate drama and gather information about it, without necessarily arriving at any knowledge through such an exercise. At best, they say, literature can entertain (Nwahunanya 2012: 1). For me, this argument is a non-issue because, criticism should go beyond the entertainment function of drama and see how it relates to the social, political, economic, cultural and educational concerns of people it is written for. Theory thereby should take into account the very decimal of the commitment of art, not in the parnasian meaning of the word, but in its cartesian meaning. On the contrary, many scholars believe that increasing attention that drama works have attracted to themselves, and the establishment of theatre studies as a serious discipline that is approached intellectually with a certain detachment and objectively and so far, with amazing results, gives legitimacy to the claim that African drama can and should be studied on theories. For one thing, the objects of drama are visible and tangible and have ontological situs, a certain autonomy or independent existence. Drama, when thus approached, can assault our sensibilities with certain contradictions and confront the reader with social realities that sets him/her thinking (Nwahunanya 2012: 1). African drama has numerous sub-forms, a factor that makes it nebulous and elusive as a subject of study, despite its independence, even if taken as monolith. Taken as a monolith verbal construct, drama could defy unilateral, unpatterned approaches to it. It would thus become difficult to study if approached in a disorderly, unsystematic and unpatterned manner. A theory of African drama is therefore a sine qua non for a proper appreciation of literature.

1.1. The Focus of Critical Theory of African Drama

Literary theory and critical theory can be used interchangeably to mean the theory and philosophy of the interpretation of literature and literary criticism. To bend Jonathan Culler to my purpose, it involves the systematic study of the nature of literature and of the methods used in the practical reading of literature (Culler 2000: 3). By drama literary theory, I refer not to the meaning of a play or a work of literature, but to the theoretical interpretations and meaning constructions that reveal what African drama can mean. One can trace its roots to the classical Greek poetics and rhetoric and chart its trajectory to contemporary aesthetic and hermeneutic theories. Although the roots of drama critical theory run as far back as the ancient Greeks (Plato and Aristotle) and ancient Rome (Longinus and Horace), it became a profession only in the twentieth century.

In the same perspective, let's note with Nwahunanya (2012: 1) that since drama is a complex area of human cultural development, many critics since Aristotle have tried to evolve theories that would help the literary adventurer explore the labyrinthine nature of the literary experience and gain a better understanding of the substance of literary artifacts. At the rudimentary stage of literary study during the classical period, Aristotle swathed the need for a comprehensive theory, so he decided to go back to 'first principles'. These principles of analysis are the theoretical foundations upon which any useful and meaningful critical analysis must stand, and from them must emerge useful views that would sustain contemporary and future critical practices. Aristotle went ahead to work out a critical theory, using basic principles, into what he called poetics. After reading Aristotle's poetics, one can assert that a theory of criticism in the context of African drama is the one whose principles apply to the whole of literature and account for every valid type of critical procedure. Aristotle, one can say, is the first serious critical theorist and literary critic, although his literary criticism was confined to some few existing plays of his time.

Having arrived at the definition of theory, I will introduce critical theory by presenting issues and debates rather than schools. Jonarhan Culler has written that Literary theory is not a disembodied set of ideas but a force in institution (Culler 2001). Theory exists in communities of readers and writers, as a discursive practice, inextricably entangled with educational and cultural institutions. Three theoretical modes in African literature readings whose impacts since the 1960s, has been greatest are the wide-ranging reflection on language, representation, and the categories of critical thought undertaken by deconstruction and psychoanalysis (sometimes in concert, sometimes in opposition); the analyses of the role of gender and sexuality in every aspect of literature and criticism by feminism and gender studies; and the development of historically oriented cultural criticisms (new historicism, post-colonial theory) studying a whole range of discursive practices, involving many objects (the body, the family, race and ethnicity) not previously thought of as having a history. What relationships do these theoretical trends entertain with African drama? How is African drama read through the lenses of these critical tendencies? And what implications do these critical engagements and analyses have on the new orientations of the studies of African drama and theatre? These are the questions that will hold my attention in this chapter.

1.1.1. Theoretical Schools and Movements

1.1.1.1. *Structuralism, Poststructuralism and the Afrocentric Schools of Thought*

Structuralism opines that elements of human culture must be understood by way of their relationship to a larger, overarching system or structure. It works to uncover the structures that underlie all the things that humans do, think, perceive, and feel. Alternatively, as summarized by philosopher Simon Blackburn, structuralism is "the belief that phenomena of human life are not intelligible except through their interrelations. These relations constitute a structure, and behind local variations in the surface phenomena there are constant laws of abstract culture". The structuralist mode of reasoning has been applied in a diverse range of fields, including anthropology, sociology, psychology, literary criticism, economics and architecture (Blackburn 1998: 32).

Afrocentricity is a literary and philosophical thought that centres of the African personality as the subject of interest and knowledge. It approaches society past, present and future from the perspective that takes into account the historical confrontation of Africans with the imperialist Europe and America in the context of slave trade, colonization and neocolonialism. There are basically three schools of thoughts that can be classified as Afrocentrist: the Panafricanists, the nativists and the bolekeja.

1.2.1.1. *Structuralism and Panafricanist Critical Theory*

The term "structuralism" is a related term that describes a particular philosophical/literary movement or moment. The term appeared in the works of French anthropologist Claude Lévi-Strauss and gave rise in France to the "structuralist movement," which influenced the thinking of other writers such as Louis Althusser, the psychoanalyst Jacques Lacan, as well as the structural Marxism of Nicos Poulantzas, most of whom disavowed themselves as being a part of this movement.

The origins of structuralism connect with the work of Ferdinand de Saussure on linguistics, along with the linguistics of the Prague and Moscow schools. In brief, Saussure's structural linguistics propounded three related concepts.

1. Saussure argued for a distinction between *langue* (an idealized abstraction of language) and *parole* (language as actually used in daily life). He argued that the "sign" was composed of both a *signified*, an abstract concept or idea, and a "signifier", the perceived sound/visual image.
2. Because different languages have different words to describe the same objects or concepts, there is no intrinsic reason why a specific sign is used to express a given signifier. It is thus «arbitrary».
3. Signs thus gain their meaning from their relationships and contrasts with other signs. As he wrote, "in language, there are only differences 'without positive terms (Saussure 1932: 2)."

Prominent thinkers associated with structuralism include Claude Lévi-Strauss, linguist Roman Jakobson, and psychoanalyst Jacques Lacan.

Structuralist thinking relates to African cultural and dramatic studies in many ways: Firstly, the Afrocentric theorists like Wole Soyinka, Ngugi wa Thiong'o, Ola Rotimi, Efua T. Sutherland, Ama Ata Aidoo, Athol Fugard all have an inclination towards the expansion of African theatre to larger related disciplines, say African cultural anthropology, African linguistics, African phylosophy. Secondly the language of African drama pertains to a larger structuralist body of knowledge that cannot be understood when it is disjuncted from the mainstream cultural paradigm of cultural philosophy and religious thought.

Structuralist panafricanist theorists argue for the unity of Africans all over the world. Pan-Africanism is a worldwide intellectual movement that aims to encourage and strengthen bonds of solidarity between all peoples of African descent. Based upon a common fate going back to the Atlantic slave trade, the movement extends beyond continental Africans, with a substantial support base from among the African diaspora in the Caribbean, Latin America and the United States. According to Reiland Rabaka:

> [Panafrican] or Africana critical theory is theory critical of domination and discrimination, and a social theory that simultaneously offers accessible and ethical alternatives to the key social and political problems of the present age, then, any theory claiming to be a "critical theory of contemporary society" must thoroughly theorize not only capitalism, but also racism,

sexism, and colonialism, and how each of the aforementioned overlaps, interconnects, and intersects to deform and destroy life and the ongoing prospects of liberation and democratic socialist transformation (Rabaka 2009: xiii).

That submission is true and to extend the theoretical grounds of structuralism, Chike Francis Mgbeadichie opines that Afrocentricity originally developed in African-American studies in the early 1930s with the primary aim to 'create a substantive knowledge about the African world experience.' He maintains that in recent years, it has been successfully applied to the African continent and to the black peoples in the African diaspora (Mgbeadichie 2015: 1). It was first traced to the African-American historian W.E.B. Du Bois, who employed it in some of his key works to project black experience and practices. Notable amongst these are: *The Study of the Negro Problem* (1898), *The Souls of Black Folk* (1903), *Black Reconstruction in America* (1935), *The World and Africa* (1946), and *Africa in Battle Against Colonialism, Racialism, Imperialism* (1960). African-American and subsequently, African critics and scholars have provided their own interpretations of this theory (Ibidem).

From that new perspective, Afrocentricity has become a philosophical paradigm that emphasizes the centrality and agency of the African person within a historical and cultural context. Molefi Kete Asante argues that Afrocentricity is a rejection of the historic marginality and racial otherness often present in the ordinary paradigm of European racial domination (Asante 2009: 24). What is more, Afrocentrists articulate a counterhegemonic or domination-resisting view that questions the application of epistemological ideas rooted in the cultural experiences of Europe to Africans or others as if these ideas were universal principles. In this sense, Afrocentricity is a critique of domination that aggressively establishes the agency of Africans in their own communication sphere. This critique may be discovered in the type of language, art forms, expressive styles, arguments, economics, or social ideas within an interactive situation. Thus, the Afrocentric idea is critical to any behavioral activity that involves Africans or people of African descent. One cannot very easily engage in communication study of Africans without some appreciation of the authentic voices of Africans (Ibidem). This implies, of course, a serious study of the deep structure of African philosophical thought. Necessitated by the conditions of history that have removed Africans from their traditional cultural, expressive, philosophical, and religious base, the Afrocentric idea in communication seeks to reposition Africans in the center of their own historical experiences rather than on the margins of European experiences. In essence, two political situations removed Africans from their own terms. First, the enslavement of African people brought about a massive physical and cultural dislocation of millions of Africans. Such a large-scale movement did not have mere displacement implications but more profound implications for how Africans would communicate out of the new reality and what Africans would say about their new reality (Ibidem). Thus, it was both *how* and *what* that mattered in the process of communication among Africans in the Americas. The second political situation was the colonizing of the continent of Africa itself, which left people on the continent but already endangered in their cultural, psychological, and cognitive selves. Thus, the disassembly of African ideas, ideals, standards, and methods was fundamental to the making of both enslaved Africans and colonized Africans. The Afrocentrist's claim that Africans were removed from their own terms in expressive and religious ways is an existential claim based on the reality of the European slave trade and the imperial colonization of Africa. When Africans were forbidden to speak their own languages, to dress in their own clothes, and in some cases, to use their own names, they were in the midst of the turmoil of dislocation. Those who were also separated from their familiar physical and environmental contexts were further alienated from their own cultural terms. The quest for Afrocentric location, that is, a place from which the African can view reality and phenomena associated with reality from the standpoint of Africans, is a liberating journey. One experiences the quest in the language of the best orators in the African American community. They are forever on the road to bringing into the arena of now the language and color of the African reality. Their voices, words, and cadences are those of Africans who are discovering their way back to the center of their own histories. Marginality is a place, but it is not a stable place from which to seek redefinition, relocation, and centering of one's perspective (Ibidem).

Post-structuralist philosophers like Derrida and Foucault did not form a self-conscious group, but each responded to the traditions of phenomenology and Structuralism. The phenomenological idea that knowledge could be centred on the human knower is rejected by Structuralism, which seeks what it asserts to be a more secure foundation for knowledge. In phenomenology, this foundation is experience itself; in Structuralism, knowledge is founded on the "structures" that make experience possible: concepts, and language or signs. By contrast, Post-structuralism argues that founding knowledge either on pure experience (phenomenology) or systematic structures (Structuralism) is impossible. This impossibility was not meant as a failure or loss, but rather as a cause for "celebration and liberation."

A major theory associated with Structuralism was binary opposition. This theory proposed that there are certain theoretical and conceptual opposites, often arranged in a hierarchy, that human logic has given to text. Such binary pairs could include Enlightenment/Romantic, male/female, speech/writing, rational/emotional, signifier/signified, symbolic/imaginary. In African terms colonization divided Africa and Europe into the binary opposition of dominated and dominating, periphery and center, division which translated into literatures whereby Eurpean literature became the masternarratives and African literature became austracized literatures or debased literature. In other words, it is a cultural imperialism that became the order of the day. Post-structuralism rejects the notion of the essential quality of the dominant relation in the hierarchy, choosing rather to expose these relations and the dependency of the dominant term on its apparently subservient counterpart. The only way to properly understand these meanings is to deconstruct the assumptions and knowledge systems that produce multiplicity, hence the illusion of singular meaning.

Afrocentrism in African drama and theatre was born in reaction to that form of European colonial cultural imperialism that denied cultural aesthetics to African indigenous performances. African playwrights began to write at a moment when Europeans had already colonized and imposed their cultural education. Afrocentric critics and theoreticians argue that Africa is home of drama and theatre traditions and has not imported but mere aesthetics from Europe. If drama means the use of mental and spiritual media to expand man's spirit, to reach to the supernatural and to seek solace in forces beyond human realm, then, African indigenous performances, namely ritual, festival, myth and rites are to be reckoned with as dramatic forms. The Nigerian critics Oyin Ogunba, Wole Soyinka, Ola Rotimi, Femi Osofisan, the Malian Bakary Traore are from the Afrocentrists school. Wole Soyinka's theoretical books *Myth Literature and the African World'* (1976), *Art, Dialogue, and Outrage: Essays on Literature and Culture* (1988), Bakary Traore' s *The Black African Theatre and Its Social Functions* (1971), Oyin Ogunba' s "Theatre in Africa" (1966), Joel Adedeji' s "Oral Traditional and the Contemporary Theatre in Nigeria" (1971) are all scholarly pieces that defend the idea of African indigenous drama. The second school of thought is held by Oyeka Owomoyela and Michael Etherton. Michael Etherton' s book *The Development of African Drama* (1982) and Oyeka Owomoyela' s article "Give me Drama or Argument on the Existence of Drama in Traditional Africa (1985)" have sought to establish that drama and theatre are European-imported arts. So theoretical arguments are intense in African critical circles as to whether African drama is solidely grounded on African soil and intellectual knowledge. Plays that sustain the Afrocentric ideas are Ola Rotimi' s *The Gods Are Not to Blame*, Efua T. Sutherland' s *The Marriage of Anansewa,* Wole Soyinka' s *A Dance of the Forests*. The main critical pronouncement here is that African indigenous aesthetics of drama has substances and forms that profend the ubiquitous nature of African folklore, rituals and festivals and unveil the original nature of theatre as a lived experience, the expansion of the mind and the reaching of the soul towards the discovery of the unknown.

1.2.1.2. Nativism and the Quest of Indigenous Aesthetics

Bill Ashcroft, Gareth Griffiths and Helen Tiffin define nativism as the desire to return to indigenous practices and cultural forms as they existed in pre-colonial society (Ashcroft, Griffiths and Tffin 2007: 143-144). African dramatists of the Soyinka generation and those of later period have returned to their native cultures to fetch material and inspiration. Either the South African Brett Beiley in his *iMumbo Jumbo* (1997), *The Prophet* (1999), Jane Taylor in his *Ubu and the Truth Commission* (1998), The Kenyan Ngugi wa Thiong'o in his co-authored *The Trial of Dedan Kimathi* (1976) or *I Will Marry When I Want* (1986), the Ghanaian Ama Ata Aidoo in her *Anowa* or *The Dilemma of a Ghost* or Efua T. Sutherlan in her *The Marriage of Anansewa, Edufa* and *Foriwa*, the Ugandan John Ruganda in his *The Black Mamba* (1972), *The Floods* (1979) incorporate in their plays elements of their native cultures and ingredients of oral tradition. In the specific context of African modern drama, nativism is most frequently encountered to refer to the rhetoric of decolonization which argues that colonialism needs to be replaced by the recovery and promotion of pre-colonial, indigenous ways. The debate as to how far such a return or reconstruction is possible (or even desirable) has been a very vigorous one. Postcolonial discourse theorists such as Soyinka, Ngugi, Fugard and Ruganda joined by Spivak and Bhabha argue strongly that such nativist reconstructions are inevitably subject to the processes of cultural intermixing that colonialism promoted and from which no simple retreat is possible. Spivak has more recently defended the use by post-colonial societies of a 'strategic' essentialism whereby the signifiers of indigenous (native) cultures are privileged in a process of negative discrimination. Such a strategy may allow these societies to better resist the onslaught of global culture that threatens to negate cultural difference or consign it to an apolitical and exotic discourse of cultural diversity. An even more positive defence of the nativist position has been mounted recently by Benita Parry (1994). On the other hand, the multicultural nature of most post-colonial societies makes the issue of what constitutes the pre-colonial 'native' culture obviously problematic, especially where the current postcolonial nation-state defines itself in terms that favour a single dominant cultural group. Minority voices from such societies have argued that 'nativist' projects can militate against the recognition that colonial policies of transplantation such as slavery and indenture have resulted in racially mixed diasporic societies, where only a multicultural model of the post-colonial state can avoid bias and injustice to the descendants of such groups. Minorities from these areas have thus argued against the idea that the post-colonial oppressed form a homogenous group who can be decolonized and liberated by a nativist recovery of a pre-colonial culture.

The assumption of a homogeneous, unitary concept of the state is also challenged by the historical and cultural legacies of colonialism in the form of large and long-established diasporic communities in many multi-racial post-colonial states, such as Malaysia, Singapore and Fiji, and in the Caribbean, where the present racial mixture is profound and virtually every group is in one sense or another the product of a cultural diaspora, rather than being native or indigenous in origin. Models of culture and nationality that privilege one geographical or racial originary sign (e.g. Africa or blackness) have similar problems in addressing the diverse and often creolized nature of the population. Even within less diverse states, minority religious and linguistic groups have faced similar difficulties with the simpler nativist projects of recuperation. The reconstruction of traditions based on supposed nativist models that enshrine a male, patriarchal vision of the precolonial, indigenous culture as authentic has necessarily aroused the resistance of women. For women, models of the traditional past have been seen as the product of present-day male practices which read the past through a biased sexist vision, and which are then used by a ruling élite to deny women their right to participate fully in the social model proposed (Mba 1982; Stratton 1994). In practice, simple models of nativism, like simple models of decolonization, have raised as many issues as they have resolved.

1.2.1.3. *Marxism in Africa*

Generally, Marxism in the African literary context and in the field of drama in particular refers to the aesthetization of the struggle for hegemony, dominance and self-affirmation either by a fierce search of material possession or by the accession and self-maintenance to political power. In the process, the poor, the peasants and industry workers take to the street for strike, demonstrations and movements. Hegemonies range from economic luxury, political dominion and power control, cultural imperialism and technological overuling. African countries' accession to political independence and the rapid advancement of technology, especially the industry of armament has bred a new form of Marxist struggles for supremacy and domination of the poor by the rich, a situation that is reflected in many African postcolonial plays. Marxism therefore points to the rise and fall of political, economic, social and cultural ideologies that intermittently and alternatively rule and are ruled in a tragic and semi-tragic mutual contestation. Even religious propaganda is explored by writers of Marxist drive like Soyinka and Ngugi to show that religion is also interested in classes. For Tejumola Olanyan and Ato Quayisan, the backbone of Marxist critical thought has been the definition of African dramatic literature as essentially a vehicle of class struggle (Olanyan and Quayson 2013: 461). Ngugi wa Thiong'o is known for his Marxist drama through *The Trial of Dedan Kimathi, The Black Hermit,* and *I Will Marry When I Want.* In these plays he has been critical of ways in which the dominant political and oligarchic classes have troppled the masses and strangled their rights. Femi Osofisan in *Once Upon Four Robbers, The Oriki of the Grasshopper, The Midnight Hotel* has shown that the poor are victim of excessive exploitation.

Whilst being a courageous and fearful opponent of black dictatorships, Soyinka attacks the nature of the system, both local and international, which produces and sustains them. In *A Play of Giants, Opera Wonyosi, King Baabu,* he exposes the anomy of dictatorship and its adamant repercussions on peoples and national economies with a strong Marxist iconoclasm. Bukassa was, after all, both installed and toppled by the French. Mobutu has been a loyal and not *too* embarrassing servant of the American interests which put him in power. Slenderly educated soldiers of the former colonial armies have also come to power in rather suspicious coups in countries such as Mali, Togo, and Uganda. The sort of sweeping transformation of the social and economic systems inherited from colonialism which might make this sort of leadership impossible do not always seem to be those which Soyinka would welcome. Where he does appear to address the problem, as in his post-Civil War plays *Madmen and Specialists, A Play of Giants, Opera Wonyosi,* he highlights political exploitation and class-conscience struggles. Through a historical accident which is certainly not his fault, Soyinka is the product of a colonial and elitist education. He was the product of an education through struggle in the field, which forced him to think much more radically about the possible lines of a new order.

Ngũgĩ wa Thiong'o does not haggle with exploiters, the postcolonial treators who double-cross their subjects. He has become one of the most important Marxist writers to emerge on the contemporary African scene. Ngugi's Marxism is deep in philosophical thought and engaging in social commitment. Among his most revolutionary contributions to African theater are *The Trial of Dedan Kimathi* (1976), which he co-authored with Micere Mugo, and *I Will Marry When I Want* (1982), an English translation from the Gikuyu of the play *Ngaahika ndeenda*, the result of his experiments on African theater with Ngũgĩ wa Mĩriĩ at the Kamiriithu Community Education and Cultural Center, inaugurated in 1977. *The Trial of Dedan Kimathi* is an interpretation of history. It examines the intensity and commitment of ordinary Kenyan citizens in the social mobilization led by Dedan Kimathi twenty years earlier, during the struggle for independence from the British. The play also clearly analyzes the self-interest of the Kenyan bourgeoisie, and their consequent role aborting this grassroot-inspired revolution.

I Will Marry When I Want, according to the author, "depicts the proletarization of the peasantry in a neo-colonial society" (44). It is in many ways the follow-up of the events in *The Trial of Dedan Kimathi*, especially after Kimathi's execution. It thus deals with a Kenyan society that is independent only in name, and that is materially and socially controlled and exploited by the erstwhile colonial forces. Focused on the land question, the play shows how a multinational firm owned by Japanese and European businessmen enters into an alliance with their African counterparts to deprive the Kiguunda family of their one and a half acres of land, which they depend on for subsistence. As a continuation of the Kimathi-led Kenya Land and Freedom Army revolution, the play examines how the struggle for independence in Kenya, for which thousands of its citizens died, has now been hijacked by neocolonial forces extending from America to Japan. In the process of researching the play at Kamiriithu, a town that historically was involved in the Kimathi struggle, Ngũgĩ wa Thiong'o and his creative associates had to contend with the problem of the language, the history, the social and working conditions of the people, and the artistic elements of the indigenous African theater, such as song, dance, mime, and ceremony, in their quest for an authentic African drama and theater. In 1981 they devised another production, *Maitu njugira* (*Mother Sing for Me*), which extended their search for a socialist-oriented society, using more than eighty songs from eight ethnic nationalities in Kenya to celebrate and to bemoan the joys and sorrows of the Kenyan people's struggles. Ngũgĩ's commitment to the struggle for real freedom has even prompted him to abandon the English language and to write in Gikuyu and Swahili in order to reach the vast majority of ordinary Kenyans. The English versions of his future works will therefore come only as translations. Still, he uses his essays and critical commentaries on culture and other sociopolitical issues to communicate to a wider English-speaking world. Ngũgĩ's commitment to the use of drama and theater as a potent instrument for mass education through a clearer interpretation of history is shared by his countryman Kenneth Watene.

1.2.1.4. Contextualizing Cultural Materialism in African Arts

As literary theory, cultural materialism is of interest to African dramatic studies. In substance, that theory is interested in how literature is affected by cultural artifacts, the congelation of consumer society with material capitalist intent. The African variant of cultural materialism is predicated upon the combination of different socio-cultural, political and economic forces that gave rise to and shaped the committed struggles of dramatic literature its anticolonial and neocolonial struggles for a more humane, freer and developed African continent. The theory that sustains such ideals in the patriotic sense of the term is the very pronouncement of cultural materialism. Nawal El Saadawi calls this type of drama dissidence drama (Saadawi 2013: 172). There are two implications to consider when the reader applies cultural materialism to African theatre studies. Firstly, African drama has come to entertain a close relationship with the socio-political and cultural conditions of the African people. Ngugi wa Thiong'o articulates thus the point:

> [African] literature does not grow or develops in the vacuum. It is given impetus, shape, direction and even area of concern by social, political, and economic forces in a particular society. The relationship between creative literature and these other forces cannot be ignored especially in Africa where modern literature has grown against the gory background of Europeam imperialism and its changing manifestations: slavery, colonialism and neocolonialism […] There is no area of our lives that has not been affected by the social, political and expansionist needs of European capitalism (Quoted in G. D. Killam 1984: 123).

Cultural materialism is not far from Marxist thinking. In African context, the theory is mostly interested in the sociopolitical and cultural forces that shaped modern African drama and portrands its commitment to change. These forces are embedded in the interrelationships and historical confrontations between Africa and Europe. Secondly, nowadays cultural materialism reads the present African geopolitics in the cultural diplomacy with world nations and relocates thematic concerns that plead for a total disengagement with vectors of oppression, exploitation and mental enslavement. Writers with cultural materialist inclinations are Ngugi wa Thiong' o, Frantz Fanon, Bode Sowande, Okot P' Biteck, Steve Biko, to mention but a few. If in European cultural studies cultural materialism traces its origin to the work of the left-wing literary critic Raymond Williams, in Africa that theory is culture oriented and integrated in the sociopolitical theatre narratives. Willams' describes "civilisation" as an achieved state of development in Marxism and Literature. In Africa, it is mostly interested by the colonial and postcolonial African condition. The word derives from "civil" meaning polite and orderly. However, the critic agrees with Marx and points out that civilisation is often achieved through capitalism and through "making barbarian countries dependent on civil ones" (http/www.ukessays.com). Cultural materialism makes analysis based on critical theory, in the tradition of the Frankfurt School. It emerged as a theoretical movement in the early 1980s along with new historicism, an American approach to early modern literature, with which it shares much common ground. The term was coined by Raymond Williams, who used it to describe a theoretical blending of leftist culturalism and Marxist analysis. Cultural materialists deal with specific historical documents and attempt to analyze and recreate the zeitgeist of a particular moment in history.

From this perspective, it makes sense to assert that African drama is culture-oriented and materially charged. It is culture-oriented in that every compartment of African theatre speaks about African people's cultural beliefs, philosophical outlooks and religious convictions. Beyond that episteme, it is also politically and materially charged because drama directly relates the people's material conditions and seeks to formulate strategies and suggest means to come to terms with material exploiation, political oppression and economic plunder. One needs to take a look at Athol Fugard's *No-Good Friday* (1958), *Sizwe Bansi is Dead* (1972), *Halo and Goodbye* (1965), Wole Soyinka's *Opera Wonyosi* (1984), Ngugi wa Thiong'o's *The Black Hermit* (1968), Efo Kodjo Mawugbe's *In the Chest of a Woman* (2007), Frank Ogodo Ogbeche's *Harvest of Corruption* (2007) to see how realist African modern plays are. Not only do they portray the unbecoming realities of life but they seek to stimulate the intellectual's thought about ways in which one can come out of them.

Williams viewed culture as a "productive process", part of the means of production, and cultural materialism often identifies what he called "residual", "emergent" and "oppositional" cultural elements (William Empson 1994: 80). Following in the tradition of Herbert Marcuse, Antonio Gramsci and others, cultural materialists extend the class-based analysis of traditional Marxism (Neo-Marxism) by means of an additional focus on the marginalized. Cultural materialists analyze the processes by which hegemonic forces in society appropriate canonical and historically important texts, such as Shakespeare and Austen, and utilize them in an attempt to validate or inscribe certain values on the cultural imaginary. Jonathan Dollimore and Alan Sinfield, authors of *Political Shakespeare*, have had considerable influence in the development of this movement and their book is considered to be a seminal text. They have identified four defining characteristics of cultural materialism as a theoretical device:

- Historical context
- Close textual analysis
- Political commitment
- Theoretical method (Dollimore and Sinfield 1994: 3)

These characteristics can be also found in African drama context. African cultural materialist playwrights from this perspective seek to draw attention to the processes being employed by contemporary power structures, such as the church, the state or the academy, to disseminate ideology and to dismantle through objective critical approaches the very discourses that bamboozle the emerging efforts of socio-economic, political and cultural developments. To do this they explore a text's historical context and its political implications, and then through close textual analysis note the dominant hegemonic position. They identify possibilities for the rejection and/or subversion of that position. British critic Graham Holderness defines cultural materialism as a "politicized form of historiography" (Holderness 1999).

1.2.1.5. Towards the Decolonization of African Drama and Theatre: The Bolekaja Criticism

In *Decolonizing the Mind,* Ngugi has demonstrated that under the strain of colonization, Africans have tended to develop a complex of inferiority towards their arts, cultures and dramatic forms. It is a colonization of the mind. This being the colonization of the mind, it becomes necessary to proceed to the decolonization of the African's mind, ideas and intellect so as to free them from cultural self-abasement. This same formulation was also articulated by Chinua Achebe in his article "The Novelist as a Teacher" where he lamented about the Africans' cultural inferiority complex and said that his primary function as a writer was to teach his African audiences that despite the imperfection of their history [past], they should not look at that as a long night of savagery from which the Europeans came to deliver them (Achebe 1988: 40). Chinweizu and Madubuike have formulated in their book *Towards the Decolonization of African Literature,* what some critics have designated as The Bolekaja criticism. The Bolekaja criticism seeks to identify the corrective struggle of "men and of nations" with "the stiflers of their life" (1983). In Yoruba bolekaja means "Come down let's fight!" However, there is far more to bolekajarism than intellectual pugilism. Committed to afrocentric cultural nationalism, "Issues and tasks," the final chapter of *Toward the Decolonization of African Literature* is a manifesto *for* African Literary production and interpretation. Earlier chapters consist of resolute critiques of the universalist assumptions of "eurocentric criticism" of African fiction [drama and theatre included] and poetry. In contrast to eurocentrism, they propose a "supportive" role for the critic. Supportive criticism provides writer and audience with the knowledge of "things valued in traditional African orature." A principal term in this Hermeneutics of support is imitation: just as writers must rely on African oral Discourse to simulate "the flavor of African life," so critics should sustain their efforts by providing them with the raw material – "knowledge of things valued in traditional African orature, and why" – of their craft. Given their stress on oral discourse, their preference for "20th-century diction and idiom," and their insistence on the autonomy of African literature, it is hardly surprising that Chinweizu, Jemie, and Madubuike decry the impact of the "anglo-modernist sensibility" on some African poets-dramatists and approve of the pursuit of traditionalism in others. Bolekaja criticism has been called an "ethnic model" for its insistence on the "cultural specificity" of African literature and its "pursuit and defense of difference." But missing from this appraisal is the recognition that part of its political inspiration derives from nonethnic, supraethnic "imagined communities" – the nation, the continent. Equally unacknowledged are its other debts: its cognitive (us–them) apparatus, its mimeticism, its (cultural) nationalist Ideology. Many of these are owed, either directly or not, to European history, epistemologies, and theories of art.

Bolekaja criticism is, like afrocentrism in North America, a form of nativism. Caught in the logic of eurocentrism, it cannot formulate a hermeneutic by which the generic, linguistic, and expressive eclecticism of African cultural practices can be most productively explicated (Tejumola Olanyan 2007: 84).

In line with the Bolekaja criticism, contemporary African plays, namely those from Africa South of Sahara and Black South African plays reflect the material existence of Black people under colonialism and the apartheid government. In West Africa for instance, Soyinka, Osofisan, Rotimi, John Pepper Clark, Ata Aidoo, Sutherland, Frank Ogodo Ogbeche have written and produced plays that critically examine the African colonial and neocolonial conditions in a language that goes beyond aesthetization to tell with realism the very location of the existential problems. When we take plays like *Opera Wonyosi, A Play of Giants* [Soyinka], *Once Upon Four Robbers* [Osofisan], *Our Husban Has Gone Mad Again, If... the Tragedy of the Ruled* [Rotimi], *The Raft, The Boat* [Clark] *Anowa, Sister Kiljoy* [Aidoo], *Foriwa, Edufa* [Sutherland], *Harvest of Corruption* [Ogbeche], there is a strong collective consciousness of the African citizens to struggle and achieve socio-political, economic and cultural liberation from the foreign tantacled economic domination, cultural exploitation and local political servility. Theater is considered an effective method of portraying that existence. In South Africa the advocacy of Apartheid and post-apartheid condition has preoccupied playwrights in their theorizing of performance arts. This is what John Kani and Winston Ntshona meant when in an interview they declared, "We believe that art is life and conversely, life is art" (5). Major playwrights that occupy the centre stage include Athol Fugard, Lewis Nkosi, Maishe Maponya and Jane Taylor. Fugard's *No Good Friday, My Children! My Africa!, Hello and Goodbye, Lesson from Aloes;* Maishe Maponya's *The Hungry Earth* and Jane Taylor's *Ubu and the Truth Commission* are among many others plays that appeal to the black community's consciousness to fight against Apartheid and establish a rule of equality before the law. It is also the concern of contemporary Black South African plays. Black theater artists are turning away from such white-masterminded "blacksploitation" musicals as *King Kong* and *Ipi Tombi* and creating their own powerful plays, like *Sizwe Bansi Is Dead, u Nosilimela, Shanti, Too Late, Survival, Woza Albert, Gangsters, Born in the RSA, Asinamali! Bopha!* and many others. The plays, which are mostly created under experimental or workshop conditions, collectively signify the intensification of the political struggle on the cultural front through grass-roots mobilization and consciousness raising among the urban masses. As experimental plays, they are unencumbered by Western production conventions, and this quality gives the artists the freedom to experiment with techniques with which the audience is already familiar in traditional performances. Younger Black playwrights have tended to eschew the intrusion of such personal problems by devoting their energies to raising the consciousness of their fellow Africans in the light of the historical and cultural contradictions inherent in apartheid. Steve Biko and other leaders of the Black Consciousness Movement encouraged the formation of grass-roots theater organizations in the African townships. The result has been the reinvention of old techniques essentially drawn from the traditional African performance conventions such as storytelling, music, song and dance, multiple role playing, open space utilization, and the active involvement of the audience during performance to suit the demands of an urgent guerrilla-like urban theater.

1.2.1.6. Postmodernism in African Context

What is postmodernism and how does it apply to African dramatic literature? How does postmodernism read as an outgrowth of modernism in Africa? In western literature, the main focus of postmodernism is the deconstruction of 'the true', 'the real', 'the universal', 'the reason', the 'master narratives', 'ideologies', 'the claim of reason' that prevailed as the main tendencies in modernism. It shows the fragmentation of the truth into relativity of truths and reveals the impossibility to claim a universal value. Pitched on the disintegration of the original, the deterioration of the genuine into photocopies presenting verissimilitudes of the initial ones, postmodernism arose from the advanced stage of modernism that brought with it the profound decline of values hitherto held in high esteem as uncritical acceptability. Postmodernism arose within Western literature with the works of Jean-François Lyotard, Jean Baudrillard, Jacques Derrida and Frederic Jameson.

To be exact, Postmodern drama is not far from absurdist drama. The same way as the theatre of the absurd was born in Europe from the destructive and meaningless rush of human society into the technological destruction of human life and materials and a loss of a sense of living, postmodern drama in Africa has emerged from the critical human condition of neocolonial technologized African society with the restless race to materialism, political violence, crime, debauchery, violation of human rights, corruption, bribery, child trafiquing, prostitution, pornography, occultism, sects. Postmodernism is quickly spotted in numerous African plays: Wole Soyinka' s *The Road, A*

Play of Giants and *King Baabu,* Ola Rotimi's *Holding Talks,* Femi Osofisan's *The Oriki of the Grasshopper, The Chattering and the Song, The Restless Race of Locusts,* are examples of the postmodern plays that tentalize the fragmentation of the African society.

Postmodernism elsewhere describes a broad movement that developed in the mid- to late 20th century across philosophy, the arts, architecture, and criticism which marked a departure from modernism. While encompassing a broad range of ideas, postmodernism is typically defined by an attitude of skepticism, irony, or rejection toward grand narratives, ideologies, and various tenets of universalism, including objective notions of reason, human nature, social progress, moral universalism, absolute truth, and objective reality. Instead, postmodern thinkers may assert that claims to knowledge and truth are products of social, historical or political discourses or interpretations, and are therefore contextual or socially constructed. Accordingly, postmodern thought is broadly characterized by tendencies to epistemological and moral relativism, pluralism, irreverence, and self-referentiality.

In African context and namely African dramatic literature context, postmodernism came as a movement after the disruptive invasion of European culture and civilization in Africa. The advent of colonialism brought with it a disintegration of African cultures, languages, modes of dressing, housing, communication, transportation. The first impact of European contact with Africa was the rapid emergence of modernism that produced a deep transformation of African social fabric: from communalism to individualism, from African originality to cultural alienation, from pastoral economy to industrial economy, from barter system to currency. Cultural alienation produced hybrid educated individuals who find it difficult to strike the balance between African values and western- acquired ones. They lost the sense of originality, genuineness, absoluteness, universal truth. African writers criticized European imperial hegemony and masternarratives that claimed centrality and mastery of knowledge and adopted the creative relativism. If a literature should be judged genuine, original and valuable, it should be judged in relation to its own audience. African drama has not to pass the test of western critics before being acknowledged as drama. But the most palpable effect of modernism was the rapid moral dawnfall and the disintegration of morality among the middle-class educated Africans who always shape their living standards on European models. With the importation of European movies, films and digital materials, African youth are given over to a critical consumerism of the crime and war-prone films, rotten porn movies, drug-addict clips which has thrown a collective moral depravation on the African consumers. In rural areas, the advent of modernism has seen the decline of the authority of the traditional elders hitherto the leaders of the communities and guardians of traditional wisdom. There has been a constant disintegration of moral values, fragmentation of truths with the perpetual quest of identity and reference. These fragmentations of values are depicted in dramatic literature by African playwrights.

The positions taken by Ato Quayson in his article "Postcolonialism and Postmodernism" confirms my stand here: "The key theoretical terms in postmodernism are dissemination, dispersal, indeterminacy, hyperreality, normless pastiche, bricolage, *differance,* aporia, play and suchlike" (Quayson 2007: 650).

1.2.1.7. Afropolitans

Afropolitan is a term constructed from the name Africa and the ancient Greek root -polis, which literally means city. Polis can also mean citizenship or body of citizens. It is to the latter meaning that the term Afropolitan takes its essence. It is an attempt at redefining African phenomena by placing emphasis on ordinary citizens' experiences in Africa. *Afropolitanism* is similar to the older Panafricanism ideology. However, it defines being an "African" in explicitly continent-wide and multiracial terms, and rejects all pretensions to victimhood. As Achille Mbembe and Sarah Nuttall write, "In an attempt to overturn predominant readings of Africa, we need to identify sites within the continent...not usually dwelt upon in research and public discourse, that defamiliarize commonplace readings of Africa" (Mbembe and Nuttall 2005). These sites include fields like fashion, visual art, music and spiritual concerns.

The term was popularized in 2005 by a widely disseminated essay, "Bye-Bye, Babar (Or: What is an Afropolitan?)" by the author Taiye Selasi. Originally published in March 2005 in the Africa Issue of *the LIP Magazine,* the essay defines an Afropolitan identity, sensibility and experience (https://en.wikipedia.org/wiki/Afropolitan). The critiques of the Afropolitan, as portrayed by Selasi in Bye-Bye, Babar, condemn its elitism and class biased approach. Susanne Gehrmann states that Selasi's Afropolitan "is addicted to urban hip life" and "international careers." However, the essay is important in discussing where emigrants of Africa fit into the spectrum of African. Knudsen and Rahbek suggest that Bye-Bye, Babar "is an integral part [in the] ongoing conversation about the relationship between identity and individuality" in the way that it "speaks to the individual" who may feel alone in the sense that they do not have "labels or identities" to understand their positioning in the world. In 2006 the essay was republished by the Michael Stevenson Gallery in Cape Town and in 2007 by *The Nation* in Nairobi, whereupon it went viral. Several communities, artists, and publications now use the label, most notably The Afropolitan Network, The Afropolitan Experience, The Afropolitan Legacy Theatre, The Afropolitan Collection, and South Africa's *The Afropolitan Magazine*. In June 2011 The Victoria and Albert Museum hosted "Friday Late: Afropolitans" in London. In September 2011 the Houston Museum of African American Culture convened the symposium "Africans in America: The New Beat of Afropolitans," featuring author Teju Cole, musician Derrick Ashong and artist Wangechi Mutu alongside Selasi. Ashong released an online album with the group Soulfège in 2011, titled "Afropolitan." Blitz the Ambassador will release the CD "Afropolitan Dreams" in 2013. Ade Bantu is the co-creator of the monthly concert series Afropolitan Vibes which holds at Freedom Park Lagos, Nigeria.

In African drama playwrights like Ade Solanke (2012), Zainabu Jalo (2013) have relocated the theoretical discourse of African drama by theorizing on Afropolitanism. Zainabu Jalo is the author of Onions Make Us Cry (2013). Ade Solanke wrote *Pandora's Box* in which she depicts the intricacies of in and out round trips for London-based African parents who would like to bring forth cultural identity as a a decimal of survival. The limestone of the play's thesis makes possible the belief that monolithic cultural retrieval is a must for the claim of universal citizenship.

Of Nigerian heritage, Adeola Solanke was born in London, growing up in Ladbroke Grove in the west of the capital. She earned an MFA in Screenwriting from the University of Southern California School of Cinematic Arts, where she was a Fulbright Scholar and Phi Beta Kappa international scholar. She also has a postgraduate diploma in Creative Writing from Goldsmiths, University of London, and an honours degree in English Literature from the University of Sheffield. Adeola "Ade" Solanke is an award-winning British-Nigerian playwright and screenwriter. She is best known for her debut stage play, *Pandora's Box*, which was produced at the Arcola Theatre in 2012, and was nominated as Best New Play in the Off West End Theatre Awards. Her other writing credits include the award-winning BBC Radio drama series *Westway* and the Nigerian feature film *Dazzling Mirage* (2014). She is the founder and creative director of the company Spora Stories, whose aim is to "create original drama for stage and screen, telling the dynamic stories of the African diaspora." Solanke has previously worked as an arts journalist and in radio and television, and in 1988 set up Tama Communications, offering a writing and publicity service, whose clients included the BBC, the Arts Council and the Midland Bank.

Ade Solanke's theory of Afropolitanism hinges on the statement that "I am sitting on the fence between two cultures" a catch phrase that explains her inclination towards a universal citizenship. *Pandora's Box* which is given full critical attention in chapter 18 is a play written with a strong sense of Afropolitanism. This is centered on the difficulty of the characters to definitely locate Africa, their origin as their home, not in the physical sense of the term but in the cultural pronunciation of the African identity that congeal a sense of purism. *Pandora's* Box redefines the African in terms of both his/her geographical location and also his/her economic emancipatory setting and cultural adjustments. It is from these perspectives that this book looks at theories of African drama.

In chapter one, the analysis has defined critical theory and its scope of study in African drama. The main argument there is that African drama and theatre are fertile grounds that appeal to the use of critical theory for deep understanding and serious analyses. Against the subversive Eurocentric and racist discourses, the body of knowledge that constitutes African dramatic literature admits the theoretical frameworks on the equal footing as any other literatures and disciplines. African drama entertains strong dynamic relationships with other disciplines namely cultural studies, anthropology, sociology, linguistics, stylistics, philosophy, history, to mention but a few. The sociology of African drama will by far x-ray the spectrum of that dynamism. Chapter two offers a critical examination on nativism and the quest for indigenous aesthetics. The main argument there is that African playwrights have domesticated the dramatic genre in the African contextualized mode to make it bear local color. Domestication is felt in the adaptation of plays to African setting, the discussion of African issues, the use of Afro-European languages, the abundant use of oral tradition elements namely myth, legends, folktales, proverbs, animal stories, local names, and the insertion of words in local languages. That process of domestication responds to the creative need to quinch the nostalgic thirst of originality and genuineness of African creative arts that do not bargain their authenticity with non-African aesthetic forms. Chapter three focuses on oral narratives and their anesthetization in African dramatic performance arts using the perspective of narratology. Key elements that are explored are the function of the narrator, the perspective of the stories, the representations of speech and thought.

Chapter four is a New Historicist Approach to Festival and Ritual Drama. The main objective has been to clarify the concept of drama and look at its outgrowth forms which are rituals and festivals. Contrarily to what European critical tendencis opine, that African ritual and festival cannot be called drama, research and investigations prove that such elements are solid grounds of the bourgeoning of African modern drama. If it is true that aspects of modern drama were imported from Europe within the context of colonial enterprise, it is not half-truth to assert that drama existed in religious performances in Africa and these forms have now served as the raw material on which modern drama is grafted.

In chapter five, the focus is on postcolonial critical debates on African drama and the orientations of discourses in that postcolonial space. I first sought to elucidate key terms of postcolonial critical theoris like hybridity, ambivalence, cultural difference, enunciation, and stereotype, mimicry, third space, western modernity, knowledge and universalism. The discussions in this chapter ended by offering a redefinition of Postcolonialism as the rejection of historical pessimism and the on-putting of the outlook of positivismas a new future perspective.

Chapter six looks into symbolism and naturalism as reading strategies in African drama. The dialectic of reading and interpretation involves African colonial and neocolonial experiences as the main vectors of African drama but the critical tendency to depict with realism political history has not been elucidated with the light of symbolism and naturalism as theories of drama. This study attempts to locate the dialectic of reading and interpreting symbolism and naturalism in African context as vectors that should guide critical interpretation. To what extent does African history, specifically colonialism and neocolonialism contribute to the framing of Symbolism and naturalism as major critical theories in African theatre studies?

Chapter seven titled African Perspectives on Cultural Materialism and Political Morality, constructs critical meaning of African drama, using cultural materialism. The main argument holds that the way drama operates in African political and cultural contexts can be more explained if we throw a glance at the operating mode of Ancient Greek drama. Greek drama whose hearth was at Athens is believed to have produced the first democracy on which other countries shaped their models. Ideas in Greek drama about freedom can be found in African traditional performances and contemporary plays. In dramatic literature, African democracy, like democracy in other nations, may have taken inspiration from Greek drama in the making of democratic ideas.

The burden of chapter eight is to examine through Marxist literary aesthetics the articulation of political consciousness of the masses and the vision for freedom and development, Ngugi wa Thiong'o's and Micere Githae Mugo's *The Trial of Dedan Kimathi* and Wole Soyinka's *King Baabu*. It analyses the vision for socio-political reconstruction in two different socio-political contexts: the struggle for independence in *The Trial of Dedan Kimathi* and the struggle for democracy in *King Baabu*. It reasserts that drama as Marxist literature is masses-oriented. It is a medium of expression for the oppressed. Such drama is tilted towards a better society and a redefinition of man within the ambit of humanity. Thus, it attacks man's inhumanity to man.

Chapter nine looks into the African female playwrights' feminist inclinations and their broader perspectives on women's problems, gender concerns and womanist ethics. Female playwrights in Africa have been interested in the questions of feminism in general and the positive change of their living conditions in particular. Despite this growing interest and concern on behalf of women, Feminism has been a controversial issue in African literature. The main argument of the study is that African female dramatists have been theorizing a feminist theory of their own laying emphasis on the specific political, social, economic and cultural factors that call for a contextualization of the theory and a perception of the feminist problems from the African angle. Three main feminist waves have been pointed out with specific writers who are to be reckoned with when it comes to debating women's questions: the first wave with pioneers like Efua T. Sutherland, Flora Nwapa, Ama Ata Aidoo, Nawal Al Sadawi, Ama Ata Aidoo, the second wave with writers like Chinyere Grace Okafor and Irene Isoken Oronsaye-Salami and Zainab Jalo. The Third wave of African feminist dramatists include Emerging Voices like Ade Solanke.

From a postcolonial perspective, chapter ten scrutinizes Femi Osofisan's and Leke Ogunfeyimi's aesthetic representations of masses' resistance to postcolonial imperial hegemony in their respective plays *No More the Wasted Breed* and *Sacrifice the King*. The study analyses the two playwrights' critical positions about the imperatives of resistance in a context where unjustified demand of dogmatic allegiance to "authority" is being imposed on the masses. In this respect, the study highlights resistance to oppressive and unjust victimization in society.

Chapter eleven uses psychoanalytic theory to investigate how Ola Rotimi uses the language of iconography to address Africa's neo-colonial predicament in *The Gods Are Not to Blame*. Critics in African literary circles have agreed on the fact that there is a general *malaise* with regard to Africa's socio-economic underdevelopment without agreeing on 'who is to be blamed' for that plight. While many critics tend to lay all the blame on the ex-colonial powers, Ola Rotimi using an iconological language seeks to turn the tide by repositioning the debate of Africa's predicament, putting at the centre stage Africans' own responsibility in carving the continent's present destiny. This article departs from the psychanalytical theoretical grounds to unveil the unconscious drives in the apprehension of African neocolonial plight and to make explicit Ola Rotimi's literary assessment of the causes of Africa's present socio-political and economic predicament.

Chapter twelve investigates the extent to which Femi Osofisan in *Women of Owu* explores ethnic conflicts to envision peace strategies in Nigeria. Diversities of ethnic and religious identities are contingent upon multiple intersecting factors, ethnic, linguistic, historical, demographic, politico-economic and ideological that, if badly handled, sometimes trouble peace and put into peril years efforts of socio-economic development. The present study analyses how Femi Osofisan uses drama to explore ethnic conflicts and envisage perspectives for peaceful settlement and social cohesion. The article studies how Femi Osofisan uses theatrical art to explore the consequences of ethnic conflicts, religiosity and economic disparities as potential sources of conflicts in Africa, to call for their peaceful settlement, and to project his literary message that mediation and dialogue are sustainable peace strategies in African settings.

Chapter thirteen analyses the postmodern formation of states in Africa projected by some African writers of dramatic expression like Femi Osofisan and Wole Soyinka that has caused the rising inequalities interacted with simmering grievances linked to political exclusion and economic neglect. Socio-political exclusion and economic neglect bred the mounting of crime and violence in metropolitan centers. Although literature on crime and how to deal with it has documented African fiction and drama, little attention has been paid to Femi Osofisan's approach to crime in *Once Upon Four Robbers* and Wole Soyinka's in *Jero's Metamorphosis*.

Chapter fourteen explores dramatic and novelistic conventions of time, space and the narrative voice which determine the genre of dramatic texts and novelistic text taking Ade Solanke's *Pandora's Box* and Ngugi wa Thiong'o's *Wizard of the Crow* as examples. It argues that dramatic texts, unlike prose fiction, are written for performance and tell stories by showing them. Unlike the novel where the story is told by a narrator without being shown on stage, in drama, the telling is direct and without mediation. Drama does not very often use the narrator, but whenever it chooses to do that the narrator becomes a character in the play. This unmediated nature of narration of drama affects the way dramatic texts represent time and space, and the way they use time and space to structure themselves. The specific question I am addressing is whether and to what extent drama like fiction narrative admits of the narratological concept of a narrative voice. This article presents a survey of dramatic and theatrical conventions about representing time and space, and notes how the conventions of "here and now" determine the generic limits of drama.

Chapter fifteen discusses the theatrical literary representations of conflicts and mediations techniques in Post-Apartheid South Africa from the perspectives of Maishe Maponya and Jane Taylor. The study asserts that the literary articulation of post-conflicts mediation strategies in Maishe Maponya's *The Hungry Earth* and Jane Taylor's *Ubu and the Truth Commission* tell the South African experience and constitute experimental praxis of social reconstruction. The two playwrights offer an example of the difficulties of putting in place a successful model of Truth and Reconciliation Commission capable of rallying Whites and Blacks after the long run segregationist and oppressive system. This study investigates the post-conflict reconciliation strategies as the bedrock and main stay of social peace, itself a springboard toward social cohesion and sustainable development.

This chapter sixteen examines the sociology of francophone drama. Aspects examined include the William Ponty drama, village drama, urban drama, and historical and political drama. The analyses relay the researches of French theatre scholar Alain Ricard who has done a seminal work on the functioning modes of theatre in West Africa in general and Francophoe west Africa in particular.

Chapter seventeen analyses the reflections of two Togolese playwrights Senouvo Agbota Zinsou and Kangni Alemdjrodo in the perspective of their ideological struggles for a freer, fairer and more fulfilled Togolese society. The analysis takes into account the historical evolution of the theater and the Togolese literary thoughts that support its development. Theatrical art, beside its function as an ideological weapon of thought-spreading, also functions as an instrument of cultural education, which should be elucidated on the basis of the example of the selected playwrights under consideration.

This chapter eighteen examines postmodernist aesthetics and the articulation of Afropolitanism and cultural ambivalence in Ade Solanke's *Pandora's Box*. Taking as point of departure the experience of the African immigrants in England, it asserts that in a globalized changing world marked by rapid spatial migration of individuals and cultural interpenetration, literary discourses have shifted from Afrocentrism to focus on Afropolitanism as a theory of global citizenship, giving way to the building of a new African identity in hybrid modern world. The article maintains that identity, sometimes a controversial concept, is very flexible and can be reshaped to suit with the needs of times and circumstances. Taking the example of the African immigrants living in England in *Pandora's Box*, the article asserts that cultural homecoming is also essential for the survival of African values.

Chapter nineteen studies the critical ideas of Athol Fugard in his questioning of post-apartheid legacy in *My Children! My Africa!* and *No Good Friday*. It asserts that the end of Apartheid in South Africa was supposed to bring a certain number of prerogatives to the black community, among which the erasure of colonial stereotypes, equal access to education and employment and stop to police vagaries and brutality, but unfortunately, these expectations were not met. The main question addressed is to what extent do the survival patterns of apartheid constitute human rights violation and a roadblock to peaceful coexistence in multiracial South Africa? How does Fugard's critical assessment of post-Apartheid violation of human rights read as a deconstructive strategy of white imperialist hegemony? Using postcolonial critical approach, the study brings out the interconnection between postcolonial theatre narrative strategy and the struggle for a human rights restoration in the context of South African postcolonial era.

Chapter twenty conducts a literary reflection on the necessity of environmental ethics and the preservation of the natural ecosystem, through the struggle against pollution in Wole Soyinka's *The Beatification of Area Boy*. The reflection asserts that environmental ethics being the prior condition for a wholesome and decent environment, deforestation, pollution and other unbecoming degradations of the nature are to proscribe from human behavior, if life is to continue. From a literary perspective, this study purports to make explicit Wole Soyinka's critical concern for the preservation of the natural environment and bioethics through a literary approach.

References

Achebe, Chinua. *Hopes and Impediments: Selected Essays.* London: Heinemann. 1988.
Barry, Peter. *Beginning Theory: An Intyroduction to Literary and Cultural Theory.* Manchester: Mancheser University Press. 2002.

Blackburn, Simon. *Oxford Dictionary of Philosophy*, second edition revised. Oxford: Oxford University Press. 2008.

Asante, Molefi Kete. "Afrocentricity." In Stephen W. Littlejohn Karen A. Foss, eds., *Encyclopedia of Communication Theory.* Los Angeles: Sage Publications. 2009.

Ashcroft, Bill, Gareth Griffiths and Helen Tiffin, eds. *Post-colonial Studies: The Key Concepts.* New York: Routledge. 2007.

https://www.ukessays.com/essays/english-literature/raymond-williams-theory-of-cultural-materialism-english-literature-essay.php.

Mgbeadichie, Chike Francis. *The Critical Concept of Afrocentrism in Nigerian Literature,* PhD Thesis Submitted to the University of Exeter. https://core.ac.uk/download/pdf/43098140.pdf. 2015.

Ngugi wa Thiong'o in G. D. Killam, G. D. *The Writings of East and Central Africa.* London: Heinemann. 1984.

Nwahunanya, Chinyere. *Literary Criticism, Critical Theory and Postcolonial African Literature.* USA: Arbi Press. 2012.

Olanyan Tejumola and Ato Quayson. *African Literature: An Anthology of Criticism and Theory.* New York: Blackwell Publishing. 2013.

Quayson, Ato. "Postcolonialism and Postmodernism." In Tejumola Olanyan and Ato Quayson, eds., *African Literature: An Anthology of Criticism and Theory.* New York: Blackwell Publishing. 2013. 646-653.

Rabaka, Reiland. *Africana Critical Theory: Reconstructing the Black Radical Tradition, from W. E. B. Du Bois and C. L. R. James to Frantz Fanon and Amilcar Cabral.* New York: Lexinton Books. 2009.

2

NATIVISM AND THE QUEST FOR INDIGENOUS AESTHETICS: STRUCTURALIST AND POST-STRUCTURALIST READINGS

A structuralist reading of African indigenous drama reveals it as a hybrid domesticated genre where poets and dramatists return to indigenous oral tradition to fetch material and construct typically African oriented performance. Through the lenses of Structuralism, traditional oral poetics are scrutinized in their interconnectedness with drama and the very implications that such fusion has on the critical formulation of a theory in the African context come into play.

Structuralism is an intellectual movement which began in France in the 1950s and is first seen in the work of the anthropologist Claude Levi-Strauss (1908—) and the literary critic Roland Barthes (1915-1980). It is difficult to boil structuralism down to a single 'bottom-line' proposition, but if forced to do so one would say that its essence is the belief that things cannot be understood in isolation - they have to be seen in the context of the larger structures they are part of (hence the term 'structuralism'). Structuralism was imported into Britain mainly in the 1970s and attained widespread influence, and even notoriety, throughout the 1980s. David Lodge and Nigel Wood observe that the structures in question here are those imposed by our way of perceiving the world and organising experience, rather than objective entities already existing in the external world (Lodge and Wood 2008: 1). It follows from this that meaning or significance is not a kind of core or essence *inside* things: rather, meaning is always *outside*. Meaning is always an attribute of things, in the literal sense that meanings are *attributed* to the things by the human mind, not contained within them. But let's try to be specific about what it might mean to think primarily in terms of structures when considering literature.

Imagine that we are confronted with a poem, let's say Niyi Osundare's *Village Voices* (1984). One's immediate reaction as structuralist would probably be to insist that it can only be understood if one first has a clear notion of the genre which it parodies and subverts. Any single poem is an example of a particular genre, and the genre and the example relate to each other rather as a phrase spoken in English relates to the English language as a structure with all its rules, its conventions, and so on.

2.1. Ferdinand de Saussure in Africa: Structuralist Understanding of African Drama

Bringing structuralism in African dramatic literature and theatre studies context entails many things. To begin with, structuralism is basically a theory of language, signs and symbols. From that angle, a structuralist reading of African drama cannot ignore how signs and symbols relate to dramatic language in African context where theatre rests essentially on oral tradition, the spoken word and the poetics of orature and orality. What then is structuralism and how does it apply to African dramatic art? Though structuralism proper began, in the 1950s and 1960s, it has its roots in the thinking of the Swiss linguist Ferdinand de Saussure (1857-1913). Saussure was a key figure in the development of modern approaches to language study. In the nineteenth century linguistic scholars had mainly been interested in historical aspects of language (such as working out the historical development of languages and the connections between them, and speculating about the origins of language itself). Saussure concentrated instead on the patterns and functions of language in use today, with the emphasis on how meanings are maintained and established and on the functions of grammatical structures. But what exactly did Saussure say about linguistic structures which the structuralists later found so interesting? This can be summarised as three pronouncements in particular. Peter Barry (*Beginning Theory,* 2002) has summarized this into two major points. I agree with him. Firstly, Saussure emphasised that the meanings we give to words are purely *arbitrary,* and that these meanings are maintained by convention only. Words, that is to say, are 'unmotivated signs', meaning that there is no inherent connection between a word and what it designates. The word 'hut', for instance, is not in any way 'appropriate' to its meaning, and all linguistic signs are arbitrary like this. (There is the minor exception of a small number of onomatopoeic words like 'cuckoo' and 'hiss', but even these vary between languages.) Insisting that linguistic signs are arbitrary is a fairly obvious point to make, perhaps, and it is not a new thing to say (Plato said it in Ancient Greek times), but it is a new concept to *emphasise* (which is always much more important), and the structuralists were interested in the implication that if language as a sign system is based on arbitrariness of this kind then it follows that language isn't a reflection of the world and of experience, but a system which stands quite separate from it. This point will be further developed later. It transpires from the above that a meaningful reading of African modern plays cannot ignore the place of signs, symbols and figurative languages. If one turns to Ola Rotimi's *The Gods Are Not to Blame,* Wole Soyinka's *A Dance of the Forests* or *The Lion and the Jewel* or J. C De Graft's *Sons and Daughters* signs and symbols feature prominently to describe the true African cultural and sociological aesthetics.

Secondly, Saussure emphasised that the meanings of words are (what we might call) *relational.* That is to say, no word can be defined in isolation from other words. In the context of African drama, the outreaching of that formulation is important. In African traditional societies the culmination of orality in the cultural performances leaves to the critic the possibility to see meaning of words, values, proverbs, rites and rituals within every cultural artifact in relation to the communities' beliefs and practices. Thus, meaning is related to other compartments of the cultural lives of the folk people. Even in modern drama dominated by literacy ideologies are related to playwrights' specific political and cultural problems. The definition of any given word depends upon its relation with other 'adjoining' words. For example, in plays like Soyinka's *Kongi's Harvest,* that word 'rule' depends for its precise meaning on its position in a 'paradigmatic election or political coup', that is, a chain of words related in function and meaning each of which could be substituted for any of the others in a given sentence. For one thing, the reader needs to understand that Soyinka has set his play within the context of political transition from traditional authority to modern political power but the cultural context would be needed to understand how Soyinka does not agree with forceful political transition, the one Kongi is trying to force on Oba Danlola. Power should be transferred democratically with the test of the ballots, not seized by force. The same philosophical outlook can be observed in many of Ngugi's plays (*The Black Hermit, I Will Marry When I Want*), Ola Rotimi's *Our Husband Has Gone Mad Again* where the African patriots are all the time in conflicts with European imperialist or their representatives. The paradigmatic chain in this case might include the following: "hovel shed hut house mansion palace." The meaning of any one of these words would be altered if any one of the others were removed from the chain. Thus, 'hut' and 'shed' are both small and basic structures, but they are not quite the same thing: one is primarily for shelter (a night-watchman's hut, for instance), while the other is primarily for storage: without the other, each would have to encompass *both* these meanings, and hence would be a different word. Likewise, a mansion can be defined as a dwelling which is bigger and grander than a mere house, but not as big and grand as a palace. Thus, we define 'mansion' by explaining how its meaning relates to that of the two words on either side of it. If we have paired opposites then this mutually defining aspect of words is even more apparent: the terms 'male' and 'female', for example, mainly have meaning in relation to each other: each designates the absence of the characteristics included in the other, so that 'male' can be seen as mainly meaning 'not female', and vice versa. Similarly, we could have no concept of 'day' without the linked concept of 'night', no notion of 'good' without a 'bad' to define it against. This 'relational' aspect of language gave rise to a famous remark of Saussure's: 'In a language there are only differences, without fixed terms'. All words, then, exist in 'differencing networks', like these 'dyads', or paired opposites, and like the paradigmatic chain of 'dwelling place' words given earlier.

2.1.1. What Structuralist Critics Do

Peter Barry singles out three essential things that structuralists do:

1. They analyse (mainly) prose narratives, relating the text to some larger containing structure, such as: (a) the conventions of a particular literary genre, or (b) a network of intertextual connections, or (c) a projected model of an underlying universal narrative structure, or (d) a notion of narrative as a complex of recurrent patterns or motifs (Peter Barry 2002: 39).
2. They interpret literature in terms of a range of underlying parallels with the structures of language, as described by modern linguistics. For instance, the notion of the 'mytheme', posited by Levi-Strauss, denoting the minimal units of narrative 'sense', is formed on the analogy of the morpheme, which, in linguistics, is the smallest unit of grammatical sense. An example of a morpheme is the 'ed' added to a verb to denote the past tense (Ibidem).
3. They apply the concept of systematic patterning and structuring to the whole field of Western culture, and across cultures, treating as 'systems

of signs' anything from Ancient Greek myths to brands of soap powder. Roland Barthes's 1968 essay 'Analysing Narrative Structures', has identified five codes in narrative structures:

1. *The proairetic code:* This code provides indications of actions.
2. *The hermeneutic code:* This code poses questions or enigmas which provide narrative suspense.
3. *The cultural code* This code contains references out beyond the text to what is regarded as common knowledge.
4. *The semic code* This is also called the connotative code. It is linked to theme, and this code when organised around a particular proper name constitutes a 'character'. Its operation is demonstrated in the second example, below.
5. *The symbolic code* This code is also linked to theme, but on a larger scale, so to speak. It consists of contrasts and pairings related to the most basic binary polarities - male and female, night and day, good and evil, life and art, and so on. These are the structures of contrasted elements which structuralists see as fundamental to the human way of perceiving and organising reality (Barry 2002: 39).

2.1.2. Poststructuralism

Applying poststructuralism to African drama firstly leaves the critic with the viable option of killing the author and generating meaning independently with the latter's cultural and political background. Secondly, the critic will try to deconstruct the text in line with Derrida's epistemology. But let's go back to trace the literary background of post-syructuralism first, before seeing how that theory enlightens African drama. Post-structuralism emerged in France in the late 1960s (Ibidem). The two figures most closely associated with this emergence are Roland Barthes (1915-1980) and Jacques Derrida (1930-2004). Barthes's work around this time began to shift in character and move from a structuralist phase to a post-structuralist phase. The difference can be seen by comparing two different accounts by Barthes of the nature of the narrative, one from each phase, namely the essay "The Structural Analysis of Narrative" (first published in 1966 and reprinted in *Image, Music, Text,* ed. Stephen Heath, 1977) and "The Pleasure of the Text" (1973). The former is detailed, methodological and forbiddingly technical, while the latter is really just a series of random comments on narrative, arranged alphabetically, thereby, of course, emphasising the randomness of the material. Between these two works came the crucial essay "The Death of the Author" (1968) which is the 'hinge' round which Barthes turns from structuralism to poststructuralism. In that essay, he announces the death of the author, which is a rhetorical way of asserting the independence of the literary text and its immunity to the possibility of being unified or limited by any notion of what the author might have intended, or 'crafted' into the work. Instead, the essay makes a declaration of radical textual independence: the work is not determined by intention, or context. Rather, the text is free by its very nature of all such restraints. Hence, as Barthes says in the essay, the corollary of the death of the author is the birth of the reader. So, the difference between the 1966 essay and the 1973 book is a shift of attention from the text seen as something produced by the author to the text seen as something produced by the reader, and, as it were, by language itself, for as Barthes also says, in the absence of an author, the claim to decipher a text becomes futile. Hence, this early phase of poststructuralism seems to license and revel in the endless free play of meanings and the escape from all forms of textual authority. Later there is an inevitable shift from this textual permissiveness to the more disciplined and austere textual republicanism suggested in the quotation (p. 71) from Barbara Johnson. For her, deconstruction is not a hedonistic abandonment of all restraint, but a disciplined identification and dismantling of the sources of textual power.

African drama also admits the interpretative praxis of the death of the author when the audience at a given time of performance is rhapsodied in the reality of dramatic extase and the critic or the actor constructs new meaning from the observable suprasegmentals of the textual structure. More than that in actual performance, the text no more belongs to the author. Rather, it is butchered, cut into pieces by the intellectual memorizing faculties of the actors only to be represented in a new critical awareness to the audience. So, between the text, the actors and the audience, stands a gulf generated by the fact that the author is "murdered" to give way to the absent-author interpretations and meaning. It is not superfluous to add that in the process the critic and the actor play the same role in the extermination of the playwright.

The second key figure in the development of post-structuralism in the late 1960s is the philosopherJacques Derrida. Indeed, the starting point of post-structuralism may be taken as his 1966 lecture 'Structure, Sign and Play in the Discourse of the Human Sciences' (variously reprinted, most recently in abbreviated form in K. M. Newton's *Twentieth Century Literary Theory: A Reader* (Newton 1984). In this paper Derrida sees in modern times a particular intellectual 'event' which constitutes a radical break from past ways of thought, loosely associating this break with the philosophy of Nietzsche and Heidegger and the psychoanalysis of Freud. The event concerns the 'decentring' of our intellectual universe. Prior to this event the existence of a norm or centre in all things was taken for granted: thus 'man', as the Renaissance slogan had it, was the measure of all other things in the universe: white Western norms of dress, behaviour, architecture, intellectual outlook, and so on, provided a firm centre against which deviations, aberrations, variations could be detected and identified as 'Other' and marginal. In the twentieth century, however, these centres were destroyed or eroded; sometimes this was caused by historical events - such as the way the First World War destroyed the illusion of steady material progress, or the way the Holocaust destroyed the notion of Europe as the source and centre of human civilisation; sometimes it happened because of scientific discoveries - such as the way the notion of relativity destroyed the ideas of time and space as fixed and central absolutes; and sometimes, finally, it was caused by intellectual or artistic revolutions - such as the way modernism in the arts in the first thirty years of the century rejected such central absolutes as harmony in music, chronological sequence in narrative, and the representation of the visual world in art. It will be helpful simply to list some differences and distinctions between structuralism and post-structuralism, under the four headings below.

From a poststructuralist perspective, modern African drama and poetry have been perceived as two different literary genres. Yet, at important moments of their performance, these two subjects merge into one. Analyzing the extent to which African literature admits the concept of aesthetic fusion of literary genres (poetry and drama) as an African model of artistic expression becomes necessary in the comprehension of African drama as structuralist and post-structuralist-oriented discipline. The study asserts that embedded patterns between poetry and drama obtain in context where performing art is perceived not as an end but a means to an end. The specific question I am trying to answer is: when poetry becomes drama, what implications obtain for the audience and the reader with regard to the understanding of space and time in a context where literary creativity crosses borders? The present study explores the significant incidences on time and space in the context of African poetics, dramatics and literary culture.

Structuralism and poststructuralism present several critical positions by critics who have admitted the cohabitation and mutual influences of drama and poetry in African context without however explaining the incidences of the merging of these genres on time and space. Isidore Okpewho asserts that in Africa, oral poetry is read and sung (Okpewho 1990: 10). Kofi Anyidoho adjoins that the concept and practice of performance are central to artistic expression in African tradition (Anyidoho 2007: 383). Abdul-Rasheed Na'Allah opines that it means a lot for African poetry to get fulfilled through song and performance (Abdul-Rasheed Na-Allah 2003: 314). These scholarships have expressed at various degrees the possibility for poetry to be performed like drama, but seem to overlook the incidences that poetry performance has on time and space. Drama and poetry usually classified as two distinct genres have important cultural significance in African context. The literary tradition in African was predominantly oral before the advent of literacy. Even after the advent of literacy, creative writers continue to use oral tradition as ingredients in literary texts.

2.2. Theorizing Nativism: The Elements of Domestication

Nativism refers to the turning of African playwrights to African indigenous cultural materials to be used in the plays. These materials include rituals, festivals, epics, legends, myths, folktales, animal stories, proverbs, riddles. Such materials portray the originality of African folk life, and are used in the elements like setting, plot, characters and characterization.

2.2.1. Setting

Structurally speaking, setting refers to time and place at which the story of a play is set. It also includes the socio-political mood or atmosphere in which the narrative evolves. To many extents, the African play has been domesticated and discernible features can be perceived through the presentation of the setting. Place should be seen in relation with the time when the dramatic events unfold. The setting in most African plays are African local environment, the village square or city arena, the house of the inhabitant, the street, under a big tree. Whatever the place chosen by the dramatist, the most important thing is what makes that venue typically African. In Wole Soyinka's *The Lion and the Jewel* (1963) the setting is the village of Ilunjile, and the time is early sixties. Evidence of the setting is given by the presence of Baroka the village chief, while time is testified by Lakunle the village school master who, it is said, relates the time of the day, morning to that of the history, the advent of modernity in the village. This is another way of introducing the reader to the clashes between African values and European ones, the latter threatening to engulf the former. Lakunle wears an English outfit badly ironed and is teaching the students when Sidi the village jewel appears. In *The Swamp Dwellers* (1967) the time is precolonial period and the setting is the village swamp. In J. C. De Graft's *Sons and Daughters,* the story is set in Accra and the time is after the independences. Efua T. Sutherland's *Foriwa* is set in Kyerefaso along a street. Ama Ata Aidoo's *Anowa* is set in Yebi in precolonial time. Athol Fugard's *No Good Friday* and *My Children My Africa* are set in Township Johanesburg in South Africa. It can be noticed that majority of African plays are set either in the precolonial Africa or post-independent Africa. The setting has profound implications in African understanding. The precolonial Africa as setting testifies to the will of African playwright to reconstruct the genuine and authentic traditional life and institutions before the disruptive intrusion of the colonizers. African indigenous life is perceived by most African playwrights as the life that is typically original to the African character and personality, the soul and spirit of the African tempo is found incrusted in that peculiar life where drama is at its quintessential proclivity: the precolonial time lets transpire the indigenous folk life at the stage of self-searching and discovery. The communities are engaged in the difficult exercise of interpreting and understanding their environment, offering to explain supernatural phenomena, to define the future, to interpret the world. They usually resort to divination, the consultation of the oracles, ancestors, the interpretations of the omens, dreams and the reading of signs and symbols. Natural phenomena like thunder, lightning, rainbow, floods, droughts, rainfalls hold prime importance for the traditional folks, for these are always pregnant with meanings and are perceived as the media gods pass through to speak to humans. Rites, rituals, religious festivals, initiation into adulthood form the major psycho-spiritual spaces where the individual attempts to elevate his soul beyond the local realities. The African space is the convenient place where the individual freely practices his/her religion, express faith into the forces that are believed to control destiny. Setting, then goes beyond the factual understanding of the geographical sphere where actions unfold on the stage. It includes also transcendental realm that confers on the human the double necessity of cohabitation with the supernatural and that of interrelating with himself as agent of social space. Be it in the traditional sense of African religion or in the modern Christianized meaning, man entertains privileged relationships with God, at least in his own understanding. While the ritual serves as the medium of communication with the supernatural, the rites are used to mark the initiation of the youth into adulthood. The sociopolitical mood is often tense, with episodes of dramatic impartations of the soul marking the venture of the spirit into the metaphysical. Coupled with storytelling sessions, settings in the African traditional communities suggest beyond the local understanding of the African cultural presence, the necessity to unveil a sense of belonging to the fatherland, the place where parenthood holds the value of cultural lore and the sense of attachment to Africa. Setting stories in Africa holds for the playwright the duty of cultural memory, the moral necessity to create a cultural mirror that reflects the integrity of detachment with the foreign and a reconnection with the roots, the source and the cradle of typified indigenous life. The setting also adumbrates the collective memory committed to the search of communal ties that preclude interior and exterior rejuvenation of the ethno-discursive cultural heritage that was bequeathed by the elders and needs to be preserved for the future generations. Time, one should remember is fluid, the most unpredictable and uncertain element difficult to master. When reference is made to precolonial time, reference is being made to the moment when people were still in control of their history and destiny. Yet, the configuration of the postcolonial era calls to memory the recalibration of historical pointers where, it is no more the Africans per see who control their destiny, but rather the Europeans who embody the outline of the cultural forces that redirected the destiny towards the centers of new interests. In Ola Rotimi's *The Gods Are Not to Blame* and *Our Husband Has Gone Mad Again*, there are contrasted settings. While in the former the story is set in a purely indigenous African traditional milieu, the setting in the latter is a modern local Nigerian city amidst the hustle and whistle of electoral campaign. By sharply contrasting the two settings, the playwright attempts a confrontation of the traditional environment where the forces of nature or the deities are controlling the human fate and the postcolonial milieu where, the Africans reached a stage of self-control of their destiny. Yet, by comparing the two settings, the reader, and indeed the spectator can notice that man has not fundamentally improved in terms of mature choice about the politics of his own development. In *The Gods Are Not to Blame,* it is clearly said that man is overruled by his predestined fate which was preordained by the deities, so that he cannot change things that were written before his birth. It is said that Adewale was born after the predictions of the gods who declared he would kill his father and marry his mother. By so doing, he would bring one of the biggest scandals in the kingdom. After his birth, all the efforts Adewale and his parents made in order to avert that fate rather contributed to fulfill the prophecy of the gods. Here the setting is controlled and manipulated by the deities. Man is not a happy fulfilled being since he doesn't have the mastery of his destiny. Yet, in

Our Husband Has Gone Mad Again, man is now ruling his own life. The post-independence period was one where the Africans took their own destiny, to rule the continent. When Lejoka-Brown goes into politics, his vision of it is blurred by an uncontrollable desire for material gain, a detachment from the national interest and a devotion to luxury, materialism, opulence and debauchery. Through Lejoka-Brown and the kind of lavish life he leads, Rotimi shows not only the failure of the African to successfully handle his destiny, but the realities of human nature that still needs to be domesticated to be conform to the candid pattern of life. The African leaders of the post-independence period are said to be at odd with their sociopolitical environment for failing to address the burning issues of the continent' s development. Most profoundly, Ola Rotimi consciously avaoids giving ready-made answers to the human predicament, and gives to drama the functionality of provoking thought and appealing to consciences and calling to rectitude these human habits that are curved in an unbecoming manner.

2.2.2. Characters and characterization

Character refers to the introduction of the fictional role players and characterization is the very art of describing them in their dramatic functions. From a structuralist stand point, every character is the byproduct of his/her literary setting, the cultural, economic and political environments that saw him/her be born and grow. What does characterization hail for the reader in African context and how is it perceived as a key component of domestication? In the African plays, characterization is done to reflect the daily struggles of Africans to come to terms with the intricacies of their daily lives. They are depicted in controversial yet appealing backdrop of human frailty, struggling against the temptations of life. Characters are shown in their virtues and flaws, exhibiting the very shortcomings of human beings. It is not uncommon to see them fall under the sutures and cocktail of human folly. Characters with typical African background have the African character of community, gathering, mutual help, collective and collegial decision-taking. They develop a strong sense of togetherness so that individual problems are felt and shared by the community. The sharing of jobs according to gender is strongly highlighted. The societies are stratified according to age groups with hierarchical sense of respect and honor. In African plays, chiefs are held in high esteem and are usually surrounded by a huge harem of wives. They are engaged in the ritualistic contest of life unpredictability and struggle to overcome thereafter the very adamic corrupt nature of the body and soul. With modernization, the city is presented as a place of opportunities and the youth with a strong inclination towards rural exodus, the departure to the city to find employment, like in Wole Soyinka's *The Swamp Dwellers*. Either weighed in the scale of gender, sex, education, age, profession, geographical location, physical and intellectual maturity they exhibit practically more flaws than virtues, unveiling thereof the necessity of the African character to keep looking for improvement and yearn for perfection. The African characters are engaged in the drama of life, falling and rising everyday with the local realities. They are constantly struggling against conflicts (internal and external), disease, joblessness, corruption, injustice, death, unsuccessful matrimony, childlessness, juvenile delinquency, oppression of the weak by the strong, exploitation of the poor by the rich, political anarchy and monarchy, loneliness, group pressure. These flaws are exhibited to the detriment of the virtues to show the urge to improve morality in family circle, in political arena, and in community at large. Although these flaws are shared by all human beings without restriction of the geographical space, they are however presented in a specific manner in the African plays to highlight thereby the local realities pertaining to African communities and the specific ways of approaching these problems. If these flaws are common to all mankind, yet the way to apprehend them, to approach them differs from one geographical location to the other. Africans have their ways of solving their problems. Typically, it is common to observe the following approaches. There are customary ways of arranging marriage through the bride price negotiation in Ama Ata Aidoo's *Anowa*, Efua T. Sutherland's *The Marriage of Anansewa* and *Foriwa*. Job talks and negociations are observed in Frank Ogodo Ogbeche's *Harvest of Corruption*, peace talks and conflicts mediations are observed in Jane Taylor's *Ubu and the Truth Commission*. Ritual festivals, the communing together as a tribe is observed in Wole Soyinka's *A Dance of the Forest*. Collective petitions and trade union negotiations are seen in Ola Rotimi's *Hopes of the Living Dead*. Criminality and road banditry are presented in Femi Osofisan's *Once Upon Four Robbers*. Broadly speaking, characters in African theatre can be classified into the following groups: male and females in terms of sex and gender; educated, semi-educated and uneducated characters in terms of literacy and finally urban or rural in terms of their geographical location. But one last essential criteria is age and maturity. I will start with sex categorization. Male characters in African plays are major role players. In majority of Soyinka's plays, men hold positional power, perform intellectually demanding jobs, and command the politics of their societies. Not only that, they also control the lives of their women. Emperor Boky, Chief Anikura, Professor Bamgbapo, Colonel Moses hold all power of decision in *Opera Wonyosi,* Emperor Gunema, General Touboum in *A Play of Giants;* Oba Danlola, Kongi in *Kongi' s Harvest* are conferred the authority of ruling in politics, just like Baroka who is the Chief of Ilunjile in *The Lion and the Jewel*. To say that Soyinka is not fair to women would not be abusive talk. Women generally play minor roles and worst, they intervene as sex workers, individuals of loose virtue. At the intellectual level, they have less intellectual capability. Sidi and Sadiku in *The Lion and the Jewel,* De Madam, Lucie, Suky, in *Opera Wonyosi,* Madame Tortoise in *A Dance of the Forest,* Ochuole, Aloho and the proprietress of the Okpara hotel in *Harvest of Corruption*, are of loose virtues. They either succumb to the unscrupulous sexual machination of the males or they exchange their sexual services against material profit. It is a noticeable fact that there is no balance of power as far as gender equity is concerned.

For some dramatic techniques reasons and the call of the very function of theatre which is to entertain, playwrights present their characters with a strong sense of humour and satire. Soyinka presents Professor in *The Road* as a fool, Jero in *The Trial of Brother Jero* as a comic prophet, Lakunle in *The Lion and the Jewel* a foolish, Samson in *The Road* as a nain. Yet, other characters appear in the most serious and committed dexterity of their local environment and historical time. Such characters are Kimathi in Ngugi wa Thiong' o and Micere Guithae Mugo's *The Trial of Dedan Kimathi,* Gathoni, Wangeci in *I Will Marry When I Want,* Asimong in Femi Osofisan' s *Midnight Hotel,* Adewale in Ola Rotimi' s *The Gods Are Not to Blame,* to mention but a few. These characters are associated with the African diversity of life, styles, local concerns, material and immaterial needs, various socio-political moods at different moments of its historical and political struggles. Another important aspect of characterization is dressing. Africans in traditional setting are dressed in traditional attire, use local object, inhabit houses made of local material and use local musical instruments. In Soyinka' s *The Jero Plays,* Jeroboam the prophet wears agbada, a traditional outfit sewn in gown with a red cap. He has long beard hairs descending on his knees showing he is a Nazari, a person whose hair has never been shaved due to the fact that he was dedicated to the religious priesthood. While Ochuole and Aloho in *Harvest of Corruption* would prefer modern seductive dresses to meet the desire of their lovers, Anansewa' s father in *The Marriage of Anansewa* would like to wear modern expensive clothes to be able to flaunt his material success in the church when the time comes for the natives of the various days of the week to dance and bring their gifts. In *The Jero Plays*, Chume and Amope are presented as mentally and intellectually immature, unstable and dependent upon Jero' s machinations. In Chinyere Grace Okafor's *The New Toy Toy*, Aisosa is a female who is cheated on by her husband Winile. Yet, despite the fact that her husband has abandoned her for many years, she has displayed a strong character of endurance, patience and longsuffering. Characters are also presented from the perspective of their manner of thinking. In Soyinka' s *The Road,* Samson is presented as an intellectual dwarf who cannot count pass ten. In a play-within-a play episode, when discussing with Salubi, the question is put to him (Samson) what would he do if he became a millionaire, and the answer provided is, "first, I will marry ten wives". When asked why ten, he answered that he could not count pass ten.

2.2.3. Themes as Structurally Based

There is an interconnection between themes in African plays and the time and location of the events. A structuralist reading therefore takes into account the inter-relationship between temporal location of events, their spatial deployments and the thematic articulation or ideological concerns of the playwrights. Themes in the African plays pertain to the African realities. Since colonization, Africa has engaged in a dramatic struggle for self-recovery, socio-political stability and economic take-off. At cultural level, the continent has been fighting against Eurocentric cultural debasement, and stereotypes. Cultural themes include Afro-European clash of cultures, the rapid disintegration of moral and cultural values under the spell of European modernity and postmodernity. Thus, African dramatic literature discusses issues within the scope of these artifacts. Political theatrical themes are made to reflect that spectrum of sociopolitical concerns, access to political power and its management in Africa, political office tenure, corruption, bribery and educational efforts. Themes are as numerous and varied as the preoccupations and problems that assail the continent. Topics' ranges are among many others tradition versus modernity as in Soyinka' s *The Lion and the Jewel*, political betrayal as in Ngugi wa Thiong' o' s *The Black Hermit*, resistance of the masses as in Leke Ogunfeyemi's *Sacrifice the King,* polygamy and bad political games as in Ola Rotimi' s *Our Husband Has Gone Mad Again,* the fight against cultural stereotypes and struggle for equal opportunities among whites and blacks as in Athol Fugard' s *My Children! My Africa!* Advocacy for gender equity can be observed in Rotimi' s *Our Husband Has Gone Mad Again,* Efo Kodjo Mawugbe's *In the Chest of a Woman,* the struggle against retrogressive customs and traditions can be read in Ama Ata Aidoo' s *Anowa*. Freedom from apartheid oppression can be found in the plays of Zakes Mda, especially *And the Girls in their Sunday Dresses, The Final Dance, The Mother of All Eating, How Can the Sky Fall?,* and *The Bells of Amersfoort*. Prostitution and the attendant circumstances of its practice can be found in Athol Fugard's *Hello and Goodbye*. Wole Soyinka presents in *A Dance of the Forests* the gathering of the tribe, the struggle to achieve identity and cultural stability. He tackles and treats political banditry in *A Play of Giants, Opera Wonyosi, Kongi' s Harvest, Madmen and Specialists* and *King Baabu*.

2.2.4. Dramatic Material as Structurally Grounded

Modern African drama has used two types of material. Cultural lores from oral tradition and European dramatic aesthetics. The first material consists of myths, rites, rituals, legends, folktales, animal stories. The second material consists of plot, setting, stage, make-ups, to mention but a few. Myths are essentially creation myths explaining the origin of the universe, tentative explanations of the meaning of natural phenomena like thunder, death, sickness, madness, vulcanoes, floods, droughts, rain. The repertoire of myths in that range offer comic and simple short tales in which the hidden mysteries of the target phenomenon finds simplistic answer to satisfy the inquisitive questions of the indigenous folk namely the youngsters. Equally present in that category of myths explanations are the most perceptible practices in human condition: why is a man attracted to a woman? On the issue of dramatic material, Cosmo Pieterse has this to say

> The dramatic material itself is, generally speaking of two sorts. The political, social and economic situation in a continent full of varieties, tensions and possible solutions supplies one kind. The other consists of the rich resources for excitement and climax to be found in the religious and rituals, the fables and folk tales, the epic poems and praise poems of the past and present (Pieterse 1978: 2).

Myths are used to explain the mysteries of the world: the creation and origin of man, what attracts man to the woman, and to explain things that challenge human understanding like transcendental questions, the reasons of contradictions and the issues of human mind. Legends are used to trace the origin and historical itinary of tribes, communities and peoples. Among the Moba people in Togo, it is said that the Ancient of Days created the world. Among the Kabye, it is claimed according to their legends that they descended from heaven. The Fulani, a nomadic people of Africa south of Sahara believe that the universe was created from a drop of milk. The Baoule people from Ivory Cost believe that in their legendary travel, under the leadership of Queen Poko, they were obliged to sacrifice a child at the big river to have the hippopotamus bridge the river for them to pass. The hypopotamus was thus acting under the command of a deity. African theatre uses myths as a strong material to reconstitute life before the advent of colonization. Every culture has its own folklore and myths that have been passed on from generation to generation. Because Africa is comprised of hundreds of different cultures, it is consequently celebrated for thousands of mythical stories and folklore. Many of Africa's legends and myths encompass common themes, including life after death, world creation and origin, animals, and even the geography of the land. They also often deal with multiple gods and spirits. There are also many legends and beliefs that evolve around life after death and the spirits of the ancestors. The San tribesmen, for example, believe that their ancestors who have died turn into stars. I said earlier that African drama borrowed aesthetics, namely plot, setting, character creation, from European drama. But in African theatrical aesthetics, there is one aspect of the performance that should not be ignored: it is the relationship between poetry performance and dramatic performance. At a given point, the two genres fuse into one.

Here is an example of how poetry performance metamorphoses into dramatic performance. In the northern part of Togo, during the storytelling session, the performance is carried out by the Fulani poet dressed in traditional attire, with a pair of traditional drum called *lonŋ* hung on his shoulders and held tightly under his left armpit. and the performance takes place in moonlight in the village square. The audience is composed of youngsters, women, children and a few elders who usually sit in a semi-circle. The stage is essentially made of a layer of firewood or planks on which stands the poet. He is the centre of attention for the audience whose attention is engaged by the narrative voice of the performer. The performance usually takes place at night and begins with the beating of the *lonŋ* to capture attention. What is mostly captivating in performance are the narrative tone of the poet, his gestures, his bending and stretching body, his acrobatic movement that are rhyming with the beatings of the drums. There is a certain cadence in the story's episode where the poet's voice raises or lowers in a melodious tone when a song, a verse or a musical mime is necessary to be used to punctuate or emphasize a cross section of the story. The audience's participation is vivid as they punctuate the story with regular intruding of handclapping, shouts of approval or disapproval, mimicry and gestures. Donatus Nwoga gives us the detailed version of the Fulani creation myth.

> At the beginning, there was a huge drop of milk.
> Then Doondari came and he created the stone:
> Then the stone created iron,
> And iron created fire,
> And fire created water,
> And water created air.
> Then Doondari descended the second time,
> And he took the five elements and he shaped them into man.
> But man was proud:
> Then Doondari created blindness, and blindness defeated man.
> But when blindness became too proud,
> Doondari created sleep, and sleep defeated blindness;
> But when sleep became too proud,
> Doondari created worry, and worry defeated sleep;
> But when worry became too proud,
> Doondari created death, and death defeated worry;
> But then death became too proud:
> Doondari descended for the third time,
> And he came as Gueno, the eternal one:
> And Gueno defeated death (Nwoga 1967: 25).

Thus, dramatic material of modern African theatre is immersed into folklore, mythic elements, masks and masquerade. Masquerade refers both to performances given by mask characters and mask performer. Mask dances and performing are very developed among the Igbo and Yoruba communities in Nigeria.

2.2.5. Language

Post-structuralism in African theatre advocates the deconstruction of discourse and the reconstruction of the same discourse in a different aesthetic contruction. African dramatic language shows a detachment of European model of linguistic purism and a domestication of that language to African setting and local concerns. Language is a stamp mark of domestication in different ways. First, the conversation techniques, second, the greetings and formal meeting introductions, the proverbial quotations and other figures of speech.

2.2.5.1. Greetings in Formal Meetings Introductions

In the plays of the first and second generations of African playwrights, greetings take the form of formal stoke exchange among village folks, friends, fellows and elders. The address forms are friendly, mixed with casual jokes, teasings and hilarious expressions. African indigenous people spend time to greet and inquire about neighbours' problems and concerns. It is not uncommon to see people spending about five to ten minutes greeting each other. People are concerned about and show interest into their neighbours' problems. The following example is taken from Femi Euba's *The Game* (1978):

> Awero (low voice): Idioko, wake up! ... Idioko, wake up!... Idioko!...
> Idioko (jerking): H' m? Can a poor beggar not even sleep peaceably out here – on the common pavement?...
> Awero: It is me silly fool.
> Idioko: H' m? Awero? Where are you going so early in the morning?
> Awero: shhhh! ... Don' t wake my husband up ... here ...here
> Awero: Take two shillings. I dreamt it was my lucky day today... but I thought it began with two pounds!
> Awero: Sh! Do the job well. I will reward you greatly in the evening.
> Idioko: Job? What job' s this?
> Awero: I want you to watch my husband' s movements, like a cat does a rat. And if he asks anything of you, throw him off the track as much as possible (*TG, OAP*: 85).

From the extract, it transpires that the early morning conversation, usually accompanied with greetings is painted with African local ways of expressing familiarity, tenderness, care and communal love. Apart from greetings we also have proverbs, jokes, songs which are developed in the next section.

2.2.5.2. The Paradigm of Proverbs

Proverbs are strong narrative devices in many African plays. The first generation of African playwrights have consistently drawn on African folk life with its rich galore of proverbial statements, wise allusive sayings and morality-teaching puns to construct their dramatic narratives. From Soyinka's plays *The Lion and the Jewel, A Dance of the Forests, Kongi's Harvest, Death and the King's Horseman,* Ola Rotimi's *The Gods Are Not to Blame,* Bode Sowande's *Farewell to Babylone,* John Ruganda's *Black Mamba, The Good Woman of Setzuan* and *Floods* Ngugi wa Thiong'o's *The Black Hermit* and *I Will Marry When I Want* Ama Ata Aidoo's *Anowa,* Efua T. Sutherland's *The Marriage of Anansewa, Edufa, and Foriwa,* and many other commandable plays. Proverbs are pitchy ground level materials the dramatists use to convey traditional African wisdom. In no aspect of its form is the African play more "oral" and "traditional" than in its use of proverbs, a fact that has been acknowledged by critics in essays and monographs (Lindfors 1973:73-93; Obiechina 1975:155-82; and Shelton 1969).

Narrative proverbs are autonomous stories that appear in different plays and narrative registers within different structural linguistic plans and are embedded inside larger, more inclusive narratives. They function as images, metaphors, and symbols and advance the meanings and formal qualities of the narratives in which they occur. They are extensively used in the works of African playwrights—in the plays of female and male African dramatists, in those of older and newer writers, in works produced in the different regions of Africa south of the Sahara—and they extend across broad ideological and generic divides (Emmanuel Obiechina 1993: 123). Because narrative proverbs in African plays cut across gender, genres, ideologies, regions, and generations, it is legitimate to assume that their use is an essential feature of the poetics of modern African drama, a feature that derives from the interplay of creative principles of oral and literary traditions (Ibidem). Obviously, the sort of rigid distinction that some critics aspire to establish between the story as a product of orality and the play as a product of literacy breaks down when applied to the African play. It breaks down because it does not accommodate the poetics of narrative synthesis in which oral and literate narrative forms and styles interfuse.

But Osofisan' s *Tegonni* provides a good example of dramatic embeddedness into poetry through the medium of songs and proverbs. Proverbial display twists the language into poetic verve in the sense that it brings rhetoric to bear with poetic style. Some proverbs are usually performed to the musical accompaniment of *gangan* or *gbedu* drums. Samuel Alaba Akinwotu in his approach to the plays of Osofisan's play affirms that he:

> Uses proverbs to draw home his message. Yoruba proverbs like proverbs in many other African societies, are used to embellish

and support arguments during conversation and other oratory events. In the social life of the Yoruba people, proverbs constitute a powerful rhetorical device for the shaping of moral consciousness, opinions and beliefs. ... Proverbs have aesthetic value, especially with the quality of their poetic language and richness of imagery (Akinwotu 2009: 344).

Proverbs in a play contribute to enrich the poetic style, to make the performance bear local colour and create an African atmosphere. Beyond their role as cultural devices explaining the philosophy of the speaker who uses them, they add poetic dimension to the language. Poetic language, usually loaded with figures of speech such as metaphors, similes, allegories, synecdoche, metonymy, to mention but a few, is better conveyed through proverbial statements. This particular technique is of great interest to Osofisan. He piles up poetic language through proverbs and songs to voice out his Yoruba culture.

In the play, the elderly characters such as Chief Isokun and Chief Labiyi express ideas through the medium of proverbs. For instance,

> Isokun … He is a lion who has been stung in the foot by an ant! He is shocked that it pains (T: 78). No lizard enters a house, unless there is a crack already in the wall (*T: 79*).

The two proverbs, though used in a play, highlight poetic inclination in their performance. In the first one, Chief Isokun uses the metaphorical name 'lion' to designate the governor whose authority as political leader has been downgraded by a simple girl Tegonni. The speaker Isokun is being confused and surprised by this type of insolence displayed towards the governor. The second proverb adumbrates the lack of unity and mutual solidarity among Africans, a situation that is one of the principal cause of our defeat in our battle against imperialists in colonial time. That lack of unity continues to operate in contemporary Africa where Europeans continue to pull the strings of political power to their advantage. Although the cultural implications of these proverbs are African continent-wide, the poetic inflections are of the most interest as they operate like poetic energizers.

In African context, poetry is performed more and more like drama with actor, audience, stage, dance, spectacle, mime, scenery, and an interactive actor/audience dialogue. The spectacle created can bring spectators to experience emotional tension and catharsis. Hybridism refers to the quality of something which results from the combination of different elements to form a new element. It is an heterogenous byproduct. In the context of African drama and theatre, hybridism compels great attention. Modern African drama and art form are hybrid. They combine the oral tradition elements which were predominantly in the cultural lore of traditional Africa before the advent of modern school form and literacy. Since then, oral tradition elements: myth, legend, folktales, proverbs, songs, etc, have been used as raw materials in the manufacturing of modern African literature in its written form. Drama being one literary genre, actively uses these elements of oral tradition to create storyline, shape ideas, model plot and adapt setting to match the originality of African cultural thought, and philosophy of life. Akin Odebunmi in his article "Pragmatic Functions of Crisis – Motivated Proverbs in Ola Rotimi's *The Gods Are Not to Blame*" (www.linguistik-online.de/33_08/odebunmi.pdf) has conducted the study on the socio-political and cultural functions of proverbs. His findings as released convey the following information.

The social crisis situations in *The Gods*, defined in terms of activities relating to day to day experiences of the Kutuje people including the people's encounter with nature, cover the outbreak of epidemics in Kutuje, divination/riddle of birth concerning Odewale and the contest between Odewale and King Adetusa, the former monarch of Kutuje (Ibidem). Although it bears some political colouration later in the play, the outbreak of epidemics in Kutuje, as seen at the actual point of occurrence is social as it is linked with the wrath of the gods, with no association with the political affairs of the community. But the contest between Odewale and King Adetusa is strictly social as it is over land, and not in any way, at least at the point of the contest, connected with the latter's throne (Ibidem). What is known to the two contesters at the instance is one trying to rob the other of his property. The proverbs used in these situations derive their sources from the fauna and flora resources of the Yoruba, their geography and their social structures. Driven by the exigencies of the situations already mentioned, the characters using CMPs: counsel, accuse, challenge, persuade and encourage. In the dialogue between Odewale and the priest of Ifa in Act 3 Scene3, we have the following utterances:

Voice:	You have a curse on you, son.
Odewale:	What kind of curse, Old one?
Voice:	You cannot run away from it, the gods have willed that you will kill your father, and then marry your mother!
Odewale:	Me! Kill my own father, and marry my own mother?

Voice:	It has been willed.
Odewale:	What must I do then not to carry out this will of the gods?
Voice:	'Nothing. To run away would be foolish. *The snail may try, but it cannot cast off its shell.* Just stay where you are (*TGANTB* : 60).

By the proverb, "the snail may try, but it cannot cast off its shell", Voice co-textually reiterates the earlier statement that: "You cannot run away from it, the gods have willed it [...]" and "it has been willed". He makes reference to the faunal resources of his environment, i.e. the snail and the shell of snail. The proverb rides on a metaphor. The interpretation is assisted by a shared cultural knowledge, Odewale being a member of the culture i.e. Yoruba, in which the proverb exists, and shared social knowledge, given the circumstance necessitating the use of the proverb (Akin Odebunmi 2008). All these are complemented by the relevance of the proverb to the question that stirs Odewale's mind. Odewale is thus given all these contextual factors, able to draw appropriate inferences. To him, as projected in his proverbial response move: "Continue to stay in the house of my father and mother? Oh, no, *the toad likes water but not when the water is boiling* (*TGANTB*: 60).

His interpretation of the proverbial utterance of the Ifa priest that he should leave the environment completely to avoid the tragedy is wise. What the priest of Ifa, with "the snail[...]", practs therefore is counseling: he has the fore knowledge of the danger lying ahead of Odewale and foresees him staying in his present environment as a probable solution. Other cases of counseling, using proverbs, are found on pages 14 and 60.

Many proverbs are used to accuse. Examples abound on pages 9, 10 and 46. For example, when an epidemic breaks out in Kutuje, the townspeople gather at the palace to register their protest over their assumed non-caring attitude of Odewale. Some of their spokespersons speak in the following proverbial language:

> Second citizen: *When the head of a household dies, the house becomes an empty shell.* (9)
> Third citizen: *When the chameleon brings forth a child, is not that child expected to dance?* (9)
> Second citizen: *When rain falls on the leopard, does it wash it off its spots.*
> Fifth citizen: *How long must feverish birds tremble in silence before their keeper?*
> (*TGANTB*: 10)

The proverbs largely derive from the fauna of the Yoruba. They make reference to the social structure of the Yoruba community, the genetic dancing skills of the chameleon, the permanent nature of the spots on the leopard and the relationship between birds and their keepers. Each of these demands SCK (shared cultural knowledge) and SSK (shared situational knowledge) for it to appear as an *accusation* posed to Odewale for not being caring. In fact, in the proverbial utterance of Fifth Citizen, there is a subtle pract of challenging: "How long must feverish birds [...]", implicating that their seeming undue respect for the king might soon end if he continues to be insensitive to their plights.

In his response to the accusation of his people, Odewale, first, subtly *persuades* and, later, *encourages,* also using proverbs:

> You do me great wrong, therefore to think that, like a rock in the middle of a lake, forever cooled by flowing waters, I do not know, and cannot know the sun's hotness that burns and dries up the open land. (*TGANTB*: 10)

Odewale refers to some geographical phenomena and atmospheric conditions in the Yoruba community i.e. a rock, a lake, the location of a rock in flowing waters, the hotness of the sun and its effect on the open land, the knowledge of all of which the audience are expected to share with Odewale. The proverb, which is a metaphor, states that the rock located in the middle of the lake experiences no hotness. The metaphor implies that Odewale sees his people as nursing the feeling that he luxuriates in the royal grandeur without devoting any attention to their degenerate conditions. What he practs, practically speaking, is *explain* his true position and role in the matter to them, contrary to their feeling. This point is further made in another proverb, performing the pragmatic function of *persuading*:

> Have I been sleeping? If so, I am sick in the head: for only a madman would go to sleep with his roof on fire (*TGANTB:* 11).

After he has convinced the people about the role he plays, he engages proverbs to *encourage* them to administer herbs properly and patiently. Two of these proverbs are important. The first appears in response to Third Woman's complaints:

Third woman:	I boiled mine longer – a long time I even added *dogoyaro* leaves to it.
Odewale:	And how does the body feel?
Third woman:	Not as well as the heart wishes, my lord.
Odewale:	Our talk is of illness, sister. To get fully cured one needs patience. *The moon moves slowly but by daybreak it crosses the sky.*

(14)

The proverb, "the moon [...]" reformulates, the co-textual expression: "[...] one needs patience". The clarity of the proverb is not in question, given the general social context, the co-text, SCK and SSK. Another pract of *encouragement* follows Fourth Woman's question:

Fourth woman:	My trouble is that I drink medicine from herbs, my husband drinks it too. But the children [...] I don't know how to give it to them so that they can drink it too.
Odewale:	*By trying often, the monkey learns to jump from tree to tree without falling* (*TGANTB*: 14).

Odewale evokes the SCK of Fourth Woman to link up the monkey's several attempts leading eventually to skillful acrobatics, with her own experience. This is not clearly reformulated but if SSK is appealed to in addition to SCK, no problem of interpretation would be expected.

2.2.5.3. Political Crisis-Motivated Proverbs

Political crisis-motivated proverbs in *The Gods* (describing activities that centre exclusively on the political affairs of the community, especially as related to problems surrounding Odewale's succession to the throne and the complications that attend the succession) are used during the following occasions: when Aderopo brings a message from Baba Fakunle; when the killer of King Adetusa is being sought; when the leaders of Kutuje have actual physical contact with Baba Fakunle; and after Baba Fakunle has left. These situations make the proverb user to draw on the social-cultural experiences of the people, their medical perspectives, their flora and their fauna. Practs of *cautioning, threatening, accusing, veiling, prioritizing* and *admitting* characterize the various exchanges.

The political crisis in the play begins with the message Aderopo brings from Baba Fakunle when sent to inquire about the cause of the epidemics in the land. The following transaction is very important in this regard:

Aderopo:	Very well. If the oracle says the curse, your highness is on a man.
Second Chief:	A man!
Odewale:	And who is this man?
Aderopo:	I don't know, your highness, the oracle did not say.
Odewale:	Very well. This man – the cursed one – what did he do, what offence?
Aderopo:	The man killed another man […] King Adetusa – my own father
	[…]
Odewale and chiefs:	King Adetusa!
Ojuola:	Who are we to trust, then?
Aderopo:	That was why I feared to speak, mother. *Until the rotten tooth is pulled out, the mouth must chew with caution.*

(*TGANTB*: 20-21)

Aderopo's proverb though immediately activated by Ojuola's question, "Who are we to trust?" is on the larger scale motivated by the political crisis on ground. The proverb is a medical one.

However, modern African drama uses European literary forms and traditions to create written literature and stage performance. Example of plays with elements of oral tradition like myth, legends, folktales, proverbs, songs, riddles, rituals include Ola Rotimi's *The Gods Are Not to Blame*, Wole Soyinka's *A Dance of the Forests, Kongi's Harvest, The Strong Breed*, Femi Osofisan's *No More the Wasted Breed*, Ama Ata Aidoo's *Anowa*, Efua T. Sutherland's *The Marriage of Anansewa*, Yawo Asare's *Ananse in the Lands of Idiots*, to mention but a few. The status of African theatre has been a contested terrain between Afrocentric critics and European-oriented ones. Many claims have been made by European-oriented critics about the recognition of modern African theatre as of European origin: Oyenka Owomoyela for example is in this first group. While Afrocentric critics maintain the argument that African drama and theatre were strongly established in African cultural practices long before the advent of European education literacy. Bakary Traore, Oyin Ogumba, Wole Soyinka, Femi Osofisan are in that group. On this debate, Mzo Sirayi has this to say:

> Cross-cultural influence is a widespread phenomenon. In Africa precolonial theatre and European drama traditions have had an impact on contemporary African drama. Elements of pre-colonial and European drama traditions continue to coexist in contemporary African drama. Most African playwrights build their plays on both traditions. They borrow from pre-colonial theatre because of a need to return to indigenous roots, while at the same time, drawing on European drama traditions, for African theatre cannot operate in isolation. To put it differently, indigenous and foreign influences have contributed to the development of contemporary African drama (Mzo Sirayi 2012: 136).

Contemporary drama may therefore be seen, as the meeting place of both precolonial African and European drama traditions. Many African playwrights base their plays on oral genres, such as oral history, epic, myth, animal stories, integrating these with European drama traditions, such as auditorium, stage, scenery, lights, actors, stage directions and rehearsals. Some African playwrights borrow their themes from the oral forms mentioned above, whereas others draw on indigenous cultural practices such as bride-price, marriage rituals, initiation ceremonies, ancestral sacrifices, the authority of parents over their children, juvenile rebellion and its consequences, etc. and combine them with European drama tradition.

2.3. The Interface of Interculturalism

In the context of drama in Africa, interculturalism can be described as the interaction between and fusion of both European (foreign) and African (indigenous) traditions in contemporary African drama (Fischer-Lichte quoted by Mzo Sirayi 2012: 138). One also needs to understand the fact that throughout history, all cultures of the world have tended increasingly to transplant elements of foreign theatre traditions into their own productions. Bernth Lindfors (1973: 11-12) argues that some African writers try to integrate the two cultures artistically, welding European form to African matter so skillfully that no one can tell without careful inspection precisely how and where they have been joined. This is a hybrid tradition, because it is a distinctive new tradition that has evolved from the two older traditions, that is precolonial African theatre and European drama tradition. Therefore, modern African drama is heir of two traditions: traditional African literature and western literature.

2.3.1. Cultural Performances in Africa

Cultural performances in Africa are the repositories of most communities' beliefs and indigenous folk life. Organised around traditional festivals and ritual performances they are celebrated around specific dates and calendrifications to rejuvenate and update the cultural memory of the clans and re-enact the faith in the supernatural. Despite the influences of Christianity, these performances have outlived the westernization of African societies. Theatre scholars trace the roots of African drama to these cultural performances. Martin Bentham and colleagues speculate that

> The roots of theatre in Africa are ancient and complex and lie in areas of community festival, seasonal rhythm and religious ritual as well as in the works of court jesters, professional entertainers, and storytellers. Since the 1950s, in a movement that has paralleled the political emancipation of so much of the continent, there has grown a theatre that comments back from the colonized world to the world of the colonialists, that discusses the shared experience in the shared languages and reasserts its own cultural and linguistic integrity (Benham, Hill and Woodyard 2004: 3).

In African context, performance carries a deep significance due to a number of cultural factors. First, African literature has long been rooted in oral tradition before the advent of literacy. Oral tradition brings together a huge body of artistic and cultural artifacts that are tied up to people's life and philosophical outlook. Among the body of work that sprawl into oral tradition are myths, legend, folktales, proverbs, riddles which are the heart and soul of African traditional life, wisdom and philosophy. Couched in the mythological conception and interpretation of prehistorical societies, these formulae serve to explain the dramatic mood that unfolded at the origin of human life, and to dive into life mysteries for more critical apprehension of man and his environment. Isidore Okpewho corroborates this idea by saying:

> There are many situations in which poetry was, and still is spoken or sung in traditional African society, and it would be better for us to see the poets within the context in which they operate. Some of these situations are somewhat restricted in the sense that the poet

is charged with chanting a specific type of poetry [...] Poets in this category would be found in the royal court of communities ruled by kings, or else attached to wealthy or powerful men in societies dominated by privileged men. Among the Mandika of Western Africa, the griot was traditionally a court poet attached to the king for the purpose of singing the king's glories and recording in his songs important historical events surrounding the ruling family (Okpewho 1988: 4).

In the mastery and retelling art of folktales, myths and legends, griots are versed in the oral performance. Griots are elderly people who usually serve in the traditional kings' palace. By virtue of tradition, they are trained by their forebears in the history and culture of the land and are entrusted with the responsibility to transmit them to the future generations. The means usually chosen to exercise that art of traditional pedagogy is oral performance. Griots are traditional poets who embody the entirety of the cultural information, the archives of history and master the political formula of the kingship and chieftaincy functioning mechanics. How they translate the cultural information into dramatic performance is an essential point of departure in this essay. In the African traditional pedagogy, it is believed that the audience better captures words through the representations of the images that unfold in the story and that are shown and brought forth before the audience through the medium of allusions, metaphors, similes, comparisons and explanations.

I would like to come back to the Fulani creation story to bring out a number of facts. In a literary context, this poem would have been read like a text. But a simple reading wouldn't have given to it the entire imagery that supports the cultural understanding of the Fulani myth and legend. The very mimicry of the poet playing Doondari the Divine Creator articulating the dramatic picture of creation and the first apparition of man on earth gives the audience the vitality and vibrancy of live experience. The Fulani philosophy of the creation of the universe finds artistic expression and cultural support in the dramatic-poetic performance of this poem where verbal art mixed with theatrical skills to create real drama. It is not far-fetched, considering the way two genres merge into one interpenetrated hybrid art, to say that significant incidences occur during this cultural display of the indigenous folk tradition.

The first incidence in this context is the difficulty to explain even to the very witnesses of this live performance that the artistic verve that is unfolding in their very eyes is the fusion of different esthetical genres and that in the supportive documentation of the oral performance, such genres should have been split into two entities: drama and poetry. What obtains from this critical position is that cultural tradition is able to do what literary text is not able to do. This means written literature in Western (European) understanding of the term is not able to fuse drama and poetry to obtain a third genre. This, oral tradition has done it in the African context. So, drama and poetry are embedded in a complexity of interpenetration relationship that lets the audience, the educated one especially, the embarrassment to decide on the genre of that hybridized formula of performance. Kate Mcgowan, a structuralist critic asserts that

> [...] structuralism is primarily concerned with the study of structures – that is, how things get organized into meaningful entities – as well as the structural relationships between things. Its premise is that whatever things mean, they will always come to mean by virtue of a set of underlying principles which can be determined by close analysis. The idea is that the world without structures is meaningless – a random and chaotic continuum of possibilities. What structures do is to order that continuum, to organize it according to a certain set of principles, which enable us to make sense of it. In this way, structures make the world tangible to us, conceptually real, and hence meaningful. Once discovered, so the theory goes, structures show us how meanings come about, why things seem to be just the way they are and, by implication, what might lead us to contest them (Mcgowan 2006: 4).

In clear terms, structures are the referentials that help to decode the fragmented meaning of texts. Such texts are organized around ideas, which in turn are structured into sentences and concepts. Every concept is a unit in the structuralist understanding which is bound into a whole to produce a syntactic meaning. When applied to African dramatic performance, that a structuralist reading of the poetic text meant to be performed will unveil the second incidence in which this oral performance has on time and space. I will begin with time. Time is defined as the duration in which an action or an event takes place. In the cultural memory of the Fulani, time carries a double meaning. The first meaning is the formulation of the time as a linear, unlimited space which only the cosmic force represented in the poem by Gueno controls its fluidity. Here, the spatio-temporal setting of the creation scene is unknown. People usually refer to it with unprecise formulae such as "in the beginning", "since time immemorial", "since the world was created". This mastery failure of time precision has an influence, maybe a positive one for the performer who will play on the mythological trust of the audience to credit the story with mythic realism. The space is also undetermined. The only informing fact that the performer has is that the story took place somewhere in the far distant place. The rebuttal that this story would meet in Western cultural understanding would be its lack of spatial accuracy. This means in African traditional context where oral poetry can be performed in dramatic manner – like the case of the Fulani creation story above - the abstraction of time is a gain for the performer, as the audience is carried in a sublimely distancing of facts.

The second example where one can clearly perceive embedded patterns of drama and poetry is the *halo* poetry performance among the ewe community. The ewe community inhabit the coastal line of Ghana, Togo and Benin. The *Halo* poetry is performed in dramatic aesthetics with songs, drums, dances, rattle beatings, acrobatic demonstrations:

1	2
It is in the hands of destiny	Hm! Hm! Hm! Beware
our life is in the hands of the Creator.	I will place a load on Kodzo's head
Songsters, listen.	Nugbleza informed me that
My Creator sent me this way.	It is the women of Tsiame
he gave me nothing not even looks.	Who goaded Kodzo into my song.
So the rich ones howl in the lanes -	Questioners, this becomes evil firewood
proclaiming their wealth.	He's gathered; his hands decayed
Dunyo says I know not what to do	his feet decayed.
My Creator gave me songs.	I am the poet I am not afraid of you.
I will not refuse them	Kodzo. winding the air, his anus agape.
My song came from the Creator's house	His face long and curved.
simmering in my head	like the lagoon egret's beak
Please, I say gently.	Call him here I say call him.
Whose legs are larger than the hippo	he is the man who eats off the farm
Let somebody abuse me	he hasn't planted (Ibidem).
then I will tell it to him (Campb II 2002: 45).	

These songs are performed orally since they pertain to the verbal art form. Yet, what strikes attention is their highly dramatic language load, their tonality and theatrical contour when placed within their context of performance. The two poetic songs are declamatory in tone and oratorical in mood. They are loaded with emotional tension. Poem 2 tends to be aggressive in its message. These are the typical feature characteristics of *halo* songs intended to attack the flaws of the addressee. They were composed in traditional ewe society at the time when literacy was in its primal infancy and the major part of the population was yet to learn the art of writing. What is of most interest here is their performance aesthetics which gather all the elements of dramatic performance: stage, audience, gestures, movements, musical accompaniment, costume, and make-ups. The audience is composed of two groups and every group summons its cantor or talented poet.

To explain this better, let me turn to Kofi Anyidoho, one of the most renowned contemporary Ghanaian poets. Anyidoho has distinguished three levels of dramatic performance for a poem. The first level is what he calls "dramatic reading":

> At this level, the poet and the poem are still somewhat bound to the written or printed text. But by the dramatic use of body language, voice, pause, tempo, gesture, and other paralinguistic techniques, the poetry is lifted from the cold print on a page and energized into a warm and living experience, an experience with which the audience spontaneously identifies and which it may enhance through various degrees of participation and through encouraging applause or comments [...] However, one of my basic contentions [...] is that, given the reality of poetry written in a cultural environment where the dominant mode of communication is oral, the printed word may not necessarily be the definitive act of publication (Anyidoho 2007: 384).

Anyidoho's idea comes to highlight what the structuralist critics call "a network of intertextual connection" which refers the intertextual interconnection between drama and poetry. Poetic texts merge into dramatic performance to congeal the transversality of poetic and dramatic genres. The poet becomes the theatrical actor and the audience becomes the artistic receptacle structurally bound in the creative ethos of oral performance.

The second level of performance is when poetry, music and action fuse to give birth to a live performance. This occurs in modern poetry where the poet actually reads or sings the poem in accompaniment of the drums, gong and rattle. The written text is only a reference as the poet interjectionally gets detached from the text to concentrate on his voice, dance and gestures. The type of performance there brings face to face the poet and the audience who are emotionally fully involved. The incidence it has on time is that the performance makes time fluid and less perceptible by the audience:

> The event just described takes us beyond the level one performance where the writer continues to hold on to a written or printed text. At the second level of poetic performance, the dramatic impact is frequently intensified by an ever-greater liberation from the text as cold print. Indeed, such performance is frequently marked by a situation in which, even though the poet may still be holding the text, he performs with little or no reference to it. The ideal situation occurs when the text has been memorized, or rather assimilated into an artistic design that makes for spontaneity of performance, reinforced by a more elaborate use of body language and paralinguistic devices (Anyidoho, op. cit, 385).

Here, Anyidoho brings in the idea of the poet detaching himself from the text as an important element that contribute to consolidate the performance aesthetics. Most importantly, his point can be useful in insinuating the incidence on time. The detachment of the poet from his text helps him to gain some more time, to throw the audience into a live spectatorship and make the performance less boring. In other words, direct performance without the interference of the texts impacts on the fluidity of the time in performance and engages the total attention of the audience by expelling snaps of inattention. Musical ingredients are also recommendable as they contribute to reinforce the rhythm of the poem. In addition to that, music engages the audience's attention in the performance by captivating, apostrophing, and questioning the soul of the spectators.

Another usual element of performance at this level is the use of music and simultaneous mimed enactments of the situations depicted in the unfolding poetic text. The music may in fact be incorporated into the text of the poem (Ibidem). To corroborate the importance of dramatic performance in poetry, Abdul-Rasheed Na'Allah takes the example of Niyi Osundare's poetry and asserts:

> Almost every critic of Osundare extols how wonderful a performance poet he is, usually citing the involvement of oral traditions in his poetry […] It is practically impossible for Osundare to suspend dancing, beating of drums, playing flutes, or goje, when performing his poetry – even when his refrains are not written in Yoruba language, as they often are not, like in his 'Songs of the Season' column in the *Tribune newspaper* ('Bard 1-47'), or when Osundare does not add any refrain at all. Yoruba musical rhythm is the blood that flows in his veins, as it does in African traditional drumming, fluting, and dancing. Osundare and his contemporaries … have demonstrated what it means for modern African poetry to get fulfilled through song and performance, and unfulfilled in being read or recited! (Ibidem)

This critical assertion highlights how embedded poetry and drama are through the umbilical cord of performance. Poetry and drama interpenetrate each other so that it becomes difficult to dissociate them. When poetry fuses into dramatic performance, it requires supporting apparatus of stage, audience, dialogue, and is expected to impact the spectators the way drama achieves the catharsis effect on its audience. I contend that poetry when performed on stage can be committed to the social cause the way dramatic performance is used to address social problems. Through poetic performance, the poet educates his/her audience, questions unethical behavior in society, exposes political deviationism, calls to rectitude distorted ways of people and imparts on the audience what it regards as the commendable ways of living.

Tanure Ojaide opines that

> The inherence performance quality of oral poetry has bearing on the aesthetic composition of modern African poetry. The poet and cantor, composer and performer, may not necessarily be the same person but are likely to be. Even when they are different, they are mindful of the other's presence. In other words, verbal composition and performance are intricately related. Since the modern poet is more likely to perform his/her own poetry, these performance qualities are built into the poem…The story told in a poem engenders its own dramatics. Much extemporization is still a part of written African poetry as songs or refrains are extended in poetry readings. The relationship between audience and performer

which is controlled in the West is more spontaneous in Africa. Modern Western poets attempt to involve their audience, and this also influences the compositional process (Ojaide 1996: 24-25).

The interpretative praxis of this statement points to the contact zone between poetry and drama, where both art merge, fuse and emerge into a newly aesthetically crafted model of poetic drama. What obtains here is that contemporary African poetry narrate stories, through the medium of artistic knitting of refrains, with the active participation of the audience. What emerges from Ojaide's critical observation is that, similarly to modern African dramatists' exploration of African traditions of the total theatre where song, mime, drumming, dance, and dialogue are synthesized on stage, contemporary poets are engaged in total theatre performance. Some cases in point can be Kofi Anyidoho, Niyi Osundare and Tanure Ojaide.

From a poststructuralist interpretation, Beatrice Hanssen adjoins that "Poststructuralist thought labored under the illusion of its own newness, which it posited at the expense of the cultural transmission of the past, the "semantic potential" of a past as yet unmined, as yet not fully realized" (Beatrice Hassan 2004: 282). This critical position means that cultural transmission is at the heart of domestication of African dramatic forms. I am going to give instances where drama display highly poetic inflections and corroborate the idea that domestication functions as structurally intertextual. Femi Osofisan, a contemporary renowned playwright leans on poems in his plays to display the richness of African poetry. For instance, in *The Oriki of a Grasshopper*, he writes:

> I shall sing my love
> Of a shield called freedom,
> Against which the talons of eagle breaks;
> Of a nut impervious
> To the knocking of boots, in which
> The kernels are ancient songs
> Set ablaze;
> Words felonious as the poet
> And dangerous to the sword
> Of tyrants (Osofisan 2003: 1)

This is a poem, pertaining to the category of epic theatre. The poem in the play addresses criticism against kings who display unwise behavior that downgrade them in face of their subjects. At the same time, the song attempts to elevate beggars and local tramps to the pedestal of heroes and heroines. Drama has become poetry and the performer or the singer needs to display poetic verve in the singing. Examples of such verve are voice, rhythm, the following of the line patterns, the stressed and the unstressed syllables.

From a poststructuralist perspective, it is not far-fetched to assert that domestication refers to the fact of bringing something that was formerly foreign to actually bear the local identity, colour and exhibit local behavior. It is to bring a foreign object home in such a way that it looks no more like its former self but like a newly imposed self. Modern African drama has borrowed technique and method from European orthodox playwrighting and stagecraft. The first generation of African playwrights affiliated to universities have attended and read extensively materials from European playwrights. Wole Soyinka studies at Royal Court Theatre in England and was greatly influenced by Knight and Bretch, two great British dramatists. His plays namely *A Dance of the Forest, Death and the King's Horseman, Kongi's Harvest* are replete with myths, proverbs and legends. Ola Rotimi has greatly taken elements from oral tradition to incorporate them into his plays namely *The Gods Are Not to Blame, Our Husband Has Gone Mad Again*. Ngugi wa Thiong'o's co-authored plays *The Trial of Dedan Kimathi, I Will Marry When I Want, The Black Hermit* contain ingredients of oral tradition. Efua T. Sutherland's plays *The Marriage of Anansewa, Foriwa* and *Edufa* also draw on oral tradition elements namely ritual and festival. Femi Osofisan has studied in France and has been influenced by European dramatic literature. His plays, *Morountodun and Other Plays, The Oriki of the Grasshopper, Once upon Four Robbers* are also replete with elements of oral tradition. So, these writers after reading consistent material in European theatrical traditions have set to write. They thus recaptured indigenous material from African traditional and cultural lore and used them as the raw material of their plays. Such elements are myths, legends, folktales, proverbs, animal stories, riddles, to mention but a few. So, when discussing theoretical approaches to African drama it is important to see how these elements of oral tradition help to pave the way to theory, since they offer the ground knowledge of the understanding of the subject matter of African drama and theatre. Walter J. Ong has theorized on the co-relationship between orality and literacy and stressed the importance of oral tradition in the growth of written literature:

> Speech is inseparable from our consciousness and it has fascinated human beings, elicited serious reflection about itself, from the

very early stages of consciousness, long before writing came into existence. Proverbs from all over the world are rich with observations about this overwhelmingly human phenomenon of speech in its native oral form, about its powers, its beauties, its dangers. The same fascination with oral speech continues unabated for centuries after writing comes into use. In the West among the ancient Greeks the fascination showed in the elaboration of the vast, meticulously worked-out art of rhetoric, the most comprehensive academic subject in all western culture for two thousand years. In its Greek original, *techn rhtorik* ,'speech art' (commonly abridged to just *rh torik*) referred essentially to oral speaking, even though as a reflective, organized 'art' or science—for example, in Aristotle's Art of *Rhetoric*—rhetoric was and had to be a product of writing. *Rhtorik* , or rhetoric, basically meant public speaking or oratory, which for centuries even in literate and typographic cultures remained unreflexively pretty much the paradigm of all discourse, including that of writing (Ong 2002: 9).

Here Ong sees an intrinsic relationship between speech, consciousness, and writing. In other words, he connects oral tradition, human consciousness and writing or written literature. First, dramatic speech is inspired by human consciousness in his search to expand himself, to stretch into the creative realm of human consciousness. This speech expresses at a certain point his need to liberate himself from the accumulated tensions. Dramatic discourse is therefore expected to produce catharsis. The context in which Ong is relating orality and literacy is Greek rhetoric which constitutes the backbone of Greek drama. Yet, his remark is very relevant for the birth and development of African drama as a domesticated genre. Two fundamental reasons can be advanced to support Ong' s claim. Firstly, modern African drama was born at the moment where oral tradition was the dominant mode of knowledge production and transmission. Yet, the appearance of written drama did not cancel or nullify oral tradition. It has rather been used as the raw material to nourish and flesh out written plays.

Emmanuel Obiechina' s explanation rightly comes to mind:

> To begin with a theoretical question, what happens to the development of literature when a relatively new cultural system based on the written word is superimposed upon an ancient oral traditional culture? The first discovery is that the oral culture does not immediately disappear

by the mere fact of its being in contact with writing, nor does the literature of the oral society disappear because of the introduction of written literature (Obiechina 1993: 134).

Going further, he says:

> Rather, a synthesis takes place in which characteristics of the oral culture survive and are absorbed, assimilated, extended, and even reorganized within a new cultural experience. Also, vital aspects of the oral literature are absorbed into an emerging written literature of greatly invigorated forms infused with vernacular energy through metaphors, images and symbols, more complex plots, and diversified structures of meaning. Such a happy synthesis is possible insofar as certain conditions are present at the meeting point of the oral and written traditions, including the extent to which the synthesizing artist, that is the storyteller or poet, is well rooted in the oral rhetorical forms or narrative traditions, the extent of the familiarity the artist assumes the audience to have with the oral rhetorical or narrative conventions, the extent to which the artist expects the audience to be composed of readers or listeners, and the extent of the artist's skill in controlling the literary form, in the sense of being capable of assimilating into it an experience produced in a non-literate tradition or a formal style that originally belonged to the oral traditional society (Obiechina 1993: 137).

Obiechina is right here. If one analyses the birth of modern African drama, it is very perceptible how orality has been imbricated in the written literary forms. As he also points out, the situation in modern Africa amply illustrates the point about the merging of the worlds of orality and literacy. The superimposition of alphabetic writing upon the oral cultures of Africa in the nineteenth century did not extinguish the oral traditions upon which African cultures and literatures had long been established. The immediate result was that African indigenous languages were written down and brought into the mainstream of the world repertoire of literate languages, and, additionally, a substantial body of Africa's oral literatures—from epics and extended forms to unicellular tales and verbal art—was written down, recorded, and archived. But beyond activities related to literary and cultural retrieval and preservation are the challenges and stimuli that the interface of oral and written traditions provides to creative artists practicing in the region. A large volume of written works built on synthesis of the two traditions has emerged in Africa, to which critics have given considerable attention. The conditioning of this literature by the African oral tradition has been discussed in several critical works. In recent times, critics continue to explore the deep structures of the texts, optimally forcing them to yield up their meanings and insights. It is no longer possible to undertake a meaningful critical discourse of African literature, whether written in the indigenous languages or in the languages of the former colonial powers, without seriously adverting to its oral traditional constituents in the matrix of composite forms and contents. Nor indeed is it expedient to ignore the tensions arising from the old/new, traditional/modern, oral/written, and indigenous/foreign configurations that characterize the texts and contexts of the new literature of Africa.

The African play as a representative "literary" form provides a good example of this assimilation and synthesis of the two traditions in that it more demonstrably illustrates the transformations that occur when the pressures of social and formal realism make such assimilation inevitable. For example, it is impossible to ignore orality in a form that prides itself on a life-like portrayal of reality when exploring the life and experience of people more than seventy per cent of whom at any given moment live within traditional oral societies throughout the varied contexts of precolonial, colonial, and postcolonial history, and who have continued to sustain traditional solidarities and to espouse values, beliefs, and attitudes conditioned and nourished by the oral tradition. Even those of them caught up in the modern, urban, industrial-technological sector are not infrequently in contact with their traditional and rural roots and thus are not totally divorced from a sense of their own traditions. The oral traditional impulse is therefore strong in the modern African play, which embodies these experiences, especially because the writers themselves are a product of both the oral tradition and literate education.[1]

Furthermore, a return-to-roots movement in African literature as a means of giving maximum authenticity to the writing made the writers look to their indigenous poetics to create works that will endure by drawing upon their living oral tradition to enrich forms, techniques, and styles received through

---

[1] Iyasere (1975:107) is right in his observation that "the modern African writer is to his indigenous oral tradition as a snail is to its shell. Even in a foreign habitat, a snail never leaves its shell behind."

literate education.[2] One major aspect of this interplay of the oral and literary traditions in the African play is the phenomenon of the-story within-the-story, or the *narrative proverb* as we shall more insistently refer to it in this discussion. Reflecting a habit of orality in life and literature, the playwrights introduce oral stories—myths, folktales, fairy tales, animal fables, anecdotes, ballads, song-tales, and so on—within the narrative matrices of their works, in the development of their plots and themes, and in the formulation of their artistic and formal principles. These embedded stories are referred to as narrative proverbs because they perform organic and structural functions of proverbs in oral speech and in creative literature.

Martin Benham and Jane Plastow have this to say

> African theatre is entertainment, but it can also be aesthetically, politically, socially and spiritually committed, and often it is all these things simultaneously. Moreover, much modern African theatre refuses to be compartmentalised into a particular form of presentation. Instead it draws on indigenous performance traditions including dance, music, storytelling and mime, and combines them with ideas of drama drawn from experiences of Western colonialism, to create theatre forms which are syncretic and inclusive in both form and content. At its best African theatre is a total experience of mind, body and soul which engages with, and feeds off, a highly responsive, involved and vocal audience (Benham and Plastow 1999: 3).

From their perspective, this means that modern African drama is hybrid in form and content. They carry the idea further by saying that modern African theatre coincides with the post-colonial period which began in 1957 when Ghana became independent of British rule. Pre-colonial African theatre forms still require much research. They were usually dance, music and poetry-based and served a wide range of functions including the teaching of social roles and behaviour, explaining the history of ethnic groups, social criticism, celebration and the fulfilment of religious rituals. Colonialism brought varying degrees of

---

[2]What we have here is a process akin to that identified by Ivan Illich (1972) as de-schooling, whereby writers return to their oral sources for ideas, subject matter, values, forms of thought, and styles in a move that counteracts the narrow conditioning from formal, school education. It assured a return to the idiom of African Languages and the roots of African oral tradition.

suppression of indigenous performance forms. These were less onerous in areas such as West Africa which were considered unhealthy for Western settlers and were therefore governed under a system of indirect rule; and far more repressive in parts of southern and eastern Africa, where settler states were established and efforts were made to eradicate traditional performance modes, which were often seen as antipathetic to European Christian and cultural values, as well as potentially dangerous foci for the incitement of rebellion. In many cases European forms of drama were introduced by missionaries, initially to transmit biblical messages, and later, in mission schools, in an attempt to teach metropolitan languages and inculcate European cultural values. This theatre was seldom meant for mass consumption: instead it was a means of separating off African elites and Christian converts from the mass of traditional peoples.

During the colonial period Africans were usually only allowed to publish or perform drama under the patronage and censorship of their white rulers. Early plays often have biblical themes, reflecting missionary influence; they also tend to be more or less naturalistic, since this was the form favoured by the colonisers. Above all involvement in political debate was strictly censored in almost all cases under colonial rule, so these plays are largely anodyne and imitative. All this began to change rapidly during the 1960s as many African nations claimed their independence. West Africa was the first region to come to literary prominence with many novelists and playwrights emerging on the international scene. There are a number of reasons for this regional prominence. Throughout the colonial experience local cultures in British West Africa remained vibrant. This gave a strong sense of identity and confidence to a number of writers, several of whom saw the literary reclamation of their history and culture as an urgent task. Also, there were a number of élite schools and colleges established in the region, especially in Nigeria and Ghana and these nurtured many new writers who had access to and interest in both indigenous and Western cultural forms.

Returning to West Africa, in Wole Soyinka and Femi Osofisan we have... two of Nigeria's most famous playwrights. These two have long had an interesting dialectical relationship, in which the younger Osofisan challenges Soyinka's use of myth as a validation of Yoruba society. Instead Osofisan chooses to use mythology in a much more critical manner which demands that society constantly questions and re-examines the philosophical premises which underlie traditional stories and beliefs. In both cases, however, we cannot but be aware that we are encountering a society which is steeped in rich and expressive indigenous culture which reaches back – not uninterrupted, but still vibrant – into the past as it also looks to the future. Female playwrights are still a relative rarity in Africa for a number of reasons. In many places it is considered disreputable for women to become involved in commercial performances and it is often difficult for women to combine domestic life with the demands of the theatre. These have been factors restricting women's development as playwrights in many societies across the world. Perhaps one of the most potent forces holding back African women playwrights has been the relative lack of educational opportunities for women, particularly during the colonial era.

Ama Ata Aidoo is a triumphant example of a writer who overcame a plethora of social handicaps to produce plays. She is a leading light amongst the small band of African women playwrights which includes her compatriot Efua Sutherland, the Nigerians, Zulu Sofola and Tess Onwueme, Gcina Mhlope from South Africa and Penina Mlama and Amadina Lihamba from Tanzania. She is also recognisable West African in her world view. The pantheon on gods, spirits, the unborn and the ancestors who are constantly encountered in much West African writing give the cultural productions of this region a density, and indeed difficulty for the uninitiated which is unparalleled in other parts of the continent.

When we move to southern Africa we see the results of a very different historical experience. Here for a hundred years – and for parts of South Africa for three hundred years – white settlers seized African land, forced Africans into ignominious wage slavery, derided and sought to repress African cultures and belief systems, and finally imposed the horrors of apartheid on the people. Protest against this process has never been absent but, as in many other parts of the colonized world, momentum grew after the second world war – which exposed many blacks to differing patterns of race relations – and increased as other parts of Africa gained their independence. In Zimbabwe and South Africa protest theatre became a force in the 1970s. In Zimbabwe theatre was used by the guerrilla fighters as a tool for politicization, while in South Africa plays were mounted predominantly in the black urban townships. Working against a background of poverty and struggle, this theatre developed its own style of presentation which relies heavily on the plasticity of the performed. Sophisticated staging, costume and props were not available and actors often had to be prepared to decamp quickly if security forces moved in to stop performances. Therefore, the primary tool is the actor himself who must create his whole world through mime, sound and a bare minimum of symbolic properties. Reflecting the urgency of the actors' messages and the energy of urban life, many such plays are composed in epic mode, with short scenes building up a collage picture of society.

Notes

1. The relationship of orality and literacy is discussed in all its complex ramifications by Walter Ong (1982), who observes that "writing from the beginning did not reduce orality but enhanced it" (9).
2. These criteria are taken from Foley 1986:14. From their autobiographies and gleanings from interview accounts, it is obvious that African writers have been well exposed to the oral and literary traditions and are thus able to synthesize the two in their works.
3. For a detailed discussion, see the chapter entitled "Growth of Written Literature in English Speaking West Africa" (Obiechina 1990:1-20 and also Gérard 1981).
4. Reference could be made to Lindfors 1973, Iyasere 1975, Obiechina 1975, Schmidt 1968, and Echeruo 1966.
5. For a detailed discussion, see the chapter entitled "Growth of Written Literature in English Speaking West Africa" (Obiechina 1990:1-20 and also Gérard 1981).
6. Reference could be made to Lindfors 1973, Iyasere 1975, Obiechina 1975, Schmidt 1968, and Echeruo 1966.

References

Akinwotu, Samuel Alaba "Language Use in Osofisan's *Tegonni*." In Tunde Akinyemi and Toyin Falola, eds., *Emerging Perspectives on Femi Osofisan*. Trenton: Africa World Press, 2009. 342-350.

Anyidoho, Kofi, "Poetry as Dramatic Performance." In Tejumola Olaniyan and Ato Quayson, eds., *African Literature: An Anthology of Criticism and Theory*. USA: Blackwell Publishing, 2007. 382-390.

Barry, Peter, *Beginning Theory, Second Edition*. Cambridge: Cambridge University Press, 2002.

Barthes, Roland. *The Pleasure of the Text*. Paris: Seuil. 1973

Benham, Martin and Plastow, *Encyclopedia of World Theatre: Africa*. Cambridge: Cambridge University Press, 1999.

Benham, Martin, Errol Hill and George Woodyard, *The Cambridge Guide to African and Caribbean Theatre*. Cambridge: Cambridge University Press, 2004.

Campbe II, Corrina, *A War of Words: Halo Songs of Abuse Among the Anlo Ewe*. Masters' Degree Thesis supervised by Professors Kofi Anyidoho and Mawuli Adjeyi Evanston: Northwestern University, 2002.

Derrida, Jacques. *Acts of Literature*. London and New York: Routledge. (1991).

Hassen, Beatrice. "Critical Theory and Poststructuralism: Habermas and Foucault." In Fred Rush, ed., *The Cambridge Companion to Critical Theory*. 1992. Cambridge: Cambridge University Press. 280-309. 2004.

Lindfors, Berth. *Folklore in Nigerian Literature*. New York: Africana Publishing Company. 1973.

Lodge, David and Nigel Wood, *Modern Criticism and Theory: A Reader*. New York: Routledge, 2008.

Mcgowan, Kate. "Structuralism and Semiotics." In Simon Malpas and Paul Wake, eds., *The Routledge Companion to Critical Theory*. New York: Routledge, 2006. 3-13.

Na'Allah, Abdul-Rasheed., ed., *The People's Poet: Emerging Perspectives on Niyi Osundare*. Trenton: Africa World Press, 2003.

Na-Allah, Abdul-Rasheed, "Niyi Osundare's Performance Notes." In *The People's Poet: Emerging Perspectives on Niyi Osundare*. Trenton: Africa World Press, 2003. 313-331.

Newton, K. M., *Twentieth Century Literary Theory: A Reader*. New York: St Martin Press, 1984.

Nwoga, Donatus I. *West African Verse: An Anthology*. Nigeria: Heinemann, 1967.

Obiechina, Emmanuel, "Narrative Proverbs in the African Novel." In *Research in African Literatures*. Vol. 24, No. 4, Special Issue in Memory of Josaphat Bekunuru Kubayanda. Winter, 1993. 123-140.

Odebunmi, Akin, "Pragmatic Functions of Crisis – Motivated Proverbs in Ola Rotimi's *The Gods Are Not to Blame*". 73-84 in Linguistik online http www.linguistik-online.de/33_08/odebunmi.pdf, *retrieved 17th November 2017*.

Ojaide, Tanure. *Poetic Imagination in Black Africa*. Durham: Carolina Academic Press, 1996.

Okpewho, Isidore, *The Heritage of African Poetry*. UK: Longman Group, 1988.

Okpewo, Isidore, *Oral Performance in Africa*. Indiana: Indiana University Press, 1990.

Ong, Walter. *Orality and Literacy: The Technologizing of the Word*. New York: Routledge, 2002.

Osofisan, Femi, *The Oriki of a Grasshopper*, in *Major Plays*. Ibadan: Ibadan University Press, 2003.

Pieterse, Cosmo. 1978. "Introduction." In *Ten One-Act Plays*. London: Heinemann Educational Books.

Sirayi, Mzo, *South African Drama and Theatre from Precolonial Times to the 1990s, Alternative Reading*. Bloomington: Xlibris Corporation, 2012.

3

DEFINING DRAMA IN AFRICAN CONTEXT: A NEW HISTORICIST APPROACH

African drama has been a fertile ground for critical debates regarding the designation of authentic dramatic art namely ritual and festival. Oyin Ogunba is one of the first critics to call African religious festivals and rituals drama. He was countered by his fellow Oyeka Ogunyemola who refuted the term drama to these indigenous cultural performances. Jenny Bourne Taylor's reading of New Historicism provides the grounwork for what constitutes the backbone of New historicism (Taylor 2010: 484). New Historicism is a form of textual analysis which developed in the United States during the 1980s and has now become firmly established in many English literature departments there and in journals such as *Representations, New Literary History, English Literary History*, and *English Literary Renaissance* (Ibidem). It cannot, however, be described as a unified approach or position, more a cluster of concerns which have been developed and elaborated in diverse ways – indeed the reluctance to adopt an overarching narrative of its own methodology has become one of its features (Ibidem). Like Cultural Materialism (which is often described as its "British" counterpart) New Historicism sees itself as a radical approach, growing out of critical engagement with both Marxism and Poststructuralism. It has been particularly elaborated in the works on the Renaissance, especially that of Stephen Greenblatt, Jonathan Goldberg, Jean E. Howard, Karen Newman, and Louis Montrose, although it has also permeated work in other periods: Catherine Gallagher, Nancy Armstrong, and D.A. Miller's work are examples of New Historicist analysis of nineteenth-century Culture (Ibidem). However, the claims of the *newness* of this "turn to history" (which seems strange to British readers) needs to be situated itself within the context of American academic institutions and traditions. New Historicism was first clearly defined as a critical tendency by Stephen Greenblatt in 1982 in his introduction to the collection of essays *The Forms of Power and The Power of Forms in the English Renaissance*(Ibidem). Here he contrasted the approaches expanded in these essays with the hitherto dominant procedures in American critical practice: "traditional literary history" and New Criticism. The former approach, Greenblatt maintained, exemplified in the writing of J. Dover Wilson, sought to impose an artificial unity on Renaissance Texts, making them internally coherent and reflective of an equally organic world view, both of which tended to legitimize dominant modes of power. The latter focused exclusively on a dehistoricized text, repressing its political meanings. The new method, he argued, emphasized the contradictions within the cultural formation of each historical moment, by making these contradictions their subject. Following Raymond Williams, this New Historicism eschewed distinctions between literature and the cultural and social context within which it was produced, instead seeing modes of representation as constituting rather than simply reflecting social reality.

New Historicism aimed to produce a "poetics of culture"; reading canonical texts within, and as part of, multiple forms of writing, cutting across the distinction between fiction and nonfiction in exploring the formation of specific discourses and institutions. It then represents a turn to history, but is often coy about what implied notion of historical change and social process is being invoked. Its theoretical reference points are diverse, and include Raymond Williams, Clifford Geertz, Michel Foucault, Louis Althusser, Mikhail Bakhtin, and Michel de Certeau. In some respects, it places itself in a skeptical relationship to a historical materialist tradition, invoking a set of social relations and productive forces within which texts are embedded, while being critical of the hierarchical division between a determining base and a determined superstructure.

Taking this point further and drawing on Foucault's work, New Historicism shares with poststructuralism a distrust of totalizing social theories and "grand narratives," continually problematizing the standpoint from which specific perceptions and theories are formed, though often in the process reinforcing the secure institutional base from which such deconstructing assertions are made (Ibidem).

New Historicism stresses the interdependent nature of cultural forms and institutions, and reads all traces of the past as texts, narratives to be interpreted. In refusing to give precedence to any particular story, it runs the risk of falling into complete relativism, in which history becomes an infinitely repetitive and regressing set of reflections. Stephen Greenblatt's work in particular is sensitive to these problems. In *Marvellous Possessions: The Wonder of the New World* (1991) for example, he argues that his emphasis on anecdote rather than totalizing explanatory stories mirrors the perceptions of the European encounter with America which he is analyzing. Nevertheless, he also points out that purely local knowledge is simply the underside of the totalization of which he is critical. He acknowledges that in foregrounding some of these anecdotes as representative stories, as somehow metaphoric, he is pointing to more generalized structures of power, though these often remain implied. In doing so, however, he runs the risk of reproducing the kind of "world view" that New Historicism claims to avoid.

Thus, new historicist criticism, as Louis Montrose claims, emphasizes the "historicity of texts and the textuality of history." But these two projects may entail distinct, even contradictory methodologies and notions of history itself. The "Historicity of texts" suggests that writings are produced within specific social, cultural, and economic conditions, and that at some level they are determined by those conditions, even as they contribute to their formation. The "textuality of history" emphasizes that history itself can be apprehended only as a collection of representations, open to multiple mediations, renarrations, and interpretations. However, both approaches recognize the problem of *how* to read historically – how to acknowledge one's own situatedness, yet make the conceptual leap necessary to apprehend the radical difference of the past. As modern readers we continually run the danger of reading texts anachronistically, seeing them as mirrors or projections of our own concerns rather than attempting to excavate the complex meanings they may have had when they were written. The emphasis on the "textuality of history" draws on both Foucault and de Certeau's writing in seeing history itself as a set of archaeological traces and as narratives whose meaning is compounded by the narrative of history writing itself. To some extent these approaches could be seen as epochal rather than historical, marginalizing issues of social change and determination by concentrating on particular historical moments as Epistemes – self-contained structures of knowledge which do not necessarily tally with our own. Another starting point which shares this "flattening" perspective is Cultural anthropology, particularly the writings of Clifford Geertz. Geertz's work on cultures was radically different from his own entailed reading the symbolic structures of these societies as stories which their inhabitants tell about themselves. "The culture of a people is an ensemble of texts," he wrote, "themselves ensembles which the anthropologist strains to read over the shoulders of those to whom they properly belong" ("Deep play: note on the Balinese cock fight" (Geertz 1972: 29). Much new historicist work too wishes to "read over the shoulder" of moments in the past, aiming at "thick description" of the processes at work within them by close reading of specific works. For all the stress on decentering the text, however, much New Historicist work still privileges literary over other forms of discourse, though it might expand its definition. In the first place, as many of its critics have pointed out, it does often seem to return to canonical writing and to extrapolate an entire social dynamic from the close reading of a specific work or Trope.

Second, literary, and specifically dramatic forms of playing and performance are seen as key metaphors for the society as a whole. For example, Greenblatt's *Shakespearian Negotiations* reads the Elizabethan stage as a central economic, political, and psychic institution (Greenblatt 1988). Elizabethan society was organized around theatricality, he argued; the notion of performance was central to both the shaping of individual subjectivity and the power relationships permeating society as a whole, manifested by pageant, public ceremony, and display. Renaissance drama does not simply reflect this theatricality – it produces, reproduces, and negotiates it in a much more complicated way, and thus it is impossible to draw a distinction between aesthetic and other kinds of social energy and discourse. This stress on negotiation and renegotiation, in which dramatic forms actively shape the power relationships of their society, continually subverting yet also ultimately contained by dominant forms of state ideological power, has led some critics of New Historicism to argue that it has become mesmerized by the notion of "ideological entrapment," on which it relies. Alan Sinfield, for example, argues in *Faultlines: Cultural Materialism and the Politics of Dissident Reading* that the approach does not realize its own political potential, too easily falling into the relativism and Formalism of post-structuralist rhetoric, and failing to consider how dissident reading strategies might be developed (Sinfield 1992). Some feminists have also argued that New Historicism runs the risk of reinforcing the marginality of oppressed groups, though others have developed its methods to focus on the power play of Gender. It has, some claim, simply become another professional approach, quickly engulfed and incorporated by an insatiable American literary institution.

When applied to African drama and theatre studies, what is the new meaning that can be derived from new historicist approach?

The bone of contention among scholars of African drama is whether one should apply the name drama to African traditional performances namely ritual and festival. To make explicit the functions of African ritual, festival and drama in literature it urges to read criticisms in the light of new historicism. It is to recall and revisit some theoretical trends which opt for or reject the designation of drama for African traditional performances like ritual and festival in theatre studies in African literature. This study brings a complement to the on-going debate. The problem of nomenclature of African traditional performances – ritual, festival and drama - is an on-going debate in African literature of dramatic expression. While theorizing about African drama, scholars such as Bakary Traoré (1972), Abiola Irele (1981), Wole Soyinka (1988), Tejumola Olaniyan (2004), Bayo Ogunjimi and Abdul-Rasheed Na'Allah (2005) have established the fact that drama takes its origins from rituals and festivals. These scholars have made it clear that drama existed long time ago before the advent of colonizers in Africa. Bakary Traoré (1972: 9), Oyin Ogunba (1986: 30), Wole Soyinka (1988: 190) and many other scholars have shown the existence of drama in African traditional performances. These writers have also highlighted the interweaving of ritual, drama and festivals in African traditional societies. The claim made by these scholars is to apply the name drama to African rituals and festivals, establishing thereby a parallelism in the development of Greek theatre and African dramatic art. While the aforementioned scholars argue for applying the name drama to traditional performances, namely rituals, rites and festivals, Oyinkan Owomoyela (1986: 30), Louise Bourgault (2005: 11) and Pierre Médehouégnon (2010: 13) contend that drama should be dissociated from them. I will first recall briefly the designation and function of ritual, festival and drama in African context and then tell my personal stances on when drama can or cannot be associated with ritual and festival. Before taking position, I want to point out the pros and the cons arguments about the imbrications of drama and ritual in the context of traditional performances in Africa.

3.1. Designation and Function of Ritual, Festival and Drama in Traditional African Context

3.1.1. Ritual: Designation and Function

In a broad context, by ritual is generally referred to a series of actions that are always performed in the same way, especially as part of a religious ceremony (Hornby, 2008: 1264). A ritual seen from religious vantage point in African context plays a key role in the lives of African people of traditional religion usually referred to as animism. Ritual usually associated with myth is man's creation to communicate with the supernatural or the divine as he seeks to explain the mysteries of life, to expand himself, to recollect old memories of historical significance and to confide in superior beings for protection and life security. The critic Bu-Buakei Jabbi commenting on the place of ritual in indigenous Africa takes inspiration from Chinua Achebe and opines:

> Myth and ritual complexes within living cultures tend, in their own right, to be intrinsic systems of ideas and general world-views, of modes of perception and sensibility. A more or less cohesive set of proportions about reality and life, about man's place in the world and in time, may often be deduced from them, though always as an act of interpretation. As Achebe puts it, they are created by man 'to explain the problems and mysteries of life and death, - his attempt to make sense of the bewildering complexity of existence' (Jabi, 1980: 132).

Here is suggested the definition and socio-cultural function of myth and ritual. Myths contain the sources of the cosmological components of human existence, as they foster man's understanding of his universe and the conduct of his own existence. In clearer terms, myths are created to try to explain the mysteries of man's creation, life and death, the origin of the world. Rituals are practices created by man to communicate with the supernatural, to interpret life and social events and to explain the problems and mysteries of life and death. Ritual then is integrated to human daily life and stretches deep in his religious beliefs. Communicating with the supernatural assumes certain beliefs in the existence of transcendental life and being. Ritual in many ways is associated with ceremonies and rites of initiation and passages from teenage to adult life in some communities. For Theodore W. Hatlen,

> The ceremony assumes a functional purpose when the tribe employs *sympathetic magic* to assure it of victory in warfare. It is no longer a celebration for the joy of the activity; it becomes a serious, religious ritual expressing the deepest needs and longing of the people and associating them with the supernatural. Thus, we see the progressive steps from a simple retelling of personal experience

to the establishment of a tribal ritual which is joined with religion
as man seeks to extend his power (Hatlen, 1962: 4).

Here ritual designated as ceremony is seen as a means employed to reach an end. It is performed by people in war context to enlist the help of deities to win a war. Need be to stress the fact that ritual involves man communicating with the supernatural. In addition to that, in ritual performance, the priest plays the central role, as he is the representative of the deity. The ritual actor is to some degree an incarnation of a spirit. He does not pretend in his role playing but rather he lets his total being, thought, feelings, emotions and consciousness be engaged in his communication with the supernatural. The function of ritual then is to make the god act. Man aiming at a certain goal to achieve, finds his potential abilities and resources insufficient and resort to the divine intervention, through faith which he translates into external action of ritual prayers and ceremonies. He believes in the possibility of his empowerment through his communication with the supernatural. Another perception of the function of ritual can be seen in some traditions of the Tallensi, a social group in Ghana, where, as G. K. Nukunya suggests, ritual has a role to play in the chiefly office:

> In our discussion of political organization in both centralized and non-centralized societies, we have occasion, at various points to mention the religious and ritual aspect of chiefly office […] The political head's ritual and religious duties and functions help to enhance his secular political position and raise him above ordinary citizens (Nukunya, 2003: 76).

Here ritual is seen playing key role in the enthronement of the traditional chief and as part of his daily services. Such enthronement bears the stamp of communal approval when rituals accompany it. It is also one way of saying that the elected chief will have the support of the deities in the discharge of his functions. While the chief is called upon to see to the political life of his community, he is equally attributed the religious functions of a priest, thus being required to perform ritual ceremonies among his people when they urge. Thus "ritual" seems inseparable with political life in that particular community. The function of ritual in this context is then to endow the leader of the community with more power to rule and settle difficult riddles among his people.

3.1.2. Festival: Designation and Function

Festival can be perceived as a day or period of the year when people stop working to celebrate a special event, often a religious one (Hornby, op cit: 544). Festival in the African context is a time of social gathering, a period of popular celebration, rejoicing and merriments which have also religious connotation in the belief systems of the communities that celebrate it. Festival in many African communities bring people together on occasions like harvest time, ritual dances and traditional contests, the objectives of which are to revive history, perpetuate old memories, consult seasonal calendrification, and observe rites of passage or transition. The critic Tejumola Olaniyan observes that

> In many African communities, the foremost indigenous cultural and artistic institution is the festival. Organized around certain deities or spirits, or to mark general transitions or the passage of the seasons whether of climate or agricultural production, festivals are sprawling multimedia occasions – that is incorporating diverse forms such as singing, chanting, drama, drumming, masking, miming, costuming, puppetry [...] Festivals could last for a few hours to several days, weeks or months. Each festival dramatizes a story or myth – or related set of stories or myths – connecting the particular subject of the festival be it a deity or the season of the harvest, to significant events in the life of the community and to its place in sustaining communal harmony, plenty and stability (Olanyan, 2004: 37-38).

Festival in African context as the critic points it out here, is a cultural institution in many communities and are religious oriented since they relate directly or indirectly to deities. The main reference point in this respect are harvest festivals which are usually celebrated on seasonal calendar fixation to coincide with the time of harvest, crop gathering and traditional contests and which are marked out as intensive popular gatherings and social encounters of members of the same community, tribes or ancestry. Many cultural and traditional performances requiring physical demonstrations among which singing, whistling, drumming, dancing, wrestling, handclapping, pouring libations, prayers and even incantations take place. Festivals are celebrated and celebratory, that is to say that, while religious and secular offices are being carried out during these events to show that these days or events are important in the belief system of the festive community, they mark out the commemorating of special historical events for them. During traditional festivals, sacrifices are being performed to deities, offerings given to them and prayers said on behalf of the communities concerned. It is believed according to the religious philosophy of each community that such prayers will bring protection against evil and greater harvest in coming seasons. The key function of festival then is to renew spiritual relationship with the local deities. It is to restate faith in the supernatural and to ensure peaceful relationship with the gods. In connection with the function of festivals, G. K. Nukunya takes the example of Ghana and explains this:

> Another manifestation of Ghanaian beliefs and practices associated with the supernatural is found in festivals. Annual or periodic festivals abound in Ghanaian ethnic groups and the importance of the *Adae* festival among the Ashanti has already been mentioned. In addition to the *Adae*, an annual custom is always held among the Akan in connection with the first harvests of each crop such as yam […] The chief's house and that of the head priest are refurbished by singing old women […] Then the spirits are invoked to start the new year which begins at different times in different localities (Nukunya, op cit, 64).

Through this explanation, the idea transpires that in the festival there are beliefs connected with the supernatural, since during yam festival, there are rituals and invocation of the spirits. This suggests that in that particular community as is often the case in many traditional African societies, festival and religious offices are imbricated. The functions of festival can be stated. The celebration of festival is one of the translations of religious belief and faith into external action. It is an interpretation of people's creed and religious philosophy. The underlying idea is that the communication of the priest with deities, if it does not play the determinant role in the celebration of the festival, has important role in this. In many contexts one can remember that the dates of festivals are usually fixed by the priest who is endowed with the ability to read the time from the moon position, the stars, the rainfall timetable, for example. Altogether, the overall idea emerging from the function of festivals is summarised in what Wole Soyinka calls "the social, ritual and political apotheosis of community life in a year" (Soyinka, 1988: 195).

3.1.1. Arguments in Favour of the Existence of Drama in Traditional Africa: the Example of Nigeria

The first group of scholars in African literature argues that drama takes its source from African traditional performances. Rituals and festivals are the roots from which dramatic performances stem. According to Bakary Traoré,

> If we consider that theatre finds its subject matter in folklore, that is, in an aggregate of myths, legends, traditions, stories, then, we can say that a specifically Negro-African theatre has existed since the beginning of African civilization. We know that the Mali empire for example, which stretched from the Sahara to the tropical forest, from present- day Nigeria to Senegal was a cradle of a civilization which astonished all the Arab travellers who visited these countries (Traore, op cit, 9).

Here, Bakary Traoré traces Black African theatre to the origins of African civilizations themselves because dramatic performances have their roots in cultural manifestations and folklore. During cultural manifestations, there are dances, rituals, rites, pouring of libation, songs and incantations. These performances are meant to remind the community of their origin and their cultural values. They determine the true identity of the indigenous community. This is taken to mean according to the same writer that theatre is a popular creative work, one of the factors which constitute the consciousness of a social group and acts as means of education (Ibidem). In ancient African societies, religious belief was an essential part of life. The initiation of young people into various rites usually involves active participation in music and dancing. Theatre is imitation and summary of active life. It is the representation and re-enactment of social life through the oral performances of dance, music, rituals, ceremonies in which man seeks to communicate with the supernatural. These performances which aim at perpetuating cultural values of the village folks largely borrow from myths and legends:

> How has the traditional theatre evolved? From borrowing from traditional beliefs. These tribal or national beliefs have their appointed repositories: griots who at festivals perpetuate the memory of heroes. Their roles is to recite the legends and to keep alive heroic narratives (Traore, op cit, 9).

In West Africa, griots are people who sing the praises of legendary heroes of their tribes and their achievements. They sing and tell stories about the history and traditions of their people and community. They are the people who better master the creation myths of their communities and who see to it that such stories are retold to the younger generation. Story- telling usually involves participation of an audience, the village folk around the fire at night. The participation of the audience is done with hand clapping, dances, mimes, repetition of the songs' chorus all of which constitute important aspects of dramatic manifestations. To mime the characters of their stories, the story teller from time to time takes some postures, adopt body positions and perform movements like theatrical actors on stage. The mood prevailing and the atmosphere created by the songs and stories combine to give pleasure to the participative audience, and serve as important means of entertainment and relaxation for the audience. There is not much difference between the theatrical audiences who go to theatre hall to release their tension of the day and story-telling audiences who find the same entertainment with the griots. Wole Soyinka sustains the idea that rites and rituals are integrant part of dramatic expressions in Nigerian society. As he says:

> Nigeria offers a valuable example of the dual process of cultural attenuation and resurgence. For example theatrical professionalism was synonymous by the middle nineteenth century with the artistic proficiency and organisation of a particular theatrical form which had emerged from the burial rituals associated with the Oyo monarchy, the *egungun*. The question of when a performed event became theatre as ritualism is of course a vexed one that we need not bother about in this context. It is however commonly agreed that we started out –probably – as a ritualistic ruse to effect the funeral obsequies of an Oyo king had, by the mid-century, evolved into a theatrical form in substance and practice (Soyinka, 1988: 191).

The burial rituals of the Yoruba kings and all the ceremonials included therein (rites, dances, libations) known as *egungun* gave rise to theatrical performances. How they turned into theatre is not according to Soyinka an easy question to answer. But to offer a general explanation of the transformation of burial rites and rituals into theatre, he says that the *egungun* that was performed during a king's death turned out to be an annual celebration and later on was re-enacted by artists in a theatrical form:

> From an annual celebration rite of the smuggling-in of the corpse of that king and its burial, the *egungun* ancestral play became, firstly, a court re-enactment, then a secular form of performance which was next appropriated by the artists themselves (Ibidem).

During funeral rites and rituals, contends Soyinka "indigenous musical instruments – *bata, gangan, dudan,* and so on – the very backbone of traditional theatre are used (Ibidem)". These are traditional drum, flute and gong. These instruments are used to accompany songs and dances. The performances take theatrical form because they involve the participation of actors (the drummers, the elders pouring libations or reciting incantations or even those carrying the corpse) and the spectators (the public attending the funerals).

Soyinka's idea is enhanced by John Pepper Clark's establishment of a parallel between the origins of drama in Nigeria (or Africa) and elsewhere. He observes that just as European drama developed from rites connected with Osiris and Dionysus, "Nigerian drama arose from the early religious and magical ceremonies and festivals of the country" (Quoted by Owomoyela, 1986: 30) This drama, he adds, has the special function of propitiating spirits and gods (Ibdem). By saying this, J. P. Clark provides a strong argument to sustain the existence of drama in Africa long time before the advent of colonists. By the same token, he is also showing that drama is interwoven with ritual in the African context. That is to say that drama cannot be separated from rites, rituals and festivals. These are the fertile ground on which African theatre has grown and taken shape.

3.2. Parallelism between Greek Theatre and African Theatre

Looking at African drama from its origins, the scholars in favour of African traditional drama establish a parallelism between Greek theatre and African theatre. Bakary Traoré offers the following explanation:

> We know from certain authors that both Greek tragedy, with its origins in dithyrambic narrative recitations from which the theatre developed, and the Satirical Comedy, based on jokes at orgies, developed out of the Dionysiac cult of mysteries and processions in honour of Bacchus. We know also that Athenian dramatic

performances continued for a long time to be a part of festive rituals even after had become a literary genre in its own right, independent of religion (Traore, 1972: 14).

Two essential ideas stem from the critic's analysis here. First, that Greek tragedy originates from dithyrambic narrative recitations. The dithyramb seems to have been at first an improvised choral ode, a song of spring; but it becomes enriched as a part of ceremonial rites in honour of the god, Dionysus, with addition of dance and written verses (Hatlen, 1962: 5-6). Dionysus, in whose honour drama was produced was the god of vegetation, wine and fertility (Ibidem). Second, Athenian dramatic performances continued for a long time to be part of festive rituals. That means that there is a close relationship between drama and rituals, on the one hand, and between drama and festivals, on the other hand. The two ideas put together underscore the fact that in the context of Greek theatre, drama cannot be dissociated from religion, ritual, or festival. The relationship is intrinsic between them. That relationship can also be found in the context of African theatre. As Bakary Traoré highlights it,

> In Negro-African society, the relationships between the gods and men are based on the relationships existing between man and man. The gods are ancestors, and the men, heroes. Theatrical performances are regulated by seasonal calendar and the days appointed for festival. The performances can sometimes translate itself completely into action; it is closely interwoven with ritual (Traore, op cit, 14).

It is to note here that as in the context of Greek theatre, African theatre originates from rituals, rites and festivals. They are the backbone of African drama. They provide a context of rise to it. Two examples will be used to explain the issue. For the first example, festivals in Africa are occasions for social gathering, and the re-enactment of life in community through dance and songs. Many modern dramatists take inspiration from these festivals to write modern plays. Soyinka's *The Strong Breed* and *Death and the King's Horseman* for example were inspired by Yoruba traditional festivals. Festivals in the villages are organized according to seasonal calendars. Festivals usually come after the harvests, when the villagers have finished gathering their crops. The high priest or the elders' council announces the new moon or the new yam festival. This is an important moment for social gathering. Tribes of common ancestry come together to recollect their old memories, to restate their common history and to renew their ancestral ties. They reaffirm their cultural values and the mores that govern their community. Just as the Greek cult was performed in the honour of Dionysus, the priest in African traditional context pours libations, perform sacrifices and communicate with the supernatural, the deities. Prayers and supplications are pronounced in the favour of the communities and the priest enquires blessings from both ancestors and gods. Incantations are also pronounced to discard evil and misfortunes from the society. Songs usually accompany these prayers and incantations during which the priest performs ritual dances and the audience participate with songs and handclapping. Sometimes the priest enters into trance communicates with evil spirits and performs acrobatic movements. All these elements of traditional celebration are at the centre of African drama.

Traditional calendrification for festivals is designed to coincide with the appearance of migrating birds, the appearance of the new moon, or a particular odour of the soil. In Nigerian society, the yam festival is very important due to the fact that yam constitutes the staple food of many communities. During that festival, wrestling contests are organized to determine the hero of the community. The wrestling itself is an important theatrical performance. There are the wrestlers and an audience. Just as the actors in a theatre constitute the focus of attention of the spectators, the wrestlers are the centre attention and admiration in a wrestling contest. During the wrestling special masquerade dances are performed with many cultural demonstrations. In the Yoruba community, *the egungun* is a mask dancing which occupies important place in the cultural activities of this people.

For the second example, rites of passages and initiation to adulthood are also important aspects of African drama. Theodore W. Hatlen takes the example of the West Ceram and the Iroquoi communities to explain their functions:

> What do we learn from the initiatory rites? The most interesting ingredient is the mimetic representation of death and rebirth, a common concept in the religion of primitive cultures, especially among agrarian people who see a parallel in the death of the seed in the winter and the reappearance of new growth in the spring. In his religion, man usually appeals for divine assistance in the crisis of life, particularly the biological ones of birth, adulthood, and

death. The West Ceram make use of mimetic action in their ritual *showing* the transition from puberty to adulthood, just as we have seen the Iroquoi employing sympathetic magic to supplicate for supernatural assistance (Hatlen, op cit. 4).

It is to be remembered from Hatlen's analysis here that initiatory rites and rituals are symbolically speaking mimetic representation of death and rebirth in some communities. The initiatory rites first of all are means for the young initiated to be inserted in their communities, to be accepted in the large social fabric as sons or daughters of the land. During these rites, it may happen that the neophytes shed part of their blood through incisions, and this will be a mark of their commitment to their land. During these rituals, the neophytes also take oath to defend their land and if possible to die for it (Ngugi, 1972: 28).

It is understandable, considering the arguments of critics raised above, that drama is inseparable from African traditional performances. Nevertheless, the debate is still going on in the literary circles, some writers advocating the thesis that drama should be dissociated from rites, rituals and festivals.

3.2.1. Advocates of Divorcing Drama from Ritual

If for many scholars, African drama of oral expression takes roots from traditional performances, namely rites, rituals and festivals, others advocate the argument that drama should be divorced from them (Owomoyela, op cit, 35). Several reasons are advocated to explain the necessity for dissociating drama from rituals and festivals. The first two arguments are given by M. J. C. Echeruo who analyses the differences between drama and festival on the one hand and between drama and ritual on the other hand. Festival for him is *celebration* whereas drama is "a re-enactment of life" (Quoted in Owomoyela, 36). The distinction, he writes, is useful because "it enables us to isolate as celebration those communal events which portray emotional state in a sort of *tableaux vivants,* induce certain moods, or are participative and celebrative" (Ibidem). In other words, for Echeruo, drama is the imitation of life, a pictorial representation of what has happened in real life, whereas festival portrays actual life at a specific time of a people's emotional state of hilarity. Drama, Echeruo continues, is "a public affirmation of a *mythos* or plot, whereas ritual is the translation of faith into external action. Divination, communion or baptism may be dramatic but they do not tell a story, only symbolically reassert a faith" (Ibidem). For Echuoro, therefore, the indispensable element of drama is a story or plot. Drama, as he says "allows for the re-interpretation of life through a pattern of history we usually call plot" (Ibidem).

Andrew Horn is another writer who wants drama to be dissociated from ritual, because, for him, "whereas ritual involves communication between man and the supernatural, drama involves man communicating with man, or with a human audience (Ibidem). Secondly, the function of ritual is to make the god act while drama seeks to stimulate thought, feeling, perhaps even action in the human world alone (Ibidem). Thirdly, the ritual actor is to some degree an incarnation of a spirit, while in drama, the actor is a pretender who must be aware at all times of his identity separate from the role he plays. Finally, ritual does not tell a story, although it might have suggestions of stories; drama on the other hand is essentially a story form and even at its most episodic, is plotted, is a narrative acted out. Thus, it stems from the foregoing critical analysis that agreement is not yet reached as scholars are still debating the problem of nomenclature in African drama and traditional performances. Should one apply the name drama to African rituals and festivals? My own stand on the question will be expressed after a brief analysis of the transitional phase from rituals to practical drama in the context of Greek theatre and see the pattern followed by African theatre.

3.2.2. Personal Critical Stance

My stand is that one should dissociate ritual, festival and drama in the designation and attribution of their functions. Although the three elements play key roles in solving emotional and moral crisis both at individual and social levels, the purpose of their creations are different at the beginning, and the functions that they play in modern society are not the same. I will explain my critical position in the light of what other critics think, taking inspiration from the development of Greek theatre.

3.2.3. Transition from Oral to Written Drama in Greek Theatre Context

To begin with, it is worthwhile to recall how the transition from religious celebrations to modern theatre was done in the context of Greek theatre. Theodore W. Hatlen in his *Orientation to the Theatre* has given an account of the development of Greek theatre relying on Aristotle's *Poetics*:

> In Aristotle's statement concerning the origin of Greek tragedy, he notes that 'it advanced by slow degrees; each element that showed

itself was in turn developed'. This evolution must be traced in detail [...] The transition from the improvised performance of the dithyrambs to the full flowering of Greek tragedy can be traced in the changes which took place in the structure of the plays and in the evolution of the physical theatre (Hatlen, op cit, 8).

According to Hatlen's explanation, threshing floors served probably as venues for the performance of improvised dithyrambs. With the altar of Dionysus in the centre, the dancers moved in a circular formation setting the pattern for the orchestra circle of the later fully developed theatre architecture (Ibidem). As the actors were added to the performance, he says, the emphasis of the production shifted. While at first the chorus was the essential theatrical element, as the dramatic form evolved, the playwright focussed his attention on the speech and actions of individuals, so that by the time Greek tragedy had reached its golden age, the chorus assumed a mere supporting role to the protagonists in whom the dramatic conflict was now centered (Ibidem). The evolution of the physical theatre was from the dancing circle which all the participants occupied, to three separate entities - *the orchestra circle*, for *the chorus*, the huge *theatron* for the audience which became quite remote from the performers, and the *skene*, where the actors carried on essential action of the play (Ibidem). Thus, it can be observed the emergence of Greek tragedy, emanating from the ritual: from improvisation to finely wrought masterpieces of drama; from a general communal activity to participation by proficient few; from a makeshift dance floor to a permanent and complete theatre of stone. This stage constitutes according to Hatlen's position the transitional phase to written drama and performance.

If the transition from rituals and festivals to drama is well observable in the context of Greek drama, one can seek to know how African rituals and festivals also metamorphosed in dramatic art. It is here that the difficulty of accurate description of African rituals and festivals transition to drama begins. Wole Soyinka acknowledges that difficulty by clearly saying: "The question of when a performed event became theatre as ritualism is of course a vexed one that we need not bother about in this context (Soyinka, 1988: 191)." This critical position stresses the difficulty to describe the metamorphosis of ritual and festival into drama. This, in my opinion, means that the process of transformation from oral drama (ritual and festival) to modern (written one) in African setting alone is difficult to trace without taking into account the foreign dramatic elements (playwriting and performance) introduced with

European colonization in Africa. Here, the problem posed is clearly that of when and how ritual or festival in African context has developed into drama as art. Can we say for sure that drama as an art in Africa is the by- product of the metamorphosis of rituals and festivals? Theodore W. Hatlen reasserts the same difficulty of transformation and adds that the transitional phase is proper only to Greek theatre:

> But not all ritual becomes drama. A spark is needed to bridge the gap. In most cultures, the transition is never made. The rites continue as a functional activity, never attaining the detachment necessary to transform them into works of art which can exist for their own sake, or the ceremony remains fixed in a simple, repetitive form, never elevated to a new status through creative and interpretative expression. Drama cannot begin without the disciplined construction of an orderly sequence of words and actions representing a real or imaginary experience to which has been added impersonation. It was in Greek that this most remarkable transformation took place (Hatlen, op. cit, 4-5).

The critical stance of Theodore W. Hatlen that not all rituals become drama seems justified in the sense that in the African context, from earlier civilizations up to modern ones, most rituals and festivals still keep their religious significance and have never evolved into pure artistic performances. The rituals that are not drama in essence are those created to palliate to intense social or personal crisis and whose objectives are essentially to restore well being, health, peace and normal order in the individual or the society. Festivals and rituals are well observable in most African cultures but they rather have inclination towards people's religious beliefs and convictions rather than artistic orientations. According to Louise Bourgault, ritual and theatre have similarities and differences. This means that the two are not necessarily the same. Rituals, like theatre are a source of social change. Ritual for example is performed to restore to the normal a situation of crisis, and to renew the relationship of man with his god. To explain this he takes inspiration from Turner and states that

> Social dramas contain four phases: breach, crisis, redress and either reintegration or recognition of schism. Redressive ritual operates in the third phase. It is a measure whose form is designed

> to repair an impending breach in the social fabric, or in individual life. When it works for example, when the gods are appeased through a patterned enactment of some sort, the actors of ritual are reintegrated. They have 'gotten right with the gods' – a score between human participants or between the human and the divine has been settled. The society goes back to reasonably smooth functioning or the individual is cured. When the ritual fails, the society or the individual supplicant is still in crisis (Bourgault, 2005: 111).

This statement means that some rituals are performed when there is a crisis in an individual's or a community's life. Crisis like sickness, barrenness, epidemics, drought, floods demand divine intervention. From the performance of ritual there may be redress of the situation, hence his description of four stages breach, crisis, redress and either reintegration or recognition of schism. But in the case of drama or theatre, the performance may take place without being prompted by a certain crisis in people's life. The festivals, the baptism ceremonies, the child naming ceremonies take place within a community and gather people without necessarily involving a crisis. When such spectacles are appropriated by artists who enact them in a recurrent manner to serve a social purpose, for example social education or entertainment, they become part of theatre.

That is why I personally think that drama as an art, that is the stagecraft and acting just like the novel, was introduced in Africa from European colonization time. It has been domesticated and adapted to African setting and cultural landscape by pioneers like the Nigerian Hubert Ogunde, Duro Ladipo. Kofi Awoonor's explanation is edifying here:

> Modern drama and stagecraft in African owes its basic impetus to the introduction of European dramatic technique. Many of the contemporary dramatists writing in English and French have also been involved in experimental theatre work in African Universities. The plays attempt a synthesis between traditional dramatic material and the Western stage and production technique. A few of the dramatists, however, returned to the traditional ritual for material and inspiration (Awoonor, 1976: 306).

This observation of Kofi Awoonor helps us see the growth of modern African art drama which can be traced to the introduction of literature from the colonial period. He also clarifies the fact that African rituals and festivals have served as fuel and source of inspiration in many plays written by African playwright. This is to say that African dramatic aesthetics read in the African play through the presence of indigenous cultural elements to name rites, rituals and festivals. Plays like Wole Soyinka's *A Dance of the Forests* and *Death and the King's Horseman,* Femi Osofisan's *No More the Wasted Breed* or Efua T. Sutherland's *The Marriage of Anansewa* delve in African indigenous ritual and festival ceremonies for inspiration and theme. This is to say that modern art drama appears to have a strong connection with indigenous ritual performances even if one should dissociate pure dramatic art from traditional cultural practices of ritual. Some scholars like Tejumola Olaniyan have proposed some designations which like 'ritual drama', 'festival drama', 'art drama' (Olanyan, 2004: 37).

My personal stand is with the first group of scholars who suggest that drama should not be dissociated from rituals and festivals. In African traditional society, drama is imbricated in the cultural practices of the folk communities, practices that are not necessarily understood by western drama scholars and critics. Traditional priests determine the favourable moments for sacrifices and offerings in general. These sacrifices offer avenues for big festivals, ritual dances and songs which are true theatrical scenes (Traore, op cit, 27). Yet it is important to differentiate theatre from drama. Theatre as art has as basis the creative literature body of knowledge that was imported from Europe in the heydays of colonization. Entertainment theatre based on morality plays was thus adapted from Biblical stories and books. These manifestations are essentially oral. Nevertheless, I do agree with Pierre Médéhouégnon that if these oral performances show, like Western theatre religious and secular sources of the Black African theatre, the introduction of written theatre, with its Western-like performance was done by colonizers, with the initiatives of the first Christian missionaries and colonizers themselves (Medehouegnon, 2010: 39). Oyekan Owomoyela adds that African scholars, secure in the value of their own cultures should have no difficulty in acknowledging that Africa borrowed drama, as it is conventionally known in the Western world from Europe (Owomoyela, op cit: 45). Doing so would not mean admitting the relative inferiority of the African mentality, any more than European artists' borrowing ideas from Africa would suggest the relative inferiority of the European mentality. Cultures tend to thrive from mutual enrichment.

In this chapter I have revisited the designations and functions of ritual, festival, and drama in African literature. Ritual is the type of ceremony created by man to communicate with the supernatural or the deity. Its function is to palliate to a situation of crisis through divine intervention. The festival is celebration of communal events in a state of hilarity. Its function is to recollect communal memories, reassert faith in the indigenous deities and reassert brotherhood among people of the same tribe or ancestry. Drama is the representation of social life on stage through the re-enactment of a story by actors and actresses. It plays the roles of social education, entertainment, relaxation and socio-political reforms. The debate on the problem of nomenclature in African dramatic discourse is not exhausted. Many are the scholars who advocate cultural dignity survival and insist on the necessity of maintaining the expressions "ritual drama", "festival drama" instead of simply calling ritual or festival. Nevertheless, I for one don't think we need to stick to the claim that drama evolved from ritual and festival as in the context of Greek theatre. It is really difficult to establish the bridge showing the transitional phase of these traditional performances in pure drama art.

References

Adejumo, Debo. "Myth and Drama: Modern Adaptations of Classical Tragedies." In Ernest N. Emenyonu (ed) *Critical Theory and African Literature.* Nigeria: Heinemann Educational Books. 1987. 55-68.

Ansu-Kyeremeh, Kwasi. *Indigenous Communication in Africa.* Accra: Ghana University Press. 2005.

Awoonor, Kofi. *The Breast of the Earth: A Survey of the History, Culture and Literature of Africa South of Sahara.* New York: Anchor Books. 1976.

Banham, Martin, James Gibbs and Femi Osofisan. *African Theatre Southern Africa.* Oxford: James Currey. 1992.

--------------------------. *African Theatre Plywrights & Politics.* Oxford: James Currey. 2001.

Diawara, Manthia. *African Cinema Politics & Culture.* Bloomington & Indianapolis: Indiana University Press. 1992.

Etherton, Michael. *The Development of African Drama.* New York: Africana Publishing Company. 1982.

Geertz, Clifford. "Deep Play: Notes on Balinese Cockplay." In *Myth Symbol and Culture, Journal of the American Academy of Arts and Sciences,* Winter 1972, vol 101, N0 1. 1972. 1-38.

Greenblatt, Stephen. *Shakespearean Negotiations: The Circulation of Social Energy in Renaissance England.* California: University of California Press. 1988.

Hatlen, Theodore W. *Orientation to the Theatre*. New York: Appleton-Century-Crofts. 1962.

Horby, A S. *Oxford Advanced Learner's Dictionary 7th Edition*. Oxford: Oxford University Press. 2008.

Irele, Abiola. *The African Experience in Literature and Ideology*. London: Heinemann Educational Books. 1981.

Jabbi, Bu-Buakei. "Myth and Ritual in *Arrow of God*". In Eldred Durosimi Jones (ed) *African Literature Today: Myth and History*. London: Heinemann Educational Books. 1980. 130-148.

Médéhouégnon, Pierre. *Le théâtre francophone de l'Afrique de l'Ouest des origines à nos jours (Historique et analyse)*. Jéricho-Cotonou : Caarec Editions. 2010.

Montrose, Louis. *The Purpose of Playing: Shakespeare and the Cultural Politics of the Elizabethan Theatre*. Chicago: Chicago University Press. 1996.

Morgan, Norah and Juliana Saxton. *Teaching Drama: A Mind of Wonders*. Postsmouth. New Hampshire: Heinemann. 1987.

Natoli, Joseph ed. *Tracing Literary Theory*. Urbana and Chicago: University of Illinois Press. 1987.

Ogunyemi, Bayo and Abdul-Rasheed Na'Allah. *Introduction to African Oral Literature and Performance*. Trenton: Africa World Press, Inc. 2005.

Okpewho, Isidore. *The Oral Performance in Africa*. Ibadan. Owerri. Kaduna: Spectrum Books Limited. 1990.

Sinfield, Allan. 1992. *Faultlines: Cultural Materialism and the Politics of Dissident Reading*. California: University of California Press.

Stratton, Florence. *Contemporary African Literature and the Politics of Gender*. London and New York: Routledge. 1994.

Szondi, Peter. *Theory of Modern Drama A Critical Edition*. Cambridge: Polity Press. 1987.

Taiwo, Oladele. *Female Novelists of Modern Africa*. London and Basingstoke: Macmillan Publishers. 1984.

Taylor, Jenny Bourne. "New Historicism." In Michael Payne and Jessica Rae Barbera., eds., *A Dictionary of Cultural and Critical Theory*. New York: Wiley-Blackwell. 2010. 484-487.

Tompkins, Jane P. ed. *Reader-response Criticism From Formalism to Post Structuralism*. Baltimore and London: The Johns Hopkins University Press. 1980.

Traoré, Bakary. *The Black African Theatre and its Social Functions. Translated and with a Preface by Dapo Adelugba*. Nigeria: Ibadan University Press. 1972.

wa Thiong'o, Ngugi. *Homecoming Essays on African and Caribbean Literature, Culture and Politics*. New York. Westport: Lawrence Hill and Company. 1972.

Nubukpo, Komla Messan. « La critique littéraire «africaine :» Réalités et perspectives d'une idéologie de la différence ». In *Canadian Journal of African Studies Number*

3. Canada : Canadian Association of African Studies. 1990. PP. 399-417.

Olaniyan, Tejumola. "Festivals, Ritual and Drama in Africa." In Abiola Irele and Simon Gikandi (eds) *The Cambridge History of African and Caribbean Literature, Vol 1*. Cambridge; Cambridge University Press. 2004. 35-48.

Oyinkan Owomoyela, "Give me Drama or…: the Argument on the Existence of Drama in Traditional Africa." In R. Hunt Davis (ed.) *The African Studies Review* (Los Angeles: African Studies Association, 1986. 28-45.

Pliya, Jean. « Rôle du théâtre dans le développement culturel en Afrique ». In Babacar Ba (ed.) *Quel theâtre pour le dévéloppement en Afrique*. Dakar Abidjan. Lome: Les nouvelles editions africaines. 1985. PP. 11-21

Sweney, Ellen. "Femi Osofissan and the Dialectic of Continuity". In Ernest N. Emenyonu (ed.) *Literature and Society. Selected Essays on African Literature*. Oguta: Zim Pan African Publishers. 1986. PP. 84-94.

Taylor, Jenny Bourne. "New Historicism." In Michael Payne and Jessica Rae Barbera., eds., *A Dictionary of Cultural and Critical Theory*. New York: Wiley-Blackwell. 2010. 484-487.

4

ASPECTS OF NARRATOLOGY: AFRICAN ORAL NARRATIVES AS DRAMA

African playwrights have extensively used elements of oral tradition as raw material to write modern plays. The presence of orality in written literature, the abundance of folk tradition, festivals, rituals, rites, myth, legends, animal stories, folktales, riddles speak from more than one perstectives about the corelationship between oral and written drama in African context. What this chapter is looking at is the legacies of oral narratives as springboard of drama, the cristalization of such elements that later on feed the industry of modern plays. Narratology serves as the methodological framework of this analysis.

One of the most prominent narratologists since Roland Barthes has been Gerard Genette, whose work has as its focus, not the tale itself, so to speak, but how it is told, which is to say, the process of telling itself. What is meant by this distinction will become apparent if we consider six particular areas which Genette discusses (in his book *Narrative Discourse*, Basil Blackwell, 1972). In what follows I ask six basic questions about the act of narration, and sketch under each the range of possibilities identified by Genette, with some supplementary categories of my own.

4.1.1. From Theoretical Groundings to The Basic Narrative Modes: 'Mimetic' or 'Diegetic'?

Genette discusses this mimesis and diegesis in Chapter four, 'Mood'. 'Mimesis' means 'showing' or 'dramatising'. The parts of a narrative which are presented in a mimetic manner are 'dramatised', which is to say that they are represented in a 'scenic' way, with a specified setting, and making use of dialogue which contains direct speech. 'Mimesis' is 'slow telling', in which what is done and said is 'staged' for the reader, creating the illusion that we are 'seeing' and 'hearing' things for ourselves. By contrast, 'diegesis' means 'telling' or 'relating'. The parts of a narrative which are presented in this way are given in a more 'rapid' or 'panoramic' or 'summarising' way. The aim is to give us essential or linking information as efficiently as possible, without trying to create the illusion that the events are taking place before our eyes - the narrator just *says* what happens, without trying to show it *as* it happens. In practice, of course, writers use the two modes in tandem, moving from mimetic to diegetic, and back again, for strategic reasons.

Oral narratives play a key role in the formulation, development and performance of drama in Africa. Born from the oral tradition that has long existed and sustained the unwritten literary forms, oral narratives purvey the quintessential dispatching of traditional wisdom, the very depository of social life and politics that find expression in the intellectual articulation of dramatic literature. Narratology refers to the scientific study of narratives. In African context, the place reserved for oral tradition is so important that literature just cannot exist in isolation without incorporating elements of orality, orature or oral tradition into its different utterances. Oral tradition ranges from folktales, animal stories, myths, legends, proverbs, riddles, to mention but a few. Theatrical oral narratives combine these elements into a wholistic body of narratives that call for serious artistic attention to comprehend how they speak to the audiences as dramatic formulae. Monika Fludernik in her *An Introduction to Narratology* (2009) has underlined the core importance of narratives in human society and their relationship with humans:

> As research is showing increasingly clearly, the human brain is constructed in such a way that it captures many complex relationships in the form of narrative structures, metaphors or analogies. Just as we may describe a personal relationship metaphorically as a house that one partner has built painstakingly and lovingly and which the other casually allows to deteriorate until the plaster crumbles and the roof caves in, we may also conceive of each of our lives as a journey constituted by narration. Throughout our lives, things frequently happen without prior warning and bring about radical changes in the course of events, for example the first unexpected meeting with one's future partner.

> In reconstructing our own lives as stories, we like to emphasize how particular occurrences have brought about and influenced subsequent events. Life is described as a goal-directed chain of events which, despite numerous obstacles and thanks to certain opportunities, has led to the present state of affairs, and which may yet have further unpredictable turns and unexpected developments in store for us (Fludernik 2009: 1).

The utility of the term oral narrative is based in its apparent neutrality in designating a story or narrative that is spoken rather than written or read. There are numerous types of narrative that need to be examined in order to understand the range of this term and how it applies to African verbal art forms. A story can be conceived as a string of words that conveys events having a beginning, a middle, and an end. A common type of story is found in the orally performed narrative, describing events that move a character or characters through one state of existence into another. In Africa, there are specific times and seasons for storytelling. At evenings, usually during the dry season when crops are gathered and the elders have time to spare, they gather the youth at moonlight, sometimes at the village public square or under a big village tree. Stories are told in a purely theatrical conventions and manners. The storyteller plays the role of a principal actor, the audience are all ears riveted on him. As the cantor proceeds, the audience participates vividly with handclapping, chanting in chorus. The cantor takes acrobatic body postures, bending and stretching his body, intermitting tale with songs and conflated language to create real spectacle. Narratologists would generally depict these stages as a movement from ignorance to knowledge, from poverty to wealth, from single to married status, from youth to adulthood, from death to life, or variations of these changes of state or status. These developments are at the heart of almost all known stories, from the briefest tales to the longest epics. In written literature, the short story, novel, and other postindustrial prose genres adhere to these basic elements of narrative. Narratives can be comprised of everyday speech interactions, as basic as a lone person telling another what happened that day or at some time in his or her life. Some societies preserve their significant historical information in primarily oral formats, with historians or even non-specialists being able to recount important events and characters from memory. These narratives are often in the form of heroic actions and/or significant migrations from one place to another. Individuals are able to tell their own life stories in the form of narratives of achievements and/or failures, and these, in turn, become a part of local or family histories.

Generically, oral narratives come in many forms. These have historically been labeled folktales, legends, fables, parables, *contes, fables,* myths, epics, histories, origin tales, and so on. In the study of oral societies, it is clear that each society has named its narratives and that these terms are often not exactly equivalent to the generic terms provided by outside scholars. For example, the Bemba people of Zambia distinguish two types of imaginative narrative: *ulushimi* (*inshimi,* pl.) and *umulumbe* (*imilumbe,* pl.). Though both types of tale are similar in many ways, the former often contains a song or songs and is mostly told to children, while the latter usually does not contain songs and is most often told to adults. The categories are familiar to the Bemba, although there is also no great care taken to keep the classifications "pure," in any sense of enforcement of rules of performance or strictures against certain people telling the respective stories. Narratives are also classified by the context in which they are performed. For example, certain narratives focus on past kings or spirits who are important to a society. If they are recounted at special occasions, sometimes as a part of a ritual, they are seen to have theatrical, religious or even curative significance. Certain forms of divination, such as the Yoruba Ifa system, include narratives or proverbs in their body of knowledge that are then linked into the process of establishing the appropriate responses to specific cases. Some tales of heroes or hunters may be linked to ceremonies of purification for initiation rites or specific preventative measures, such as before a hunt or a particularly hazardous journey.

In post-colonial times, these journeys may include travel to a distant town to work in mines, industry, or agriculture, or even wayfarers going abroad for study or commercial reasons. Sacred or secular, the narratives often have similar plots and activities. In some cases, the same story may take its particular value from the characters involved. In one set of tales, the characters may be animals, and all their actions, attitudes, and accomplishments may be simply seen as humorous thus creating a theatrical interest to be watched as spectacle. If the same plots and actions are carried out by human characters, the tales might be seen as more important or significant in their relationship to the world of people. Even some of the most intricate or important tales are subject to repetition by anyone who has heard them. In fact, the continuity of some narratives over time depends on this kind of transmittal and repetition. Africa is particularly replete with narratives that treat the adventures of trickster characters. Though societies from other parts of the world sometimes produce stories centered on trickster activities, many have inherited the stories from the African diaspora. Ruth Finnegan has this to say:

> The fact, however, that oral literature can also be considered on its own terms, and, as pointed out in the last chapter, may have its *own* artistic characteristics, analogous to but not always identical with more familiar literary forms, is neglected in both popular conceptions and detailed studies. The poetic, the topical, and the literary—all these, then, are aspects which still tend to be overlooked. It is indeed hard for those steeped in some of the earlier theories to take full account of them. But what the subject now demands is further investigation of these aspects of African oral art, as well as the whole range of hitherto neglected questions which could come under the general heading of the sociology of literature; and a turning away from the generalized assumptions of earlier theoretical and romanticizing speculators and of past (or even present) public opinion (Finnegan 2012: 49).

Bending Finnegan to the present argument, one needs to understand that oral narrative expands in time and space. Trickster narratives found in the Caribbean, South America, and in the southern United States can be identified as having African origins. There is a Native American tradition of trickster stories, but these are often quite different from the African narratives in terms of characteristics of the trickster and the tone and tenor of the tales. Nonetheless, African tricksters tend to be small, clever creatures, such as Kwaku Ananse, the spider of Akan tales; Sungura and Kalulu, the hares of East African and Zambian narratives, respectively; Mantis, the San trickster; or the tortoise of several Nigerian traditions. The character of the trickster, the small, clever, and, at times, amoral figure, is often diluted a bit and found in the person of the young child who is beset by ogres or brutal villains in other kinds of narrative. Narrative in Africa reaches a particularly complex, highly textured form in the performance of epic, which involves a combination of narrative, poetry, and song; the epic is often sung or chanted to musical accompaniment. The content of these narratives is usually historical, at least in part, and focuses on a crucial period in the society in question's past.

4.1.2. Narrative focalization: Oral Narratives and their Theatrically Implied Meanings

Focalisation (discussed in pages 189-94 of *Narrative Discourse*)[3] means 'viewpoint' or 'perspective', which is to say the point-of-view from which the story is told. There are many possibilities: for example, in 'external' focalisation the viewpoint is *outside* the character depicted, so that we are told only things which are external or observable - that is, what the characters *say* and *do*, these being things you would hear and see for yourself if you were present at the scene depicted. In the opposite, 'internal focalisation', the focus is on what the characters *think* and *feel*, these being things which would be inaccessible to you even if you had been present. Thus, the sentence 'Kongi stood up and called out Oba Danlola' is an externally focalized representation of this moment, for you would see and hear these things if you were present when they happened. By contrast, consider the sentence 'Kongi suddenly felt anxious that Danlola was not going to see her and would walk by oblivious on the other side of Ikebadan Cross Road.' This is an internally focalised representation of her; it reveals her unspoken thoughts and feelings, which you could be completely unaware of even if you were standing next to her. If the story is told throughout mainly with this internal focalisation on Thelma, then she can be called the 'focaliser' of the tale (or the 'reflector', in another tradition of narratological terms). Some-times a storyteller will freely enter the minds and emotions of more than one of the characters, as if privy to the thoughts and feelings of all of them. This kind of narrative can be said to have 'zero focalisation'; this occurs 'when no systematic conceptual or perceptual constraint governs what may be presented', as Gerald Prince elegantly puts it in his *A Dictionary of Narratology* (University of Nebraska Press, 1987). Prince says that zero focalisation is characteristic of 'traditional' or 'classical' narration. Its more familiar name is 'omniscient narration'.

The real question may be how can one read oral narratives or storytelling as drama? Every well-told story is rife with drama-packed features. First, it is worth recalling that human life is drama in content and form. Stories are the recapturing of life in allegorical tales intended to teach morality, to admonish, to rebuke bad behavior and to encourage good attitudes. Just like dramatice scenes unfold before the very eyes of the spectators, everyday life unfolds as dramatic scenes with people meeting one another, exchanging

---

[3]Ernest Hemingway, *The First Forty-Nine Stories* (Arrow Books, 1993)

greetings, discussing business, planning actions, remembering past incidents or events, collaborating in joint actions, sometimes clashing into petty quarrels. Anyone who chooses to watch storytelling sessions becomes active spectator. Storytelling is present in many aspects of human life. Stories are told by grandparents, parents, and other family members.

Stories are integral to the mediums of television, film, opera, and theater, and storytelling sessions sometimes take place in the business world at special meetings. Campfire tales are meant to make campers shiver. And urban legends, contemporary folktales that usually are attributed to a "friend of a friend," are told and retold. No matter how unlikely the tale may be, the teller invariably insists, "It's *true!*" formalize this sharing takes on the role of the "storyteller." A storyteller has a repertoire of tales, skill at delivering those tales, and access to an audience.

The sharing of stories serves the audience as well as the teller. For the audience, the storytelling event offers a moment of play, a shared experience, a bonding. Participation stories allow listeners to be involved in an artistic event—and, in the hands of a skilled teller, they can play their part very well. Emotionally intense stories bring a group of people closer together in a shared caring. What even testifies to the dramatic content of stories is that in such a group event, emotions that are not normally allowed to surface are released. The most wonderful gift of story is the bonding of a group. Held close under the spell of a story, the group breathes as one. The shared experience softens the edges between individuals and brings everyone closer in the warmth of the moment. Together, the members of the group enter a "story trance." Storytellers benefit, in turn, as they experience the heartwarming feeling of holding the audience's attention and nurturing the group by sharing a beloved tale. Many stories also serve the community in a broader sense. All societies use stories to pass on group values. Wrapped in the sweet pill of an entertaining story, a moral goes down easily. Stories also can be useful tools that allow individuals to chastise or expose negative behaviors without overtly speaking the truth. The Liberian storyteller Won-Ldy Paye related how Ananse spider stories have been used to "say without saying" in front of a chief. If the chief has behaved in a greedy manner, the storyteller shows Anansi in this incorrect behavior. Everyone knows whom the storyteller is talking about. The chief hears, and he knows, too. Many families draw "catch-phrases" from their favorite stories, with which they can quickly refer to a story in the course of their daily lives. A phrase, such as "It doesn't take long to look at a horseshoe," can bring family members back to the original story, as well as remind them of the moral of the tale. Communities and families also may wrap their history in stories in order to remember details of events long past. A moment in time can be preserved by creating a story and telling it a few times. The story format bundles the facts into a neatly tied packet that is more readily stored and retrieved than a number of separate details. Stories also help to broaden awareness of other cultures. The folktale genre, in particular, reflects many traditions and helps to familiarize people with world cultures. Stories also can be used for educational purposes. Stories can help to develop a child's literary sensibilities, and listening to tales impresses a sense of story structure into a child's mind. Stories aid in stretching vocabulary, and children who are able to tell stories often gain advanced verbal ability and an increased sense of self-worth. Storytelling provides other growth opportunities, as stories help listeners to see through another's eyes and to share the protagonist's feelings of anger, fear, or love—all from a safe place. Stories provide role models who show us how to face demons and overcome adversity. Perhaps best of all, stories stretch the imagination. The teller takes the listener to distant places where remarkable things happen. And once stretched, an imagination stays stretched. There are many different story categories, ranging from true adventures to tall tales. All stories can be organized roughly into four genres: true stories, folklore, fiction and literature, and fairy tales.

4.1.3. Who is Telling the Story: Narrative Realism

Of course, the author/cantor/storyteller is, but not necessarily in his or her own voice or persona the teller or narrator. One kind of narrator (the kind that often goes with a zero-focalised narrative) is not identified at all as a distinct character with a name and a personal history, and remains just a voice or a tone, which we may register simply as an intelligent, recording consciousness, a mere 'telling medium' which strives for neutrality and transparency. Such narrators may be called 'covert', 'effaced', 'non-intrusive', or 'non-dramatised'. We may impatiently insist that it is simply the author speaking to us directly, but it is worth remembering that this is not in any sense the author's 'true' voice, since he or she only uses this precise tone, pace, degree of detail, and so on, when narrating a work of fiction. If we met the author at a party or in a bar we wouldn't be able to tolerate this narrative style for more than a couple of minutes. Hence, it makes sense to think of this kind of disembodied narrator as an 'authorial persona', rather than as the author in person. The other kind of narrator is the kind who is identified as a distinct, named character, with a personal history, gender, a social-class position, distinct likes and dislikes, and so on. These narrators have witnessed, or learned about, or even participated in the events they tell. They can be called 'overt' or 'dramatised' or 'intrusive' narrators.

A true story may be a personal account or a recounting of a historic event. The story may be embellished or exaggerated, but the facts generally are unaltered. News stories fall into this category, and newscasters, with their deliberate style of delivery, definitely can be called storytellers. There are also folk performers, such as the *plena* singers of Puerto Rico, who present the news of the day and social commentary in music. Like the traditional town crier, who strolled the streets calling out the day's news, these storytellers provide information in communities that lack ready access to television or recent newspapers. Family stories usually are shared among the members of a nuclear or extended family.

These tales may include factual history, shared memories, family jokes, and exaggerated tales about the exploits or mishaps of family members and friends. In the past, family histories were fabricated to trace back the ancestry of a ruler, or a particular clan, to a deity. This gave early leaders and dominant peoples credibility among the masses. The types of family stories range from personal memories to general family histories that include a family's shared beliefs, customs, and folklore. Stories of personal memories tend to be less complex than family histories. Personal memories might include seemingly trivial events, such as how a sister had a "bad hair day" on the day of a big date and what she did about it, or how the teller first planted a garden. In the right hands, however, this same material can be crafted into an engaging tale. Family stories or histories generally encompass a larger view of the world. They might tell of how the family survived a famine, a flood or an epidemic.

The genre of folklore predates written literature and can be broken down into the following categories: folktales, nursery rhymes and some nonsense rhymes, myths, religious stories, epics, ballads, fables, and legends. A folktale is literally a tale of the folk, or the people, that has no known author. Folklorists separate folktales into basic categories, such as wonder tales, moral tales, tales of fools, and *pourquoi,* or how-and-why, tales. A wonder tale generally is a story of adventure and magic with familiar themes, such as the triumph of the third son, the magic sword, the talking animal helper, and so on. An example of a moral tale is the "Grateful Dead" tale type, in which a ghost rewards the man who gave his earthly remains an honorable burial. Fool tales, also known as noodle or numbskull tales, generally are good-natured tales of foolish or downright stupid people, such as the Jewish folktales of the people of Chelm, "to whom foolish things keep happening." Pourquoi tales explain the how-andwhy of things that are too ordinary to be the themes of true myths, such as the West African story of "Why Mosquitoes Buzz in People's Ears" or the Indian story of "Why the Blue Jay is Blue." Nursery rhymes are ideal for entertaining young children. There are many collections of nursery rhymes available, and the rhymes usually are in the public domain. Some storytellers invent their own rhymes. But the classic rhymes have been around for ages for good reason: They are fun for children to repeat and effectively use humor and musical language.

Nonsense rhymes are also favorites with the younger age group. Myths address daunting themes such as creation, life, death, and the workings of the natural world, answering major life questions such as "How did the world begin?" and "Why does the Sun rise and set?" Myths often include deities and other supernatural beings in their lists of characters, and they may tell of cosmic events, such as the birth of the universe. Myths are closely related to religious stories, since myths sometimes belong to living religions. In addition to explaining questions about the world around us, these stories create a sense of community among believers, often giving comfort to the listeners. Religious stories are likely to be retellings from sacred books, such as the Christian *Bible* and the Hindu *Bhagavad Gita*. Religious stories also may take the form of parables, or tales intended to teach a lesson, such as the Christian parable of the prodigal son. Epics are long narrative poems about the adventures of legendary figures. While Homer's *Iliad* may not sustain the interest of a youthful audience, the tales of King Arthur and his knights or the adventures of the African heroking Sundiata would be appropriate. Shorter epic tales that are full of adventure and heroism are ideal for children. Ballads are poems that tell a dramatic story in verse. Longer ballads may be too much for a younger audience, but a great many of the ballads—for instance, those about Robin Hood—can easily be told as stories. Fables are short stories that teach a lesson. Many of the characters in fables are animals that talk and act like humans. Some fables, such as those written by the eighteenth-century French writer Voltaire, were meant for adults. Others, such as Aesop's fables, are more popular with children, because of the clear examples of right and wrong. In Aesop's "The Fox and the Grapes," the fox is unable to reach the grapes and so decides they are sour. The moral of this fable is, "It is easy to despise what you cannot get." Legends are about historic or quasi-historic people or places. American legends, to take some familiar examples, include stories about larger-than-life but real people, such as frontiersman Davy Crockett (who invented many of his legends himself) and riverboat man Mike Fink. A legend may feature a real person but not celebrate an actual event. The American legend of George Washington and the cherry tree is based on an incident that never occurred. The legend has lasted, because peo Fiction and Literature Storytellers often turn to fiction when searching for source material. Nonfiction books do not lend themselves as well to storytelling. The genre of fiction ranges from novels based on historic events to total fantasy. Fantasy and science fiction describe adventures in both realistic and fantastic settings.

Mysteries engage listeners young and old, as the unraveling story leads the audience to discover "whodunit." Children's mysteries generally do not feature murders or other gruesome crimes, and early mystery series. Animal stories can be about either wild or domestic animals. Within this genre are stories about the bond between animals and humans. These stories have long been favorites of children and have long been used by storytellers. Adventure tales feature brave and clever heroes and dangerous villains. Early adventure stories might feature brave swashbucklers and pirates, while heroes in modern works may triumph over terrorists. Historical fiction is exciting as well as educational, since it provides a glimpse of life ways and traditions from long ago. Realistic novels, also called problem novels, deal with real world issues, such as drugs and pollution. These have a more limited audience than some of the other "lighter" genres.

Stories both realistic and far-fetched that are set in foreign lands give listeners a look into other traditions and cultures that add an exotic touch. Fairy Tales Fairy tales are stories in which a series of fantastic events befall the protagonist and almost always lead to a happy ending. The bestknown fairy tales are those written by the nineteenth-century Danish author Hans Christian Andersen.

4.1.4. The Handling of Time in the Story

Oral narratives often contain references back and references forward, so that the order of telling does not correspond to the order of happening. Sometimes the story will 'flash back' to relate an event which happened in the past, and such parts of the narrative can be called 'analeptic' (from 'analepsis', which literally means a 'back-take'). Likewise, the narrative may 'flash forward' to narrate, or refer to, or anticipate an event which happens later: such parts of the narrative can be called 'proleptic' (from 'prolepsis', which literally means a 'fore-take'). Typically, writers make strategic use of both **analepsis** and **prolepsis** in telling a story, for the beginning is seldom the best place to begin - stories tend to begin in the middle *(in medias res,* as the theorists of classical times said), with analeptic material sketching out what went before, and proleptic devices hinting at what the outcome will be, and thereby engaging the reader and generating the basic narrative momentum. These matters are discussed in Genette's first chapter, 'Order', under the sub-heading 'Narrative time'.

Fairy tales usually open with the conventional, "once upon a time," which still holds power over listeners. Other beginnings from around the world include (origins are listed if known):

- It all happened long ago, and believe it or not, it is all absolutely true . . . (Ireland)
- Long years ago, in the early ages of the world . . . (Hungary)
- In a place neither near nor far, and a time neither now nor then . . . (Denmark)
- Once there was, twice there was, and once there was not . . . (Scotland)
- Long ago, so long ago I wasn't there or I wouldn't be here now to tell you . . . (Ireland) Not in your time, not in my time, but in the old time, when Earth and the sea were new . . .
- At a time when people and animals spoke the same language . . . (Navajo)
- Once there was and once there wasn't . . . (Slavic)
- Back when it was a sin to talk too much . . .
- In the days now long departed . . . (Scandinavia)
- Long ago, when some folk were dead and others weren't born yet . . . (Tartar)
- It happened, it did not happen, it could perhaps have happened in the tents of our neighbors . . . (Arabic)
- Many years ago, in a time when memory was young . . . (India)
- Before the beginning of time, before the beginning of everything, before there was a beginning . . .
- Once, on the far side of yesterday . . .
- Once upon a time, and a very good time it was . . . (England)
- In a time not your time, nor my time, nor indeed anyone's time . . . (England)

- In a time when your grandfather was a wee baby, and turnips could talk ... (Ireland)
- Long, long ago, in the days when animals talked like people ... (used by many indigenous peoples)

All fairy tale plots follow a basic structure: The initial setup is a description of the setting and main characters—such as the poor farm and the poor family or the royal palace and the ugly princess. Then, a complication is presented—for example, the poor family's only son must leave home to find a fortune before his family starves, or the ugly princess must find a way to break the curse she lives under before she reaches her sixteenth birthday or she will never be free of it. The setup and complication are followed by a quest. This could be the son's efforts to succeed with royalty or rich merchants or the ugly princess's hunting to find the fairy who cursed her or a magician who can help her. Finally, there is the outcome, in which all problems are resolved and there is a happy ending. There are also certain conventions that pertain to fairy tale characters.

4.1.5. Speech and Thought Representations

Genette discusses this matter in his 'Mood' chapter under the sub-heading 'Narrative of Words'.

Genette's terms for representations of speech in a narrative are actually slightly more generalised than those just described, envisaging three layers, which get progressively further away from the actual words spoken, as follows:

1. 'I have to go', I said to her. (Mimetic speech)
2. I told her I had to go. (Transposed speech)
3. I informed her that it was necessary for me to leave. (Narra-tised speech)

As Genette says (172), transposed speech isn't quite the same as free indirect speech: to be precise, it's indirect, but it isn't free (since it has the declarative verb 'I told', which is a form of tagging). The essential difference between transposed and narratised speech is that the former allows us to deduce the actual form of words used ('I have to go'), whereas the latter conveys the *substance* of what was said, but not the actual verbal formula (which could have been 'I've got to go', 'I am obliged to go', 'I have no option but to go', etc.).

Effectively, this converts living speech into narrated event, and interposes the maximum distance between the reader and the direct impact and tone of the spoken words.

Listeners expect the characters to be somewhat familiar. The protagonist generally is possessed of one or more of the following attributes: He or she is young, is either of common or of noble birth, is the third son or daughter, has a good heart and is well mannered, and/or is a human without magical powers. Similarly, villains generally fall into one of the following categories: He or she may be a wicked or insulted fairy, witch, or warlock, an evil aristocrat wanting the throne, a miserable miser, an officious official, a greedy or envious ruler, or a demon or devil (sometimes in disguise). Descriptions of characters are minimal in fairy tales, as they are in folktales and myths. It is enough for readers to know that a character is kind of heart or fair of face. Peripheral characters often are not even given names but are placed in a story to move the action along.

They simply go by descriptive monikers such as "the blacksmith" or "the tailor." Other detailed physical descriptions or identifications also are not included. In the Greek myth of Jason and the Argonauts, the Golden Fleece is never actually described. And further details are not required for such story elements as the "golden apples" or the "honest farmer." Most, though not all, fairy tales include some element of the supernatural. When the hero is kind to an old woman, he may be given a magic box of never-ending coins or a flying carpet. These gifts are always taken in stride by fairy tale characters who accept the existence of magic without question. Again, fairy tales almost always end happily, and villains are ultimately punished. The penalties generally are not described in graphic, sadistic detail, as they often are in folktales, but there is a feeling of satisfaction and justice achieved at the story's end. Interestingly, what is considered a happy ending may vary, depending on the tale version. For instance, modern fairy tales do not always end in the traditional way, with the princess marrying a handsome prince. Instead, the princess might choose to start a democracy and run for public office. As with the variable outcome, there are many variants of the familiar ending, "and they lived happily ever after" from around the world (origins are listed if known):

- Snip snap snout, now my tale is out. (Caribbean)
- Wires bend, stories end. (Caribbean)
- Crick! Crack! (Caribbean; also may be used to open a story)
- And maybe they did all live happily ever after, but how you and I live is up to us. (Western Europe and United States)

- And they lived happily ever after, but you and I are left here sucking on our teeth. (Eastern Europe)
- And that's the end of that. (Ireland)
- And the party lasted four days and four nights, and I've only just come away from it to tell you this tale. (Eastern Europe)
- And if you don't believe this story is true, go see for yourself.
- And ever since then, that's the way it has been. (widespread)
- And what happened next? Well, that's another story for another day.
- And so it was, and so it is, to this very day. (Ireland and Western Europe)
- Such things do happen, you know.
- And they lived happily ever after, or if they didn't, it's none of our business. (United States)

4.1.6. The Packaging of Stories

Stories are not always presented 'straight'. Often storytellers make use of 'frame narratives' (also called 'primary narratives'), which contain within them 'embedded narratives' (also called 'secondary narratives'). For instance, the main story in Ola Rotimi's *The Gods Are Not to Blame* is embedded within a frame narrative of Baba Fakunle telling the story of how the kingdom of Adewale got defiled by the misdeed of the king who killed his father to marry his mother. One of the stories told by one of the characters in Femi Osofisan's *The Oriki of the Grasshopper* in these circumstances is the one which forms the substance of Osofisan's tale. Notice that here 'primary narrative' really just means the narrative which comes first, rather than the *main* narrative, which in fact it usually isn't. The 'secondary narrative' is the one which comes second and is embedded into the primary narrative. The secondary narrative is usually the main story.

It is possible, too, to go a little further and sub-classify frame narratives as 'single-ended', 'double-ended', or 'intrusive'. A 'single-ended' frame narrative is one in which the frame situation is not returned to when the embedded tale is complete.

Oral performance and literature are often regarded in contrast to one another. The relationship between the two types of discourse is a complex one and depends in many cases on the researcher's interest and what he or she is seeking. On the one hand, studies from the 1960s onward have been exploring the concept of "orality" as opposed to "literacy." On the other hand, there are many qualities of narrative, form, and imagery that clearly overlap between the spoken and written word. It is important to emphasize the differences between oral performance and literature because, for many years, the former was seen as the progenitor (and less "advanced" relation) of the latter. This relationship is clear in the earliest evidence of literary activity, from the Dead Sea Scrolls, to the Epic of Gilgamesh, the Old Testament, and Homeric epic. At the same time, these seminal works posed problems in form and style that were only answered when scholars began to see them as products of oral societies. Qualities often seen as flaws in contemporary literature—repetition, parallel constructions, episodic structure, rambling speeches, or apparent digressions—were common in these early texts.

Work begun by Milman Parry in the 1920s, and later carried on by Albert Lord and others, compared a living epic tradition from Yugoslavia with the remnants of the oral epic tradition of the Homeric corpus. The similarities were impressive enough to allow scholars to solve some of the oldest questions about Homer's compositions. The repetition, digressions, even the obvious errors due to losing one's train of thought, were explained by the dictates of narrating and composing poetic narrative as the performer went along. Methods of composition were discovered that were based upon the rhythmic activities of bardic in-struments such as the lute. Oration, furthermore, came to be seen as a living, interactive art form. (Lord 1960)

Later scholarship by Walter Ong (1967) pointed to similar qualities of composition and performance in other literary works, in particular, the Bible, and went further to hypothesize an entirely different sensory mode of perceiving the world. Oral societies were based in an orally and aurally dictated environment that was three-dimensional and founded on sound and its various emotional/intellectual properties. The literate world had evolved into a visual culture, depending on the private and isolating environment of reading and writing to keep history, store knowledge, and even argue ideas. The oral world was a communal one, where ideas had to be voiced in order to be understood, argued, and perpetuated. The great orators were also among the most respected intellectuals, the most powerful people in society. In the literate world, ideas flowed in books and on paper, and they could be read repeatedly for understanding and critical examination. The spoken word was powerful, though vaporous. Once spoken, it disappeared. It is difficult for someone to say the exact same thing more than one time. Therefore, ideas were subject to perpetuation only if they were spoken over and over again.

Some scholars argued that orally composed and performed narratives were, in fact, not prose at all. Tedlock (1977) and his contemporaries in the field of ethnopoetics contended, that prose is a product of literacy. What oral performers of narrative did was much closer to what literary scholars call poetry. The rhythms of speech, the types of imagery, the power of the spoken word, and the close proximity of song to speech in oral performance all moved towards poetic composition rather than prose. This is a particularly valuable way to discuss the dynamics of performance, which often include many techniques and interactions that allow speech to approach song and body movements to approach dance. Yet it is also important to acknowledge the elements of spoken narratives and poems that approach literary production. In imaginative narrative, there are crucial elements of plot, character, action, and theme that are linked to the appreciation of these performances. Some scholars acknowledge this vital connection by referring to the art forms as *oral literature*. Other scholars, treating mostly African verbal arts, who are wary of a certain degree of ethoncentricity intrinsic in even the term literature, choose to call the activity and its products *orature*. Both schools of thought explicitly acknowledge the equivalent processes of creativity in language, character development, intricacies of plot or structure, and related factors that go into orally performed narrative or poetry. Oral performance and literature employ symbolic forms that create metaphor and allegory.

Both oral and written arts are potentially transformative in the ways they can move audiences/readers. Early African writers, mission-educated and often working in their own languages, reproduced tales, proverbs, and riddles as subjects of their literary efforts. Although they lacked evidence of the dynamic oral spontaneity and verbal interactions between audience and performer, these works did, in an inadequate way, suggest the themes, characters, and concerns of African oral traditions. Contemporary African writers, working in English and French, often include elements of oral traditions in their literature. In his novels, Nigerian Chinua Achebe has made the proverb a key formal and thematic device of his art. Nigeria's Nobel laureate Wole Soyinka combines ideas from Yoruba myth, religion, song, and ritual within modernist frameworks in his plays, novels, and poems.

Oral performance is the means by which numerous genres of verbal arts are externalized through the interaction between performer(s) and audience(s). There is no verbal art outside of performance. Storytelling, singing, formal orations of any type exist only in people's minds until they are spoken, shared. The techniques employed by performers and the context within which the performances occur comprise the dynamics of oral performance. On one level, performance dynamics are linked to the methods or techniques the performer employs in externalizing the particular genre at any one time. A simple example of these techniques is the choice of demeanor by a storyteller or bardic performer of epic poems. This choice is often dictated by the individual's personality: serious or comical, authoritative or open to audience concerns. This demeanor is also influenced by the context of the performance: tied to an important ritual/festival, an informal gathering around a fire, a competitive situation between performers, and so forth. Both the qualities of the individual and the elements of context of performance are also mediated by the expectations of the audience. Do they know the performer and expect him or her to satisfy their expectations of style or technique? Does the context suggest a well-known performer should, for reasons of decorum, alter his or her approach in deference to the situation?

Looking more specifically at techniques that make up any one performer's style, certain elements can be catalogued. Does the performer prefer the lengthy exposition of certain commonly known kernels of imagery, plot, or character development, or is he or she prone to concise evocation that allows the audience to fill in details on their own based on past performances? A simple example can be seen in the performance of the epic *Sunjata* among the Mande people of the Gambia. One bard performed the epic in the framework of 1305 lines, while another extended the same basic plot and events into an exposition of 2065 lines (Innes 1974). Some people opt to chant rather than sing their performances, while others avoid the poetic genre entirely in favor of songless narratives or the more concise, more compact genres of proverb and riddle. Another dimension of performance is the methods by which performers learn their skills and shape them into individual styles. Basically, performers learn in two ways: formal and informal. The latter is by far the most common for most types of oral performance. The most common genre of performance is probably song, and songs are sung at many occasions, from solemn rites to boisterous beer-drinking gatherings. Singers simply learn from hearing certain songs repeatedly sung over time. Since some individuals are creatively gifted or inspired, they become singers and composers of songs.

A similar process holds true for storytellers, who learn tales by listening and participating in the various contexts that spur performances. Most storytellers have heard narratives performed since birth and begin by repeating tales, some going no further than telling the same few stories they know over and over. Other performers move to more intricate manipulation of tales by adding new scenes or episodes and altering them to fit certain occasions or conditions of performance. The formal education of oral performers is not common in all African societies, but the instances of such education are not rare. Often this kind of education is dictated by the nature of the art form or genre. For example, the singer of Yoruba Ijala poetry often is apprenticed to an experienced bard. The apprenticeship begins with the student listening to and learning to repeat what the master sings. After a while, the student is allowed to perform in concert with the bard, singing along during performances. The final stage is reached when the student is allowed, or decides, to go out on his or her own (Okpewho 1992). This kind of training is most often tied to the more esoteric forms of oral traditions: genres such as divination, epic singing, forms that require instrumental accompaniment, or specialized ritual performances. The question of audience response and interaction is vitally tied to the notion of performance dynamics. The oral performer must share the art, or there is no performance; and part of the sharing is in the response of the audience and the counter response of the performer. Some generic forms by definition require immediate and continual response.

This includes songs that employ the well-known call-and-response pattern, in which the singer depends on a chorus to either repeat or augment the lyrics he or she sings. There are narrative genres that often employ antiphonal cooperation between storyteller and audience. The riddle and proverb genres depend almost entirely on responses to initial statements or problems set out by the performer. In fact, in these particular art forms, the distinction of who is a performer and who is the audience is almost completely blurred. Further, audiences respond to performers in widely varied ways. This again depends on the context of the situation and the relationship between the individuals involved. Sometimes audience support for the performer is strong and encouraging, egging him or her on with positive comments. On other occasions, the performer is discouraged from continuing in no uncertain terms. Although the term *oral performance* suggests a verbal activity, there are important nonverbal techniques employed by performers. These are termed by some "histrionics This term is made up of two words. *Oral* is associated with the spoken or sung word, as well as the verbalization of sound in general. It is also associated with the reception of those sounds, that is, the aural activity of listeners. Modes of speaking and interacting verbally are often given the generic term *orality*. This term is often opposed to, or seen as the opposite of, *literacy,* the latter concept having to do with the written word. *Tradition* has historically been employed by several scholarly disciplines. The word is most commonly used to refer to long-term practices and beliefs of groups of people. It was often contrasted to the notion of "modern" or contemporary practices. Therefore, when one spoke of a people's traditions, the implication was that these were practices located in the past that had persisted over time, somehow fixed in the social memory, and at times outlasting their practical relevance into the present. In early anthropological discourse and later folkloric designations, traditions were associated with the idea of "survivals" from antiquity. Long seen as a product, the term *tradition* has come to be applied to processes since the later twentieth century. In ethnography and related disciplines, there is a current of thought that focuses on the ways tradition is continually created and adapted by contemporary, living cultures. Rather than static, fixed anomalies, traditions are considered to be linked to the activities that allow cultures to grow and change in order to perpetuate themselves. If the products of societies are the result of ongoing creation and transformation, both the products and their processes can be considered traditions.

When the words *oral* and *traditions* are therefore combined, the resulting term connotes the verbal arts of a society *and* the creative activities that surround their production. The range of oral traditions is therefore broad. It includes imaginative oral narrative, song, proverbs, riddles, and epics. It also designates the more "realistic" verbal genres such as history, personal narrative, formalized speech, and informal daily speech that employs tropes or standardized explanations. In all cases, the notion of transmission by performance and preservation in living memory are important elements of oral traditions.

These traditions conform to the tenets of verbal arts, whereby they must be performed in order to be experienced. They otherwise exist only in people's memories, until they are verbalized. This is not to say that the traditions are exclusively learned through memorization or internalization of the words and images that comprise the specific traditions. In fact, some sources of stories or histories may originate in books, radio broadcasts, films, or formal schools. The material is, however, transformed into oral knowledge when it is presented as part of a larger store of ideas, imagery, or forms. Most genres of African oral traditions generally conform to the categories found in other parts of the world. One form of oral tradition, which today is not often found outside of Africa, is the epic narrative. These long, intricate poems, intended for performance, have been recorded in West, central, and East Africa. Generally, they are tales of individual heroes who founded states or created new social orders. Most recorded African epics are sung or chanted to the accompaniment of music.

They are, therefore, impressive combinations of narrative, poem, and song. A genre that exists on the border between epic and poetry is the praise poem, which, in some cases, can reach epic length, but sometimes does not have the linear continuity of a narrative. This genre is found in many areas of Africa, most notably in southern Africa.

Oral traditions perform several societal functions. On the one hand, they constitute living representations of significant cultural information: history, values, instructions, and ritual activities. On the other hand, they are a dynamic form of entertainment based on the development and appreciation of artistic skills of speech, song, mime, gesture, dance, and instrumental music. Indeed, the elements of social function and aesthetic pleasure combine in oral traditions to make a highly effective network of cultural expression, educating and entertaining at the same time. The blurred line between artifice and reality is the space in which individuals create their statements on cultural issues, confirming or challenging old and new assumptions, depending on their respective points of view. These ongoing statements and debates are the means by which the culture renews, reaffirms, and regenerates itself in words and music.

4.1.7. Epic Performance

Stephen Belcher's approach to Epic in Africa is edifying here. In Africa, the term *epic* is applied to a wide range of lengthy oral poetic narratives, usually performed by a specialist, often with musical accompaniment. (2009: 25) The subject of the narrative is usually seen as historical, although the nature of the history involved will vary from myths and legends of origin to recent historical anecdote, and the characters are considered heroic in local terms. Performances will often incorporate songs, as a part of the action or as praise of characters within the story (and their descendents among the audience), and in some cases may include dancing. Recorded lengths of performances range from half hour to a continuous seven-night narrative.

Traditions of oral epic performance are found across Africa, and for convenience may be divided into three groups on the basis of geography, content, and performance features. One group, probably the smallest, represents African adaptations of Arabic epic traditions: this includes the cycle of the Bani Hilal through northern Africa, especially in Egypt and Tunisia, whose hero, Abu Zayd, is a black poet (Connelly 1986), and along the east coast a number of Swahili epics known generically as *utenzi* (Knappert

1983). Some Swahili epics are translations of Arabic texts *(Herakili, Ras al-Ghul);* at least one, *Liyongo Fumo,* represents an adaptation of local material to this imported form. Liyongo was a prince and a poet, and his preserved songs seem to provide the core of his narrative. Performance of these epics has not been exhaustively documented, but appears to be principally a recitation of a memorized text, and manuscripts play an important role in the diffusion of stories. The texts employ an adapted Arabic metrical scheme.

Throughout central Africa, and extending west and south, there is an epic tradition that is the vehicle for traditions of origin centered on a culture hero such as Mwindo of the BaN-yanga, Lianja of the Mongo, or Ozidi of the Ijo. Myth overpowers history in these epics, and the biography of the hero provides the matrix in which the numerous (and variable) episodes of the cycle may fit. The Swahili Liyongo and the Malagasy Ibonia may be connected to this tradition, as also might southern African trickster figures such as the Zulu Hlakanyaka. The hero is typically a precocious, almost monstrous, child who is born to avenge his father or to struggle with him. The hero also engages in a number of adventures that may carry him into the heavens, below the earth or the waters, and to the land of the dead. The hero is typically accompanied by a female relative who serves as protector, inspiration, and manager. Performances typically feature a master-singer (who has been initiated into the practice through occult means) accompanied by an ensemble, and take place in a relatively public space. The master-performer narrates, sings, and mimes the action with a considerable degree of audience participation. The verbal element consists of a mix of prose and songs.

A subgroup of these central African traditions is found among the Fang peoples of Gabon and Cameroon, and is known as the *mvett*. The term designates the instrument (a bamboo chordophone) and the genre. The *mvett* centers not on a given hero, but on an entire world (of times gone by) in which the immortals of the clan of Engong confront the mortals of the clan of Oku in a never-ending series of conflicts. The performer is thus free to plot the story and to embellish it in any effective way. Warriors struggle through magical obstacles rather than against weapons, and the magic is clearly a counterpart to modern technology. The *mvett* plays somewhat more than do the hero-centered cycles with romantic complications; the women who often accompany the men on their adventures are lovers rather than siblings.

Throughout West Africa, in a region centered in the Sahel and bounded roughly by Niger and Senegal, is the third and largest group of epics, unified by the social position of the performer, internationally known as the griot and at home by a variety of local terms: *jeli* or *jali, gawlo, mabo, gesere, gewel*. The performers are members of an endogamous status group, and this institution is shared among a number of neighboring peoples: various Mande groups such as the Soninke, the Mandinka, and the Bamana, as well as the Fula, the Wolof, and the Songhay. The practice of singing epics also seems to have spread among the groups, although each shows a distinct repertoire of stories and an idiomatic style of narration. Political history provides the narrative foundation for these epics, although in many cases the historical element is purely a veneer. The action, however, is human centered and takes place in something close to the immediate past: Mwindo's visits to other planes do not recur here. Magic serves to protect or destroy warriors, and to bring victory, and where magic does bring victory it is almost always associated also with treachery.

The best-known epic of this region is certainly the epic of Sundiata, founder of the empire of Mali. An influential prose version was published by D.T. Niane in 1960 (English translation in 1965) and has inspired further work. There are dozens of published accounts of his life and a growing body of recordings from Mali, Guinea, and the Gambia. This story is centered on a hero, although a "full" epic will usually begin well before his birth with a migration from Mecca or some account of the creation of the world. In childhood, Sunjata is crippled by hostile sorcery, and the high point of the epic may be the moment when, impelled by his fury at an insult to his mother, he rises to his feet and takes his first steps to uproot a baobab. He later goes into exile to avoid conflict with a brother, and, while he is absent, Sumanguru the sorcerer-blacksmith invades the Mande and oppresses the people. Sunjata is summoned back to defeat him, which he does with the help of his sister. After her brother has been defeated a number of times, she seduces Sumanguru to learn the secret of his power, and so Sunjata is able to overcome him. The traditions of Segou provide another corpus whose wealth is of a different order. The epics of Segou constitute a rough cycle, which is based on a selective king-list (Wolof epics offer the same organization) and recount the history of the kingdom from the early eighteenth century to the early 19th century. Many of the most popular pieces deal with the conquests of the last king, Da son of Monzon, and establish an almost conventional pattern: a vassal or neighbor insults Segou, and after initial setbacks a way is found (often through seduction) to defeat him. The Bamana traditions of Segou interact very closely with the Fula epics from the adjacent region of Massina, and there seems some evidence for Soninke contribution as well. In this polyglot environment, epics lose much of their historical weight and develop along purely narrative and artistic lines. A number of other groups in this broad region also offer documented epic traditions: the Songhay, the Mandinka of the Gambia, and the Wolof. Many of these focus upon nineteenth-century heroes upon one side or another of the Islamic movements of the period.

Performance practice varies somewhat from group to group and over time, but is centered upon a male master-narrator who in the Mande is accompanied at the least by his *naamu-sayer,* an apprentice who responds at each line with encouraging words, and possibly by accompanists. Women often participate for lyric passages and clan-praises, which in some sense are their special domain. Musical instruments include the *balafon,* the wooden xylophone, and various sorts of harp-lutes: the *kora,* the *ngoni* (a widespread four-stringed instrument also known as the *molo* or the *hoddu*) and now also guitars. This region also offers a nonhistorical corpus of epics best documented among the Mande peoples: that of the hunters. The late Malian hunters' bard Seydou Camara has bequeathed a considerable body of recorded material, which is now being increased by others. Hunters' epics focus on the condition of the hunter, as defined in terms of society rather than natural history. While a staple plot element involves a monstrous beast that a hunter must slay, the resolution often turns on the hunter's relations with his wife, and she is the key to his success. Many of these narratives occur as folktales rather than epics among neighboring peoples. Although the earliest attempt to convey an African epic in print goes back at least to 1856, and the collector Leo Frobenius devoted a volume to the "minstrelsy of the Sahel" (1921), doubts have persisted until relatively recently about the existence of African epic.

The growing mass of collected and published material dispels those doubts, and the challenge now is one of analysis and appreciation. A valuable early survey is that of Daniel Biebuyck (1976), somewhat amplified with additional Swahili material by Knappert (1983). In his dissertation (1978) and in his published edition of the *Epic of Son-Jara,* John W. Johnson has attempted to define the criteria of African oral epic, while Isidore Okpewho has approached epic traditions from the perspective of the Parry-Lord school of oral composition. Working in French, at first with Bamana traditions, Lilyan Kesteloot has produced a number of valuable analytic essays and editions, and in collaboration with Bassirou Dieng has produced a study and anthology (1997).

References

Beltcher, Stephan, "African Epic": https://www.birmingham.ac.uk/.../African-Epic-Stephen-Belcher.p.. *2010.*

Finnegan, Ruth. *Oral Literature in Africa.* New York: Routledge. 2012.

Fludernik, Monika. *Introduction to Narratology.* New York: Routledge. 2009.

Okpewho, Isidore. "Rethinking Epic" in *Storytelling, Self, Society*, Vol. 5, No. 3. USA: Wayne State University Press. 2009. 218-242.

Peek, Philip M. and Kwesi Yankah, eds., *African Folklore: An Encyclopedia.* New York: Routledge. 2011.

Sherman, Josepha. *Storytelling: An Encyclopedia of Mythology and Folklore.* New York: Sharpe Reference. 2008.

5

POSTCOLONIAL THEATRE IN SEARCH OF A REFERENTIAL FRAME OF THEORY

Post-colonial theory involves discussion about experience of various kinds: migration, slavery, suppression, resistance, representation, difference, race, gender, place, and responses to the influential master discourses of imperial Europe such as history, philosophy and linguistics, and the fundamental experiences of speaking and writing by which all these come into being. None of these is 'essentially' post-colonial, but together they form the complex fabric of the field (Bill Ashcroft, Gareth Griffiths and Helen Tiffin 2003: 2)

5.1. An Outline of Postcolonial Theory in African theatre Studies

In African critical dramatic theory, the formulation of a postcolonial critical theory that strikes the balance of African dramatic assertion as both a body of knowledge and artistic expression has been a subject of intense debates in literary circles. Eurocentric theorists who speculated the non-existence of genuine African theatrical forms were later challenged and counter-attacked by Afrocentric scholars who claimed critical space for the exhibition of African drama in its artistic forms. Yet the intellectual debate went beyond to advocate a new search for critical tradition that strikes the balance between the Afrocentric self as a critical entity and the Eurocentric other as its counter balance. The latter theoretical tendency ignites the searchlight for theoretical multiculturalism that admit hybrid forms of theatrical aesthetics as the new model for postcolonial African dramatic literature. Adopting a metacritical approach, this analysis focuses on the revisitation of these different theoretical orientations and attempts to address the question: what is postcolonial critical theory and how does it apply to African drama? To what extent does postcolonial African dramatic theory admit time sequences as a referential frame in its development?

Postcolonial literary criticism refers to the critical analysis in literary texts of the full implications and effects of colonialism on the Third World countries. Three waves of postcolonialism can be observed: the Eurocentric discourses, the Afrocentric discourses, the afropolitan discourses. Eurocentric colonial discourses held that Europe was the center of the production of knowledge, culture and civilization. In addition, they also claimed that such values produced in Europe have universal stamp of approval and quality. These two epistemes made Eurocentric writers claim for the centrality, the mainstream line of thought. From this claim, they claim that every cultural value has to be compared with the European model or pattern to receive the stamp of approval as valid. Being the centre, Europeans saw as a humanitarian mission to extend to the rest of the world the benefits of their civilization and culture. These Eurocentric discourses were actually prevalent in the hey days of colonization and cultural imperialism. In Africa for instance, local languages were banned from schools, syllabuses on local subjects and studies rejected to the benefit of European subjects. The nationalist protests were born out of patriotic feeling and the desire for political independence. Once African nations became independent, they sought to reverse the literary and cultural tendencies by revisiting colonial claims and ideologies. So, in reaction to these Eurocentric arrogance, postcolonial writers and critics sought to reposition debates, reverse discourses and decentralize the canon. Bill Ashcroft, Gareth Griffiths and Helen Tiffin's *The Postcolonial Studies' Reader* (1994) Gayatri Chakravorty Spivak' s A Crtitique of the Postcolonial Reason: Toward a History of the Vanishing Present (1999). Or *The Empire Writes Back* (2004) are major works that discuss in details the political, cultural and ideological implications of colonization and the attendant retaliation of postcolonialism. Some writers, critics and scholars are considered as major theorists include Edward Said with his three books *Orientalism* (1978), *Culture and Imperialism* (1993), *Representations of the Intellectual* (1996). In the academy, *Orientalism* became a foundational text of the field of Post-colonial studies, for what the British intellectual Terry Eagleton said is the book's "central truth ... that demeaning images of the East, and imperialist incursions into its terrain, have historically gone hand in hand." Said's friends and foes acknowledged the transformative influence of *Orientalism* upon scholarship in the humanities; critics said that the thesis is an intellectually limiting influence upon scholars, whilst supporters said that the thesis is intellectually liberating. The fields of post-colonial and cultural studies attempt to explain the "post-colonial world, its peoples, and their discontents", for which the techniques of investigation and efficacy in *Orientalism*, proved especially applicable in Middle Eastern studies.

Orientalism proposed that much Western study of Islamic civilization was political intellectualism, meant for the self-affirmation of European identity, rather than objective academic study; thus, the academic field of Oriental studies functioned as a practical method of cultural discrimination and imperialist domination—that is to say, the Western Orientalist knows more about the Orient than do the Orientals. That the cultural representations of the Eastern world that Orientalism purveys are intellectually suspect, and cannot be accepted as faithful, true, and accurate representations of the peoples and things of the Orient; that the history of European colonial rule and political domination of Asian civilizations, distorts the writing of even the most knowledgeable, well-meaning, and culturally sympathetic Orientalist.

> I doubt if it is controversial, for example, to say that an Englishman in India, or Egypt, in the later nineteenth century, took an interest in those countries, which was never far from their status, in his mind, as British colonies. To say this may seem quite different from saying that all academic knowledge about India and Egypt is somehow tinged and impressed with, violated by, the gross political fact—and yet *that is what I am saying* in this study of Orientalism (*Introduction, Orientalism*: 11).

Homi K. Bhabha has been very influential in the development of postcolonial theory with particular attention paid to key concepts like hybridity, ambivalence, cultural difference, enunciation, stereotype, mimicry and third space in the postcolonial theory. His major works, *Nation and Narration* (1990), *The Location of Culture* (1994), *Edward Said and Continuing Conversation* (co-ed. with W. J. T. Mitchell, 2005) confirm him as a great theorist of postcolonialism.

5.1.1. Hybridity

African modern drama is hybrid in content and form in that it combines material forms and oral tradition into modern literary artistic forms. One of his central ideas is that of "hybridisation," which, taking up from Edward Said's work, describes the emergence of new cultural forms from multiculturalism. Instead of seeing colonialism as something locked in the past, Homi K. Bhabha shows how its histories and cultures constantly intrude on the present, demanding that we transform our understanding of cross-cultural relations.

> If cultural diversity is a category of comparative ethics, aesthetics, or ethnology, cultural difference is a process of signification through which statements *of* culture or *on* culture differentiate, discriminate, and authorize the production of fields of force, reference, applicability, and capacity. Cultural diversity is the recognition of pre-given cultural 'contents' and customs, held in a time-frame of relativism; it gives rise to anodyne liberal notions of multiculturalism, cultural exchange, or the culture of humanity. Cultural diversity is also the representation of a radical rhetoric of the separation of totalized cultures that live unsullied by the intertextuality of their historical locations, safe in the Utopianism of a mythic memory of a unique collective identity. Cultural diversity may even emerge as a system of the articulation and exchange of cultural signs in certain… imperialist accounts of anthropology (Bhabha 1995: 206).

Bhabha submits that the postcolonial subject is never a purist one. He is culturally hybrid and cannot escape that condition. A postcolonial is in cultural contrainst of syncretization. His [Bhabha's] work transformed the study of colonialism by applying post-structuralist methodologies to colonial texts (Ibidem). He also shows that in postcolonial space, hybridity is inherent to all human cultures since humanity is engaged into rapid mobility, cultural interpenetration. The postcolonial subject holds double education. His indigenous education and the education of his/hr colonial master. He/she cannot scape none. Modernity is accompanied with formal education and the postcolonial citizen is no more defined in terms of his geographical space, his linguistic belonging or his political and religious convictions. The postcolonial subject is a global citizen, hybrid in content and form. People move from local belonging to global one. In that perspective, one should live locally but see the world globally.

5.1.2. Ambivalence

Ambivalence is close to hybridity. The idea of ambivalence sees culture as consisting of opposing perceptions and dimensions. Bhabha claims that this ambivalence—this duality that presents a split in the identity of the colonized other—allows for beings who are a hybrid of their own cultural identity and the colonizer's cultural identity. Ambivalence contributes to the reason why colonial power is characterized by its belatedness. Kole Omotoso in Martin Benham's edited volume *A History of Theatre in Africa* (2004) asserts:

> This domestication can only take place when African languages are the medium of encounter between student and the known world. Indeed, this is the only means by which the knowledge contained in his language and the knowledge brought by the European languages of colonial experience can co-mingle and cross-fertilise one another (Omotoso 2004: 6).

In connection to Omotoso' s ideas, it is plausible to theorise that ambivalence is the adjunct and outgrowth African European educated intellectual playwrights. Ola Rotimi has theorized ambivalence in critical essays and in plays. In "African Literature: To Be or to Become" he argued for a theory of ambivalence that militates for an emerging complex identity of African indigeneity and European modes of aestetic modes. Lejoka-Brown, Sikira and Liza are symbols of cultural ambivalence. While Lakunle in Soyinka' s *The Lion and the Jewel* are ambivalent combining African ideologies and western. Colonial signifiers of authority only acquire their meanings after the "traumatic scenario of colonial difference, cultural or racial, returns the eye of power to some prior archaic image or identity. Paradoxically, however, such an image can neither be 'original'—by virtue of the act of repetition that constructs it—nor identical—by virtue of the difference that defines it." Accordingly, the colonial presence remains ambivalent, split between its appearance as original and authoritative and its articulation as repetition and difference. This opens up the two dimensions of colonial discourse: that which is characterized by invention and mastery and that of displacement and fantasy (Ibidem).

5.1.3. Cultural Difference, Enunciation, and Stereotype

Bhabha presents cultural difference as an alternative to cultural diversity. In cultural diversity, a culture is an "object of empirical knowledge" and pre-exists the knower while cultural difference sees culture as the point at which two or more cultures meet and it is also where most problems occur, discursively constructed rather than pre-given, a "process of enunciation of culture as 'knowledgeable'" (Bhabha 1994). Enunciation is the act of utterance or expression of a culture that takes place in the Third Space. Since culture is never pre-given, it must be uttered. From Soyinka's submission in *Myth, Ritual and the African World* (1976), it is recommendable to argue that modern African drama from this perspective should be read as the enunciation of complex hybrid modes of cultural performances that ignit the difference between European congellations of theories and African variants of theories. The enunciation of dramatic theory that berefts western standards and recalibrates with African standards purveys the contours of its self-valorisation. It is through enunciation that cultural difference is discovered and recognized. The enunciative process introduces a divide between the traditional a stable system of reference and the negation of the certitude of culture in the articulation of new cultural, meanings, strategies, in the political present, as a practice of domination, or resistance. Therefore, cultural difference is a process of identification, while cultural diversity is comparative and categorized. The foregoing can be read in Ngugi's theory of cultural differences, enunciation and stereotypes. In *Moving the Centre: Struggle for Cultural Freedoms* (1993) and *Something Torn and New: An African Renaissance* (2009) the theory of cultural difference, enunciation and stereotypes is recurrent. Moreover, it is that possibility of difference and articulation that could free the signifier of skin/culture from the fixations of racial typology, however, the stereotype impedes the circulation and articulation of the signifier of "race" as anything other than that. An important aspect of colonial and post-colonial discourse is their dependence on the concept of "fixity" in the construction of otherness. Fixity implies repetition, rigidity and an unchanging order as well as disorder. The stereotype depends on this notion of fixity. The stereotype creates an "identity" that stems as much from mastery and pleasure as it does from anxiety and defense of the dominant, "for it is a form of multiple and contradictory beliefs in its recognition of difference and disavowal of it."

5.1.4. Mimicry

Like Bhabha's concept of hybridity, mimicry is a metonym of presence. Mimicry appears when members of a colonized society imitate and take on the culture of the colonizers. Lacan asserts, "The effect of mimicry is camouflage… it is not a question of harmonizing with the background, but against a mottled background (Lacan 1936/1966: 73)." Colonial mimicry comes from the colonist's desire for a reformed, recognizable Other, as a subject of a difference that is, as Bhabha writes, "almost the same, but not quite". Thus, mimicry is a sign of a double articulation; a strategy which appropriates the Other as it visualizes power. Furthermore, mimicry is the sign of the inappropriate, "a difference or recalcitrance which coheres the dominant strategic function of colonial power, intensifies surveillance, and poses an imminent threat to both 'normalized' knowledges and disciplinary powers" (Ibidem). In this way, mimicry gives the colonial subject a partial presence, as if the 'colonial' is dependent for its representation within the authoritative discourse itself. Ironically, the colonists desire to emerge as 'authentic' through mimicry—through a process of writing and repetition—through this partial representation. On the other hand, Bhaba does not interpret mimicry as a narcissistic identification of the colonizer in which the colonized stops being a person without the colonizer present in his identity. He sees mimicry as a "double vision which in disclosing the ambivalence of colonial discourse also disrupts its authority. And it is a double vision that is a result of what [he has] described as the partial representation/recognition of the colonial object...the figures of a doubling, the part-objects of a metonymy of colonial desire which alienates the modality and normality of those dominate discourses in which they emerge as 'inappropriate colonial subjects" (Ibidem). The colonists' desire is inverted as the colonial appropriation now produces a partial vision of the colonizer's presence; a gaze from the Other is the counterpart to the colonizer's gaze that shares the insight of genealogical gaze which frees the marginalized individual and breaks the unity of man's being through which he had extended his sovereignty. Thus, "the observer becomes the observed and 'partial' representation rearticulates the whole notion of identity and alienates it from essence" (Ibidem).

5.1.5. Third Space

The Third Space acts as an ambiguous area that develops when two or more individuals/cultures interact (compare this to urbanist Edward W. Soja's conceptualization of thirdspace). It "challenges our sense of the historical identity of culture as a homogenizing, unifying force, authenticated by the originary past, kept alive in the national tradition of the People". This ambivalent area of discourse, which serves as a site for the discursive conditions of enunciation, "displaces the narrative of the Western written in homogeneous, serial time." It does so through the "disruptive temporality of enunciation". Bhabha claims that "cultural statements and systems are constructed in this contradictory and ambivalent space of enunciation." As a result, the hierarchical claims to the innate originality or purity of cultures are invalid. Enunication implies that culture has no fixity and even the same signs can be appropriated, translated, rehistoricized, and read anew. Karma R. Chávez made the following account of postcolonialism:

Broadly speaking, postcolonial theory or postcolonialism looks into processes of colonization and decolonization.[4] Postcolonial theory engages questions about how cultures create identities after colonization, about the subjugation of colonized peoples' knowledge and histories, about the use and misuse of knowledge about colonized peoples by Westerners, and about the creative ways in which colonized and formerly colonized peoples respond to their oppression. Additionally, postcolonial theory extends beyond traditional geographical colonialism into neocolonial relationships between nations, questioning why such relationships exist. Communication scholars have taken up postcolonial theory primarily in order to critique the Eurocentrism of both scholarship and beliefs about communicative and rhetorical practice and to center knowledge produced from other locales and subjects. Many parts of the world have been impacted by colonialism and continue to be shaped through neocolonial relationships and various kinds of cultural imperialism. One historical trajectory of contemporary postcolonial theory marks its origins at World War II, with Indian independence from Britain as one of the hallmarks of the scholarly enterprise. The third-world migration to cities and the emergence of English-speaking formerly colonized academics in the Western academy created the push for postcolonial theorizing. Specifically, postcolonial theorists asked the West to confront its colonial history and refused what Dipesh Chakraborty calls a waiting room version of history where colonized and formerly colonized peoples are configured in a liminal, or threshold, space in relation to the West. This is, however, only one version of the emergence of postcolonial theory. Other scholars such as Angelita Reyes, mark the emergence of something called postcoloniality in the 19th century. Frantz Fanon is sometimes credited for the earliest postcolonial writing in books such as his 1952 text, *Black Skin, White Mask.*

Still other scholars contend that Edward Said's 1978 book, *Orientalism,* is the hallmark text in postcolonial theory. Other key figures in postcolonial theory include Gayatri Spivak, Homi Bhabha, Albert Memmi, and Aimé Césaire. Though there are disagreements about the origin of postcolonial theorizing, a number of similarities exist across versions of postcolonialism.

---

[4]Karma R. Chávez in Stephen W. Littlejohn and Karen A. Foss, eds., *Encyclopedia of Communication Theory* (California: Sage Publication, 2009), p. 768.

Foremost, postcolonial theory is a transformative stance, focused on reconfiguring epistemic or knowledge structures and making connections to groups' and cultures' obliterated pasts. This is not simply an intellectual endeavor, although much good work remains to be done in the academy. In that vein, postcolonial theory challenges established disciplinary knowledge that has been created through the force of modernity and long histories of imperialism. Postcolonial theory thus provides historical and transnational depth to understandings of culture and power.

5.6. Western Modernity

Although not its only focus, a central concern for postcolonial scholars centers upon the impact of Western modernity. Although the modern has been characterized a number of ways, the characteristics associated with Western modernity have often been taken as the standard by which all other nations are evaluated, and those nations that are radically different from the West often are imagined to be exotic, backward, or wrong. No other playwright than Wole Soyinka, Ola Rotimi, John Pepper Clarck have portrayed with craft the impact of western modernity on the African character. Soyinka's *The Lion and the Jewel*, Rotimi's *Our Husband Has Gone Mad Again,* Clarck's *The Raft* all portray how modernity has transformed the African character from communalism to individualism, from attachment to African cultural values to a detachment of these values and alienation from the folklife. One way the primacy of Western modernity persists is through what Said calls orientalism, which he describes as functioning in the dichotomy between the occident, or Western European countries and more recently the United States, and the orient, or non-Western, typically Asian regions. Orientalism is not only a simple geographic distinction that the world is made of two unequal parts called the orient and the occident, but it also engenders a range of interests. As an occidental construction, orientalism creates and also maintains an intention to know, or even to control and manipulate, what is a very different world. Whether in politics, media, or literature, orientalism has led to very limited representations of the orient. Such depictions fashion people in exotic and sometimes passive ways that work to remove their agency or ability to be considered fully human actors in the Western imaginary. Most fundamentally, postmodern thinkers challenge two aspects of Western Modernity—knowledge and universality.

5.1.7. Knowledge

The dominance of Western modernity promotes a very narrow construction of what can count as knowledge and who is a valid producer of knowledge. Within Western modernity, Europe and the United States get constructed as subject, or active knower, whereas subaltern, or subordinated, peoples get positioned as object or other, that which is known about. This means that too often, in the best scenario, texts produced by subaltern peoples are not considered knowledge, but rather an object for Western scholars to create knowledge about. More typically, however, anything produced by subaltern peoples is simply ignored as not worthy of being knowledge at all. Western scholars, however, have long relied upon the other for production of knowledge. In her 1988 book, *A Critique of Postcolonial Reason,* Spivak uses the notion of the native informant to critique philosophical, literary, and cultural history (and present), showing the ways that this figure has been used in colonial discourse studies. The native informant is not a celebrated figure, but both the necessary and foreclosed, or denied, figure of the West, which means that all knowledge production in the West always already relies upon the native's story at the same time that that fact is denied. A task, then, of postcolonial theory is to avoid re-inscribing, or rewriting, the position of neocolonial knowledge in a way that locates imperialism and colonialism safely in the past, when neocolonial knowledge itself assumes a continuous connection between past (colonialism) and present (postcolonialism). This is especially important because many foundational Western texts that continue to undergird Western thinking sanction colonialism and imperialism. In this way, the legacy of Western knowledge production very much impacts the present moment, which renders quite complex the West's relationship with its colonial past and post- and neocolonial present.

5.1.8. Universalism

Knowledge gets produced within Western modernity in a way that assumes the universalism of Western thought and the Western subject. Postcolonial theory challenges this universalism on a number of fronts. Initially, in critiquing Immanuel Kant's depictions of culture, Spivak shows how this view overlooks the possibility of a geo-politically differentiated subject. This universalism permits subjectivity to be solidly configured in a way that perpetuates and justifies further exclusion of subjects who are left out of this way of constructing knowledge. The Western subject within Western thought re-inscribes and reaffirms itself by making use of certain kinds of colonial subjects as evidence for knowledge claims. Because the Western subject is the standard, all others who might be subjects are evaluated in relation to the criteria of the West. This means that many non-Western peoples would fall short of the Western standard of subjectivity that requires certain peoples be cast as other in order for Western knowledge to have meaning.

Although postcolonial theorists contend that historically Western thought has been universalist in this way, they also maintain that contemporary thought continues to mark the Western subject as the standard. Postmodern thought has devoted much attention to the decentering of the Western subject. A premise of this decentering, however, is that the Western subject is currently the center of knowledge, demonstrating that even attempts to rupture the historical line of Western thought still assume that its lineage is universal. Alternatively, postcolonial theorists use other kinds of subjects as the starting points for their critiques, which implicitly decenters the Western subject without centering it in the first place. For instance, an assumption within much Western communication theory about subjectivity is that silence demonstrates a lack of agency. In an analysis of mothers in South Asia, however, Radha S. Hegde challenges this taken for granted assumption by showing how a variety of geo-political, interpersonal, and historical factors make silence a rich source of agency in certain cultural contexts. Postcolonial theorization of culture has offered some of the most poignant critiques of Western universalism. Because many formerly colonized peoples exist in widespread diasporas (geographical dispersion), for example, their relationships to their home cultures and their new cultures challenge any kind of cultural essentialism. Similarly, Bhabha's notion of cultural hybridity highlights the ways in which oppressed peoples make use of the oppressors' cultural artifacts in new and unfamiliar ways. A song that might have one meaning in the oppressors' country can be completely refashioned in the oppressed country to create a hybrid text that combines old and new. The practice of colonial mimicry, where colonized peoples learn to perform civilized or European manners of dress, talk, and comportment to gain privilege, directly challenges both the universalism and the superiority of Western culture and subjectivity. Postcolonial theorists have centered analyses of culture(s) in order to highlight the creative cultural practices and productions of subaltern peoples in order to obliterate the strongholds of Western modernity.

5.1.9. Postcolonial Theory in African theatre Studies

Wole Soyinka is a major voice in the African postcolonial literary theory and criticism. His attention is turned towards the alienation of African institutions by European cultural imperialism. In 1963, he had already published *The Lion and the Jewel* which critically assessed how European imperial legacy sought to anhilate African cultural values. His critical books *Art, Dialogue, and Outrage: Essays on Literature and Culture* (1988), *The Burden of Memory – The Muse of Forgiveness* (1999), *New Imperialism* (2009), and *Of Africa* (2012) address the burning issues of cultural imperialism, neocolonialism, international terrorism, African dictatorship and the implication of European powers in helping and maintaining such oligarchic dictatorship. Soyinka has made known through theatrical works namely *Opera Wonyosi, A Play of Giants, Kongi's Harvest, Madmen and Specialists, King Baabu, The Trials of Brother Jero,* to mention but a few that European cultural imperialism has gone beyond the pervasion of African cultural values. It has actually reproduced another form of colonialism in Africa where African political leaders simply act as puppets of western colonial powers to safeguard European interests, mortgage African economies, plunder African resources and create a state of terror, unrest and helplessness. African masses are left impotent in the face of repression, imposition of political powers, dictatorships and the dwindling purchase power. For Soyinka, postcolonial discourses should debunk the theoretical praxis of European imperial legacy, interrogate the survival patterns of colonial rule in a modern Africa where the masses are toiling to meet daily needs and garner means of survival. In an earlier study, I showed that Soyinka's postcolonial theory of drama questions the African condition. He objects to the failure of the continent's leaders to end with European imperialism and specifically address the burning issue of the continent's development. Soyinka observes that Africa is rich enough to ensure the economic development and intellectual emancipation of all her citizens. The only problem according to Soyinka is the incapacity of its leaders to think beyond their selfish ambitions. In clearer terms, I submit that Soyinka writes back to self, self being Africa. In *King Baabu* Soyinka has shown signs of economic delay and underdevelopment to be the impacts of corruption. The first major sign of economic delay in the play is the heavy national debt under which the whole country of the play stagnates. The banks are heavily indebted and their accounts are now far insufficient to help the country survive, lest alone, to pay back the debt to the international financial institutions. The managing director of the Sankofo Heritage Bank reports that not less than "fifty million dollars payable in hard currency" (*KB:* 55) has to be paid, which money was borrowed to finance King Baabu's (formerly called Basha Bash's) project "Fill the Stomach" (*KB:* 14). The major part of the borrowed money which constitutes the national debt today was in fact embezzled and squandered by the royal family, because, as Baabu himself says, "all banking now" is "in the hand of palace government" who sees to its "accountability" (*KB:* 56). The whole nation is undergoing a serious economic delay, and the very concern of the whole population, especially the specialist of economics is how to help the country to elaborate a reliable programme for the national recovery. Basha himself talks about "a serious matter for (our) economy" (*KB:* 37). Shoki argues that "the banking system needs to be overhauled" (*KB:* 37), because of the "economic sabotage" (*KB:* 97). All these statements are making reference to the state of bankruptcy and economic recession in which the country has deeply sunk because of the corrupt practices of the leaders. For the spokesman of the Central Bank of Guatu,

> […] the banking sector is more than prepared to play its role in the programme for national recovery. But we are to account to our shareholders and investors. We must know how much we are contributing here and there and then we know how to justify it to those who really own the bank. (*KB:* 54)

The words of the spokesman express the good will of the economic experts to play active role in the country's economic recovery. But they also make allusion to the difficulty they have to play such a role, because, in the present economic recession due to King Baabu's mismanagement and corruption, many economic partners who used to help the country financially, have retrieved their help. The few economic partners who remain require clear and faithful accounts of their investments as one of the prior conditions of their economic cooperation. But under King Baabu's regime, such transparent accounts seem difficult, if not impossible, because of the high degree of corruption. As a result, the national debt remains unpaid and the economic condition of the country goes from bad to worse. This has repercussions on the development of the country which continues to remain underdeveloped and backward. In *King Baabu,* other signs of under-development are hunger and squalor.

In Soyinka's critical positions on postcolonialism, he analyses the African societies flaws and expresses his views on where changes need to be made.

His postcolonial attention is inflected towards the reflection of the under-development on the lives of the citizens in his *The Open Sore of a Continent A Personal Narrative of the Nigerian Crisis* (1996). Taking Nigeria as an example, he exposes the symptoms of under-development -which itself is the effect of corruption- as follows:

> The agony of a nation is observable largely in material reality, which alone records its proof of existence. Now, how is that reality actually experienced by the Nigerian people on a daily basis? […] The health services of that Nation are nonexistent; mothers die in childbirth for the lack of the most basic drugs and a hygienic environment for labor. Infant mortality has reached epidemic proportions. The simplest, easily curable disease worsens for lack of treatment and kills. Three year ago even a military governor, a pillar of the establishment, lamented that the hospitals in that country had become mere consulting clinics, so desperate had become the dearth of basic drugs and hospital equipment. Two years later, that is last year, a medical specialist, also in the service of government, was compelled to return to that statement, updating it with the comment that the nation's hospitals could no longer claim even that downgraded status but had become virtual mortuaries (Soyinka 2006: 123.).

The emphasis in these statements is laid on poor amenities of health; health being one of the basic needs of people in the society. Soyinka points out the problem of hunger as another feather characteristic of under-development:

> Hunger stalks the streets and, with it, desperation. Thus, security of individuals has become a game of Russian roulette: One never knows whose turn it is. Even diplomats have been compelled to lead protest delegations to the seat of government in Abuja as, be it on the open road, in the heart of the city, or in their residences, they regularly discover the limitations of diplomatic immunity. […] Yet, the country that serves us here as a model is poor neither in human nor in material resources (Soyinka 2006: 125).

Soyinka's laments for the Nigerian population here concerns the lack of food. Nigerian population is affected by hunger while in fact, judging from the material resources available in the country, the nation should be self-reliant. Soyinka here puts on the mantle of a Marxist critic. The logic of his observation is that, the resources that should have been used to alleviate starvation and hunger are mismanaged and wasted in corruption. The country's wealth is unequally distributed among the population. The upper class gets the lion's share and the lower class which normally works to produce that wealth starves. The consequence of that wastage is the continual prevailing of hunger and under-development. Judging from Nigeria's material resources, the country is supposed to be self-sufficient in terms of basic valuables like food. Soyinka's diagnosis goes to the transportation system too:

> Public transportation is so inadequate that it provides a study in collective masochism, degenerating often into a contest of survival of the fittest at the arrival of the lone tumbrel. In certain suburban areas –Oshodi, Apapa, Ipaja, for instance, -workers on a seven-thirty to five o'clock shift must leave home at four in the morning and are lucky to be home at eight or nine in the evening. The sight of in-between commuters listlessly awaiting some form of locomotion on a blistering Lagos afternoon at improvised stops without shelter, while the latest off-the-line models in private automobile cruise by, strikes visitors no less forcibly than those who still guard their conscience among the privileged of such a national space (Ibidem).

The transportation system plays some important role in the development process of a country because, for work in the civil service or elsewhere to be efficient, the workers need to be on time. The lack of transportation facilities, the jamming of the traffic, or the occurrence of road accidents can probably affect the workers diligence to service and as a result, it can reflect on the productivity of the country and lead to underdevelopment. Other problems include lack of potable water and the failure of the press to expose these problems. Concerning potable water, Soyinka writes:

> Potable water, even in the heart of the nation's capital, has become a commodity that is left to the dispensation of the skies, from where, perhaps, it is also hoped that Sango, the god of lightning, would perform the miracle that has so far eluded an infamous institution known as NEPA, the Nigerian Electric Power Authority. (Nigerians

> have even become bored with the game of finding new readings for that acronym, the best known being 'Never Electric Power Anytime'.) Many small businesses have collapsed as a result of this failure and often join domestic households in mourning the periodic vengeful surges of power that incinerate their appliances and even their homes, as if the god of lightning has indeed taken personal charge but remains unschooled in the elementary laws of voltage distribution (Ibidem).

It is my belief that Soyinka does not expose the foregoing problems for the sake of exposing them, but he intends to draw the attention of the readership the effects of corruption in African countries. The image of Nigeria is also that of many African countries. If the leaders are willing, they can initiate change. Soyinka's plea with the African leaders for the future of the continent is to open their eyes and see the conditions of underdevelopment of African nations. Change is central to Soyinka's social vision. Put more clearly, Soyinka envisions a new image for the African continent, which is an image of development and prosperity. Taking Nigeria as example, he states:

> If one accepts Nigeria as a space that must move beyond what a politician once described as "a mere geographical expression" to what my vision dictates as a humanized space of organic development, then I may be moved to stop quibbling over mere nomenclatures. Until then, that unfulfilled promise, Nigeria must remain only a duty. And it is that the same duty that we, on our part, must continue to urge upon those same "governments of African countries," challenging them to realize their own pronouncements, denouncing them before the entire world when they fail to do so, and insisting in that case that they be treated, as pariahs, as the real traitors to their own kind and to humanity in general (Soyinka 1988: 133-134).

Here, Soyinka reveals his social vision of Nigerian society as a "humanized space of organic development." It is a society different from "a mere geographical expression". In other words, Soyinka is more concerned with the improvement of people's conditions of life. People's conditions of life should be improved. The social environment in which people are living should reflect an emancipated society. Soyinka's vision, we may say, is a developed society, where problems like corruption, hunger, lack of health care, lack of potable water and electricity are solved. To arrive at that level of development, Soyinka reminds the reader of his commitment to that cause and his combative strategy. For him, as a writer, he must write to "continue to urge upon those same 'governments of African countries', challenging them to realize their own pronouncements." Having in mind that the playwright's concern goes beyond Nigeria and encompasses Africa as a whole, we believe that, the foregoing statements translate the desire for Soyinka to urge political authorities to see to the development of their countries. It is taken to mean that Soyinka plays the role of eye opener who reveals through drama the very social evils which cause African predicament and cripple its development. In the words of Patrick Ebewo, "Soyinka's theatre has become not only a critic of prevailing society, but an attempt to change it, by contributing, as directly as art can ever allow, to the struggle for human rights and a meaningful existence (Ebewo 2002: 195)." Changing the society is, as said the critic Ebewo the end objective of Soyinka's plays' message. We have been so far discussing the impacts of corruption on society, with emphasis laid on the economic recession in *King Baabu*.

Postcolonial theory gained legitimacy in theatre studies in the 1980s. Raka Shome's 1996 germinal essay, "Postcolonial Interventions in the Rhetorical Canon: An 'Other' View," which focuses on how rhetorical scholars could benefit from an engagement with postcolonialism, is a significant introduction of postcolonial theory to the field of communication. One of the most important contributions of postcolonial theory to communication has been its critique of the limits of critical theories. Shome and Hegde contend that critical theories in communication have focused on axes of power such as race, class, and gender mostly within the context of the United States and without attention to other factors outside of the nation. Postcolonial theory unearths specific historical, geopolitical, and geographical aspects of several forms of modernity within which other sites of power such as race, class, and gender reside. This transnational layering adds richness to discussions of power axes and has led communication scholars to ask questions pertaining to issues such as media representations in global contexts and hybrid communication practices that challenge typical assumptions about race and nation.

5.10. Criticisms

Postcolonial theory has been subject of controversies. For example, some scholars have argued that postcolonial theory focuses too much on the West and its colonial impact while denying the colonial-style relations between, for example, Arabs and Africans. The Western emphasis can function to continue to project the West as the site of knowledge production and civilization. Additionally, other scholars have suggested that postcolonial theory overemphasizes the impacts of culture while denying or ignoring the relevance of economics. Such criticisms maintain that postcolonial theory's import remains minimal until it wrestles with the material factors that compel colonial relations. Scholars of globalization have critiqued postcolonial theory for construing all unequal global relationships as remnants of past colonialism, which, they argue, is an inadequate depiction of globality.

Although much of the earliest postcolonial theorizing emerged from Asian, African, and Middle Eastern scholars living in various diasporas, postcolonial theorists from parts of Latin America have also suggested the regional and experiential limitations of this work. Since more than one colonizer colonized many Latin American countries, postcolonial theorists working from these locations demonstrate the complex layers of colonization- decolonization that is arguably elided in other kinds of postcolonial theory. Additionally, these theorists often center indigenous and mestizo/a cultures as central to understanding the impacts of colonization. This focus has introduced the importance of religious conflict and translation to understanding the continual impacts of colonialism and imperialism. Despite criticisms, postcolonial theory offers different ways of reading and understanding that are guided by postcolonial subjectivities, historical and geo-political contextualization, and alternatives to Western modes of meaning making.

Indeed, if the common designation "postcolonial" obligates cultural theorists from various Third World nations to reflect on their relation to each other, that is something to be welcomed, not dreaded. Finally, the criticism that postcoloniality is a misleading context for Third World cultural practices that do not directly engage with it is often met with the rejoinder that Texts produced within a larger political context can be read in its terms, whether or not the texts anticipate such a reading or, more generally, such a positioning of themselves. As these debates should make clear, the rapid institutionalization of postcolonial studies has resulted in an ongoing and close scrutiny of its scope and method. For postcolonial studies to retain its oppositional charge, it will be necessary that the ambiguity of the prefix "post" be kept in sight; that specific differences within its rubric be actively mobilized and understood not just in terms of national origins but also of Class, Gender, race, sexual and ethnic orientations; and finally, that increasingly complex and rigorous ways be found to read cultural practices in their political contexts. An older but recurring debate within postcolonial studies is over Third World discourses of pan-nationalism, nationalism, and diaspora. Each offers one way for Third World communities to construct cultural and political identities in opposition to Western imperial prescriptions. Pan-nationalisms, which arose in the early phases of some anti-imperial struggles, were short-lived but powerful movements that added a great impetus to cultural production. An example is *Negritude*, which called on people of African descent across Africa, Europe, and the Americas to forge a collective identity beyond national boundaries, recognize their shared history of oppression and resistance, and celebrate and preserve a common culture rooted in Africa. Although *Negritude* attracted prominent literary and political figures such as Leopold Senghor (Senegal) and Aimé Césaire (Martinique), it was also, from its inception, criticized from other revolutionary perspectives, for instance, that of Frantz Fanon (Martinique). Although he was drawn to the affirmatory politics and creative energies of *Negritude*, Fanon found its oppositional political stance to be a mere reversal rather than a fundamental displacement of Western ethnocentrism; as such, it remained locked in the essentialist terms dictated by that ethnocentrism. Marxists such as Fanon believed that anti-imperial struggles would necessarily be organized on the model of the nation-state; if a cross-continental resistance had to be chosen, it would need to be based on class rather than race.

Pan-nationalisms generated a vast literary and cultural archive, much of it committed to reviving "authentic" and "classic" precolonial indigenous practices, often in direct challenge to imperial/colonial pronouncements on the cultural impoverishment of the colonized. While appreciating the energy of this cultural project, critics such as Fanon questioned its nativist rhetoric of authenticity, and its petrification of culture into static, essentialized, and classicized forms outside the reach of the masses. The debate over authenticity has often been revived in postcolonial studies, for instance, with the incorporation of Western Critical theory (see Appiah, 1984; Bhabha, 1994; and Ngugi, 1986). The majority of anti-imperialist struggles, especially in the twentieth century, have been organized not on pan-nationalisms but the model of the nation-state. Recent discussions of nationalism have historicized this model as something not ordained in nature but produced in response to specific needs of European economies during their industrial phase. Critics of nationalism argue that the nation-state model, held out to Third World cultures as their only entry into the global economy after decolonization, did not necessarily address their specific needs. Further, nationalist movements were led by middle-class Western-trained leaders who, in their efforts to present a united front to colonialism, often curbed the more radical demands of feminists and subalterns, and were thus unable fundamentally to transform the oppressive political structures they inherited from colonialism. Like pan-nationalisms, nationalist struggles and discourses have been immensely productive in the cultural sphere, although their own rhetoric of authenticity has also raised some questions from Third World feminist and subaltern critics. In their efforts to preserve an untainted, classic, precolonial, and indigenous tradition, these discourses sought to ward off the influence of living and Popular cultures. As is frequently the case, they called on women to assume the role of the keepers of tradition, thus reimmersing them in the rhetoric of purity and sanctity, and assigning them the most passive, secondary, and privatized spaces in the official narrative of nationalisms (see Jayawardena, 1986; Mohanty, 1991).

The critique of these discourses from the viewpoint of those excluded by it, such as subalterns and women, is an increasingly powerful strain within postcolonial studies. This criticism is sometimes misrepresented as a nostalgia for colonial Ideology and institutions, and sometimes reduced to a tradition versus Modernity debate, with indigenous practices being seen as traditional and therefore oppressive for women and the subaltern, and the Western as modern and more emancipatory. In fact, however, few Third World subaltern and/or feminist critics of nationalism are apologists for Western imperialism, and few endorse its claims of having eradicated oppressive feudal and patriarchal indigenous practices. Instead, scholars such as the subaltern collective in Indian, Ngugi wa Thiong'o in Kenya, and Rey Chow in China have read imperialism as not only actively suppressing the more feminist and egalitarian of indigenous institutions and cultural practices, but also as driving indigenous Patriarchy to increasingly reactionary excesses against women and subalterns in an effort to maintain its strength *vis-à-vis* the colonizers. Third World feminist and subaltern histories/cultural studies have thus been engaged in a dual task: close analyses of colonial *and* indigenous patriarchal power, and crucial archival work to recover lost/neglected female and subaltern cultural texts and resistances. This work has been tremendously effective in opening up the closed, official narratives of nationalism, and clearing the space for a study of popular cultural practices, including film and music; street and creolized languages; oratures (or oral literatures); and politicized and agitprop genres such as testimony, prison memoirs, and street theater.

To be exact, Ngugi is to reckon with when it comes to postcolonial critical theory. The general philosophy guiding the literary commitment of Ngugi wa Thiong' o is the improvement of the living conditions of Africans and the change from destitution to emancipation. This change should start from the rupturing of neocolonial legacies, namely European imperialism and African leaders' connivance with it. Ngugi thinks that African postcolonial predicament is the direct result of European colonialism which, African leaders have connived with European imperialists to perpetuate. In *Homecoming: Essays on African and Caribbean Literature, Culture, and Politics* (1972), he has shown how British rule turned the Kenyan living conditions sour. This theme is reproduced in plays namely *This Time Tomorrow* (1970), *The Trial of Dedan Kimathi* (1976), *The Black Hermit* (1963) and *I Will Marry When I Want* (1982). One important critical point stands firm in all these plays: the havoc of African socio-economic institutions by European colonialism and the necessity thereof to combat, the injust dispossession of African property by colonial and neocolonial imperialists. His critical book *Moving the Center: Struggle for Cultural Freedoms* (1993) comes to reinforce his authorial ideology in the plays. Ngugi thinks that African heroic leaders of the Kimathi kind, should hold strongly to the one political goal: the liberation of the masses, the poor peasants and workers, and the underpaid factory workers. Equally important for Ngugi is the fact that there is imperious necessity to move the European center from the hegemonic priviledged Europe to Third world nations. For Ngugi, Europe and America owe their prosperity in major part to African labour and African resources (from plantation slave trade down to colonialism). But what is most alarming is the fact that Europeans still hold the centre of literary discourses, the epiteme of the production of knowledge. They still claim their universal orthodoxy of values where by all other values have to be judged in comparison of what Europe has, before being validated. For Ngugi, moving the center is not an option, it is an imperious necessity. He explains this in a 1996 conversation with D. Venkat Rao:

> I use the phrase "moving the center" in the context of moving the center from its assumed centrality in the West to where it should be in a multiplicity of centers all over the world. Because each of our own experiences can be a center from which you look at the world – our language, our social institutions very important as basis for looking at the world. I was also thinking about this moving the center from its assumed locationwithin a nation or nationality,

from its assumed place among a minority class strata [sic] into what I mean is its creative base among the people. But once having said that, we must be prepared to learn. Quite frankly, one of the most important things is how we must be prepared to self-renew ourselves by interacting even with the thought which are hostile to our own situation. Because one can learn more from hostility at times than from friendly advice. So even when conditions are hostile to ours, we can learn from them. It is the same for literature. We must be prepared to learn from different literary inheritances of our people and other people… We must be prepared to learn from criticism – sometimes hostile critical evaluations, sometimes friendly, imaginative and sympathetic interpretation of our own work (Sander and Lindfors 2006: 372).

This he suggests is a necessity for the survival of nations' cultures:

Thus, cultures that stay in total isolation from others can be crippled, deformed, or else die. Cultures that change to reflect the ever-changing dynamics of internal relations and which maintain a balanced give and take with external relations are the ones that are healthy. Hence the insistence in these essays on the suffocating and ultimately destructive character of both colonial and neo-colonial structures. A new world order that is no more than the global dominance of neo-colonial relations policed by a handful of Western nations, whether through the United Nations Security Council or not, is a disaster for the peoples of the world and their cultures. While there is a need for cultures to reach out to one another and borrow from one another, this has to be on the basis of equality and mutual respect. The call for western-based new world order should be countered by a continued call for a new, more equitable international economic, political and cultural order within and between nations, a world order that reflects the diversity of world peoples and cultures. Hence the struggle for cultural freedoms (Ngugi 1993: xvi).

Ngugi wa Thiong'o has a worldwide recognition as one of the spearheads in African literature in English. By this time, his writing career to date runs about forty-three years dating from the publication of his debut play in *The Black*

Hermit in 1963. This is just a half-way assessment, as Ngugi is very active in literary production and will do so as long as he is alive. Writing fiction, drama and criticism, he has problematized the African condition as a triple legacy: the colonial legacy where Europeans play a determinant role in the shaping of black continent's predicament, the neocolonial legacy where some African oligarchic bandits of the ruling class acting as puppets of European and American imperialism have taken the continent's economy in hostage, and the gender legacy where colonial and neocolonial patriarchies have enslaved women to the dependency policy.

Along the years of his literary activities and political commitment Ngugi has been a keen observer of African political life and a defender of her culture. His creative vision has kept pace with the development of sociopolitical and cultural lives of Africa in general and Kenya in particular. Although European colonialism has been a continent-wide phenomenon, African countries experienced it differently and colonial experience in Kenya is much telling in its scope, its propensity, its vibrancy and its impartation. The land issue – the confiscation of Kenyan citizens' properties by European colonialists and the bloody wars Kenyans had to fight before getting them back – cannot be excluded from the writings of Ngugi, who has been an active advocate of African people's rights in all their nitty-gritties. He has devoted his literary production to one fight: European imperialism and its tentacles. Even his most recent book, *Birth of a Dream Weaver: A Memoir of a Writer's Awakening* (2016) bears the burden of denouncing the abuses of imperialism. The history of Africa is so interlocked with that of Europe that one cannot discuss past and present African conditions without viewing the European colonialism behind the screen. One would rather say that African history past and present – and very likely future – has been decided, shaped and remodeled at will by Europe. The land issue keeps on recurring in Ngugi's writings just like a painful experience that one had and that has shaped his life. Ngugi's literary ideology and his political vision have been acknowledged and classified as a literature of resistance by many critics. Abdul JanMohamed (1983), Modhumita Roy (1995), Anders Breidlid (2002), G. D. Killam (2004), Dul Johnson (2007), Chinua Achebe (2009), Robert Dale Parker (2015) at various degrees view Ngugi as a resistance writer.

The long and perseverant struggle that Ngugi wages against European imperialism and the relentless efforts he makes to promote African cultural diplomacy deserve a serious attention. Mala Pandurang has given the following account of him:

> Ngugi wa Thiong'o is one of Africa's most prolific intellectual activists. A versatile novelist, playwright, essayist, journalist, film maker and academic, Ngugi has inspired an entire generation of [...] postcolonial scholars by his undeterred commitment to the processes of cultural and linguistic decolonisation; his consistent interrogation of the ambivalent position of the postcolonial writer-in-English; his persistent call for a radical reinterpretation of Kenyan 'nationalist history; and his insistence on the power of the story as a weapon against multiple structures of oppression. Ngugi has led the way in questioning of the epistemological criteria of western scholarship, and has been ruthless in his interrogation of the pressures of international capital and neo-colonial forces on cultural formations within the third-world milieu. Ngugi's entire oeuvre is the outcome of his participation in the larger socio-political processes of the Kenyan nation state (Pandura, 2007: 11).

Pandura's assessment of Ngugi is a testimony to the artistic commitment of Ngugi. He is the East Africa's first and best known writer. He has published prolifically over forty books including fiction, drama, criticism, short stories, political and cultural commentaries and is still active in literary creativity. He was in exile from his country, Kenya, since 1982. Despite this fact he has remained a famous critic of and spokesperson of Kenya's political and cultural life. Ngugi's cultural diplomacy cannot be separated from his life, his work and his political convictions. His vision has been a moving target. Yet, Afrocentric vision of the world is an unshakable pillar that has crystalized his ideological struggle for a better continent. From the rigidity of the 1970s and 1980s, the verve of his criticism has been moderated as he revisited the colonial legacies in the light of the 21st century demands of globalization that imposes cultural dialogue as a necessity to charter peace for a better Africa. This does not equate with an ideological conversion of the man who is known for his impatience towards imperial overlords and their African accomplices. Rather, Ngugi's critical ethos can be identified as strategic way to promote curtesy in cultural conversations, a way of enriching self and other in the world exchange of ideas and values.

Contemporary discussions of nationalism have also had to address the question of postcolonial Diasporas. Earlier colonial institutions of slavery, indenture, and forced migration, and more contemporary divisions of labor between the Third and First Worlds have scattered large groups of the colonized across the globe. Left to negotiate new ethnic identities for themselves *vis-à-vis* both the European-descended majority populations and groups of non-European displaced and disenfranchised people, various diasporas from Africa, Asia, and the Caribbean have given rise to questions about multiple-rooted ethnic identities and languages. Diaspora theorists such as Homi Bhabha, Rey Chow, Stuart Hall, Wilson Harris, and Trinh T. Minh ha focus on cultural production within communities almost exclusively populated by displaced Third World populations, such as the Caribbean, as well as on Third World immigrant cultures within the First World, such as the black British. From a variety of theoretical perspectives, these critics have proposed that identity and language be read not as closed, static, and imbued with essences, but rather as performative, "hybrid," "creolized," and existing "on the borders" of various interpellating systems. The focus on diaspora has also led feminists such as Chandra Mohanty to call for a dialogue between theorists of gendered subalternity in the Third World and First World women of color. The concept of diaspora has emphasized the need for postcolonial studies to enter a sustained dialogue with Afro-American or native American studies, again without presupposing an entire coincidence or a complete discontinuity of interests. Unfortunately, however, such efforts have often been thwarted in the academy by the phenomenon of various marginalized studies being made to compete for resources. In diaspora communities, the question of language of course takes a very different form from that of the indigenous cultures of Africa or Asia. In the latter, activists and theorists such as Ngugi, who himself turned from writing in English to writing in Gikuyu, have called for postcolonial writers to return to indigenous languages. While acknowledging that postcolonial writing in European languages has subverted these languages with oral and written indigenous traditions, and thus displaced colonial literary Paradigms and genres, Ngugi argues that the most scrupulous and innovative efforts to Africanize the English language will still not make that language accessible to the majority of Africans. Further, if writers continue to work within colonial languages and structures in an effort to subvert them, they will run the risk of being recuperated as minor strains and Subcultures within European cultural traditions. In a similar vein, Subaltern studies in India have focused not on the history and cultural production of a Western-trained middle class writing in English or classicized indigenous languages, but of disenfranchised Indian masses working in the vernacular. However, in the context of Caribbean or black British diasporas, where the language of the majority is a European one, there is clearly less impetus for returning to the original language of one's culture than for creolizing European languages. This difference notwithstanding, diaspora theorists and theorists of subalternity in the Third World share the common goal of studying the languages not of high culture, but of the people. Underlying the debates over the rubric of postcoloniality and over nationalism, pan-nationalism, and diaspora are various theories of identity and the production of culture. A central impetus in postcolonial studies has been the resistant reading of power – in its complex colonial, neocolonial, patriarchal, discursive, and material manifestations – so as to unsettle its epistemology, its claims to truth, and its strategies of representation.

An attentiveness to the ways in which meanings are produced and value-coded in language has always marked postcolonial studies, exemplified in landmark works such as Edward Said's *Orientalism* (1978). Although formalist universalist claims that culture and language are produced autonomously of the political context have sometimes been internalized by Third World writers and critics, especially when postcolonial scholarship was organized under the rubric of "commonwealth studies," these claims have been contested from their inception. As a result, the theorizing of language and culture has been central to postcolonial studies, notwithstanding vast differences between various theoretical perspectives. The role of Western(ized) theories in postcolonial studies has been the first subject of debate. With the proviso that postcolonial cultural texts have always themselves theorized meanings and values, critics such as Barbara Christian have attacked the inaccessible languages of Western theories; their refusal or inability to speak to the situation of the Third World; and their institutional effect of distracting postcolonial studies from crucial archival work and political praxis. Those opposed to this view maintain that Western theories, which themselves criticize the closures of Western systems of thought from their margins, can be disengaged from any leanings towards patriarchal or imperial ideology and thus made useful for postcolonial studies. Such postcolonial theorists question the residual nativism being the blanket rejection of Western theories, and argue against the polarization of theory and praxis, or theoretical and empiricist scholarship, urging that while one kind of work cannot replace the other, each must be used productively, in Spivak's words, to "interrupt" the other and bring it to crisis. A variety of theoretical approaches characterizes postcolonial studies at present, of which the three most prominent, the Marxist, the psychoanalytic, and the deconstructive will be briefly described below. It is important to note that postcolonial theory takes variety of meanings depending on the geographical space. In South Africa, postcolonialism has been associated with the struggle against apartheid and white hegemony. Theatre works have been devoted to debunk the apartheid legacy and to show in practical terms how white imperialism, racism and discrimination have impacted the black communities and created distance in the social interactions between blacks and whites. Athol Fugard, Lewis Nkosi, Jane Taylor, Reza de Wet and many other playwrights have positioned postcolonial discourse within the ambit of the struggle against Apartheid. I will briefly illustrate this critical stance with two plays by Athol Fugard.

Mwihia Margaret Njoki and Collins Ogogo in their article "A Critical Analysis of Athol Fugard's Social Vision in Four Selected Plays" have explained how Apartheid has influenced Athol Fugard's postcolonial social vision in his plays. In *Hallo and Good – Bye*, the playwright makes use of two characters Johnnie and his sister Hester together with absent and dead characters as their parents. These two also represent the two races in South Africa. The play begins with Johnnie who is alone in an empty room. This is symbolic in that Johnnie has an only sister who is also lonely but they cannot live together (Njoki and Ogogo 2014: 77). The empty room is symbolic of the emptiness in the lives of the blacks in South Africa. Hester is only interested in inheritance from her father but Johnnie takes care of his ailing and crippled father. When the father dies he feels so lonely and desperate that he doesn't know what to do. Fugard makes use of flashbacks and monologues to explain why certain circumstances are the way they are (Ibidem). An example is the reason why Johnnie's father is a cripple. It is because of an accident he got and he had one leg amputated. He walks with the help of clutches. When he dies his son can only inherit the clutches (Ibidem). This is symbolic of apartheid in that it is crippling and there is nothing worthy inheriting from the system. If there is anything to be inherited from apartheid it is the crippling effect on the citizens. Johnnie is lonely and alienated to his sister Hester. When she arrives expecting a warm welcome from her brother she is shocked to realize that he is neither excited to see her nor interested in talking with her.

> Johnnie: I've been sitting here minding my own business…
> Hester: I've started to wonder if it was the right place
> Johnnie: Surprised of course. I mean, put yourself in my shoes
> I'm sitting here, reading a Comic, passing the time and then you!
> Suddenly you're here too.
> Hester: Not even a word of welcome.
> Johnnie: Welcome. (*HAGB*: 11)

That conversation is in itself cold. "The welcome" statement is only said after Hester demanded it. Hester has been away for twelve years and her brother is not excited at all about her visit lonely as he may be. The exclamation mark in the conversation "… you!" shows unfriendliness. This is abnormal for a brother who is now an orphan and so lonely. He ought to be excited to see his sister (Ibidem). Fugard is showing us that the relationship between the blacks and whites in South Africa is so sore that they don't so much care what happens to the other. The blacks have always been in South Africa and have never left because this is their home. Johnnie has been at home and has never left even when his crippled father becomes so impossibly dependent on him he doesn't desert him. Hester goes away leaving his brother who is actually younger than her with a huge responsibility of taking care of an ailing crippled father. No wonder Johnnie is not interested in her. The whites are interested with the material wealth they get from South Africa like Hester (Ibidem).

When asked how long she would be staying in the house, Hester ignores the question and starts talking about the twelve years she has been away in a flashback. Out there she is not comfortable and she has really suffered. Like Morris in *Blood Knot*, Hester comes back to her brother. She is back because out there she has no money and she needs to live. She has come to see if her father has anything for her to inherit since she is his child. The whites need South Africa as much as the blacks. The only difference is that they want to take what they have not worked for. Hester has not cared for her ailing father and yet she wants to get inheritance (Ibidem). Johnnie has been looking after the father and is not asking for anything. He has been doing it as a duty to her father as a son. Johnnie insists on asking his sister why she has come back.

> Johnnie: Why have you come back?
> Hester: It is also my home. I've got a right to come here if I want. I'm still his daughter. How is he?
> Johnnie: How long you staying?
> Hester: What you worried about? I will buy my own food.
> Johnnie: Is this a holiday? Back home for old times' sake sort of thing. Two weeks annually.
> Hester: In here? I got better things to do with my holidays. (*HAGB:* 11)

This conversation shows mistrust between Johnnie and his sister Hester which is symbolic of the mistrust in the blacks and whites for each other.

Johnnie doesn't trust his sister at all and suspects she is up to something. Hester was not at all interested in her father. Her relationship with her father is sore and she doesn't care about it. All she needs from her father is her inheritance (Ibidem). Johnnie also tells Hester that when she left, her father had said that no one was going to speak of her again. He hated her and had said that she was not a real Afrikaner like him by nature as she had the English blood of her mother (Ibidem). When she asks Johnnie whether the old man still hates her and he replies in the affirmative, her response is "So what? Just remember mom didn't hate me and half of this house is hers so I'm entitled to be here" (*HAGB*: 11). It is ironical that such words can be spoken by a daughter (Ibidem).

Johnnie pesters his sister further by also asking her whether she has actually come back for something to which she does not give a direct reply but goes round and round by replying that she hadn't stated it. She is hypocritical. She doesn't disclose her mission at first but later she makes her advance by telling Johnnie to bring her all the boxes in the house she needed to search for something. She claims that their father was paid hundreds of pounds for compensation after the accident that crippled him and it was hidden somewhere and that is why she needed to ransack all the boxes in the house (Ibidem).

Through Hester the theme of greed is explored and through the father racism is expressed by the fact that he hates his daughter and adores the son who he claims to have inherited his Afrikaner blood.It is then that Johnnie realizes and asks the sister "So that's it? That's why you've come back!" (*HAGB*: 25) There is racism in South Africa and through Hester, it is evident that one race is only interested in exploiting the other (Ibidem). Hester goes further than that and asks her brother what would have happened to her half share if the father had died in her absence. Johnnie urges her not to mention their father's death but she doesn't care saying that "…I'm still alive, you see. He is passing away but I'm still alive. And I'm his daughter. So, half of that compensation is mine" (*HAGB*: 26) The search for the treasure begins and goes on for a long time but finally there is nothing to be inherited showing the futility of the regime (Ibidem).

Third World feminisms have intervened powerfully in each approach, insisting that it addresses the concepts of gender, sexuality, and varied discourses of patriarchy not merely as secondary issues within the larger inquiry, but rather as questions that could transform the terms of the inquiry. Marxist and feminist-Marxist critics have asked persistent questions about the institutional apparatuses through which postcolonial cultural texts are produced and circulated; about the hegemony of high literary aesthetics over popular culture; about the vanguardist and "native informant" roles postcolonial intellectuals sometimes assume *vis-à-vis* the masses; and, following the intervention of Marxist-feminists, about the role of gender and sexuality in the production of culture. Although Western Marxists such as Marx, Mikhail Bakhtin, Antonio Gramsci, and Louis Althusser have strongly influenced postcolonial studies, for instance, the work of Fanon, Spivak, Ngugi, Hall, Chow, and the subaltern studies collective, some Western Marxists have also been criticized for their minimal engagement of postcoloniality, and for their periodization, which positions the Third World in a time lag in relation to the First, reading it as the historical past of the First World present (see, for instance, Fanon's critique of Jean Paul Sartre; Said's critique of Marx; and Madhava Prasad's critique of Jameson). Aspects of psychoanalytic theory have also powerfully influenced theorists such as Fanon and Homi Bhabha, feminists such as Trinh T. Minh ha and Rey Chow, and postcolonial Althusserians, who have used Psychoanalysis to complicate Marxist teleological narratives of power and resistance. Such critics are drawn to psychoanalysis for its ability to position power and resistance in the contexts of desire, psychic investments, and the processes through which identities are constructed in language. Psychoanalytic critics approach identity as not given or static, but as performative and staged within language. By mobilizing Freudian and Lacanian concepts such as "fetish" and "mimicry" in the context of postcoloniality, theorists such as Bhabha have drawn attention to the ambivalences within colonial stereotypes and within various subject positions occupied by any one "consciousness." While Third World psychoanalytic feminists share these interests, they have also criticized some of the male approaches, including Fanon's, for their inability or refusal to address questions of gender, sexuality, and sexual orientation, and to go beyond the patriarchal subtexts of thinkers such as Freud. Psychoanalysis continues to have a strong appeal for Third World feminists such as Trinh and Chow because of its sustained interest in questions of sexuality, and its narrativization of sexed and gendered identity. However, like Western Marxisms, Western psychoanalysis has not been embraced uncritically. The larger Marxist critique of the psychoanalytic approaches is that they have not theorized beyond individuated psychic resistances to collective action. An early instance of the unease generated by the more ahistoricized forms of psychoanalysis is Fanon's critique of O. Mannoni, who isolated such static Paradigms as the "dependency complex" of the colonized with little reference to the systemic material exploitation of colonialism. Third World Marxist feminists such as Spivak have pointed to the Orientalism, ahistoricism, and even antifeminism of Freud as well as of some contemporary French feminists such as Kristeva, while still suggesting that French feminism can be usefully extended to a postcolonial context. Finally, Derridean Deconstruction (rather than its US version) has strongly influenced the work of Spivak and translation theorists such as Tejaswini Niranjana. The appeal of deconstruction for political resistant readings is precisely its persistent questioning of the kind of originary and foundational thinking that has characterized Western universalist, humanist, and colonial discourses. Spivak also describes deconstruction as a reading strategy that consistently questions the objectivity and innocence of the reader, and is thus of immense use to postcolonial readers as a reminder of their own complicity in the structures of thought that they critique.

African drama has known different stages in the postcolonial development: colonialist discourses based on Eurocentric claim of universalism of knowledge and the refutal of Africa as home to theatrical arts. That period was followed by the phase of cultural nationalism from 1850-1950; the consolidation of theatrical literature and art through performance for independence from 1951-1970; the theatre of the post-independence politics from 1971 to the present day. Yet critics are divided in their different approaches to the emergence of dramatic theory and especially on its search for referential frame. According to Hansel Ndumbe Eyo, "Critical assessment of many of the leading first-generation playwrights of Anglophone Africa, especially Soyinka, J. P. Clark, Ene Enshaw, Sarif Easmon, Joe de Graft, Ngugi wa Thiong'o and Guillaume Oyono Mbia, has been mixed." (Eyo, 2001: 26). He adds that "The search for some universal frame of reference has often resulted in works which are sterile and emasculated (Ibidem)." One major book that guides theory is Michael Etherton's *The Development of Drama in Africa* (1983). The major theoretical pronouncement of that book is that African drama has emerged from the combination of several contrapuntal forces, historical, socio-political, economic, and cultural that have shaped and molded the modern theatrical orientations. African drama has emerged as the heir of triple cultural heritages: indigenous traditions, western Christian civilization and mid-west Islamic waves (Etherton, 1983: v). Michael Etherton's analyses have left a gap with regard to the theoretical articulation of that satisfies the canon with regard to its search for a referential frame.

The second major book is *Precolonial and Postcolonial Drama* (2001) edited by Lokangaka Losambe and Devi Sarinjeive. This book gathers twelve essays around the themes of precolonial indigenous forms of drama and postcolonial formulation of African theatre. Various contributors have centered their arguments around the ideological discursive line of thought that sustain a critical theory for indigenous theatrical forms in Africa. In the introduction to the book the editors assert: "this book also seeks to emphasize the existence of a link or a sense of organic continuity within African literary tradition between pre-colonial and post-colonial forms of African drama" (2001: vii). But going deep inside these books, they do not satisfy the demand of theory concerning the referential frame as the reader cannot locate the relationship between criticism, theory and the diachronic evolution within the neocolonial space. Even a look at topics in journals like *Critical African Studies* especially in its 2015 and 2016 volumes reveals the absence of theoretical approaches that discuss the theoretical aspect of African drama and theatre. It follows that critical theory is left unattended on this question of referential frame. That is why I submit that literary theory of drama taking into account its evolution across the time and its major theoretical orientations in the precolonial and postcolonial trajectories needs deep critical analyses.

5.11. Postcolonial Critical Configurations

5.11.1. The Phase of Cultural Nationalism 1850 - 1950

The search for a frame of reference in African critical theory of drama starts from the recognition of what trajectory drama has followed with regard to theory and criticism. Research on African theatre in the precolonial and colonial African societies was carried out in the main by anthropologists. As a result, the field of theatrical accomplishment and dramatic lore has suffered from the absence of expertise eyes on what was the cultural wealth of the African peoples. In *The Expansive Moment: Anthropology in Britain and Africa 1918—1970 (1995),* Jack Goody examines aspects of cultural life in Africa without any identifiable major statement on how African theatre operates and the theory that sustains its critical attention.

Henri Morton Stanley in his article "The Meeting with Stanley", declared "Africa possessed no theatres, newspapers, or agreeable societies" (Stanley [1886] 2009: 42), and disseminated dangerous and derogatory statements about African dramatic performances.

This first generation of scholarship was challenged and counter-attacked by later scholars and researchers who did some investigations on African cultures, theatres and literatures. The work of anthropologists was taken over by drama specialist Peter Brook who journeyed to Africa in 1973 to search on "a universal language of theatre" which goes beyond the division of nationality. Yet, the account given by Peter Brook leaves the reader unsatisfied, for he established that African theatre does not equate European dramatic forms and concludes to a non-effectiveness of a theory of drama in indigenous Africa. Biodun Jeyifo in assessing Peter Brook's work asserts:

> Brook's text turns to be ambiguous, it turns out to be solidly inscribed in an established tradition of critical discourses of the Nigerian and African theatre whose apprehension of the phenomenon of interculturalism is the subject of this essay, especially as this apprehension pertains to the interactions and oppositions between, on the one hand the 'Western', 'the foreign' and on the other hand, the 'African', the 'indigenous' (Jeyifo, 2002: 458).

This critical assessment of Brook by Biodun Jeyifo reveals a dissatisfaction in the search of a critical theory that sufficiently examines the threatre field in Africa. What makes Jeyifo to take Brook to task is the scholar's (Brook's) classifying African theatre as "Other" and European one as "Self". Serious debates in literary circles were engaged to discuss the evidence of the existence of drama in Africa prior to the advent of European colonization. In theorizing the origin of African drama, critics have not found a ground for agreement on two points: firstly, whether festivals and rituals constitute drama, and secondly which birth date attribute to drama as a body of performance. On the designation of drama, two major critical tendencies emerged. In the first group, scholars like Bakary Traore (1975), Wole Soyinka (1988), Biodun Jeyifo (2002), Mineke Schipper-de Leeuw (1984), and Mzo Sirayi have strived to establish African festival forms, rituals and rites as important dramatic forms, while other scholars like Oyenka Owomoyela (1985), Ruth Finnegan (1970/2012) and Pierre Medehouegnon (2006) contend that African drama dates back to the colonial penetration in Africa. Wole Soyinka in defense of the recognition of African drama writes:

> Festivals, comprising as they do a variety of forms, from the most spectacular to the most secretive and emotionally charged, offer

> the most familiar hunting-ground. What is more, they constitute in themselves *pure theatre* at its most prodigal and resourceful. In short, the persistent habit of dismissing festivals as belonging to a 'spontaneous' inartistic expression of communication demands re-examination. The level of organization involved, the integration of the sublime with the mundane, the endowment of the familiar with properties of the unique (and this spreads over days) all indicate that it is into the heart of many African festivals that we should look for the most stirring expression of man's instinct and need for drama as its most comprehensive and community-involving (Soyinka, 1988: 138).

Through this statement, Soyinka seeks to demonstrate that African festivals speak in themselves about the existence of drama and theatrical traditions in Africa. In this perspective, he admits that African drama does not need to look at the outside models of dramatic performance for reference, but the recognition of its artistic manifestation in different cultural activities should find ground of justification in the fact that African dramatic performances are autonomous and satisfy the required features for the purpose for which it was created: the expansion of the African's spirit as a catharsis fulfilment. The Finnegan school of thought that emerged in the 1970s has built its critical approach along the line of non-conformity of African traditional performances with Greek or European models of drama. They rate African festivals, rituals and myths as insufficiently dramatic and conclude that poetry fits their designation, not drama or theatre. Ruth Finnegan has formulated a counter argument in which she repudiates in bloc the dramatic values of African festival and artistic performances as theatrical body:

> How far one can speak of indigenous drama in Africa is not an easy question. In this it differs from previous topics like, say, panegyric, political poetry, or prose narratives, for there it was easy to discover African analogies to the familiar European forms. Though some writers have very positively affirmed the existence of native African drama (Traoré 1958, Delafosse 1916), it would perhaps be truer to say that in Africa, in contrast to Western Europe and Asia, drama is not typically a wide-spread or a developed form (Finnegan, [1970] 2012: 485 web).

From an oral literature perspective, the argument advanced by Ruth Finnegan constitutes for the theorist of African drama an unacceptable proposition, because, African literature traces its roots to oral tradition, the manifestation of which stretches in different ramifications, drama, poetry, song, fiction. For Finnegan, African drama has to be positioned, measured and judged in the scale of European dramatic tradition before one pronounces its fitness as drama. Never border to know if European drama itself has a barometric regulator that decided when its own was fit to be conferred the title of drama.

Critical theory arguing in favor of traditional myths, festivals, rituals and rites as the prime level of drama in Africa, has established parallel standard of indigenous African drama with the ancient Greek ceremonial elements found in the cult to Dionysus, the Greek god of fertility, wine and vegetation (Oyin Ogunba, 1967). Such examples are festival and myth. Myths and festivals have existed in every culture, every civilization and every community in Africa since early civilizations till date. For instance, every community has its creation myth that explains the origin of the world and human life on earth. Such creation myths are often times recounted in certain conventional manners around the storyteller, who involves the audience through handclapping, mimetic gestures, chanting, drum and gong beating, and the dance. The village square that shelters such myth narratives are solicited by large audiences who sit in the round like in theatre halls. In these kinds of oral performances, the concept of performance itself takes a very important meaning.

The Nigerian critic Biodun Jeyifo has observed in *Modern African Drama, a Norton Critical Edition,* (Jeyifo, 2002: 459), that the period (1850-1950) was marked by the desire of the African playwrights to assert African presence in world literature and cultural politics due to the circulation of defamatory arguments about the non-existence of an indigenous African theatre. That was the time when the main literary discourses were Eurocentric in theme, tone and style. Literatures of minority groups were denied recognition and momentum when they did not fit in with the cultural philosophies of Western literatures. Drama and theatrical performances in Africa were under the spell of colonial rules and adopted hybrid forms blending African themes with Christian religious stories. Elleke Boemer in *Empire Writing: An Anthology of Colonial Writing 1870-1918* has offered a broad perspective on colonial Eurocentric literature that arbitrarily denied African drama and theatre the fundamental backbone of artistic craft (Boemer, 2009). Many arguments hold the tenets that only literature produced by the mainstream Europe passes the test of recognizable referential body of theory. As a result, the drama and theatrical performances of other people, essentially deriving from cultic traditions where chanting and dancing are the predominant modes of expressions are downgraded and rated non-theoretical. The argument advanced is that there was no indigenous form of theatre in Africa. Rabindranath Togore (1861-1941) writes:

> Leave this chanting and singing and telling of beads! Whom does you worship in this lonely dark corner of a temple with doors all shut? Open thy eyes and see thy God is not before thee! He is there where the tiller is tilling the hard ground and where the pathmaker is breaking the stones. He is with them in sun and in shower, and his garment is covered with dust. Put off thy holy mantle and even like him come down on the dusty soil (Tagore, 1912: 378).

In the face of this types of statements, many African scholars feel offended and would like to retaliate by developing a theoretical body of criticism that deconstruct and off-shoot the discursive tenets of Eurocentric criticisms. Challenging the European canons these critics of African inflection repudiate theories that hold African dramatic theory at bay. They also seek to restore the body and soul of African critical discourse that looks deep into the past to bring out on the theory side information that were lost to the human memory and bring to rectitude the pageant of African theatre.

The first generation of postcolonial African writers, the majority of whom attended European and American universities shaped their playwrighting techniques according to European dramatic forms. They looked in African traditional and cultural lore for referential elements that could be akin to Greek original festival ingredients to build an Afrocentric drama parallel to Greek tragedies. Before Wole Soyinka, dramatists like Hubert Ogunde, Duro Ladipo, Kola Ogunmola, Ene Henshaw have adapted local and traditional stories to European theatrical traditions. With plays like *Africa and God* (1944), *Strike and Hunger* (1945), and *Worse than Crime* (1945), Ogunde dived into the heart of African traditional culture to purvey the quintessential indigenous material of storytelling, myths and religious beliefs to map out hybrid texture that is adjacent to European tragi-comedy. These elements point to the search for a theoretical frame that blend African dramatic forms with European theatricality. What obtained from the primacy of these hybrid textures was an aesthetic ethos that reconfigured art in the mainstream collective literary discourse, the adjuncts of which was to become later the recapturing of first hand material into contemporary African dramatic force. In the same line of thought, Dapo Adelugba and Olu Obafemi observe:

> It consists of a dynamic interplay of the visual, verbal and kinetic elements of music, dance, poetry and song with invited audience participation, as in traditional festival theatre. The initial aesthetic format of this theatre as composed by Hubert Ogunde from 1944 was a syncretization of the Native Air Theatre's disposition employing Yoruba cultural adjuncts with Yoruba music and dances. The Aladura movement, one of the secessionist churches that grew out of the cultural Renaissance of the late nineteenth century, used theatre to propagate its doctrine, 'basing church plays on stories taken from the Bible and setting them to music and dance with a uniquely innovative Yoruba cultural influence […] The structure of the traditional travelling theatre – the opening glee, the play proper, and the closing glee – is the major aesthetic plank of Ogunde's theatre (Adelugba and Obafemi, 2004: 148).

Pursuing postcolonial discourse later Nigerian playwrights namely Wole Soyinka and John Pepper Clark, produced plays which contain traditional material of myth, ritual and festival. Soyinka's *A Dance of the Forest*, *The Strong Breed* and *Swamp Dwellers* having African rituals and festival imprints, demarking them as ritual-based plays. The concern of Soyinka was to produce an African drama calqued on Greek tragedy. John Pepper Clark also produced *The Song of a Goat* that is ritual centered and that parallelled the Greek tragedy. In Ghana, Efua T. Sitherland's *The Marriage of Anansewa* also has ritual and African funerals as its central focus. In South Africa, Herbert Dhlomo was significant in defining South African theatre. His creative work focused on his need to articulate the African experience. He integrated the Bantu traditional festivals and rituals to his plays as can testify *Cetshwayo* (1936), *Dingana* (1937) and *Moshoeshoe* (1937).

Many of Wole Soyinka's early plays demonstrate this kind of derivation with obvious Shakespearian echoes, although he is more imaginative in transforming his sources and instilling them with freshness and verve. Soyinka has been able to develop a more eclectic style, the result of a thorough process of experiential distillation.

Martin Banham's volume *A History of Theatre in Africa* (2004) brings together eighteen seminal essays that update information about theory of drama and theatre in Africa. Research has centered on a continentwide submissions of what drama hails to the various inhabitants of the African continent from prehistoric time to the contemporary period, a search whose main thesis is:

> The roots of African theatre are ancient and complex and lie in areas of communal festival, seasonal rhythm and religious ritual, as well as in the work of popular entertainers and storytellers. Since the 1950s, in a movement that has paralleled the political emancipation of so much of the continent, there has also grown a theatre that comments back from the colonized world to the world of the colonists and explores its own cultural, political and linguistic identity. *A History of Theatre in Africa* offers a comprehensive yet accessible account of this long and varied chronicle and is written by a team of scholars in the field (Banham, 2004:i).

Perceptible features of that type of drama was the will of the African playwrights to valorize their cultures and traditions albeit the colonial propaganda to debunk them. Significant theatrical pointers of that periods circulated the theories of African subordination to the White man. Due to the low literacy level in majority of African societies at that periods, dramatic literature was eclectic, freelance enterprise, although cultural traditions have always sheltered inside them gorgeous theatrical aesthetics. The theatrical display, and cultural performances were done solely to please the whims of the colonial master, to conform to his ideological standards. Important referentiality from this cultural fragmentation is testified by Chinua Achebe who points out:

> the result of the disaster brought upon African psyche in the period of subjugation of subjection to alien races. I remember the shock felt by Christians of my father's generation in my village in the early 1940s when for the first time the local girls' school performed Nigerian dances at the anniversary of the coming of the gospel. Hitherto they had always put on something Christian and civilized which I believe was called the Maypole dance (Achebe, 1988: 29).

The refusal of some local leaders to the teenage girls in Nigeria to perform local dances to the detriment of European dance can be explained as a lack of confidence in the value of African performances. They look down upon African indigenous drama as non-conform to the European standard of theatre. Shall we say, analyzing from Achebe's comments on African drama that dramatic art was in a dubitative stage, as it didn't have yet an independent critical standard to defend a theory on itself. Dramatists were speculating between African traditional aesthetics and European-based model of drama. Wole Soyinka explains that "This period may also be justly said to constitute the lowest ebb in the fortunes of traditional theatre, participation in cultural life even in the villages being subjected to lightening descents from the fanatical hordes of the prophetic sects" (Soyinka, 1988: 142). In addition, drama suffered from the lack of literary theory that sufficiently documented and sustained its visibility. The second half of the nineteenth century and the first half of the twentieth century were periods when many documents written on African cultures and histories were in Arabic and not not translated. The only literary documents available were books written with Eurocentric approaches, denying Africans their past and civilizations. Ali Mazrui in *Africans a Triple Heritage* refers to this as "de-Africanizing Africa" which he explained as "turning Africa's back on previous centuries" (Mazrui, 1986: 11). Mazrui's interpretation completes Achebe's on the basis that the critic looks at how African drama both suffered from literary records, imprecision of theory and the effect of colonial psychological debasement. The colonial cultural denial of African dramatic art was later to produce the counter-effect of the intellectual awakening leading to political agitation for independence. It began in the form of cultural nationalism which Wole Soyinka explains in the following words:

> Cultural nationalism was, however, constantly at work against a total usurpation of imported forms. Once again, religion and its institutions provided the base. Unable to accept the excesses of the Christian cultural imperialism, such as the embargo on African instruments and tunes in a 'universal' church, and the prohibition of drumming on tranquil Anglican Sundays, the breakaway movements began. The period 1888 to the early 1930s witnessed a proliferation of secessionist movements, mostly inspired by the need to worship God in the cultural modes of the

forefathers. And now began also a unique 'operatic' tradition in West Africa, but especially Lagos, beginning with church cantatas which developed into dramatizations of biblical stories until it asserted its independence in secular stories and the development of professional troupes (Soyinka, 1988: 141).

Soyinka describes the burden of African theatrical disavowal by colonial adjuncts as a colonialist literary enterprise intended to off-shoot the premises of intellectual theory of theatre in Africa, at the time when orality had primacy over written records. The first reason is that school education at that period was not the benefits of many African citizens and seemed not to be enough reason to justify the denial of a theory that explains the past in agreement with the historical records of the body of theatrical art present in the very cultural industry of the African communities. A second reason that can be advanced to explain the search of a theoretical frame of reference, is the failure of scholarship to document, record and store in public and private universities and other institutions of higher learning the cultural products that emanated from the works of theatrical productions pertaining to indigenous cultural lore. Soyinka theorizes this by saying: "The process, reminiscent of the evolution of the 'miracle' or 'mystery' plays of medieval Europe, is identical with the evolution of the Agbegijo theatre (then temporarily effaced) from the sacred temporal funeral rites of the Alafin of Oyo to court entertainment and, thereafter, independent existence and geographical dispersion" (Soyinka, 1988: 141). From this belief, it makes sense to submit that it is the search for identity affirmation that informed the awakening of consciences for cultural nationalism that was to be the backbone of intellectual claims for political independence. Frantz Fanon advances the argument that:

> The historical necessity in which the men of African culture find themselves to racialize their claims and to speak more of African culture than of national culture will tend to lead them up in blind alley. Let us take for example the case of African Cultural Society. This society had been created by African intellectuals who wished to get to know each other and to compare their experiences and the results of their respective research work. The aim of this society was therefore to affirm the existence of an African culture, to evaluate this culture on the plane of distinct nations, and to reveal the internal motive forces of each of their national cultures (Fanon, 2002: 416).

Three key ideas emerge from Fanon's position in this excerpt, and which from dramatic theoretical perspective respond to the idea of the search for a theoretical frame of reference. firstly, the necessity for African intellectuals to assert their cultural identity not simply as national citizens of the countries they belonged to, but to actually go beyond by posturing their citizenship as Africans, a way of framing for themselves an identity that will fit in the universal. Put otherwise, the African intellectuals saw their battle beyond the confinement of a country as the struggle was continental. The implication of this interpretive praxis from dramatic scholarship is that the struggle for cultural identity assumed greater importance when it was continent-based, not country-based; thus, the perspective of a universal frame of reference. Secondly, since drama partakes for hundred per cent to the cultural life of a people, the formulation of a theory of the universal bearing African imprints would give impetus, shape and character to the body of knowledge that reads itself as a genre in African literature. Due to the fact that drama combines text and stage, to say performance, it is closer to the people, the masses, and suites better to address day-to-day common struggles and life intricacies of the people whose very common experiences are represented and reflected in there. What obtains from this ideological perception of the drama utilities is the relocation of the cultural referential within the ambit of visual arts, not in the sense of abstract epistemology, but in the very construction of knowledge in practical use of promoting social education. Thirdly, every literature, when it is interpreted and backed with theoretical anchors better stands as a scientific discipline that resists the test of time and space. One can remember that the very inadequate and derogatory postulates pondered by colonial Eurocentric literatures about the non-existence of African drama and cultures were informed by the scarcity of written records that backed and explained African life and cultural performances to the outside worlds. As a matter of fact, the lacking cultural information gave way to distorted and displaced interpretations of African literary forms. The articulation of a theory that serves as a universal frame of reference will most definitely serve the utilitarian needs as a cultural memory for future generations, rebuff the shackles of docile acceptance of any form of inferiority and engage African theatre on the ground of intellectual propensity.

5.11.2. The Consolidation of the Canon: Postcolonial Theory from 1951-1970

The search for a postcolonial theoretical frame of reference continued in the periods preceding and following political independences in Africa. First, the period preceding African countries' independences was a period of intense political activities, of abundance cultural performances and deep intellectual reflections. One would say that in literature, there was a bourgeoning of critical theories. Now, how was theory of drama to bend on universal frame of reference? First, one needs to approach the question from the perspective of the literary ideologies of that period. In fact, pure indigenous drama that was under censure and were banned in many colonies were being reopened and authorized as one of the claims of independence. It followed that the literary harvest of these periods in terms of the cultural pronouncement and theoretical reformulations were rather on the bloom pace. In this perspective, Ngugi wa Thiong'o states:

> The result of this has been more research on oral traditions and also attempts at collecting some of these traditions as well as critical commentaries on these traditions. Quite recently about three books have come out on the different oral literatures of the different nationalities in Kenya. But this is only the beginning. Massive work will have to be done to ensure the preservation of the oral tradition as well as creating the basis for further development (Ngugi, 2006: 227).

African dramatic literature took the body of theoretical expression as writers began interrogating the colonial administration, the direct and indirect rules imposed on them and the exclusion of the educated elite from the prerogatives of employment in civil service. Political agitation for independence began in Anglophone Africa earlier than Francophone one due to the fact that the British did not develop an employment policy in their territories to absorb the educated African youth. A different policy, though inefficient too, was adopted in Francophone territories where assimilation was applied. Drama being an excellent means of expression, many writers turned their gazes to theatre to voice their criticism and make their claims heard.

But most importantly, African schools of drama majority of which were built incorporated to the universities shaped the critical traditions of African drama. In Francophone Africa, William Ponty in Sengal played a key role in the shaping of Francophone theatre. The major contributors of dramatic literature and theory from the francophone world were trained in that school. The case in point being Bernard Dadie and Bakary Traore. Bakary Traore in *Black African Theatre and Its Social Functions* has theorized and defended the existence of dramatic art in oral narratives and folktales performed by the griots and other storytellers. He has also examined the functionalities of myths and rituals as the mediums of spiritual and religious expansions of traditional communities (Traore, 1972: 50).

On the Anglophone side, the plays of Wole Soyinka (*Kongi's Harvest*), Ngugi wa Thiong'o (*The Trial of Dedan Kimathi*), Kateb Yacine (*Circle of Repression*), Athol Fugard (*People Are Living There*), and Ama Ata Aidoo (*The Dilemma of a Ghost*) can be associated with protest drama and a claim for independence. As a matter of fact, major theoretical positions taken by critics like Ngugi, Soyinka, Don Rubin, Joachim Fiebach and David Kerr bring dramatic theory on more secure ground and consolidates its canon. These critical positions will be analysed one by one. For instance, Wole Soyinka's *Art, Dialogue and Outrage* bears the tonality of iconoclastic articulation of protest against the colonial empire and verges on the claim for African freedom. One essay in that collection, "Between Self and System: The Artist in Search of Liberation", critically asserts the need for liberation of both Africa as an oppressed continent, and the artist himself in what he calls the crisis of Euroamerican racism:

> If I do not exercise great caution, I know that I may end up with no persuasive defense against some kind of declaration… in the early seventies a certain African notorious playwright underwent a crisis of racism. Certainly, I am aware that my pronouncements on Euroamerican society and culture have become more abrasive, less compromising, while recourse to the contrast provided by mine has tended, even by the very fact of comparison, to magnify its virtues. Perhaps, basically, the artist is an insecure being. Even when he says: 'This work is not open to disput (Soyinka, 1988: 41-42).

Soyinka's reexamination of the harms done by colonialism to Africa and Africans reverberates throughout the book. But most tantalizing and abrasive is his reclaiming of the restoration of cultural freedom to Africans. This freedom entails for Africans, the freedom to create, to organize and manage their internal affairs without the intrusion and perpetual disturbance of the colonial master. Ngugi wa Thiong'o in *Decolonizing the Mind, the Politics of Language in African Literature* purveys African theatrical theory:

> The revolt of the sixties and early seventies had a more nationalist flavor. Kenyan playwrights (like Francis Imbuga, Kenneth Watene,

> Kibwana and Micere Mugo) and Kenyan directors (like Seth Adagala, Thirus Gathwe…) emerged with a growing circle of actors around Voice of Kenya radio and television, the Kenyan national theatre and the University….The revolt took many forms: one was the sheer African petty bourgeois assertion in the very fact of writing and directing and performing plays. It also took the form of a more and more nationalistic patriotic and anti-neocolonial, anti-imperialist content in the plays, this trend perhaps best exemplified in Micere Mugo's and Ngugi wa Thiong'o's *The Trial of Dedan Kimathi*… (Ngugi, 1987: 39)

Ngugi's theoretical pronouncement turns to assert an anticolonial struggle that purveys Africa's historical contestation with European colonialist forces around the discursive ethos of one ideal: the liberation from the colonial yoke and the cultural regeneration of African masses. Dramatic theory reverberates the necessity to confer on African literary art, namely drama its methodological framework of an art that partakes to the essential development of society and the rejuvenation of its cultural lore. It also advocates a critical agency that renegotiate productive space in favour of the artists in their support to the masses and their ideal of freedom. The implication of this critical agency being that theory blends with practice to produce the fundamentals of theatre for liberation, itself couched in the compulsive frame of art as a committed tool. Don Rubin from this perspective has cleared the ambiguities that may arise in the field of theatrical theory from the assertion and recognition of the consolidation of theory in its fundamental assertion as a canonical force that sufficiently documents the scholarship. In his article "African Theatre in a Global Context", he asserts:

> It is at the root of the new interdisciplinary science of theatre anthropology, an extraordinary late-twentieth-century investigation into the nature of the performative being created by groundbreaking theorists and practitioners in this growing field such as Victor Turner, Richard Schechner Eugenio Barba… All are seeking to recognize and understand the role of the performative in daily life, to enlarge the notion of the theatrical to make all of us realize that theatre is not necessarily limited to a few hours in a closed, darkened building with a carefully prepared text.… It is an attempt to make us aware that theatre, the theatrical and the performative are

quintessentially connected to universal human experience: birth, death, rites of passage, marriage, namings and even funerals (Rubin, 2002: 470).

The main argument in this statement is that African theatre has consolidated its place in the global context where formerly opinions were dubitative about the presence of a critical theory that sustains theatrical literature and art. Noticeable is the fact that drama in Africa enjoys a substantial support from theory and such theory entertains good relationship with other close disciplines like anthropology and sociology. What mostly compels attention in Rubin's submission is not only that drama has the support of theory, but also and especially that it has come to be vested with the authority of transdisciplinary body of knowledge. The construction of such critical standard renegotiates in its constituency the thematic approach of drama as bourgeoning discipline in Africa and the theory that sustains its viability. Its backbone is the analytical tool that prunes and sprawls its reproductive cells. It may make sense in this critical outlook to postulate that dramatic theory now attends a dislocation and a relocation of creative abode that transcends the unidisciplinary approach to resume a larger proportion of creativity and reproductivity. At this level, Joachim Fiebach has described what he refers to as the theoretical "dimensions of theatricality in Africa" by saying:

> My understanding of theatricality in this all-encompassing, expansive sense is similar to views and notions that have been advanced mainly by western theatre people, social and cultural historians, anthropologists, sociologists… There is a rich body of material (e.g., description of travelers, analyses of anthropologists) to support my contention that large portion of public communication (sociopolitical interaction) in many African countries, before and during the period of full-scale colonization that began in the nineteenth century have been structured in similar theatrical ways (Fiebach, 2002: 475, 477).

There is a connection between Rubin's statement and Fiebach's. First, the two of them see in African theatrical theory a possibility of interdisciplinary stature. They advocate a close relationship between anthropology, sociology and drama. Their argument can be justified in the sense that cultural manifestations and performances serve as backbones of these disciplines.

Thus, to theorize on drama means to theorize on culture and by extension on anthropology and sociology. But most importantly, the theory of African drama at this stage conceptualizes a canonical reception of the interplay between the materials of dramatic literature, rituals, rites and festivals, the body of texts that recreate these integrative elements and the final consumption of the performance through the audience's appropriation of the content. It makes sense from this perspective to say that the material of dramatic inspiration, the text of its materialization, the performance of its visibility and the theory of its interpretation form together a whole. David Kerr complements this argument by saying:

> This is not a place to attempt a genealogy of Arts for Development, a text which would require tracing the various indigenous adaptations African cultures have made to the dialectic elements within their own art forms. It would also entail describing the attempts made by colonial educators to mobilize African communities through a variety of imposed or transformed, indigenous art. Instead, I offer a much narrower historical framework:
> 1. Research into a community's problems;
> 2. Using a workshopped technique to create a play contextualizing those problems;
> 3. Presenting the play to the community; using the post-performance discussion as the basis for initiating action to solve the problems (Kerr, 2002: 487).

David Kerr summarizes the methodology of African community-based theatre and from this point builds a theoretical approach of this theatre as an utilitarian practice. From the theoretical perspective, theatre responds to the needs of the community and the artistic production that seeks to display performance should take into account its social function an as instrument of education, sensitization and admonition. The theory of African drama that problematizes, questions and reflects intellectually on problems surrounding the community bears the stamp of approval as commitment dramatic theory.

5.11.3. Postcolonial Theory from 1972 to the Present Day

Postcolonial dramatic theory turns to the African *arrivists* in power who have hijacked political power, seized the national treasury and made their political office a private property. Most theorists entered in confrontation with political leaders because of their critical denunciation of political deviationism. The theory of African drama sought to position itself as the recorder of these critical tendencies that crystalize the dramatic momentum of literary inflections towards the deconstruction of oligarchic leadership and labyrinthian corruption. At the pinnacle of theorists stand firm the second generation of African playwrights namely Femi Osofisan, Ola Rotimi, Wole Soyinka, James Gibbs, Ngugi wa Thiong'o, and Athol Fugard. Here their critical books give posture and reference frame of post-independent theory to their plays. Osofisan's *The Nostalgic Drum, Essays on Literature, Drama and Culture* (1999), Ola Rotimi's *African Drama Literature: To Be or to Become* (1991), Wole Soyinka's *The Open Sore of a Continent, a Personal Narrative of the Nigerian Crisis* (1995), James Gibbs (editor)'s *Nkyin-Nkyin Essays on Ghanaian Theatre* (2009), Ngugi's *Something Torn and New An African Renaissance* (2009), Toyin Falola and Tunde Akinyemi (editors)'s *Emerging Perspectives on Femi Osofisan* (2009) most definitely secured African drama and theatre its place within the canon.

These critics and playwrights have at different levels and from different sociopolitical and cultural contexts assessed the political, economic, cultural, and intellectual dynamisms of their countries from 1972 onwards and produced theories that reassert the African presence in world geopolitics. What makes the particularity of these theoretical body of texts is their address of past and contemporary socio-political issues and their future outlooks. I will select and analyze Osofisan and Rotimi's positions. Speaking from the intellectual perspectives of the struggles that tantalize the histories of their nations, they went far to produce theoretical discourses that engage African socio-cultural and political dynamism on the challenging terrain of literary bargain which, if not entirely, but at least essentially renegotiate the place of African dramatic theories and stage performances on the platforms of world literary debates. Femi Osofisan's *The Nostalgic Drum, Essays on Literature, Drama and Culture* has oriented his critical theory towards an iconoclastic assessment of post-independent African politics. His theory conceptualizes drama as a barometer that measures and seeks to regularize and balance the power relationships between political functionaries, the economic problems and the social needs of the masses. On this account, he opines:

> The tropes of discourse have altered, and nowadays, carry some deep imprints of sadness…But I do not want to stop the story

> there... Let us examine the implications on the national plane. I say nothing new, I am sure, when I underline here that the imbalance which as we have seen existing on the international plan exists, even more crucially, within the shell of the nation itself, in reflection of the forces of power which govern our individual countries. Power of course as we know, has been confiscated since independence by politicians, the military and the urban elite. Thus, if you were to read our newspapers, and listen to the radio or television, you would quickly notice how the news items is almost entirely devoted to the activities of soldiers and politicians, and to their urban constituency. The same injustices complained by the Third World against the developed world are almost exactly the same as these which our urban-based media inflict on the rest of the nation's populace. Thus, for instance, our farmers and peasants, who compose the majority of the population, are mostly absent and unheard...By 'alternative theatre', I mean of course a theatre which exists largely outside the orbit of the officially sanctioned culture... (Osofisan, 2001: vi,112)

Osofisan builds his theory on the re-examination of African politics in the postcolonial space. For him, theatre at this point of African history should have as primary task of questioning the political agendas of the African leaders and their actual implementation in African nations.

Osofisan advocates what Evan Maina Mwangi calls "Africa writing back to self" theatre. It is a theatre that seeks first and foremost to question the despondent attitude of an oligarchic leadership that has supplanted national interest by its egocentric upsurge, especially as it continually embezzles money from national treasury and leave the masses in abject destitution. To say that Africa is in search of a theoretical frame of reference is to advocate for an intellectual critical discourse that postulates theoretical viability and adumbrates the international tentacles of what was many decades ago the unique prerogative of European hegemony: the international recognition of drama as a discipline of cultural knowledge, a body of theoretical and critical discourses and a genre that engages both the attention of audiences and scholars.

Ola Rotimi has identified three major contributions he brought to the consolidation of African dramatic theory: Negritude discourse, culture conflicts discourse and the anger and protest discourse, as he explains in the following excerpt:

> Yet another contribution which I have made to African Dramatic Literature is the consolidation of a new theme. It would be recalled that at the earlier stage of this lecture, I identified THREE broad themes that have engaged African Dramatic Literature, from colonial times to the present, and promised to elaborate on the fourth. The three themes are: the theme of Negritude; the theme of culture conflict, and the theme of ANGST (anger and protest). The last two are post – independence themes. If the theme of "culture conflict" has focused more on situations involving "normal" personages caught in some social or domestic contretemps or other, the theme of ANGST has dwelt pungently on rulers of modern Africa. Without exception, works of Dramatic Literature dealing with the theme of ANGST, have all been damnatory. They customarily depict embodiments of insatiable lust for power, of misrule, and of betrayal of the people's cause. They all display NEGATIVE heroes. It seems that despite these negative mirrorings, not much has impaired misrule in modern Africa. No sooner would a reckless ruler be overthrown, than a new one came forth, exuding recklessness more vicious than his predecessors. The virulent cycle goes on (Rotimi, 1991: 26).

Rotimi has put at the centre of his theoretical framework sociopolitical themes that reflect the African predicament of post-independent era. I will start by the last thematic approach, anger and protest. This theme is the same as the one developed by Femi Osofisan when he advocated in the extract I analyzed earlier, the necessity for drama theory to expose and denounce the excessive corrupt practices of the contemporary African leadership. Yet what makes Rotimi's theory particular is his use of satirical comedy as a mode of theatrical expression to deconstruct African political deviationism. Such mode is easily discernible in his major plays, *Our Husband Has Gone Mad Again* and *The Gods Are Not to Blame* through the characterization of political arrivists like Lejoka-Brown and the infamous King Odewale. In *Holding Talks* he has turned to the absurdist dramatic technique to satirize corrupt practices and the irrational waste of time in Africa. The second theme, culture conflicts represents not the least theoretical issue. By theorizing on culture conflicts, Rotimi shows that during the historical confrontation with Europe, Africa lost an important part of her cultural values. Now, with first theme, negritude he constructs the theory of Africans' identity affirmation and the defense of black culture. He problematizes and critically questions the Eurocentric literary discourses that negate Africans in their fundamental rights to be independent and to develop. That theoretical approach is readable in *Hopes of the Living Dead*. The ideas of the Negritude movement insisted on the recognition of African cultural values, the preservation of black identity and the fundamental establishment of African self. The ideological orientation of negritude movement that promoted African theatre was mostly perceived in Francophone Africa with the advent of writers like Sembene Ousmane and Aimé Césaire. It is perhaps useful to review the background of negritude oriented drama. The combat front on which Francophone playwrights built the theory of negritude was the struggle for the recognition of Black identity and culture. In the 1920s, a group of Francophone intellectuals among whom Césaire, Damas, Senghor gathered in Paris to relay the Pan Africanist struggle movement that was vehiculating W. E. Dubois' ideas about the African unity. The rear glance that counteracted the racially informed denigration and oppression of Africans from the continent and the diaspora gained momentum in the first half of the twentieth century, more precisely in the 1920s in the United States' Harlem Negro Renaissance that was spurred up by the assertive Pan African duo, Marcus Garvey and W. E. Dubois. Negritude theorists sought by all means available to express in literature what they felt was the part of African self that was negated and denied to them by the cultural forces of European colonialism: the African identity. Drama and theatre became a privileged tool for communicating the ideas of the philosophy of negritude and by aiming at gathering as many Africans as possible to adhere to that philosophy. The celebration of black cultural achievement became the focus of the dramatists and the plays written and produced emerged as the literary tools that the African writers of the negritude movement used as critical responses to the downgrading subjection inflicted on black race by Europeans, thus constructing a theory that discarded racism and asserted the African presence in world politics.

Patrick Corcoran in his approach asserts:

> Negritude appealed to the notion of a universal 'black essence' and a brotherhood of black peoples. The argument that black culture had a specific contribution to make to humanity was simultaneously a promotion of a new conception of civilization and a rejection of the dominant world view promoted by the West, according to which Western values were generally presented as universal. The positive side of its message reverberated through the colonial world as

a model and an example of a newly self-confident, liberating discourse that empowered other oppressed minorities to proclaim their own worth and distinctiveness. The critique of Western (colonial) domination it also conveyed fed into forms of counter-hegemonic resistance that shaped the decolonisation struggles of subsequent decades (Corcoran, 2007: 184 Web).

The contemporary theoretical orientation in African theatre has left the claim for theatrical purism and advocates now a postcolonial hybrid formulation as it transpires in Chinyere Nwahunanya's *Literary Criticism, Critical Theory and Post Colonial African Literature* (2012). This book focusses on the evaluation of African dramatic criticism after fifty years of independence. His theory examines the contribution of dramatic literature in four spheres of African life: tragedy and tragic vision, the playwrights as preachers and the theatre of the absurd in Nigerian context. The major tendencies that emerge are that African contemporary drama is very much in the image of politics and culture where western and African identities fuse and mix up to produce a new hybridized form. Theory and criticism still examine the thematic development of post-independent ideologies by focussing on the challenges after the political independence. These challenges are essentially economic, cultural, and political. Another major book that theorizes the critical tendencies of African theatre is Damlegue Lare's *Diction and Postcolonial Vision in the Plays of Wole Soyinka* (2016) where the author looks at Soyinka's socio-political struggle for a democratic Africa along the years of his dramatic writings. Nwahunanya's and Damlegue's criticisms look at the reflections of cultural demands, political control and the economic incidences of Africans affairs as conveyed by dramatists. They submit that dramatic tragedy is more than ever a reflection of the socio-political anomies that besiege African countries and slow down their development. Forms of oppression that nurture contemporary drama include political, economic and gender. The dramatists practises aesthetic syncretism by selecting materials from different environments to satisfy the demands of audiences but also to keep the tune of his authorial ideology. Theory also sustains syncretisation of cultural forms as a creative mode.

5.11.4. Towards a Redefinition of Postcolonialism: The Theory of Afropositivism

African drama is in the remaking process. If one agrees with Ngugi that literature does not develop in the vacuum, a theory of Afropositivism is created to direct critical discourses into identifying in dramatic literature the various socio-cultural and political forces that condition the change from pessimism to uplifted development. Soyinka in *Of Africa* (2012) has already formulated the wish to see African nations use historical events to remake African history in the utilitarian meaning of the word. He also pondered over that issue in *The Burden of Memory: The Muse of Forgiveness* (2009). He charts art with the uplifting of human lfe. Ngugi wa Thiong'o is of the same view in *Birth of a Dream Weaver: A Memoir of a Writer's Awakening* (2016). My contention here is that Africans have been locked up in the legacy of colonialism and neocolonialism to the extent of side-tracking the future development of African dramatic discourse. Afropositivism is the theory that seeks to move beyond the historical pessimistic legacies and obscure images that colonialism and neocolonialism have depicted about Africa and show that a new continent can emerge from the ashes and havoc created there in by imperialist Europe. Positivism in African present context advocates not a tabula razza of the historical facts – for no one can erase history – but a visionary outlook that stretches into the future to foresees an emerging African continent leading the world. It remains a fact that there are dark ages in the history of every nation, continent or people. But these dark episodes pertain to the evenmential prune tools that should serve to carve out a positivist look of life both in the present and future perspectives. Critics and theatre scholars should orient their critical positions towards a positivist outlook of the African continent. Afropositivismin drama outgrows from the combination of the cultural theories that portrand African renaissance not only in the ideology of panafrican philosophy, but the blending of such an ideology and the new perceptive outlook of the world as global entity in which the African is both citizen with full rights and a world inhabitants with autonomous prerogatives. Physical displacement, geographic space, cultural reconnections with the roots, the struggle for identity and dignity are defined with the Afropositivist thinking as the aggregats of self-fulfilment if within these parameters the African sees his dreams fulfilled. To be specific, Afropositivism should combine political, social, economic and educational views of a new African continent that is recreated in the image of the solver of the future challenges. With regard to politics, Lwarence Mukaka has this to say:

> The role of enlightened people, especially the young men and women who have a lot to gain from a politically stable and productive economy, should be to advise the economic and political

leadership and encourage and support those structural reforms that are aimed at economic growth and national development. In addition, they should be willing to share their knowledge and vision about the future and development with as many people as possible inside and outside of their own countries; encourage and monitor improvements in their countries' policies and programs; undertake research studies and advisory activities which facilitate and empower different stakeholders to accomplish mutually beneficial goals and objectives, and enable policy makers and program implementers to set new priorities for state-formation, institutionbuilding and national development (Mukaka 2001: 121).

This Afropositivism is multidimensional and multipurpose in theory and practice. The total improvement of the human condition is the central concern of the theory. The main focus in African dramatic theory should be the reorientation of discourse in a committed way for the new millennium development goals. Afropositivism theory is not far from theatre for development theory, the main focus being the social change and political reforms.

To conclude this chapter, let' s say that the main argument has propounded that African drama has been in a dynamic search of referential frame due to the fact that there has been an intellectual series of assertion and contestation of the critical frame that strikes the balance between theoretical tendencies and dramatic discourses as they function diachronically. Three stages have been observed: the phase of cultural nationalism from 1850-1950; the consolidation of theatrical literature and art through performance for independence from 1951-1970; the theatre of the post-independence politics from 1971 to the present day. In the first period, theory has focused on writing back to the Eurocentric critical canon that negated Africa and the recognition of her field of dramatic fertility. The second phase has taken theoretical discourses further by returning the writing to African self as it has been established that African scholarship has to question the problematic mismanagement of the postcolonial state. The final stage has relocated the theoretical debate within the scope of an evaluation of cultural and literary achievements after fifty years of independence. Criticism has insisted on the recourse to hybrid forms of creation and a syncretic aesthetics that select material from different items: cultural lore, political life, economic pressures and religious ingredients. Further theoretical perspectives will offer a universalist view of African theory in the age of globalization.

Notes:

1. Information about Hubert Ogunde's plays, Duro Ladipo's contribution and Ene Henshaw's stage work is taken from Dapo Adelugba and Olu Obafemi's article "Anglophone West Africa: Nigeria" in Martin Banham, ed., *A History of Theatre in Africa.* Cambridge: Cambridge University Press, 2004. 148-149.

References:

Achebe, Chinua. *Hoppes and Impediments Selected Essays 1965-87.* Nigeria: Heinemann. 1988.

Adelugba, Dapo and Olu Obafemi. "Anglophone West Africa; Nigeria". In Martin Banham, ed., *A History of Theatre in Africa.* Cambridge: Cambridge University Press. 2003. 138-158.

Ashcroft, Bill, Gareth Griffiths and Helen Tiffin, eds. *The Post-colonial Studies Reader.* New York: Routledge. 2003.

-------------------------. *Postcolonial Studies: The Key Concepts, Second Edition.* New York: Routledge. 2007.

Banham, Martin, ed. *A History of Theatre in Africa.* Cambridge: Cambridge University Press. 2004.

Beresford, Alexander, ed. *Critical African Studies. Volume 8 Number1.* Abingdon: Taylor & Francis. 2015.

Bhabha, Homi K. *The Location of Culture.* New York: Routledge. 1994.

-------------------------. "Cultural Diversity and Cultural Differences." In *Bill Ashcroft, Gareth Griffiths and Helen Tiffin,* eds., *The Post-colonial Studies Reader.* London and New York: Routledge. 1995. 206-212.

Boehmer, Elleke. *Empire Writing: An Anthology of Colonial Literature 1870-1918.* Oxford: Oxford University Press. 2009.

Bourne, Taylor Jenny. "New Historicism." In Michael Payne and Jessica Rae Barbera., eds., *A Dictionary of Cultural and Critical Theory.* New York: Wiley-Blackwell. 2010. 484-487.

Corcoran, Patrick. *The Cambridge Introduction to Francophone Literature.* Cambridge: Cambridge University Press. 2007.

Damlegue, Lare. *Diction and Postcolonial Vision in the Plays of Wole Soyinka.* Berlin: Verlag. 2016.

Etherton, Michael, 1983. *The Development of Drama in Africa.* London: Hutchinson.

Falola, Toyin and Tunde Akinyemi, eds. *Emerging Perspectives on Femi Osofisan.* Trenton: Africa World Press. 2009.

Fiebach, Joachim. "Dimensions of Theatricality in Africa". In Biodun Jeyifo, ed., *Modern African Drama, a Norton Critical Edition.* New York: WW Norton and Company. 2002. 471-486.

Finnegan, Ruth. *Oral Literature in Africa.* Cambridge: Open Book Publishers. Web. 2012.

Gibbs, James, ed. *Nkyin-Nkyin Essays on Ghanaian Theatre.* New York: Rodopi. 2009.

Goody, Jack. *The Expansive Moment: Anthropology in Britain and Africa 1918—1970.* Cambridge: Cambridge University Press.

Hasse, Fee-Alexandra, 1995. *Conceptions of Criticism: Cross-Cultural, Interdisciplinary and Historical Studies of Structures of a Concept of Values.* Madrid: Ediciones E-Theoria, Universidad y Complutense. 2007. Web.

https://en.wikipedia.org/wiki/Homi_K._Bhabha

Jeyifo, Biodun. *Modern African Drama, a Norton Critical Edition.* New York: Norton and Company. 2002.

Kerr, David. "Art as Tool, Weapon or Shield?: Arts for Development Seminar, Harare". In Biodun Jeyifo, ed., *Modern African Drama, a Norton Critical Edition.* New York: WW Norton and Company. 2002. 486-493.

Lewis, Herbert. *Social and Cultural Anthropology and the Study of Africa.* Nebraska University Press. 2014.

Losambe, Lokangaka and Devi Sarinjeive, eds. *Precolonial and Post-colonial Drama and Theatre in Africa.* Trenton: Africa World Press. 2001.

Mazrui, Ali A. *The Africans: A Triple Heritage.* Boston: Little, Brown and Company. 1986.

Mukaka, Lawrence. "A Vision for the Future of Zambia and Africa." In Olugbenga Adesida Arunma Oteh, eds, *African Voices, African Visions.* Uppsala: The Nordic Africa Institute. 2001. 110-123.

Ndumbe Eyoh, Hansel. "Anglophone Africa". In Don Rubin, Ousmane Diakhate and Hansel Ndumbe Eyoh, eds. *The World Encyclopedia of Contemporary Theatre: Africa.* New York: Routledge. 2001. 25-29.

Ngugi, wa Thiong'o. *Something Torn and New, An African Renaissance.* New York: Basic Civitas Books. 2009.

---------------------------. *Moving the Center: Struggle for Cultural Freedoms.* London: Heinemann. 1993.

----------------. *Decolonizing the Mind, the Politics of Language in African Literature.* London: James Currey. 1987.

Njoki, Mwihia Margaret and Collins Ogogo. "A Critical Analysis of Athol Fugard's Social Vision in Four Selected Plays." In *Journal of Educational and Social Research Vol. 4, No 1.* Rome: MCSER Publishing. 2014.

Nwahunanya, Chinyere. *Literary Criticism, Critical Theory and Post Colonial African Literature.* Bethesda: Arbi Press. 2012.

Osofisan, Femi. *The Nostalgic Drum: Essays on Literature, Drama and Culture*. Trenton: Africa World Press. 2001.

Pandurang, Mala. *Ngugi wa Thiong'o: An Anthology of Recent Criticism*. New Delhi: Pencraft International. 2007.

Rotimi, Ola, ed. *Issues in African Theatres*. Ile-Ife: HP Humanities Publishers. 2001.

--------------. *African Drama Literature: To Be or to Become, Inaugural Lecture*. Port Hartcourt: University of Port Harcourt Inaugural Lecture Series. No 11. 1991.

Said, Edward. *Orientalism*. New York: Routledge. 1978.

---------------. *Cultural Imperialism*. New York: Routledge. 1993.

---------------. *The Representations of the Intellectual*. New York: Routledge. 1994.

Sanders, Reinard and Bernth Lindfors, eds. *Ngugi wa Thiong' o Speaks: Interviews with the Kenyan Writer*. Trenton: Africa World Press. 2006.

Soyinka, Wole. *The Open Sore of a Continent: A Personal Narrative of the Nigerian Crisis*. Oxford: Oxford University Press. 1995.

----------------. "Theatre in Traditional Cultures: Survival Patterns". In Biodun Jeyifo, ed. *Modern African Drama, a Norton Critical Edition*. New York: Norton and Company. 2002. 421-433.

----------------. *Art, Dialogue and Outrage, Essays on Literature and Culture*. New York: Pantheon Books. 1988.

Stanley, Henry Morton. "The Meeting with Livingstone". In Elleke Boehmer, ed., *Empire Writing: an Anthology of Colonial Literature*. Oxford: Oxford University Press. [1886] 2009.

Stephen W. Littlejohn and Karen A. Foss, eds. *Encyclopedia of Communication Theory*. California: Sage Publication, 2009.

Rubin, Don. "African Theatre in a Global Context." In Biodun Jeyifo, ed., *Modern African Drama, Norton Critical Edition*. New York: W.W. Norton & Company. 2002. 468-470.

Tagore, Rabindranath. "Poems from Gitanjali Song Offering, 1912". In Elleke Boehmer, ed., *Empire Writing: An Anthology of Colonial Literature 1870-1912*. Oxford: Oxford University Press. 2009. 377-381.

Traore, Bakary. *Black African Theatre and Its Social Function*. Translated by Dapo Adelugba. Ibadan: Ibadan University Press. 1972.

PART TWO

SYMBOLISM, CULTURAL MATERIALISM, POLITICAL MORALITY, MARXISM, FEMINISM, RESISTANCE THEORIES

6

SYMBOLIST AND NATURALIST READINGS OF AFRICAN DRAMA

This chapter looks into symbolism and naturalism as reading strategies in African drama. Within the field of theory, critical emphasis has not been put on the possibility to read traditional and modern African drama as symbolically and naturally oriented. The dialectic of reading and interpretation involves African colonial and neocolonial experiences as the main vectors of African drama but the critical tendency to depict with realism political history has not been elucidated with the light of symbolism and naturalism as theories of drama. This study attempts to locate the dialectic of reading and interpreting symbolism and naturalism in African context as vectors that should guide critical interpretation. To what extent do symbolism and naturalism contribute to frame meaning for African drama and theatre? In addition, how does African history namely colonialism and neocolonialism contribute to the reading of symbolism and naturalism as major critical theories in African theatre studies?

6.1. Symbolism, Naturalism and Realism

In the usage of literary historians, Symbolist Movement designates specifically a group of French writers beginning with Charles Baudelaire (*Fleurs du mal,* 1857) and including such later poets as Arthur Rimbaud, Paul Verlaine, Stéphane Mallarmé, and Paul Valéry (Abrams 1988: 152-154). Baudelaire based the symbolic mode of his poems in part on the example of the American Edgar Allan Poe, but especially on the ancient belief in **correspondences**—the doctrine that there exist inherent and systematic analogies between the human mind and the outer world, and also between the natural and the spiritual worlds. As Baudelaire put this doctrine: "Everything, form, movement, number, color, perfume, in the *spiritual* as in the *natural* world, is significative, reciprocal, converse, correspondent" (Ibidem). The techniques of the French **Symbolists,** who exploited an order of private symbols in a poetry of rich suggestiveness rather than explicit signification, had an immense influence throughout Europe, and (especially in the 1890s and later) in England and America poets such as Arthur Symons and Ernest Dowson (see *Decadence)* as well as W. B. Yeats, Ezra Pound, Dylan Thomas, Hart Crane, e. e. cummings, and Wallace Stevens. Major symbolist poets in Germany are Stefan George and Rainer Maria Rilke (Ibidem). The *Modern Period,* in the decades after World War I, was a notable era of symbolism in literature. Many of the major writers of the period exploit symbols which are in part drawn from religious and esoteric traditions and in part invented. Some of the works of the age are symbolist in their settings, their agents, and their actions, as well as in the objects they refer to. Instances of a persistently symbolic procedure occur in lyrics.

Naturalism is sometimes claimed to be an even more accurate picture of life than is realism. But naturalism is not only, like realism, a special selection of subject matter and a special literary manner; it is a mode of fiction that was developed by a school of writers in accordance with a particular philosophical thesis. This thesis, a product of post-Darwinian biology in the mid-nineteenth century, held that a person inherits personal traits and compulsive instincts, especially hunger, the accumulative drive, and sex, and is then subject to the social and economic forces in the family, the class, and the milieu into which that person is born. The French novelist Emile Zola, beginning in the 1870s, did much to develop this theory in what he called "le roman experimental (that is, the novel organized in the mode of a scientific experiment). Zola and later naturalistic writers, such as the Americans Frank Norris, Stephen Crane, Theodore Dreiser, and James Farrell, try to present their subjects with an objective scientific attitude and with elaborate documentation, sometimes including an almost medical frankness about activities and bodily functions usually unmentioned in earlier literature. They tend to choose characters who exhibit strong animal drives such as greed and sexual desire, and who are victims both of their glandular secretions within and of sociological pressures without. The end of the naturalistic play is usually "tragic," but not, as in classical and Elizabethan tragedy, because of a heroic but losing struggle of the individual mind and will against gods', enemies', and circumstance. Instead the protagonist of the naturalist plot, a pawn to multiple compulsions, usually disintegrates, or is wiped out. There is a close relationship between naturalism and realism.

Realism is used by literary critics in two chief ways: (1) to identify a literary movement of the nineteenth century, especially in prose fiction (beginning with Balzac in France, George Eliot in England, and William Dean Howells in America); and (2) to designate a recurrent mode, in various eras, of representing human life and experience in literature, which was especially exemplified by the writers of this historical movement.

Realistic fiction is often opposed to romantic fiction: the romance is said to present life as we would have it be, more picturesque, more adventurous, more heroic than the actual; realism, to present an accurate imitation of life as it is. This distinction is not invalid, but it is inadequate. Casanova, T. E. Lawrence, and Winston Churchill were people in real life, but their histories, as related by themselves or others, demonstrate that truth can be stranger than literary realism. The typical realist sets out to write a fiction which will give the illusion that it reflects life and the social world as it seems to the common reader. To achieve this effect the author prefers as protagonist an ordinary citizen of Middletown, living on Main Street, perhaps, and engaged in the real estate business. The realist, in other words, is deliberately selective in material and prefers the average, the commonplace, and the everyday over the rarer aspects of the social scene. The characters, therefore, are usually of the middle class or (less frequently) the working class-people without highly exceptional endowments, who live through ordinary experiences of childhood, adolescence, love, marriage, parenthood, infidelity, and death; who find life rather dull and often unhappy, though it may be brightened by touches of beauty and joy; but who may, under special circumstances, display something akin to heroism.

Many critics have offered theoretical approaches to African drama without showing the contributions of symbolism and naturalism in the construction of meaning. Biodun Jeyifo asserts that postcolonialism is the only theory that meaningfully reads modern African drama. His argument is that postcolonialism responds as a deconstructive theory to debunk "dominant Eurocentric or colonialist perspectives from a powerful, imperializing scholastic western critical orthodoxy deployed in debates on the existence or non-existence of indigenous African theatre tradition" (Jeyifo 2002: 459). Michael Etherton opines that no critical theory is suitable to interpret indigenous African drama (Etherton 1982: 35). These statements seem to establish the fact that African theatre is not theoretically intelligible to be interpreted with theatre theory. I disagree with such critical tenets and suggest that drama is symbolically and naturally oriented. For the two critics, all critical analyses should be theory-free, an idea that overlooks the implications of theory in the construction of meanings of African drama. J. C. de Graft holds that "the dynamics of dramatic development" is informed by "the cumulative result of over five hundred years of the subjection of African cultural system to colonialism, the most ruthless forms of domination and exploitation" (DeGraft 1976: 19). Alpha I. Sow declares: "After a period of direct colonial domination during which the values of its cultural heritage were denied, Black Africa seeks to assert its personality, to resist the intellectual control of the Western powers [...]" (Sow 1979: 30) These approaches to the development of African literature do not offer an elucidating explanation about the contribution of symbolism and naturalism in the reading and articulation of African drama as theories of theatre in Africa. It follows that aspects of reading strategies of how colonial history shaped and oriented African drama towards symbolist and naturalist movements is missing. That is why I propose to re-examine in the first part, African drama as cultural community-based, using symbolism as methodological approaches. In the second part, I will read African drama with naturalist approach, showing how it is politically oriented and historically grounded. I specifically want to address the question how do symbolism and naturalism stand as privileged theoretical frameworks in African theatre studies?

6.1.1. An African Variant of Symbolism: Theory and Reading Strategy

Symbolism is a theory of theatre that reads in literature the interconnection between objects, facts, ideas or entities and their allegoric or metaphoric meanings in the metaphysical realm. Symbols allude to deeper or transcendental realities that go beyond the physical world to refer to deeper metaphysical realities according to their properties, so that the words of action and facts may be explored by analogy using symbols.

A. I. Sow states:

> Symbolism *adds* a new value to an object or an act, without thereby violating its immediate or 'historical' validity. Once it is brought to bear, it turns the object or action into an 'open' event:

> symbolic thought opens the door on to immediate reality for us, but without weakening or invalidating it; seen in this light the universe is no longer sealed off, nothing is isolated inside its own existence: everything is linked by a system of correspondences and assimilations (Sow 1979: 30).

The point made here is that symbolism is grounded in the interpretation of symbols, which are present as signs, ideas, objects, facts or entities and their meanings. Symbolism is an important critical theory to be used in trying to understand African drama. I use critical theory to mean a plausible set of acceptable principles offered to explain the birth and development of African theatre. African traditional drama rests essentially on elements of oral tradition namely rituals, festivals, myths, legends, and figurative language (proverbs, riddles and folktales) which are not to be ignored in the formulation of theory and interpretation. Festival, ritual and myth in African drama reflect the transcendental aspects of performance which contain codified messages that need the priest's initiated knowledge of the mystic world to decipher their symbolic messages. Indigenous theatre performance uses symbols and symbolic language to impart meaning.

Despite the salient features of symbols in indigenous drama performance, some critics who approach it have ignored them. Some books have been written with the intention to meet that need, but theoretical approaches offered have left interpretive gaps with regard to theory. One major book that guides theory is Michael Etherton's *The Development of African Drama*. The author sought to solve the problem of critical theory in African drama through the examination and interpretation of essays and plays that sustain the canonical works of African theatre scholars but didn't achieve the goal. What is missing in his book is the formulation of a critical theory that can be used to understand and interpret African drama. Etherton's reading does not clearly formulate a critical theory on which a reader can build meaning. He was expected to elucidate the critical theory orientation that applies to African indigenous and modern dramas. He has only shown that African drama has emerged as the heir of triple cultural heritages: indigenous traditions, western Christian civilization and mid-west Islamic waves (Etherton 1982: 35), without specifically naming out the theory that reads comprehensively African drama and theatre. Etherton's thematic approaches to indigenous African drama has left out its symbolic dimension. He declares:

> [African] drama may well become a key methodology for developing thought across a board front... The process of turning a problem of social analysis into a play is achievable but complex. Experiments so far have resulted in only limited achievements both in Africa and elsewhere.... This process requires skills, but at the same time a demystification of those skills (Ibidem).

First, Etherton does not show why precolonial indigenous drama essentially rests on symbolism. His approaches to what he calls "ritual traditions for drama and theatre" are vague and not theoretically based. In the first chapter of the book titled "traditional performance in contemporary societies", he asserts:

> If much tradition-based critical analysis of African drama is limited by focusing exclusively on the artistic product and omitting its social and economic organization from the discussion, so too are a number of sociological and anthropological studies of African societies severely limited by their exclusion to the plastic and performing arts from their analyses. The sociologist's definition has been narrowed down to include that which can be assessed scientifically: descent groups, lineages, kingship patterns, the functioning of magic and religion... (Etherton 1982: 35)

This statement means Etherton acknowledges the insufficiency of theoretical approaches to indigenous African drama which he promised to solve in his book and yet the book ends with no theoretical examination of indigenous African theatre. He limits his analysis to generic definitions of drama and tradition, proceeds to show that African traditional societies were attached to their customs and concludes that "the phenomenon of African drama developing out of traditional art is complex..." and in the various critical approaches, there are limitations manifest in the various methodologies... (Ibidem).

For me I think that the major theory that best applies to the indigenous African drama is symbolism and naturalism. A look at symbolist movement in European drama can help make the point. In European drama, Symbolism was a 19th century drama movement that sought to go beyond the natural empirical description of events in literature and focus on metaphorical and allegorical meanings of facts. Reacting against the rationalism and materialism that had come to dominate Western European culture, symbolism proclaimed the validity of pure subjectivity and the expression of an idea over a realistic description of the natural world. Marvin Carlson in *The Theories of Drama: A Historical and Critical Survey* opines that that Symbolism is "the evocation of thoughtful life" which "touches the depth of human condition. Symbolic drama gives suggestion instead of reality. A symbol instead of an imitation" (Carlson 1993: 303). The symbolic interpretation incorporates the poetic aesthetics, conveys the conviction that reality is best expressed through symbols because it seeks to understand nature through metaphysical medium of communication. The symbolic approach seeks to touch realities that are not apparent in the physical world, and this becomes a central tenet of the movement. How man relates to gods can be understood only through symbolic approaches to spiritual realm. In African context, symbolism regulates and govern drama.

I will give specific domains where symbolic understanding of life is reflected in dramatic literature, both oral and written. First, traditional folk life: religious festivals, ritual dances, folktales, creation myth stories, proverbs and popular sayings in day-to-day exchange talk, dressing styles and other cultural practices are replete with symbols. One would say that life in African culture rests on symbols and allegories. In traditional Africa, traditional drama was deeply entrenched in the cultural practices of the folk communities.

Several reasons can be advocated to sustain the necessity of using symbolism as the main theoretical tool for understanding African indigenous or traditional drama. The first reason is that African indigenous drama emerged out of rituals, festivals, myths legends, folk life and language.

Drama in traditional Africa rests on a body of symbols and signs that metaphorically stand for values, entities, facts and events that are meaningful to the indigenous population who practice and use them as remedy to approach life. Such symbols like eating the new yam on the new moon, purification rites, harvest festivals, ritual murder, wrestling contests, dirge and eulogy, initiation into adulthood, funeral dances to mention but a few, bear symbolic meaning. In West Africa, these symbols are the backbone of African indigenous drama that dominated the theatre field before the advent of European colonialism. Theodore Hatlen shares this logic when he says: "It is in such rituals that we find the basic elements of drama – music, song, dance, costuming, mimetic action and communal performance. Religious ritual expresses the deepest needs and longings of the people and associating them with the supernatural". Ritual is used as a communicative mode to talk with supernatural forces to expand human spirit and reach metaphysical realm. Myth is used as an interpretative medium to explain life mysteries. For instance, creation myth stories give tentative answers to the origin of the world, the meanings of life and death. Festivals are used as celebratory modes to commemorate the gathering of the tribes, rejoice over abundant harvest, assess human values and commune within the same community. Talking especially about ritual, this communicative mode is used to perform sacrifices and offer prayers to deities in moments of trouble, sickness, to conjure evil predictions and to seek protection from them. Ritual is also used to exorcise evil spirits or to attempt to cure mental diseases. Behind the symbolic act of ritual stands a strong faith in the divine intervention of transcendental forces that traditional communities resort to as their ultimate refuge when human efforts fail to yield the expected solutions to human predicaments. J. C. De Graft corroborates this critical stand by saying:

> One must never forget those threats posed by forces that lie deep within our souls (as some would put it), forces like pride and anger, greed and lust, jealousy and fear...It was the awareness of these many threats that led 'primitive' man to those rituals of apprehension, propitiation, purification, and exorcism of which impersonation was often such a cardinal feature. It was this same awareness that animated the drama in such widely different cultures as those of fifth-century Greece (BC) and medieval Europe. Indeed, it is impossible to read accounts of the origins and development of Ancient Greek drama and theatre, or medieval European drama, without being deeply impressed by this fact (DeGraft 1976: 4).

It would be short-sighted to theorize on African drama without taking a holistic connotation of symbolism. All traditional performances shelter symbolic connotation beyond their physical appearances. Symbolism governs life and its meaning in Africa and drama is one of the major ways in which this symbolic interpretation and understanding of life finds expression.

The second reason why symbolism stands out as a suitable theory to understand and interpret African traditional drama is that the symbolic ingredients find ways of expression in the day-to-day language through the use of proverbs, puns, riddles and imagery talks. Such imagery language borrows words, names, diction and illustrations from animal kingdom, ancestral world, and human experience to talk about realities that apply to human condition. For instance, Wole Soyinka extensively quotes from Yoruba proverbs in his plays to establish the symbolic dimension of proverbs which allude to deeper social realities. For instance, in *Kongi's Harvest,* he quotes the following proverbs: "the pot that will eat fat, its bottom must be scorched. The squirrel that will long crack nuts, its footpad must be sore. The sweetest wine has flowed down the tapper's shattered shins" (Soyinka 1967: 1). In these proverbs, squirrel, the pot and the wine are used as symbols to designate human beings. These proverbs mean that in the life of a human being, success is predicated upon time-consuming hard work and every desired end exacts its price. Here, symbols are metaphorically employed to utter codified strong moral lessons and express ethical philosophical outlook. In *Swamp Dwellers,* he quotes proverbs like: "Every god shakes the beggar by hand" (Soyinka 1964: 35), "The hands of the gods are unequal" (Ibidem). These two proverbs mean that human beings are subjected to the unpredictable whims of the gods who hold power of life and death on humans. This was a strong belief among precolonial African societies. Ola Rotimi adjoins this ideology by creating fate oriented story in *The Gods Are Not to Blame* in which Adewale is doomed to fulfill the gods' predictions by killing his father and marrying his mother. He illustrates this tragic fate through a proverb quoted by Baba Fakunle the Soothsayer to Adewale: "The snail may try, but it cannot cast off its shell" (Rotimi 1971: 40). The snail and its shell are symbolically alluding to Adewale who cannot escape from the predictions of the gods, the very manipulators of human life. If one refers to African communities every culture is predicated on the belief in ritualistic mode of communication with the deities or the ancestors. The Igbo proverb "When a man says yes, his chi or personal god also says yes" (Achebe 1958: 40) is quoted by Chinua Achebe to explain how human fate is interconnected with the divine will. Thus, symbolism and symbolic interpretation of life are inherent to African traditional life.

 A third reason why symbolism is relevant as a theory in approaching African drama is that dreams and their symbolic interpretations occupy a central place in African traditional life and also the fact that many African playwrights have explored that reality in their plays. Sleep and dreams are part and parcel of human life and in Africa the interpretation of dreams and visions rely heavily on symbols. Elders endowed with traditional wisdom resort to symbols, images, metaphors and allegories to give tentative meanings to dreams. It is believed that dreams come in the form of codified messages that need to be decoded and put in meaningful words through the symbolic analysis of facts that occurred in dreams. Even in modern societies dreams remain mysterious.

As a matter of fact, their interpretations strongly rely on symbolism and cultural beliefs. Sigmund Freud's attempt to use psychanalysis as a theory to interpret dreams has shed some light on the functioning mode of human subconsciousness and its relationship with the world of dreams but there are still imprecisions as to the prophetic aspects of dreams and their fulfilment. As an adjunct of African drama, traditional wisdom which transpires in African literary texts uses symbolism to decipher possible meanings of dreams and has established in communities, belief systems that use these symbols to give meanings to dreams. For instance, it is believed among the Igbo community West Africa that rainwater in a dream is a good omen presaging good luck, happy events like the finding of employment or marriage; while termites generally presage bad omen like destruction, accident, or even death (Chinua Achebe 1960: 102). It is also believed that eating in dreams has bad symbolic meaning as it is specifically associated to initiation into witchcraft and sorcery.

Modern African dramatists recapture beliefs and their culture-related understandings in plays. For instance, in Wole Soyinka's *A Play of Giants*, Gunema a Head of State has had one of his subjects executed because he had a nightmare about an impending danger in his country and concluded about a potential coup that this citizen was allegedly believed to be plotting. He didn't have proofs of the realist fulfilment of the dream but relied on the symbolic interpretation of images he saw that was decoded as a coup being plotted against him. Equally important are the roles of dreams and their symbolic meanings in Ngugi wa Thiong'o and Ngugi wa Mirii's *I Will Marry When I Want* and Ama Ata Aidoo's *Anowa*. In Ngugis' *I Will Marry When I Want*, dreams are presented as unrealizable beliefs, the belief of Kiguunda that his daughter Gathoni will marry Kioi's son John, once he agrees to mortgage his piece of land and organizes a church wedding. Unfortunately, this belief, the Ngugis' show, is a mere dream as John abandons Gathoni after impregnating her. Symbolically that dreamlike story represents the exploitative strategies of western imperialists who use neocolonial strategies like foreign aid and structural adjustments to exploit African countries. In Ama Ata Aidoo's *Anowa*, the dream of the protagonist Anowa reads both like a psychological fulfilment of her strong desire for children and a metaphor of trans-Atlantic slave trade to which Africa has been subjected for many centuries. Anowa narrates her dream thus:

> I dreamt that I was a big, big woman. And from my insides were huge holes out of which poured men, women and children. And the

sea was boiling and steaming. And as it boiled, it threw out many, many giant lobsters, each of whom as it fell turned into a man or woman, but keeping its lobster head and claws. And they rushed to where I sat and seized the men and women as they poured out of me, and they tore them apart, and dashed them on the ground and stamped upon them (Aidoo 1965/2003: 71).

Here Ama Ata Aidoo has Anowa tell a dream she had, but has left to the reader to construct its symbolic meaning from the main story of the play. I personally look at the meaning of this dream from Freud's psychoanalytic theory. Anowa is a barren woman whose marriage with Kofi Ako is running the risk of tearing apart due to the lack of children. Her dream in which she sees herself as a big woman from whose insides ran big holes out of which poured out men, women and children may be the subconscious fulfilment of the strong desire to bear children. But this dream can also have a deep symbolic meaning in which the protagonist Anowa's childbirth stands for a prophetic human and socio-economic recovery of Africa after ravages of centuries of slavery and colonialism. Delia Kumavie offers the following explanation:

> In this passage, Anowa associates herself with the traumatic experience of the trans-Atlantic slave trade, which occurred in an earlier time in history. She maps slavery and the slave trade onto her physical being as though she had a personal experience of it. Anowa's dream positions her at the heart of the slave trade as the woman out of whom the men, women, and children are born, and whose progeny are seized and destroyed. The sea both represents Anowa's loss and separation from the past and connects her to the roots of pan-Africanism. Indeed, Anowa's return to this imagery in her own moment of personal crisis foregrounds the depth of the diasporic connection that Aidoo pursues in her subsequent work (Kumavie 2015: 61).

This critical interpretation which consists in viewing Anowa as a symbolic representation of Africa which has been the suffer head of slavery when her children were captured, but whose future recovery is possible. Bearing in mind that Ama Ata Aidoo is a Pan-Africanist writer, it is plausible to infer that the men and women coming out of Anowa are symbols of present and future generations, the manpower of the continent who will work for its development. As a matter of fact, approaching her play from a symbolist perspective is realistic. So, approaching African drama through symbolism enables the critic to offer deeper and broader perspectives on both traditional drama and modern drama.

The fourth reason for the need of Symbolism in approaching African drama is that majority of the first and second generations of African playwrights have turned to traditional folk life with its operative modes to reconstruct life in precolonial Africa. They redefined African identity by creating the theory that asserts black identity as valuable, precious, and original. Several playwrights have recaptured oral tradition as first hand material to redefine Africans' identity. Soyinka's *Kongi's Harvest* highlights the organization of Yoruba kingdoms with hierarchized structures, festival dances and cultural practices. Ola Rotimi's *Ovonramwen Nogbaisi* describes cultural life and social organization in the Benin Kingdom before the colonial incursion. The play underscores the ability of African people to live in an organized community, manage political affairs and develop democratic institutions. Ebrahim Hussein's *Kinjeketile* also displays well organized socio-political life in Tanzania before the colonial penetration.

Another reason why symbolism suits as theory in approaching African drama is the presence of magical realism in drama. Magical realism is the belief in the potency of magic as effective tool to obtain a desired result. The desired results range from change of situation from bad to good or vice-versa, the protection against misfortune, or the access to good luck. According to African traditional belief system, magic can also be used to make money, to get somebody's favour, to succeed in an exam. But it can also be used for negative ends, by for instance harming a person by causing them to become sick or invalid. Magical realism is abundantly present both in real life and in dramatic literature. In many communities in West Africa, it is believed that festival drama and ritual drama are performed side by side with exorcism, the chasing out of evil spirit through incantatory recitation of prayers. It is also believed that magical lotions or substances can make a woman fertile. Magical realism is also missing in Etherton's treatment of theory. I prefer using magical realism in this text because this terminology better describes the manifestation of the supernatural which comes to the surface structure of humans' lives and becomes part of their living experience. Whatever the context in which magical realism operates, many symbols are used to perform action. From the gathering of items needed for its performance to the very results to be obtained, symbolism operates to hide aspects of its significance to the common spectator. In an earlier article, I explained that dramatic symbols transpire in Act Two, Scene two of Wole Soyinka's *King Baabu*. For instance, when King Baabu goes to consult an Oriental Mystic and a Marabout it is because he believes in the potency of magic to perpetuate his rule (Lare 2013: 181). Several symbols are used by Soyinka to explain deeper realities in the belief system of African politicians. When Baabu goes to the Marabout, every item prescribed has symbolic meaning. His kingship is metaphorically labelled a dynasty, because, he wants to secure the throne for him and his descendants alone. In the process of the Marabout's divination, mythical objects are presented and their meaning revealed to the king.

> Marabout […] Baabu must sit on the skin of a freshly sacrificed goat for forty days and forty nights. A spotless white he-goat. A new one will be sacrificed each day and Baabu must consume its testicles. Nobody whose eyeballs are red must come near the palace. No red kola nuts, only white or yellow. (KB: 60)

The skin of a freshly sacrificed goat and the act of sitting on it for forty days and forty nights symbolically mean securing the throne for forty years with the magical potency that the sacrifice of the goat will procure. Consuming the goat's testicles is believed to increase the king's ability to resist foreign attacks and white kola nuts are also symbols of life and prosperity. King Baabu is further requested to sacrifice a spotless white he-goat (*KB*: 60), to provide forty hunchbacks and forty albinos who must be buried alive with padlocks through their lips (*KB*: 62). The Marabout explains this through a simile, "just as the camel's hump stores the power of water that sustains the camel over long distances in the arid desert, the human hump can do even better by sustaining the king's throne for many years" (*KB*: 63). Considering how magical realism operates in African drama, it is therefore essential to approach it from symbolist theoretical perspective.

Through symbolism one can understand that magical realism seeks to effect the course of action through the involvement of the supernatural. Man searching to expand his spirit reaches out for security and protection and looks into the spiritual worlds elements of reference that can help him reach his full potential. Playwrights with magical realism ideology have theorized on history and society as continuously undergoing a cyclic turn of fate. Man in such dramas becomes a mere pawn in the hands of the gods or fate. This theoretical outlook has far reaching implications in the understanding of African traditional mindset where there is a strong belief that human beings entertain ontological and cosmological relationships with ancestors and deities. Wole Soyinka, Oyin Ogunba and Abiola Irele are important voices in the development of magical realism. In *Theatre in Africa* they defend the thesis that magical realism is inherent to African indigenous life. Soyinka's critical books *Myth, Literature and the African World* and *Art (1976), Dialogue, and Outrage: Essays on Literature and Culture* (1988) sustain this thesis. My premise here is that magical realism in African drama entails a defacement of the scrounging masses who cannot compete with these domineering gods, spirits and kings. They [the masses] must continually pay allegiance to their gods and appease them with enormous sacrifices. But magical realism has a symbolical and more profound meaning because playwrights like Femi Osofisan and Ola Rotimi use the interaction between humans and gods respectively in *No More the Wasted Breed* and *The Gods Are Not to Blame* to talk about the European colonizers shaping Africans destiny and present the African present condition of economic dependence on European nations as an inescapable fate that history imposed on Africans. This theoretical interpretation also transpires in their critical essays, especially Rotimi's "The Attainment of Discovery: Efua Sutherland and the Evolution of Modern African Drama" (2000) and Osofisan's book *The Nostalgic Drum: Essays on Literature, Drama and Culture* (2001).

Another dimension of magical realism is seen when ritual becomes a type of language. Rituals are normally operational on symbolic and metaphorical levels. But when rituals are enacted by human beings in theatrical representations rituals must, as language, be grounded in social and cultural matrices of human lived experience. The meaning of this argument is that in theatrical representation, ritual symbolism blasts its symbolic shell, merges with concrete social, cultural and historical matrices and becomes specialized to selected, formalized, repeated and enacted human activities with an undercurrent human intentionality.

6.1.2. Naturalism and Realism in the Context of African Drama

The second theory which in my opinion best suits with African drama is naturalism. Naturalism is a literary theory and movement that seeks to depict in theatre works human living conditions as close to reality as possible.

As Theodore Hatlen put it, "naturalism is an exaggerated form of realism" (Hatlen 1962: 157). In other words, naturalism is an advanced form of realism. In European context, naturalism was a movement in late 19th-century drama that aimed to replace the artificial romantic style with accurate depictions of ordinary people in plausible situations. In attempting to create a perfect illusion of reality, playwrights and directors rejected dramatic conventions that had existed since the beginnings of drama (Carlson 1984: 158). In African context, naturalism is not ascribed within a specifically historical period, but it has taken form and developed as a literature of African consciousness since the time after colonial rule began until the present time.

I will give three reasons why African drama needs to be read with naturalist theoretical outlook. Firstly, modern African drama developed as a realistic literature that chronicles Africa's historical struggles with the European colonialism and developed a consciousness that dislocates western imperialist discourse as the center of cultural production and knowledge. As a matter of fact, in African context, naturalist movement has been both keen observer of the socio-political development of African history and the chronicler of the continent's predicament. Writing about African history offers the playwright the possibility to help the readers understand the past. History becomes reference and playwrights use that reference to frame ways of understanding the present. They assess the continent's present conditions in the light of history, and theorize about a better future. Naturalism critically assesses historical drama as a medium for rewriting Africa by recasting the continent's identity and aspirations. Drama being creative literature, ideas about ways to avoid past mistakes can be pondered over in plays and on stage. On this issue, David Kerr has this to say: "It [Naturalism] would also entail describing the attempts made by colonial educators [African playwrights] to mobilize African communities through a variety of imposed or transformed, indigenous arts" (Kerr 2002: 486). To mobilize here means to prepare intellectually people to know their history and be willing to change. The critical analysis has an important implication on the naturalist reading of plays. The implication is that naturalism entertains close relationship with history and politics and the main objective is to read historical plays as efforts to historical education to readers and spectators through a realistic depiction of socio-political reality. Naturalism as a critical theory would read African drama as a realist literature that articulates the colonial brutality highlighting the tragic aspect of the encounter where Africa became the suffer head with the loss of its human and economic resources. Plays in that perspective include Ngugi wa Thiong'o's *The Trial of Dedan Kimathi,* Wole Soyinka's *Death and the King's Horseman,* Athol Fugard's *My Children! My Africa!* and *People Are Living There.* These plays portray with realism the colonial brutality and the expected violent reactions of Africans who opposed with fierce resistance the colonial penetration. Reading these plays with naturalist inclination will prepare the cultural memory of the reader to reflect on African past critical moments and better apprehend the continent's present condition.

Secondly, in African context, naturalism has gone beyond the historical documentary recording of past frustrations to project the possible and the plausible picturesque orientations of socio-political life and events projecting thereby in the future the possibility of optimistic outgrowth of events. Drama has been used to anticipate the future. Playwrights have creatively projected a construction of sociopolitical life that transcends the historical frailties of African continent to foresee ways of avoiding past mistakes. On this point, Wole Soyinka asserts that:

> The writer is the visionary of his people, he recognizes past and present not for the purpose of enshrinement but for the logical creative impulse and statement of ideal future. He anticipates, he warns. It is not enough for the writer to be involved in the direct physical struggle of today, he often cannot help but envisage and seek to protect the future which is the declared aim of contemporary struggle (Soyinka 1988: 20).

This statement by Soyinka reinforces my view that naturalism goes beyond the historical description of life. It analyses the past, uses this to understand the present and anticipates the future by predicting through plausible projections things which may happen in the future.

From this perspective, I see naturalism as both descriptive and predictive in content. Naturalism is descriptive in the sense that it delineates African history and chronicles the continent's endeavor to come to terms with colonial forces. It is also prescriptive in that it seeks to project in literature the possible ways of future events reading from past experiences, and from there prescribe attitudes to adopt to avoid in the future mistakes that occurred in the past. The prescriptive aspect of naturalism in interested in showing how postcolonial affairs should be run in order to build a meaningful future for Africa. From that perspective, it takes lessons from history to anticipate sociopolitical events by constructing fictional possible ways that future events may occur. Naturalism as a theory seeks to locate in drama the ability of the artist's creative mind to anticipate with realism what may occur in the future, by constructing stories, scenes and episodes that are close to real future.

Thirdly, naturalism offers the possibility to relocate in drama aspects of the African values, objects and characters that were dislocated by the colonial discourse. The central concern of African drama as a literature of consciousness has been the strategic writing style that can change the African condition from bad to good. A naturalist approach to African theatre engages theory and criticism to reading the representation of historical tragedies in Africa from realist perspective but tries to reconstruct that part of life that was lost. That reconstruction is what I refer to as relocation of the dislocated values. Dislocation affects all those value systems that because of colonial hegemonic practices, need, in a sense, to be 'reinvented' in language, in narrative aesthetics, or myth. African drama in the main developed as a critical response to European colonialism which negatively impacted African theatrical traditions and weakened its literary documentation. In the 19th century, African identity was constructed by Eurocentric writers and was reflected in literary works as stereotypical and derogatory due to the fact that they assimilated African cultural practices with primitive, superstitious and barbaric ways. African playwrights in their theoretical approaches have attempted to redefine and recast that identity to provide an objective image of Africans.

Fourthly, naturalism helps to read trends in African drama that establish a link between social ethics and the established laws of human conduct that regulate them. Despite the naturalist tendency of critical theory, few critics advocate the reading strategy that locates the historical experience of colonialism as drama itself. Drama here is taken to mean the interplay between the social construction of life and the ironical deconstruction of its tenets by colonial agents. Naturalism as a theory looks at particular national contexts where the independence struggles that were expected to yield true socio-cultural, economic and political freedoms became shattered dreams with the disillusionment that followed these struggles. As a matter of fact, dramatists rewrite African postcolonial stories with the desired oriented ideologies that restore justice. I am going to illustrate with examples starting from reading plays to articulating their theoretical approaches.

For instance, Frank Ogodo Ogbeche in *Harvest of Corruption,* Chinyere Grace Okafor in *The New Toy Toy,* and Irene Isoken Salami-Ogunloye in *Sweet Revenge* have created situations whereby evil doers are punished by human laws and by the laws of the nature while benefactors are rewarded according to their good deeds. Naturalist approach to these plays show the relationship between ethical norms in human society and the laws of nature that punish trespassers. For instance, in *Harvest of Corruption,* Chief Aladu Ade Amanka faces trial and loses his job as a consequence of his embezzlement of public funds and his immoral deals with Aloho who died during abortion. Naturalism verges on realism and provides ingredients for teaching morality to social actors. Since then such theory has provided staple ingredients for reforming society, it can be said that naturalism is fundamental to postcolonial theory as the main setting in these plays are the postcolonial African states and the main discourse is the deconstruct of the hegemony of imperialism operated by the African rallies of the European ex-colonialists. In modern African drama, naturalism and realism are theories built on practical guidance on right action, the outlook of natural jurisprudence highly influential in ensuring a continuous focus on rationality of the postcolonial state and the constant and uniform accessibility to the human rights as a shared privilege of citizens. I suggested that naturalism as a theory of modern African drama is both descriptive and prescriptive. Another such understanding is that it is descriptive in that it describes in plays the imaginative genius of moral interplay between social actors and the code of ethics that guides and sanctions their actions. It is also prescriptive in the sense that it shows through the inductive analysis of the stories created the moral frame that people living in society are supposed to abide by in order to live in peace and harmony. Naturalism in modern African drama arose as a response to the general malaise felt about the mismanagement of the postcolonial state by political juntas, some oligarchic corrupt leaders who side-tracked ethical norms in their ruling and broke loose with regard to political morality without yet being sanctioned by the state judicial apparatus, a mechanism they have created and are controlling. I infer that naturalism is sustained by morality plays. Behind every morality play one can find a strong naturalist ideology. This critical stand is shared by Charles Uji who asserts:

> There is currently an aesthetic, philosophic tangentiality in the African literary dramatic and theatrical arts with particular emphasis on the English idiom. On the one hand there exists the drama of bourgeois, idealist aesthetics which predominates the scene, while on the other hand one notices the drama of revolutionary, Marxist poetics... It is my contention that the principal characteristics of Nigerian drama of bourgeois aesthetics

include uncomfortable fact that they project a cyclical view of history and development (Uji 2001: 44).

The critic Uji is describing the relationship between the theatre of the oppressed and the theatre of the oppressor in the Marxist tradition without making it explicit that Marxism itself is the product of naturalism. Marxist literary approach describes in plays class struggles and ideological contestation for hegemony between the masses, or the working class and the ruling bourgeois in economic conditions of exploitation and oppression of the former by the latter. From this perspective, Marxism is predicated on naturalism or realism in that it describes real social living conditions. Ngugi wa Thiong'o's *I Will Marry When I Want* responds to the Marxist and naturalist ideology in that the story brings the factory workers of the Kigunda type in contestation and class struggles with the bourgeois Kioi.

There is a close relationship between naturalism or realism, the theatre of absurd and existentialism. In other words, naturalism is also the ability to tell the truth when things go wrong. This desire to tell the truth especially when things are wrong gives sometimes the playwright a pessimistic view of the society. This pessimistic view may verge on existentialism. So, a playwright with naturalist orientations may be develop existentialist ideas. I will use examples to make the point clear. Naturalism took over from the theatre of the absurd campaigned for many decades by playwrights like Wole Soyinka, Ola Rotimi and Athol Fugard in which good characters with strong moral intent never get their way until they die and are buried with their dreams, and the society is described upside down as people are engaged in self-destructive adventure. Wole Soyinka's *The Road,* Ola Rotimi's *Holding Talks* and Athol Fugard's *People Are Living There* narrate stories with characters in an absurdist engagement. For instance, Professor's insanity in *The Road* is coupled with the existentialist mood in which people strive to get rich only to die in road accidents, an apt metaphor to the postcolonial civil warfare that damaged many African countries including Nigeria. Athol Fugard's *People Are Living There* highlights the inhuman living conditions under the Apartheid regime where human life is trapped in the snare of ablaze violations of human rights with infernal cycles of killings, rape, arsons. Fugard's existentialist praxis comes in the form of a question as to what good end serves life in South African society if one should strive to build only to see all property including human life dwindle in a smoke of arson and police mortal brutalities? In other words, Fugard develops a naturalist ideology that practically unveils an existentialist intent to criticize South African Apartheid regime for reducing life to an infernal cycle of birth and death with no possibility for black Africans to realize their full potentials as human beings and citizens of the world. Existential philosophical outlook becomes a constituent in the African drama and theoretical formulation of such drama needs to be aware of its tenets. It is not far-fetched to say that the tragic history of African continent which was tested successively by slavery, colonialism and neocolonialism informs the existentialist vision of many playwrights. Wole Soyinka's *Madmen and Specialists,* Bode Sowande's *Farewell to Babylon* and Femi Osofisan's *Farewell to a Cannibal Rage* are all written with existentialist outlook. The three writers draw on Nigerian civil war to articulate the tragic self-destruction of human societies and question the meaning of life trapped in the vicious circle of birth and premature death. Soyinka in *Of Africa* states:

> ... the resolution of the existential dilemma... or indeed to global survival if only they were known about or permitted their proper valuation. There is also of course the aspect of negative attributes, one whose very nature constitutes a burden on others. We are speaking here of a condition where the unravelling of a part can menace the health or survival of the whole (Soyinka 2012: 7).

Soyinka in this statement brings out the fact that existentialism and naturalism correlate. Naturalism in modern African drama also reads from the perspective of realist vision of the society that orients the playwright and the ability of the critic to theorize of that vision. Drama is seen as a means by which objective reality is reflected upon. Gyorgy Lukacs observes:

> If literature [drama] is a particular form by means of which objective reality is reflected, then, it becomes of crucial importance for it to grasp that reality as it truly is, and not merely to confine itself to reproducing whatever manifests itself immediately on the surface. If a writer strives to represent reality as it truly is, i. e. if he is an authentic realist, the question of totality plays a decisive role, no matter how the writer actually conceives the problem intellectually (Lukacs 2001: 1033).

This critical view means that realism and naturalism are if not two faces of the same coin, but at least. Drama as a literary genre offers a practical avenue for diagnosing and discussing society's problems, to grasp socio-political and cultural realities and fictionalize them on stage and plays. In African context, the historical factor plays a key role in understanding the birth, the rise and the theoretical frames of drama in Africa.

Michael Etherton in seeking to solve the theoretical problem of African drama did not take into account the dramatic aspect of African history, an aspect which nevertheless comes to reinforce the theoretical understanding of drama in Africa. A referential frame of theatre theory refers to the contending ideas and opinions about theatre and interpretation. Interpretation has been conceptualized to designate an objective textual analysis, critical assessment and response to colonialism and neocolonialism. African colonial past provides a frame of African theatre theory as a naturalist delineation of intellectual reaction to construct African identity, and political agendas. These conceptualizations brought in African theatre context contribute to read plays as critical responses to imperialism and neocolonialism. Taken together, theorists adhere to very different often contradictory understandings of theatre and interpretation. As a matter of fact, critics have often arrived at converging but conflicting formulations of theory regarding the development and status of African theatre. Such conflicts point to the vitality, the excitement, and the complexity of the field of theory and criticism whose expansive universe of perennial issues and problems engages ideas not only about theatre as literature, its language, interpretation, genre, style, meaning, and tradition, but also about subjectivity, ethnicity, race, gender, class, culture, nationality, ideology, institutions and historical periods.

In this chapter, the objective was to elucidate the reasons why symbolism and naturalism emerge as the suitable critical theories that best apply to African drama. Two key ideas have emerged: African drama due to its contextualized predication on indigenous performances make an extensive use of symbols in every aspect of its performance and expression. The use of symbols and symbolic language makes it meaningful to view African drama in the light of symbolism and naturalism. Drama in Africa is symbolically oriented and naturalistically grounded. Symbolism becomes a fundamental theoretical tool suitable for interpreting the intrinsic dimensions of drama. Secondly, naturalism in the context of African drama is a literature of consciousness that developed in response to Eurocentric imperial discourse and critical lenses for assessing postcolonial politics. From this perspective, naturalism comes to reinforce symbolism as critical tools in the examination of drama.

References

Abrams, M. H., *A Glossary of Literary Terms, 5th Edition*. San Francisco: Holt, Rinehart and Winston, Inc., 1988. 152-154.

Achebe, C. *Things Fall Apart*. Heinemann Educational Books. [1958] 2001.

Aidoo, A. A. 1970. *Anowa*. London: Longman. 1970.

Banham, M. ed. *A History of Theatre in Africa*. Cambridge: Cambridge University Press.

Carlson, M. *Theories of the Theatre: A Historical and Critical Survey, From Greeks to the Present*. Ithaca: Cornell University Press. 1993

Damlegue, L. "Political Consciousness and Social Reconstruction: Ngugi wa Thiong'o and Micere Githae Mugo's *The Trial of Dedan Kimathi*." In *Geste et Voix: Revue Scientific, No 17*. 2013. 165-185.

De Graft, J. C. "Roots in African Drama and Theatre". In Eldred Durosimi Jones, ed., *African Literature Today: Drama in Africa, No 8*. London: Heinemann Educational Books. 1976. 1-25.

Etherton, M. *The Development of African Drama*. New York: Africana Publishing. 1982.

Jeyifo, Biodun. 2002. *Modern African Drama*. New York: W. W. Norton sand Company.

Kerr, D. "Art as Tool, Weapon or Shield?: Art for Development Seminar, Harare". In Biodun Jeyifo, ed., *Modern African Drama*. New York: W. W. Norton and Company. 2002. 486-493.

Kumavie, D. "Ama Ata Aidoo's Woman-Centered Pan-Africanism: A Reading of Selected Works". In Amina Mama and Hakima Abbas, eds., *Feminist Africa, Issues 20, 2015 Pan-Africanism and Feminism*. African Gender Institute: University of Cape Town. 57-68.

Lukacs, G. "Realism in the Balance". In Vincent B. Leitch, ed., *The Norton Anthology of Theory and Criticism*. New York: W. W. Norton & Company. 2001. 1033-1058.

Ngugi, wa T. and Ngugi wa M. *I Will Marry When I Want*. London: Heinemann. 1982.

Nwahunanya, C. *Literary Criticism, Critical Theory and Postcolonial African Literature*. Mayland: Arbi Press. 2012.

Obiechina, Emmanuel. *Themes in African Literature*. Cambridge: Cambridge University Press. 1975.

Olaniyan, T. and Ato Quaysan. *African Literature: An Anthology of Criticism and Theory*. New York: Blackwell Publishing. 2013.

Rotimi, Ola. *The Gods Are Not to Blame*. London: Oxford University Press. 1971.

Sow, A. I. "Prolegomena". In *Introduction to African Cultures: General Aspects*. Paris: UNESCO. [1973] 1979. 9-31.

Soyinka, W. *Death and the King's Horseman*. London: Eyre Methuen Ltd. 1975.

- ------------. *A Play of Giants*. London: Methuen Ltd. 1984.

- ⸻. *Art, Dialogue and Outrage: Essays on Literature and Culture.* Ibadan: New Horn Press. 1988.
- ⸻. *King Baabu.* Oxford: Oxford University Press. 2002.
- ⸻. *Of Africa.* Oxford: Oxford University Press. 2012.
- Uji, C. "Sowande's Revolutionary Socio-Aesthetic Ideal". In Ola Rotimi, ed., *Issues in African Theatre.* Ibadan: HP Humanities Publishers. 2001. 44-66.

7

AFRICAN PERSPECTIVES ON CULTURAL MATERIALISM AND POLITICAL MORALITY

7.1. Understanding Cultural Materialism

There is a strong relationship between cultural materialism and the political philosophy. The British critic Graham Holderness (quoted by Peter Barry) describes cultural materialism as 'a politicised form of historiography' (Barry 2009: 121-124). We can explain this as meaning the study of historical material (which includes literary texts) within a politicised framework, this framework including the present which those literary texts have in some way helped to shape (Ibidem). The term 'cultural materialism' was made current in 1985 when it was used by Jonathan Dollimore and Alan Sinfield (the best-known of the cultural materialists) as the subtitle of their edited collection of essays *Political Shakespeare*. They define the term in a foreword as designating a critical method which has four characteristics: it combines an attention to:

1. historical context,
2. theoretical method,
3. political commitment, and
4. textual analysis.

To comment briefly on each of these: firstly, the emphasis on *historical context* 'undermines the transcendent sigificance traditionally accorded to the literary text'. Here the word 'transcendent' roughly means 'timeless'. The position taken, of course, needs to face the obvious objection that if we are today still studying and reading Shakespeare then his plays have indeed proved themselves 'timeless' in the simple sense that they are clearly not limited by the historical circumstances in which they were produced. But this is a matter of degree: the aim of this aspect of cultural materialism is to allow the literary text to 'recover its histories' which previous kinds of study have often ignored. The kind of history recovered would involve relating the plays to such phenomena as 'enclosures and the oppression of the rural poor, state power and resistance to it … witchcraft, the challenge and containment of the carnivalesque' (Dollimore and Sinfield 1994: 3).

Secondly, the emphasis on *theoretical method* signifies the break with liberal humanism and the absorbing of the lessons of structuralism, post-structuralism, and other approaches which have become prominent since the 1970s. Thirdly, the emphasis on *political commitment* signifies the influence of Marxist and feminist perspectives and the break from the conservative-Christian framework which hitherto dominated Shakespeare criticism. Finally, the stress on *textual analysis* 'locates the critique of traditional approaches where it cannot be ignored'. In other words, there is a commitment not just to making theory of an abstract kind, but to practising it on (mainly) canonical texts which continue to be the focus of massive amounts of academic and professional attention, and which are prominent national and cultural icons. The two words in the term 'cultural materialism' are further defined: 'culture' will include *all* forms of culture ('forms like television and popular music and fiction'). That is, this approach does not limit itself to 'high' cultural forms like the Shakespeare play. 'Materialism' signifies the opposite of 'idealism': an 'idealist' belief would be that high culture represents the free and independent play of the talented individual mind; the contrary 'materialist' belief is that culture cannot 'transcend the material forces and relations of production. Culture is not simply a reflection of the economic and political system, nor can it be independent of it'. These comments on materialism represent the standard beliefs of Marxist criticism, and they do perhaps point to the difficulty of making a useful distinction between a 'straight' Marxist criticism and cultural materialism. However, it is added that the relevant history is not just that of four hundred years ago, but that of the times (including our own) in which Shakespeare is produced and reproduced. Thus, in cultural materialism there is an emphasis on the functioning of the institutions through which Shakespeare is now brought to us – the Royal Shakespeare Company, the film industry, the publishers who produce textbooks for school and college, and the National Curriculum, which lays down the requirement that specific Shakespeare plays be studied by all school pupils.

Cultural materialism takes a good deal of its outlook (and its name) from the British left-wing critic Raymond Williams (Ibidem). Instead of Foucault's notion of 'discourse' Williams invented the term 'structures of feeling': these are concerned with 'meanings and values as they are lived and felt'. Structures of feeling are often antagonistic both to explicit systems of values and beliefs, and to the dominant ideologies within a society. They are characteristically found in literature, and they *oppose* the status quo (as the values in Dickens, the Brontes, etc., represent human structures of feeling which are at variance with Victorian commercial and materialist values). The result is that cultural materialism is much more optimistic about the possibility of change and is willing at times to see literature as a source of oppositional values. Cultural materialism particularly involves using the past to 'read' the present, revealing the politics of our own society by what we choose to emphasise or suppress of the past. A great deal of the British work has been about undermining what it sees as the fetishistic role of Shakespeare as a conservative icon within British culture.

7.2. Applying Cultural Materialism to African Drama

To clearly see the implications and meaning of cultural materialism on African drama from their theoretical perspective, it urges to see in concrete terms what cultural materialist critics do. To move a step further, it is necessary to understand what cultural materialist critics do taking into account Barry's explanation:

1. They read the literary text (very often a Renaissance play) in such a way as to enable us to 'recover its histories', that is, the context of exploitation from which it emerged.
2. At the same time, they foreground those elements in the work's present transmission and contextualising which caused those histories to be lost in the first place, (for example, the 'heritage' industry's packaging of Shakespeare in terms of his-tory-as-pageant, national bard, cultural icon, and so on).
3. They use a combination of Marxist and feminist approaches to the text, especially in order to do the first of these (above), and in order to fracture the previous dominance of conservative social, political, and religious assumptions in Shakespeare criticism in particular.

4. They use the technique of close textual analysis, but often employ structuralist and post-structuralist techniques, especially to mark a break with the inherited tradition of close textual analysis within the framework of conservative cultural and social assumptions.
5. At the same time, they work mainly within traditional notions of the canon, on the grounds that writing about more obscure texts hardly ever constitutes an effective political intervention (for instance, in debates about the school curriculum or national identity).

From the perspective of cultural materialism, one should see how the struggles of the masses for political freedoms directly relate to Marxist ideals and feminist inclinations. In the study and research of African drama, the literary dimension of political liberation tends to be marginalized. Criticism has often emphasized on the cultural liberation that informed the nationalist movements of the independence period without specifying how the political praxis of African drama played a key role in the rising and shaping of African nationalism and the struggle for independence and democracy (Ansu-Kyeremeh 2005: 1). According to Michael Etherton, African literary criticism should be more interested in the growing tension in African countries between playwrights and the political leaders (Etherton 1982: 26); a statement which denotes the non-perception by African critics of the phenomenon of African drama as a sociopolitical process that reflects the intellectual affirmation of peoples' struggle for democracy. Oyekan Owomoyela seems to be of the same ideological perception as Etherton by inferring that Africa does not have drama as an art form in its indigenous cultures (Owomoyela 1985: 28); he claims a European origin of African theatre. David Kerr in his approach takes a different critical stand and suggests that the dissatisfaction of drama debates expresses itself as a feeling of shame about writing African literary drama (Kerr 1991: 57).

Kwasi Ansu-Kyeremeh posits that in the field of dramatic "communication in particular, and more so in mass communication, indigenous forms …are often dismissed as 'inconsequential' or only casually mentioned in the mainly Eurocentric mainstream research (Ansu-Kyeremeh 2005: 1)." These critics have, at various degrees, expressed what constitutes the neglected aspect of African drama studies and the possible reasons to explain these but seem to overlook the contribution of its theory and criticism to the enhancement of democracy taking Greek theatre and African theatre for development as paradigms. Reading Cultural materialism as theory, I set forth to re-evaluate the contributions of African drama to the expression of the masses' aspirations for freedom and democracy by drawing analogies from Ancient Greek tradition.

7.2.3. Cultural Materialism in African Drama Context

The theory of cultural materialism seeks to examine in literary texts the cultural values of African people that sustain culture in Africa as the fundamentals sustaining life and seeking to change it for the best (Gibson 1984: 10). According to Brad West, "[An African] cultural theory is one that gives primacy to the dynamics of culture in its analysis, foregrounding the logics and power of ideas, symbols, myths, discourses and emotions that people use in understanding the world and acting within it" (West 2010: 188). It is also "a historically transmitted pattern of meanings embodied in symbols, a system of inherited conceptions expressed by which men communicate, perpetuate, and develop their knowledge about and their attitudes towards life" (Ibidem).

That theory recognizes the universalism of human values based on politics, culture and economics and the ethics as guide. African cultural theory acknowledges diversity, pluralism and inclusion. It advocates cultural tolerance as a way of accepting self and other in a contextual framework of mutual understanding. It lays emphasis on serious effort to understand African cultural life; to develop a compendium of values and belief systems within African cultures and other cultures of the world. It recognizes the reader as an active agent who imparts "real existence to the work and completes its meanings through interpretation" (Damlegue 2016: 16).

The way drama operates in African political and cultural contexts can be more explained if we throw a glance at the operating mode of Ancient Greek drama. Greek drama whose hearth was at Athens is believed to have produced the first democracy on which other countries shaped their models (Taplin 2003: 3). Ideas in Greek drama about freedom can be found in African traditional performances and contemporary plays. In dramatic literature, African democracy, like democracy in other nations, may have taken inspiration from Greek drama in the making of democratic ideas. I foreground this argument because in the development of literature and culture, disciplines cross borders and influence each other. In addition, oral and written literatures in Africa have been so much influenced by external factors like colonial encounter and migration movements. This idea is sustained by Mineke Schipper-de Leeuw who claims that

> in the history of literature and culture, it is never possible to bring about a clear separation between areas, periods and movements, because they always influence one another [...] Likewise, in the case of drama, it would be absolutely incorrect to treat traditional drama-forms as one thing and the so-called modern drama as another thing. The oral tradition continues partly in the written and literature and traditional drama influences very much written drama in our time (Leew 1985: 57).

Thus, drama, as it was performed in Ancient Greek has influenced and continues to influence world democracies, the African included. Greek drama is showing the extent to which drama was religious festivals, an exploration of political identity, or an engaging piece of popular entertainment, but was used at the same time for expressing people's aspirations for democracy (Stoey and Allan 2005: 47). Ian C. Storey and Arlen Allan in *A Guide to Ancient Greek Drama* have explained with accuracy how drama in Ancien Greek was a medium for forum talk, panel discussions about issues related to democracy, political life, and public affairs:

> [Drama], then, has a great deal in it that we would identify as political content. But to what degree can this content be called primarily or essentially "democratic" in orientation rather than "about the polis" in more general terms? Tragic drama was traditionally instituted in the Athenian polis under the tyranny of Peisistratos, and after the tyrant's overthrow and the first democratic reforms had been established, comedy, too, had its place in dramatic competitions of the City Dionysia... (Leew 1985: 70)

Here, it is perceptible that Greek tragedies referred to as tragic drama, originally an institution of the king, became a popular theatre used for political actions, mass sensitization as religious festivals. Mixed with sportive competitions, it drew large crowds who gathered to deliberate on political issues of the polis. Athens is often associated with the first hearth of democracy a strong inspiration for modern democracies. There, the populations gathered to choose their leaders at universal ballots. More clearly reflective of the political life are the mechanics behind the organization of the festival and the events which are noted as taking place in the opening days of the competition. Greek festivals were cosmopolitan organizations that included religious worship, sportive competitions, political debates and social recreations. Here is where the idea of "context" of performance comes into play, for the figures involved and the type of events enacted have far more in common with the city's public life and political interests than with anything we would recognize as "religious" (Ibidem).

Public affairs, namely, how to implement development strategies of the city to the benefits of the majority were at the center of debates, as Ian C. Storey and Arlen Allan further explain:

> While a festival honoring a god might strike us as wholly religious in orientation, participation in religious festivals was an essential part of civic life in every Greek community. Since all religious festivals were at least in part directed toward the protection and prosperity of their participants, when those festivals were community-wide, they all might be said to serve political ends in the broadest sense of that term, that is, to be of benefit to the polis. On this most basic of levels, then, the two Dionysiac festivals at Athens at which drama was produced can be said to serve both religious and political purposes (Ibidem).

More telling though is the manner in which drama itself is granted the freedom to question and criticize the values and socio-political institutions of the Athenian polis in the guise of the mythological reenactments of tragedy and the farcical representations of contemporary civic life in comedy. We do not know whether this challenging of normally unquestioned values and practices was always part of tragic drama at the City Dionysia (Ibidem). But we might suspect it was, given that the City Dionysia, was also a period of "sacred time" in which liberties not normally granted to citizens were made available. Part of the reason why tragedy in the fifth century had the liberty to address political issues in the form it did may be located in the fact that the festival took Dionysos Eleuthereus as its patron (Ibidem).

Under democracy more citizens had been released to participate in the affairs of the city than under any other previous form of administration. But this freedom seems to have generated some perhaps unexpected problems. In the fifth century Athens, the city's decision-makers and leaders were, in principle if not in fact, the people (Ibidem). Ever since Homer and Hesiod, it had been a taken-for-granted assumption that those in positions of power had an obligation to honor the gods, which by extension meant to honor the law of the polis, often presented as divinely inspired. The problem with these divinely inspired laws and the socio-political institutions which they supported was that they were an inheritance from a period of aristocratic rule and in many cases ill-suited to the emerging ideals of a democratic polis. Couched in the equally traditional and aristocratic myths of the past – in the case of tragedy (and also some comedies) – or in the humorous fantasies of comedy, drama became the vehicle through which the city could celebrate its freedoms while it simultaneously challenged and interrogated some of its most cherished ideals. Storey and Allan offer the mind picture of the polis to help us understand the notion of politics and political administration in the Ancient Greek context:

> "Polis," of course, is the Greek term from which is derived the terms "politics" and "political," but it remains notoriously difficult to convey the depth and complexity of its associations in a single English term. Most frequently translated "city-state," in Greek sources polis serves to identify both a town as administrative center of a territory and the territory itself. [...] But more than this, polis also embraced the people resident in its territory and in the case of Athens/Attica, whether they lived in the city proper or dwelt in an outlying community, these people bore the name Athenians, if they qualified for citizenship. The Greek term for "citizen" was polites, and signified one who possessed certain rights in a polis (Leew 1985: 70).

Thus when someone claimed to be an Athenian citizen, he was not making claim to a particular nationality, nor was he necessarily revealing the town of his residence; rather he was identifying himself with a particular collective, a polis, in which, according to its constitution, he was entitled to certain benefits and obligated to fulfill certain responsibilities in and to the larger community. Different constitutions set different qualifications and restrictions on who could claim citizenship and on what their rights and duties might be, but generally these rights and duties were loosely framed around four activities – defense (military service), policy-making (voting), administration (holding office) and resource management (owning land).

> To consider drama in relation to the polis of Athens is inevitably to raise the question of drama's relationship to ta politika ("the affairs of the polis"), its politics, its laws, and its political identity. Was drama "political," that is, "about the polis"? Did it contribute to the creation of an Athenian identity, or help to define what it meant to be an Athenian polites? Was drama a form of mass education, a vehicle for the instruction of the citizens in matters of "good" and "bad" citizenship? Or was it a vehicle for the airing of concerns that could not be given expression in other public forums? The answers to these questions are not mutually exclusive, for as we will see, drama can speak to its spectators on several levels simultaneously. But to address the issues raised by these questions requires that we view the institutionalization of drama from two perspectives, the context of its performance and the content of the plays, for each may be politicized in different ways (Ibidem).

This extract suggests that drama was playing both a political function and a socio-cultural function. At the political level, drama was a forum for political debates, for deliberating on issues concerning the political live of the city, the choices of the leaders and the constitutions that should rule the city's political life. At the level of socio-cultural function, drama was expression of the civic culture of the people, entrenched in their religious celebrations, ritual festivals, the use of myths for explaining the world mysteries. Entertainments were encrusted in the sportive competitions organized jointly with religious festivals. This account of Ancient Greek Drama constitutes a springboard for me to draw similarities with African theatre for development and see how drama is used in the African context as a means for democratic expression.

7.2.3. Theatre for Liberation in Africa

Drama in Africa has served as a means of expressing people's socio-cultural and political aspirations for democracy and freedom. Not only have people used it as a means of entertainment and relaxation, but they have used it for political struggle along political actions led by elites in political parties and organizations.

It is important to recall the context in which theatre for liberation was born in Africa before highlighting its major contributions to democracy strengthening. From a historical perspective, Africa has been part of the nations of the world that have suffered political domination, cultural alienation and economic exploitation on behalf of European countries. A quick glance at African history informs us that African societies went through slave trade and colonization before breathing the air of political freedom in the nineteen sixties for majority of African countries (Anene and Brown 1999: 326). After political independence, dramatic concerns turned unto the leadership incompetence problems of African nations. Eugène van Erven takes position to assert that

> A new pragmatically oriented political theatre has come into being in the developing world [Africa]. Some observers refer to it as 'People's Theatre'. Others label it 'Popular theatre for Social Change.' Both terms, unfortunately, evoke echoes of previous, unsuccessful Western attempts at creating a political theatre for the underprivileged; therefore, I prefer to call this type of political theatre from the developing world the 'Theatre of Liberation'. The term's association with 'Liberation Theology' and 'Pedagogy of the Oppressed' are quite deliberate, since the activilties and the methods of the theatre of liberation have been inspired by similarly oriented activities in the religious and educational sectors of developing societies. As such it differs fundamentally from most western political theatre practices, for it is process-oriented and does not focus on the performance as the sole purpose of theatre (Erven 1991: 11).

The proviso advanced by Eugène van Erven can be summarized as follows: liberation theatre was given impetus and stamina in Africa in the political context of liberation struggles which saw many African countries' protest against the colonial yoke and claim for political independence. Just like the Ancient Greek Athenians rebelled against their tyrant to ask for freedom of expression, liberation as a political concept was appropriated by Africans in the 1960s when a worldwide solidarity movement took shape in support of all the oppressed and exploited peoples who, according to Eugène van Erven, ranged from Blacks in South Africa to Africans in other parts of the black continent (Ibidem). Liberation drama in Africa is born in a context where the economies of the post-independent countries fell under the control of local elites, whose members not only were educated in the ex-colonizers' mindset to be dependent on transnational corporations, western foreign aid, and military support. They did nothing to improve the lot of the toiling masses who don't have the minimum means of survival. It is in this context that theatre of liberation took shape and materialized into a political praxis of claiming for freedom and democracy. That drama was to raise the awareness of the rural masses in Africa about their unbecoming social conditions and the possibilities of liberation.

In Third World African context, freedom was to be achieved at two levels. Firstly, the revolutionary drama targeted liberation from hunger, thirst, political violence, homelessness and physical abuse. Secondly, it also aimed at the kind of social reforms that would create the economic, political, educational, social, psychological and cultural conditions that would ensure a maximum realization of human potential. These performances were sketched and debates were organized in forums; sometimes after performances, workshops were also organized. Before the mounting on scene of contemporary dramatists like Wole Soyinka, Ngugi wa Thiong'o, Andrew Horn, James Gibbs, Michael Etherton, Fay Chung and David Kerr who helped to develop a tradition of African theatre in the universities in Nigeria (Etherton 1982: 344), Kenya, Zambia and Malawi, pioneering popular theatre practitioners like Hubert Ogunde, Duro Ladipo and Kola Ogunmola from Nigeria, Gibson Kete from South Africa, J. C. DeGraft and Efua T. Sutherland from Ghana struggled to make the voices of the masses heard. According to Erven, military and civilian millionaires from the Third World African countries allowed emergent middle classes to enjoy a modicum of material comfort and hold out promises of greater wealth in the future (Eugène van Erven, op. cit., p. 13). Yet, because their own fortunes depend on the continued exploitation of peasants and workers, the rulers of these countries found it necessary to silence dissidents and control social unrest by creating an extensive, corrupt and brutal paramilitary apparatus. Yet, with increasing social polarization, a new revolutionary radicalism has slowly taken root among the impoverished masses with the support of intellectual artists, dramatists who bear the burden of socio-political reforms for the benefits of the masses. In fact, the idea of liberation and true democracy grow almost naturally out of unbearable socio-economic predicament. Jean Pliya, a Beninese drama scholar and literary critic, asserts that

> les grandes préoccupation du théâtre africain sont à l'image des préoccupations sociopolitiques de l'Afrique. En d'autres termes, le théâtre accomplit sa véritable fonction en collant à la réalité,

tout en libérant l'imagination et le rêve, en mettant en scène la vie vécue ou la vie rêvée, la vie élaborée ou la vie souhaitée. Voilà pourquoi, après 1960, avec les indépendances politiques, les thèmes fondamentaux du théâtre africain ont porté sur la lutte nationale, - la résistance anticoloniale, …la dénonciation des tares de nos jeunes sociétés (dot exorbitants, corruption des cadres, mythe des diplômes, patrons vénaux et véreux – le besoin de poser des problèmes moraux, de satiriser les institutions nouvelles mises en place « au soleil des indépendances […][5]

Jean Pliya explanation is about the political contexts – motivations and objectives – of African drama of the post-independent period. It was essentially a politically motivated theatre, and freedom or democracy underpinned the themes and fledged the contents of the plays. Aristotle defined drama as the mimesis of "people in action," wherein an actor makes us believe that he is someone other than himself, the desire to represent the words, vocal inflections, posture and gestures, first, of someone known to us, and later, of some imagined or imaginary figure. Contemporary Radical and Experimental African Drama and Theater offer a critical survey of contemporary drama and theater scene in English-speaking African countries. J. Ndukaku Amankulor has observed that

> In a number of countries a style of dramaturgy [developed], that does not merely describe the contemporary situation but appears to interpret sociopolitical phenomena in such a way as to educate the reader or spectator on the desirability of mass enlightenment and commitment to the issues raised. The task of tackling those

---

[5]Jean Pliya, « Introduction : Le rôle du théâtre dans le développement culturel en Afrique », in *Quel théâtre pour le développement en Afrique* (Paris: Les nouvelles éditions africaines, 1965), p. 15.
[the major preoccupations of African theatre are in the image of socio-political themes in Africa. In other words, theatre fulfills its genuine function by adding to the reality, and by releasing the imagination and the dream, by staging the lived life or the life aspired to, the elaborated life or the wished life. This informs why after 1960, with political independences the fundamental themes of African theatre bore on national struggle, anticolonial resistance, …the denunciation of the vices of the new states (excessive dowry charging, corruption of the senior civil service staff, myths of diplomas, dishonest and mischievous bosses – the need to pose moral problems, to satirize the new institutions put in place under the radiations of independences [*Translation mine*].

> issues has been the major burden of African drama and theater since the 1970s. In the independent African countries, where the powerful ruling military, political, or religious classes appear to have generated more poverty and social strife than existed during colonial times, the playwrights engage in historical or social analyses of the situation to arrive at an enlightened interpretation (Amankulor 1993: 160).

The critic here is giving credence to the idea that in the African socio-political context, it is the vibrancy of political instability, social strife caused by poverty and unemployment that dictates to the playwright his critical orientations: the more problems undermine the society, the more acute the dramatist becomes in struggling for change.

C. L. Innes acknowledges that in *The Wretched of the Earth*, it is drama, rather than poetry or the novel that Frantz Fanon advocates as the best means of raising the consciousness of peoples involved in an anti-colonial struggle (Innes 2007: 19). Fanon, we remember pioneered the psychology of the oppressed as it applies to the colonial and neocolonial world. His book *The Wretched of the Earth* "dissects the mentalities of the colonial settlers, slaves, and neocolonial bourgeoisie, thereby enriching ideas on freedom by placing them unequivocally in a third-world context" (Eugène van Erven 1991: 17) Critic Lyn Innes further infers that in cultures where literacy has been confined mainly to a small elite group and where there is a continuing oral culture with roots in precolonial traditions, drama and performance provide a means of reaching a much wider indigenous audience and tapping into forms and conventions which are already familiar to them (Innes 2007: 19). British colonialism came down heavily on indigenous African cultures, especially the performing arts. The reaction of the indigenous theater to colonial efforts to gag it was similar in many African countries. The Igbo in Nigeria created new plays featuring British colonial officers—administrators, police, missionaries—and their families as characters to replace the banned traditional characters. The new plays were satiric comedies imitating the manners and foibles of the European in a very broad sense, but also more incisively where historical circumstances provided materials on such characters. J. Ndukaku Amankulor explains that

> The colonial district commissioner, popularly known as "Nwa D.C." (*nwa* being an Igbo term for "child," which the elders used in

this context to draw attention to the young administrative officers who were made to rule over and command their elders, contrary to the Igbo system of authority), has become a stock character in contemporary indigenous theater. He can be seen in a variety of performances strolling along with his aides and muttering instructions to them. The policeman is another stock character, frequently sheepish in his execution of authority (Amankulor 1993: 60).

Put in another way, in searching for strategies to counterattack the derogatory treatments of imperial powers, African people resorted to cultural performances of dramatic expressions where communication was achieved by means of stagecraft actions which operated as signals, signs and symbols. In some forms of theatrical communications, the expressive actions of the oppressed populations beckoned to the audiences' collective desire to achieve true freedom. All art forms communicate but drama communicates by telling stories and showing images on stage. Performance is central to African cultures. More so are the cultural performances during traditional festivals, masks dancing and carnivals parades. Some of these performances were used by African theatre practitioners to impart messages among Africans themselves and decoding it to enable colonial impostors to get it. This was done especially in contexts where the actors were miming these colonial agents. Amankulor further observes that

> Colonial Europeans, men, women, and children, feature in the *Ijele, Uzoiyi, Odo, Omabe,* and *Ikoro* performances, to mention only a few in Igboland. In Ikoro the repertoire of European characters includes the King and Queen of England, the Governor General in Lagos, the Residents and District Commissioners in the provinces and districts, and the law enforcement officers. The performance takes the form of an official visit by the King and Queen of England to their subjects at Ngwa in Igboland and the ceremonies and protocols performed to receive them, including the presentation of the welcome address and the response to it. In spite of the obvious satire of the performance, the *ikoro* drum, the original symbol of the performance before colonial intervention, still occupies the center of the arena stage, surrounded by a chorus of dancers (Amankulor 1993: 160).

Given the derogatory representations of Africans in Eurocentric literature, it was the role of African national theatres to restore the dignity of Africans and their culture, to promote self-respect and remind audiences of a heroic African history and a tradition of ancient times. Elsewhere in Africa, the *Nyau* cult leaders in Malawi reacted to colonial interference in their *Gule wa Mkulu* (big dance) "by incorporating stereotypes of colonial political and religious figures into the satire of the anthropomorphic masking tradition, and in the Bamana puppet plays in Mali the characters include colonial as well as modern-day police" (Ibidem). The contradictions of colonial contact that led to the incorporation of European characters into indigenous African plays have become a regular, albeit anachronistic, feature of the performances. Their place within the total structure of the performance, however, shows that although they form a constellation of history, they are only peripheral to the people's lives and worldview. Thus, in the variety of festival and other performances where they are featured, the colonial figures yield the center of the performance space to the enactment of the original myths or stories at the basis of the performance. The foregoing is only a brief overview of indigenous theatrical performances in Africa.

The scholarly debate on the question of indigenous theater and drama in Africa has been conducted by such scholars as Ruth Finnegan (2012: 490), Wole Soyinka (1988: 191), Oyekan Owomoyela (1986: 32), Alain Ricard (1986: 40), Oyin Ogunba (1978: 5), J. Ndukaku Amankulor (1993: 168), Bakary Traoré (1972: 18), and Kofi Awoonor (1976: 69), to name but a few. Indigenous theater and drama are alive and well in contemporary African culture, conflicting theories of the drama notwithstanding. Two main critical tendencies emerge here: the first one held by Wole Soyinka, Bakary Traoré, Oyin Ogunba, and Kofi Awoonor pleads for the recognition of drama in its full meaning in African indigenous performances namely, ritual festivals, initiation rites, masquerades and carnival processions. The second critical position, which dismisses the existence of drama from African cultures *per see*, relocates the emergence of theatrical tradition in Africa within the ambit of European education introduced in colonial days. I side with the second theoreticians. But what engages my attention in this article is not so much the true origins of African drama, but rather the appropriation of it to promote democracy, to dismantle forces of oppression, to rebuff the shackles of unjust domination and struggle for true freedom. In those parts of Africa where Africans are still politically dominated, the need for such social education becomes even more urgent. I will examine the phenomenon of experimentation as a crucial factor in the development of modern African drama and theater. Experimentation flourished in the 1970s and 1980s and promised to significantly affect the African theater for liberation and democracy in the twenty-first century. Examples include Ngugi Soyinka, Osofisan and Maponya.

For instance, J. Ndukaku Amankulor explains in "English Language Drama and Theatre" how Ngugi wa Thiong'o has become one of the most important writers to emerge on the contemporary African scene (Amankulor 1993: 60). Among his most revolutionary contributions to African theater are *The Trial of Dedan Kimathi* (1976), which he co-authored with Micere Mugo, and *I Will Marry When I Want* (1982), an English translation from the Gikuyu of the play *Ngaahika ndeenda* prominently feature in his anti-imperialist plays. *The Trial of Dedan Kimathi* is an interpretation of history. It focuses on Kenyans' heroic struggle for independence. It examines the intensity and commitment of ordinary Kenyan citizens in the social mobilization led by Dedan Kimathi twenty years earlier, during the struggle for independence from the British. The play equally unveils the self-interest of the Kenyan bourgeoisie, and their consequent role aborting this grass roots inspired revolution. *I Will Marry When I Want* according to Ngugi (quoted by Amankulor) "depicts the proletarization of the peasantry in a neo-colonial society" (Amankulor 1993: 161). It is in many ways the follow-up of the events in *The Trial of Dedan Kimathi*, especially after Kimathi's execution. It thus deals with a Kenyan society that is independent only in name, and that is materially and socially controlled and exploited by the erstwhile colonial forces. Focused on the land question, the play shows how a multinational firm owned by Japanese and European businessmen enters into an alliance with their African counterparts to deprive the Kiguunda family of their one-and a-half acres of land, which they depend on for subsistence. As a continuation of the Kimathi-led struggle, for freedom, the play examines how the struggle for independence in Kenya, for which thousands of its citizens died, has now been hijacked by neocolonial forces. Ngugi's commitment to the struggle for real freedom has even prompted him to abandon the English language and to write in Gikuyu and Swahili in order to reach the vast majority of ordinary Kenyans. The English versions of his future works will therefore come only as translations. Still, he uses his essays and critical commentaries on culture and other sociopolitical issues to communicate to a wider English-speaking world. Ngugi's commitment to the use of drama and theater as a potent instrument for mass education to the principles of freedom and democracy through a clearer interpretation of history is great. In *Dedan Kimathi*, the playwright brings the hero down to earth by exposing the suspicious and autocratic dispositions that prompt him to kill Nyati, his best friend and ritual leader of the Mau Mau.

In Nigeria, Wole Soyinka has brought a major contribution to the development of theatre for liberation. In creating *The 1960 Masks*, to stage and perform his plays, Soyinka intended to bring about socio-political reforms in Nigerian society and to create more room for freedom and democracy. According to Oladele Taiwo, Soyinka's troop has stimulated interest in drama and shown that stage can be used as an instrument of social change (Taiwo 1967: 72). It has also demonstrated that stage-acting is not a pastime reserved for irresponsible or unemployed members of the community. *The 1960 Masks* successfully produced *A Dance of the Forests, Dear Parent and Ogre* and *The Republican*. When *The 1960 Masks* became inefficient in performing socio-political plays for reform, Soyinka created the *Orisun Theatre* another troop which performed *The Lion and the Jewel, The Trials of Brother Jero* and *Before the Blackout*. Soyinka's criticism of colonial and neocolonial leadership that shaped the African present destiny characterized by underdevelopment, poverty and squalor is reflected in his political plays. *Opera Wonyosi, A Play of Giants, Kongi's Harvest* and *King Baabu* all criticize and question the contemporary African leadership which has done little to promote the masses freedom from the yoke of poverty, corruption and dictatorship. Mpalive-Hangson Msiska opines that

> The general reconstruction of the development of Soyinka's work with regard to the problem of history and myth closely follows Frantz Fanon's model of literary historical change in the post-colony, whereby the African writer, who during the struggle for liberation from colonialism relies on the past as a way of legitimizing the drive towards political autonomy, counter-identifies with the political elite, who have by this time begun to reproduce an acquisitive bourgeois ideology (Msiska 2007: 3).

This analysis of Soyinka shows the dramatist as a social reformer whose creative vision goes beyond art for art sake as he takes freedom to mean liberation from oppression. Soyinka's vision for freedom is described as a central pillar, pivotal to contemporary efforts to sustain efforts for sustainable development and envisage the possibilities of self-liberation. His works conceptualize democracy in ways that promote and modify critical perceptions of theatre as an instrument of entertainment, to look at it as an effective political tool for sensitization, education and political reforms. Overall, what emerges from analyzing Soyinka's theatre for liberation is the postulation that theatre has the capacity to assume personal and collective agency of self-liberation, and the strengthening of democracy in a context that determines the trajectory of change and ultimately the nature of post-colonial political existence itself. Soyinka's art in this context of performance reveals the content of plays like *King Baabu* as the translation of the dramatist's criticism of dictatorship and the call for democracy implementation. What Soyinka attacks and tries to change is what Kofi Awoonor calls "a system of exploitation without responsibility" (Awoonor 2014: 46).

Femi Osofisan leads the group of new playwrights advocating radical social change. Unlike his predecessors Wole Soyinka, J. P. Clark, and Ola Rotimi, Osofisan is unequivocal in his sympathies with the working masses, and even when they use myth as their backdrop for dramatic action it is manipulated in such a way that the message comes out clearly in favor of radical change. From the early social farce *Who's Afraid of Tai Solarin*, in which Osofisan takes a roll call of corrupt Nigerian citizenry, to the more mature political plays such as *Once upon Four Robbers, Morountodun*, and *The Chattering and the Song* (),[6] he has demonstrated a commitment to social justice and political change. *The Chattering and the Song* is ideologically situated to reflect the struggle of the farmers—the neglected masses of the population—to be free. Their freedom will not materialize until such a time as "everyone's a farmer." In *Morountodun* the playwright demystifies an ancient Yoruba myth by transforming Moremi, the mythical heroine whose self-sacrifice saved Ile-Ife from its erstwhile marauders, into a sympathizer and advocate for the peasants after sharing their material condition. The class war continues in *Once upon Four Robbers*. A group of armed robbers forms a syndicate under the spiritual leadership of Asafa, a babaláwo (seer). As it turns out, the syndicate becomes an instrument for fighting the overprivileged military class. Their principle of robbing public places only but never the poor or private homes demonstrates their sympathy with the underprivileged in society, and the subversive ideological import of the play. The important contribution of Osofisan to the emergence of democracy in Nigeria has probalby informed many critics' claim of him as an emerging voice of African democracy and freedom:

---

[6]Femi Osofisan, *Who Is Afraid of Solarin?* (Ibadan: Ibadan University Theatre,1978), *Once Upon Four Robbers* (Ibadan: BIO Educational Services,1980), *Moruntodun and Other Plays* (Ikeja: Longman Nigeria, 1982), *The Chattering and the Song* (Ibadan: Ibadan University Press, 1977).

> Femi Osofisan's dramaturgy elicits the trajectory and temperament of coming to terms with the contemporary problems and challenges of Africa. These range from military dictatorship, political perfidy and economic corruption, ethnic nationalism, violation of fundamental human rights by the state, to official injustice, mass pauperization through decadent economic policies… The issues Osofisan contends with remain the same: the re-humanization of our dehumanized world through the creative process (Tsaaior 2009: 44).

As said here, not only does Osofisan's dramaturgy elicit the trajectory and temperament of the dramatist's commitment to democracy but it also sets him as a mediator for justice and peace. It is Osofisan's relentless struggle for Nigerian masses' rights for democracy both in drama and society that confers on him the title of a contemporary giant for freedom.

The critic Etherton describes Kabwe Kasoma from Zambia as a committed playwright for freedom and democracy (Etherton: 1982: 178). He has an overriding commitment to creating episodes that talk for the masses. A committed political activist, he uses dramatic art to promote his political ideas about freedom; he was member of the United National Independence Party (UNIP) in Zambia. His *Black Mamba Plays,* a trilogy (Kasoma 1975) is based on Kenneth Kaunda's *Zambia Shall Be Free* and therefore represents the same sort of artistic extension of a political freedom in historical struggle as is observable in the plays of Ngugi . Kasoma means the trilogy not only to portray Kaunda as a political leader but also to propagate his views among the people of Zambia. His interest in theatre that informed the writing of *Black Mamba Plays* springs from his love of the performing arts as a tool for promoting ideas for change, freedom and development. Moreover, Kasoma believes in the potency of drama as a revolutionary tool to impact his society, especially in the use of appropriate linguistic registers to drive home the points of his plays:

> Theatre which engages in art for art's sake is a luxury in Africa. Our theatre must therefore be totally committed to national development. I have always regarded it as a most powerful communication tool in national development plans. I have always seen it as a vehicle for critical appraisal for government plans that are faulty [with all the dangers that this entails for the social health of the dramatist] (Kasoma quoted by Etherton 1982: 179).

Drama is for promoting change from oppression to freedom. The three *Black Mamba* plays may be roughly divided into the three crucial stages in Kaunda's struggle for Zambian nationhood: (I) colonial domination and the inability of even the most qualified Africans to secure suitable jobs in the colonial administration; (2) the political struggle by Africans for independence, including the arrest of the Black Mambas: Nkumbula, Kaunda, Kapwepwe, Kalulu, and Kamanga; and (3) the emergence of an independent Zambian nation. *Black Mamba One* reflects the limited horizon and non-existent job opportunities for even the most intelligent Blacks during the colonial period. *Black Mamba Two* shows the hero Kaunda organizing strikes and protests with the leader of the African National Congress. It shows the Party and Congress being established in rural areas, a sign beckoning to the dramatist's desire to extend democracy to the village folks. *Black Mamba Three* is concerned with the last stages of the struggle for independence, during the Central African Federation, and the final achievement of Zambian nationhood. The struggle for independence and freedom is not only between Africans and white colonialist, but also between Africans themselves in the context of post-independence disillusionment.

Inside South Africa Black drama and theater have been prominent and successful on the cultural front of the war against apartheid. The theatre for liberation against apartheid is better illustrated in Maponya's *The Hungry Earth*. That play focuses on different aspects of apartheid oppression, showing how bad racial segregation can generate many other problems inside the society. Helen Gilbert pinpoints problems like child labour and poverty, family breakdown, dangerous working conditions, state-sanctioned and legally enshrined racism and the restless quelling of strikes (Gilbert 2001: 13). The play reveals apartheid as a servant of capital that supports an ideology of racial superiority to justify industrial exploitation and human subjugation. From this perspective, *The Hungry Earth* is a political play, a lament for the dehumanization of workers and a call for resistance to, and rejection of the oppressive state apparatus. Helen Gilbert estimates that Maponya's theatrical technique partly derives from Bretch and that his play has much in common with African theatre's desire to stimulate debate and encourage community scrutiny. It is a call for racial unity and a symbol of the struggle against white oppression.

Three key ideas have emerged from this analysis: First, drama in the African and Greek contexts has been an important tool for dramatists to express the masses' struggle for democracy. In Greek context, drama was organized around religious festivals and forums organized to debate issues related to public administration of the city, democracy and political leadership. Secondly, in the African context, drama, from religious festivals to the modern plays and stagecraft, has served as a forum for African artists and indigenous practitioners to promote ideas of freedom from colonial yoke and liberation from modern dictatorship; it definitely calls for democracy. Thirdly, perspectives on criticism of African drama reveal the manifestation of art as an instrument beyond entertainment, a medium for fostering theories of cultural materialism about the African neocolonial predicament. The result is that drama still remains a potent instrument for political expression.

References

Amankulor, J. Ndukaku. "English Language Drama and Theatre". In Oyekan Owomoyela (ed.) *A History of Twentieth Century African Literatures.* Lincoln: University of Nebraska Press, 1993. PP. 137-171.
Anene, Joseph C. and Godfrey Brown, (eds.), *Africa in the Nineteenth and Twentieth Centuries.* Ibadan: Ibadan University Press, 1999.
Ansu-Kyeremeh, Kwasi. *Indigenous Communication in Africa: Concept, Application and Prospects.* Accra: Ghana University Press, 2005.
Awoonor, Kofi. *The Breast of the Earth: A Survey of the History, Culture and Literature of Africa South of Sahara.* New York: A Doubleday Anchor Books, 1976.
Bose, Brinda. "Lewis Nkosi". In Pushpa Naidu Parekh and Siga Fatima Jagne, (eds.), *Postcolonial African Writers: A Biobibliographical Critical Sourcebook.* Westport: Greenwood Press, 1998. PP. 332-346.
Chifunyise, Stephen. *I Resign* in *Medicine for Love and Other Plays.* Gweru: Mambo Press, 1984.
Damlègue, Lare. *Diction and Socio-political Vision in the Plays of Wole Soyinka,* thèse de doctorat unique en littérature de l'Afrique Anglophone. Lomé : Université de Lomé, 2011.
Dollimore, Jonathan and Alan Sinfield. *Political Shakespeare: Essays on Cultural Materialism.* Manchester: Manchester University Press, 1994.
Etherton, Michael. *The Development of African Drama.* New York: Africana Publishing Company, 1982.
Finnegan, Ruth. *Oral Literature in Africa.* UK: Open Book Publishers, 2012.
Gibert, Helen. *Postcolonial Plays: an Anthology.* London and New York: Routledge, 2001.
Hussein, Ebrahim N. *Kinjeketile.* Dar es Salam : Oxford University Press, 1985.
Innes, Lyn. *The Cambridge Introduction to Postcolonial Literatures in English.* Cambridge: Cambridge University Press, 2007.

Kasoma, Kabwe. *Black Mamba Two,* in Michael Etherton (ed.), *African Plays for Playing II.* London: Heinemann Educational Books, 1975.

Kerr, David. "Participatory Popular Theatre: The Highest Stage of Cultural Underdevelopment?" In Richard Bjornson (ed.) *Research in African Literatures.* Indianapolis: Indiana University Press, 1991. PP. 55-75.

--------------. "Unmasking the Spirits: Theatre in Malawi". In *Drama Review 31, N°2.* Ibadan: Ibadan University Press, 1987. PP. 105-121.

Msiska, Mpalive-Hangson. *Postcolonial Identity in Wole Soyinka.* Amsterdam: Rodopi, 2007.

Ngugi, wa Thiong'o and Ngugi wa Mirii. *I Will Marry When I Want.* London: Heinemann Educational Publishers, 1982.

------------------------- and Micere Githae Mugo. *The Trial of Dedan Kimathi.* London: Heinemann Educational Publishers, 1982.

Nkosi, Lewis. *The Rhytm and Violence.* London: Oxford University Press, 1964.

Nunley, John. "Purity and Pollution in Freetown Mask Performance". In *Drama Review 32, N°2.* Ibadan: Ibadan University Press, 1988. PP.102-122.

Ogunba, Oyin. "Traditional African Festival Drama". In Oyingunba and Abiola Irele (eds) *Theatre in Africa.* Ibadan: University of Ibadan Press, 1978. PP. 3-26.

Osofisan, Femi. *Once Upon Four Robbers.* Ibadan: Heinemann Educational Books. 1991.

------------------. *Moruntodun and Other Plays.* Ibadan: Longman, 1982.

------------------. *Who Is Afraid of Solarin?* Calabar: Scholar Press. 1978.

------------------. *The Chattering and the Song.* Ibadan: Ibadan University Press, 1977.

Owomoyela, Oyeka. "Give Me Drama or…The Argument on the Existence of Drama in Traditional Africa." In R. Hunt Davis (ed.) *The African Studies Revue,* Vol 28, N°4. California: University of California Press, 1985. PP. 28-43.

Pliya, Jean. « Introduction : Le rôle du théâtre dans le développement culturel en Afrique ». In *Quel théâtre pour le développement en Afrique* ? Paris: Les Nouvelles Editions Africaines, 1965. PP. 11-21.

Ricard, Alain"Theatre Research: Questions about Methodology". In Richard Bjornson (ed.) *Research in African Literatures.* Indianapolis: Indiana University Press, 1986. PP. 38-52.

Schipper-de Leeuw, Mineke. "Origins of Drama in the African Context". In Basil T. Kossou (ed.) *La Tradition orale : Source de la littérature contemporaine en Afrique.* Dakar : les Nouvelles Editions Africaines, 1985. PP. 55-64.

Soyinka, Wole. *King Baabu.* London: Methuen Drama. 2002.

------------------. *Art, Dialogue and Outrage: Essays on Literature and Culture.* Ibadan: New Horn Press, 1988.

------------------. *Opera Wonyosi.* Bloomington: Indiana University Press, 1981.

------------------. *The Jero Plays.* Oxford: Oxford University Press, 1964.

------------------. *The Lion and The Jewel.* Oxford: Oxford University Press, 1963.

Storey, Ian C. and Arlene Allan. *A Guide to Ancient Greek Drama.* New York: Blackwell Publishing, 2005.

Taiwo, Oladele. *An Introduction to West African Theatre.* Lagos: Thomas Nelson and Sons Ltd, 1967.

Taplin, Oliver. *Greek Tragedy in Action.* New York: Routledge, Taylor & Francis Group, 2003.

Thompkins, Jane P. (ed.) *Reader-Response Criticism from Formalism to Post-Structuralism.* Baltimore and London: The John Hopkins University Press, 1984.

Traoré, Bakary. *The Black African Theatre and its Social Functions.* Ibadan: University of Ibadan Press.

Tsaaior, James Tar. "The Postcolonial State and its Texts of Meanings: Femi Osofisan's Dramaturgy as Paradigm". In Tunde Akinyemi and Toyin Falola (eds), *Emerging Perspectives on Femi Osofisan.* Trenton: Africa World Press, 2009. PP. 37-52.

Van Erven, Eugène. " Revolution, Freedom and Theatre of Liberation". In Richard Bjornson (ed.) *Research in African Literatures.* Indianapolis: Indiana University Press, 1991. PP. 11-27.

West, Brad. "Cultural Social Theory". In Anthony Elliott (ed.) *The Routledge Companion to Social Theory.* London and New York: Routledge, 2010. PP. 188-202.

8

MARXIST PERSPECTIVES ON NGUGI WA THIONG'O'S & MICERE GITHAE MUGO'S *THE TRIAL OF DEDAN KIMATHI* AND WOLE SOYINKA'S *KING BAABU*

The burden of this chapter is to examine through Marxist literary aesthetics the articulation of political consciousness of the masses and the vision for freedom and development, Ngugi wa Thiong'o's and Micere Githae Mugo's *The Trial of Dedan Kimathi* and Wole Soyinka's *King Baabu*. It analyses the vision for socio-political reconstruction in two different socio-political contexts: the struggle for independence in *The Trial of Dedan Kimathi* and the struggle for democracy in *King Baabu*. It reasserts that drama as Marxist literature is masses-oriented. It is a medium of expression for the oppressed. Such drama is tilted towards a better society and a redefinition of man within the ambit of humanity. Thus, it attacks man's inhumanity to man.

8.1. Background to Marxism

Karl Marx (1818-1883), a German philosopher, and Friedrich Engels (1820-1895), a German sociologist (as he would now be called), were the joint founders of this school of thought called Marxism. Marx was the son of a lawyer but spent most of his life in great poverty as a political exile from Germany living in Britain (he was expelled after the 1848 'year of revolutions'). Engels had left Germany in 1842 to work in Manchester for his father's textile firm. They met after Marx had read an article by Engels in a journal to which they both contributed. They themselves called their economic theories 'Communism' (rather than 'Marxism'), designating their belief in the state ownership of industry and transport, rather than private ownership. Marx and Engels announced the advent of Communism in their jointly-written *Communist Manifesto* of 1848. Marxism literary criticism comprises: (i) a general theory of human history, postulating the ultimately determinant role therein of successive "economic formations" or modes of production; and (ii) a particular theory of the development, reproduction, and transformation of the capitalist mode of production, identifying one of its principal antagonistic social classes – the proletariat – as the potential historical agency of a transition to communism.

The aim of Marxism is to bring about a classless society, based on the common ownership of the means of production, distribution, and exchange. Marxism is a *materialist* philosophy: that is, it tries to explain things without assuming the existence of a world or of forces beyond the natural world around us, and the society we live in. It looks for concrete, scientific, logical explanations of the world of observable fact. (Its opposite is *idealist* philosophy, which *does* believe in the existence of a spiritual 'world elsewhere' and would offer, for instance, religious explanations of life and conduct). But whereas other philosophies merely seek to understand the world, Marxism (as Marx famously said) seeks to change it. Marxism sees progress as coming about through the struggle for power between different social classes. This view of history as class struggle (rather than as, for instance, a succession of dynasties, or as a gradual progress towards the attainment of national identity and sovereignty) regards it as 'motored' by the competition for economic, social, and political advantage. The exploitation of one social class by another is seen especially in modern industrial capitalism, particularly in its unrestricted nineteenth-century form. The result of this exploitation is *alienation,* which is the state which comes about when the worker is 'deskilled' and made to perform fragmented, repetitive tasks in a sequence of whose nature and purpose he or she has no overall grasp. By contrast, in the older 'pre-industrial' or 'cottage industry' system of manufacture, home and workplace were one, the worker completed the whole production process in all its variety, and was in direct contact with those who might buy the product. These alienated workers have undergone the process of *reification,* which is a term used in Marx's major work, *Das Kapital,* but not developed there. It concerns the way, when capitalist goals and questions of profit and loss are paramount, workers are bereft of their full humanity and are thought of as 'hands' or 'the labour force', so that, for instance, the effects of industrial closures are calculated in purely economic terms. People, in a word, become things.

In the drama and fiction of Ngugi wa Thiong'o and Wole Soyinka, Marxist aesthetics are salient. Freedom from oppression stands as a yardstick that can be used to gauge the social aspirations of characters. The attainment of a better society where social disparities and injustices are reduced to the maximum is the target of the struggles of these writers. Although time and space may separate *The Trial of Dedan Kimathi* (1976) and *King Baabu* (2002), these two plays seem to read as a protest against oppression expressed by the poor peasants and masses against their political leaders. Political independence from white imperialists in Ngugi wa Thiong'o's & Micere Githae Mugo's *The Trial of Dedan Kimathi* and democracy and reduction of corruption in Wole Soyinka's *King Baabu* are the subject matter of masses' struggle in the two plays. For the authors of the two plays, as suggests Adebola Adebambo Ademeso "man is the bedrock and the mainstay of society; he determines the economy, politics and religion of his society" (Ademeso 2009: 54) and the society "is filled with oppressive conditions in the form of class disparity, unequal distribution of wealth and material means, corruption of all forms, killing and assaults, lawlessness, and injustice" (Ibidem). The implication of these statements is that the playwrights project their societies' images with realistic socio-political ills and intend to change them through a positivist vision, from the state of underdevelopment to that of development.

Emphasis will be laid on the articulation of political consciousness of the masses and the ideas of social reconstruction in *The Trial of Dedan Kimathi* and *King Baabu* in two different contexts: the struggle for independence and the struggle for democracy and development. I will bring to the fore the playwrights' ideas of socio-political reconstruction through characterization and the use of dramatic symbols. They are ideas which seek to dismantle the machine of oppression in human life created by fellow human being. I will show that Ngugi's and Soyinka's plays are committed to the up-lifting of the masses. Drama as Marxist literature is masses-oriented. Traditional Marxist literary theory in this approach is helpful to highlight the socialist visions of Ngugi wa Thiong'o and Wole Soyinka. Marxist theory argues that the way characters think and the way they experience the world around them are largely conditioned by the way the political and socio-economic life is organized (Bertens 2001: 82). Thought is subservient to and follows the material conditions under which it develops. If the way people experience reality and the way they think about it – their religious, political, and social views – are determined by the sort of economy they happen to live in, then, there is no such thing as unchanging human condition.

8.1.1. The Birth of Political Consciousness and the Imperatives of Freedom in *The Trial of Dedan Kimathi* and *King Baabu*

8.1.1.1. *Reading History for Socio-political Reconstruction in The Trial of Dedan Kimathi*

Ngugi wa Thiong'o and Wole Soyinka write Marxist literature inclined towards the improvement of the social conditions of the masses. Imperialism and its twin sister capitalism and their corollaries have been a great source of inspiration for Ngugi wa Thiong'o in his literary productions. He has co-authored *The Trial of Dedan Kimathi* with Micere Githae Mugo and has devoted the play to championing the masses' revolts against oppressive state structures (Akinyemi and Falola 2009: 4). He charges the poor and the downtrodden to shake off the shackles of docile acceptance of the tyrannical authority of the White imperialists and rebuff the capitalist oppressors. In the introductory notes to *The Trial of Dedan Kimathi,* the authors Ngugi wa Thiong'o and Micere Githae Mugo inform the reader that the play is an attempt to reproduce in literature the history of "the grandeur of the heroic resistance of Kenyan people fighting foreign forces of exploitation and domination, a resistance movement […] (Ngugi and Mugo 1976: ii). This statement suggests that the struggle of the heroes for political independence from European imperialism by the freedom fighters which culminated in the Mau Mau revolutionary war in Kenya has fuelled thought lines of the play. The play then, is a literary representation of the political struggle for political and economic independence.

Although European colonialism has been a continent-wide phenomenon in Africa, its experimentation has not been the same in all parts of the continent. The colonial yoke imposed by European imperialists on people in East Africa, Kenya namely has included the exploitation and expropriation of the lands from natives with the turning of peasants and workers into labourers on their own lands. These ideas read in the first leader / crowd conversation of the introductory scene entitled First Movement. This implies that Africans have to produce crops on their own lands that eventually belong to European settlers. Africans produce riches on their own lands to give their European masters. This abnormal situation of unjust exploitation and misappropriation of lands, the only indigenous heritage meant to ensure livelihood and survival for majority of peasants creates unhappiness and protest among the masses. That situation has inspired Ngugi wa Thiong'o and Micere Githae Mugo who co-authored *The Trial of Dedan Kimathi*:

> This led us back to Mau Mau, the actual subject of our discussion: was the theme of Mau Mau struggle exhausted in our literature? Had this heroic peasant armed struggle against the British Forces of occupation been adequately treated in our literature? Why was Kenyan literature on the whole so submissive and hardly depicted the people, the masses as capable of making and changing history? […] The writing of *The Trial of Dedan Kimathi* has been both challenging and exciting. It has put as through a lot of education in connection with the continuing struggle against economic and other forms of oppression. (*TTODK:* i-ii)

The writers through this statement present British imperial occupation, their oppression exercised on Kenya citizenry and the masses' reaction for self-liberation as subject matter of the play. Freedom stands as the main target of the masses in uprising against the British imperialist. This seems to be the reason why consciousness awakening becomes crucial. For Ngugi, this point is crucial because, in literature human beings are offered the opportunity to learn from the past, to improve the present so as to better the future (Owonibi 2009: 99). One may be justified to say that literature serves as a means through which the link between the past, the present and the future are highlighted as a way of facilitating a positivist oriented growth of the society (Ibidem). The engine that stirs the wheel of revolution is an acute political consciousness of the masses about their social plight. That consciousness revitalises the senses and mental powers of the masses to understand what is happening around them and undertake actions to come out of their predicament. The birth of political consciousness about oppression in the play is perceived through the statement of Kimathi, the hero of the struggle.

> KIMATHI: The jungle of colonialism? Of exploitation? For it is there that you'll find creatures of prey feeding on the blood and bodies of those who toil: those who make

> the earth yield. Us.
> Those who make the factories roar
> Those who wait and groan for a better day tomorrow
> The maimed Their backs bent Sweat dripping down
> their shoulders […] (*TTODK: 26*)

The speech of Kimathi above highlights the unbecoming conditions or the social plight of the peasants and masses marked by their overexploitation and oppression and continual impoverishment. It depicts the toiling masses in their abject poverty and squalor overworking themselves to produce wealth for the European bourgeois. The African poor peasants and masses work for European landlords and rulers against very meagre wages. They actually produce the riches for which they don't have their share of wealth. That plight has been made bitter by the connivance and betrayal of some Africans crooks who act like middlemen between the European settlers and their African compatriots.

The relevance of a writer is determined by the useful role he or she plays in the portrayal of the social realities of his or her time. Ngugi's commitment to the uplifting of the oppressed masses is demonstrated in *The Trial of Dedan Kimathi* where he has taken upon himself the primary responsibility of educating and orienting the downtrodden of the society. The masses' struggle for independence in East Africa seems to have been fierce, harsh, long and tedious considering how reluctant colonizers were to relinquish their power and grant freedom to Africans. To achieve this, Ngugi and Mugo have depicted characters waging war in bloodshed and swearing oaths of loyalty to their native land and sometimes paying with their own lives. It is in this context that freedom fighters who distinguish themselves through their bravery in independence guerrilla warfare became historic heroes and had their names recorded in the legend of the country, Kenya. In the introductory notes to the play, the playwrights mention names: "Take the heroes and heroines of our history: Kimathi (the hero of the play), Koitalel, Me Kiulini, Mary Nyanjiru, Waiyaki. Why were our imaginative artists not singing songs of praise to these and their epic deeds of resistance" (*TTODK*: i)? Literature here is seen as a mirror that reflects the efforts of people in their combative struggle for freedom. The aspiration of people to freedom and the yearning for liberation come from the articulation of a consciousness which has been itself shaped by the social conditions in which people are living. It is in this context that Michael Etherton a Marxist critic states that:

> It is not the consciousness of men that determines their being, but, on the contrary, their social being that determines their consciousness. What we understand about life has been fabricated in our minds by the way our social and economic system works. In a given social system, the way we relate to people [...] is an expression of that system and makes us think in certain ways (Etherton 1982: 1965).

This suggests for example that, when people are subjected to many years of exploitation and oppression, it appears logic that they develop a consciousness that yearns for freedom. It is to note that in the capitalist system of the play's society, two antagonistic classes emerge from the social tensions created by exploitation of the masses: the bourgeoisie and the proletariat respectively the upper class and the lower class. In *The Trial of Dedan Kimathi,* the bourgeoisie class is made of European colonial settlers like Shaw Henderson judge and prosecutor, Waitina the district officer, British soldiers, Bankers, Business Executive, Politician, and the proletariat essentially made of peasants and labourers like Kimathi, Woman, Boy, Girl, the Crowd, the Guerrilla fighters who are peasants and workers. The struggle is permanent between the two classes, with the masses trying to get a reversal of situation, to get back their lands and obtain fairer deals in the sharing of the wealth they produce. As the critic Za-Ayem Agye posits,

> In a society where capitalism is the dominant mode of production, the two classes continually wage an ideological struggle for the control of production and the distribution of resources. The struggle is a historical necessity inherent in the contradictions within the capitalist relations of production where the producer-majority classes of the working people are exploited and oppressed by the tiny but dominant idle class which controls production. Africa where this exploitation and control of production are being done for the interest of the European bourgeoisie, the struggle for national liberation becomes the more imperative (Agye 1986: 128).

The key idea suggested here is that in a capitalist system as depicted in *The Trial of Dedan Kimathi,* the stratification of society in two antagonistic classes, the bourgeoisie and the proletariat is a noticeable fact. The bourgeoisie owns the means of production, hires the labourers for very low wages and accumulates wealth they produce for themselves. In the case of the Kenyan society of the play, the peasants who own the lands are turned in daily underpaid workers and overwork themselves to yield wealth for their European bosses. It is to note that lands are not bought from Africans but snatched from them. For the Kenyan citizens in the play, the idea that the true landowners have to toil on their land to earn daily their livelihood creates in them dissatisfaction and a political consciousness for revolt and revolution. The actual wealth they produce is being concentrated in the hands of the European capitalists at the apex of power. The masses are embittered against their oppressors and yearn for freedom. As Woman, a character sharply utters it,

> WOMAN: [...] The same old story. Our people... tearing one another
> And all because of the crumbs thrown at them by
> the exploiting foreigners. Our own food eaten
> and leftovers thrown to us in our own land,
> where we should have the whole share. We
> buy wood in our own forest; sweat on our own
> soil for the profit of our oppressors. Kimathi's
> teaching is: unite, drive out the enemy and
> control your own riches, enjoy the fruit of your
> sweat. (*TTODK: 18*)

The woman's complaints in this extract indicates that there is a general dissatisfaction among the population due to the widening gap between the rich and the poor, with as results the continual impoverishment of the masses and the enrichment of the strangers. Few grow richer and richer and many grow poorer and poorer. In addition to that, it is to note that different laws are being used to judge Whites and Blacks, so that social injustice is common practice, with heavy court sentences and penalties weighing on Africans. This unjust system is being outcried and denounced by Kimathi.

8.1.1.2. The Birth of Political Consciousness and the Imperatives of Development in King Baabu

Although the context of the struggle in *King Baabu* is different from the one in *The Trial of Dedan Kimathi* in time and space, there are converging points in the nature of the struggle and the objectives being pursued in the two plays appears to be the same. *The Trial of Dedan Kimathi* is set in a fictional Kenyan society in the years preceding its independence, while Soyinka's *King Baabu* is set in the post-independent contemporary Nigerian society during the Sani

Abacha rule (Habila 2006: 139). Soyinka's subject matter in *King Baabu* is a revolutionary struggle of the masses against the oppression and exploitation of implacable dictator rulers. But more than that, the playwright depicts an ideological class struggle between the bourgeoisie – exemplified by the political leaders and their army officers and the proletariat epitomized by the suffering masses, workers and peasants (*KB: 87*) Unmistakably, the society is stratified in two social classes, the upper class and the lower one in perpetual conflicts of interests. The criticism being levelled at the bourgeois by the proletariat is what they call "bourgeois deviationism and criminal adventurism" (*KB: 87*) which means their capitalist tendency to trample down and over-exploit the working class of poor peasants and workers.

The play *King Baabu* reflects the temper and sensibility of a society where there is a gulf of separation between the rich and the poor. In the words of the critic Henri Oripeloye, Soyinka reveals the reality of existence in the contemporary world where avarice, unbridled lust for wealth and power, and class discrimination are prevalent (Oripeloye 2009: 112). Soyinka's intention is to reform society and, in his pursuit of anti-capitalist ideology he shows the potentials of drama as a tool to reshape the African societies, if not in a Marxian activist way, at best in an analytic, gradualist method which strives towards the ideal of human perfection (Oripeloye 2009: 112). Class struggle is ideological and aims at the kind of revolution that will turn upside down the proletariat and bourgeois present positions. That is the kind of social change Rout qualifies as "revolutionary justice" (*KB: 87*). The playwright doesn't conceal his portraiture of the main character Baabu whom he qualifies as a power-drunk king blinded by thirst for dominance and master of megalomania (*KB: 61-62*). There is much in common with the struggle of the masses in *The Trial of Dedan Kimathi* because in *King Baabu*, the imperialist tendency of the dictators like King Baabu (formerly named Basha Bash), General Potipoo, General Rajinda seems inherited from British imperialist system, tracing its source back to the colonial period. The nature of oppression seems to be the same because it is political and economic. It is political because the rulers in the play have set up mechanisms to prevent the masses' participation to political life and power management; and it is economic because capitalism is the order of the day; a system in which the masses work hard only to yield wealth for the bosses while they themselves remain poor. According to the comments of *The Observer,* a magazine which reviewed the play,

> *King Baabu* chronicles the debauched rule of General Basha Bash,

who takes power in a coup and exchanges his general's uniform for a rob and crown. In the manner of Alfred Jarry's *Ubu Roi*, this is a ferocious, crackpot satire of the plague of dictatorship on the African continent. Waving together burlesque comedy, theatrical excess and story telling, it has been hailed as a brilliant parody of political regimes in Africa and beyond.[7]

Through this excerpt, Soyinka is revealed as a social reformer exposing the flaws of African leadership with the aim to change it from bad to good manners. In the oppressive regime of Basha Bash – who later takes the title of King Baabu- , people are exploited and oppressed. One form of oppression is the violent repression of all forms of protest or disagreement with authority. Under Basha Bash people do not have freedom of speech or expression. The ruler wants absolute authority and submission of the whole nation. Expressing an opinion different from the king's is interpreted as a rebellion or mutiny and must be severely repressed:

> BASHA: Those who disagree with authority are mutineers and only
> One answer to mutineer (*KB: 34*)

If disagreeing with authority is synonymous with mutiny, then, Basha Bash's regime is dictatorial and oppressive. In other words, Basha's regime is despotic and a despotic regime is inclined to oppression. Soyinka here is exposing a system privative of freedom of people and expression and, as the critic Helon Habila says,

> Soyinka's writings have always been consistent in condemning all forms of despotic and irresponsible regimes in Nigeria and Africa as a whole [...] *King Baabu* is more direct in its handling of its subject matter than his other works that treat a similar theme (Habila 2006: 139).

This enhances my critical stand that oppression and exploitation are of date in the society depicted in the play and Soyinka wants this situation to change. Exploitation is also seen through the huge taxes imposed on them by the

---

[7]This information is taken from the backcover page of the play *King Baabu*.
Wole Soyinka, *King Baabu* (London: Methuen Publishing Limited, 2002)

king, the destination of which is the enrichment of the royal purse. Taxes are not collected to finance development projects or improve the masses' living conditions but to make the king and his family rich. The masses are compelled to pay heavy taxes without being told the final destination of these taxes. But when an inquisitive citizen Tikim, an officer and brother to the king's wife, wants to know about them, the king is outraged and rejects the question as being foolish:

> KPOKI: King Baabu, what of the per capita war levy you imposed on the entire population, man, woman and child? Where is all the dedicated account from the oil revenue?
> BAABU: Dedicated to the royal purse – don't waste my time with foolish questions. (*KB: 67*)

Oppression features in the play when observed from the way in which mutinies and uprising groups are being repressed by the military men. The birth of political consciousness about oppression among the masses and their decision to claim for freedom come from the awareness of the common plight and the aspiration to the same objective: freedom. King Baabu's own perception and opinion of rebellion is that it is indigestible and inimical to the state and as such, should be severely repressed:

> BAABU: Nothing can make a rebel palatable, mind you. A rebel is the stringiest mammal of God's creation, totally indigestible and inimical to state and stomach. (*KB: 82*)

Comparing *King Baabu* and *The Trial of Dedan Kimathi*, there are common features. Firstly, the writers depict society from the vantage point of Marxist thinking, where the masses – peasants and workers – are being exploited by oppressive capitalist leaders and protest in unison to free themselves from such oppressive bosses. Secondly, the struggle is revolutionary in nature because peaceful negotiations have failed to meet satisfactory answer. Thirdly, the struggle has been possible through intellectual organization of the masses by heroes: Kimathi in *The Trial of Dedan Kimathi* and Rout, the Trade Union leader in *King Baabu*.

8.1.2. Marxist Dramatic Symbols Expressive of Political Consciousness

In *The Trial of Dedan Kimathi*, the playwrights' depiction of characters and their actions provide another approach to drama through Marxist symbolism. Not only language but also events of the play may be infused with symbolic meanings. Marxist symbols are the language, objects and tools that the lower-class use to express their anger against political leaders. J. L. Styan, a theorist of symbolic drama has highlighted that idea by saying that "a verbal symbol is intended to evoke feelings and ideas greater than those the words usually stand for, suggesting a meaning beyond its immediate and concrete reality" (Styan 1981: 1).

Dramatic symbols are the bedrock on which rests the true meaning of a play. In *The Trial of Dedan Kimathi*, the events are woven around three movements which have symbolic meanings: the first movement is a recall of the historical context of the present struggle against imperialism. Salient events are the Mau Mau war, especially the critical phase of the war and Kimathi's arrest and detention in Nyeri. War here is the symbol of revolution and change. It took place in mountains and forests. The mountains symbolise obstacles in altitude and forests stand for vertical barriers. The playwrights are presenting Kimathi as the hero and symbol of the revolution, the true leader of the masses, the father of independence. He incarnates the hopes of freedom and is the epitome of development. A true patriot and nationalist, he is leading the Kenyan people from the oppression of the colonial yoke to independence and true development. If we analyse the war armaments used by the war leader Kimathi and his fellow freedom fighters, we can see tools like shield, guns, bullets, spears, and machetes. The shield used by the freedom fighters in the Mau Mau revolution is represented on the Kenyan flag, and we need to comment on it. The flag is symbolic. It was officially adopted on December 12, 1963. The design of the Kenyan flag is a horizontal tricolour of black, white-edged red, and green with two crossed white spears behind a red, white, and black Maasai shield. The colour black symbolises the black majority in the country, red stands for the bloodshed during the fight for freedom, and green for land; the white fimbriation was added later and symbolises peace and honesty. The black, red, and white traditional Maasai shield and two spears symbolize the defence of all things mentioned above (En.wikipedia.org/wiki/Flag_of_kenya#Symbolism). These symbolical images on the flag trace their roots back to the Mau Mau revolution of the Kimathi days.

The Trial of Dedan Kimathi is a play for revolution. Since Kimathi is the hero and leader of the revolution, his capture is symbolic and stands for the seizure of the Kenyan people's freedom. He is the eponymous character of the play. His trial is memorial and eventful. It is memorial and eventful because, while the British colonialists see in this trial an occasion to condemn and silence the Africans' resistance forces, for Kimathi and his people, it is a rendez-vous with history, an opportunity to tell the truth about the unjust exploitation of the African resources, the wicked snatching of the Africans' lands, and the inhuman nature of the oppression to the White imperialists. The final objective of this public revelation of the truth to the Colonizer is to urge him to grant independence to Africans, to re-establish justice and return the stolen lands and properties to Africans. Kimathi also sees in this trial an opportunity to teach Africans the sense of political resistance, the price to pay for commitment to social change for those who have come to witness the trial. History records him as the hero of independence, and his name and feats will go down in the annals of Kenyan history. He becomes a reference and an icon for future generations. He becomes the inspiring model for the future patriots. He will inspire the younger generations in their nationalist struggles for development. He has laid a solid foundation and set up the pillars on which the country's future leaders will build the edifice of economic, social and political development. He is also the symbol of unity and bravery. He rallies the people to act like one man and to speak with one voice. That is why during his trial the masses have come in great number to support him. Drama being the representation and enactment of social life on stage, the watching of the images created by the playwrights will most definitely instil in the Kenyan spectators the republican virtues of patriotism and nationalism. It will foster in them the ideals and values of patriotism. The critic J. L. Styan's opinion is in line with mine when he says that " […] the existence of drama itself suggests there is an abiding need for symbolic representation. Symbolism in the theatre can therefore exist alongside realism, or it can eliminate realistic illusion entirely" (Styan, op. cit: 1). This points to the fact that dramatic symbols lend full meaning to a play. In the context of *The Trial of Dedan Kimathi,* the representation of the hero Kimathi on stage will instigate in the minds of the youths the desire to serve their country and to develop it. History being the mirror of human existence, in it, we look at the past to understand the present and to prepare for a better future. I maintain that Ngugi wa Thiong'o and Micere Githae Mugo have written an anti-imperialist drama for development and social reconstruction.

The second movement presents another phase of the court in session where the Africans enter the court clad in rags. Symbolically, the rags stand for deterioration and deprivation but the dressing in rags or torn clothes stands for the resistance efforts made by Africans to oppose the Whiteman's oppression. Thus the total meaning is that the masses can resist against oppression even in the midst of poverty and squalor. The flashbacks in this movement reveal Kimathi's explanation of Eurocentric ways: there exist two kinds of laws in the same country, one for "the man of wealth," and another for "the poor" (*TTDK*: 25-26). This system is unjust and needs to change, and Kimathi has said it to the White judges. The third movement brings together the portrait of Kimathi and the story of how the Woman brings Boy and Girl into the struggle. It is a metaphor, which describes the rally of the masses for a stronger resistance and an eventual victory for freedom. These characters display wisdom and courage and metaphorically stand for the future potentials in the nation. Kimathi can rest assured that there are among the young people in the crowd some imbued with patriotic virtues and nationalist bravery, who can take over from him, for the struggle to continue.

The Trial of Dedan Kimathi is a play for socio-political reform. It aims at social reconstruction. Such drama presents characters who represent a larger humanity and their actions are endowed with significance beyond the immediate story being played on the stage. The woman, the boy and the girl simply called Woman, Boy and Girl in the play are symbols and are established as representatives of the oppressed. They are archetypes symbolising the masses behind the hero Kimathi. Their objective is to give moral and material support to the leader of revolution. In other words, they are vectors of change. Objects are also symbols: the bread that Woman holds represents food or agriculture. It indicates that the revolution aims at the re-conquest of the lands from where food is to be produced. The gun is the tool to be used to fight the White imperialist; and it symbolises the legitimisation of violence in the context of the struggle for political freedom. The female characters metaphorically stand for fertility, the hope for the fertilization of people and their efforts to generate freedom and development. In analysing *The Trial of Dedan Kimathi*, social uprising and claims for freedom come as a resultant of consciousness awakening where the role played by heroes and the masses is crucial.

The sharpening of political consciousness is the result of mass sensitization done by the hero Kmathi and can be noted both in the leader and the masses. Such consciousness aims at the liberation of African peoples worldwide from the incapacitating effects of colonialism and neo-colonialism. To achieve that liberation, Ngugi and Soyinka believe that there is an urgent need for the re-education of African peoples and drama is the way *par excellence* to achieve that goal (Anyidoho 2012: 81). The force of the masses is in their number. The more numerous they are behind their leader, the more effective is the toning of their voice to be heard. As a result Kimathi has achieved independence, one of the important steps towards development. At the same time, that consciousness is the tumbler that can spur out and liberate the energy potentials for true change and development. The achievement of social development among the working peasants and masses is the rational behind uprising and protest movements in the play. Chidi Amuta, a Nigerian critic believes that "This development, which is a logical consequence of the relative explosion in social development in the decade […], has also been characterized by an unprecedented awakening of political consciousness […] (Amuta 1989: 53). In *The Trial of Dedan Kimathi*, the strategies and methods of the struggle are designed by the legendary hero Dedan Kimathi having the support of the masses. The hero plays the role of intellectual in society by sensitizing the masses about their unbecoming social plight and the possibility of change:

> KIMATHI: We stood on Githuri hill […]
> We asked ourselves
> How long shall we […]
> Allow our people to continue
> Slaves of hunger, disease, sorrow
> In our own lands
> While foreigners eat
> And snore in bed with fullness? (*TTODK: 38*)

Here Kimathi plays the role of a leader defending the cause of the masses. He is the head of the people planning and working out strategies to implement to obtain social reforms. He starts by questioning the duration of their plight, by asking when people's sufferings will end. That question presupposes that the leader is concerned with the social liberation of the masses. He has the burden of planning and initiating a social agenda for revolutionary struggle for people's freedom and better living conditions. He has implemented that social agenda by organizing his fellow freedom fighters into troupes who fought and re-conquered the lands. His statements above reveal social disparities which need to be reduced; disparities seen in the luxurious and opulent living of the capitalist bosses – White men essentially - and the abject poverty and squalor of the masses. His thinking is a Marxist one because it is readable from his statements that he has a socio-political vision, a desire to overhaul, and even to somersault the prevailing order of the social classes and to have the masses take the social lead. As critic G. D. Killam says,

> Dedan Kimathi fought for the total liberation of the Kenya people from foreign domination and oppression. He did not achieve this in his lifetime: the struggle continues and Kimathi is the legitimate hero of the revolution. Ngugi and his colleague Micere Githae Mugo have collaborated in writing a play with a number of specific purposes. It is a song of praise for the feats of leadership and resistance of the most brilliant of the generals of independence struggle […] (Killam 1980: 86).

Through this critical stance of G. D. Killam, the qualities of Kimathi as a hero, a leader, a patriot and an intellectual are well stated. He is hero because of the courage and bravery with which he speaks for the masses in the play. He is a leader because he is at the top of the masses and actually shows them the way, that is the manner in which they can better organize themselves. He is a patriot because he loves his country, for which he takes an oath of loyalty and fights for its liberation. He is an intellectual because he uses his knowledge to enlighten his compatriots, to shed light on people in society. In the play, we note that the very reason why Kimathi is standing trial after his arrest by the British armed forces is his protest against white imperialism and his attempt to organize people to fight for liberation. He acts in public in defiance to white authority which he looks upon down. Kimathi, then is a committed political activist of his society and time. As a leader, he has the support of the masses. His sense of social organization as a strategy for effecting change is readable in his address to the masses:

> KIMATHI: [Addressing the people]
> So, go!
> Organize in your homes
> Organize in the mountains
> Know that your only
> Kindred blood is he
> Who is in the struggle

> Denounce those who weaken
> Our struggle by creating ethnic divisions
> Uproot from you those
> Who are selling out to imperialism
> Kenyan masses shall be free! (*TTODK:* 83-84)

Here, the role of the masses is determinant in the struggle, for they are numerous and united behind Kimathi. The masses are called and urged to organize themselves. The social organization should be done in homes and outside and unity must prevail. Through his message unity transpires as a cornerstone that can sustain lasting efforts for freedom achievement. That is probably the reason why he urges his fellow citizens to uproot and erase ethnic discriminations among them and to fight like one man. Here, the call still bears some social relevance even though the message was delivered to people in colonial time. For one thing, ethnic cleavages, sources of social tensions are still a burning problem in our contemporary society and there is need for a peaceful coexistence and harmonious development in society to erase them through mass sensitization. Thus, Ngugi's and Micere's play can be classified as theatre for development, in that it calls for constructive social reforms. By extolling the legendary feats of the hero Kimathi the playwrights are possibly suggesting the need for contemporary African citizens to cultivate a sense of patriotism, the kind that will urge them to work hard to develop their nations.

In Soyinka's *King Baabu* the struggle for freedom comes from the masses whose representative shows diligence in matters related to their claims. Soyinka also uses dramatic symbolism. He uses caricature and metaphors to expose the autocratic rule of Basha Bash, whom he ironically names King Baabu. Soyinka uses a lot of metaphors to poke fun at the present Nigerian rulers. Reviewers of the play and critics argue that Basha Bash (King Baabu) is a satirical depiction of Sani Abacha (Habila 2006: 138), who led the country from November 1993 to June 1998 (Soyinka 2006). In fact Soyinka gives the title king to Basha Bash because that characters wants to remain president for life. It is a metaphor in the sense that he substitutes the title president to that of king. It is also satire because, in Hausa language, "baabu" means "nothing or emptiness", so Soyinka is presenting his character as a king who has nothing in terms of competence to offer to the population, but yet is asking to remain a ruler for life. Dramatic symbols transpire in Act Two, Scene two where King Baabu goes to consult an Oriental Mystic and a Marabout. The crown symbolises Baabu's royal authority. His kingship is metaphorically labelled a dynasty, because, he wants to secure the throne for him and his descendants alone. In the process of the Marabout's divination, mythical symbols are presented and their meaning revealed to the king.

As the philosophy critic Kwame Gyekye points it out, symbolism is a potent medium of artistic production, expression, or appreciation; meaning and ideas are given expression through symbolic art (Gyekye 2003: 127). Soyinka uses these devices to emphasize irony and satire in the delineation of that character. King Baabu resorts to divination and magic to make himself invincible. But ironically, his actions in society contradict sharply with what he should normally do to be loved by his people. He starves the population. He uses force to repress the people when they up-rise. There is no democracy in the country. But the popular masses aspire to freedom, democracy and development. Soyinka shows through these symbols the gap between a leader and a ruler. A leader seeks to gain the masses' confidence through his competence and wisdom to manage people but a ruler seeks power through superstition. These symbols highlight Baabu's short-sightedness as a ruler.

Since King Baabu relies on magic and superstition to make his kingship indestructible, Soyinka is showing these symbols as the elements that make him become too self-confident in his magical powers and to fearlessly oppress the masses. King Baabu relies on his magical powers to exercise his tyranny on the masses. At the same time it is this tyrannic attitude that makes the masses suffer and rebel against him.

It is Baabu's resort to magic to rule for life and the cumbersome social conditions he creates for people to live in that constitute the object of social grumbling and unhappiness among the population. Then, I can say that the resort to magic in which many symbols transpire constitutes the far-reaching element that will provoke the consciousness awakening in the masses, since Baabu relies on his magical powers to believe that he is untouchable and therefore he can inflict sufferings to his people without being punished or challenged. Thus, mythical symbols can be seen as vectors contributing indirectly to the birth and awakening of political consciousness in the masses. They also stand as the remote causes of Baabu's failure as a leader, because, being blinded by superstition, he disregards the rules of democracy and this causes the population to rebel against his autocratic rule.

Revolution in the play comes as a solution to call back to reason the abusive malpractices of a ruler, King Baabu who promises much but gives little. Rent and Dope have organized the masses for a social revolution. Through protest, mass rallies, sitting they have brought King Baabu to revisit his leadership. Baabu is a demagogue and does not keep his promises. I make this critical statement because, at the early period of his seizure of power, he promised democracy, freedom of speech, equal chances and opportunities to all citizens, fair share of the country's wealth to citizens, but such promises never materialized. On the contrary, the masses note the worsening of living conditions. Patrick Ebewo's critical approach falls in this line: "This promise never materialised as Gatu's citizens are only open to poverty. His rule is the most damaging to the nation as the economy stagnates and several rebellions are brutally crushed" (Ebewo 2002: 166). This makes Rout openly state that "Revolution begins from the grass roots, never from the top" (*KB: 14*). The underlying meaning of this statement is that, masses are those who will most definitely initiate revolution as their top leaders show no volition to change. The revolutionary slogans are being chanted by the masses in unison and change is readable in the very words they utter:

> CROWD: Enough of army rascals.
> Down with Rajinda
> Down with Potipoo
> Away with Basha Bash.
> Down with the Army
> Long live Democracy. (*KB: 41*)

By saying "enough of", "down with", "away with" the crowd is making bold statements about its desire for change, its longing for revolution. Three names are mentioned, Rajinda, Potipoo and Basha Bash/King Baabu, three political leaders who have successively assumed political power without bringing the expected socio-political reforms in the country, Gatu and alleviating the sufferings of the masses. The military rule instituted by these rulers has not given chance to democracy to grow, the result of which is the unhappiness created in the people. The organization of the crow deserves some attention here, because, it shows some maturity of people who, in spite of the fact that the leader or representative is not there, they are able to organize themselves and claim for democracy. Elsewhere in the play, the masses scan slogans showing dissatisfaction with the leaders:

> RENT: Our people are groaning.
> DOPE: The heavens are weeping
> RENT: The earth is wailing
> DOPE: The very stones are bleeding

> RENT: Our ancestors have spoken. Their anger is in the thunder
> DOPE: Their lamentations are rains of fire [...]
> DOPE: Our women are violated (they exchange glances) Indeed Why hide it?
> RENT: Why hide what is known to the entire nation? Even men and Have not been spared. (*KB: 88-89*)

Here, it is perceptible that there is a certain organization of the masses by their representatives, their leaders who carry their petitions to the ruler. Rent, representative of the Royal Estates, Nominal and Traditional and Dope, the representative of the Divine Order of Prelates Ecumenical have carried their petitions to Potipoo. It is to note that the masses have a common leader. Like in *The Trial of Dedan Kimathi*, protest against oppression and struggle for the liberation of the masses in *King Baabu* is being organized by masses' representatives. Here, Rent and Dope appear to play the same role as Dedan Kimathi, the hero of Mau Mau revolution in *The Trial of Dedan Kimathi*. In both plays, the reading shows a development of political consciousness in the masses who strive to attain liberation from the imperialism of capitalist bourgeois. The common point in Soyinka and Ngugi is the shared hatred of capitalism and oppressive regimes as the causes of the continuing poverty and despair of the working masses and of the peasants in the third world. The socialist view is related to the struggle for independence in Kenya and that for democracy and development in Nigeria. Through drama, group behaviour can be influenced and the playwrights are using the stage to reinforce patriotic values.

In my analysis of *The Trial of Dedan Kimathi* and *King Baabu* I have laid emphasis on three key ideas. First, the social conditions in which people live shape their political consciousness in a certain way, and they undertake actions to free themselves from their oppressor and to write their own history. Second, drama serves a social purpose in that it is a tool used to speak for the masses. Ngugi wa Thiong'o & Micere Githae Mugo and Wole Soyinka have used their art to uplift the downtrodden of the society. Through the representation of social problems on stage, scenes of revolution are re-enacted, symbols and their meanings are explained and the theatre audiences draw important teachings. Third, social reconstruction may pass through an objective reading of history, and as such, past events should help a people to readjust their present actions in order to build a positive and meaningful future. In a context where man is the torturer of his fellow man, man-made oppressive structures can be dismantled by fellow man if there is good will.

Works Cited

Soyinka, Wole. *King Baabu*. London: Methuen Publishing Limited. 2002.

Ademeso, Adebola Adebambo. "National Development and the Concept of Compassion in Osofisan's *Esu and the Vagabond Minstrels*." In Tunde Akinyemi and Toyin Falola eds. *Emerging Perspectives on Femi Osofisan*. Trenton: Africa World Press. 2009. 53-63

Agye, Za-Ayem. "Towards a People's Literature of Socio-political Awareness in Ernest N. Emenyonu (ed.) *Literature and Society: Selected Essays on African Literature*. Nigeria: Zim Pan African Publishers. " 1986. 127-145

Akinyemi, Tunde and Toyin Falola. *Emerging Perspectives on Femi Osofisan*. Trenton: Africa World Press. 2009.

Amuta, Chidi. "The Nigerian Woman as a Dramatist: The Instance of Tess Owueme" in Henrietta C. Otekunefor and Obiageli C. Nwodo (eds) *Nigerian Female Writers: A Critical Perspective*. Lagos: Malthouse Press Limited. 1989. 53-59.

Anyidoho, Kofi. "Literary Visions of a 21st Century Africa: A Note on the Pan African Ideal in Ghanaian Literature" in Anne V. Adams ed. *Essays in Honour of Ama Ata Aidoo at 70 A Reader in African Cultural Studies*. UK: Ayebia Clarke Publishing Limited. 2012. 80-85.

Bertens, Hans. *Literary Theory The Basics*. Routledge: Taylor & Francis Group. 2001.

Ebewo, Patrick. *Barbs A Study of Satire in the Plays of Wole Soyinka*. Kampala: JANyeka Publishing Center. 2002.

Etherton, Michael. *The Development of African Drama*. New York: Africana Publishing Company. 1982.

Gyekye, Kwame. *African Cultural Values An Introduction*. Ghana: Sankofa Publishing Company. 2003.

Habila, Helon. "Drama and Poetry by Wole Soyinka". In Ernest N. Emenyonu, ed. *New Directions in African Literature*. Oxford: James Curry. 2006. 138-142.

Hatlen, Theodore W. *Orientation to the Theatre*. New York: Appleton- Century- Crofts. 1962.

Killam, G. D. *An Introduction to the Writings of Ngugi*. London. Nairobi. Ibadan : Heinemann Educational Books. 1980.

N'Dah, Pierre Ayoun. *Regard sur… moderniser l'état africain*. Abidjan : Les édition du CERAP. 2003.

Ngugi, wa Thiong's & Micere Githae Mugo. *The Trial of Dedan Kimathi*. Nairobi: Heinemann Educational Book. 1976.

Ogunjimi, Bayo and Abdul-Rasheed Na'Allah. *Introduction to African Oral Literature and Performance*. Trenton: Africa World Press. 2005.

Oripeloye, Henri. " Reordering Humanity: Femi Osofisan's Backward Glance in *One Legend, Many Seasons*" in Tunde Akinyemi and Toyin Falola (eds). *Emerging Perspectives on Femi Osofisan*. Trenton: Africa World Press. 2009. 108-112.

Owonibi, Sola. "The Political Consciousness in African Literature: A Critical Analysis of Selected Plays of Femi Osofisan" in Tunde Akinyemi and Toyin Falola eds. *Emerging Perspectives on Femi Osofisan*. Trenton: Africa World Press. 2009. 99-106

Styan, J. L. *Modern Drama in Theory and Practice 2 Symbolism, Surrealism and the Absurd*. London. New York Sydney: Cambridge University Press. 1981.

Ngugi, wa Thiong'o. *Homecoming Essays on African and Caribbean Literature, Culture and Politics*. New York. Westport: Lawrence Hill and Company. 1972.

Soyinka, Wole. "The Critic and Society : Barthes, Leftocracy and Other Mythologies" in *Arts, Dialogue & Outrage Essays on Literature and Culture.* Ibadan: New Horn Press. 1988. 146-178

----------------- . *You Must Set Forth at Dawn*. USA: Random House Trade Paperbacks. 2006.

Traoré, Bakary. *The Black African Theatre and its Social Functions* (Translated by Dapo Adelugba). Ibadan: Ibadan University Press. 1972.

Webliography

En.wikipedia.org/wiki/Flag_of_kenya#Symbolism.

9

FEMINIST PERSPECTIVES OF AFRICAN FEMALE DRAMATISTS

This chapter looks into the African female playwrights' feminist inclinations and their broader perspectives on women's problems, gender concerns and womanist ethics. Female playwrights in Africa have been interested in the questions of feminism in general and the positive change of their living conditions in particular. Despite this growing interest and concern on behalf of women, Feminism has been a controversial issue in African literature. The main argument of the study is that African female dramatists have been theorizing a feminist theory of their own laying emphasis on the specific political, social, economic and cultural factors that call for a contextualization of the theory and a perception of the feminist problems from the African angle. Three main feminist waves have been pointed out with specific writers who are to be reckoned with when it comes to debating women's questions: the first wave with pioneers like Efua T. Sutherland, Flora Nwapa, Ama Ata Aidoo, Nawal Al Sadawi, Ama Ata Aidoo, the second wave with writers like Chinyere Grace Okafor and Irene Isoken Oronsaye-Salami and Zainab Jalo. The Third wave of African feminist dramatists include Emerging Voices like Ade Solanke.

9.1. Conceptualising Feminism

As feminism originated from the West, African female scholars have been reluctant to accept the Western meaning of the word feminism and have bargained for an African variant. It then became imperious to define an African variant of feminism that takes into account the specificity of African cultures, political and economic conditions under which women live. Feminism of global sisterhood has been contested as unrealistic and inappropriate to local realities, regional differences based on history, culture, politics, education and economy. However, the fundamentals of the feminist ideology, that is, the liberation of women from oppressive structures and unjustly imposed living conditions have been of interest to women worldwide, including the African woman. Not until recently in Africa, before the famous hue and cry of the Nigerian contemporary female writer Chimamanda Ngozi Adichie that "We Should All Be Feminists" (2014), African creative writers were not outspoken in their identification of themselves as feminists. Yet, when analyzing plays written by African women, feminism emerges as a tantalizing force that sustains women's theatrical creativity and the fuel that move the engines of their literary inspiration. From this perspective, what are the feminist dramatic poetics that command critical attention from scholars and how do African female playwrights express their visions of the world free from women's subjugation and oppression? Carole R. McCann and Seung-kyung Kim in *Feminist Theory Reader: Local and Global Perspective* (2013) assert that in a broad sense,

> feminism refers to political activism by women on behalf of women, the objective of which is the liberation of females from patriarchal oppression and from all forms of injustice perpetrated by male-ruled society and institution. The term originated in France in the 1880s. It combines the French word for woman "femme", with the suffix meaning political position, "ism". And was used in the time and place to refer to those who defended the cause of women. Widely used in the US women's movements beginning in the 1970s, it indicated opposition to women's subordinate social positions, spiritual authority, political rights, and/or economic opportunities. However, beyond that general descriptions, the meaning of feminism has never been historically stable or fixed. For all its ambiguity and limitations, the term signals an emancipatory politics on behalf of women. It contends that the prevailing unjust conditions under which women live must be changed. Moreover, it assumes that a group of historical agents – women – will take action to change them (McCann and Kim 2013: 1).

She further explains that feminist theories, like other political philosophies provide intellectual tools by which historical agents can examine the injustices they confront and build arguments to support their particular demands for change. Feminist theories apply their tools to building knowledge of women's oppression. That knowledge is intended to inform strategies for resisting subordination and improving women's living conditions. Feminist theories formulate questions of the following kind: How do gender difference structures subordinate women because of their nature as women? How can one understand the ways in which specific events result from gender oppression rather than unique individual misfortune? How is women's subordination as women connected to related oppression based on race, ethnicity, nationality, class and sexuality? The critical analyses that follow will attempt to discuss these issues in the light of the selected African female playwrights' works.

Drama has been a privileged tool of expression of feminist ideals by African female playwrights. Perhaps, one of the reasons of that privileged choice is the capacity of drama to reach the masses, both the educated and uneducated. Pioneers like Zulu Sofola, Buchi Emecheta, Tess Onwueme, Efua T. Sutherland, Micere Githae Mugo, have used dramatic literature to claim for more voice and space for women. Contemporary female playwrights like Chinyere Grace Okafor, Irene Isoken Oronsaye-Salami and Ade Solanke equally see in dramatic art a powerful critical medium to be used to proclaim women' s liberation discourse, to highlight women' s feminist petitions and to echo gender equality message. In examining their works, I will explain what African feminist literary theory entails and channel it with African dramatic literature by women. African Feminist critical theory examines in literature the socio-political and cultural forces that inform the subjection and oppression of women and from there advocate positive change for them. The main target of African feminist struggles has been patriarchy, male phallocentric hegemony and power structures. Feminism as a political and social movement has been a response to injustices done to women throughout the time and cultural geographic spaces. Such injustices include the refusal of the right to vote, the inequalities in salaries, refusal to education, and sexual harassments. Let us note that feminism comes into different phases and different historical periods with relatively different objectives. African women and Third world women have claimed different variants of feminisms that apply to their specific cultural differences and historical realities. Alison Bailey and Chris Cuomo posit that:

> At the heart of feminism is a moral judgment from the perspectives of the subjugated—usually women—and an argument that the systematic mistreatment and devaluation of females cross-

culturally is a paradigmatic human harm with grave and pervasive consequences. Feminism is therefore also a positive judgment that with emancipation for women will come widespread human improvement. Feminist philosophy is grounded in the premise that in patriarchal, sexist, or male-dominated contexts, women's wisdom on the matters that affect them is crucial. However, in such contexts, "woman" is seen as a diverse social category, not a universal experience or body type, because women and their interests are immeasurably diverse. Instead of promoting a female essence, feminist philosophers investigate the patterns, histories, and systemic nature of women's oppression and feminist resistances (Bailey and Cuomo 2008: 1).

African Feminism is a struggle to end sexist oppression. Therefore, it is necessarily a struggle to eradicate the ideology of domination that permeates Western culture on various levels as well as a commitment to reorganizing society so that the self-development of people can take precedence over imperialism, economic expansion, and material desires. A commitment to feminism so defined would demand that each individual participant acquire a critical political consciousness based on ideas and beliefs. Its aim is not to benefit solely any specific group of women, any particular race or class of women. It does not privilege women over men. It has the power to transform in a meaningful way all our lives. (24-25)

The movement is not about being anti-male. It makes it clear that the problem is sexism. Female and male have been socialized from birth on to accept sexist thought and action. To end patriarchy (another way of naming the institutionalized sexism) we need to be clear that we are all participants in perpetuating sexism until we change our minds and hearts, until we let go sexist thought and action and replace it with feminist thought and action.

A fundamental goal of feminist theorists is to analyze gender: how gender is constituted and experienced and how we think—or equally important—do not think about it. The study of gender includes but is not limited to what are often considered the distinctively feminist issues: the situation of women and the analysis of male domination (patriarchy)....Because within contemporary Western societies gender relations have been ones of domination, feminist theories have compensatory as well as critical aspects. Feminist theories recover and explore the aspects of societies that have been suppressed, unarticulated, or denied within male-dominant viewpoints. The histories of women and our activities have to be written into the accounts and self-understandings of entire cultures. Feminist theories call for a transvaluation of values—a rethinking of our ideas about what is just, humanly excellent, worthy of praise, moral, and so forth.

Feminism from the African woman's perspective is a literary and social movement that militates for the visibility of women, the restoration and full grant of their rights, their freedom from patriarchy and their redemption from colonial memories. A regain of identity and dignity in the social sphere, more representativity in political decision areas and greater participation in public debates affecting the life of the nation, education for all women are on the agenda of African women's struggle. These claims find expression in the literature of combat written by the first, second, third and fourth generations of African female writers. Postcolonial African drama has been the fertile grounds of the bourgeoning of feminist and womanist ideas, philosophies and modes of thoughts. The fundamentals in the opening of minds to the feminist philosophy has been the regaining of awareness of gender equality, the balance in the biological nature and gender roles. Chikwenye Okonjo Ogunyemi's standpoint is useful here in explaining what has emerged as the main agenda of African feminism:

> What does a black woman [...] go through as she comes in contact with white feminist writing and realizes that Shakespeare's illustrious sisters belong to the second sex, a situation that has turned them into impotent eunuchs without rooms of their own in which to read and write their very own literature, so that they have become madwomen, now emerging from the attic, determined to fight for their rights by engaging in the acrimonious politics of sex? Does she precipitately enter the lists with them against Euro-Amercican patriarchy and, in their victory further jeopardize the chances of her race in the sharing of the political, social, and economic power? Does she imitate their war effort and throw the gauntlet down to challenge black patriarchy? Does she light sexual war some of the time and the racial war at other times? (Ogunyemi 2006: 21)

Ola Rotimi in *Our Husband Has Gone Made Again* (first performed in 1966) has Liza outspeak the mind of women by claiming "Man and Woman are created equal (*OHHGMA*: 56)". That very statement produced the expected results, for, just after the sentence is uttered, Sikira the second wife of Lejoka-Brown opened her eyes to the uneven prejudice being done to her and not long after that, asked for divorce to her husband. Rotimi's ideological stand convenes the reader to a meeting point between how western education can open women's minds and the actual awareness point they reach is actually positioning themselves as dissidents of patriarchal mainstream wheel-stirrers. Liza has the profile of an educated woman whose competence goes beyond book knowledge. She trained as a medical doctor, an achievement which is not common among women in developing countries. Medicine is symbolically the potency that is used to cure ailments, disease and curse. Having her train as a medical doctor implies therefore the endowment of women to heal the sick, to bring life and maintain it. Her advocacy that men and women are created equal is the nexus that seals her enlightening function as an eye opener, the torch bearer and path-paver. Liza therefore is the very embodiment of feminist philosophy, ideals and ideology. The breakaway of Sikira from the marital abode reads as the woman's capacity to actually depart from the male-made societal structures that militate against women's happiness. She does not advocate divorce as a solution to women' s social plight, nor does she beckon marital breakup as a doorway to women' s emancipation, but she actually stands against the very structure of polygamy, a social institution that downgrade women and demean their value both at socio-political and intellectual levels. Polygamy, the fact of marrying more than one wife is an injustice done to women and a despise of their stature as human beings. Two reasons can be given here to actually show how polygamous institutions function as injustice and prejudice to women. Firstly, women under polygamy are cheated on their right of equal partnership with men, that makes them share their time and be programmed according to the husband' s schedule on the time (it may be days or weeks) they have to be with the husband. This very programming makes women waste their time waiting for their turn to come. By the same token, it makes women engage in a contest to be the most loved woman for their husband. It has been proved that in polygamous marriages, not all women are loved equally by their husbands. In Wole Soyinka' s *The Lion and the Jewel* a play in which Baroka the Lion of Ilunjile is surrounded by the harem, the youngest wife is the most loved. The very argument Sadiku advances to conquer Sidi for her husband is that if she [Sidi] becomes a member of the harem, she will enjoy Baroka' s favours as the youngest wife. Where women are engaged in contest to gain their husband' s favour, the risk is high for them to thrust in open conflicts, suffer jealousy deals and betrayal on behalf of their co-wives. The second reason showing how polygamy operates as a prejudice done to women is that polygamous men have a false sense of superiority toward women and as a matter of fact tend to despise them. For instance, Lejoka-Brown has married Sikira purely for political reasons. It is said that Sikira' s mother, Madam Bambina Ajanaku is the president of the Nigeria' s Market Women' s Association and Brown saw in marrying her an opportunity to use her mother' s rally to compete for and actually win the elections. Such an attitude denotes not only a disrespect toward Sikira as a respectable person, a betrayal on the part of Lejoka-Brown, but also felony, despise of the woman' s personality and improper marriage contract deal. Marrying Sikira for political reasons actually means he would end the marriage contract the day he wins the elections or even the day he fails them. These are to my standpoint the very reasons why Rotimi has made Sikira break away from that marriage.

Ama Ata Aidoo' s *Anowa* vehiculates feminist philosophy from many standpoints. From one perspective, Anowa' s behaviour equates the rebellious attitudes of the radical feminists but the only difference is that her rebellion first goes against patriarchy, the elders, custodians of the priesthood office and her parents who agree with its philosophy. Anowa has rebelled against the elders' decision for her to enter traditional priesthood as a dancer. Ama Ata Aidoo has encrusted in the character Anowa a feminist consciousness that questions the logic of patriarchal institutionalization of imposed marriage, enslaving traditions and customs detrimental to women' s well-being. Aidoo also criticizes the colonial enterprize in Africa that was itself preceded by slavery.

9.2. The first Wave of African Feminism: Adverting Radicalism

The first wave of African feminism has been the ground work of the first generation of African female dramatists namely Nawal Al Sadawi, Flora Nwapa, Zulu Sofola, Tess Onwueme, Efua T. Sutherland, Ama Ata Aidoo, to mention but a few. Nevertheless, it has been at the centre stage of African female writers of the first generation to voice their dissidence from the European and American radical feminism that sought to completely break away from men. Concentrating on problems specific to African women, these female dramatists at varying degrees have spotlighted areas of victimization of the African woman by patriarchy in general and by the phallocentric male writers and critics in particular. Areas of the victimization include genital mutilation, rape, wife battering, domestic violence on women, sexual harassment, abusive sacking as a result of the woman's refusal to yield to sexual exploitation, women's under-representativity in education sector, public administration and political decision-making area, women's short lived political office tenure. These issues have been raised, discussed and debated upon by these writers seeking to restore justice for women, earn voice for females and have them emerge both in literature and society.

9.2.1. Nawal El Saadawi (Egypt)

The Egyptian feminist activist Nawal El Sadawi has been a strong voice in the proclamation of the message of women's liberation and a gender sensitive writer who strongly advocates the restoration of women's rights. She uses drama and prose fiction as main weapons in creative literature to speak out her mind about women's rights to freedom and development. Female - circumcision generally referred to as excision - forced marriages on women, religious oppression are some of the topics in her literary agenda. In the introductory notes to a critical book on herself, *The Nawal El Saadawi Reader,* she writes: "Women pay dearly with their freedom and dignity to obey the laws of marriage and then patriarchal class system that dominates society. Women also pay dearly in order to become free and escape domination" (Saadawi 2010: 49). It is with these catch words that Saadawi expresses her desire to fight for women's liberation in the Arab world. Maureen N. Nke opines that she describes herself as one whose initial purpose for writing was to release her anger against women's oppression: "What angered me most" she writes, was oppression: oppression of women and oppression of the poor" (Quoted by Nke 2010: 49). The initial principle has remained central to her writings over several decades and has gained her a collective of followers and detractors. "I have always felt that the pen was an effective weapon that I could use against injustice and oppression." Saadawi founded the Arab Women's Solidarity Association in 1982; the objective of which was to promote the advancement of Arab women. In other words, Saadawi sees a link between creativity and political activism and through the two, she hopes to empower women by helping them to unveil their minds. It is therefore not surprising that her narratives and plays depict various ways in which dominant patriarchal and other social structures like religion, marriage and traditional practices disempower women. Consequently, the female characters often interrogate or resist those social structures which marginalize them, engaging in either over resistance or employing subversive means to destabilize patriarchy and male tyranny.

Maureen N. Nke submits that "Patriarchy imprisons women and downgrades them by denying them rights as individuals and as members of large collective. Through imposed cultural practices, women are repressed, contained, and monitored under the constant gaze of males, first the father, then the brother, (where there is one), husband and sometimes the son" (Nke, op. cit, 50).

Adele S. Newson-Horst has offered a critical reading of Nawal El Saadawi's feminism and her combat for the Arab women (Newson-Horst 2009). From her account, Nawal El Saadawi has to her credit seven dramatic works published in Arabic by Madbouli publishers. Part of a larger series of works, these plays are *Isis, God Resigns at the Summit Meeting, Children Singing for Love, Twelve Women in a Cell, The Torn Picture, The Ruler in the Name of God, The Blue Female*. In his introduction to the series, the publisher notes: "In the past fifty years, Dr Nawal El Saadawi has given her Arabic readers and Arabic thought a complete project characterized by courage, in speaking her mind, discussing many issues that most of the writers are afraid to address. Her works changed the mentality of our region" (As quoted by Adele S. Newson-Horst 2009). *Twelve Women in a Cell*, has allowed to reverse the position of women in literature and "lift the veil of ancient civilizations and view them in the light of liberating female gaze". Her two plays collection has centered on the question of the dissolution of feminine power. Her works are works of moral, mental, physical recovery. The first play *Isis*, was written in Cairo, Egypt in 1986. It draws on the Egyptian myth. Isis, one of the triumvirate Osiris, Horus and Isis who in ancient Egypt were seen as gods of nurture. In the play, Isis is the central figure and plays the role of wife, mother, and actively struggles for diversity, wisdom and compassion against patriarchy:

> Priest: And how do I eat if the people do not offer sacrifices in the temple?
> Isis: You eat by working like us and all these peasant men and women.
> Priest: But I do not belong to these people… I am a priest… and priests belong to the rank of masters, not slaves…
> Osiris: There are no masters and slaves in the villages… We are all humans. People are all equal. This is Isis, the daughter of the goddess Nut and the god Geb, and she works with us…she married

me, a poor sailor man whose father and mother were peasants (Quoted in Ernest Emenyonu 2004: 95).

In this conversation between Priest and Isis, the fundamental feminist principle is unveiled by Isis: people [men and women] are all equal, all must work, and the voice belongs to the masses, the peasants. Jane Plastow believes that "Religion and patriarchy both mean that the priest cannot accept the radical vision of equality while the god Isis, holds the opposite view. In a society where gender disparity is reduced to the maximum, great will be the chances that social cohesion and peace prevail. Feminist ideas replete the other plays too. The following interview with Nawal El Saadawi conducted by Elizabeth Bekers shows her preoccupation with women' s liberation:

> E. B. What I like about the way you address female genital excision in your novels is that you attack the practice from within the protagonist's society. A lot of writers when they denounce female genital excision, they bring in western point of view: they introduce a western character, or their African protagonist starts thinking about the practice when she moves to the United States or to Europe, or they present the west as a safe haven for women who have been or may be subjected to genital operation. In your novels, the critique against female genital excision is contained within the protagonist' s culture. It is not through contact with the outside world, or somebody else' s opinions, but it is really the women themselves who come to denounce female genital excision.
> N. S. Exactly.
> E. B. So you formulate an intra-cultural rather than inter-cultural critique.
> N. S. Brilliant! That is a really very important point and I am happy that you make this point, for not everybody is able to discover that in my work.[8]

One of the feminist combat Saadawi is engaged in is the battle against female circumcision, a practice common in many parts of Sub-saharan

---

[8] Interview with Nawal El Saadawi by Elisabeth Bekers, Indianapolis, 26 October 1998, recorded in Ernest N. Emenyonu, ed., *Emerging Perspectives on Nawal El Saadawi* (Trenton: Africa World Press, 2010), p. 263.

Africa and the Islamic countries. Saadawi' s *Woman at Point Zero* is devoted to denounce genital excision of women, a practice intended to keep women faithful to their husband. Saadawi finds excision intolerable, cheating and humiliating for women as it affects them psychologically and emotionally and renders them frigid. The literary campaign against excision is relayed in dramatic works and her plays exhibit several aspects of the message contained in *Woman at Point Zero*. If Saadawi turns to dramatic literature to make her ideas known, this medium is surely one of the widely publicized that gathers larger audiences. Drama charts with the receptive capacities of the masses as the telling is associated with the showing of the stage.

9.2.2. Zulu Sofola (Nigeria)

Zulu Sofola, the first published female playwright in Nigeria has broken and pulled tremendous weight on a male-dominated arena. Sofola's feminism adumbrates the necessity to revisist men's attitude in patriarchal societies where most privileges including public talk, decision-making process, community and political leadership, modern education better jobs in civil service are firmly concentrated in the hands of men. In an interview with Adeola James, Zulu Sofola pondered:

> […] there is this problem which the educated African - male or female - has as regards himself. With European exposure, the African educated person has been led to believe that the female is an after-thought, a wall-flower, and the man is heaven-sent, the controller of everything. When you look in our literature, you find this is how our women are portrayed. Even where it is a woman in her own right, within the traditional setting, she is going to be portrayed half-way her strength (Sofola 1990: 145).

As can be perceived here Sofola has revealed her feminist commitment to the injustice done to women both in society and in literature. To see a woman as an 'after-thought' is the derogatory expression most men label on women in bid to assert male dominance over females.

In *Wedlock of the Gods,* the reader is introduced to Uloko and Ogwoma, the radical couple, who are genuinely in love but cannot marry because Uloko cannot afford the bride-price. Despite the fact that some critics like Henrietta C. Otekunefor and Obiageli C. Nwodo read Sofola as a traditionalist playwright (Otekunefor and Nwodo 1989: 61), I think that here, Sofola is already commandable for aspects of her feminist ideology by emasculating the male Uloko who cannot afford the bride-price. Since Ogwoma's parents badly need money to cure her sick brother, she is given into marriage to Adigwu, a higher bidder much against her wish. Shortly after the marriage, Adigwu dies and the lovers get married, not waiting for the traditionally prescribed mourning period to lapse. Thereupon, the mother-in-law gets enraged. In order to enable tradition to run its course and also to avenge the death of her son whom she believes is killed by the lovers so they might have their way, she uses her magical prowess to destroy Ogwoma. Uloko also later commits suicide after having avenged Ogwoma's death by killing Odibei. This looks dangerously reactionary. What transpires here is a bourgeois romanticizing with the past, the feudal past. The reader encounters in *Wedlock of the Gods*, Sofola's artistic construction of the plot that brings out, the centrality of women's conditions in traditional Africa. Women are objectified by male-made customs and traditions that pin down women and deprive them from enjoying freedom. Sofola goes into feminist war against such erected barriers that cripple women in their endeavor to emerge on the stage of modern emancipated women. She critically rejects dogmatic submission to the whims and caprices of age-old demigod (patriarchy) or custodians of bogus tradition analysing things from the tragic consequence they may generate, because, for those who kick, there is no restitution. There is no redemption from the tragic consequences of dissent. Neither Emene nor Okebuno has any respite till they die. Central to the spirit of Sofola's feminism, is her stance that the African woman must become free from traditional customs and patriarchal yokes. The woman tied to tradition and customs is a slave to patriarchy, since male elders are the very custodians of these customs. She questions the rationale behind harmful traditions that make its offenders perish without remedy. Her position is radical. It is clear from *Wedlock of the Gods* that the playwright herself believes it is unjust to snatch Ogwoma from Uloko simply because he cannot afford the bride-price. At the same time she does not sympathize with emasculated men who want to devalue women to the extent of marrying them free of charge. When Ogoli cries of shame after it has been discovered that his son had impregnated Ogwoma while still in her period of mourning, Uloko queries her:

> It was in your presence that Ogwoma was forced from my hands and given away to Adigwu. Did you speak for me? Did you let

Ibekwu know that an injustice was being done to you by his action? Did you let anyone know that, for money, your wife, whom you had planned for your son was being forced from your hands and being given to someone else (*WOTG*: 43)?

This declaration showcases the real preoccupation of Sofola in showing the way in which Ogwoma the female victim of both tradition and patriarchy suffers the moral and psychological torture when she was prevented from marrying her lover and commodified to garner money to pay out her brother's healing. One question Sofola would like the audience to reflect on and possibly answer is whether Ogwoma's brother could also be sold to fine her treatment if she were sick. If the answer is negative, then there is injustice, in that women are being used as commodities to serve men's interest.

Even in her non-tragic plays, Sofola is always unequivocal about her defense of women's rights and her criticism of male chauvinism. *The Sweet Trap* is a fairly comic play where she exposes sexism against women and condemns the traditionally held supremacy of the male, especially over his wife or collection of wives. In a demonstration of brute force and male chauvinism, Femi Sotubo refuses to allow Clara his wife to celebrate her birthday. The docile, submissive good housewife Clara agrees initially. But a friend whose own matrimony has previously collapsed (someone to be shun obviously) advises Clara to hold the party at another avenue. The party is eventually disrupted, and, for resolution, Clara takes the advice of Dr Jinadu, her elderly uncle, and apologizes to her husband with her knees firmly on the ground. This shows Sofola's impatience with male chauvinism and her ideological assertion of the necessity for women to actually rebuff the docile acceptance of docility and servility. Clara is brought cringing on her knees for trying to defend her right. Her husband is right even when he is being stupid. Elements of myth, magic and ritual are heavily drawn from and espoused in Sofola's plays. *The Sweet Trap* is intentionally set in the period when Ok-da-Badan, an age-old-male festival is being celebrated.

Mary E. Modupe Kolawole has read the plays of Sofola and Onwueme as true feminist manifestoes that adumbrate the epistemological quintessence of the woman's feminist fierce struggle for self-assertion, intellectual visibility, political emergence and economic self-reliance. Her reading projects Zulu Sofola and Tess Onwueme on the pulpit of assertive feminists who spearhead the struggle for women's liberation in Nigeria and Africa as a whole:

Zulu Sofola has become more overtly vocal in creating women in the process of social change in her most recent plays. Sofola and Tess Onwueme represent the two generations of female African writers who have the priviledge of the restless spirit of creating heroes and heroines who are impatient and with tradition and eager to change the nervous conditions erected by male centered ideologies. Sofola as well as Onwueme are cultural agents and appear through their plays as gender sensitive, feminist conscious and womanist inclined by unveiling progressive radical commitments to positive change for women. Zulu Sofola is arguably the first Nigerian playwright/dramatist with no less than twelve plays over a period of twenty years. Iconoclastic, she is critical of the indoctrination of dogmatic imposition of traditional customs to women, for whom these practices are very detrimental and prejudicial. *Wedlock of the Gods* conceptualizes the social predicament and fate of a woman who puts personal love above collective ethos. Ogwoma's tragedy stems from her being liberated ahead of her time. Her true love for Uloko is thwarted because her parents need a lot of money to care for her sick brother. She is forced to marry a richer man since Uloko is too poor to pay a huge bride price. The death of Ugwoma's husband shortly after the marriage gives her and Uloko a chance to have their dream fulfilled. Nevertheless, tradition becomes a roadblock. She is expected to enter into a Leviathan union with a brother-in-law. To avoid this, Uloko begins to visit her before the end of the three months mourning period. This is considered an abomination by the society and Ogwuma's mother-in-law avenges her son by destroying Ogwuma. In a multiple tragic situation, Uloko kills the latter and commits suicide (Mary E. Modupe Kolawole 1997: 143).

Sofola believes in taking the best from tradition and resisting the society whenever necessary. The tragedy in this play is that of individual woman confronting society, which appears to be stronger than the individual woman. Sofola is of the view that Uloko and Ogwoma should have been more decisive in preventing forced marriage. She says the fight should not have been fought alone. She does not reject the whole tradition as she explains:

> I have always said that the only way the African woman of today, with her European orientation which we call education, can be

liberated is to study the traditional system and the place of the woman as defined by it. There was no area of woman's endeavor in the traditional system where the woman did not have a role to play. She was very strong and very active (Quoted by May E. Modupe Kolawole 1997: 144).

From this perspective, Sofola is viewed as a conscious feminist woman commissioned to the uplifting of the African traditional woman torn between modern values and traditional customs. She advocates a kind of intellectual approach to tradition that selects from the cultural lore useful things and values and rejects negative and retrogressive practices. The African feminist of Sofola's caliber embodies a whole range of philosophies that sustain the visionary emancipation of the African woman who should forge ahead by all means. The women in *Sweet Trap* seize power and authority in a phony manner. Clara Sotubo's insistence on having a birthday celebration creates tension in her home, as her husband, a doctor, insists that they cannot have the birthday party for economic reasons. Her personal problem becomes the concern of the circle of friends who take it up as a gender war. They agree to defy the men by shifting the venue of the party to the home of Fatima Oyegunle. The party becomes a disaster because of the intrusion of ruffians and this creates conflicts between men and women. The struggle of the women is from a cultural void that has made no provision for them to enjoy freedom. Sofola believes that the struggle against women's marginalization should be contextualized and purposeful. Her political voice and cultural nationalism are balanced as she critiques various forms of extremities. Womanist consciousness no doubt pervades the works of that playwright whose themes vary consistently. In other plays namely *The Showers* and *Lost Dreams,* Sofola launches an overt feminist campaign, and her ideas sparkle as ideologically charged propaganda. From the opening scene of *The Showers,* a gender battleline is drawn. The remark of the female nurse, Nurse Odigie, against men, reveals this tension when a woman in labour is brought into the Shasha hospital under emergency conditions:

> They always do
> It is when their wives need them most
> That they are conveniently absent (*TS: 3*).

This extract brings to the fore the feminist imprecation against unconscious male chauvinist carefree attitude. Men are supposed to cooperate with women, and if they are missing at the very moment they are mostly needed, there is an indication of tragic neglect of responsibility. This critical thought is even more perceptible in the context where it becomes a necessity to adopt a culturally valid women's theory. Sofola is interested in a womanist's ideology that addresses their specificity and she is unequivocally convinced that some brands of western feminism are too uncompromising to apprehend the African cultural peculiarity.

9.2.3. Flora Nwapa (Nigeria)

Flora Nwapa has published three remarkable plays posthumously: *The First Lady* (1993), *Two Women in Conversation* (1993) and *The Sycophants* (1993). Ernest N. Emenyonu' s critical reading of these plays provide a sparkling insight to the study conducted here (Emenyonu 1998: 357-390). In these plays, namely *The First Lady* and *Two Women in Conversation,* Nwapa firmly asserts that women' s empowerment is the key to gender equilibrium by which universal harmony can be assured. The new woman of Nwapa' s plays who had been already in gestation in her prose fiction resembles in essence the mystical *Uhamiri* – a paradoxical mixture of motherly tenderness and masculine fierceness. The plays diagnose other maladies and proffer other solutions. These solutions are bitter pills for men already trapped within the sexist ideas of the familiar status quo. Through these plays Nwapa has projected for her society the inevitable final stage of the chaos which had become the order of the day in Nigeria. In *The Sycophants,* the mind has vegetated beyond remedy but the physical man seems to enjoy and relish in the stupor. In *Two Women in Conversation* the society has reached a state of anarchy but the men who run its affairs seem oblivious of the ever-ticking time bomb. Marital war is at its zenith. Unlike what happens in her novels, the women combatants in Nwapa' s plays are poised for a fight which no longer seems uneven or predicably conclusive. Women are no longer waiting for their oppressors to bequeath freedom on men' s own terms. They are poised to wrench it from their grips. In *The First Lady,* female assertions of responsibility and leadership are uncompromisingly evident. The plays are windows through which the reader perceives Nwapa' s new women and their world. The decay in the old order is dramatized in all its putrefaction but there are persistent dreams of a new dawn. Nwapa shows flickers of hope, of restoration and of rebirth. Each play reflects a particular social dimension and a particular dream. Ogunyemi states that Her (Nwapa' s) call is for action among the rulers and the ruled and among men and women to heal the sick society...she wants the treacherous old ways buried to make possible the rebirth of the country and its people (quoted by Emenyonu 1998: 360).

Nwapa's *The First Lady* is elaborate play in which she highlights her feminist ideologies combined with multifaceted thematic variety and stylistic diversity. It is about illusions, appearances, greed, vaulting ambitions, torn hopes and metaphorical cleansing. It is also about identity and conflicts in values and standards. Equally present as themes are corruption – corruption of the state of womanhood- and the battle for regeneration and ascendancy. It seeks to set straight the records of the status of women in the traditional society vis-à-vis the misconceptions of contemporary society. Nwapa addresses eloquently such issues as women's leadership, and political activism, education and universal suffrage, accountability and individual freedom, patriotism and individual honour. The author's technique in communicating these calls for attention. There are vivid and elaborate stage directions, flashbacks, ironic twists, linguistic code-switching and use of native idiom at tense moments.

Flora Nwapa in *The First Lady* ridicules and satirizes the unelected leadership among women, but uses the play to expose the government's strategy of muzzling women's voices in local and national issues. She questions through the female characters some fundamental tenets of patriarchal authority unheard of before, such as when they argue with a local traditional chief on the role of women in politics and society:

> Chief Akuma: In our tradition, the wife should stay home, welcome the husband when he returns home, and…
> Barrister Egenti: No. That is not our tradition. If by 'our tradition' you mean Igbo tradition, then, you should put it to you that you got it wrong. The traditional Igbo woman is not the stay-at-home. She goes to the farm. She trades. She does many other things.
> Chief Akuma [*lamely*]: Yes, but things have changed.
> Barrister Egenti: And human beings have not changed?
> Chief Akuma: There was no politics in Igbo traditional society. I mean in our traditional past, our traditional way of life.
> Barrister Egenti: Did women not set up and run their own councils? Did those councils not oversee both women's affairs and men's affairs?
> Chief Akuma: I don't mean this kind of thing. Listen to me. I am running for a high political office. Our ancestors did not have this

type of thing. Now, I return home, and what do I find? I find that my wife is away campaigning. I go to bed hungry. Before I am up the next morning, my wife is already out. I don't see her for days. She does not know whether I eat or not…
Barrister Egenti: And you have no cook?
Mrs. Nkana (a woman leader): Easy, Barrister. Chief, what you have just said can cost you dearly if we should reveal it to the women. We have come a long way in this country, and in this age chief. Whether you like it or not, neither you nor any other man can set back the hands of the clock. You can no longer do without us….
(*TFL*: 100-101)

The climax of this encounter comes when Nwapa reports a gesture and body language which has serious cultural implications. In the middle of their verbal exchanges, the chief and the two women pause but in the interval, the women show mitigating acts of contempt towards male authority: "He pauses, looks at them. They look back at him, looking him straight in the eye. He is one who looks down first. Then he raises his face and begins…" (*TFL*: 101).

The focus of *The First Lady* is change, the inevitability of change, and no one can turn back the hands of the clock. Ironically, when the chief asserts that things have changed, he does not seem to understand the full import of this statement; for change also affects the females' perception of women's rights and roles in the changing world. Expressions such as 'listen to me' and 'this is my home' are all sexist, used for coercion and intimidation, while the invocation of our ancestors was a decisive way of asserting the age-long patriarchal authority and silencing female agitations which, obeying the status quo, should have been voiceless. Also, the expression that a man (married) "went to bed hungry" was an implacable way of drawing attention to the absolute failure of a wife in the home. But those assertions and expressions no longer shocked the women in the play, since they are galvanized against male chauvinism. In the highest cultural manifestation of feminine revolt shown through innuendo, the women look him (chief) straight in the eyes, signifying not just an assertion of equality but also a determination to upset down patriarchal structures. In some African cultures, facial confrontation, that is, looking straight to someone in the eyes may suggest un uncompromising way of eliciting the truth, but in the cultural setting of the play, women cannot look men, let alone the chief of the community, straight in the eye, as this signals the flaunting of constituted authority.

9.2.4. Tess Osonye Onwueme (Nigeria)

Internationally renowned for her award-winning plays, Dr. Tess Onwueme is Africa's best-known female dramatist, whose writing and speaking often poke into taboo and controversial subjects, revealing the untold hidden stories of young women and the poor, who remain caught in various crossfires with; family, tradition, race, class, gender, culture and politics. But then in the growing stampede for material wealth and power in both Africa and the global community today, their striving for voice, place and identity still remain unheard, thus provoking Tess Onwueme who commits herself as "a writer with an active conscience" to constantly "stage-a-hearing" for them through her inspiring provocative writing and speaking. That the BBC recently adapted and produced Onwueme's 2001 award-winning play, *Shakara: Dance-Hall Queen* as a major feature of their BBC World Drama Service for the Fall of 2004, is only one of such recent testimonies, marking the enriching value of Onwueme's creative work as a steady staple for the international public, as well as schools, colleges, and universities in international contexts, where her creative writings continue to impact and transform the academic curricular as scholars and teachers continuously adapt as primary teaching texts and tools for teaching, scholarship, theses, and dissertations.

The prolific Onwueme, who is married with five children, earned her Ph.D. from the University of Benin, Nigeria in 1988, following both her Masters and Bachelors degrees from the university of Ife, Nigeria in 1982, and 1979, respectively. Dr. Onwueme has won numerous international awards for her creative writing and contributions, including: the Drama Prize of the Association of Nigerian Authors, which she has broken all records to win four times with various plays, *Then She Said It* (2003), *Shakara: Dance-Hall Queen* (2001), *Tell it to Women* (1995), and *The Desert Encroaches* (1985), two substantial awards from the Ford Foundation in both 2000 and 2001, the 1988 Distinguished Authors Award, and the Martin Luther King / Caesar Chavez Distinguished Writer/Scholar Award, 1989/90. In 2009 she was awarded the prestigious Fonlon-Nichols Award at the African Literature Conference in Burlington, Vermont. Since joining the University of Wisconsin, Eau Claire Wisconsin in 1994 as a Distinguished Professor of Cultural Diversity and Professor of English after her years of teaching in both Nigerian and American universities, Tess Onwueme continues to gain her steady strides, not just as a role-model for women and youths in the world, but also as a remarkable international writer and speaker, whose inspirational work and talent is steadily shaping and transforming public consciousness of issues impacting black women and youths in postcolonial societies today, while providing the critical resources and texts for scholars, who derive inspiration for their theses and dissertations from her writing in such multidisciplinary contexts as: Women/Feminist Studies, Cultural Studies, Studies of African, Diasporan, Black, Postcolonial, World, Literature, and Drama, together with those critically engaged in vital studies of Gender, Race, Class, especially as these impact underclass women and youths today.

Onwueme is fervently committed to the sociopolitical transformation of her immediate society (Nigeria) and the world at large. She has published sixteen plays and they include: *Then She Said It* (2002), *Shakara Dance Hall Queen* (2002), *The Missing Face* (1997), *Tell It To Women* (1994), *Riot in Heaven* (1996) and *Three Plays: The Broken Calabash, Parables for a Season* and *the Reign of Wazobia* (1993). The protagonists of most of Onwueme's plays are women, no doubt about that. However, Onwueme's dramaturgy is not limited to discussing the problems of women in a patriarchal society. Onwueme is a woman and it is natural to see the problems of her society with the eyes of a woman. As a writer, she is no different from all other writers whose concern has been to cry out against man's inhumanity to man. Her dramaturgy covers issues of governance to freedom, fairness, justice and equality. These are not problems peculiar to women. Therefore, her dramaturgy interrogates issues germane to human society at large, with Nigeria as her primary setting. Of course, her plays attain universality because the issues of oppression, inequality, injustice and inequitable distribution of the commonwealth which she cries against are problems which plague human societies everywhere. Her proposals for change have been known to work in many places.

A careful reading of her plays show that they are, at once, historical and contemporary, traditional and modern, dramatic and lyrical, visual and verbal, tragic and comic. She bridges these contrasts and by so doing manifests hope and optimism for the future if only the poor oppressed people protest and resist oppression. In her exploration of contemporary issues, she crosses boundaries and break down barriers to the utter chagrin and infuriation of those strongly wedded to silencing not only the gendered but also the poor, alienated and powerless in society. Because she does not refrain from stirring the pot, she has been unjustly criticized for being too political. In recent works such as *The Reign of Wazobia, Tell It To Women, Shakara Dance Hall Queen* and *Then She Said It*, Onwueme has cricticised the Nigerian patriarchal system that leaves freedom to women.

9.2.5. Efua T. Sutherland (Ghana)

Efua T. Sutherland has been a pioneer in drama and theatre studies and the body of her work reveals her as a strong feminist voice for women's emancipation, empowerment and their total liberation from the clutches of patriarchy and male domination. Her attack has been on the institutionalization of material exploitation of women by men, the commodification of female children and girls, issues that tanspire in her three plays *Edufa* (1967) (based on *Alcestis* by Euripides), *Foriwa* (1967), and *The Marriage of Anansewa* (1975). In addition, Sutherland experimented creatively with storytelling and other dramatic forms from indigenous Ghanaian traditions. Her plays are often based on traditional stories, but also borrowed from Western literature, transforming African folktale conventions into modern dramatic theatre techniques. Many of her poems and other writings were broadcast on *The Singing Net*, a popular radio programme started by Henry Swanzy, and were subsequently published in his 1958 anthology *Voices of Ghana*. The 1960 first issue of *Okyeame* magazine contains her short story "Samantaase", a retelling of a folktale

In *Edufa* the eponymous character seeks to escape death by manipulating his wife, Ampoma, to the death that has been predicted for him by oracles. In the play, Sutherland uses traditional Ghanaian beliefs in divination and the interaction of traditional and European ceremonies in order to portray Edufa as a rich and successful modern person who is held in high esteem by his people. The play uses traditional ritual and symbolism, but the story is told in the context of Edufa's capitalistic abandonment of his moral commitment to his wife, while his wife and the other women favour the morality of the past.

In *Foriwa* the eponymous character, who is the daughter of the queen mother of Kyerefaso, and Labaran, a graduate from northern Ghana who lives a simple life, bring enlightenment to Kyerefaso, a town that has become backward and ignorant because the town's elders refuse to learn new ways. *Foriwa's* main theme is the alliance of old traditions and new ways. The play has a national theme to promote a new national spirit in Ghana that would encourage openness to new ideas and inter-ethnic cooperation.

The Marriage of Anansewa: A Storytelling Drama (1975) is considered Sutherland's most valuable contribution to Ghanaian drama and theater. In the play, she transmutes traditional Akan Ananse Spider tales (*Anansesem*) into a new dramatic structure, which she calls *Anansegoro*. *Nyamekye* (a version of *Alice in Wonderland*), one of her later plays, shows how she was influenced by the folk opera tradition.

In the 60's women seemed to be second rated in Ghana and when men talked, women did shut up in submission or say just a little, that is if they speak at all. It was a period in which males dominated and unfortunately, the women seem to accept the trend of things. Since women were not very much regarded within the era, if a man wants to protect or preserve himself, he could choose to use a woman anyhow he liked to satisfy his interests. Having observed this trend, Sutherland wants to use the play to help women emancipate themselves. It is possible the playwright is only being subtle so as not to incur unnecessary negative reactions from the men in her level- the educated at that time. In order to change a person, let the person know who he is; that is what Sutherland is doing for women through *Edufa*. She wants women to observe how men consider and treat them so as to liberate themselves from the hegemonic tendencies of their male counterparts. Again, Martin Owusu and Benjamin Asante in "an interpretative analysis of Efua T. Sutherland's *Edufa*" state that:

> As a product of a male-dominated society, Efua Sutherland uses her plays to create an awareness among women to change their situations in a dynamic society. She portrays the nature of human power as used against African women. She, therefore, creates a conducive environment for the necessary changes. (2002:4-5).

9.2.5.1. Feminist Inclinations in Foriwa

The portrayal of women in Sutherland's *Foriwa* shows the playwright's indebtedness to her Fante matrilineal cultural background where women command greater power than in the patrilineal societies. Both Queen Mother and her daughter Foriwa are very strong women and have tremendous influence on the men with whom they work. But, as can be observed from the old Sintim's hostile attitude towards Queen Mother, the play is based on general African communities in which conservative men do not readily accept women's leadership. The success of the two women in winning the respect of the male citizens is due not only to their determination but also to the selfless nature of their leadership. Their portrayal illustrates Sutherland's strong belief in women's potential in leadership which is dedicated to the advancement of society rather than to personal aggrandizement.

Queen Mother is an embodiment of Sutherland's idea about the answer to Africa's transitional cultural problems, a synthesis between what is vital from the traditional African culture and what is relevant from the Western culture. Queen Mother combines her traditional royalty with Western education. Notice, from Sintim's attitude, the playwright's criticism of men who feel threatened by educated women. Queen Mother's leadership is distinguished by her commitment to real down-to-earth cultural progress for her community as opposed to meaningless personal pomp and exhibitionism. It is this dedication to meaningful progress which makes her disregard the usual props and customary jargon at the festival and instead conduct the ceremony in a way which initiates new life in Kyerefaso. Her strength and determination as a leader make her risk her people's rebellion when she topples their expectations at the festival. But her people cannot help being moved to shame after her convincing outline of their shortcomings in building their community; they have engaged in words rather than deeds. Queen Mother attacks this superficial progress when she tells the people at the festival:

> Sitting here, seeing Kyerefaso die, I am no longer able to bear the mockery of the fine, brave words of this ceremony of our festival. Our fathers earned the right to utter them by their deeds. They found us the land, protected it, gave us a system of living. Praise to them. Yes. But is this the way to praise them? Watching their walls crumbling around us?
>
> ...
>
> Unwilling to open new paths ourselves, because it demands of us thought and goodwill and action? No, we have turned Kyerefaso into a death bed from which our young people run away to seek help where, the promise of life we've failed to give them here (*F: 45*).

Queen Mother's confidence as she shakes idleness out of her people so that they can engage themselves in meaningful progress at Kyerefaso wins her even the support of the old Sintim, the representative of the conservative males who hitherto have been opposed to a woman's leadership. It is also Queen Mother's impact at the festival which makes Foriwa decide to leave her teaching job away from Kyerefaso and join in the development projects here. Like Queen Mother, Foriwa is portrayed as an embodiment of Sutherland's idea of progress. Foriwa represents the younger generation of women who have to continue with the work of development started off by Queen Mother and her generation. "More than a representative, Foriwa is presented as a symbol of the future progressive culture. Foriwa is for down-to-earth meaningful progress rather than the superficial exhibitionist progress. It is in this spirit that she rejects entering into marriage with the wealthy Anipare. The latter, like Edufa in the play discussed above, represents the nouveaux-riche- whose values about life are distorted; they judge human beings and human relationships in material terms. Foriwa's rejection of him and his wealth is therefore a rejection of these values and her choice of Labaran instead of Anipare shows the extent of her dedication to meaningful and selfless development. On a superficial level, Labaran has very little to offer as compared to Anipare; he is poor and he is also a foreigner at Kyerefaso.

But as far as development is concerned, he has a wealth of potential to offer. He is educated where Anipare is not, and in addition, he is committed to using this education for development projects that are beneficial to the community. In this light, he is the male counterpart of Foriwa as a representative of the future generation on whose shoulders the task of Africa's progress lies. The marriage between Labaran and Foriwa represents Sutherland's idea of the role of men and women in Africa's post-independence cultural development. This marriage symbolizes the co-operation of men and women which Sutherland views as crucial to the development of her country and that of other African states. The presentation of the relationship between Labaran and Foriwa offers an illustration of the difference between the depiction of the co-operation of men and women by female playwrights and that by their male counterparts.

9.2.5.2. *Women's Images in Edufa*

The way and manner in which Ampoma is viewed goes for all the women in the play, who in turn represent the entire female faction in Ghana. The level of disrespect for women at the time is nothing to write home about. Though not meant to denigrate the line of Kankam, Edufa's father goes a long way to confirm the notion formed about women around the sixties. Kankam refers to her as "...poor, doting woman" *(Edufa: 2-3)*. A doting person is somebody who is foolish or weak-minded; it could also mean a person who is excessively fond of someone. The playwright uses Ampoma's helpless condition to warn women to realise their status in order to rise up for their right. Ampoma is a wife to Edufa and the mother of his children; it is her health that gets everybody busy in the household in order to restore back to her, good health. The efforts to me are vain because it is obvious that this rich husband does nothing extraordinary to show the urgency of his wife's situation. In the prologue of the play, Abena laments on why more potent help is not being sought. She highlights the fact that:

> ...True that Ampoma ... is unwell; but
> If she is unwell, should we not open our
> gate? She is not mortally ill; but even so,
> just let it be known, and sympathy and
> comforting gifts will flow in from every
> home. So much does the whole town hold
> her dear (*E*: 3).

Ampoma is a wife who shares everything with her husband but could not look him in the face to refute Edufa's request of dying in his place but swore her life away for her husband, (*E*: 17). The relationship between Edufa and Kankam his father is of blood tie; therefore the love between them cannot be said to be less than that of Edufa and his wife. However, Kankam is able to look into Edufa's demand and rejects his request outright but Ampoma fails in doing same. Sutherland might have kept her silent in order to show the voiceless and subservient condition of most of the women in those days which made the men walk over them as if they were non-entities. It is not as though they knew not what is right or wrong but accepted everything with the intention to avoid any castigation from their men and spouses respectively.

9.2.6. Ama Ata Aidoo (Ghana)

The works of the Ghanian playwright, poet, and teacher Christina Ama Ata Aidoo expose the despotism of Africa's patriarchal roots. Born a chief's daughter in Abeadzi Kyiakor, she had a proud heritage and grew up in a royal compound. During the nation's struggle for freedom, she was educated at the University of Ghana and, under the influence of evolving concepts of freedom, wrote her first short fiction in her undergraduate years. In 1965 she published the whimsical courtship comedy *The Dilemma of a Ghost*, which dramatizes the cultural clash of native customs with competing Western values. At the climax, Eulalie Rush saves the family through her witty patter. In a reworking of the "Whither thou goest" speech from the biblical book of Ruth, the playwright contrasts the humble Jewish heroine to the outspoken Ghanian mother who demands respect. Education gave Aidoo the tools to become a force for good. After completing her education at Stanford, she came under the mentorship of Efua Sutherland, founder of the Ghana Drama Studio. As minister of education Aidoo later applied her vision of literacy and knowledge to the elevation of rural Ghanian women. As she explained in an interview, her motives were nationalistic:

> 'The decay of Africa's social, political, and economic systems is directly related to the complete marginalization of women from developmental discourses'. She asserted that equality in learning and opportunity could save sub- Saharan Africa (Needham 123).

In a period of rapid social and economic changes, Aidoo settled in Zimbabwe and began challenging the abasement of African women with vernacular writings that equate the ravages of imperialism with the destructiveness of sexism. Her strongest feminist themes enliven the song play *Anowa* (1970), which depicts a young woman's rebellion against feudal marriage by choosing a man whom she can help to achieve a good life. An opinionated crone honors the spunky Anowa, a representative of Africa's New Woman, for listening to her own tales, chuckling at her own jokes, and following her own advice. In the last scene Anowa describes traditional female Silencing under old-style marriage: "In order for her man to be a man, she must not think, she must not talk" (Aidoo *1987*: 64). Unlike Western feminist writers who decry inequality in politics and workplace sexism experienced by career women, Aidoo focuses on the grassroots frustrations of rural wives and mothers, the hardships of feeding a family, and the terrors of domestic abuse. In 1995 the *Feminist Press* reprinted her collection of stories, *No Sweetness Here* (1970), a survey of African women's lives during a time of a dizzying cultural shift to Western values and behavior. Her style relies heavily on the oral ambience of the Fanti language and a blend of prose with lyric verse. A standout story, "Something to Talk about on the Way to the Funeral," ponders the age-old dilemma of the pregnant woman whose lover is too immature to commit to marriage and family.

9.3. Second Wave Feminism: Chinyere Grace Okafor's *The New Toy Toy* (2007) and Irene Isoken Oronsaye-Salami's *Sweet Revenge* (2007)

The postcolonial literary discourses have engaged African theatre criticism towards a redefinition of relations between men and women and by large between ex-colonizers and ex-colonized. In this respect, critical discourses have examined patriarchal hegemonic deals towards women by asserting that if African countries were victims of colonization, the African women were victim of double colonization from patriarchy on the one hand and from colonization on the other hand. This chapter purports to make explicit the use of hegemonic masculinities as postcolonial articulation of African women's rights' violation. The specific question addressed is to what extent does the display of male chauvinism read as an extension of colonialism for women?

Many critics have emphasized the patriarchal abusive treatment of women without however viewing such ill-treatment as an extension of colonialism. The first generation of female writers namely Efua T. Sutherland, Ama Ata Aidoo, Tesse Owueme, Zulu Sofola, insisted on the women' s conditions from the perspective of patriarchal oppression and heavy traditions, ancestral customs. What comes under attack with the contemporary African female playwrights is marital unfaithfulness, betrayal and disappointment of a lover, and the desire to revenge:

> Aisosa: What did you expect? Abandoned by a husband, no job, on a meagre allowance of ₦ 10, 000 a month lost my dear parents who were so supportive, struggling to build a house for you and saddled with four children, did you expect to return home to meet a model? If you did, wouldn't you have been surprised? *(SR:* 32)

Aisosa is accusing Sota her husband for marital neglect and abandonment as he travelled for about ten years without being in good touch with her. This form of neglect has had moral, psychological, physical and emotional impacts on her. Morally, she has been affected through the lack of moral comfort, psychologically, the physical displacement brought about the nostalgic longing for a loved one. Physically, Aisosa must have surely lost some weight due to the lack of love. From this perspective, one can agree with the play' s reviewers that Irene Isoken Salami-Agunloye' s *Sweet Revenge* explores the subjugation of women by patriarchal system and the attempt of women to subvert it. She specifically elaborates critical issues namely motherhood by experience, power, female resistance, diasporic issues, nationalism, sexism, and shows possibilities of women' s empowerment. Spousal neglect is a relevant problem in some areas of Africa and other parts of the world, and the choice of drama as a medium to expose and discuss such issues testifies about the playwrights' social commitment to bring about reforms that take into account women' s freedom from gender oppression, sexism, and economic self-reliance. From another perspective, it can be said that Salami-Ogunloye sees women's social plight from the perspective of women's docility. It is a fact that, Aisosa has waited for her husband for more than ten years and the husband turned out to disappoint her. The logic of such a fact is that the wife could have gone to another man without expecting him:

> Winile: There are many jobs a girl can do here in the city. You said your father is doing small jobs. Why couldn't you do odd jobs? Cleaning, vending food, washing. No. The jobs are too dirty for your type. You cannot do dirty work to help yourself, and help your parents? You chose to marry a rich man with wives, so that you can wear fine clothes (*TNTT*: 38).

Here, Chinyere Grace Okafor shows that women's subjugation to men is partly due to their low economic income and their inability to garner sufficient money to meet their needs. Economic exploitation of women is still rampant in many modern African societies like Nigeria where women are being used in informal sector, housemaids, barmaids, waitresses in restaurants, washwomen, babysitters, to mention but a few. The playwright's feminist thrust spurns from the vista that women should battle for their personal economic autonomy, their intellectual attainments and their cultural liberation. The secondary jobs mentioned are underpaid jobs and do not offer women the expected self-reliance socially and economically speaking. As a matter of fact, women, especially youngsters still dive in economic mendicancy and by doing that ensnare themselves in sexual debauchery and exploitation orchestrated by men. Examples can be given from Frank Ogodo Ogbeche's *Harvest of Corruption* (2007) where Aloho and Ochuole are held in the clutches of sexual slavery, exploitation and economic dependence by Chief Ade Aladu Amanka the minister of foreign affairs. Such girls are the target of macho men, sick from megalomania, who use embezzled money from public treasures to flaunt themselves in disproportioned luxuries before these victimized women. Grace Okafor ascribes to the feminist ideology which perceives the woman not from the perspective of a victimized being only, but also from that of one who can actually regain consciousness, decide to free herself and empower her fellow women. That is the hue and cry of Thami a female character who suddenly becomes aware of the unbecoming situation she is in: "Some evil thing is hanging in the air. Can we escape from the air" (*TNTT*: 15). The very 'evil' being referred to here is the victimization of women. Such victimization tantalizes in the male-oriented dark socio-political environment that leaves little space for women to enjoy freedom. To be specific, Okafor unleashes her critical shads against every social structure, political fiefdom, economic barrier, mental enslavement and cultural retrogradation that hold women in dungeon and blur their sights. She underpins the tantalizing idea that women should rebuff all the shackles of docile acceptance of unjust oppression and fight with the fierce energy the economic subjection that maintains them under the lordship of men. This critical stand comes as a denunciation of what is exactly wrong with young females in African societies: "This girl is a victim of poverty. Poverty is also a disease. So, let us fight the disease whether it is in the body, in the mind, or in the food that is no longer enough (*TNTT*: 38)." Poverty is a fact created by man and what is man-made can be unmade by man. She is clear in her submission: poverty being a disease, should be cured either such disease is in the body, the mind or the food. In clear terms, Okafor is saying that there should be no solace for economic barriers like poverty. It should be extracted and fought against. The playwright sees too narrow a sphere of entertainment for African women. In fact, she believes that the well-being of every individual should be whole and the fact that women are deprived of the potential of entertainment is a serious threat to their well-being: "Thami: African women do not have time for tea parties. No time for wear high-heeled shoes. No time for ballroom dancing. African women have no time to enjoy life like Madam" (*TNTT*: 15). This is a complaint of an African woman about their lack of recreational and entertainment time. Such precious entertainments like tea paties, high-heeled shoes and ballroom dancing, though pivotal to women' s welfare, are defaced by men.

> Zanele: I have been married for one year two months and seven days, yet I have not missed my period. I have cough and body weakness and fever. An I think 'I must be pregnant.' I go to the hospital. They tell me that I am not pregnant. They also tell me to bring my husband. But Magagula refuses to go to the hospital, and I cannot do anything about it. I am too young, too small for him, and he does not need more children. But I want a baby, my own baby (*TNTT*: 39).

Zanele is a female character whose husband is careless, boastful and indifferent to her problems. She has been to the hospital because of mental depression, and anxiety. The moral torture has been so rude that it impacted on her menstruation. She thought she was pregnant but this was not the case. Okafor shows that the moral torture inflicted by men on women can actually make them sick. She also highlights the idea that when women are ill-treated, they can actually take initiatives to upset the oppressive structures. It is my contention that Okafor has used metaphor to underpin and upload ideologically charged ideas about feminism, the necessity for women to assert themselves, to actually challenge culturally rooted cumbersome traditions and practices and rewrite a new page of women's emancipatory paradigms. Furthermore, it can be argued that Ntombi's injunction that "When it is time to marry the law will protect me" (*TNTT*: 43) is an intellectual way of perceiving women as citizens in need of the protection of the law. What most African traditional cultures suffer from is the absence of legal dispositions that protect women. One needs to add that determination and perseverance are used in Okafor's *The New Toyi Toyi* as metaphorical symbol to explain the probability of women's success in the struggle. Ntombi pursues: "I am prepared to suffer any kind of hunger as sacrifice for what I shall enjoy in the future" (*TNTT*: 44). The speaker here is referring to the social, political, economic and cultural liberation of women. The idea that freedom comes after a fierce battle with oppressive institutions transpires as a point of departure for the building of determination. If it is acknowledged that every desirable end exacts its price, women like Ntombi and Zanele are well determined to pay that price and reach the goal. The use of the bride-price referred to as lobola by male parents to get rich is denounced and criticized. Women have opened their eyes to the benefits of education. Nomsa, a young girl asserts: "If I marry Samson, my father will no longer pay school fees for me, and he will get another lobola from Samson's father. He will expand my mother's shop. He can even stop doing odd jobs, and become a rich man" (*TNTT*: 46). This is the expression of a girl's consciousness about the way patriarchy works to jeopardize the prospective emancipation of women. Nomsa comes to full awareness of the ways in which her own father is predisposed to actually sell her out for a huge bride-price, to use that money for personal upkeep and for expanding her mother's shop. Such awareness, Nomsa has gained from her ability to decipher materialist inclinations in her father who adores money to the detriment of his female children. This critical stance is reinforced in the play by the statement of Kenneth: "Going after girls can lead you into trouble, but working hard on your studies can earn you a passport to a better life (*TNTT*: 47)". This statement comes in a conversation between Kenneth and Samson two friends who are used to sharing companionship. In fact, Grace

Okafor has created women who are fully aware of the whims of the evil men. But such awareness they also use it to educate their children in the values that should govern the society and the intellectual decisions are made by women. The playwright believes that when women's eyes are open to the awareness of their own liberation, this benefits both men and women. In the logic of the play, she creates teenage male characters with the sense of understanding that women hold their future from the collaborative participation of both sexes. For one thing, women are well aware of one social plight that is AIDS, a plague that kills both men and women, but where women are mostly victims. Social mobilization, demonstrations and protestations are used to sensitize fellow women against the disease and against patriarchy:

> Bongani: If you are with me, come with me to the market and drinking parlor, where we will get more followers for the demonstration. We shall join forces with the women. No matter the name we give to DISEASE, whether AIDS or hunger or cough or plague, it is a disease and we must kill it. Like the *lunwabu*, it can hide under different colors like cough, fever, and running stomach (*coughs*) but we shall recognize all the colors and expose it (*TNTT: 55*).

Here, Bongani has spoken plainly about the agenda of women who are now supported by few men. Three ideas emerge. Firstly, the presence of the disease is real. But the disease here is a metaphor for women's predicament with regard to poverty, enslavement to customs, subjugation to patriarchy and the frequent lack of access to education and decent jobs. This metaphorically designated disease should be exposed, and treated. Secondly, Killing the disease requires the active collaboration of both men and women. This suggests that gender collaboration has not left the vicinity of African feminism. Thirdly, the political authorities must be involved in the struggle against all forms of the disease. So, for Okafor, women's liberation from patriarchy, oppression and poverty requires a concerted action both from the masses and the authorities. Intellectuals, politicians and the masses should collaborate to succeed.

Zeinab Jalo is another Playwright who can be classified among the second wave feminists. She has already embarked on the journey of feminist revolution against women's domestic violence in her play *Onions Make Us Cry*. She believes that Nigerian women and Africans in general are victims of injustice from men. For that reason, she thinks that creative drama should be used to rectify the incongruencies of life. Daniella Menezor gives the following account: *Onions Make Us Cry* (Livelibooks, London, 2009), which featured in the February 25 edition of Rainbow Book Club reading, is a play about domestic violence and its effects. It is set in ward 6 in a hospital or more specifically in 'the first room of ward six.' At first glance, the hospital seems like an unlikely setting for a play on domestic violence until you think of domestic violence as a disease for which a cure must be sought.

The two major characters in the play are women suffering varying degrees of domestic violence; Malinda Jandayi is a patient at the hospital suffering from post traumatic stress disorder having killed her abusive husband by striking him with a pestle. She is in the hospital for evaluation as she awaits her trial for homicide (Daniella Menezor 2011). Lola Gambari, a clinical psychologist at the hospital and Malinda's psychiatrist, is also a victim of domestic violence but when we first meet her, she is in denial about her situation, making up all sorts of excuses to cover up the abuse, especially from her patient's prying questions and comments leading Malinda to make the statement from which the play gets its title '… it's the onions that make us weep…' In what appears to be a reversal of roles, Malinda is able to accurately diagnose Lola's problem, seeing past her excuses, denials, fear and administering a cold dose of reality: "You stare at yourself each time you come here. Except of course, you didn't slay anyone… not yet at least…you fear it won't get to that eh? …you yearn for my company yet you despise it. You are frightened; me or anyone else will see through you…sadly your worst fears are being borne out… wouldn't even let your best friend know…cos every union should be heavenly…a haven, glorious eh? Wrong! Untrue!" (*OMUC*: 32).

In the end, Malinda empowers Lola to face up to her situation and stand up for herself. Lola and her husband agree to seek counseling, yet, as a counselor Lola, doesn't appear to help Malinda. Malinda is disillusioned in marriage; the hospital that is to evaluate her and supposedly help her instead makes her worse, because everyone around her is 'mad.' Finally, her lawyer cannot offer any hope that she'll get her kids back, let alone be acquitted. Domestic violence is a complex issue with no simple solutions and Jallo does not set out to offer the audience any.

9.4. Third Wave African Feminists

Third Wave African feminists think that there is a necessity to enlarge the scope of vision of the African woman and see her as a global citizen.

They advocate the universalist values of material, technological and spiritual conditions that can make the African woman comfortable everywhere she lives on the globe. The philosophy of common space, different grounds that was the philosophical trends of the first and second waves of African feminists needs to be reconsidered with the specific claim of the freedom for the African woman to move everywhere duty calls, to be treated with the rights and prerogatives that all universal citizens enjoy. Amon Third Wave African feminists can be mentioned Chimamanda Ngozi Adichie who launched the debate of global feminism from African perspective in her *We Should All Be Feminists* (2014). But before her published talk, Ade Solanke, a London-based African playwright had already undertaken a theatre campaign to discuss the universal conditions of African women taken in the webb of globalization. In her *Pandora's Box* (2012) which I discuss in chapter sixteen, she started literary reflections on the necessity to revisit women's conditions from a global perspective. That play met a considerable success in the literary world. Taiye Selasi is another African feminist who has global views on African women. The idea of Afropolitanism was proposed by Achille Mbembe and relaunched by Taiye Selasi.

Afropolitan is a term constructed from the name Africa and the ancient Greek root -polis, which literally means city. Polis can also mean citizenship or body of citizens (https://en.wikipedia.org/wiki/Afropolitan). It is to the latter meaning that the term Afropolitan takes its essence. It is an attempt at redefining African phenomena by placing emphasis on ordinary citizens' experiences in Africa. *Afropolitanism* is similar to the older Panafricanism ideology. However, it defines being an "African" in explicitly continent-wide and multiracial terms, and rejects all pretensions to victimhood.

As Achille Mbembe and Sarah Nuttall write, "In an attempt to overturn predominant readings of Africa, we need to identify sites within the continent… not usually dwelt upon in research and public discourse, that defamiliarize commonplace readings of Africa" (Mbembe and Nuttall 2002: 352). These sites include fields like fashion, visual art, music and spiritual concerns.

The term was popularized in 2005 by a widely disseminated essay, "Bye-Bye, Babar (Or: What is an Afropolitan?)" by the author Taiye Selasi. Originally published in March 2005 in the Africa Issue of *the LIP Magazine*, the essay defines an Afropolitan identity, sensibility and experience. The critiques of the Afropolitan, as portrayed by Selasi in Bye-Bye, Babar, condemn its elitism and class biased approach. Susanne Gehrmann states that Selasi's Afropolitan "is addicted to urban hip life" and "international careers." However, the essay is important in discussing where emigrantes of Africa fit into the spectrum of African.

Today, the forces of global engagement are helping some people identify as global citizens who have a sense of belonging to a world community (https://en.wikipedia.org/wiki/Global_citizenship). This growing global identity in large part is made possible by the forces of modern information, communications and transportation technologies. In increasing ways these technologies are strengthening our ability to connect to the rest of the world— through the internet; through participation in the global economy; through the ways in which world-wide environmental factors play havoc with our lives; through the empathy we feel when we see pictures of humanitarian disasters in other countries; or through the ease with which we can travel and visit other parts of the world.

Those of the African women who see themselves as global citizens are not abandoning other identities, such as allegiances to their countries, ethnicities and political beliefs. These traditional identities give meaning to their lives and will continue to help shape who women are. However, as a result of living in a globalized world, women understand that they have an added layer of responsibility; they also are responsible for being members of a world-wide community of people who share the same global identity that they have.

Global citizenship is the rights, responsibilities and duties that come with being a member of the global entity as a citizen of a particular nation or place. The idea is that one's identity transcends geography or political borders and that responsibilities or rights are derived from membership in a broader class: "humanity". This does not mean that such a person denounces or waives their nationality or other, more local identities, but such identities are given "second place" to their membership in a global community. Extended, the idea leads to questions about the state of global society in the age of globalization. In general usage, the term may have much the same meaning as "world citizen" or cosmopolitan, but it also has additional, specialized meanings in differing contexts.

References:

Adichie, Chimamanda Ngozi. *We Should All Be Feminists.* New York: Anchor Books. 2014.

Aidoo, Ama Ata. *Anowa*. London. London: Heinemann Educational Books. 1970.

--------------------. *The Dilemma of a Ghost.* London: Heinemann Educational Books. 1965.

Bailey, Alison and Chris Cuomo. *The Feminist Philosophy Reader.* Boston: McGraw Hills. 2008.

Emenyonu, Ernest N. *Emerging Perspectives on Nawal Al Sadawi.* Trenton: Africa World Press. 2010.

Emenyonu, Ernest N. "Portrait of Flora Nwapa as A Dramatist." In Marie Umeh, ed., *Emerging Perspectives on Flora Nwapa.* Trenton: Africa World Press. 1998. 357-390.

https://en.wikipedia.org/wiki/Afropolitan.

McCann, Carole R. and Seung-kyung Kim. *Feminist Theory Reader: Local and Global Perspective.* New York: Routledge. 2013.

Meneza, Daniella. "Zainab Jalo Decries Woes of the Nigerian Women". 2011. http://www.nigerianbestforum.com/blog/zainab-jalo-decries-woes-of-nigerian-women/

Ogunyemi, Chikwenye Okonjo Ogunyemi. "Womanism: The Dynamics of the Contemporary Black Female Novel in English (1985)." In Layli Phillips, ed., *The Womanist Reader* (New York: Routledge. 2006. 21-36.

Okafor, Chinyere Grace. *The New Toy Toy.* Trenton: Africa World Press. 2007.

Oronsaye-Salami, Irene Isoken. *Sweet Revenge.* Trenton: Africa World Press. 2007.

Otekunefor, Henriette C. and Obiageli C. Nwodo. *Nigerian Female Writers: A Critical Perspectives.* Nigeria: Malthouse Press. 1989.

Rotimi, Ola. *Our Husband Has Gone Mad Again.* London: Heinemann. 1977.

Solanke, Ade. *Pandora's Box.* London: Oberon Books. 2012.

Sutherland, Efua T. *Edufa.* London: Heinemann. 1967.

----------------------. *Foriwa.* London: Heinemann. 1967.

----------------------. *The Marriage of Anansewa. London:* Longman. 1975.

Umeh, Marie. *Emerging Perspectives on Flora Nwapa.* Trenton: Africa World Press. 1998.

10

POSTCOLONIAL RESISTANCE IN FEMI OSOFISAN'S *NO MORE THE WASTED BREED* AND LEKE OGUNFEYIMI'S *SACRIFICE THE KING*

Resistance Theory

Resistance theory is an aspect of political thought, discussing the basis on which constituted authority may be resisted, by individuals or groups. In the European context it came to prominence as a consequence of the religious divisions in the early modern period that followed the Protestant Reformation. Resistance theories could justify disobedience on religious grounds to monarchs, and were significant in European national politics and international relations in the century leading up to the Peace of Westphalia of 1648. They can also underpin and justify the concept of revolution as now understood. Resistance theory of the early modern period can be considered to predate the formulations of natural and legal rights of citizens, and to co-exist with considerations of natural law. Any "right to resist" is a theory about the limitations on civil obedience. Resistance theory is an aspect of political theory; the right of self-defence is usually taken to be a part of legal theory, and was no novelty in the early modern period. Arguments about the two concepts do overlap, and the distinction is not so clear in debates. Resistance theory has been formulated as "resistance to the magistrate", where *magistrate* stands for authority in the legal form. In effect "magistrate" here may stand for head of state, but the modern concept of state grew up alongside the early modern resistance theories, rather than preceding them. Reference was made, for example by Althusius to classical history: to the ephors of the Spartan Constitution, as "lesser magistrates", or to the *optimates* of the late Roman Republic.

One of the objectives of postcolonial literature is to reposition the debate about the power relationships between African leaders and their subjects and by large between Western imperialists and their Third World subjects. This analysis attempts to scrutinize Femi Osofisan's and Leke Ogunfeyimi's aesthetic representations of masses' resistance to post-colonial imperial hegemony in their respective plays *No More the Wasted Breed* and *Sacrifice the King*. The study analyses the two playwrights' critical positions about the imperatives of resistance in a context where unjustified demand of dogmatic allegiance to "authority" is being imposed on the masses. In this respect, the study highlights resistance to oppressive and unjust victimization in society.

Postcolonial literature of resistance champions in literary texts the dismantling of forces of oppression by dissenting voices against the structures of domination and oppression. The selected plays of Femi Osofisan and Leke Ogunfeyimi, respectively *No More a Wasted Breed* (1982) and *Sacrifice the King* (2012) are a literature of resistance that exposes the unjust practices by undermining the power of the dominant structures and eventually carves out an acceptable place for the underprivileged masses of the society. Many critics have tried to characterize the nature and function of Osofisan's drama in *No More a Wasted Breed* without insisting on his aesthetics of resistance, and a rejection of unjust victimization. Criticism has also neglected Leke Ogunfeyimi's *Sacrifice the King* from that angle. According to Chris Egarevba (1987), Osofisan's *No More a Wasted Breed* is a critique of Wole Soyinka's *The Strong Breed* and seeks to criticize the tradition of the ritual carrier (Egharevba 1987: 25). For Elen Savory (1998), Femi Osofisan "criticizes tradition as a romantic escapism" (Savory 1998: 376). Helen Gilbert excludes Leke Ogunfeyimi from his sphere of criticism and talks about Osofisan's acute historical consciousness that emerges through a re-interpretation of the past and an engagement with traditional Yoruba performance (Gilbert 2001: 69). Tunde Akinyemi and Toyin Falola (2009) overlook Leke Ogunfeyimi as a post-colonial anti-imperialist writer, and opine that the central issue of Femi Osofisan's drama is his desire to fight for the marginalized masses and to create a better society for all to live in" (Akinyemi and Falola 2009:3). These critics rarely mention Osofisan's play *No More the Wasted Breed* and Leke Ogunfeyimi's *Sacrifice the King* as ideological tools for a post-colonial critique of Western Imperialism and African post-independent politics. That is why I think both plays need a re-examination that sheds new insights on their anti-imperialist perspectives.

10.1. The Aesthetics of Resistance of Femi Osofisan and Leke Ogunfeyimi

Resistance according to *Longman Dictionary of English Language and Culture* is the fact of opposing or fighting against something (Summers 2003: 1133). In this chapter I use resistance to mean disobedience to authority, religious and political, especially when their dictates are irrational and oppressive. Post-colonial theoretical approaches negotiating Femi Osofisan's dramaturgic and theatrical output show that he has consistently questioned the post-colonial African condition. He has developed in his drama a post-colonial theory of resistance to imperial authority and capitalist oppressors. His pen is sharp in showing through theatrical creativity social disparities and class dichotomy as the profound causes of the masses' grudge and revolt against their "gods". He uses many metaphors in drama to address the contemporary African society's problems. Myth is one such metaphorical device which he uses to make the gods interact with the indigenous population. Muyiwa Awodiya a a post-colonial resistance theoretician posits that

> Femi Osofisan's basic material is the expression of rebellion, an element that recurs overtly or covertly in his work. Discontented with old and static forms, Osofisan finds it impracticable to identify with the existing art forms, government system, or program, or even to ally himself with any leftist revolutionary vanguard. His revolt against human forces of oppression, corruption and injustice is a means of engaging the status quo and agitating for moral, social, artistic, religious, and political transformation. His theatre reflects both his sympathy for human suffering and his outrage of human absurdity (Awodia 2006: 50).

This critical appraisal reveals the theoretical orientations of Osofisan's art which puts resistance and rebellion to unjust oppressive masters at the forefront. The agenda of his post-colonial resistance theory is more specifically political which, in the words of Helen Gilbert and Joanne Tompkins is to "dismantle the hegemonic boundaries and the determinants that create unequal relations of power based on binary oppositions" such as "us (the poor) and them (the rich)", "first world and third world", "white and black", "colonizer and colonized" (Gilbert and Tompkins 2002: 3). A conspicuous aspect of his theory responds to more than the merely chronological construction of post-independence and becomes a discursive experience of anti-imperialist struggle. To consolidate his theory, Femi Osofisan uses myth and rituals to talk about the African predicament. He creates human characters as well as deity characters. *No More the Wasted Breed, Red Is the Freedom Road, Many Colours Make Thunder King* are few examples where characters of human attributes intermingle with gods. My analysis focuses on *No More the Wasted Breed*. His use of symbols, metaphors, and traditional images according to Helen Gilbert,

> [...] all converge and translate into semiotic essence, becoming a poetic language conveying his message of resistance to oppression. Even from the cover pages and titles the reader encounters semiotics as it plays itself out at varying levels of symbol, icon, index, image and metaphor (Ibidem).

In Osofisan's theatrical epistemology, the oppressive rulers to be resisted are voracious gods who like to prey endlessly on the menial pittance of their worshipers. At this point, the playwright has these worshipers counter-attack with a language of resistance and denounce the abuses of the gods. To better understand how Femi Osofisan uses myth as metaphor to describe power dichotomy between Western imperialist forces and African post-colonial states on the one hand and the masses and their leaders in Nigerian society on the other hand, it is important to give a particular attention to Osofisan's post-colonial theory of resistance. His theory is foregrounded in his ideological inclination towards social justice, as he has Olokun say it: "I am condemned always to be on the side of justice (*NMTWB: M AOP: 89*). Osofisan's predilection for social justice is confirmed in Biokun's indictment of the leaders who connive with the European imperialists to over-exploit the masses:

> BIOKUN: What is justice when you hack a tree down and blame the handle of the axe? You complain of pollution, but who brought the ships of merchandise from across the ocean to our shore? You complain of being abandoned, but who brought the predators who impoverished our people and turned them into groveling slaves? *(NMTWB: M AOP: 108).*

The two extracts above reveal Femi Osofisan's concern about social justice and his belief that in the face of capitalism, resistance against authority is not an act of rebellion. To begin, he dislikes African leaders conniving with European imperialists to maintain African nations in economic dependency through the conduit pipes of capitalism and imperialism.

Femi Osofisan's post-colonial theory of resistance is an anti-imperial language engaged in contestation with capitalist and imperialist discourses, power structures and social hierarchies rampant in African societies. It posits that capitalism, the twin sister of Western imperialism is insidious in that it invades far more than political chambers and extends well beyond independence celebrations. Its effects shape language, education, religion, artistic sensibilities, and, increasingly, popular culture. Osofisan's post-colonialism is politically motivated, historically analytical and engages with imperial discourses, resists and seeks to dismantle the effects of Western imperialism, neocolonialism, and African oppressive capitalism in material, historical, cultural, political and textual domains.

Some metaphors and dramatic symbols are used to address the theory of African post-colonial resistance imbedded in the masses' social predicament. Wendell V. Harris endorses that a metaphor is "the rhetorical device of giving something a name that belongs to another thing for the purpose of emphasis (Egharevba 1987: 222)." It is also "a trope in which one thing is referred to in terms of another in a way semantically inappropriate and in which the inappropriateness triggers a meaning not derivable from semantics, that is, dictionary senses alone (Ibidem)." From these definitions I posit that metaphors and tropes are used interchangeably to mean in literary creation the fact of attributing something the name and meaning belonging to another thing by way of rhetoric or by way of concealing its meaning to a common observer. I will be using trope and metaphor interchangeably. Let us go a step further to provide a reliable chart summarizing Femi Osofisan's and Leke Ogunfeyimi's metaphorical character representation and the plays in which they are described:

Some binary representations of oppressing and oppressed characters:

Oppressor	Oppressed	Play (source)
Maggot, Stray Dogs, Predators	Crabs, Scorpions, Preys	*NMTWB, MAOP*: 93, *100*, 108
The Gods	Mortal Humans	*SK*: 16, 17
The King	The subject	*SK*: 46
Policeman	Prisoner	*NMWB; MAOP*: 20
Medicine Man	Madman	*SK*: 68
Slave master	Slave	*NMTWB; MAOP*: 118; *SK*: 80

This table represents the social class dichotomy of symbolic characters in the positions of oppressors and oppressed. They provide concrete images of the predatory relationships between the rich and the poor. While the men in power are delineated as immortal gods, masters, kings, lions, slave masters, and medicine men, the masses are presented as slaves, mortal subjects, prisoners, subjects, crickets, toads. These representations highlight unequal power relationships since the former are far more powerful, economically and socially speaking, than the latter. On the other hand, a binary opposition can be seen between these metaphorical characters. In each play, a predatory person or animal is matched with its easy prey, so that we assist to a life of a jungle where the powerful creatures feast on the weak ones. For instance in *No More the Wasted Breeds,* the crabs and scorpions are put together with dogs and maggots (*NMTWB, MOP: 93*), their easy prey; while in *Sacrifice the King*, the slave is doomed to share space with his master (*SK: 80*). The rich devour all the resources while the poor are left with the crumbs.

The belief that gods are the sole responsible for human social conditions is being rejected here by the playwright who relocates the destiny of man within the ambit of his own struggle for positive change. All expectations of socio-economic change from the divine powers alone without the active participation and cooperation of man, the stakeholder of the change is bound to fail. Osofisan and Ogunfeyimi reassert that dogmatic allegiance to deities who endlessly require sacrifices of body and soul from human beings will unquestionably result in disappointment. As the critic Chris Egharevba posits, "Femi Osofisan, like several folks out here is a supplicant at the shrine of the gods. But true to the spirit of the age, he would not mind emptying the washbasin on the scalp of any god (or goddess) who misbehaves" (Egharevba: 1987: 32). This critical analysis gives credence to my claim that Femi Osofisan's art is expressive of the masses' aspirations to autonomy and self-government. This is conveyed through a certain language that deserves critical attention.

10.1.2. *Sacrifice the King*: Leke Ogunfeyimi's Poetics of Resistance

Leke Ogunfeyimi's poetics of resistance is incrusted in his dismantling of oppression through the artistic representation of the masses' demand that the king be sacrificed. His message complements Femi Osofisan's in that he thinks that for the survival of the nation's interest, it is the king who must be sacrificed. Resistance in *Sacrifice the King* rests essentially on the population's contestation of their king's illegitimacy. It is a way for the masses to criticize dictators' undemocratic ways of coming into power, especially through rigged elections or military coups. On the other hand, the playwright Leke Ogunfeyimi artistically puts resistance at the level of the scapegoat allegory. The major philosophical question that he tries to ask is "who should die for the African nations to survive?" Who should be sacrificed for the interests of the nation? His answer is "sacrifice the king". He thinks that a leader is there to serve the nation, defend its interests, and promote its welfare no matter what it costs him in terms of money, energy, time and dignity. In fact, a true leader cares for his people. He should be able to sacrifice himself for the nation to survive. A leader who cannot rise to that nobility of humanitarian task for his population does not deserve the allegiance of his people. The people must resist him. Thus, Leke Ogunfeyimi's aesthetics of resistance falls in line with Femi Osofisan's, for both think that the masses should resist their leader when he/she doesn't rise to the responsibility of true leadership: the promotion of the poor people's welfare. Given the irresponsible attitude towards leadership which bedevils most countries of the African continent, *Sacrifice the King* details the brazen assumption of power which most unscrupulous African leaders misuse to tyrannize and brutalize their subjects. The playwright succeeds in articulating the "disease" of African leadership, or the body politic which can be summarized as the thirst and hunger for wealth accumulation, power drunkenness, personality cult, and the immoral lust for women. This is exemplified in the play through the dialogue between King and Arugbo:

> King: […] Lead him out of this land. He shall spend the rest of his days in exile. Two bosses cannot row the same boat of cassava. They will capsize it.
> Arugbo: (*Shouts*) People of Iseluwa, it is a great honour to temporarily be on exile for my soul to gain permanent rest than endure the pain of perpetual servitude … (*SK: 11-12*)

Here, Arugbo is in contestation with the King about the courageous denunciation of King as the real cause of the drought in the kingdom. Outraged, the king orders him to quit the kingdom or he shall be killed. This sudden threat takes a political tune in that, Arugbo has become a political prisoner, a prisoner of opinion. He is refused the right of residence. For the king, Arugbo must, in addition to living in the kingdom with restricted freedom, pay taxes to the king's treasury. Here, Leke Ogunfeyimi has introduced another dramatic element: the King's legitimacy is contested both by the oracles and by his citizens. Despite that contestation of legitimacy, the king forces things to remain in power. This dramatic episode is an allusion to the very much contested enthronization of African leaders who come to power through military coups and seek to remain in power for life. To achieve that goal he resorts to dictatorship:

> King: […] Tell them to bring that fool who thinks he can toy with the edge of my sword! (*Servant leaves.*) If indeed I am not who I am, why am I no longer what I am? Elders toy with my crown; my whisk, my scepter are what children use for their panks and other games of fun. My name rings no longer with fear but fun […] Awolalu…is it true that the oracle did not lend credence to my appointment as the Asalu of Iseluwa? (*SK*: 46)

Here, the king does not accept that his office mandate is over and that there should be a political alternance. For him, he must continue to rule the kingdom despite his illegitimacy. That is the reason why his population contests his rule. That is why it develops a philosophy of resistance to his leadership. Leke Ogunfeyimi, like Femi Osofisan, develops a theory of post-colonial resistance pointed towards the masses' aspiration to self-government. His dramaturgy elicits the trajectory and temperament of coming to terms in a visceral sense with the contemporary problems of leadership and challenges of Africa. These range from military dictatorship, political perfidy and economic corruption, ethnic nationalism, violation of fundamental human rights by the state, official injustice, mass pauperization through decadent economic policies. The issues Femi Osofisan and Leke Ogunfeyimi contend with remain dominantly the same: the re-humanization of our dehumanized world through creative art. Ogunfeyimi and Osofisan's dramaturgies evince the post-colonial spirit which is quintessential of all post-colonial literatures.

10.2. The Language of Resistance in *No More the Wasted Breed* and *Sacrifice the King*

10.2.1. Diction

Diction in this study refers to the artistic use of language through a careful choice of words to represent postcolonial imperatives of resistance. Helen

Gilbert and Joanne Tompkins have established that "Post-colonial stages are particularly resonant spaces from which dramatists articulate linguistic resistance to imperialism" (Gilbert and Tompkins 1996: 116). This analysis is relevant to my approach to Femi Osofisan's *No More the Wasted Breed* and Leke Ogunfeyimi's *Sacrifice the King* in that language in these plays functions both as a basic medium through which meaning is filtered, and also as a socio-cultural vector that has meaning in itself by conveying Osofisan's postcolonial ideology as a writer. The post-colonial stage acts as a principal arena for the enunciation of such a linguistic system. In Osofisan's *Red Is the Freedom Road* just like in *No More the Wasted Breed,* the playwright uses diction borrowed from the linguistic lore of fishing to adapt to the stage. Sentence styles and vocabulary are referring to resistance to oppression: "Freedom or death!" (*RITFR: MAOP*: 131) is a parody of war cry connoting the hardcore resistance. Grammatical structures, adjectives, adverbs, exclamations, interrogations, imperatives, interjections all converge to highlight the playwright's ideology of resistance to imperialism and unjust capitalist exploitation of the poor by the rich: The solution to oppression is "the rebellion, the revolt, the *coup d'état* (*RITFR: MAOP*: 133) which are nominals conveying violence: "red runs the freedom road" (*RITFR: MAOP*: 133) is a pun denoting how hard freedom acquisition is. Other instances of resistance language are: speak with "bitter tongue" (*NMTWB: MAOP*: 96). This locution refers to the masses' cursing the gods; "walking on the back of a crocodile" (*NMTWB: MAOP*: 96) is a metaphor alluding to the resistance from the masses to give sacrifices. "Carrying a mole" is the image of resistance of the masses to obey. The mole symbolizes delay (*NMTWB: MAOP*: 97). The construction of the plot, characters' actions and reactions to situations are focal strategies deployed by the playwright to bring out the ideas of resistance. To begin with, Biokun and Saluga both fishermen, are radical in their belief in the power of the gods as the inflictors of their predicament. Biokun's only son, born after waiting for ten "seasons", is about to die, one of the victims of Elusu's vengeance. But unknown to him, he is the sacrifice needed, for, as revealed later, Biokun is of the line of Carriers: he bears the mark of the foredoomed. Thus there is a gradual understanding or a realization of a tragic destiny; that he has to offer himself for the survival of the community:

> ELUSU: Let her carrier go, and all will be restored. The water will withdraw and the fishes return. All the dying will live again.
> [...] BIOKUN: I have no choice but to take the risk. Look at so much suffering in the land. If I could do so little to end it –
> (*NMTWB: M AOP: 103*)

Here, the playwright uses a language of resignation to start. But this will not last before the character's eyes open to the necessity of resisting to the gods, demand with a critical language. They operate a language shift to adopt a discourse that criticizes the excessive demands of sacrifices from the gods. One can see that the gods endorse the imperative that the only solution to end the flood that threateningly kills the inhabitants is that a human being (Biokun's son) be sacrificed to the river goddess, because, he has been chosen as ritual carrier. A human sacrifice as demanded by the deity is the sine qua non condition to restore life to the normal. In this perspective, we see Biokun acquiesce to the tragic destiny of self-sacrifice in the moral belief of providing salvation for his community. It is in this perspective that Chris Egarevba suggests that in Femi Osofisan's portraiture, it is perceptible that despite the optimistic tag attached to it by some critics like Chris Egarevba, the play does not end with this type of tragic acceptance of a doom through a radical look at the essence of the ritual carrier. For Femi Osofisan, allegiance to the gods must be backed up by a certain rationality. After sacrificing to the deities, the problem of man must find solution, otherwise, the god becomes a cruel dictator. In that case, his worshiper can stop sacrificing. As Saluga puts the question, "What do they add up to, except that one day he'll (Biokun's son) be ripe for the long teeth of a goddess" (*NMTWB: M AOP*: 104). But Biokun, still urged on by the feeling of saving his people through his self-sacrifice, refuses to listen to Saluga's tirades:

> SALUGA: […] Tell me, why is it always us who give our lives? Why is it always the poor who are called to sacrifice? Why is it always the wretched, never a wealthy man, never the son of a king, who is suddenly discovered to bear the mark of destiny at difficult moments, and pushed on to fulfill himself in suicidal tasks? Why?
> TOGUN: You must ask the gods, who decide such things (*NMTWB: M AOP*: 105).

The questions raised by Saluga here are objective and rational: "why is it always us who give our lives?" "Why is it always the poor who are called to sacrifice?" "Why is it always the wretched, never a wealthy man, never the son of a king?" From this dialogue, one idea to underscore is that the gods in the land of Saluga and Biokun have one intolerable attitude: that of demanding endless sacrifices from the poor, not from the rich. For these deities the wretched of the land, the downtrodden and the needy are those who must always sacrifice to the gods to maintain the rich people alive and prosperous. Such an attitude is unjust and wicked. Femi Osofisan does not conceal his indignation and protest to the system where allegiance to divine decree is a matter of one social group, the underprivileged.

Here it is the issue of unjust victimization of innocent citizens which is questioned. The playwright allies with the masses and uses his art to effect change in their favour. That is why he puts penetrating questions in the mouth of his character Saluga to call to attention the subjectivity and injustice of the autocratic deities. These penetrating questions can only arise from the perspective of a writer who allies himself with the suffering masses in his society.

In *Sacrifice the King,* Arugbo's language of resistance is predicated on exile: "People of Iselua, it is a great honour to temporarily be on exile for my soul to gain permanent rest than endure the pain of perpetual servitude" (*SK:* 12). Exile here is an escape way to resist servitude.

I endorse that Saluga has acquired a new awareness about the intractable character of the deity Elusu. Here Femi Osofisan puts into question the philosophy of dogmatic allegiance to imperial authorities, for the playwright is using the religious language to address socio-political questions. The critic Hope O. Eghagha advances the thesis that "in his plays, Osofisan has transformed the mythopoeic concerns contained in traditional Yoruba cosmology into a tool of radical conscientization" (Eghagha 2009: 106). In other words, the playwright is raising the point whether disobedience to an authority that cares little for its subjects in spite of their loyalty to it can be interpreted as an act of rebellion and be morally condemned. From my perspective, I think that a worshipper who refuses to pay allegiance to his deity because the god has unleashed cruel punishment on him/her cannot be blamed for that. It seems self-contradictory to flog a child and prevent it from crying. Another critic, Henri Oripeloye puts it this way, "The play in many ways is an act of social change, a concept bound up with Osofisan's belief that positive consciousness is attained through spiritual purgation" (Oripeloye 2009: 106). This suggests that a person's physical well being is commanded and controlled by his spiritual fitness. But the spiritual exercise cannot be performed without a balanced body, well fed and well clothed. As the saying goes, a wholesome spirit must live in a wholesome body. Hope O. Eghagha's stance is relevant here when he says that in most of his dramas, Femi Osofisan's thematic preoccupations are firmly and consistently rooted in a strong didactic interrogation of the power relations and class conflicts that control the African societies, conflicts between the forces of capitalism and the oppressed people of society (Eghagha 2009: 65). These are the powers of capitalism and the forces of the oppressed masses of the society. Leke Ogunfeyimi on his part uses some proverbs "It is death that can remove the shoes from the feet of a goat" (*SK:* 51). It is a proverb which points to the masses' determination to resist capitalist oppressors till death. Another proverb is "The orange that fails to give its sweetness, to the farmer, birds will make a waste of it" (*SK:* 53). That proverb means, a leader (king) who fails to work for the welfare of his subjects will be deposed by the masses. *Sacrifice the King* is thus replete with an artistic use of a language of postcolonial resistance.

The unjustified killing of Saluga has awoken the radical spirit in Biokun. Chris Egharevba remarks that Biokun's consciousness awakening becomes real and thus "begins his self- realization which includes a historical realization of the societal problem" (Egharevba 2009: 32). That problem is the precarious living conditions of the indigenous population characterized by extreme poverty, abject lack of food, clean water and money indispensable for decent living. Biokun thinks that in such a context, spiritual worship to their deity is not possible, for one must live before worshipping:

> BIOKUN: I was blind, just like my father.... But my eyes are clear now. Saluga told the truth [...] The people, goddess, they abandoned your cult because you failed us. Because you take and take, and give nothing back, except betrayal, except a great betrayal! They did not kill you, you killed yourself. *(NMTWB: M AOP:* 108*)*

And Biokun's sparkling remark is that "we will never survive... as long as such gods as these are around" *(NMTWB: MAOP: 108)* is pragmatic and true. It is a sparkling remark which denotes the character's consciousness awakening of the abnormal living conditions they are in and his decision to change, to shift from one attitude to the goddess to another attitude. In other words, Biokun is saying that they have to break away with traditional worship which has pulled them backwards for years, and resume a pragmatic attitude in life, an attitude that consists into taking their destiny in their own hands. One important remark here is that Osofisan has made his characters change. He has had Saluga and Biokun shift from their primitive naïve obedience to traditional deities to a pragmatic attitude of self-defense and the prime belief that man is the shaper and carver of his own destiny, not the god only. That change of mind is translated in the refusal of the worshippers to obey the goddess henceforth. They have refused to bring sacrifice to her again. Osofisan has brought his characters to maturity. The characters have undergone what Hope O. Eghagha calls "character metastasis", which he explains as "a predilection to move on, to abandon ship once the milieu becomes inclement" (Ibidem). This means that one needs to be realistic and objective about the conditions in which one lives. For instance obedience to authority is good insomuch as the rules issued by that authority fit in with the well being of the social fabric one lives in. Nevertheless, rules issued with the only intention to crush, to squash and to squeeze the poor masses need simply not to be obeyed, and the masses are not accountable for civil rebellion. It is the rationale behind the philosophical questions raised by Eghagha as follows:

> Why do people change? What accounts for a repudiation of past values and the embrace of new ones? Is character change simply a psychological experience or something determined by one's social class? Is it a manifestation of one inherent weakness? When can character change be said to be progressive? (Ibidem).

In fact these questions are pivotal to the understanding of Femi Osofisan's logic and his dramaturgy. To better apprehend a character's social behavior one needs to dig deep into the past life of that character and see the contingency of diverse forces that have come to junction to shake the fundamental prime values of that character to bring him to life crisis. The quest for the resolution of these crises determines him or her to repudiate old values and embrace new ones. To make the point clearer, one may apply these questions to the lives of the two characters Saluga and Biokun as they happen in *No More a Wasted Breed*. When the inhabitants of the land (the setting is a seashore in one of the Yoruba ancient kingdoms) have given all they could give to their goddess Elusu to obtain the restoration of life threatened by the floods and came to no results; and when the priests continued asking for more sacrifices, they found enough reason to change from allegiance to that goddess to rebellion. For Chris Egharevba, "the voice of Biokun becomes the voice of the people who have suffered economic hardships, and as a result, he questions the essence of such cultural values; one has to survive to think of culture or tradition (Egharevba 2009: 33)." He carries his analysis a step further by saying that "What we find here is a certain new awareness, the realization that the economic base of the society determines the political structure which in turn influences the cultural outlook of the people" (Ibidem). What the reader can hear from Biokun is not a strident voice of frustration *per se* but an ideological analysis of what is fundamental to the advancement of our contemporary society. In a proverbial rhetoric, he asks the question of the responsibility of the goddess who punishes the worshippers with a stick and blames it on the very handle she has used to hold the stick: "What is the justice, when you hack a tree down, and blame the handle of the axe?" *(NMTWB: M AOP:* 108). The meaning of this proverb is fully stated in the next intervention of Biokun where he explains clearly the bone of contention between their goddess and her worshippers:

> BIOKUN: Only a happy people pay homage to their gods. We fed you with the best of our seasons, praying for peace and abundance. But instead, you brought us the white slavers, who carried off our best men to the far plantations to anguish and humiliation. You did not shake your head, and overturn their ships on the way. You did not ask your tides to lead them astray before they reached us. They rode on your shoulders and they brought the terror of guns, corruption of cowries, they brought their venereal diseases. And now they have seized control of the main land over there, have seized our richest lands, and are busy carting off to their brethren back at home the most precious of our natural resources. (*NMWB: MAOP*: 108-109)

In this excerpt, the "deities" [African leaders] are accountable for the painful memories of African history, for showing the way to Europeans during slave trade, colonization and neocolonialism that gave open hand to Europeans to capture Africans to American plantations, to loot her Africa's economic and cultural resources. Some African leaders have connived with foreign agents to bring woes in the land, especially slave raiders, colonizers, White merchants to loot and pilfer all the natural resources and the wealth of the indigenous population. She has also conspired with white oppressors and European capitalists to snatch the lands from African poor peasants. These devices are purposefully introduced by the playwright to denounce what Loy Tyson calls "cultural imperialism" (Tyson 2006: 425) and I will add socio-economic imperialism. By the time Biokun is speaking, it seems that Africans are still bearing the scars of the slave raiders' whips. In such a situation the worshippers, no matter how docile they are, cannot continue paying allegiance to their deity, the one who betrays her worshippers to foreign invaders. Allegiance therefore does not pass the test of rationality. This critical stance is shared by Derek Walcott who calls it "the muse of history, a deep thought about historical facts that have shaped one's social existence" (Walcott 2003: 370). Let me stress here that Femi Osofisan's sympathy lies with the masses and his concern is the improvement of their living conditions, which should start by the change of their economic life. In a given society, economy determines the nature of socio-political relations between individuals and their leaders and unless people get fairer deals of the wealth they generate, there will always be social tensions between the leader and the led. When the economic life is whole, social relations are good but they start going sour when the economy is in trouble. "The problem of that community", points out the critic Chris Egharevba "is more economic than moral and does not arise from the sins of the people but from the nature of the gods in the society" (Egharevba 2009: 33). Similarly, he pursues," their survival lies not in the procurement of a yearly scapegoat willing or unwilling as Carrier to appease these gods, but in the rejection of these gods who "take and take and give nothing back except betrayal" (Ibidem). Osofisan thinks that the concept of allegiance needs a new definition in that community. The people in power, symbolized by the gods have made it a hell for their subjects to pay homage to them and the playwright uses this trope to call back to rectitude the morals of a society that has been curved and hackneyed. The gods support the robbers of the nation:

> BIOKUN: Those are your friends, the ones you protect. They can go and come as they will across your waters, and across the skies of your brother Orun. You ask no sacrifice of them, no token of allegiance. They are rich and few... But we are numerous and nameless, like the sand of the beach, we are wretched and expendable. (*NMWB: MAOP*: 108-109)

By accusing the goddess to be on the side of the rich oppressors, to the detriment of the masses, Biokun has a point. For him, the goddess is corrupt because she doesn't judge fairly between the rich and the poor; being the friend of the former and neglecting the latter. But what is more interesting is that Osofisan has had these characters (the worshippers) be united in their act of disobedience to the goddess. They are unanimous in their refusal to bring sacrifices to her. That unity has achieved some results, because the goddess has taken note and changed her attitude towards the worshippers.

10.2. 2. Dramatic Symbolism Fostering Resistance

Both Femi Osofisan and Leke Ogunfeyimi use myths and symbols to foster postcolonial resistance of the masses against their double crossing leaders, that is leaders who make promises they never keep. Myth serves as an important symbolic dramatic device. It is used to explain the world beyond human control. Among the many functions attributed to metaphor, that of Bayo Ogunjimi and Abdul-Rasheed Na'Allah who propose that "Myths deal with forces above man and of course man himself" (Ogunyemi and Na' Allah 2005: 55) is edifying. Starting with Osofisan, I will borrow words from J. C. Cirlot to assert that the basic ideas that allow me to conceive of symbolism together with literary creation and vitality are the following: firstly, the 'cesspit' is the symbol of the masses rejection of their "god" (*NMWB, MAOP*: 89); nothing is meaningless or neutral, everything is significant (Guirlot 2001: xxxvi). Secondly, 'the flotsam' represents the goddess reduced in a pile of garbage (*NMWB, MAOP*: 89), her worshipers resisted to her will, making her skirm in the depth of humiliation (*NMWB, MAOP*: 92). Symbols operate both at quantitative and qualitative levels. "The quantitative symbols", according to J. E. Cirlot, "become the qualitative in certain essentials which, in fact, precisely constitute the meaning of the quantity (Ibidem)." This means that numerical numbers of symbols reinforce the strength of their meanings. Many symbols are there to reinforce theatrical meaning. For instance, the deities stand for Western powers who have forged Africa's present destiny. But looking closely, the deities also stand for the political leaders who have shaped the destiny of the Nigerian nation. His characters are in pairs. The deities are in couple, male and female. The playwright is using the idea of binary opposition with the gods to point to the fact that both men and women in power are to be blamed for the prevailing social plight of the nation. The human beings are in a team of two. The number "2" in the play speaks about class dichotomy. The Nigerian society is split into two classes: the rich and the poor, with sharp antagonism on their living conditions. The rich people, who are also the men in power, arrogantly display their wealth to the annoyance of the poor. Ultramodern luxury cars, splendid mansions, extravagant dressings, first class home-use appliances, expensive parties, festivities and birthday celebrations, a life of debauchery with women in hotels, ultramodern fashion wedding celebrations are some of the manifestations of the luxury of the oligarchic leading class to which Femi Osofisan has seen suitable to attribute the transcendental attribute of gods. Indeed these leaders consider themselves above fellow human beings, since they demand constant allegiance and worshipping from the underprivileged class.

As the critic Chris Egharevba points out, "Osofisan's sensibility at the time of writing *No More the Wasted Breed* was shaped by the frustrations of the masses in the face of a blatant exploitation" (Ibidem). In Osofisan's play, there is a thorough revisitation and reassessment of the parameters of the old mythology so as to reassert the rights and claims of a society that has been for too long dispossessed by her leaders. Femi Osofisan's dramatic techniques also bear to some extent significant meaning. *No More the Wasted Breed* is a tragedy. The actions of the play are treated seriously. Characterization, I have said is infused with symbolic meaning. In the prologue, the gods appear, disguised in human forms of Old Man and Woman. This appearance reinforces the technique of theatre where actors pretend in their roles. But at a deeper level, the disguise of the gods in human form is a metaphorical representation of the hypocritical behavior of the leaders. When they want to appear before the population, they masque themselves with humanistic attributes, language and actions, to gain the confidence of the masses, but after that they change their behavior again. For instance, during electoral consultations, leaders display hypocritical kindness with ponderous promises of happy life to the masses. To have their ballots they offer gifts and make promises. But once elected, they never fulfill their promises. When they return in their strongholds, they resume their superhuman wicked lifestyle.

The gods and the humans, respectively leaders and masses, live in different environments: the sea for gods and the land for humans. The sea is symbol of abundance and plenty. In in like manner that water never dries in the sea, in the same manner wealth never lacks in the palaces of the leaders. The same way that gods hold power of life and death on humans, the way autocratic leaders hold supreme power on their subjects. The same way gods are demanding about sacrifices to their shrine, the same way oppressive leaders demand from the masses extra efforts to supply their needs through taxes and other contributions but they resist to their demands. In the first movement of the play, the stage direction shows Biokun over a "narrow muddy path, carrying a pot, earthen, chalked white" (*NMWB, MAOP*: 91) on his way to perform a sacrifice. The narrow muddy path is the symbolical representation of the hardships of life for the average citizen. Not only is life difficult but it is full of pressures, symbolized by the mud. The masses undergo constant pressures from their leaders without having the right to protest or disobey them. The pot is symbol of the heavy underpaid or unpaid jobs that the workers do for the rich from where they derive their wealth. Biokun's own "face is partially chalked white too, his body naked, save for a white wrapper round his waist. He walks in slowly, solemn manner, seeming to count his steps" (*NMWB, MAOP*: 91). The tattooing in white is a ritual act and symbolically stands for obedience to the gods' spiritual principles. In clear words, the masses must do all they can, including physical acrobatic feats to please their leaders. The appearance in naked body symbolizes the material poverty of the population. They lack everything from money to clothes, passing by food and potable water, for the gods have defiled the inland waters.

An investigation conducted by Festus Igu Idoko reveals that the major theatrical strategies Femi Osofisan uses to capture audience's attention include dance, music, proverbs, myths and legends – all these take inspiration from the rich Yoruba tradition of South Western Nigeria (Idoko 2009: 136). Osofisan's dramaturgy speaks for the masses and is very popular not only among the Yoruba axis but also in other Third World countries. Although his constituency is the Yoruba, his audience is a mixed one, and this shows that his works are not only for the Yoruba audience, but for all the nationalities and races around the world because of its universal application. In this perspective it is not far-fetched to say with Festus Igu Idoko that "these universal applications are evident from the thematic strands that run through his play" (Ibidem). Though writing a tragedy, he is tactful and humorous in his surreptitious and subversive treatment of Yoruba traditional materials and motifs.

The underlying perspective of Leke Ogunfeyimi's play *Sacrifice the King* emphasizes what Chidi Amuta calls "a certain projection of the masses as the real makers of history, a clamor for a revolutionary transformation of society and the abandonment of the capitalist economic framework" (Amuta 1989: 57). One of his major means towards achieving this purpose is the creation of what David Cook refers to as "mythical figures, types, generalized personae" (Cook 1977: 200). Although the playwright attributes names to these characters, he wants us as readers to identify ourselves and with others whom we know with these prototypes. If this terminology is to be adopted, there is need to clarify the meaning of myths. In *Sacrifice the King*, the slave/master symbolism is ever present to explain the fact that postcolonial forces relationships between leaders and masses are lopsided with the leaders weighing heavily on the scale while the masses are so weak and light. As David Cook points it out, though the masses may speak panegyric in the presence of officials or leaders, in the streets when evening comes in the village, the bitter disappointment of the people, their despair but also their unceasing anger makes itself heard (Ibidem).

Through their arts, Femi Osofisan and Leke Ogunfeyimi are spokespersons in defense of the masses causes. Their dramas are verged towards a re-education of the masses to the republican values of democracy, human rights and freedom. Their languages are revelatory of committed artists whose emerging perspectives take into account the embitterment of indigenous masses.

In this study, I have focused on two main points. The first one is that Femi Osofisan and Leke Ogunfeyimi have written a drama of resistance that takes position for the masses in the debate on the question of victimization and resistance. Secondly, resistance is normal when oppression is unjustified. I came up with the results that African contemporary drama is still dynamic in representing the masses in contestation with their leaders. Through a careful handling of language and theme, Femi Osofisan and Leke Ogunfeyimi convince the reader that in the face of oppression, the masses should be left free to make up their own minds. They are good debaters; unobtrusively yet firmly, who guiding the direction of the reader's thoughts.

References

Akinyemi, Tunde and Toyin Falola. *Emerging Perspectives on Femi Osofisan.* Trenton: Africa World Press. 2009.

Amuta, Chidi. *The Theory of African Literature: Implications for Practical Criticism.* London: Zed Books Ltd. 1989.

Awodiya, Muyiwa. "Celebrating Femi Osofisan at Sixty:" In Soda Adeyemi (eds.) *Portraits for an Eagle.* Bayreuth: Bayreuth African Studies. 2006. PP. 49-52.

Cirlot, J. E.. *A Dictionary of Symbols.* London: Routledge. 2001.

Clark, Timothy. *The Cambridge Introduction to Literature and Environment* Cambridge: Cambridge University Press. 2011.

Cook, David. *African Literature: A Critical View.* London: Longman Group Limited. 1977.

Egharevba, Chris. "The Carrier Ritual as Medium of Vision in Nigerian Drama: the Examples of Soyinka and Osofisan". In Ernest N. Emenyonu (ed.) *Critical Theory and African Literature.* Ibadan: Heinemann Educational Books. 1987. PP. 25-36.

Elen Savory, Elen. "Femi Osofisan". In Pusha Naidu Parekh and Siga Fatima Jagne (eds) *Postcolonial African Writers: A Biobibliographical Sourcebook.* Westport: Greenwood Press. 1988. PP. 374-381.

Gilbert, Helen. *Postcolonial Plays: an Anthology.* London and New York. 2001.

Harris,Wendel V. *Dictionary of Concepts in Literary Criticism and Theory.* New York. Westport. London: Greenwood Press. 1992.

Gilbert Helen and Joanne Tompkins. *Post-colonial Drama*. London and New York: Routledge. 2002.

Idoko, Festus, Ogu. "Femi Osofisan: Popularity of his Audience or Audience of his Popularity? A Survey of Two Nigerian University Communities". In Tunde Akinyemi and Toyin Falola (eds.) *Emerging Perspectives on Femi Osofisan*. Trenton: Africa World Press. 2009. PP. 133-150.

Iness, C. L.. *The Cambridge Introduction to Postcolonial Literatures in English*. Cambridge: Cambridge University Press. 2007.

Obiechina, Emmanuel. *Language and Theme: Essays on African Literature*. Washington, D. C: Howard University Press. 1990.

Ogunfeyimi, Leke. *Sacrifice the King*. Yaba: Wealthsmith Global Services Ltd. 2012.

Ogunjimi, Bayo and Abdul-Rasheed Na'Allah. *Introduction to African Oral Literature and Performance*. Trenton: Africa World Press. 2005.

Oripeloye, Henri. "Re-ordering Humanity: Femi Osofisan's Backward Glance in *One Legend, Many Seasons*". In Tunde Akinyemi and Toyin Falola eds. *Emerging Perspectives on Femi Osofisan*. Trenton: Africa World Press. 2009. PP. 106-112.

O. Eghagha, Hopes. "A Wasted Breed and a Grsshopper's Oriki: Interrogating Ideological Concerns and Character Metastasis in Selected Plays of Femi Osofisan". In Tunde Akinyemi and Toyin Falola (eds.) *Emerging Perspectives on Femi Osofisan*. Trenton: Africa World Press. 2009. PP. 65-77.

Osofisan, Femi. *No More the Wasted Breed in Moruntodun and Other Plays*. Ibadan: Longman. 1982.

Slemon, Stephen. "Unsettling the Empire Resistance Theory for the Second World". In Bill Ashcroft Gareth Griffiths and Helen Tiffin (eds.) *The Post-colonial Studies Reader*. London and New York: Routledge. 2003. PP. 104-110.

Soyinka, Wole. *The Strong Breed*. Oxford: Oxford University Press. 1979.

Summers, Della. *Longman Dictionary of English Language and Culture. Sixth Impression*. England: Pearson Education Limited. 2003.

Tong, Rosemarie. *Feminist Thought: A More Comprehensive Introduction, Third Edition*. USA: Westview Press. 2009.

Tyson, Lois. *Critical Theory Today: A User Friendly Guide*. New York and London: Routledge. 2006.

W. Hatlen, Theodore. *Orientation to the Theatre*. New York: Appleton-Century-Crofts. 1962.

Walcott, Derek. "The Muse of History". In Bill Ashcroft, Gareth Griffiths and Helen Tiffin (eds), *The Post-colonial Studies Reader*. London and New York: Routledge. 2001. PP. 370-374.

PART THREE

PSYCHOANALYTIC CRITICISM

ETHNICITY AND CONFLICTS POSTMODERNISM

INTERTEXTUALITY

BLACK CONSCIOUSNESS AESTHETICS

11

A PSYCHOANALYTIC APPROACH TO OLA ROTIMI'S *THE GODS ARE NOT TO BLAME*

This chapter uses psychoanalytic theory to investigate how Ola Rotimi uses the language of iconography to address Africa's neo-colonial predicament in *The Gods Are Not to Blame*. Critics in African literary circles have agreed on the fact that there is a general malaise with regard to Africa's socio-economic underdevelopment without agreeing on 'who is to be blamed' for that plight. While many critics tend to lay all the blame on the ex-colonial powers, Ola Rotimi using an iconographic language seeks to turn the tide by repositioning the debate of Africa's predicament, putting at the centre stage Africans' own responsibility in carving the continent's present destiny. This article uses psychoanalytic critical approach to unveil the unconscious drives in assessing African neocolonial plight and in making explicit Ola Rotimi's literary assessment of the causes of Africa's present socio-political and economic predicament.

11.1. The Tenets of Psychoanalitic Theory

Psychoanalytic criticism is a form of literary criticism which uses some of the techniques of psychoanalysis in the interpretation of literature. Psychoanalysis itself is a form of therapy which aims to cure mental disorders 'by investigating the interaction of conscious and unconscious elements in the mind' (as the *Concise Oxford Dictionary* puts it). The classic method of doing this is to get the patient to talk freely, in such a way that the repressed fears and conflicts which are causing the problems are brought into the conscious mind and openly faced, rather than remaining 'buried' in the unconscious.

This practice is based upon specific theories of how the mind, the instincts, and sexuality work. These theories were developed by the Austrian, Sigmund Freud (1856-1939). There is a growing consensus today that the therapeutic value of the method is limited, and that Freud's life-work is seriously flawed by methodological irregularities. All the same, Freud remains a major cultural force, and his impact on how we think about ourselves has been incalculable. Freud's major ideas include those italicised in the next three paragraphs. All of Freud's work depends upon the notion of the *unconscious,* which is the part of the mind beyond consciousness which nevertheless has a strong influence upon our actions. Freud was not the discoverer of the unconscious: his uniqueness lies in his attributing to it such a decisive role in our lives. Linked with this is the idea of *repression,* which is the 'forgetting' or ignoring of unresolved conflicts, unadmitted desires, or traumatic past events, so that they are forced out of conscious awareness and into the realm of the unconscious. A similar process is that of *sublimation,* whereby the repressed material is 'promoted' into something grander or is disguised as something 'noble'. For instance, sexual urges may be given sublimated expression in the form of intense religious experiences or longings. Later in his career Freud suggested a three-part, rather than a two-part, model of the psyche, dividing it into the *ego,* the *super-ego,* and the *id,* these three 'levels' of the personality roughly corresponding to, respectively, the consciousness, the conscience, and the unconscious.

11.1.1. What Freudian Psychoanalytic Critics Do

1. They give central importance, in literary interpretation, to the distinction between the conscious and the unconscious mind. They associate the literary work's 'overt' content with the former, and the 'covert' content with the latter, privileging the latter as being what the work is 'really' about, and aiming to disentangle the two.

2. Hence, they pay close attention to unconscious motives and feelings, whether these be (a) those of the author, or (b) those of the characters depicted in the work.

3. They demonstrate the presence in the literary work of classic psychoanalytic symptoms, conditions, or phases, such as the oral, anal, and phallic stages of emotional and sexual development in infants.

4. They make large-scale applications of psychoanalytic concepts to literary history in general, for example, Harold Bloom's book *The Anxiety of Influence*

(1973) sees the struggle for identity by each generation of poets, under the 'threat' of the greatness of its predecessors, as an enactment of the Oedipus complex.

5. They identify a 'psychic' context for the literary work, at the expense of social or historical context, privileging the individual 'psycho-drama' above the 'social drama' of class conflict. The conflict between generations or siblings, or between competing desires within the same individual looms much larger than conflict between social classes, for instance.

11.1.2. Lacanian Psychoanalysis

Jacques Lacan (1901-1981) was a French psychoanalyst whose work has had an extraordinary influence upon many aspects of recent literary theory. Lacan began his career by taking a medical degree and then training in psychiatry in the 1920s. In the 1930s he worked on paranoia, publishing his thesis on his patient Aimee. His famous theory of the 'mirror stage' (explained later) was first presented at a conference in 1936. Subsequently his ideas were influenced by figures who successively dominated Parisian intellectual life, such as the anthropologist Claude Levi-Strauss (1908-2009), and the linguists Ferdinand de Saussure (1857-1913), and Roman Jakobson (1896-1982). Only in the 1950s did Lacan begin to challenge the orthodoxies of his subject field. In 1955 at a conference in Vienna he called for a new 'back-to-basics' Freudianism. But he meant, not a new attempt to understand the 'conscious personality' (the 'ego') and interpret its behaviour in the light of an understanding of the workings of the unconscious (which many would take to be the whole point of Freudianism), but rather a new emphasis on the the unconscious itself, as 'the nucleus of our being'. In 1959 these unorthodox views resulted in his expulsion from the International Psychoanalytic Association (a kind of World Congress of Freudian analysts) and in 1964 in Paris he set up his own breakaway Ecole Freudienne and published a section of his training sessions under the title *Ecrits*. By this time he himself was one of the most prominent Parisian intellectuals. Lacan's reputation, then, rests on the published 'seminars', the *Ecrits*. A French seminar is not a group discussion but a kind of extended lecture for graduate-level students. The intense atmosphere of these occasions is suggested in an eyewitness account of Lacan's seminars in the 1950s:

> He speaks in a wavering, syncopated or thundering voice, spiced with sighs and hesitations. He notes down in advance what he is

> going to say, then, before the public, he improvises like an actor from the Royal Shakespeare Company ... he fascinates his audience with his impressive language ... Lacan does not analyse, he associates. Lacan does not lecture, he produces resonances. At each session of this collective treatment, the pupils have the impression that the master speaks about them and for them in a coded message secretly destined for each one.
> (Quoted by John Lechte 1990: 36-7)

So the unconscious, in Lacan's famous slogan, is structured like a language. But how is a language structured? Modern language studies, he goes on, begin with Saussure, who shows that meaning in language is a matter of contrasts between words and other words, not between words and things. Meaning, that is to say, is a network of differences. There is a perpetual barrier between signifier (the word) and signified (the referent). He demonstrates this built-in separation with a diagram showing two identical lavatory doors, one headed 'Ladies' the other 'Gentlemen'. This purports to show that the same signifier may have different signifieds, so that (Lodge, p. 86) 'only the correlations between signifier and signifier supply the standard for all research into meaning'. Hence, 'we are forced to accept the notion of an incessant sliding of the signified under the signifier' (Lodge, p. 87). That is, words and meanings have a life of their own and constantly override and obscure the supposed simplicities and clarity of external reality. If signifiers relate only to one another, then language is detached from external reality, and becomes an independent realm, a crucial notion in post-structuralist thinking (see Chapter 3, pp. 64—5). But what evidence is there that the unconscious is 'linguistic' in structure as Lacan alleges? He argues that the two 'dream work' mechanisms identified by Freud, *condensation* and *displacement* (Chapter 5, pp. 98-9) correspond to the basic poles of language identified by the linguist Roman Jakobson, that is, to *metaphor* and *metonymy*, respectively.

The correspondence is that:

1. In metonymy one thing represents another by means of the part standing for the whole. So twenty sail would mean twenty ships. In Freudian dream interpretation an element in a dream might stand for something else by *displacement*: so, a person might be represented by one of their attributes; for instance, a lover who is Italian might be represented in a dream by, let's say, an Alfa Romeo car. Lacan says this is the same as *metonymy,* the part standing for the whole.

2. In *condensation* several things might be compressed into one symbol, just as a *metaphor* like 'the ship ploughed the waves' condenses into a single item two different images, the ship cutting through the sea and the plough cutting through the soil. The use by the unconscious of these linguistic means of self-expression is part of Lacan's evidence for the claim that the unconscious is structured like a language.

What meaning can we derive from a Freudian and Lacanian psychoanalytic reading of Rotimi's *The Gods Are Not to Blame?*

A conspicuous aspect of Ola Rotimi's preoccupation with contemporary African sociopolitical reality is the searchlight which he throws on the relationship between African neocolonial predicament and Western imperialist hegemony. In *The Gods Are Not to Blame*, he has adopted an anti-imperial discourse, a discourse attacking neo-colonialism's agenda, seeking to dismantle the hegemonic power structures of imperial ideology and the socio-political encroachment of the "First world countries" into the cultural, the socio-political and economic affairs of Africans. But Ola Rotimi's discourse is a reaction to the African leadership's coward international diplomacy that has paid and continues to pay dogmatic allegiance to Eurocentrism as a universal culture, a model to be copied uncritically. African economic life, its political leadership, its educational systems and cultural values are gauged on Western standards and pronounced fit or unfit according to the White man's taste. Even our democracy should follow Western model. As Africans, our destiny then, is decided for us by Westerners. Colonialist literature scholars like Lord Milverton, David Hume, W. H. Bentley and Arthur Gobineau (Onwubiko 1982: 3) had disseminated a Eurocentric theory of African people's inferiority. Despite the oldness of such theories, in practice Eurocentric hegemony continues to reverberate both in politics and in literature. Theorists like Ola Rotimi (1975/2002), Keith Green and Jill Lebihan (1996), Lois Toyson (2006) and Rosemary Tong (2009), have counter-attacked these Eurocentric theories in literature. I will analyse Rotimi's Afro-centric criticism as African leaders have let the continent's destiny be shaped by foreigners. I will analyse *The Gods Are Not to Blame* as a deep metaphorical analogy to the post-colonial counter discourse of imperial control to which African leaders have sold Africa, its resources and cultural lore; and are trying desperately to conform to the Eurocentric model of universal cultural standard. I discuss Ola Rotimi's play in the light Freudian and Lacanian psychoanalytic theories. As Roman Jakobson has pointed it out, 'the poetic function of language, by promoting the palpability of signs deepens the fundamental dichotomy of signs and objects (Jakobson 1968: 358). He sees metaphor and metonymy as characteristic modes of binary opposed polarities which between them underpin the twofold process of selection and combination by which linguistic signs reformed. Metaphor, to apply Ferdinand de Saussure's concepts as reused by Terence Hawkes is generally "associative" in character and exploits language's "vertical" relations (Hawkes 2003: 60). Psychoanalytic theories seek to question Eurocentric discourses and discursive strategies from a privileged position within pre-colonial, colonial and post-colonial worlds; to investigate the means by which Europe imposes its cultural and material domination to the third world countries.

11.2. Psychoanalytic Discourse Analysis in Ola Rotimi

By choosing to read Ola Rotimi's *The Gods Are Not to Blame* in the light of psychoanalytic literary criticism, I propose that Ola Rotimi writes a literature of resistance. In developing his theory of psychosexuality, Freud closely linked the pairs activity/passivity [and masculine/feminine], which he sometimes used as synonyms. In some texts, in fact, Freud's clinical observations show them to be nearly indistinguishable, for example, in the WolfMan's regression from passive desires to masochistic and feminine desires toward his father (1918b [1914]). Later and in a context less closely associated with individual clinical analysis, Freud insisted on the importance of not "identify[ing] activity with maleness and passivity with femaleness" (Freud 1930a: 106). That means that the main debate that engages his attention as a postcolonial psychoanalytic writer critic is the rejection of the idea that colonialism is a thing of the past. In reality it is not. Colonialism has resumed another form nowadays, neocolonialism, and it is in the effort to counter the neocolonialist discourse in literary texts that Ola Rotimi has used Yoruba folktale tradition and myths to criticize European neocolonialism.

By iconography I refer to the use or study of metaphors, metonymy, images or symbols in art. Ola Rotimi is an iconographer who delves into dramatic imagery and symbolism to bring out an iconoclastic appraisal of Africa's postcolonial predicament, looking from the perspective of its causes, to assert that "the gods are not to blame." In this respect Rotimi has Baba Fakunle foretell the bad news of an incestuous boy's birth; a boy who will kill his father to marry his mother (*TGANTB: 3*). This is a highly symbolic *mise-en-scène* telling how Westerners have "raped" and continue to "rape" our mother continent

Africa, looting abusively her most precious resources. In literary debates, two theoretical tendencies have emerged in the discussion about colonization and imperialism. The first theorists, supporting imperialist ideology include old writers like Lord Milverton (Owubiko 1982: 3), W. H. Bentley and Arthur Gobineau (Ibidem) who have stayed in the ideology of Joseph Conrad (*Heart of Darkness* 2010 reprinted) and Niccolo Machiavelli (Machiavelli 2011: 36) to defend that all means are good to be used to dominate and exploit weaker nations, provided that one serves personal interest. The second theorists include Frantz Fanon (quoted in Biodun Jeyifo 2004: 196), Ngugi wa Thiong'o (1993), Chinua Achebe (1988) and Edward Said (1978) who deconstruct colonial discourse to assert African identity. Edward W. Said is one of the major postcolonial theorists who adheres to Ola Rotimi's philosophy by acknowledging the topicality of Western imperialism and interventionism in the Third World countries (*TGANTB: 60*). For the scholar Said, African countries' political independence is but a mere formalist garment put on them by Europe, but in actual facts, she continues to manipulate African destiny. In *Culture and Imperialism* (1993) Said has theorized that western imperialism is a long story that has involved the dominant European powers' oppression on these ex-colonial subjects:

> Neither imperialism nor colonialism is a simple act of accumulation and acquisition. Both are supported and perhaps even impelled by impressive ideological formations that include notions that certain territories and people require and beseech domination, as well as forms of knowledge affiliated with domination: the vocabulary of classic nineteen-century imperial culture is plentiful with words and concepts like 'inferior', 'or subject races', 'subordinate peoples', dependency, 'expansion' and 'authority' (Said 1993: 9).

This statement by Edward W. Said summarizes the imperialist ideology of the Western powers in their conquest of African territories, and position the debate of controlling African destiny from a distant place, a debate Ola Rotimi engages the reader in *The Gods Are Not to Blame*. European imperialism started even before colonization and has continued till date in the form of neocolonialism. What Said wants to bring out here, which is very relevant in the approach to Ola Rotimi's *The Gods Are Not to Blame* is the connivance of some African leaders with the imperialists in destroying Africa's heritage and the refusal to take action for Africa's liberation. In Said's own words, "For one, the theory and theoretical structures suggested by writers on liberation are rarely given the commanding authority – I mean the phrase quite literally" (Ibidem) In this perspective, I propound that Ola Rotimi's has a deep concern for the sense of human life in general and that of the African in particular. In *The Gods Are not to Blame,* an adaptation of Sophocles' *Oedipus Rex* to the African context he uses myth to reassert ironically and metaphorically the fact that if man commits his own destiny to other people, they will take advantage of this to enslave him forever. To corroborate this truth, he quotes a proverb: "When the wood-insect gathers sticks on its own head, it carries them" (*TGANTB: 72*). This means one must be ready to bear the consequences of his actions. Africans believe in their incapability to govern themselves, to rule themselves and to shape their own destiny, that is why they entrust the Western powers with their destiny. All important decisions affecting African future are being taken by Europeans outside Africa.

As for the role of active and passive in the theory of the ego, Freud, in 1915, emphasized that transformations of the drive by repression and reversal protect the psychic apparatus. These transformations depend on "the narcissistic organization of the ego and bear the stamp of that phase. They perhaps correspond to the attempts at defense which at higher stages of the development of the ego are effected by other means". The transformations between active and passive imply a narcissistic consistency and a drive that is also no longer "poorly connected and independent" (Freud 1915c: 132). In consonance with this claim, It is not far-fetched to see that our destiny as African is predetermined by "the gods" (Western powers). The "gods" appear as the wheel stirrers of man's destiny and Africans stand aloof observing them to reshape the pre-ordained fate they have to undergo (*TGANTB: 10*). It is in this context that Kerstin W. Shands' question "so where are we now?" (Shands 2008: 7), becomes crucial. African leaders' absence of protest against Western imperialists is equated to death in the following proverb: "When the head of a household dies his house becomes an empty shell" (*TGANTB: 9*). Africans seem to have lost the way and Western powers should show it to them. This story is used by Rotimi to explain a deep truth about African postcolonial predicament. As a postcolonial writer, he is critical of how the developed nations' apparent "endeavour" to improve developing nations' economies is but an attempt to expand their imperial hegemony in Third World countries.

As a result we continually witness chaos and disaster in African political life, its economic structures and social fabric. Africans continue to regard themselves as inferior and non entities, people who need to be guided by the universalist model of the West. Africans need to be aware of these and exercise self-criticism about their responsibilities in Africa's present sociopolitical challenges. The playwright uses the metaphor "the gods" to designate Western powers and "humans" to name Africans. Reading *The Gods Are not to Blame* as a metaphor on the causes of African sociopolitical woes amounts at showing how Ola Rotimi has been concerned with the African post-independent predicament and has critically addressed the question "to whom should the responsibility of shaping Africa's destiny belong?" This is due to the countless post-colonial interferences of western powers in African public and private cultural, socio-political and economic life. Just like the character Adewale, some Africans have come to believe in the inescapable fate of Africans as subjects who need to be controlled, by western ideology, thus the belief that African destiny should be decided in western international conferences and world summits.

In Freudian theory, agency plays a key role; and I will explain how Ola Rotimi uses elements of African oral tradition to underscore the functional system of agency. The term "agency" denotes a part of the psychic apparatus that functions as a substructure governed by its own laws, but that is coordinated with the other parts. In Freud's work this term first appeared in chapter VII of The Interpretation of Dreams (1900a), as a synonym or near-synonym for the term system, which he had been using for several years: "Accordingly, we will picture the mental apparatus as a compound instrument, to the components of which we will give the name of 'agencies' or (for the sake of greater clarity) 'systems.'" (Freud 1900: 536–537) The term apparatus, used in a sense that never changed in Freud's work, explicitly gives the psyche a status comparable to that of the major organic systems (respiratory, circulatory, etc.). Adaptation is not part of Freudian vocabulary. The idea of adaptation, however, is present throughout Freud's work. In the same perspective,

Martin Okyere Owusu's reading of *The Gods Are not to Blame* is inspirational in the kind of approach I am offering (Owusu 2002: 1). Africa, traditional drama takes inspiration from myths, festivals, rites and rituals. Ola Rotimi henceforth uses Yoruba myths, folktales and legends as material to metaphorically address African problems and call to rectitude some moral and social deviances of human conducts. It is therefore a fact that the presence of mythological characters and representations are important narrative elements used by him to convey the message of Africans' responsibility vis-à-vis their future destiny. He explains: "It is in the process of exercising my mind to create meaning for *The Gods Are Not to Blame* that, I focus on social metaphors, namely the concept of destiny or fate, the eponymous characters the gods, and the conflicts that underpin the play's plot". Many critics of *The Gods Are Not to Blame* have given much thought to the concept of destiny as directed by supernatural forces like gods. In this respect, Michael Etherton (1982) holds the view that Ola Rotimi's play is an adaptation of Sophocle's *Oedipus Rex* and as such, he (Ola Rotimi) attempts to assert "the inexorability of fate, and the divine order" (Etherton 1982) and Martin Okyere Owusu (2002) has established that

> Ola Rotimi observes an important religious fact of life among the Yoruba: when the gods will man's destiny, though he may try to escape from it, he will fulfill it. Whether he fights against the will of the gods or not, he will become what he has been destined to become… One may then ask 'why then should man worry his head struggling or fighting against his fate as King Odewale does?' (Okyere 2002: 6).

The point made by Martin Okyere Owusu brings to the fore the idea of inescapable fulfillment of man's fate as destined by the gods. That idea suggests that Odewale's destiny was pre-ordained by the divine order, the decree of the gods. Looking into that character, it is not farfetched to say that Odewale suffers his tragedy because of his inner shortcomings, his tragic flaw, the fact of his pride and one shouldn't blame external forces for it. Odewale himself acknowledges this at the end of the play by admonishing:

> ODEWALE: No, no! Do not blame the gods. Let no one blame the powers. My My people, learn from my fall. The powers would have failed if I Did not let them use me. They knew my weakness: the weakness of a Man easily moved to the defense of his tribe against others. I once Slew a man on my farm to Ede. I could have spared him. But he spat on my tribe. He spat on the tribe I thought was my tribe. The Man laughed, and laughing, he called me 'a man from a bush tribe of Ijekun'. And I lost my reason. Now I find out that that very man was my… own father, the king who ruled this land before me.
> (*TGANTB*: 71)

From the reading of these statements, it transpires that man is the main responsible of his social predicaments. The problems surrounding human beings have their sources in the very nature of people's behaviors. Human beings at different social levels have to do self-criticism and adjust their ways to conform to ethics, rather than finding excuse with supernatural forces teleguiding their actions. This social philosophy is highlighted by a number of thinkers like Christopher Heath Wellman who writes "There are a number of controversies surrounding responsibility, but few doubt that there is anything conceptually confused or morally problematic about holding competent adults responsible for their free and informed actions" (Wellman 2007: 736). This view comes to stress my point that human beings should be held responsible for their actions; and as a matter of fact, they should also be accountable for their consequences. On this issue, Lois Tyson has this to say:

> *Colonialist ideology* often referred to as *colonialist discourse* to mark its relationship to the language in which the colonialist thinking was expressed, was based on the colonizer's assumption of their own superiority, which they contrasted with the alleged inferiority of the native (indigenous people), the original inhabitants of the land they invaded… Because their technology was more highly advanced, the colonizers believed that their whole culture was more highly advanced, and they ignored and swept aside the religions, customs, and codes of behavior of the peoples they subjugated. So the colonizers saw themselves at the center of the world; the colonized were at the margins (Toyson 2004: 419).

This critical stance is in my view the beginning of African predicament, because, from the way European ex-colonizers continue to view their ex-colonies, they seek to control every sphere of their lives from distance.

Ola Rotimi has projected in drama the social image of man in a desperate struggle to escape the prediction of the gods about the unfathomable adventure of Odewale who will kill his father to marry his mother. It is in his relentless efforts to escape that curse that he plainly fulfills the prophecy. That very social condition makes man an appendage of the gods because he cannot depart from the life trajectory traced by them.

An informed postcolonial psychoanalytic reading of Ola Rotimi enables me to assert that what is fundamentally at the heart of creative drama in

The Gods Are Not to Blame is the question whether man should maintain a dogmatic allegiance to the unpredictable gods till death because they own and manipulate his destiny? In other words, the issue being addressed is to what extent does man a common mortal hold or does not the orientation of his destiny? From my personal stand point, Ola Rotimi is writing an allegory as he wants to expose through the stage the barbarous evils of corruption, kleptocracy, racketeering crime and general moral decay that bedevil the Nigerian society, and the African in neocolonial era. Man in society never wants to put himself into question but continues to indulge in the bottomless gulf of inhuman practices, accusing by the same token Mother Nature and laying the blame on his fellow man, while he himself has the potentiality and capability to redefine life in society and provide his environment with new meaning. The African, says Ola Rotimi, does not need constant allegiance to the "gods" or to the world super powers to solve the problem of peace. The Divine Creator has endowed him with the capacity of wholesome reflection to construct a decent environment and make life enjoyable. The gods are not to blame if man does not question himself on his destiny and if he does not show concern into adopting responsible attitudes to avoid evil doings. Man must shun evil and pursue peace and sustainable development. He should stop destroying the environment and his fellow man. Ola Rotimi is inviting man to rationality, the use of logic to redefine a new philosophy of life for his general well being. Take for instance war that man carefully plans around the globe knowingly, fully aware of its disastrous consequences on himself, his fellows and the environment. The playwright thinks man should prefer peace to war. Ola Rotimi subsequently suggests in a published interview that the play was an allegory of the civil war in Nigeria which was raging when the play was first performed. According to Michael Etherton,

> the gods are the European powers who were, accordingly, not to blame for the conflict; Odewale represented tribalism in Nigeria; and the civil war was caused not by the intervention of the superpowers, but by Nigeria's tribalism: 'the powers would have failed if I did not let them use me. But what is seen at the end of the play is the tragedy of one man, not of Kutuje or of Yoruba kingdom; and the civil war was fought on a regional basis in which the Yoruba role itself was not clearly defined. There are many tangled issues caught up in the war, and to reduce it to a single cause is trite (Etherton 1982: 127).

Thus, the invitation of the playwright to the humans in general and the Africans in particular is to pose and reflect. The reflection should go in the streamline of reshaping values and redefining new set of goals that will go with the upkeep of general interest rather than personal selfish ambition. The invitation to rationality consists also in freeing one's mind of the dangerous belief that it is the outside world that can procure one's happiness without one's personal initiative and full implication. If all these ideas are reproduced on the stage, the audience will most definitely do an exercise of reflection and meditation. I hold this critical stand because drama does double work: it tells the story and shows the images. Since drama combines telling and showing, the story will prick the audiences' consciousness and the picturesque representations will bring catharsis in the spectators.

11.3. Metaphors of Alienation: Africa' Neocolonial Predicament

More than Freud, Lacan has amply theorized on metaphors. The specific aspect of Lacanian use of metaphor that interests me here is the metaphor of alienation in Lacanian sense and how to channel it to Rotimi' s own advocacy. Inscribed in the opposition between the Same and the Other, alienation describes the condition of the subject who no longer recognizes himself, or rather can only recognize himself via the Other. The philosophical background of this concept derives from Hegel and then Marx. Classical psychiatry used the term to classify any mental illness in which the subject no longer knew who he was. Thanks to Jacques Lacan's study of Hegel's master/slave dialectic, the term no longer refers only to mental alienation, but retains the meaning it has in philosophy. For Lacan, who followed Hegel on this point, human desire is constituted by mediation: "Man's desire finds its meaning in the other's desire, not so much because the other holds the keys to the desired object, but because his first objective is to be recognized by the other" (Lacan 1936: 58). Specifically, the objective is to be recognized by the Other as a desiring subject, because the first desire is to have one's desire recognized. The conclusion is Lacan's well-known formula: "Man's desire is the desire of the Other," which doesn't mean that one desires another as object, but that one desires another desire, and wants to have one's own desire recognized by the Other. This is an echo of Hegel's master/slave dialectic (a struggle for pure prestige) where each consciousness wants to be recognized by the Other without recognizing it in turn ("each consciousness seeks the death of the other").

Lacan one would say has a deeo concern for iconographic language, as he constantly uses metaphors to speak about deep psychic realities. So iconography occupies a center stage in lacanian psychanalitic theory and it compells attention to see how such theory reads in rotimian dramatic discourse.

Iconography is the use or study of images or symbols in art (Horby 2009: 738). Ola Rotimi' s extensive use of metaphors provides a ground for me to look into the iconographic dimension of *The Gods Are Not to Blame*. The similarity view of metaphors holds that a metaphor is a departure from the literal, that is what a competent speaker experiences as the standard use of language which serves as a condensed or elliptical simile in that it involves an implicit comparison between disparate things (Abrams 2005: 163). This explanation is further enhanced by Keir Elam who quotes Roman Jakobson: "advances a highly influential theory according to which metaphorical substitution forms one of the fundamental poles not only of language use but of semiotic and artistic activity in general" (Elam 2005: 18). This statement points to the fact that every element in a dramatic work - from characters to the stage ornaments passing through the language used by the dramatist- is an icon, a symbol or sign.

The play is a social metaphor, a symbolic representation of African continent's predicament. It is a critical reading of Africa's socio-political woes caused by inter-tribal or ethnic conflicts, political and ethnic intolerance rampant throughout the continent that Ola Rotimi propounds. The metaphor also alludes to the way people resort to violent means to settle conflicts. The unwise resort to ways in which people perpetrate social injustice, corruption, sycophancy, political blackmail are symbolized by the ostentatious behavior of the chiefs in the presence of the king (*TGANTB*: 54). There is a general tendency to resort to rash and violent means to settle scores and disunity, and for decades, African countries have not been able to broker real economic and political unity, in spite of the existence of the African Union. In today's world while Europe and America are striving to unite their economic, social and political structures for a more formidable strength, Africa is busy disintegrating herself. Some political leaders exploit the economics of their fragile situations for personal reasons, including dictatorial entrenchment, corruption and nepotism, all at the expense of their suffering poor. Having acquired arms and ammunition for man's self-destruction from the 'big powers', America, Britain, France and Russia, Germany, Japan, China, the gods metaphorically, they, like Odewale search for the cause of their problems outside of themselves. This is the very trouble beleaguering Africa according to Oluchi Joyce Igidi (Igidi 2011: 16). Africa after Independence still has many challenges to take up. These challenges are essentially at economic, cultural, and even political levels. Ola Rotimi explores the possibility of collective struggle, a continent wide struggle against Western imperialists in his plays. Plays like *Hopes of the Living Dead* (2001) and *If... A Tragedy of the Ruled* (1983) put across that message of African collective struggle.

If it is true that independence has been achieved at the political level, this is not the case at economic level. African economy is being controlled in the main by Europe. For example, Europeans continue buying cash crops from Africa at the very low prices they fix themselves. Examples include coffee, cocoa, cotton, timber and resources like oil. Africa still enlists the help of technical experts from Europe for the mining of mineral resources like gold, diamond, copper or oil. These experts charge the Africans at very high prices. Our financial institutions are controlled by European multinational firms. Even our currency is dependent on the European monetary system. It is as if Africa doesn't have her identity as independent continent, because, as Michelle Harris puts it, "If identity is real, then others will know it (Harris 2013: 12.)" Africans do not manage their economic and financial resources well. Corruption and bribery are the order of the day in Africa. At political level there are many challenges. There has been much hesitation to take the step of democracy in Africa after the independence. Dictatorship has taken advantage over democracy. Post-independence Africa has been characterized by coup –d'états and political violence during elections. Leaders manage their countries as if it were family heritage, seeking to preserve their political chair for life and even bequeath it to their sons after their death. As there is democratic immaturity, Africans still enlist help from Europe during elections. Many elections are undemocratic and stained with violence, corruption and rigging.

The task ahead to be done at political level is to achieve full democracy in Africa. Culturally speaking, Africans are not independent. European languages are being used in all the teaching institutions and cultural manifestations. This may have some positive gain. But that European languages should transplant African languages even into our home education, this leaves some worries for our African cultural heritage. It is true that the European languages enable Africans to communicate easily and freely in multi-linguistic settings. Here Ngugi wa Thiong'o is one of the leading figures in the struggle for linguistic pluralism in Africa where priority should be given to African languages:

> That is why I still believe that despite the hue and cry about reductionism, nativism, backwardlookingness from the Europhonist opponents of this development, writing in African languages still holds the key for the positive development of new and vital traditions in African literature as we face the twenty-first century. [...] African languages must not be afraid of also borrowing from the best of world culture. All the dynamic cultures of the world have borrowed from other cultures in a process of mutual fertilization (Ngugi 1993: 21-22).

The relevance of Ngugi's statements dwells in the fact that Africans tend to forget their indigenous languages; even look down upon them as inferior and regard European ones as the best. As Africans, we should keep our own values and borrow what is good from others. But Africans are living a kind of life one may describe as "cultural enslavement". Africans are copying from Europe, even practices they know are bad. There is a kind of cultural dependence at many levels of African lifestyle: Western belief systems are the religion in fashion as it has integrated all the aspects of Africans' lifestyle. For instance some bad religious practices of sectaries are blindly adopted by Africans as good simply because they come from Western countries. When Africans integrate these sects they are confronted with such bad practices as pornography, human sacrifices, genital mutilations, incest, trans-sexualism, sexual promiscuity; practices that are at odd with African ethics but they indulge into them simply because they come from 'Europe' or 'America'. Dressing styles, haircuts for women, food and eating fashions are often being adopted from Europe. I am not saying that if a Western value is good Africans should not copy it, but I am critical about values that are perverse and destructive but that Africans blindly adopt them for the fact that they come from the West.

Rotimi uses elements of traditional Yoruba religious practices and folklore not only to make Oedipus African, but also to make his play a comment on modern African political responsibilities. It is a criticism of modern Africa's political woes and an invitation to see were the problems really lie in Africa. The plot of *The Gods Are Not to Blame* is based on a classical Greek tragedy *Oedipus Rex* by Sophocles. When asked whether he does not feel it a waste of energy if a playwright goes outside his cultural context for material, since many African playwright choose their themes from traditional sources, Rotimi replies:

> Well, I thought a playwright should, by all means, react to the prevailing social, political conditions in the setting in which he exists and, as far as I know, the Nigerian setting is such as one would describe as far from being relaxing… what with the civil war now at our doorstep and so on – and I thought something must be done to express one's feelings about these happenings around the writer. That was why I chose *Oedipus Rex* as an idiom for conveying my emotions, my feelings, my ideas about existing conditions in Nigeria. Now you might ask what these ideas are that are conveyed. Well the title itself bears this out: *The Gods Are not to Blame*. Brought down to in mundane terms, the gods simply mean world powers (Owusu 2007: 16).

Ola Rotimi's points is even clearer as he adds:

> What I am saying is that these powers cannot be held responsible for our own downfall, the downfall of underdeveloped nations, the downfall of Nigeria, for instance, if we, by our own errors allow them to exploit our flaws. The flaw of tribalism is a foregone conclusion as the bane of modern Africa, and as the hero in this play says at the end of the play, "The Gods Are not to Blame." Do not blame the gods. The gods would have failed if I did not let them use me. They knew my weakness, the weakness of one easily moved to the defense of his tribe against another (Ibidem).

The social metaphors contained in Rotimi's *The Gods Are not to Blame* are readable in his explanation above. Reading from the title, there is a tension between the gods and the man Odewale. Just as it happened in Oedipus, man attempts to thwart what the gods have ordained. Odewale stands as a symbol. He represents Africa, a continent full of tribal intolerance, nepotism, precipitous actions, violence of war, corruption and perfidy. The gods stand for the "Super Powers" namely America, Britain, France, Germany, China, Russia who continue to control and exploit African natural and human resources because, as a people, Africans allow the looting and the exploitation to happen due to their weakness of disunity and intra-continental conflicts. King Odewale is to a great extent, to blame for his downfall – his intolerance, his hot temper and his rash suspicions. But the gods certainly play an active role in Odewale's misfortunes. They are shown to be powerful and uncompromising in their demands on man. The Iroko tree in the story of Olurombi emphasizes this power. The import of the gods however is not a question of sharing responsibility in the downfall of Odewale. To "blame" here means to hold someone responsible for a reprehensible act. As playwright Rotimi infers above, the gods are strong and they know the weakness of a man who is easily aroused to anger in defense of his tribe, and this is his tragic flaw; so they exploit that weakness. It is of no use to sit by, blaming the gods while man's tribal prejudices exist.

Applying lacanian psychoanalytic theory to the text of Rotimi, I think like Wolfgang Iser that the picturing that is done by our imagination is only one of the activities through which we form the gestalt of a literary text (Iser 1980: 58). My interpretation here is that, by grouping together the written parts of the text, we enable them to interact, we observe the direction in which they are leading us, and we project onto them the consistency which we, as readers require. Ola Rotimi uses the tragic flaw in Odewale to represent African tribalism, which has contributed a great deal to social and political failures in many African states. *The Gods Are not to Blame* then is symbolic. It is a commentary on the African political and social imbroglio generated by such factors as a feeling of tribal superiority and social injustices within the societies themselves, nepotism and favoritism, especially among the ruling class. Yet the irony is that people often times feel the urge to put the blame on some outside forces. The gods in Yoruba religion and contemporary life are symbolic of "the big powers" who are aware of the weakness that has been crippling African nations: tribalism and attendant divisionism, nepotism, favoritism and corruption. They make use of this weakness for economic and political exploitation. King Odewale is symbolic of these African dictators, leaders of nations who must revisit their ways of behaving, and his tragic flaw represents the weakness of tribal intolerance. On this issue, Christopher Heath Wellman has this to say:

> To begin, notice that dictators are typically able to impose their oppressive regimes upon the unwilling masses only because they ruthlessly use their military power to suppress any and all opposition. What is more, staying in power requires a vicious cycle because despots are typically able to retain the military's loyalty only as long as they have the money to pay the soldiers, and rulers can acquire the necessary funds only if they continue to exploit their political power. Some of the revenue comes from taxes that (insofar as the funds are used to benefit the ruler rather than the people themselves)

essentially enslave the political subjects. Another large source of income for rulers, especially pertinent to our discussion, is selling the country's natural resources: personal, collective, corporate 743 to foreign companies. If a dictator's country has extensive oil reserves, for instance, then she can sell this oil and use the money to secure her military stranglehold over her subjects (Wellman 2007: 742).

Here, two points clearly emerge. First and most obviously, the mere fact that a dictator effectively controls access to the country's natural resources does not make him / her *morally entitled* to those resources any more than a slave-owner's effective control over her slaves implies that she is morally entitled to the fruits of these slaves' labour (Ibid 746). Second, and more relevant to the point at hand, foreign companies are an integral part of the problem because, in seeking to acquire natural resources as cheaply as possible, they are giving undemocratic leaders the money necessary to continue their unjust domination over their political subjects. In a very real sense, it is as if these companies were buying cheap cotton from slave-owners who were using this money to buy more guns with which to subdue their slaves (Ibidem). (Of course, as in the times of slavery when the legal institutions protected the rights of slave-owners, a key part of the current problem is that legal systems the world over recognizes these companies' ownership rights in the natural resources solely on the basis of their having purchased them from tyrants.) These observations, in tandem with our earlier discussions, put us in a better position to assign responsibility for world poverty. First and most obviously, Ola Rotimi is right about the extent to which the problems stem from the actions of suitably organized groups like private companies, political states and international organizations such as the World Trade Organization (WTO) and International Monetary Fund (IMF), then these organizations can and should be held responsible for the damage they do (Ibidem). Pressure should be put on them to reform their practices and to offer restitution for the suffering they have caused. And as we have seen, concluding that these groups are responsible in a non-distributive sense is consistent with also claiming that various persons may also be responsible, as individuals, for their actions. Most obviously, those executives who played the greatest roles in directing these companies, countries and international organizations should be held responsible for the massive pain and suffering they have caused.

It is up to each of us, in other words, to hold the international organizations accountable by, among other things, bringing pressure to bear upon those executives who have the greatest control over what policies are put in place. If the preceding arguments are on target, then it is easy to see why the literature on group responsibility is so important and controversial (Ibidem). It is important and controversial for the same reason: it suggests that our responsibilities are much more extensive, demanding and inescapable than we might have supposed (and hoped). Political theorists commonly assume that every competent adult has a natural duty to promote justice. This assumption is attractive because it seems reasonable to think that each of us should strive to make the world more just or, at the very least, not to make it a less just place (Ibidem). However, once one recognizes (1) the gravity of injustices currently being perpetrated by today's most powerful governments and international organizations and (2) each individual's accountability for her role in these group actions, it becomes apparent that we cannot adequately discharge our moral duties in an atomistic fashion. Instead, we have an obligation vigilantly to monitor any organization of which we are a part and to work aggressively to ensure that these organizations do not perpetrate injustices. And because every social actor is a participant in the global economy, each reader has a responsibility to work to reform those organizations which render so many of the world's population imperiled by poverty.

The morality in this symbolic drama in that light is basically this: as long as African leaders remain full of suspicion, distrust and hatred, getting into the conflicts with each other on the basis of tribalism, no progress is ever possible. According to Rotimi, it is futile to lay the blame on external powers. In creating this political dimension he departs from a major theme in the Greek play, which is the futility of man's attempt to thwart the will of the gods. In the context of *The Gods Are not to Blame,* Rotimi emphasizes this departure by making Odewale a source of inspiration for his people in their struggle to survive the plague. The protagonist Odewale has always been a fighter and a winner; he leads the people of Kutuje to defeat the Ikolu invaders (*TGANTB*: 5-7); his charms prove more potent than his assailant's; and when he recalls the reason for his running away from his parents in Ijekun, he again defies the so-called inability of the gods' will.

11.3.2. An Interaction View of Metaphors

The interaction view of metaphors is a conceptual approach introduced by I. A. Richards who proposed that "a metaphor works by bringing together the disparate thoughts of the vehicle and tenor so as to effect a meaning that "is a resultant of their interaction…" (Abrams 2005: 163). Applied to Ola Rotimi's drama under scrutiny, I infer that the interaction view refers to the dramatic conflicts and their significance in the development of the plot. Conflicts in the play are also metaphors which explain the nature of life as an everlasting struggles for survival. Conflicts are the struggle, fight or clash between opposing characters or forces that cause tension or suspense in the plot. It grows out of the interplay of the two opposing forces, providing and heightening interest as the action develops. At least, one of the opposing forces is usually a person or if an animal or an inanimate object is treated as though it were a person. This person, usually the protagonist may be involved in conflicts of three different kinds: 1) a struggle or fight against another person, usually the antagonist, or against a whole society; 2) a struggle against nature, and 3) a struggle against himself/herself that means a struggle for mastery by two elements within the person.

In *The Gods Are not to Blame,* all three kinds of conflicts operate effectively throughout the action.

11.3.2.1. Man Against Man: a Metaphor of Colonization

Here, there is a confrontation between Odewale the protagonist and several individuals as well as the society as a whole. Here, I am going to reverse roles, to have Odewale stand for Europe and Adetusa for Africa. For instance, the conflict between Odewale and King Adetusa on the farm near Ede is a metaphor of the confrontation of Africa and Europe in the context of colonization. Odewale has become strong and powerful because he has killed Adetusa by giving him a mortal stroke and taking his land. This is the metaphor of how Europe has looted African natural resources and exploited lands to enrich herself. The way the confrontation between the two men has been violent and fatal to the weaker party, that of Adetusa, the same way European incursion in Africa has been stormy, violent and fatal for African people, their culture and their natural resources. The confrontation between the two antagonists is therefore an epitome of colonialism. In its literal meaning colonialism is a form of imperial domination of one country/continent (the colonial power), over others (its colonies) for political, economic or strategic purposes (Lee 1994: 160-161). The main period of colonial rule was 1870-1960, when European powers 'scrambled' to gain control over territories in Africa. The French and British had the largest colonial empires. They partitioned the African cake and laid indelible marks upon African history. Colonialism is said to have established a system of dependency in the colony, whose economy and political administration served primarily not its own needs, but those of the colonial power. This has made it difficult for the colony to develop on its own terms and in its own direction. This situation prevails even after the granting of independence, and these dependent countries make up the underdeveloped Third World.

Three main points have been stressed in this chapter. Firstly, the two theoretical tendencies in African drama that debate on the African colonial and post-colonial rapports with the West have been entertaining conflicting views on the responsibility of Africans to determine their fate. Secondly, Ola Rotimi has opted for a philosophy of psychanalisis and self-appraisal, that is, Africans are responsible for their postcolonial predicament. Third, it is high time Africans woke up to think out development. African neocolonial predicament's solution dwells in the hands of Africans themselves. Self-consciousness awakening seems to be the proviso proposed by the dramatist Ola Rotimi in the struggle towards Africa's liberation.

References

Abrams, M. H. *A Glossary of Literary Terms* (Australia. Canada. Mexico: Thomson Wadsworth, 2005.

Achebe, Chinua. *Hopes and Impediments*. London: Heinemann, 1988.

Barry, Peter. *Beginning Theory: An Introduction to Literary and Cultural Theories.* Manchester: Manchester University Press, 2009.

Conrad, Joseph. *Heart of Darkness. Reprinted.* New Delhi: UBS Publishers, 2010.

Elam, Keir. *The Semiotics of Drama.* London and New York: Routledge, 1980/2005.

Etherton, Michael. *The Development of Drama in Africa.* New York: Africana Publishing Company, 1982.

Fanon, Frantz. *The Wretched of the Earth.* New York: Grove Press, 1978.

Gilbert, Helen and Joanne Tompkins. *Post-colonial Drama Theory, Practice, Politics.* London and New York: Routledge, 1996.

Green, Keith and Jill LeBihan. *Critical Theory and Practice.* London and New York: Routledge, 1996.

Harris, Michelle. "Emergent Indigenous Identities : Rejecting the Need for Purity" in Michelle Harris, Martin Nakata and Browny Carlson (eds), *The Politics of Identity: Emerging Indigeneity.* Australia: UTSePress, 2013. PP. 10-25.

Hawkes, Terence. *Structuralism and Semiotics.* London and New York: Routledge, 2003.

Igili, Oluchi Joyce. *Social Commitment in Ola Rotimi's Plays Understanding an African Playwright's Passion for Societal Transformation.* Verlag: Lambert Academic Publishing, 2011.

Iser, Wolfgang. "The Reading Process: a Phenomenological Approach". In Jane P. Tompkins (ed.) *Criticism from Formalism to Post-Structuralism.* Baltimore and London: the Johns Hopkins University Press, 1980. PP. 50-69

Jakobson, Roman "Closing Statement: Linguistics and Poetics" in Thomas A. Sebeok (ed.) *Style in Language.* Baltimore: John Hopkins Press, 1968. PP. 354-360.

Machiavelli, Niccolo. *The Prince. Reprinted.* Hammersmith: Collins Classics, 2011.

Onwubiko, K. B. C. *History of West Africa.* Onitsa: Africana –Fep Publishers Limited, 1982.

Ngugi, wa Thiong'o. *Moving the Center: The Struggle for Cultural Freedoms.* London: Heinemann, 1996.

Owusu, Martin Okyere. *Analysis and Interpretation of Ola Rotimi's The Gods Are Not to Blame.* Accra: Sedco Publishing Ltd, 2002.

Rotimi, Ola. *The Gods Are not to Blame.* Ibadan: Oxford University Press, 1976.

-------------- . *Hopes of the Living Dead.* Ibadan: Spectrum, 2001.

----------------. *If... A Tragedy of the Ruled.* Ibadan: Heinemann, 1983.

Said, Edward W. *Culture and Imperialism.* New York: Ventage Books, 1993.

Shands, Kerstin W. *Neither East Nor West: Postcolonial Essays on Literature, Culture and Religion* (Sweden: Södertörns Högskola University College Press, 2008.

Tiffin, Helen. "Post-colonial Literatures and Counter-discourse". In Bill Aschcroft, Gareth Griffiths and Helen Tiffin (eds.) *The Post-colonial Studies Reader.* London and New York: Routeledge, 2003. PP. 95-98.

Tong, Rosemarie. *Feminist Thought A More Comprehensive Introduction, Third Edition.* USA: Westview, 2009.

Tyson, Lois. *Critical Theory Today A User Friendly Guide* (New York and London: Routledge, 2006.

Wellman, Christopher Heath. "Personnal, Collective, Corporate" in Robert E. Goodin, Phillip Pettit and Thomas Pogge (eds.) *A Companion to Contemporary Political Philosophy.* USA: Blackwell Publishing, 1993/2003. PP. 743-744.

12

ETHNICITY, CONFLICTS AND PEACE STRATEGIES IN FEMI OSOFISAN'S *WOMEN OF OWU*

One of the particularities of the post-colonial African societies is their multi-ethnic dimensions and their pluralistic-religious groupings. This chapter investigates the extent to which Femi Osofisan explores in *Women of Owu* (2008) ethnic conflicts to envision peace strategies in Nigeria. Diversities of ethnic and religious identities are contingent upon multiple intersecting factors, ethnic, linguistic, historical, demographic, politico-economic and ideological that, if badly handled, sometimes trouble peace and put into peril years efforts of socio-economic development. The present study analyses how Femi Osofisan uses drama to explore ethnic conflicts and envisage perspectives for peaceful settlement and social cohesion. The approach shows how Femi Osofisan uses theatrical art to explore the consequences of ethnic conflicts, religiosity and economic disparities as potential sources of conflicts in Africa, to call for their peaceful settlement, and to decode his literary message that mediation and dialogue are sustainable peace strategies in African settings.

12.1. Ethnic Studies School of Thought in Africa

Originally emerged from the United States, Ethnic studies is the interdisciplinary study of difference—chiefly race, ethnicity, and nation, but also sexuality, gender, and other such markings—and power, as expressed by the state, by civil society, and by individuals. An academic field that spans the humanities and the social sciences, it emerged as an academic field in the second half of the 20th century partly in response to charges that traditional disciplines such as anthropology, history, literature, sociology, political science, cultural studies, and area studies were conceived from an inherently Eurocentric perspective. Its origin, then, lies in the civil rights era, when ethnic studies was originally conceived to re-frame the way that specific disciplines had told the stories, histories, struggles and triumphs of people of color on what was seen to be their own terms. In more recent years, it has broadened its focus to include questions of representation, racialization, racial formation theory, and more determinedly interdisciplinary topics and approaches.

In African context, ethnic studies have gained increasing awareness due to the fact that Africa is home to many ethnic conflicts. Ethnicity is more than skin color or physical characteristics, more than language, song, and dance. It is the embodiment of values, institutions, and patterns of behavior, a composite whole representing a people's historical experience, aspirations, and world view. Deprive a people of their ethnicity, their culture, and you deprive them of their sense of direction or purpose. Traditionally, African societies and even states functioned through an elaborate system based on the family, the lineage, the clan, the tribe, and ultimately a confederation of groups with ethnic, cultural, and linguistic characteristics in common. These were the units of social, economic, and political organizations and inter-communal relations (Deng Francis M. 1997: 1). In the Great Lake region (Democratic Republic of Congo, Uganda, Ruwanda, Central Africa), in Somalia ethnic conflicts and tensions have been rife for years. In Nigeria, the 1966 saw the country sink into rivalery between the Igbos and other ethnic groups. Ethnic conflicts are even long intrenched in Nigerian history and Femi Osofisan has used dramatic literature to ponder over such ethnic conflicts in Nigeria.

Much literary documentation on conflicts has examined the multifaceted aspects of African conflicts without paying due attention to the problem from ethno-religious vantage point, taking history as reference. Going from the grassroots of the causes of Nigerian ethnic conflicts, Femi Osofisan offers a dramatic perspective of their remote causes and explores their impacts on modern African societies. Some critics of Osofisan have spotted out the corroding aspect of conflicts in his art, but seem to overlook the necessity of mediation in a context where ethnicity and religiosity stir the wheels of sociopolitical cleavage. Chidi Amuta (1989) asserts that Femi Osofisan's new writing is characterized by his accent on political commitment and by a certain ideological predilection that is class-partisan, as he sees socio-political salvation mainly in terms of the revolutionary transformation of society (Amuta 1989: 169). He overlooks ethnic conflicts in Osofisan's art.

J. Ndukaku Amankulor (1993) on his part thinks that Osofisan is a leading voice of new generation of playwrights who advocates radical social change (Amankulor 1993: 162), a position that does not include Osofisan's mediation policy in literature. Elaine Savory (1998) goes a step further to propose that Osofisan's commitment to social change in Nigeria has been evident since his earliest writing (Savory 1998: 376), without however specifying the aspect of social change targeted by his art. Alexander Kure (2012) takes a different position to points out that violent conflict in Femi Osofisan are "a recurring decimal" and that they can be mediated through a spirit of forgiveness (Kure 2009: 80). It appears that in the ecology of their readings, only Alexander Kure slightly touches conflict mediation as important issue in Osofisan's work; thereby making a new critical analysis that will offer in-depth examination of conflicts and their mediation necessary. From a postcolonial perspective, Femi Osofisan in *Women of Owu* and *Farewell to a Cannibal Rage* has shown the harmful aspects of ethno-religious and tribal conflicts and calls for peaceful mediation. My analysis will focus on the nature and causes of conflicts in Africa as viewed by Osofisan in *Women of Owu* and the solutions suggested in there.

12.1.1. Ethnic Diversity: The Informing Rationales of Tribal Conflicts in Nigeria

Postcolonial ethnic theory offers to the reader the possibility to apprehend in Femi Osofisan's literary texts the cultural and political impacts of European conquest and partition of Africa, foregrounding the ethnic problematic. Approaching ethnic problem from post-colonial theoretical perspective, Siân Jones quotes Wallman S. to make the point that Ethnicity frames ethnic identity and that identity involves the active maintenance of cultural boundaries in the process of social interaction (Jones 1997: 28). Simply put, it means that ethnicity which is supposed to be a source of cultural enrichment can become a source of conflict if it is not well handled. The critic goes further to state that "As a *process* ethnicity involves a consciousness of difference, which, to varying degrees, entails the reproduction and transformation of basic classificatory distinctions between groups of people who perceive themselves to be in some respect culturally distinct" (Ibidem). The points made by Siân Jones enable the reader to understand that ethnicity which entails cultural differences among different ethnic groups can be source of conflicts especially when conflicting interests divide stakeholders.

Many of the postcolonial conflicts in Africa are of ethnic or religious origins. That theory serves as a lens for me to examine in Femi Osofisan's plays *Women of Owu* and *Red Is the Freedom Road* the aftermaths of the ethnic groupings in African countries issued from the Berlin Conference (1884-1885) partition of Nigerian nation by the British. To be exact, Africans were never consulted nor associated to the partition of the continent. It follows that the partition of Africa was done in conditions that ignored African realities related to ethnicity, religiosity and tribe, to be modeled on the sole desires and wish of the colonizers. In such conditions the smearing divisions of people of the same ancestry and the grouping of different ethnic groups under the same national bordering seem to have done more harms than good to Africans, considering the upsurging of inter-tribal and inter-religious conflicts that undermine African societies to the present date. In search for definitional orientation of the Post-colonial theory, Bill Ashcroft and Pal Ahluwalia write that

> Postcolonial [ethnic] theory investigates, and develops propositions about, the cultural and political impact of European conquest upon colonised societies, and the nature of those societies' responses. The 'post' in the term refers to 'after colonialism began' rather than 'after colonialism ended', because the cultural struggles between imperial and dominated societies continue into the present. Post-colonial theory is concerned with a range of cultural engagements: the impact of imperial languages upon colonised societies; the effects of European 'master-discourses' such as history and philosophy; the nature and consequences of colonial education and the links between Western knowledge and colonial power (Ashcroft and Ahluwalia 2002: 14).

In particular, add the critics, it is concerned with the responses of the colonised: the struggle to control self-representation, through the appropriation of dominant languages, discourses and forms of narrative; the struggle over representations of place, history, race and ethnicity; and the struggle to present a local reality to a global audience. Although it has been heavily oriented towards literary theory, since it was prompted by the flourishing of literatures written by colonized peoples in colonial languages (particularly English), it is becoming widely used in historical, political and sociological analyses as its relevance to these disciplines grows (Ibidem).

Femi Osofisan has chosen ethnic and social conflicts and their aftermaths as subject matter in *Women of Owu* and *Farewell to a Cannibal Rage*. It seems undeniable fact that ethnic conflicts in Africa have done harm to people and society more than any other type of social crisis. But the manner leaders look at these conflicts and the mediation they opt for have proved inefficient to remedy that evil. Conflicts for some critics have important role in literary works since they help develop the plot. But beyond that role, the representation of conflicts in drama is first and foremost a means of initiating debate for social problems because, in literature, we find an opportunity to talk and to give our critical appreciation of the conflicts being presented.

The Nigerian society like any other society in Africa shaped by the ex-colonizers is cosmopolite and diverse, with multi-ethnico-linguistic groups living together and sharing the same geographic zone. This situation can be traced back to colonization where the Whiteman – the British colonizer-partitioned the African countries without paying respect to ethnic groupings. The first step towards conflict resolution is the awakening of awareness that conflicts are piece and parcel of humanity. Conflicts are inherent to human society, and scrutinizing the history of Africa, the continent has always faced conflicts. In seeking the informing spirit of conflicts in Nigeria, just like in any other African country, it is not farfetched to say that they are due to the diversity of interests among people of different ethnics, tribes or region, interests which are often time opposed to each other and the stakeholders positioning themselves to defend such interests, collide with one another, a situation which usually degenerates into open conflicts. Chinua Achebe corroborates this critical stand by saying that "Nothing in Nigeria's political history captures her problem of national integration more than the chequered fortune of the word *tribe* in her vocabulary" (Achebe 1983: 5). Femi Osofisan staying in the logic of Achebe sees tribalism as a serious problem that deserves to be addressed with a due attention in art, especially in a way of peaceful settlement. From the worldwide conflicts to quarrels inside a family tissue, people have always been called upon to sit down and talk about conflicts resolution. In *Women of Owu,* Femi Osofisan insists of the aspect of neighboring conflicts as generated by opposing interests. The notes on the play's genesis reads thus:

> In 1821, the combined forces of the armies of Ijebu and Ife, two Yoruba kingdoms in the south of what is now known as Nigeria, along with mercenaries recruited from Oyo refugees fleeing

> downwards from the Nigerian savannah land, sacked the city of Owu after a seven-year siege. Owu was a model city- state, one of the most prosperous and best organized of those times. The Allied Forces had attacked it with the pretext of liberating the flourishing market of Apomu from Owu's control. Owu closed the gates of its formidable city walls, but it soon had to face the problem of drought when the rain stopped in the third year of the siege. (*WO*: vii)

And commenting on the havoc and destructions engendered, he adds that:

> This was a boon in the Allied Forces of course, and finally, in the seventh year they entered the city, and it was all over. The Allied Forces, determined that the city must never rise again, reduced the place to complete rubble, and set fire to it. They slaughtered all the males, adults and children, and carried away the females into slavery. Owu was never rebuilt. So it was quite logical therefore that, as I pondered over this adaptation of Euripides' play, in the season of Iraqi War, the memories that were awakened in me should be those of the tragic Owu War… (*WO: vii*).

This is an outline of the historical event and facts that have inspired and fuelled the storyline of Osofisan's *Women of Owu*. At the center of this conflict stands the Apomu flourishing market, which opposes the population of Owu to those of Ijebu. Owu has built its prosperity on that market and is enjoying the bliss of life before being attacked, wrecked and vandalized by the Allied Forces of Ijebu. What is being said here is history, a way for Osofisan to underscore the importance of history in the writing of literature. History serves as a mirror in which human beings can look to understand the past, to interpret the present and to construct the future. Past mistakes that have caused ruination to society should be corrected and avoided in the present and future times. Osofisan shows that Literature and history entertain important relationships and in literature we are given the opportunity to learn from other people's mistakes to improve our lives.

Femi Osofisan berates war and decries its dehumanizing nature on humans. *Women of Owu* is a personal and communal tragedy. A tragic play deals with grave issues and often ends in deaths or grief while leaving on the audience a sense of feeling of sorrow and a deep thought about life (Nwachukwu-Agbada

2010: 138). As the play opens, there has been a tragic consequence of the seven-year siege laid at the gates of Owu city by her enemies, the Allied Forces of Ijebu, Ife and Oyo. There has been massive destruction of the property of the people as well as of the environment. There is a smouldering over there and the proud city of Owu reduced to ruin yesterday *(WO: 1)*. Lives have also been decimated. But more crucially, "not a single man is left now / in Owu except those who escaped the night before / With our king, Oba Akinjobi (*WO: 3*). Even those who are seen late are rounded up and slaughtered. Not even shrines and groves of respected gods and goddesses have been spared. The major grievance of Lawumi against the Allied Forces is that upon the Owus running into her shrine for protection, "the allied soldiers did not care for that, they seized them all and finished them" and to cap the insult, complains Lawumi, "they set fire to my shrine." The play is a personal tragedy because, certain individuals take the brunt of the tragic ruination. The Oba Akinjobi family seems to have been the most affected as individuals. He is not only killed, his five sons, two daughters and a grandson are killed in cold blood as well. As Scene two opens, we observe Erelu Afin, the wife of Oba Akinjobi "sprawled on the ground…/ in the dust, like a common mongrel. She has lost her splendor as a king's wife and asks rather rhetorically, "who will look at me now, and remember / I was once a queen here in this broken city…" (*WO: 10*). Erelu does a lot of talking in the play, which is justifiable, judging by the weight of the tragedy that has laid indelible scars on her psyche and mind. As the play is about to end, she considers herself already dead by asserting that "This is no longer the Erelu you knew but just another corps still talking. Erelu suffers the indignity of being allocated to one of the victorious generals, notwithstanding her age, her sorrows and her status before the conquest of Owu city.

At communal level, the tragedy reads in the fact that, apart from the destruction of the entire environment of Owu city as well as setting fire to cultural sites and religious groves, norms and communal ethos have been trampled upon. Women are raped and later distributed out to various generals of the Allied Forces. Because of the crisis, the dead hardly receive their due reverence as demanded by custom. Hence, as soon as Adumaadan informs that she has performed the ritual of pouring sand on the dead body of Adeoti, Erelu is very thankful to her daughter-in-law: "Thank you again, I wish I knew what deity to pray to now to reward you / for the kindness you show to my daughter." Later Erelu herself is called to perform the ritual of pacifying the dead meant to forestall future eternal damnation of the people. This ritual, it seems, is the provenance of appropriate males but since there are no more males, Erelu takes up the role saying that "it shall not be sent while I live".

The entire breadth of the play is tragic. The songs, the dirges, dances and dance movements evoke sadness and despair. All that is heard from time to time is the death of one person or the other or the suspected madness of somebody. Part of the tragedy is also manifested in the loss of respect for the gods. Apart from chasing victims into shrines and killing them there, the gods' underbelly has been exposed by the war. For instance, Erelu remarks that she has just observed that "the gods are not worth much! They lie and lie all the time / and deceive us" (*WO: 59*).

War dehumanizes, because in war no infringement or misdeed is really considered indecent if it is committed against the losing side. This is what Erelu Afin calls "the law of combat" or "the law of defeat" (*WO: 16*). Let's note the unprecedented wickedness of the victorious forces transpiring in the amount of destruction they unleash on the conquered people. On that point, it is propitious to see the relevance of Wole Soyinka's lament over violent ethnic conflicts perpetrated by leaders, an atrocity which he terms ethnic cleansing which the Ogoni were victims of (Soyinka 1996: 6). Not only is the city of Owu on fire as the play opens, but also desperate Owu men and women who run into sacred shrines for protection are not spared. It is not just in the current Owu war that this kind of thing has happened, but even in the war the Owus had fought with the Ife people earlier, "recklessly, The [Owus] looted the stalls of Ijebu, killed many / and sold the others into slavery (*WO: 20*). At war, human beings turn maniacal and devilish. We are told that the invading forces not only cut off the heads of male Owus, they stick these heads on stakes and dance away with them in their camps. Adding to that, they killed the "five splendid sons of Oba Akinjobi, killed himself and raped his daughters, before sharing out the surviving women to some officers among them. Erelu Afin hitherto the queen of the city is about to be sold into slavery. She wonders if she will be "sold to the flesh merchants of Kano or Abomey" or "straight to the White masters in the cold Castles of Cape Coast (*WO: 16*). At war, men develop strange tastes. Later we hear that Erelu a very old woman with fallen breast (WO: 25) is to be given out to Balogun Derin as his own war booty. Orisaye, the half-mad daughter of Erelu and the vestal votary of Obatala is to be inherited by Balogun Kusa who is "determined to taste the food/ Reserved for the god" (*WO: 32*). Ordinarily this desire would have been unthinkable because a god does not share anything with a human, least of all a wife. War not only dehumanizes the loser, but it also turns the victorious into a monster.

I hold this critical stance because the soldiers' dashing the head of toddler Aderogun against a tree just to ensure that no sun or heir to the Oba Akinjobi survives is a crude revelation of human mischief.. This, they do by crushing the boy's little skull because "it is a taboo to shoot him/Or cut his skin with a blade" (*WO*: 45). It is the extent of the dehumanization of the invaders that has resulted in the current heated argument among the winning generals as to the acceptable sharing formula for the loot out of the war.

12.1.2. A Literary Spectrum of War Trauma

From postcolonial ethnic theoretical approach, I suggest that Femi Osofisan has shown that many mental disorders occur in African societies in general and the Nigerian in particular as effects of tribal wars; and this apprehension reads from his representation of mental and psychosomatic disorders in the play *Women of Owu*. Such disorders include, hysteria, melancholy, fright, hallucinations, shame, disgrace, cries, sorrows, despair, all these culminating into madness, a state of uncontrollable psychosomatic-disorder. War is the real cause of trauma and bewilderment. Due to the havoc done by the Ijebu soldiers to Owu population, many characters especially women have developed the symptoms of mental disorders, ailment near schizophrenia. My target character will be Orisaye, presented as the half-mad daughter of Erelu, votary of the god Obatala. Jean Du Verger in his essay " *Hamlet* and Melancholy" has shown how a situation of disarray, worry and anxiety can lead to madness:

> If the heart became over-contracted under the effect of a cold and dry passion (coldness and dryness were believed to be hostile to life), it would draw off the vital spirit from the rest of the body. Sorrow, fear and despair, cold and dry passions would then rise through the body, which would obscure the clearness of reason (Verger 1997: 84).

This critical stand traces the sources of madness to over-contraction of the heart under the pressure of sorrow, fear and despair. That is what has exactly happened to Orisaye, who lost his brothers and sisters in the hideous Owu/Ijebu war. From fear of facing facts of her life, she has progressively developed the symptoms of melancholy which later becomes madness. I totally agree with critic Jean Du Verger's position that melancholy is an illness whose most potent form is madness (Ibidem). Femi Osofisan represents this image on stage in *Women of Owu* through the mental disorders afflicting Orisaye, now half-made due to the accumulation of emotional tensions of fear, sorrow, and despair. This argument finds justification from the play where Erulu acknowledges that melancholy is a sickness which borders on madness in her daughter Orisaye (*WO*: 23). Isolation is indeed another symptom of the melancholic disease of Orisaye, since she seeks to avoid the society of men. The melancholic's attributes are also shrewdness and secrecy and these are a response to a diseased world seen as hostile to her. The full depiction of that character (Orisaye) in her insane state emphasizes the victimization of the mentally sick as discriminated people of the society who must avoid public places for fear of exposing their life incoherence.

> ERELU: [...] At least, let my poor Orisaye continue to remain inside, out of sight for now. These events, as you know, have made her Even more delirious than she was, and her state of incoherence would only worsen to see her mother like this (*WO*: 16).

Two states of mind of Orisaye are important for me to underline here: delirium and incoherence of mind. Incoherence of mind here is what French critics term *"la maladie de l'âme"* (Verger 1997: 86) to mean man's existential bewilderment before a world in which all is evanescent and in which he has lost his central position. On the basis of this testimony, Femi Osofisan gives to Orisaye a careful etiological description of the progress of the disease – fear, depression, insomnia, delirium, debility, delusion and finally raving madness. He shows that the resort to violence to settle such conflicts has always been chaotic and disastrous. Femi Osofisan is one of the drama scholars who believes that art can be used to raise awareness among the populations on the nefarious consequences of unsettled human conflicts. His grudge is against the resort to violence instead of peace talks to address quarrels of the same nature. Among the many plays that Osofisan has written to attract attention on the havoc of war and conflicts *Red Is the Freedom Road, Farewell to a Cannibal Rage* and *Women of Owu,* occupy a place of choice. The vibrancy and vitality of his art shows a propensity of the playwright's criticism of the negative aspect of recourse to violence in conflicts resolution and gives a couple of ideas on the advantages of peace maintenance. I maintain that it is the future that one needs to look into to better weigh the need to settle peacefully conflicts.

12.1.3. Self-Indexation /Criticism: A Step toward Appeasement

In human affairs, oftentimes they tend to rely on the gods and to ascribe their fortune or misfortune to supernatural forces. Osofisan is trying to make the point that this tendency by humans is misplaced. In such tragedies like war, human beings are unquestionably responsible for all the havoc and damage that come out of these. From fabricating war armaments to bombing a whole city reducing it to ashes, man is at the center of the drama. Therefore it is out of question to transfer the responsibility of disastrous conflicts on the supernatural forces. Osofisan conveys this message through several images. For instance, in creating a character god who totally ignores that there is war in the land where he is god, while in fact he was supposed to be omniscient about the conflict: "I don't understand" he replies to the women informing him about the actions of the Allied Forces, "you said all this happened only yesterday?" (*WO:* 2) Not only do the women give him an update information about how Owu males have been decimated "whether old or young", they even draw his attention to the desecration of his own shrine. "All your shrines drenched in the blood/ of your worshippers /All your sacred symbols wiped out by fire" (WO: 6). Anlugbua takes the news just as a typical human being could have done. In other words, it is wrong for human beings to rely on the gods to save them from all the misfortunes which may visit them from time to time. Before coming to art, Femi Osofisan has already indicted the political leader for standing aloof in front of the devastating effects of inter-ethnic wars: "Those were, you all recollect the decades of harsh suppression of human rights everywhere, when to dare to speak out at all was more or less to put your neck in the nooze in the face of horrendous laws and decrees" (Osofisan 2012: 364). The revelation by Chorus Leader when she admonishes her fellow women "to stop wailing and brace yourselves" is instructive here. According to her,

> CHORUS LEADER: No, Stop the wailing and brace yourselves My dear women. The lesson is clear. It is us not the gods, Who create war. It's us, we human beings, who can kill it.
> *(WO: 15)*

It transpires from this extract that the cause of the war and the level of destruction are the results of human folly. Owu which is now on the receiving end had once been brutish to the Ife people when they conquered the latter. This was in spite of the fact that Ile Ife played a role in her establishment as "one of the seven kingdoms/of Yorubaland (*WO: 19*). After their founding and flourishing as a city, the Owus took to arrogance, "an insufferable display of arrogance" *(WO: 18)*. According to Lawumi, Owu forgot its history, forgot its origins! They began to sell other Yoruba into slavery (*WO:* 19). Upon sacking the Ife army and taking back the Apomu market, the Owus looted the stalls of the Ijebu, killed many and sold the others into slavery. In response, the IIjebus sent their dreaded army up against the city, thus resulting in the present military siege against Owu city (*WO:* 20). Another reason for the current impasse is Maye Okunade's sworn stand to punish Owu people for one of her sons, Adejumo, taking his wife away during the attack on Ife. Because of the disgrace and the humiliation, Okunade caused this havoc (*WO: 5*). He has abandoned his vocation as an artist and embraced violence as his next calling. For seven years he mounts a military campaign against the Owus, and when he achieves the purpose, all the Owu men are slaughtered and their women shared to the officers with whom he captured the Owu city. Osofisan conveys the message that Human beings are the architects of their own woes; a message he releases through Anlugbua: "You human beings always thirst for blood, always eager to devour one another, history will teach you. I hope you will learn *(WO: 67)*.

Another discernible message Femi Osofisan highlights in the play is one which appeals to all the oppressed and the cheated to do something to rescue themselves from their downtrodden and repressed status. This is more than calling for self-reliance, it calls for people's discovery of the source of their burdened state and thereafter to dismantle it. The gods in Femi Osofisan's plays essentially stand for political leaders, and, and the master/servant relationship between human beings and the gods (their leaders) is emphasized. The playwright energetically condemns man's folly in his promotion of war and violence. By so doing, man does not realize that love is superior to war. One of the oppressors whose antics would have to be discouraged is exulted, comprising the generals, the rich and the rulers. Gesinde complains about the generals who sit back and give their orders while "we poor ones face the victims and spill the blood (*WO:* 45). Chorus Leaders also complains that it is the rulers who write history just as the hunters compose the story of the hunt and the revelers record the fable of the feast (*WO:* 66).

In *Red Is the Freedom Road,* Femi Osofisan has complemented the message of *Women of Owu* by laying emphasis on the aftermath of war as experienced by families. Osofisan has brought down the message close to individuals' understanding by showing that war split couples, divide father and children, sisters and brothers. For instance, Akanji and Ibidun once a harmonious couple have been separated by a civil war and Ibidun spends years without seeing her husband Akanji. Akanji's mother dies out of grief because of the disappearance of her son. These are the facts that Situation One highlights (*RFR: 116*). Due to war atrocities, says Ibidun, "we have our wounded slaves; … We have only our wounded slaves… we have only our empty hands, hands all graunt and hollow (*RFR: 124*). War can reduce the whole of a king into slave. War can reduce even an army general to a slave. For instance, Jengboran, a king who once owned thousand slaves has been captured a slave himself:

> Akanji: You, soldier, I see your marks, and they are foreign, not of this land I know you well. Your house is at Akatan, home of heroes. Why, only Yesterday…your name rocked us like thunder. So you are fallen too? You were a king wherever you came from. I think your name is Jengboran, the One who owned a Thousand Slaves. Is that you, just another Slave? (*RFR*: 130).

In this excerpt, it is perceptible that war pulls people down. From a high position one can totally decline to nothingness. During war, people easily lose their relations, even the dearest ones. War annihilates all efforts of development. Femi Osofisan may have taken inspiration from the Nigerian civil war to ponder over the content of *Red Is the Freedom Road*. For the same way characters suffered death, hunger, deprivation, wastage of property, it is the same way people are suffering in the play. And the central question remains, until when will the populations who are the true victims of war ever find relief? The soldiers themselves who are the war emissaries are aware of the hell fire that the civil war has rained on the innocent victims:

> 1st SOLDIER: O when will men learn the truth? War is not the only means of Dialogue.
> 2nd SOLDIER: Nor can peace be won by warriors.
> 1st SOLDIER: No prosperous harvest from battlefield.
> 2nd SOLDIER: But corpses only. Stench and horror. But corpses therefrom.
> 1st SOLDIER: And the wailing of widows, of children abandoned?

> 2ⁿᵈ SOLDIER: Hunger and horror, disaster and death. When will men learn the simple truth?
> 1ˢᵗ SOLDIER: You cannot reap cocoyams when you plant blood. All feet flounder When the road runs red. The flower must wither in its season. O when shall we learn?
> (RFR: 135)

Here, we note that corpses, stench, horror, disaster, plunder and contrition are the reflections of war in society. The soldiers are leveling a criticism on the corrosive nature of war, but especially on human beings' unwillingness to learn, to draw teachings from the past. All people on the human planet agree on the fact that war is evil and anti-life. No society can ever develop in an atmosphere of belligerent tensions. Yet, the alarming remark is that the more people become aware of the evil of war and its destructive nature, the more they perpetrate scenes of violence and resort to war to look for peace. It is contradictory and appears nonsense to seek peace through war. Femi Osofisan's art is meant to teach readers these important lessons. The recurrent question in the soldiers' conversation is 'when will men learn the truth?' This question is raised oftentimes because human beings are unable to change their behavior by learning from the past.

12.1.4. Conflict Resolution, A Means for Pacific Coexistence

Osofisan's drama is geared towards socio-political change, a complete overhauling of the mental decay that belittles the fundamental values of peace strategies. His art recommends that one goes at the root of conflicts to dig out their causes for a complete cure. In his selected plays under consideration, *Women of Owu* and *Red Is the Freedom Road,* he condemns the tragic use of armed forces to repress, kill and oppress. He locates the responsibility of the human lives wastage within the realm of political power. Osofisan's ideology falls in line with Edmund Burke's proviso that the failure of Nigeria so far as political experiment is concerned can be traced to one essential source, "The fact that the politicians played too much politics, often ignoring national interests in their quest for power or personal or regional aggrandizement" (Burke 1976: 113). This can be perceived as the fundamental, though not excluvive factor that informed the disparaging forces that conflicted to breed the cocktail of Biafran war. Ethnicity, religious grouping and linguistic formations when they are not objectively managed and sanctioned by the state may breed the relics of conflicts. Referring to Nigeria, Alex Thompson goes in the same line by adjoining that:

> In terms of ethnicity, the Third Republic has been associated with political violence in the oil-producing Niger Delta region of the country. Activists, invoking sentiments of ethnicity, have mobilised against the federal government, complaining that local people gain little economic or social benefit from the oil extracted on their land. Profits, they argue, are siphoned off by federal authorities and transnational corporations. The struggle is portrayed as central government exploiting the local minority ethnic groups that inhabit the delta. Once again, political conflict over inequality has taken on an ethnic dimension. Low-intensity insurgency, including the kidnapping of oil workers, has been the result (Thompson 2010: 78)

To my understanding, there has been an unequal redistribution of the national riches not just because the delta oil-mining region is firmly controlled by the state, but also because the government has not been enough mindful about sharing equally the outcomes of the national riches among the population. For instance, local people gaining little of the very produce mined on their soil is synomous with injustice, especially when it is known that an oligarchy holds the biggest share. David Bloomfield while asserting that democracy is a system for managing difference without recourse to violence means a profound understanding of a pacific coexistence that uses cultural differences, diverging political opinions and contradictory social interests as sources of mutual enrichment, to achieve viable human society (Blommfield 2003: 12). Though difficult in practice, pacific coexistence amidst differences is not impossible to achieve. Femi Osofisan in *Women of Owu* develops the philosophy of pacific coexistence as the prior condition informing the bedrock and mainstay of a viable development in Nigerian social fabric. If war is anti-social and anti-life, peace is the cornerstone for enjoyable social life and development. The starting point is reconciliation. Reconciliation is both a goal and a process; it is an over-arching process which includes the search for truth, justice, forgiveness, healing and possibly compensation. In this respect, educating young generations of the twenty-first century to the ideals of pacific coexistence in multi-ethnic regions is fundamental. Jean Bosco Habiarimana's suggestions of strategies for attaining sustainable peace compel attention. I am indebted to that critic in the following ideas he develops. For him, there should be a fostering of culture of peace through education by promoting education for all, focusing especially on girls, revisiting curricula to promote the qualitative values (Habyarimana 2012: 78). Education should also aim at developing attitudes and behaviours inherent to a culture of peace, and training for conflicts prevention and resolution, dialogue, consensus-building, and active nonviolence. A sustainable peace seeking strategy should also include the promotion of long lasting economic and social development by targeting the eradication of poverty, focusing on the special needs of children and women, working towards environmental sustainability , fostering ethnic and inter-ethnic cooperation, national and international cooperation to reduce economic and social inequalities. In this perspective, social justice resting on the meritous rewarding, not on ethnic favoritism or regionalism should be encouraged. Chinua Achebe, a Nigerian writer and critic himself, acknowledges the presence of the virus of nepotism in the country's social fabric and recommends its destruction:

> The motive for the original denial [of merit] may be tribal discrimination, but it may also come from sexism, from political, religious, or some other partisan consideration, or from corruption and bribery […] it is sufficient to state that whenever merit is set aside by prejudice of whatever origin, individual citizens as well as nation itself are victimized (Achebe 2012: 78).

Achebe's prophylactic remark on the denial of merit to those who deserve it is in line with Osofisan's critical position, a position that helps to explain the propensity and persistence of ethnic conflicts in Nigeria and Africa in general. If ethnic rivalry is to stop, nepotism and regionalism, inhibiters of intellectual and professional excellence must be discouraged. A step towards sustainable conflicts mediation is the promotion of respect for human rights, at least the inalienable ones. This proceeds by vulgarizing, disseminating and explaining in details the Universal Declaration of Human Rights at all levels of society and fully implementing international instruments on human rights. For this reason, it urges to ensure equal opportunities between men and women by integrating gender perspectives and promoting equity in economic, social and political decision-making; eliminating all forms of discrimination and violence against women; supporting and aiding women in crisis situations resulting from war and all other forms of violence (Ibidem). To successfully arrive, Jean Bosco proposes that one should foster democratic participation, by educating responsible citizens, reinforcing actions to promote democratic principles and practices, establishing and strengthening national institutions and processes that promote and sustain democracy (Ibidem). A further step will be the advancing, and understanding of tolerance and solidarity by promoting dialogue among civilizations, ethnics, and tribes. It also includes undertaking actions in favour of vulnerable groups, migrants, refugees and displaced persons – indigenous people and traditional groups; and respect for difference and cultural diversity. In *Women of Owu* many such people pain to find asylum. All these can be possible if there is supporting participatory communication and the free flow of information and knowledge. In the process this should be done by means of concrete actions, say by supporting the media in the promotion of a culture of peace. For an effective and efficient use of media and mass communication, measures to address the issues of violence should be taken and knowledge and information sharing through new technologies encouraged (Ibidem). Local peace will last long only if it ascribes to a global policy of international peace and security. Through actions like the promotion of general and complete disarmament, greater involvement of women in prevention and resolution of conflicts, and the promotion of a culture of peace in post-conflicts situations, African societies can attain peace and development. There should be initiatives in conflicts situations, to encourage confidence-building measures and efforts for negotiating peaceful settlements.

The essentials read that Femi Osofisan shows through *Women of Owu* that ethnicity is a delicate problem in Africa. Its mishandling can breed inter-ethnic conflicts with dire consequences like manslaughter, division and property destruction. Africans can exploit their ethnic diversities to make them a source of enrichment. Peace attainment should be a participative struggle. By creating conflicts and resolving them, Osofisan conveys the message that amicable settlement of conflicts can only be better achieved through the acceptance of the spirit of forgiveness and accommodation.

References

Achebe, Chinua. *There Was a Country: A Personal History of Biafra.* USA: Penguin Books 2012.
-------------------- (1989). *The Trouble with Nigeria:* London: Heinemann, 1983.

Amankulor, J. Ndukaku. "English Language Drama and Theatre". In Oyekan Owomoyela (ed) *A History of Twentieth Century African Literatures.* Nebraska: University of Nebraska Press. 1993. 138-172.

Amuta, Chidi. *The Theory of African Literature: Implications for Practical Criticism* (London and New Jersey: Zed Books Ltd 1989.

Ashcroft, Bill and Pal Ahluwalia (1999), *Routledge Critical Essential Guide for Literary Studies: Edward Said* London and New York: Routledge. 2002.

Bloomfield, David et al. *Reconciliation after a Violent Conflict: A Handbook.* Sweden: IDEA 2003.

Burke, Edmund. *Reflections on the Nigerian Civil War : Facing the Future* (Ibadan: Spectrum Books Limited 1976.

Du Verger, Jean. "Hamlet and Melancholy". In Pierre Iselin ed. *William Shakespeare Hamlet.* CNED: Didier Erudition. 1997. 81-106.

Habyarimana, Jean Bosco. "Educating for Twenty-first Century : Peace Education for the Post-genocide Rwanda". In Samuel Kale Ewusi (ed) *Weaving Peace: Essays on Peace, Governance and Conflict Transformation in the Great Lakes Region of Africa.* USA: Trafford Publishing. 2012. 75-92.

Osofisan, Femi. *Women of Owu.* Ibadan: University Press PLC. 2006.

Siân Jones, Siân. *The Archeology of Ethnicity: Constructing Identities in the Past and Present.* London and New York: Routledge. 1997.

Kure, Alexander. "Conflict Resolution in Femi Osofisan's *Another Raft* and *Farewell to a Cannibal Rage:* Models for the Attainment of Peace in Kaduna State, Nigeria" in Kinde Akinyemi and Toyin Falola (eds) *Emerging Perspectives in Femi Osofisan.* Trenton: Africa World Press. 2009. 80-98.

Nwachukwu-Agbada, J O J et al. *Exam Focus Literature in English.* Ibadan: University Press. 2010.

Osofisan, Femi. "African Theatre and the Menace of Transition: Radical Transformations in Popular Entertainment". In Anne V. Adams (ed.) *Essays in Honour of Ama Ata Aidoo at 70: A Reader in African Cultural Studies.* UK: Ayebia. 2012. 362-373.

Savory, Elene. "Femi Osofisan". In Pushpa Naidu Parekh and Siga Fatima Jagne (eds.) *Postcolonial African Writers: A Bio-Bibliographical Critical Sourcebook.* Westport: Greenwood Press. 1998. 374-381.

Soyinka, Wole. *The Open Sore of a Continent: A Personal Narrative of the Nigerian Crisis.* Oxford: Oxford University Press. 1996.

Thompson, Alex. *An Introduction to African Politics,* Third Edition. New York: Routledge. 2010.

13

THE AESTHETICS OF MARXISM AND POSTMODERNISM IN OSOFISAN'S *ONCE UPON FOUR ROBBERS* AND SOYINKA'S *JERO'S METAMORPHOSIS*

Postmodernism then becomes an activist strategy against the coalition of reason and power. 'Postmodernism', Frank Lentricchia explains 'seeks not to find the foundation and the condition of truth, but to exercise power for the purpose of social change.' The task of postmodern professors is to help students spot, confront and work against the political horrors of one's time (Ricks 2004: 3).

13.1. Theory in Context: The Vanguards of Postmodernism

A major 'moment' in the history of postmodernism is the influential paper 'Modernity - an Incomplete Project' delivered by the contemporary German theorist Jiirgen Habermas in 1980. For Habermas the modern period begins with the Enlightenment, that period of about one hundred years, from the mid-seventeenth to the mid- eighteenth century, when a new faith arose in the power of reason to improve human society. Such ideas are expressed or embodied in the philosophy of Kant in Germany, Voltaire and Diderot in France, and Locke and Hume in Britain. In Britain the term 'The Age of Reason' was used (till recently) to designate the same period.

The so-called Enlightenment 'project' is the fostering of this belief that a break with tradition, blind habit, and slavish obedience to religious precepts and prohibitions, coupled with the application of reason and logic by the disinterested individual, can bring about a solution to the problems of society. This outlook is what Habermas means by 'modernity'. The French Revolution can be seen as a first attempt to test this theory in practice. For Habermas this faith in reason and the possibility of progress survived into the twentieth century, and even survives the catalogue of disasters which makes up this century's history. The cultural movement known as modernism subscribed to this 'project', in the sense that it constituted a lament for a lost sense of purpose, a lost coherence, a lost system of values. For Habermas, the French post-structuralist thinkers of the 1970s, such as Derrida and Foucault, represented a specific repudiation of this kind of Enlightenment 'modernity'. They attacked, in his view, the ideals of reason, clarity, truth, and progress, and as they were thereby detached from the quest for justice, he identified them as 'young conservatives'.

The term 'postmodernism' was used in the 1930s, but its current sense and vogue can be said to have begun with Jean-Francois Lyotard's *The Postmodern Condition: A Report on Knowledge* (Manchester University Press, 1979). Lyotard's essay 'Answering the Question: What is Postmodernism?', first published in 1982, added in 1984 as an appendix to *The Postmodern Condition* and included in Brooker's *Modernism/ Postmodernism, 1992,* takes up this debate about the Enlightenment, mainly targeting Habermas, in a slightly oblique manner. Lyotard opens with a move which effectively turns the debate into a struggle to demonstrate that one's opponents are the real conservatives (a familiar 'bottom line' of polemical writing on culture). From every direction', he says, 'we are being urged to put an end to experimentation', and after citing several other instances he writes (obviously of Habermas): I have read a thinker of repute who defends modernity against those he calls the neo-conservatives. Under the banner of postmodernism, the latter would like, he believes, to get rid of the uncompleted project of modernism, that of the Enlightenment (Brooker: 141)

Habermas is simply one voice in a chorus which is calling for an end to 'artistic experimentation' and for 'order ... unity, for identity, for security' (Brooker: 142). In a word, these voices want 'to liquidate the heritage of the avant-gardes'. For Lyotard the Enlightenment whose project Habermas wishes to continue is simply one of the would-be authoritative 'overarching', 'totalising' explanations of things – like Christianity, Marxism, or the myth of scientific progress. These 'metanarratives' ['super-narratives'], which purport to explain and reassure, are really illusions, fostered in order to smother difference, opposition, and plurality. Hence Lyotard's famous definition of postmodernism, that it is, simply, 'incredulity towards metanarratives'. 'Grand Narratives' of progress and human perfectability, then, are no longer tenable, and the best we can hope for is a series of 'mininarratives', which are provisional, contingent, temporary, and relative and which provide a basis for the actions of specific groups in particular local circumstances. Postmodernity thus 'deconstructs' the basic aim of the Enlightenment, that is 'the idea of a unitary end of history and of a subject'.

Another major theorist of postmodernism is the contemporary French writer Jean Baudrillard, whose book *Simulations* (1981, translated 1983) marks his entry into this field. Baudrillard is associated with what is usually known as 'the loss of the real', which is the view that in contemporary life the pervasive influence of images from film, TV, and advertising has led to a loss of the distinction between real and imagined, reality and illusion, surface and depth. The result is a culture of 'hyperreality', in which distinctions between these are eroded. His propositions are worked out in his essay 'Simulacra and Simulations' reprinted in abridged form in Brooker, 1992. He begins by evoking a past era of 'fullness', when a sign was a surface indication of an underlying depth or reality ('an outward sign of inward grace', to cite the words of the Roman Catholic Catechism). But what, he asks, if a sign is not an index of an underlying reality, but merely of other signs? Then the whole system becomes what he calls a *simulacrum*. He then substitutes for *representation* the notion *of simulation*. The sign reaches its present stage of emptiness in a series of steps.

Firstly, then, the sign represents a basic reality: let's take as an example of this the representations of the industrial city of Sal-ford in the work of the twentieth-century British artist L. S. Lowry. Mid-century life for working people in such a place was hard, and the paintings have an air of monotony and repetitive-ness - cowed, stick-like figures fill the streets, colours are muted, and the horizon filled with grim factory-like buildings. As signs, then, Lowry's paintings seem to represent the basic reality of the place they depict.

The *second* stage for the sign is that it misrepresents or distorts the reality behind it. As an example of this let's take the glamourized representations of cities like Liverpool and Hull in the paintings of the Victorian artist Atkinson Grimshaw. These paintings show the cities at night, wet pavements reflecting the bright lights of dockside shops, the moon emerging from behind clouds, and a forest of ships' masts silhouetted against the sky. Life in these places at that time was presumably grim, too, but the paintings offer a romantic and glamourised image, so the sign can be said to misrepresent what it shows.

The *third* stage for the sign is when the sign disguises the fact that there is no corresponding reality underneath. To illustrate this, take a device used in the work of the surrealist artist Rene Magritte, where, in the painting, an easel with a painter's canvas on it is shown standing alongside a window: on the canvas in the painting is painted the exterior scene which we can see through the window. But what is shown beyond the window is not reality, against which the painting within the painting can be judged, but simply another sign, another depiction, which has no more authority or reality than the painting within the painting (which is actually a representation of a representation).

The *fourth* and last stage for the sign is that it bears no relation to any reality at all. As an illustration of this stage we have simply to imagine a completely abstract painting, which is not representational at all, like one of the great purple mood canvases of Mark Rothko, for instance. I should emphasise that I'm not suggesting that these four paintings are examples of the four stages of the sign, merely that the four stages can be thought of as analogous to the four different ways in which these paintings signify or represent things.

13.1.1. What Postmodernist Critics Do

1. They discover postmodernist themes, tendencies, and attitudes within literary works of the twentieth century and explore their implications.

2. They foreground fiction which might be said to exemplify the notion of the 'disappearance of the real', in which shifting postmodern identities are seen, for example, in the mixing of literary genres (the thriller, the detective story, the myth saga, and the realist psychological novel, etc.).

3. They foreground what might be called 'intertextual elements' in literature, such as parody, pastiche, and allusion, in all of which there is a major degree of reference between one text and another, rather than between the text and a safely external reality.

4. They foreground irony, in the sense described by Umberto Eco, that whereas the modernist tries to destroy the past, the postmodernist realises that the past must be revisited, but 'with irony' *(Modernism/ Postmodernism,* ed. Peter Brooker, p. 227.

5. They foreground the element of 'narcissism' in narrative technique, that is, where novels focus on and debate their own ends and processes, and thereby 'de-naturalise' their content.

6. They challenge the distinction between high and low culture, and highlight texts which work as hybrid blends of the two.

Having seen what postmodernism means and how it urges to have a close look at the implications of postmodernist ethics and aesthetics in Femi Osofisan's and Wole Soyinka's plays, respectively *Once Upon Four Robbers* and *Jero's Metamorphosis*. Postmodernism seeks to bring socio-political reforms by displaying the frailty, the weaknesses and the flaws of a modern fragmented and criminality-prone society. It views the inefficacy of death penalty as a measure to curb the intractable menace of armed robbery in African societies, through their plays *Once Upon Four Robbers* and *Jero's Metamorphosis* taking Nigeria as a model. It addresses the underlying and stifling socio-economic factors responsible for the prevalence of crime in Nigerian society. Such factors include among many others unemployment, hunger, poverty, corruption, depravation, injustice, and ridiculous salary structure. The study contends that in a society where class disparities and overexploitation of the masses are deeply rooted in the social fabric of the nation, it takes more than coercive legal proceedings to solve the problem of moral decay whose roots can be traced back to the very unjust system created by social inequalities. The problem, more than social, needs to be approached at the aetiological (causative) level.

The postmodern formation of states in Africa projected by some African writers of dramatic expression like Femi Osofisan and Wole Soyinka has caused the rising inequalities interacted with simmering grievances linked to political exclusion and economic neglect. Socio-political exclusion and economic neglect bred the mounting of crime and violence in metropolitan centers. Although literature on crime and how to deal with it has documented African fiction and drama, little attention has been paid to Femi Osofisan's approach to crime in *Once Upon Four Robbers* (1980) and Wole Soyinka's in *Jero's Metamorphosis* (1994). Critics like Helen Gilbert and Joanne Tompkins assert that Femi Osofisan in *Once Upon Four Robbers* has made the central conflict between robbers and soldiers end in a stalemate (Gilbert and Tompkins 2004: 128). Gordon Douglas Killam and Alicia L. Kerfoot (2008) reject this idea and contend that "Osofisan's work attacks political corruption and injustice" (Killam 2008: 238), without however specifying his critical position on criminality. Victoria O. Adeniyi (2009) also stays in the logic of Killam and Alicia and states that religion, corruption and democratic Nigeria are the subject matter of Osofisan's *Once Upon Four Robbers* (Adeniyi 2009: 154) and adds that the criminals have taken to robbery because of unemployment (Ibidem). These critical positions about Femi Osofisan's work do not take into account the playwright's pragmatic approach to criminality, approach in which he shows how death penalty reveals to be inefficient to curb the intractable menace of armed robbery in African societies. About Wole Soyinka's *Jero's Metamorphosis*, Mpalive-Hangson Msiska (2007) writes that he (Soyinka) focuses on civil society, demonstrating that it is in an equally bad state (Msiska 2007: 92). It stems from these critics' views that Osofisan and Soyinka address the problem of criminality by condemning it, but critics fail to tell in practical terms how the two playwrights think the problem can be solved, and invite for a further analysis that will take into account the aetiology of crime, that is, its remote causes and suggest solutions. With a postmodern formulation, I will show how Soyinka and Osofisan relate crime to social inequalities and corruption, suggesting thereby that these problems need to be approached not through capital punishment but through an overhauling of the very unjust treatment of citizens and the corrupt practices of the rogue state.

12.1.2. Postmodern Inflections in Femi Osofisan

Postmodernism lays the claim of the lack of the original, the true and the real. Going deeper into the philosophy of that theory, it seeks to analyse the discourse of oppression between classes in confrontation, namely in terms of opreessor and oppressed. Stephen R. C. Ricks has this to say:

> Postmodern accounts of human nature hold that individuals' identities are constructed largely by the social linguistic groups that they are part of, those groups varying radically across the dimensions of sex, race, ethnicity and wealth. Postmodern account of human nature also consistently emphasize relations of conflicts between those groups and given the de-emphasized or eliminated role of reason, postmodern accounts hold that those conflicts are resolved primarily by the use of force, whether masked or naked; the use of force in turn leads to relations of dominance, submission and oppression. Finally, postmodern themes in ethics and politics are characterized by an identification for and sympathy with the group perceived to be oppressed in the conflicts and the willingness to enter the fray on their behalf (Ricks 2004: 6-7).

The substance of this formulation reveals the quintessence of postmodernism as a theory that emphasizes the bipolarization of society in dichotomic structures ruled essentially by binarism between the rich and the poor, the strong and the weak, men and women whereby class becomes object of struggle. To say that postmodernism and Marxism have many embedded patterns that are interlocked into a congelation of finality is not an overstatement.

In line with postmodern ethics, Femi Osofisan sees society from the perspective of the rich and the poor, the strong and the weak. He is in the postmodern critical line of thought. For him, criminality stems from the lopsided management of economic resources. He purports that for an effective control of criminality in African societies, as reflected in *Once Upon Four Robbers* and Wole Soyinka's *Jero's Metamorphosis,* there is need to tackle the problem at causative level. The most prominent preoccupation of Osofisan and Soyinka's dramatic arts is in their functions as a tool for social change. It results that if drama cannot be designed to diagnose society's problems, it becomes what a theorist of Marxist ideology of literature Eagleton Terry calls "a wasted enterprise" (Eagleton 1976: 3). Their plays, basing on historical, political, social, religious, and economic events of Nigerian society come to grip with the in-depth causes of criminality and the attendant solutions of the authorities using capital punishment as a punitive resort (Ademeso 2009: 53). *Once upon Four Robbers* reads as an attack to the phenomenon of armed robbery which seems to be an apt metaphor for our age (Gilbert 2001: 69). The playwright seeks to dismantle the gross material inequities characteristic of post-independent Nigerian society as the fundamental root of this kind of crime, suggesting that, the rich are themselves robbers of the country's oil wealth (Ibidem). The Nigerian society in the play is replete with crime. Four robbers, Angola, Hasan, Major, and Alhaja, have organized themselves into a rapacious band of criminals, robbing and killing the citizens who come their way.

A postmodern reading pictures out the most helpless victims, the market women who have little defense mechanism to confront their torturers. Robbery and crime then become like an instituted mechanism which leaves no chance of survival to the wretched victims. The generalized psychosis created by the havoc and damages done by the robbers bring the government, the political authorities to adopt death penalty, a public execution of any arrested robber to be carried out publicly on the beach at the full sight of the population. But by using this social image where the leaders play the judge administering death sentence to the armed robbery culprits, Femi Osofisan is addressing a more profound and serious social matter: the outcome of social disparities in the distribution of the national wealth. This problem is corollary of a series of other inequities such as ridiculous salary structure, unemployment, hunger, poverty, inflation, greed, hoarding, graft, corruption, depravation, injustice. Osofisan the playwright complains:

> Take a look at our salary structures, at the minimum wage level, count the sparse number of lucky ones who even earn it... and then take a look at the squalid spending habit of our egregious 'contractors', land speculators, middlemen of all sorts, importers, exporters, etc. Or take a look at our sprawling slums and ghettos, our congested hospitals and crowded schools, our impossible markets... and then, take another look at the fast proliferation of motorcars, insurance agencies, supermarkets, chemist chops, boutiques, discotheques etc. The callous contradictions of our oil-doomed fantasies of rapid modernization. It is obvious that as long as a single, daring nocturnal trip with a gun or machete can yield the equivalent of one man's annual income, we shall continue to manufacture our own potential assassins (Gilbert 2001: 69).

Probing into the remote causes of criminality in Osofisan's fictionalized society, it reveals itself as a stratified society where the country's wealth is being kept by one fraction of the society. Such overprivileged people are so selfish that they never share their privileges with the less fortunate people. The playwright indicts his characters for being too selfish with one another. Alhaja remarks that their main concern is to reduce social disparities: "Rob the rich, feed the poor", "Each man for himself" (*OUFR, PP:* 84). This is a social system which does not favour the development of moral uprightness, for robbery is first and foremost a result of moral decay. In a society where the wealth is generated by the working class or the masses only to profit the few members of the oligarchic self-elect, these working masses will but continue to grumble until they find an outlet for their grudge. Such outlet may go against morality as the resort to crime for instance. There is a schism in the social tissue where the poor are set against the rich. Hasan, one of the robbers complains:

> HASAN: We are doomed, my brother, and only our solidarity can save us [...] What else do they recount but the unending tales of the powerless Against the strong. And it is a history of repeated defeat, oppression And nothing changing (*OUFR, PP: 89*).

The idea corroborated in this statement is that the powerless who constitute the masses are deprived of their right to decent living and resort to crime in the form of armed robbery. For them, it is a way of unleashing their suppressed desires of decent living in a dignified acceptable social condition. Sigmund Freud's Psychoanalytic theory on human behavior explains that when we suppress our desires in the sub-consciousness, such desires find a way of expressing themselves which can be translated in abnormal social behavior (Abrams 2005: 257). Theorists of Psychoanalytic criticism, Temma F. Berg argues that when unfulfilled desires have been internalized rather than released in a sublime way, the individual will surely manifest acts of deviationism (Berg 1987: 248). The robbers in Osofisan's *Once Upon Four Robbers* take to robbery because they live in abject poverty while the bourgeois class continues to display their wealth – luxury cars, expensive clothes, ultra- modern storey buildings, money show – at the nuisance of the "wretch of the earth." The image of modernity highlights the sense of anomy caused by neo-colonial and technological developments that benefit only a select few, leaving the majority condemned to poverty and crime (Gilbert op cit, 69). Osofisan is indirectly pointing at the wide spread corruption engendered by successive political systems in a country where a cycle of failed civilian government and subsequent military coups have become the norm. Adjacent problems hovering in the administration are bribery, unemployment, hunger, poverty, inflation, injustice and ridiculous salary structures, summarized by the playwright in a song:

> Yes, I gave them the right reply
> To this your modern world
> Money-grabbing has made you mad
> Money, empty money
> Evil doing to amass property
> Buildings upon buildings
> Wife-stealing, home-destroying
> Teaching by the hard way of pain

> A modern tale I will tell you
> A tale of four armed robbers
> Dangerous highwaymen
> Freebooters, source of tears
> Like kites, eaters of accursed meals
> Visitors who leave the house in wreck
> Dispatchers to the heaven of slumber […] (*OUFR, PP: 95-96*)

This song illustrates the social problems which have made life intolerable for the average citizen, problems that have equally led the robbers to resort to robbery and criminality for their daily survival. Such problems are the aforementioned, from bribery to unpaid jobs passing through unemployment, hunger and corruption. Brief, the general life is stuffed by an atmosphere of dystopia. To draw people's thinking on the dire consequences of these problems on the society, Osofisan organizes his ideas around the negotiation table of drama.

His concern with class oppression and social injustice lies at the heart of *Once Uppon Four Robbers* one of the well known plays in a wide-ranging dramatic corpus which consistently demonstrates the playwright's conviction that drama as an artistic weapon can be used as efficient tool to initiate important debates on society's problems. Femi Osofisan's art is characterized not just by his accent on political commitment but on a certain ideological predilection that is class-partisan and sees sociopolitical salvation mainly in terms of the revolutionary transformation of society (Amuta 1989: 167-168).

Postmodernism also reveals the contradictory orientation of social structures with the contradictory situation of a few who pilfer the resources and many who are reduced to abject poverty, mendicancy and who develop strong inclination towards crime. In *Jero's Metamorphosis,* Soyinka complements Osofisan's message by adding that exploitation and oppression can breed criminality in postcolonial society. It is not far-fetched to say that criminality is the granddaughter of oppression. Characters like Ananias have practiced armed robbery all their lives before coming to prophet Jero's church for salvation. But what they see there is not spiritual salvation but a more subtle form of exploitation which was at the grassroots of their very criminal acts:

> And the dum, gross, incompetent all-muscle-and-no-brain petty criminal left a hefty thumbprint on the kerosene tin on the refuse heap near bye. They also know that that dirty great print matches the thumbprint of a certain ex-convict. The only thing they don't

know is where he is hiding out after crimes and arson, unlawful wounding, attempted murder... Even the tin kerosene was stolen from a nearbye shop...that was robbery (*JM, JP*: 54).

Criminality here is being retorted by capital punishment, but the criminal Ananias has just escaped from that punishment to find solace in Brother Jero's church. In a soul cleansing session, Jero obtains from his confession the list of all the crimes he committed out there in society. During his confession he also confides that their criminal acts were committed in search for livelihood means, which State authorities were supposed to provide. In fact, many workers in *Jero's Metamorphosis* are really underpaid, which constitutes a major cause of their poverty and destitution. As a result, to have ends meet, many of these exploited workers turn to criminality and robbery at night and go to their jobs in the day. Another character, Rebecca also beckons to the same malpractices as evil by saying: "Shameless sinners who acquire wealth from the misfortunes of others? Will you make money off sin and iniquity? (*JM, TJP*: 58).

Exploitation from Soyinka's marxist perspective is not only taking place between the rich and the poor, but also between the poor themselves, especially when the exploiter thinks he masters one aspect of life which the other doesn't. Here, spiritual worship takes the form of business and prophet Jero preys on his converts to get rich at their expense. Not only that, the spiritual leader has a hand in the executions (capital punishment) of the convicted criminals of the society, for the political leaders ask him to pray before they carry out the firing squad. Such prayers are believed to expel the guilt on the executioners' consciousness so they still hold their esteem. It is, to believe Soyinka not only abnormal to exploit people in the name of religion, but also abnormal to resort to capital punishment as a cure of criminality. As the critic Mpalive-Hangson Msiska writes,

> Wole Soyinka offers the example of micro-exploitation of the poor by the poor, which shows that one cannot regard the oppressed or exploited class as homogeneous or as a class for itself, collective in its will to transform the conditions of its subordination and disadvantage. In this respect, any hope of a worker's or peasant's revolt cannot be expected to emerge spontaneously from the condition of oppression itself, since some members of the oppressed group have themselves invested in the exploitation of their own class (Msiska 2007: 94).

This excerpt releases the truth that the poor also do exploit the poor if they are given the opportunity to do so. Another important information that stems from this extract is the proviso that criminals are preying on their victims out of a revolt of their violent repression by the armed forces. In other words, exploitation in that fictional society of *Jero's Metamorphosis* is institutionalized by society and their leaders. As a matter of fact, any person put in the position of power is prone to exploit his fellows, because Jero the prophet exploits his church members as he is in the position to do so. Then, the real problem is not with the culprits' acts, but with internal motives of their criminal acts.

In this chapter I lean on critic Chidi Amuta's approach to explain that Osofisan's play is an intellectual attempt to use the medium of drama to proffer materialist explanations of the major contradictions in Nigeria's neo-colonial society. I contend that the Nigerian society is but a microcosm of the larger African society where criminality has become the order of the day and governments have failed to diagnose and identify the real origin of such social plague. In this regard as goes the logic of Amuta, such contemporary issues as bureaucratic ineptitude, indiscipline, armed robbery, and peasants' revolts have formed the major preoccupations of the play. In his attempt to provide a fictional representation of the social scourge of violent robbery which has engulfed Nigeria since the end of the Civil war in 1970, the playwrights relocate the responsibility of the social anomy in the ranks of the leaders. It seems that the robbers act out of necessity than out of criminal inclinations or intents. Successive leaders have insisted on dealing with armed robbery at symptomatic rather than at causative level, and this has been bound to failure (Msiska 2007: 168). The state has resorted to public execution of robbers backed by draconian decrees. Such executions have been carried out in full view of the public either as a live audience or as a television audience.

> HASAN: A corpse! (*laughs suddenly*) Forget it, the death mark is on all of us Even if we never reach the bar beach (OUFR, 83)

For Major,

> MAJOR: (*Breaking off*) But alas it is finished. I knew it that day we failed to rescue the Leader from prison. (*ALHAJA starts to dirge softly, he faces her.*) Sing on Alhaja, sing on but we shall not mourn! Tears are useless, they screen off the truth of sight. We built a world and they tore it

> down. Think, that night! The lives wasted, the blood spilt.
> How many men did we lose, how many of us left now of a
> whole army of warriors! (*OUFR: 84*)

It reads from the perspective of these statements that armed robbers are publicly killed by firing squad at the beach show in full view of the public. Osofisan therefore is making an attempt to counteract and challenge the government's position which is informed by the perspective of the ruling class (Ibidem).

More specifically I contend with Chidi Amuta that the artistic theses that form the basis of *Once Upon Four Robbers* are that a) armed robbery is the product of a system rooted in inequality; b) that the way to controlling armed robbery and associated societal problems lies in a revolution that redefines production relations, thus removing the sources of inequality and aggressive competition. c) The violence with which the State confronts violent robbers cannot but beget greater violence on the part of robbers and others whom objective conditions compel to defy the terrorism of the state (Ibidem). Here the playwright is asking whether it is right to kill a group of defaulters when those that sit in judgment to determine their fate are worse, looting millions of francs in their official positions, yet pronouncing death sentences on those who steal peanuts. Tunde Akinyemi and Toyin Falola posit that "he sees crime and armed robbery as the product of bad leadership" (Akinyemi and Falola 2009: 4). The robbers are produced by the politicians as they equip them with sophisticated weapons and use them as tools to rig their way into power. These thugs are immediately disown after election. These armed thugs graduate into armed robbers as soon as they win or lose elections because, they would no longer be relevant. In pursuit of their own brand of politics, the robbers take up arms against the government and the society at large (Ibidem). It seems from my perspective that Femi Osofisan is insistent on these points, for, his materialist socialist perspective may be traced in part to his own experience of poverty as a child; however, his caustic portraits of a dystopian culture also reflect the deep distress of Nigeria's failure to foster a more democratic society after it had officially cast off the shackles of colonialism only to resume the cape of neocolonialism. Crime and robbery can be then considered as the by-products of neocolonialism.

This logic is shared by postcolonial critics like Edward Said who contends that " the culture of opposition and resistance suggest a theoretical alternative and a practical method for reconceiving human experience in non imperialist terms" (Said 1993: 276). Still staying in the logic of Chidi Amuta, it is not far-fetched to ponder over the issue of class dichotomy and assert that Osofisan explores these propositions through an artistic strategy that places the armed robbers at the center of action thereby revealing their motivations and thought process. Contrary to the propaganda of the state, it is revealed that the robbers, like other members of the society act out of love of life, that is they see robbery as a means of survival, though not morally good, robbing can procure them some pittance, a temporal means of survival. They seek to live by robbing and killing others. More importantly, they show a keen awareness of the mechanism of a system that breeds criminals and seek survival and identification through stealing and violence. All this amounts for them to think that in a world characterized by aggressive competition, private property, crass materialism, unemployment and poverty for the weak majority, the underprivileged who crave a good life must resort to violent action.

> MAJOR: Stop! Don't move any of you (*kicks out the sack*) Alhaja, take This sack and collect all the money. You heard me! (Reluctantly, She does so.) And I warn you no one else is to move. I love you all But I won't hesitate to shoot any of you (*OUFR; PP: 83*).

Femi Osofisan is not doing the apology of evil in a capitalist society, but he is drawing our reflection to the fact that social dystopia generally has more profound causes which need to be cured at the roots level. Leaders and all the people in power should be able to read the causes of the problems objectively and anticipate far reaching and sustainable solutions to problems. Curing a social disease like robbery only at symptomatic level cannot sanitize the society. Cure should begin at causative level. As a matter of fact, the violence which attends the operations of the robbers is a form of political protest against the inequalities in society. Angola one of the robbers has it that "There are many citizens who must be made to account for their wealth, and the poverty of the workers. Such accounts can be settled only one way." That way for him is violence. Critic Adejumobi S. in his appraisal of the causes of civil violence in Africa focuses on the question of citizenship and rights as its main cause:

> The construction and nature of the state in Africa, tend toward the institutionalization of ethnic entitlement, rights and privileges,

which creates differentiated and unequal status of citizenship. This tendency de-individualizes citizenship and makes it more a group phenomenon. Rather than the state providing a common bond for the people through the tie of citizenship with equal rights, privileges and obligations, both in precepts and practice, people's loyalties are bifurcated. The result is usually tension and contradictions in the public sphere as claims of marginalization, exclusion, and domination among individuals and groups are rife (Adejumobi 2006: 251).

The critical stance expressed here by Adejumobi S. puts at the forefront ethnicity and class problems as the real causes of most social tensions in African societies. This is where I think that awareness raising and education to the culture of peace are essential in postcolonial African multiethnic societies. To be exact, Femi Osofisan here strives to emphasize a strong class consciousness among the robbers, thereby exonerating them from that kind of sponsored official prejudice which dismisses them as bloodthirsty vagabond and anarchists. Throughout the play, all the robbers see their actions as a means to settle a score with a society whose ruling and propertied classes, often one and the same, deprive the majority of fair chances and opportunity. For Angola, "Too many people ride their own cars along the sore ridden back of the poor". In spite of the probability to meet death on their way, the robbers see their actions as the early signs of the possibility of a revolutionary overthrow of the parasitic bourgeois class.

13.1.3. A Way to Controlling Armed Robbery

From aetiological perspective, a sickness is never wholly cured unless its real causes are diagnosed and treated. All possibilities must be explored even digging into the patient' s subconsciousness. Where I depart from the critic Chidi Amuta's position is that in every society, there must be laws and regulations to govern the society and ensure good conduct and life of decency to all citizens. My first premise here is that, no matter the misrule to which a political leader can subject his/her society, no defendable rationale can inform criminality and excuse those who abhor honest work to prefer dishonest gain like stealing. Secondly, every evil deed creates conflicts in society and to bring peace, the state which is the legally established authority has the responsibility to intervene to settle the conflict. Therefore, it is not an abuse of power for the state to punish no matter the means used, the criminals whose actions by no means can bring development and peace to the society. Thirdly, if there must be a social revolution leading to the change of leaders, I don't think that robbery is the way to proceed to engender desirable revolution. To be objective, robbery is after all the illegal manner of dispossessing someone of his/her property using violence especially. Nowhere in the world do people acquire wealth or property without suffering through hard work first. Every desirable end exacts its price. It is therefore inhuman to pretend to earn one's living by robbing fellow citizens. Criminality itself is an outgrowth of postmodernism. Political misrule also is hinged upon the a postmodern cocktail of moral decay. Concerning social inequalities, the state is not hundred per cent responsible for them, because, even in situations where people are given equal opportunities and chances, they come up with different results. Some succeed in making a profit, while others end up gaining nothing. For instance, when people are given the same opportunity to sit for an exam giving entrance to the civil service, some pass while others fail. In that case, those who fail cannot hold the state responsible for their failure, and therefore should not complain if life treats them unequally compared with their fellows who have made it to the exam to work in the civil service. Likewise, in business, if people are given the same amount of money to start their own business, within a relatively acceptable period of time, some will have generated enough profit to continue a prospering business while others will go bankrupt. So, the state has to give equality of chances and opportunities to citizen, but the state cannot guarantee that life will treat people equally. That principle cannot be defined by a democratic government anywhere. Therefore it is irrational to purport that the state is responsible for everybody's unbecoming social plight.

What then can the government do in the face of social evils like crime and armed robbery? I think that first, the leaders must tackle the problem at two levels: both at the causative level and at the symptomatic level. To approach the problem at the causative level is to have the youth be inserted socially either by giving them the means to go to school and have proper school and professional education, or by having them train as professional workers. School leavers should be be given employment, even if it is to start with volunteering jobs, which progressively should lead to paid employment. At symptomatic level, the government should punish criminality, not by death penalty as is the case in the play, but through ways that enable the culprits to sincerely change from bad ways to good behavior. In this perspective, social and religious educations should be encouraged because, these types of education cleanse the morality of the individual and equip him/her with moral values that can deter him/her from bad or criminal intents. Efforts should also be made by the government to maintain transparency in the management of the national resources, devoting the major part of the wealth generated to the achievement of social amenities profitable to all citizens. Hospitals should be well equipped to enable citizens to have access to decent quality treatment. Schools and universities should also be well equipped, well financed and teachers well paid to ensure quality of teaching and training to school attendants. Financial institutions should be given means to function and ensure allocations and loans to the citizens who wish to start their own business.

13.1.4. From Text to Context: Exploring Osofisan' s and Soyinka's Postmodern Languages

Postmodrnism rests on a language of symbolism, the simulation of the real and the display of intensive metaphoric fragmented language. Femi Osofisan uses lot of metaphors to address the ills of his society. He quotes proverbs to speak metaphorically about the bad behavior of the leaders and their accomplices, the soldiers who are sent to execute publicly the robbers. He compares the execution of the robbers to the sacrifice of Jesus-Christ on the cross, where the Son of God died for mankind to survive. For the playwright, the robbers sacrifice their lives so that the rich people live:

> MAJOR: There was a Messiah, once, and one was enough! For all the centuries One great monumental mistake and nobody since has been in any hurry to repeat it. They crawl to the cross, they fall on their faces, wail and moan, but no worshipper asks to mount it and leave his life there. No! The nails and blood, the crown of thorns, all is a charade, kept for tourist value and the ritual of house cleaning. *(OUFR, PP: 84)*

In this excerpt, the playwright has used humour to make the reader understand the scope of the robbers' death by firing squad. Not many people do pay with their lives the price of community survival. People attempt actions of self-sacrifice but never go till the end. They simply content with miming the action of dying on the cross. They never truly die for others to survive. Words like "crawl, wail, moan" are verbs of action, but they are a language of mimesis.

They are never followed by the concrete action of dying. In the Christian orthodoxy, the only person who willingly died as a sacrifice to save mankind was Jesus-Christ. Since then, no other human has never dared to pay the price of salvation with his life. Though people may from time to time mime the action of the cross, in real facts, they never die. But the robbers are being publicly executed just as Jesus was publicly executed. The metaphor of the cross is being reinforced by the similarity in the manner of execution. Jesus was killed by Roman soldiers and here, the robbers are also being executed by the Nigerian soldiers.

The play is divided in three parts punctuated with prologue, interludes and an epilogue. In each part there are figurative language, proverbs and metaphors. In part one for example, significant proverbs are quoted to allude to the social realities of the contemporary society. Among the proverbs that allude to the social reality one can quote the following: "The dog boasts in town, but everybody knows the tiger's in the bush" (OUFR, PP: 75). This proverb is quoted by Major, one of the robbers to explain the fact that in their country, leaders are only there for the name, although they are so boastful about being the guides of the nation. Actually the true 'pillars' that sustain the population through their hard work are the working masses. For these people who sweat for the rich leaders to enjoy, their reward is nowhere to be seen. Their efforts are not acknowledged nor encouraged by the men in power. The tempo of that social condition is evidenced by another proverb Osofisan has the same character quote: "You can only walk that far on the edge of the blade" (*OUFR, PP: 75*). To walk on the edge of the blade is a metaphor meaning to live a very difficult and complex life. The social system of *Once Uppon Four Robbers* does not tolerate free enterprise. One cannot prosper by undertaking personal business, since every structure and every economic tunnel are firmly controlled by the leaders who make and unmake the rules to suit their selfish ambition with the connivance of the soldiers. The robbers are saying that the men in power fool the masses and belittle them as they play on their submissiveness and spirit of dogmatic allegiance. They are aware of these cunning ways but for the sake of respect, they do not protest, and they quote a proverb to explain: "They think chameleon is a dandy, but if he were to talk what strategies of dissimulation he'd teach our cleverest spies" (*OUFR, PP: 77*). The proverb is a warning to the leaders, not to abuse of the docility of the masses to perpetuate their evil deeds with them.

"The bat has no eyes but it roams with ease in the dark" (*OUFR, PP: 77*). This proverb stresses the life philosophy of the playwright that with good will one can achieve tremendous results even if the means to reach this are inefficient. Osofisan indicts the leaders for not showing concern for the improvement of the masses' living conditions. If only they were willing to initiate development programmes to change the society, those could help reduce no matter how little, the criminality adamant in that society. It takes more than a name to be a leader, and unless the leaders work for the development of the nation, they become totally irrelevant. This seems to be the message of the playwright in this proverb.

"Nobody quarrels so much with his head that he wears his hat on his knees" *(OUFR, PP:* 77). The philosophy of this proverb is that criminals are citizens of a country, and from this vantage point of view, efforts have to be made for their socio-professional insertion. Crime must be punished, but criminals must be salvaged from their evil practices. They shouldn't be ostracized. No matter how virulent a criminal may be, leaders have to see to it that after the prison, ex-criminals are given occupations that will divert them from pursuing their former life. The major pivot around which Osofisan's drama revolves is life (Owonibi 2009: 99).

"When fools mistake a beard for the moustache of impertinence, then they must pay the penalty" (*OUFR, PP:* 77).

Femi Osofisan's and Wole Soyinka's language beckon to the postcolonial Marxist aesthetics and focus on an intellectual discourse of the fierce urgency of political reforms in African societies giving priority to social cleansing of crime and robbery. Their language use enables a renewed perception and understanding of modern society where every member has his/her rightful place and personal identity. Human dignity and the right to a decent living occupy center stage in both writers' arts. This is perceived through their use of metaphors, their quotation of proverbs and sometimes their story telling techniques. An example of metaphorical statement by Major, one of the robbers in Osofisan's *Once Upon Four Robbers* is the injunction that in a rogue Society, "You can only walk on the edge of a blade. Sooner or later, the blade cuts in" (*OUFR, PP:* 75). To walk on a blade here refers to the insecurity conditions in which both the robbers and their victims live. Robbers are acting in insecurity because they can fall at every time in the grips of the police and thus end up in capital punishment. At the same time, the morally honest citizens also live in fear of sudden attack from the criminal robbers. As a matter of fact, fear hovers like a pale on the souls of every inhabitant of the fictional Lagos. But the question is who is responsible for the terrorism created and the fearful environment? The answer is obviously "everyman"; and to add, everybody is at the same time a social actor and can be an efficient agent of change for a better society.

It is to emphasize this point that Onyeka Iwuchukwu holds the stand that Osofisan reject the recourse to gods for solution to societal problems. He insists that man is the originator of his own problems, so, the solution to these problems lies within the scope of man. In other words, man is his fellow man's torturer. But it is the downtrodden, the poor masses who become the suffer- heads. That is why Aafa an enlightened characters tells Alhaja: "Truth is a bitter thing" and add "When fools mistake a beard for the moustache of impertinence, then, they must pay the penalty" (*OUFR: PP: 77*). The wisdom of this proverb verge on the truth that the robbery practiced in the play is remotely caused by hunger and extreme poverty, not by the rottenness of mind inclined to evil acts. Major corroborates this by saying "We are honest, we only steal from the rich" (*OUFR, PP: 77*).

Their cultural background as Yoruba playwrights gives them the privilege of apprehending the real problems of society in African setting. It can be said without overstatement that Osofisan's and Soyinka's plays mirror the very Nigerian – say African – society in very concrete terms through the interaction of characters with their socio-political environment. Their art is a harbinger of a creative genius which views society into a praxis of consciences renewal, a regeneration of people's minds with integrative policies of development. Drama is a living tool for carving out a revolutionary consciousness and igniting hopes for a better future society. Far from doing the apology of violence, Osofisan and Soyinka promote change through revolt. Revolt, explains Onyeka Iwuchukwu is an act of protest against or a rejection of an existing authority, concept or idea (Iwuchukwu 2009: 161). To revolt against something is to oppose or to refuse to do or accept that thing. The revolt these dramatists refer to in creative art is the awakening of characters' consciousness to ask for the demise of their suffering.

For Onyeka Iwuchukwu they use their art not just to protest against inequality, injustice, or oppression in the society, but insist on a revolt against the perpetrators of injustice (Ibidem). Their aim is to rectify and reduce to the maximum the social inequities. Revolt in Femi Osofisan's perspective is to be viewed here in the streamline of the legitimate claiming of one's due. It is the rightful demand to the implacable authority to relinquish what is due to the masses. In the process of seeking to establish the normal order of things, frictions may occur and parties in contention disagree on a number of issues. Nevertheless, national interests should prevail on individualistic selfish interests. By the same token those who pertain to the lower class today should strive through hard work to climb the social ladder.

Wole Soyinka's critical language in *The Jero Plays* is used to denounce the evil of capital punishment of the criminals. It is almost the same evil that Femi Osofisan denounces in *Once Upon Four Robbers*. Yet Soyinka's language is satirical and is directed against the false prophets who use religion to exploit the docile worshipers and possibly make them become renegades like Chume and turn criminals like Ananias. Soyinka uses a language of defamiliarization as a form of revolutionary language in *The Jero Plays*. Defamiliarization is a language that creates a distance between either the author and his audience, or between the main character and the other characters in the play. When Jero says for instance that "I am a shop keeper waiting for customers" (*TTOBJ; JP: 20*) his church members who understand the full implication of the money metaphor being used to allude to the prophet's materialistic exploitation of religion to make money will only distance themselves from him. That is why Ananias an ex-crime convict tells him: "That is because you are a clever man, Jero, not even your worst enemy will deny you that" (*JM; JP: 51*). It is therefore incontestable from my perspective that Soyinka uses comic and satirical language to write diatribe. Diatribe is a long and angry speech attacking and criticizing somebody (Hornby 2008: 403). To borrow words from Mpalive-Hangson Msiska, in *The Trials of Brother Jero,* Soyinka focuses on civil society, especially religion, demonstrating that it is an equally bad state (Msiska 2007: 92). The play stages the appropriation of the language and symbolism of Christianity for the exploitation of gullible postcolonial citizens. Soyinka has his main character use the language of infatuation to underscore the diatribe. Brother Jero's infatuated language outcries the other characters in the play when he claims to be born a supernatural prophet (*TTOBJ; TJP: 9*). Through his infatuated language Brother Jero has desacralized the Christian religion transforming it into a trade. "I grew to love the trade" (*TTOBJ; TJP: 9*). It is this greed and excessive love of money that bring Jero to exploit his church members. There has been a lot of critical work done on Jero's language style, but my emphasis here is on the impoliteness of Jero that is incongruous with the politeness of his church members. In dramatic terms, Soyinka has Jero use impolite language turns to generate the disharmony and conflicts between him and other characters especially his renegade Chume; a device which generates audience interest and contributes to develop the theme of discord between sociopolitical leaders and the masses. The critic Jonathan Culpeper observes that impoliteness, a form of language defamiliarization is used as a linguistic strategy to attack face – to strengthen the face threat of an act in dramatic dialogue. By the same token, politeness can be used as a strategy to maintain or promote harmonious social relations (Culpeper 1998: 85).

A character like Jero act under the cover of religion to perpetrate crime and robbery. That is why critics do not spare him their attack. Mpalive-Hangson Msiska writes that when Brother Jero senses an opportunity to make money from execution spectators, he convenes a gathering of all the prophets, and, as expected, it is more a gathering of thugs and men of violence than anything resembling conventional religious congregation (Msiska 2007: 97). *Jero's Metamorphosis* shows Jero not only as a better and more skilful swindler than other beach prophets, but also as more accomplished than corrupt government officials, who must still hide their dees under the cover of complicated government discourse and procedures. That is why I think as a critic that Soyinka suggests another way of controlling criminality, as capital punishment has become a money enterprise for characters like Jero (Ibidem). It is the overhauling of the sociopolitical system that I think the playwright Soyinka recommends. Soyinka's message is complemented by Osofisan's creative message that change should come from the very social fabric of Africa.

The perception of criminality and the ways designed to eradicate it from African social environment is projected differently by Femi Osofisan and Wole Soyinka as postmodern playwrights. While Osofisan looks at social inequalities as a far-reaching cause of crime and robbery, Wole Soyinka looks at religious hypocrisy imbued with material gain as a plausible catalyst for crime and robbery. Robbing others out of hunger and material poverty can be however tolerable to some extent more than robbing people in the name of God or Providence. In either case every playwright echoes the message that the cure of criminality and robbery should start from the grassroots.

References

Abrams (M. H.). *A Glossary of Literary Terms,* Australia, Canada, Mexico, Thomson Wadsworth 2005.

Adebambo (Ademeso Adebola). "National Development and the Concept of Compassion in Osofisan's *Esu and the Vagabond Minstrels*". In Tunde Akinyemi and Toyin Falola eds., *Emerging Perspectives on Femi Osofisan* . Trenton, Africa World Press, 2009. 53-63.

Akinyemi (Tunde and Toyin Falola). *Emerging Perspectives on Femi Osofisan* Trenton, Africa World Press. 2009.

Amuta (Chidi). *The Theory of African Literature: Implications for Practical Criticism,* London and New Jersey, Zed Books Ltd, 1989. PP. 167-16.

Culpeper (Jonathan). "Impoliteness in Dramatic Dialogue", in Jonathan Culpeper, Mick Short and Peter Verdonk (eds.) *Exploring the Language of Drama: From Text to Context,* London, Routledge, 1998. PP. 83-95.

Eagleton (Terry). *Criticism and Ideology: A Study in Marxist Literary Theory* London, Humanities Press. 1976.

Evans (Dylan). *An Introductory Dictionary of Lacanian Psychoanalysis.* New York and London: Routledge. 2006.

F. Berg (Temma). "Psychologies of Reading." In Joseph Natoli ed. *Tracing Literary Theory,* Urbana and Chicago: University of Illinois Press, 1987. PP. 248-277.

Freud (Sigmund). *A General Introduction to Psycho-analysis.* Pdf Books World. 1920.

Gilbert (Helen and Joanne Tompkins). *Postcolonial Drama: Theory, Practice, Politics,* London, Routledge. 1996/2004.

Gilbert (Helen). *Postcolonial Plays: An Anthology.* London and New York, Routledge. 2001

Heyns (Christof and Karen Stefiszyn eds). *Human Rights, Peace and Justice in Africa: A Reader.* South Africa, Pretoria University Law Press, PULP. 2006.

Hornby (H. S.). *Oxford Advanced Learner's Dictionary* 7th Edition Oxford, Oxford University Press. 2008.

Killam (Gordon Douglas). *Student Encyclopedia of African Literature,* Westport, Greenwood Press. 2008.

O. Adeniyi (Victoria). "Religion, Corruption, and Democratic Nigeria in Femi Osofisan's Drama", In Tunde Akinyemi and Toyin Falola eds., *Emerging Perspectives on Femi Osofisan,* Trenton, Africa World Press, PP. 151-165. 2009.

Msiska (Mpalive-Hangson). *Postcolonial Identity in Soyinka.* Amsterdam, Rodopi Publishers. 2007.

Onyeka (Iwuchukwu). *Introduction to Nigerian Literature I* , Lagos, National Open University of Nigeria. 2009

Osofisan (Femi). *Once Upon Four Robbers,* Ibadan, BIO Educational Publishers. 1980

Owonibi, Sola. "Political Consciousness in African Literature: a Critical Analysis of Selected Plays of Femi Osofisan" . In Tunde Akinyemi and Toyin Falola eds. *Emerging Perspectives on Femi Osofisan,* 2009. Trenton, Africa World Press, 2009 PP. 99-106.

Ricks, (Stephen R. C.) *Explaining Postmodernism: Skepticism and Socialism from Rousseau to Foucault.* New Berlin: Scholargy Publishing. 2004.

Rivkin (Julie and Michael Ryan). *Literary Theory: An Anthology,* Second Edition. USA, Blackwell Publishing. 2004

Said (Edward). *Culture and Imperialism,* New York, Vintage Books. 1993

Soyinka (Wole). *The Jero Plays,* Ibadan, Spectrum Books. 1964/1994

14

AN INTERTEXTUAL READING OF TIME, SPACE AND NARRATIVE POETICS IN ADE SOLANKE'S *PANDORA'S BOX* AND NGUGI WA THIONG'O'S *WIZARD OF THE CROW*

This chapter uses intertextual approach to explore dramatic and novelistic conventions of time, space and the narrative voice which determine the genre of dramatic texts and novelistic text taking Ade Solanke's *Pandora's Box* and Ngugi wa Thiong'o's *Wizard of the Crow* as examples. It argues that dramatic texts, unlike prose fiction, are written for performance and tell stories by showing them. Unlike the novel where the story is told by a narrator without being shown on stage, in drama, the telling is direct and without mediation. Drama does not very often use the narrator, but whenever it chooses to do that the narrator becomes a character in the play. This unmediated nature of narration of drama affects the way dramatic texts represent time and space, and the way they use time and space to structure themselves. The specific question I am addressing is whether and to what extent drama like fiction narrative admits of the narratological concept of a narrative voice. This article presents a survey of dramatic and theatrical conventions about representing time and space, and notes how the conventions of "here and now" determine the generic limits of drama.

Intertextuality was proposed by Julia Kristeva, drawing on Mikhail Bakhtin's notion of dialogism ("the necessary relation of any utterance to other utterances") to indicate a text's construction *from texts*: a work is not a self-contained, individually authored whole, but the absorption and transformation of other texts, "a mosaic of quotations" (Kristeva, 1967). This is a matter not of influence (from one author or work to another), but of the multifarious and historically variable relations between works as heterogeneous textual productions ("influence" is simply one limited and limiting figure of intertextuality). Kristeva developed this perception in a generic study of "the text of the novel" as resulting from the combination or transposition of several different Sign systems (Kristeva, 1970), while Roland Barthes analyzed a single Balzac story as a tissue of "voices," redeploying and recasting fragments from a range of discourses on which it depends for its intelligibility (Barthes, 1970).

Such an approach through intertexuality situates literary structure within social structure as itself textual. Nothing is given other than constituted within discourse and a text is not the reflection of some nontextual "exterior" but a practice of writing that inscribes – and is inscribed in – the social as just such an intertextual field, a mesh of textual systems. In a move characteristic of poststructuralism, intertextuality displaces intersubjectivity: the reading of a text is seen not as a subjectto- subject exchange between author-source and reader-receiver, but as the performance by author *and reader* of a multitude of writings that cross and interact on the site of the text. A text is thus never finished, written once and for all; it exists in the continuing time of its intertextual production, which includes the texts of its future (those that will be brought to its reading) – as intertext it has, in Barthes's words, "no law but the infinitude of its recurrences." Though the condition of all texts, intertextuality may also be used evaluatively, distinguishing texts which attempt to cover up their intertextual nature from those which acknowledge and display it. Where Balzac refers his novels to the truth – the depiction – of an externally grounded reality, Joyce, self-described as "a scissors-and-paste man," offers *Finnegans Wake* as "stolen telling," an accumulation of bits and pieces of writing from the world as infinite text. Modernism in this distinction marks exactly the break from which the problem of intertextuality is posed *as such*.

Michael Riffaterre, defining intertexuality as the reader's perception of the relations between a text and all the other texts that have preceded or followed it, is concerned to allow both for *aleatory* intertextuality (the reader brings the text into play with his or her familiar texts) and *obligatory* intertextuality (the "hypogram" or core intertext that is a work's matrix, presupposed in its reading) (Riffaterre, 1979). Gérard Genette proposes five types of *transtextuality*, his overall term for the relations a text may hold with others; with intertextuality limited to the specific relation of *copresence*, the effective presence of one text in another through quotation, plagiarism, or allusion (Genette, 1982). A particular intertextual history is provided in Henry Louis Gates's account of the Afro-American literary tradition as characterized by Signifyin(g): texts talking to and from other texts in a self-reflexive process of repetition and revision that seeks to make representational space for "the so called Black Experience" (Gates, 1988a).

Reception-oriented theories of fiction namely intertextuality and narratology while theorizing on narratives have neglected the role of mediating narrator, and the impacts that his presence or absence may have on the representation of time and space. Critics seem to have agreed on the indispensability of time and space in narratives and the relationship these devices entertain with the plot without agreeing on the agenda of bringing narratology to bear on theory and analysis of plays. Mikhail M. Bakhtin talks of the temporal and spatial relationships that are artistically expressed in literature and adds that "what counts for us is the fact that it expresses the inseparability of space and time… Time as it were thickens, takes flesh, becomes artistically visible; likewise, space becomes charged and responsive to the movement of time, plot and history" (Bhaktin 1981: 84). H. Porter Abbott holds the view that narrative time comprises of a succession of necessary events that leads up to, and accounts for what we see (Abbott 2002: 6). Susan Stanford Friedman postulates that "Space restored to its full partnership with time as a generative force for narrative allows for reading strategies focused on the dialogic interplay of space and time as mediating constituents of human thought and experience" (Friedman 2005: 195). For Monika Fludernik, simultaneity and anachrony are two features that are specific to time referencing: "Simultaneity plays a significant role in locating a narrative in time. It often serves to bring together various strands of action […] Spaces are static; what needs to be stressed is changes of scene" (Fludernik 2009: 43-44).

A synthesis of these critics' assertions on the functionality of time and space seems to leave out the dramatic representation of time and space, how theatrical texts differ from novelistic texts and especially the way the unmediated nature of narration of drama affects the way dramatic texts represent time and space and how the convention of "here and now" determines the generic limits of drama. Taking examples from Ade Solanke's *Pandora's Box* (a play) and Ngugi wa Thiong'o's *Wizard of the Crow* (a novel), my present analysis will focus on three points: the differences of dramatic and novelistic texts, the voice of the author and the mediating narrator and the natures and representations of time and space in drama.

14.1. Dramatic Texts and Novelistic Texts: Showing versus Telling

From an intertextual perspective, I submit that the claim that dramatic texts also tell stories just like fictional narratives of novels is already established. Linda Hutcheon and Michael Hutcheon write that opera, a form of drama, is literally the embodied telling of a story (Linda Hutcheon and Michael Hutcheon). Yet, despite the fact that dramatic texts tell stories, the mode of narration is quite different from that employed in the novel. A distinction needs to be made between telling which is the prerogative of the novel and showing which is the technique of drama. The novel tells stories in narrative form using the narrator, while drama tells stories by showing them on stage during actors' performance. In the play, the showing is direct, without the intrusion of the narrator to explain what is going on in characters' minds, while in the novel, the telling is mediated through the comments of the narrator who, with omniscient eyes and ears can tell what is going on in characters' minds, and even bring back their past memories. While in the novel everything is told to the reader through the medium of the narrator, in the play, the story is told through what characters say. This makes the drama narrative direct and factual, with the profuse use of the present tense. As Marjorie Boulton points it out, the playwright unlike the novelist, cannot step in with comments to describe for instance what is happening in the minds of characters or what happens behind the stage (Boulton 1977: 87). He cannot describe past events that happened in characters' lives in a narrator's voice. The dramatist's intrusion in the play is done through stage directions, and his comments are often very brief, selective and with few details. The stage directions insist on settings (place and time at which the story takes place), the characters' dressing and costumes and never go into details to show their private lives. Examples can be shown from dramatic text and extracts from novels. The following extract is an introductory from Ade Solanke's *Pandora's Box* which is a play:

> SCENE ONE: *Adelabu street, Surulere, Lagos. August. A large and opulent front room, filled with expensive furniture. The wall at the back is dominated by a large window. It's open and from the street, the sounds of early evening Lagos life waft in: the traffic, the hawkers, the Fuji music. The other walls are lined with family portraits and photos, as is an elaborate oak sideboard.*

> *A clock on it says 7 pm. The room is so quiet we can hear its loud ticking [...] A woman, Toyin (late thirties) is kneeling before it, praying feverishly* (PB: 23).

On the contrast the opening passage from Ngugi wa Thiong'o's *Wizard of the Crow*, a novel reads:

> There were many theories about the strange illness of the second Ruler of the Free Republic of Aburĩria, but the most frequent on people's lips were five. The illness so claimed, was born of anger that once welled up inside him; and he was so conscious of the danger it posed to his well being that he tried all he could to rid himself of it by belching after every meal, sometimes counting from one to ten, and other times chanting *ka ke ki ko ku* aloud (*WOTC*: 3).

In the first extract, the playwright Ade Solanke has opened the play with the setting, limiting herself to the place, time and the presence of a character, Toyin, without actually describing her, while Ngugi the novelist has insisted on the description of the character without going into details about the physical setting. Just after the stage direction, Solanke has the character Toyin talk: "Please, God, please, please, let me be doing the right thing." (*PB*: 23) while in the case of the novelist Ngugi, his character hasn't talked until in the middle of the chapter: "Dr. Yunice Immaculate Mgenzi", he called out." (*WOTC*: 20). While the novelist Ngugi has the possibility to fully describe the private lives of the characters, their physical appearances, their minds and thoughts, and the various settings in which they move, the playwright often limits himself / herself to the setting and a brief introduction of the characters. The rest of the characters' lives including their thoughts, their past lives, present experiences and future plans are shown by letting them talk in dialogue. The showing in drama is of outmost importance. The absence of a narrator with omniscient eyes on the private lives of characters makes their talking indispensable.

Basing on the experience of Greek tragedy, comedy and epic, Plato and Aristotle clearly established the distinction between simple narrative, which I refer to here as telling, and a narration through imitation or representation, which I refer to as showing. Drama is *mimesis*, "imitation" or "representation". Ian C. Storey and Arlene Allan put it this way:

> Drama is action. According to Aristotle, (*Poetics* 1448a28), dramatic poets represent people in action", as opposed to a third-person narrative or the mixture of narrative and direct speech as done by Homer […] For both Plato and Aristotle, the two great philosophers of the fourth century, drama is an example of mimesis, "imitation" or "representation", but each took a different view of the matter. *Mimesis* is not an easy word to render in English. Neither "imitation" nor "representation" really get the point. […] Drama then is "doing" or "performance" and in human culture performances can be used in all sorts of ways (Ian C. Storey and Arlene Allan 2005: 1-2).

In this extract, the very nature of drama and fiction narrative is used to explain the difference between the text in the novel and that in the play: the novel's text or story is written to be read while the play's text is written to be performed on stage. In other words, in drama, showing matters more than telling. Some scholars of drama like Bernard Beckerman would say that a play is incomplete until it is shown (performed) on stage (Beckerman 1970: 50). But this is not taken to mean that telling is of least importance. But the stage lays emphasis on showing. This is justified by the abundance of gestures, mimicries, facial expressions, signs and symbols, which are silent language speaking sometimes more than verbal utterances. Drama tells stories by showing them on stage (*PB: 23*). The showing is done through the talking and the images. This is fundamental in theatre because orality and oratory are at the heart of drama. The showing is usually sustained by oral utterances. In addition, all necessary measures are taken to make sure that the various elements of dramatic techniques including the language of characters, the tones of their voices, their actions and mimicries transpire on the stage for audiences to see and hear. Even the costumes worn by characters, their colours, the appearance of the stage, the lights and darkness must be shown to the audiences, not only told. To corroborate these ideas I will borrow words from Oliver Taplin, another drama scholar, to say that:

> All students of the theatre – indeed anyone who has thought about human communication must be aware that the written quotation of any spoken sentence is a very incomplete transcript of what was conveyed by the utterance itself. On one level we miss the tone of voice, nuance, pace, stress; and we miss facial expression, gesture

and physical posture and positioning of the speaker and addressee even more profoundly, the transcript does not convey the roles and social relationships of the real people involved, their past, their shared assumptions, the full circumstances of the speech-act (Taplin 2003: 2).

The point to stress here is the relevance of live experience present in drama which is missing in novels. Such live experiences in *Pandora's Box* are the tone of voice, nuance, pace, stress, facial expression, gesture and physical posture and positioning of both speaker and addressee. These elements which are more visible in performance nevertheless play also crucial role in plays texts. They denote the dramatist's visual techniques, the way he /she translates their meaning into theatrical terms and, as Oliver Toplin puts it, drama must be visualized, must be seen to be believed (Ibidem). The fact that dramatic texts are meant to be performed has some implications on the presentation of the texts. To begin with, characters are listed in full details at the beginning of the play. As a matter of fact, plays are written in dialogues, with an introductory list of characters, their identities, their relationships with other characters, their roles in the play. Some playwrights include prologue to introduce the audience or the reader to the general context of the play and epilogue to draw a moral lesson or a conclusion from the story unfolded. The fact that drama tells by showing brings some scholars to state that, a play is incomplete until it has been performed. Performance is the only way in which dramatic world is constructed. Keir Elam for instance is inflexible in his insistence that performance must accompany dramatic text and that a reader of a play cannot get the same understanding that a spectator gets:

> The effective construction of dramatic world and its events is the result of the spectator's ability to impose order upon a dramatic content whose expression is in fact discontinuous and incomplete. It should not be thought that a reader of dramatic texts constructs the dramatic world in the same way as a spectator: not only does the latter have to deal with more varied and specific kinds of information (through the stage vehicles), but the perceptual and temporal conditions in which he operates are quite different. The reader is able to imagine the dramatic context in a leisurely and pseudo-narrative fashion, while the spectator is bound to process simultaneous and successive acoustic and visual signals within strictly defined time limit (Elam 1980: 60).

Here Elam wants to show that the dramatic world that the spectator constructs when watching a play's performance is much more real, vivid and tangible than that represented by a reader of that play in his mind. It follows that performance fleshes out the play's meaning while reading is merely conveying literal facts without going deep in the emotional aspects of the play. I shall come to the exploration of spatio-temporal aspects of drama in the next section but for the meantime I would like to elaborate on some intertextual narrative conventions in plays and novels which distinguish them as two different narrative genres. One of the major differences between dramatic texts and novelistic texts – between *Pandora's Box* and *Wizard of the Crow* - is that in the novel, the story is intended to be read and with very few exceptions, novels are not performed on stage. The first consequence of that aspect is that the novelist Ngugi has the ability to choose the way he introduces his characters, to choose the time of narrations with the possibility to be going to and fro with different time aspects (preterit to present, present to future, and vice versa). Ngugi uses introspection as narrative technique. For instance, "Sikioku stood up and again walked about the office, deep in thought. How was he to know for certain that his sorcerer had not heard what he said so indiscreetly? How could he be certain that the mirror had not retained traces of his treason? (*WOTC*: 416). Here the mediating narrator is explaining what is happening in Sokoiku's mind. With that technique he can explore the characters past lives explain their present worldviews and give details of their future plans. He also chooses the narrator and the narratee, the focalizer, the discourse modes (direct discourse or free indirect discourse), characters' thought perception (for example free indirect thought). He chooses the point of view (first-person narrative, second-person narrative or third-person narrative). As a matter of fact, he has the possibility to step in the story through the narrator's voice and explain in detail the minds of characters, their inner thought through the technique of introspection. Some would say that the novelist is like a god who creates the novel's universe, designs and shapes the characters the way he/she likes. To give information about the characters' lives, the novelist can choose between direct narrative – stepping in the story through the narrator's voice – or indirect narrative – having characters release information about the lives of their fellow characters (*WOTC*: 407).

There are several intertextual implications that need to be considered. Firstly, all opportunities are not given to the dramatist who must convey every information in the play by having a character say it himself/herself. When for instance Ade Solanke wants her character Sis Ronke to express an opinion about Nigeria, he has her say it aloud to Toyin: Sis Ronke: Look? Nigeria has problems, yes" (*PB:* 52). She cannot have the character do introspection. In addition, to release information concerning characters' lives, their past and present experiences and future perspectives, the playwright must have characters say this, and this is done either through a dialogue – two or more persons conversing - or an interior monologue – a character speaking to himself / herself or thinking aloud. This makes the showing extremely crucial in drama. That is why Manfred Jahn stresses the point that despite their divergences, reception-oriented theorists agree on the fact that plays must come in two forms of realization, texts and performance (Jahn 2001: 660). The dramatist resorts to telling the story through the technique of "here and now" narrative (having characters tell everything in the present tense), or having these characters utter facts about their fellow characters. Both novelists and dramatists choose soliloquy or interior monologue to tell stories. Even in that case, they do this from time to time, because, as Marjorie Boulton points it out, "soliloquy is a relatively primitive form of dramatic expression and is not generally accepted as a dramatic device today without some further trick to soften its artificiality" (Boulton, op cit: 85) This critical position is in line with Keir Elam's explanation that in dramatic text, the world is presented to the spectators or readers without 'narrative mediation'; the world is apparently shown or ostended, rather than being stipulated or described (Elam 1980: 110). Secondly, intertextuality implies that when a novel is read, the reader does not expect – and hence is not conscious – of the possibility that the events and people represented in it are to be shown on stage, but a dramatic text always keeps the reader alert, reminding him that the text is to be performed. It is not to be told as a story is told by a narrator, but the narrator is also to be shown telling that story.

14.1.1. The Narrative Voice or the Mediating Narrator: Where Intertextuality Matters

Intertextuality has a complex imbeddedness in the readings of plays and novels. In dramatic texts, the author's voice is always present but its mode of mediation is significantly different from that in the novels. In the novel, the narrative voice is usually assimilated to that of the narrator. To sense Ade Solanke's voice in the play, one should remember that all the arrangements made in the play – the creation of characters, their names, the roles assigned to them, the choices of settings, the very conversations they are engaged in, the scenic arrangements, the costumes designed, the masks to be worn, the mimes created – are all the making of the playwright or author. Thus, the author's voice comes to us through what the spectator or the reader sees unfold before his/her eyes. Yet, there is a major difference to note between dramatic narrative and novelistic narrative. While in the novel Ngugi tells the story through the narrator's voice, in the play, the narrator seems to be absent. When the playwright chooses to introduce the narrator, he becomes part of the characters in the play. It is also commendable to point out that in the play, the places where the mediating narrator can intervene are prologues and epilogues. On this point, Ian C. Storey and Arlene Allan have this to say.

> […] the Greek tragedians had a repertoire of formal scenes to use in constructing their dramas […] We may prefer a catalog of series of types of scene: prologue, episode, *kommos*, choral song, and monody. Prologues are almost always in the iambic trimester, the closest to ordinary speech in Aristotle's view, and as the name implies, open the drama (Friedman op cit: 88).

The point made here is that historically, drama and theatre have developed rhetorical conventions about the presence of a narrator and about the nature of his or her mediation. In some medieval plays, the mediating narrator was directly present in the play. Such medieval drama which took place in streets, market places, at courts or in the halls of a lord's house used a number of presentation techniques, the most important of which was the presence of a presenter whose function was to open up the play through the recitation of the prologue, a function very similar to that of the chorus in Greek theatre. The same presenter would usually come back at the end of the play and conclude or close with the epilogue stating the moral lesson. In this perspective, the narrative quality of drama becomes progressively recognized. It is in this context that Manfred Jahn asserts that

> […] the narrative quality of drama is now accepted by many post-Genettean critics. However, while the story dimension of a play readily submits to a "story narratological" or "deep structural treatment, it remains an unsettled issue whether drama should also fall under the sway of what Thomas Pavel has termed discourse narratology, the discipline that theorizes narrative acts and narrative situations, modes of presentation and the functions of narratorial voice (Jahn 2001: 670).

From these grounds, it seems the question of mediating narrator in plays, though accepted for many scholars, is still a topical issue in literary debates. The question is whether a play's narrative agent whom I refer to as mediating narrator shows up as an overt teller figure or remains an impersonal, covert-shower or plays' arranger function. To this question Manfred Jahn answers in the affirmative (yes), but proposes a redefinition of a narrative agent or mediating narrator. For him, the narrator is not so much the one who answers to Genette's question: who speaks or who betrays himself or herself by using the first-person pronoun but the agent who manages the exposition, who decides what is to be told (especially from what point of view and in what sequence), and what is to be left out. Of course, this is not to deny that a narrator will often overtly speak or write, establish communicative contact with addressees, defend the tellability of the story... (Jahn 2001: 670) This is especially true about some African plays in which the dramatists use the story telling techniques to put across the message. In Ama Ata Aidoo, *The Dilemma of a Ghost* (1964) and *Anowa* (1970) the playwright uses several characters of the fictional community to act as choric story-tellers who relate current issues to traditional contexts (Helen Gilbert and Johanne Tompkins 2002: 131). Aidoo's works are concerned with morality and the ways in which people ought to operate within a social structure; hence, those who disobey the established rules or threaten the survival of the traditions are punished. As Helene Gilbert and Johanne Tompkins say about story-tellers in *The Dilemma of a Ghost* the female elders who comment on and advance the action in that play reinforce the strength of women and the ineffectiveness of the men whose access to western education has if anything, diminished their useful archive of locale knowledge (Ibidem). This assertion corroborates my claim that the play doesn't bear with the presence of a mediating narrator per see, but that once the dramatist opts for a narrator, that narrator is part of the characters whose role is to read out the prologue and the epilogue.

Another narratological device that underscores the difference between showing in drama and telling in prose fiction is the aesthetic representation of silence. The way silence appears in prose fiction differs from how it does in drama. To represent a character's silence in a novel the novelist Ngugi generally resorts to the technique of introspection and in some cases to stream of consciousness, while in drama the playwright Ade Solanke uses soliloquy, mime, facial expression or muteness. In Ngugi's *Wizard of the Crow,* characters that are silent spend time reminiscing their past experiences in a form of introspection. On the contrary, in Solanke's *Pandora's Box,* when characters do not talk, they mime, show facial expression, or bodily gestures which are all the same expressive and meaningful. Helen Gilbert and Joanne Tompkins quote Rajeswari Sander Rajan to assert that "there is silence that speaks, and speech that fails as communication" (Helen Gilbert and Johanne Tompkins 2002: 190). It follows that the natures of speech and silence are more complex than is often assumed and that silence can be more *active* than passive, especially on stage where a silent character still speaks the language of the body and of space (Ibidem). Here, silence enacts more than a problematic absence of voice; rather, it is a discourse in its own right and a form of communication with its own enunciative effects.

These effects emerge through the length and depth of the silence; through its tenour in relation to the volume, tone and intent of the speech which circumscribes or interrupts it; and through the gestures and postures of silence (Ibidem). Helen Gilbert and Joanne Tompkins stay in the same logic to demonstrate that while language is commonly misperceived to be the loudest and clearest mode of theatrical communication, there are at least three 'silences' that are expressively deployed on the post-colonial stage: inaudibility, muteness and refusal to speak. Basing on Elaine Showalter's concept of "muteness" which illustrates itself from the way women's lack of voice in patriarchal societies can act as a type for the ways in which silence communicate in post-colonial drama, Gilbert and Tompkins maintain that muteness transmits meaning in several ways, given that the muted groups (women) mediate their beliefs through the allowable forms of dominant structures. Thus muted characters do often communicate through normative discourses as well as speaking. The oppressed women accustomed to the position whereby they are unheard, not listened to, or even prevented from speaking, have found ways to exploit this muteness, transforming it into a language of resistance.

14.1.2. Time, Space and Narrative Poetics

14.1.2.1. Time

The intertextual analysis of time bears on the time perception of the reader. As forms of telling, dramatic narrative and novel stories exist in time and space. A narrative takes place within a geographical space and uses time to tell about sequence of events (Friedman op cit: 193). Space and time referred to as setting are pivotal to the development of narratives. One would say that they are the breath of narrative in that every story takes place within the limits of time and space. Despite the multiplicity of techniques in representing time and space used by writers, what all narratives have in common is the presence of timing and spacing in fiction and drama. A story wouldn't deserve the name of narrative if it didn't have the spatio-temporal references. Creative writers always situate their readers within the scope of time span and spatial delimitation. Gerard Genette (quoted by Susan Stanford Friedman) identifies three main components of narrative discourse for analysis: tense ("temporal relation between narrative and story"), mood ("form and degree modalities of narrative 'representation' "); and voice ("the narrative situation...: the narrator and his audience, real or implied").

The most important feature of time in dramatic texts is its "here and now" nature; the action and events unfold 'here and now', to mean in the immediate presence of the audience. In Ade Solanke's *Pandora's Box*, this immediate present is usually reflected in the present tense of the verbs used to describe the actions of the characters; the extra-dialogic text is always written with verbs in the present tense: "There is nothing wrong with my son" (*PB*: 35); "To him, we are foreigners" (*PB*: 35).

The absence of a mediating narrator in drama affects the representation of time in plays. As a result, the playwright has to make characters utter dialogue in the present tense. This technique is referred to as the "here and now" of drama. The immediacy of the present time in dramatic text is reflected in the dominance of the present tense. Some critics like Keir Elam argue that the very fact that dramatic time has to be rendered in present tense makes the sequences of events continuous both synchronically and diachronically: "Synchronically at a given point, in the performance continuum – theatrical discourse is characterized by the density of signs. Diachronically – in its temporal unfolding on stage – the text is characterized by the discontinuity of its various levels" (Elam, op cit: 27). This assertion basically means that even in those situations in which past events are narrated, reported or represented on stage, the act of narration and representation takes place in the fictional "now" or the fictional present time. Another major difference between dramatic time and novelistic time is that, because dramatic texts are written for performance, they bear the marks of the constraints imposed by performance time. The playwright, the spectators and readers are aware that the text will come to a physical end within a finite period of time, for instance within 'a single revolution of the sun' for the Greek tragedies and within about three hours in contemporary theatre (2005: 8). The author of dramatic text being aware of these limits writes the text keeping in view the prevalent conventions about the performance time. In many plays this finite period of time, during which the events have to reach their climax is announced clearly in the prologue. Keir Elam thinks that the spectators' or the readers' awareness of these limits adds to the tension associated with the plot time (Elam 1987: 27).

The dramatist cannot easily dive into the past and tell events and actions that happened weeks, months and years ago without resorting to the techniques of flashback. The immediate consequence of this in dramatic narrative according to Seymour Chatman is the interruption of the flow of thought (Chatman 2005: 274). The narrative flow is momentarily interrupted as characters are battling to recover memory, to search for words, and are trapped in the ebbs and flow of their past dreams, remote experiences, and their feeling uncertain. The telling is done in the first person narrative. Mostly, every character tells his/her story in drama. But in novels, the writer resorts mostly to speech report. Monika Fludernik refers to this by asserting that "In contrast to free indirect discourse and indirect speech which both preserve the propositional content (the message) of an utterance, speech report reduces a prior utterance to the fact of its articulation or gives the overall gist of the remark" (Fludernik 2009: 160). The way flashbacks are presented in drama differs neatly from the way they are done in a novel. In drama, every character's past experiences are retold or relived by himself/herself. It is a lively experience and the dramatist must show them in the reality of time and space. Flashbacks are often presented in the form of dreams, recollections, with picturesque representations which demark themselves from novelistic texts. In novels the narrator can render characters past lives and experiences in mediated way by telling in the third person narrative. Mediation or mediacy is the central defining characteristic of narrative in the novel, a concept proposed by Stanzel and explained by Monika Fludernik:

> In contrast to the representation of the fictional world in drama, in which the actions of the protagonists are shown in an unmediated fashion (in other words, the spectators see the actors before them, without any mediating instance, in novel narrative there is mediation by the narrator or the narrative discourse. This can be mimetic as the result of there being a teller or chronicler (teller mode) or it can be focused through the consciousness of one of the characters in the novel (reflector mode). The latter means that an impression of immediacy is created, but the representation is

not really unmediated Fludernik (1996) extends mediacy to the prototypical scenarios of conscious-related cognitive perception – *telling* schema; *viewing* or witness schema; *experiencing* schema; *reflecting* schema (Ibidem: 155).

Fludernik's explanation gives credence to my stance that the absence of mediating narrator in drama affects the rendering of time in plays. For one thing, in drama, the actions of the characters are shown in an unmediated fashion, so that even the past events are to be revived, not told, a condition which is not the case in the novel. Time then, I can argue, is ever present, real, actual and unmediated in drama. The rendering of time in novels is fluid, fluctuating between the past, the present and the future. For instance, Ngugi's narration reads: "Sikiokuu did not take the challenge to come up with a mirror… At first, he thought it an easy matter… 'Ii is our duty to let you know of any threat to the security of the State…" (*WOTC*: 419). Here the time fluctuates between the past and the present. Dan Shen has explained how Gérard Genette in *Narrative Discourse* classifies discourse into three basic categories: tense (the relation between story time and discourse time), mood (forms and degrees of narrative representation), and voice (the way in which the narrating itself is implicated in the narrative). The first category tense comprises three aspects: order, duration and frequency. In clear terms the order deals with the relation between the chronological sequence of story events and the rearranged textual sequence of the events. But what interests me in Dan Shen's discussion of temporal aspect proposed by Genette is what he refers to as "narrative frequency" (Shen 2005: 138). A narrative, he says, "may tell once what happened once, *n* times what happened *n* times, *n* times what happened once, once what happened *n* times" (Ibidem: 138). Now whether to tell an event once or more than once is not the prerogative of drama. A dramatic scene is not usually shown several times unless the actors repeat the show on stage. This marks the difference between a reader of the novel and a theatre spectator. A reader can come back several times on his texts, (and indeed a narrator can tell his story several times in the novel), but a spectator cannot see the same picture in performance on stage unless he sees a second show of the same play. Mick Short, another drama scholar posits:

> Reading and watching plays both appear to have advantages and disadvantages. When you read, you can try things more than one way in your head, and you can go back to something you didn't

understand. You can't do this in performance, but the acting, lighting, etc (a) help you feel more vividly what is in the play and (b) help you understand what is happening more easily as you have both visual *and* aural information to help you. When you see a play while reading it, the 'performance' is always perfect: the actors never fluff their lines, for example. On the other hand you can never be pleasantly surprised (Short 2002: 9).

Short is bringing out two essential ideas which ascribe to my critical position. First that a reader of a play or a novel has the possibility to re-filter the narrative in his mind, by going over and over again to his text, while the spectator cannot bring the performance back to better see or follow what he didn't picture well. In other words, the spectator has a live performance unfolding before his eyes while the reader has a mediated narrative which he/she can revisit again and again.

14.1.2.2. Space

Space is the geographical setting where narrative events take place. The ways a playwright and a novelist represent space are not the same. If space is an essential element in the structuring of all literary narratives, it is even more important for a dramatic text, because it is written for theatrical performance and cannot be read only diachronically, that is within the temporal sequence. It must be spatially arranged or spatialised. Some critics hold the view that the art of theatre is the art of space. For instance, Susan Stanford Friedman asserts that "space within the story told – the space through which characters move and in which events happen – is often the site of encounter, of border crossing and cultural mimesis" (Friedman op cit: 196) If other narratives like the novel and poetry represent space verbally, dramatic texts take into account the fact that the space has to acquire concrete visual forms, so that when mounted on the stage, it will become a concrete place in which real living human beings will be enacting the story. In narratives such as the novel, the voice of the author or the narrator is the main instrument of representing space. In a dramatic text, however, this is achieved through a secondary text [stage directions for instance] or through the actions and verbal exchanges of the characters. If in a novel, the place and the setting are described with painstaking details, in dramatic texts, this description is sketchy, because its main function is not the construction of an imaginary space, but to help stage directors to reconstruct it physically on the stage.

According to Susan Stanford Friedman, space, restored to its full partnership with time as a generative force for narrative allows for reading strategies – I will add performance strategies – focused on the dialogic interplay of space and time as mediating constituents of human thought and experience.

> In this sense, space is not passive, static or empty; it is not as it is in so much narrative theory the (back)ground upon which events unfold in time. Instead, in tune with current geographical theories about space as socially constructed site that are produced in history and change over time, the concept of narrative as a special trajectory posit space as active, mobile and full (Friedman, op cit: 195).

For me, the meaning attributed to space here is that space as the milieu of existence and becoming of characters allows for understanding reality as a question not of history alone but also of orientations, directions, entries and exits. It is a matter of geography of becoming. It refuses not only to privilege time over space but to separate time and space. Space in drama is quintessential to the display of plot. I will begin my demonstration by foregrounding the prime relevance of stage in dramatic performance. Stage is the symbolic representation of space in drama. Many of the spaces created by Ade Solanke in *Pandora's Box* are symbolic. By symbolic I mean that theatre performers manage to bring all spatial elements – scenes occurring in houses, on streets, in offices, in cars, in planes, on the sea, on mountains, etc – on stage. Thus, no matter the place where a scene has taken place, arrangements have to be made on stage for it to be represented. Space is the bedrock and the mainstay of dramatic action. Stage in drama makes it differ considerably from the novel. As the novel is not meant to be performed, it doesn't incorporate stage in its texts. This makes the representation of space in the play differ enormously from the way it is done in the novel. No single action can take place outside a spatial setting. Every action is happening somewhere. What also gives space its momentous importance within a dramatic world is the fact that characters' behaviours most often take contextual meanings within a specific spatial setting; and the same character can change his/her worldview, opinion, decision, future plans, depending on the place where they are. In clearer terms, space has incidence on character's behaviours. To give examples, in Ade Solanke's *Pandora's Box*, in scene four, Tope is complaining about the change in the behavior of her mum who has become hardcore (in this context it means greedy with regard to money) since her mother came back in Lagos

- from London. The way the playwright has presented the incidence of space on Tope's mumu's character is telling:

> *We're outside Mama Amaka'a 'Takeaway' chop shop. Tope and Timi are sitting on a bech taking photos with the phone. Lagos traffic blares past. Fuji music by Pasuma (Nigeria's answer to 50 Cent) is playing somewhere in the background. Snatches a conversation in Yoruba waft by.*
>
> TIMI: My mum is soft. Your mum is hardcore. A female Mr T.
> TOPE: When she left here, I didn't talk to her for three months.
>   she wasn't hardcore when she left you here, though. She was crying at our house for days. (*PB: 72-73*)

The place described by the playwright is Lagos. The characters, two teens, Timi and Tope are in front of a shop and the subject matter of their conversation is the way their mothers are treating them since they came back from London. Timi qualifies his mother as soft, kind, gentle and care-giving. Tope describes her as hardcore, that is stingy, greedy with regard to money, strict in her ways of dealing with her. Tope thinks that some time ago when they were still in London, her mother used to treat her well, but since their arrival in Lagos, the mother changed her behavior towards her. A possible explanation that I can provide for that change is that she doesn't want Tope who is a teenage girl to share the company of wayward children and copy bad ways from them. But what interests me the more is the fact that the playwright has conveyed the message that space influences characters' behaviours. The same character can behave differently in two different settings. Another major difference between the way space is presented in plays and the way it is done in novels is that in drama, playwrights can present "a play within a play", a device very common in drama, but which doesn't often occur in novels. "A play-within-a play is a device in which, a character mimes or plays out another character to obtain a desired reaction or response from his or her audience. For instance in Wole Soyinka's *The Road*, Samson has played a millionaire in the presence of Kotonu for comic purpose. When he plays a millionaire, his friend asks him what he will do with his money and he retorts, "first, I will marry ten wives" (*TR: 5*). This play -within- a play occurs at a road-side shack. Possibly, Soyinka produces this device at a roadside because he knows many passers-by will be around the scene to watch and comment on its humoristic accent. In the novel, the play within a play device is replaced by the technique of analepsis and prolepsis and of streams of consciousness. This shows again that drama and narrative fiction do not have the same modes of space representation.

13.2. Symbolic Representation of Space

Another intertextual interest is the symbolic representation of space. Space in dramatic texts can carry symbolic meaning. As the playwright cannot tell as much as he/she can about the place or space in the play the way a novelist does in the novel, he/she sees to it that the scenic elements selected to represent space are much telling. When space is used as a symbol, the reader or spectator has to bear in mind the connotative meaning inferred by the playwright. In the novel, the writer has the opportunity to comment on space, to explain to the reader the implied meaning that he/she wants the reader to get from its depiction. The post-colonial spaces in the African novel like Ngugi's Free Republic of Aburĩria in *Wizard of the Crow* are represented with the novelist's craft. The telling dominates more than the showing: "Any person who threatens the peace and stability of this nation should be done away with, even if that person is the wife of who is who in Aburĩria" (*W OTC*: 240).

In post-colonial context, theatrical space can be used symbolically to dramatise the dialectic of place and displacement which are depicted as key issues in societies affected by imperialism. For instance in Ade Solanke's *Pandora's Box,* London symbolizes a place of cultural uprooting while Lagos stands for home for the characters like Toyin, Sis Ronke and Principal Osun. London is a place of cultural exile or uprooting because that place has caused them, especially Toyin to forget about their Yoruba culture to the detriment of English. The playwright asserts "At one point I feel awkward about being born abroad in the company of Nigerians, I hated my accent, and my typical English reserve which stood out a mile amidst African spontaneity (*PB:* 15)". Due to the fact that they are descents of Nigerian parents living in London, they have spent the most important part of their lifetime in England, and as a result, they feel totally strangers or alien when they came back home in Lagos. As Toyin says, the only thing that makes them feel Africans is their African names: "Just because we have African names and relatives… that doesn't mean that we belong [to Nigeria] or that they [our people] accept us" (*PB:* 36). They blame their cultural alienation on their long stay in England. On this issue, Gilbert Helen and Joanne Thompkin have this to say:

> Post-colonial special histories dramatise the 'dialectic of place and displacement' which has been identified as a key issue in societies affected by imperialism (Ashcroft *et al.* 1989:9). Such histories work against models of theatre which subordinate spatial signifiers to other thematic and generic concerns, and/or which present the landscape merely as a scenic device, designed at best to heighten narrative emplotment and, at worse, to recede as a naturalized backdrop for signal events. In settler colonies, spatial histories can effectively dismantle the myth of *terra nullius* by revealing the land as object of discursive and territorial convention, as well as an 'accumulative text' that records in multiple inscriptions the spatial forms and fantasies of both settler and indigenous cultures (Helen Gilbert and Johanne Tompkins 1996: 156).

The quintessential point raised here is that the symbolic representation of space by post-colonial dramatists bears much significance when these symbolic spaces are gauged against the backdrop of their referential meanings. But what mostly strikes is that in the context of African post-colonial drama space bears much significance when looking at the theatre of political struggle like Ngugi wa Thiong'o's political plays. In *The Trial of Dedan Kimathi,* Nyeri is not a mere geographical space when Dedan Kimathi's trial is taking place, but it is the symbolic representation of African people's historical struggle against European imperialism, where they are determined to fight for freedom, to the cost of their lives. So when the reader reads about that place in the play or when the spectator watches this on stage, it is directly speaking to his mind as a talking symbol of freedom struggle. *I Will Marry When I Want, The Black Hermit*, and Wole Soyinka's protest plays – *Madmen and Specialists, Kongi's Harvest, A Play of Giants* and *King Baabu.* In *King Baabu* for instance Soyinka presents Gatu as a post-colonial kingdom where the military juntas grab the power by force and refuse to leave. It is also a place where democracy is put into peril by the oligarchic ruling class. Thus, due to their symbolic parlance, the way these places will appear on stage will tell the spectator that these places are highly symbolical and their interpretation should go beyond immediate perception.

This study on narratological and intertextual perceptions of time, space and narrative poetics in drama and fiction has resulted into three findings. First, drama and prose fiction do not share the same experience of narrative mode. In the former the telling is direct and is done in the present tense, while in the latter the telling is mediated. This unmediated nature of narration of drama affects the way dramatic texts represent time and space, and the way they use time and space to structure themselves. Secondly, the performing nature of drama confers on it a potency that fiction texts do not have. The performance aspect adds a plus in the understanding and reality perception of theatrical texts, which is the prerogative of the spectator. Third, the representation of silence and the way it is exploited by the novelist and the playwright are not the same in the novel and in the play. Due to the techniques of mimicry, facial expressions and bodily gestures, silence in drama tends to be more active and showing than in the novel where introspection and stream of consciousness are deployed.

References

Abbott, H. Porter. *The Cambridge Introduction to Narrative*. Cambridge: Cambridge University Press. 2002.
Ata Aidoo, Ama. *The Dilemma of a Ghost and Anowa*. UK: Longman. 1985.
Bakhtin, Mikhail. *Questions of Literature and Aesthetics*, (Russian) Moscow: Progress. 1975.
---------------- *[The] Aesthetics of Verbal Art*, (Russian) Moscow: Iskusstvo. 1979.
---------------- *The Dialogic Imagination: Four Essays*. Ed. Michael Holquist. Trans. Caryl Emerson and Michael Holquist. Austin and London: University of Texas Press. 1981.
Beckerman, Bernard. *Dynamics of Drama: Theory and Method of Analysis*. New York: Alfred A. Knopf. 1970.
Boulton, Marjorie. *The Anatomy of Drama*. London: Routledge & Kegan. 1977.
Chatman, Seymour. "Mrs. Dalloway's Progeny: The Hours as Second-Degree Narrative" in James Phelan and Peter J. Rabinowitz (eds.) *A Companion to Narrative Theory*. USA: Blackwell Publishing. 2005. PP. 269-280.
Elam, Keir. *The Semiotics of Theatre and Drama*. London and New York: Routledge. 1980.
Fludernik, Monika. *An Introduction to Narratology*. London and New York: Routledge. 2009.
Friedman, Susan Stanford. "Spatial Poetics and Arundhati Roy's *The God of Small Things*". In James Phelan and Peter J. Rabinowitz (eds.) *A Companion to Narrative Theory*. USA: Blackwell Publishing. PP. 192-205. 2005.
Gilbert, Helen and Johanne Tompkins. *Post-colonial Drama: Theory, Practice, Politics*. London and New York: Routledge. 1996/2002.
Hutcheon, Linda and Michael Hutcheon, "Narrativizing the End: Death and Opera". In James Phelan and Peter J. Rabinowitz (eds), *A Companion to Narrative Theory*. USA: Blackwell Publishing. 2002. PP. 441-450.

Jahn, Manfred. "Narrative Voice and Agency in Drama: Aspects of Narratology of Drama" in Ralph Cohen (ed.) *New Literary History: Objectives in Ethics, Politics and Aesthetics.* Baltimore: John Hopkins University Press. 2001. pp. 659-679

Michael Holquist ed. *The Dialogic Imagination Four Essays by M. M. Bakhtin.* Austin and London: University of Texas Press. 1981.

Ngugi, wa Thiong'o & Micere Githae Mugo. *The Trials of Dedan Kimathi.* Nairobi: Heinemann Educational Books. 1976.

Ngugi, wa Thiong'o. *Wizard of the Crow.* New York: Anchor Books. 2006.

Rifaterre, Michel. *Essais de stylistique structurale*, (présentation et traductions par Daniel Delas), Paris, Flammarion. 1970.

---------. *La Production du texte*, Paris, Le Seuil. 1979.

Shen, Dan. "What Narratology and Stylistics Can Do for Each Other" In James Phelan and Peter J. Rabinowitz (eds.) *A Companion to Narrative Theory.* USA: Blackwell Publishing. 2005. pp. 135-149

Short, Mick. "From Dramatic Text to Dramatic Performance" In Jonathan Culpeper, Mick Short and Peter Verdonk (eds.), *Exploring the Language of Drama: From Text to Context.* London and New York: Routledge. 2002. PP. 7-18

Solanke, Ade. *Pandora's Box.* London: Oberon Books. 2012.

Soyinka, Wole. *The Road.* Oxford: Oxford University Press. 1965.

Storey, Ian C. and Arlene Allan. *A Guide to Ancient Greek Drama.* USA: Blackwell Publishing. 2005.

Taplin, Oliver. *Greek Tragedy in Action.* London: Routledge Teylor and Francis Group. 2003.

15

BLACK CONSCIOUSNESS AESTHETICS IN MAISHE MAPONYA'S *THE HUNGRY EARTH* AND JANE TAYLOR'S *UBU AND THE TRUTH COMMISSION*

This chapter discusses the theatrical literary representations of post-conflicts and mediations techniques in Post-Apartheid South Africa from the perspectives of Maishe Maponya and Jane Taylor. The study asserts that the literary articulation of post-conflicts mediation strategies in Maishe Maponya's *The Hungry Earth* and Jane Taylor's *Ubu and the Truth Commission* tell the South African experience and constitute experimental praxis of social reconstruction. The two playwrights offer an example of the difficulties of putting in place a successful model of Truth and Reconciliation Commission capable of rallying Whites and Blacks after the long run segregationist and oppressive system. This study investigates the post-conflict reconciliation strategies as the bedrock and main stay of social peace, itself a springboard toward social cohesion and sustainable development.

The dramatic literary images projected by Maishe Maponya and Jane Taylor of South African post-conflict society reveal peace and development strategies in African societies as an important literary project to achieve. Post-conflicts reconciliation in South Africa has preoccupied Maishe Maponya in *The Hungry Earth* (Maponya 1976/2014) and Jane Taylor in *Ubu and the Truth Commission*, (Taylor:2007). Yet few critics view these two South African playwrights as peace mediators whose literary contributions to the promotion of reconciliation and peace in South African literature can no more be overlooked and ignored. Michael Etherton in examining the development of South African drama concentrates only on the works of pioneers like Gibson Kente and Credo Mutwa, ignoring contemporary playwrights Maishe Maponya whose play does an in-depth analysis on different aspects of apartheid's oppression, showing its state-sanctioned and legally enshrined racism (Etherton, 1982: 52). Helen Gilbert and Joanne Tompkins (1996) overlooking these writers, concentrates on the works of Alan Lawson andStephen Slemon to assert that post-colonial drama resists imperialism and its effects (Gilbert, 1996: 1). Charles E. Nnolim (2006) contends that the African writer in the 21st century is challenged to envision a new Africa which has achieved parity politically, technologically, economically and militarily with Europe and America (Nnolim, 2006: 9). And, making a further comment, he adds that protest literature over apartheid irrigates Africa's tears without addressing the issue of post-apartheid national reconciliation (Ibidem). It is Olga Barrios (2008) who has given careful thought to the South African post-conflict reconciliation problem by stating the socio-political commitment of the Black Theatre Movement in its struggle for equal rights between Whites and Blacks (Barrios, 2008: 59). The fact that critics have side-tracked the literary contributions of Maishe Maponya and Jane Taylor to peace seeking strategies through post-conflict national reconciliationin South African literature gives me the opportunity to study how national reconciliation can be used as a means to attain sustainable development. In this article I will analyse how Maponya and Taylor critically address the atrocities of apartheid regimes in South African and by so doing call for reconciliation and peace as strategies to attain national cohesion and development. My methodological approach is New Historicism. New Historicism focuses on issues of power – with a particular interest in the ways in which power is maintained by unofficial means such as the theatricality of royal display in the Court (Rivkin and Ryan, 2004: 506).

15.1. Conceptualizing South African Conflicts in Maishe Maponya's Dramatic Aesthetics

Conflicts in South African Apartheid contexts and the way to handle them have fuelled theme and subject matter of several South African playwrights' theatre works. Maishe Maponya and Jane Taylor advocate in their respective plays *The Hungry Earth* and *Ubu and the Truth Commission* interracial conflicts between Black and White communities as one of the social decimals that inform the necessity of mediation. Using drama as a means of communication, they seek to address the fundamental question of how to find back a peaceful society after violent conflicts. Theatre for Black African consciousness emerged in a context of post-apartheid injuries that needed to be healed. Olga Barrios has shown how Black theatre emerged in South Africa parallel to the Black Consciousness Movement, which reached its peak in the 1970s and had Stephen Biko as its main spokesperson (Barrios, 2008: 145-146). Yet Black theatre suffered from continuous banning and theatre artists were imprisoned most of the times. Therefore, Black South African artists were prevented from formulating in a written manifesto the principles that were already establishing the birth and subsequent development of Black Theatre. Olga goes on to show how after the Soweto students' uprising in June 1976 and Biko's death in 1977, Black theatre took the torch kindled by Biko's spirit (Ibidem). Olga also informs us that Black artists raised their torch with a tremendous sense of power, as if the bloodshed of the Soweto children and Biko had infuriated and given them an invincible strength to fight back. Nevertheless, every attempt pursued by Black South African artists in theatre was hindered (Ibidem).

Black theatre of the 1970s and 1980s is comprised in this study under the denomination of Black Theatre Movement because the playwrights of this time sought the same principles and goals although they were not written in a manifesto (Barrios, 2008: 146). Black theatre developed out of the Black consciousness concept and its artists were committed towards the same objective: to raise Black people's consciousness about their need to take an action in their liberation struggle and that of their country through the recovery of Black history and self-affirmation. Black consciousness aesthetics expressed in Maishe Maponya 's *The Hungry Earth* and Jane Taylor's *Ubu and the Truth Commission*, then, are ascribed within the theatrical Aesthetics of self-affirmation that equally defines the African American theatre of the 1960s and 1970s.When studying the two plays of the black consciousness movement, I will examine the specific sociopolitical and historical situations faced by black theatre artists in South Africa. In spite of the aforementioned restraints, theatre continued to exist and demonstrated to be a powerful weapon for action and social change, as the two playwrights Maponya and Taylor have aestheticized regarding the situation in theatre and poetry performances. They were successively discontinued by police force, a situation which confirms that theatre was a dangerous threat to the White government's policy of apartheid because it conveyed the power to move the masses into action.

Taking the Truth and Reconciliation Commission as inspiration, they showed that social cohesion would be possible only if citizens could forgive and forget past wounds in a context of national conflicts. The Truth and Reconciliation Commission in South Africa has spawned the bold imaginative artistic works of Jane Taylor's *Ubu and the Truth Commission* which is lauded as the touchstone artful work of social reform. The playwright brings to the fore the guilt of those who committed atrocities during the apartheid regime. According to Helen Gilbert, "In doing so, the play enters a politically volatile terrain, asking difficult questions about the moral value and social effectiveness of reconciliation as an official nation-building strategy, but refusing to provide easy answers (Gilbert, 2001: 25)." No other time than during the anomy of apartheid were acts of atrocities and unheard barbarism like killings, rape, genital mutilations, limbs chopping, burning people alive, child labour and trafficking committed. The character Pa Ubu in *Ubu and the Truth Commission* is one of the male characters who witnessed such inhuman barbaric acts:

> Pa Ubu: They put the makarov pistol to the top of his head and pulled the trigger. The gun jammed. We got another gun from one of the askaris. That didn't work either, so in the end, we beat him to death with spade. Then, we each grabbed a hand and a foot, and put the body on the pyre of tyre and wood, poured petrol on it, and set it alight. Now of course, the burning of a body to ashes takes about seven hours; it is – ah – and – ah – whilst that happened we were drinking and even having a braai next to the fire (*UTC, PP*: 40).

This is a living testimony of how uncivic citizens committed reprehensible acts of ultimate barbarism on their fellow citizens. Brutality, beating, torture, killing, mutilations chopping, and many other crimes were committed. Now the conflict is over and the victimized people must outlive the pains of their mental torture. For the society to continue to exist and progress toward development, reconciliation and forgiveness become imperious necessity. Jane Taylor's approach is conciliatory, seeking to raise consciousness about the intricacy and delicacy of post-conflict reconciliation, as the moral and psychological scars are still rife in the minds and souls of the victims. For that playwright, reconciliation must proceed from forgiveness, a desire to overlook others' guilt and forget. Reconciliation is more than a concept, it is an act of volition and the insightful decision of people who envision to live together as a nation looking into the future. The people must see themselves as bound by fate and history to live together. According to David Bloomfield et al, reconciliation means different things to different people. It is both a goal - something to achieve - and a process – a means to achieve that goal (Bloomfield et al, 2003: 19). Reconciliation prevents the use of the past as the seed of renewed conflict. It consolidates peace, breaks the cycle of violence and strengthens newly established or reintroduced democratic institutions. There is necessity to commit reconciliation problems to the Truth Commission: "My advice would be to pre-empt it all. I hear there is to be a Commission to determine Truths. Distortions and proportions" (*UTC, PP*: 32). The role of such commission is to investigate on the immediate and the far-reaching causes of violence in the society in havoc, going back into history to dig up facts and propose solutions for sustainable reconciliation and peace.

From a historical perspective, a glance at the political millstone of South Africa reveals that Blacks had been governed by White minority and remained foreigners in their own homeland (Barrios, 2008: 29). Most violent conflicts in South Africa as fictionalized by Maishe Maponya and Jane Taylor have historical origins and can be traced to the refusal of the transfer of power by White colonizers to the African post-independent leaders. In *The Hungry Earth* Maishe Maponya establishes that the White community's settlement and power mismanagements were printed with incompetence mistakes marked by accusations of ethnocentrism, economic corruptions, money embezzlement, religious conflicts, and dictatorship. In the context of South Africa the Apartheid regime spearheaded by White minority gave little power to Black communities and created social strife and political tensions. Political power being concentrated in an oligarchic White minority's hands, Black majorities were marginalized and cheated in their rights. The character Matlhoko attempts to reconstruct the context of that socio-political dystopia through the explanation of the past memories:

> Matlhoko: When this land started giving birth to ugly days, things started going wrong from the moment of dawning and peace went into exile, to become a thing of wilderness. Yes, we experienced the saddest days of our lives when umlungu first came to these shores called Africa, a total stranger from Europe. We received him kindly, we gave him food, we gave him shelter, we adopted his ideas and teachings […] Whilst we were still smiling, he set up laws,

organized an army and started digging up the gold and diamonds; and by the time our forefathers opened their eyes, umlungu was no more - he had moved to Europe. He had only left his army behind to 'take care of the unruly elements that may provoke a revolution' (*THE, PP: 17*)

This passage is a literary reconstitution of the historical apartheid settlement in South Africa with its discriminatory practices. Maponya like all South Africans had been personally affected by the discriminatory practices of the apartheid system. Land expropriation, looting of gold and diamond, over-exploitation of mines workers, arbitrary arrests and detentions without trial, properties seizures, torture, killings and abuses of authority by the state are rampant practices. The social atmosphere is replete with terror, violence, insecurity, fear and mistrust. It results that the social peace is put in peril and the climate of insecurity and terror has settled in the society for years. Helen Gilbert explains that the playwright Maishe Maponya has developed an increasing interest in the political theatre that emerged in the 1970s and became actively involved in the Black Consciousness Movement (Gilbert, 2008: 16). A combination of socialist and essentialist ideology, this movement owed as much to black American cultural politics as it did to the Third-World theories of liberation inspired by such scholars as Frantz Fanon. As Olga Barrios explains,

By the end of the 1950s Frantz Fanon had established a revolutionary line of thought that African Americans, Africans and other people of the Third World countries would adopt in their political, social and artistic agendas. Fanon was determined to change the status, identity and history imposed upon Black people by Western Culture. He advocated self-determination for his people and the people of the Third World against an intellectual and political imperialism that had colonized their land and their minds. He proclaimed the need for national consciousness that could help the colonized unveil the lies by which they had been subjected to a dominant culture which had denied and/or undervalued theirs. He insisted on the need to look at their own past and to study and find new strategies for their present in order to build their future. He envisioned the necessity for a re-evaluation of their history by breaking myths and stereotypes dictated by colonizers by searching and discovering their true selves (Barrios, 2008: 47).

Here, the key idea that transpires is the contribution of Fanon to the sensitization of Africans to the appropriation of black consciousness struggle for freedom in a context of social violence and injustice caused by apartheid. It is a

For the African Black Consciousness Movement, pursues the critic Gilbert, political and cultural liberation were inextricable. Black Consciousness theatre is a kind of committed literature that launches an offensive literary attack on the social injustices bred by the apartheid regime, seeking to overhaul the political apparatus of White oligarchy, the military junta who, like cankerworm, palmerworm or locust ate up all the rights and prerogatives of the Black community including decent living, access to education, employment, land and property owning, to mention but a few. David Bloomfield et al observe that it is necessary to understand the past, and to understand how people interpret their past [...] The intensity of violence that has taken place directly affects the depth of response of those involved and partly defines the scale of the problem to be addressed... (Bloomfield 223: 40). Maishe Maponya in Scene One of *The Hungry Earth* calls for an urgent militancy of all the African Black Community to arise and protest against the ravages of apartheid. The central role that such art form plays is the dissemination of ideas to debunk the superstructure of racial discrimination. It seeks to dismantle the ill-practices due to social disparities, oppression, corruption, arbitrary imprisonment and detentions without trial as the message is encrusted in the introductory passage of *The Hungry Earth*:

> Stand up all ye brave of Afrika
> Stand up and get to battle,
> Where our brothers die in numbers
> Afrika you were bewitched
> But our black blood will flow to water the tree of our freedom
> (*THE, PP:* 18).
> ....
> Wake up MotherAfrika
> Wake up
> Time has run out
> And all opportunity is wasted
> Wake up Mother Africa
> Wake up
> Before the white man rapes you.
> Wake up Mother Africa. (*THE, PP:* 16)

It is against such background that political violence took place in South Africa, according to the play's storyline. Thus, the sociopolitical turmoil set up by the discriminatory violent apartheid regime informs the turn in the historical upsurge and violent black/white communities conflicting interactions over the years. The literary message conveyed here by Maishe Maponya is that violence breeds violence and inter-racial hatred nurtures hatred. Such a situation is anti-life and can never help society to make progress:

> TWO: If we would really feel, the pain would be so great that we would stand up and fight to stop all the suffering.
> THREE: If we would really feel it in the bowels, the groin, in the throat and in the breast, we would go in the streets and stop the wars, stop slavery, destroy the prisons, stop detentions, stop the killings, stop selfishness – and apartheid we would end. (*THE, PP:* 16)

If community life should be made enjoyable, it urges that social actors under the supervision of political actors commit themselves to promote peace and social cohesion, human values that are the bedrock and main stay of development. The vibrancy and vitality of Black South African theatre inscribes in its cultural agenda peace seeking strategies as the pivotal point that sustains the masses, struggles against the oppression of apartheid. Art here is being used to sustain political struggle, to boost and galvanize the socio-political aspirations of the people towards the achievement of decent living environment where black community and white community can be weighed on an equal social scale of human value. Looking closely at life in society, one can infer that social strife, anomy and mistrust impinge on the atrocities committed by some citizens against their fellow citizens during the apartheid period, and which the victims are unable to forgive and forget. Therefore, it urges that true reconciliation begins by a mass sensitization on the necessity of social cohesion. To arrive there, the playwrights Maponya and Taylor think that there should be a cultural revalorization that restores Black South African cultural values in the concert of other nations'. The cultural disruptions caused by apartheid prone white communities that crippled the blossoming of dramatic performances is also a remote cause of social tensions, for the Whites overvalue their cultural practices and disparage Africans'. It is to advance the postulate that cultural equation is a source of social cohesion while cultural chauvinism demotes all efforts of peace building strategies in society. The evidence of such a critical stance is adumbrated in the following position taken by J. Ndukaku Amankulor. According to him,

> The vibrancy and vitality of contemporary Black South African theater is the result of an ideological commitment to promote the image and views of Black people in their struggle against apartheid. The creative vigor that has flourished in the 1970s and 1980s corresponds with the heightening of awareness of the role art must play in the fight for freedom and a distinct identity (Amankulor, 1993, 170).

This statement underscores the propitious assertion that Black South Africans use theatre as a tool for seeking freedom. In the struggle for cultural freedom, theatre becomes an ideological weapon that serves for self-affirmation in the face of unjust White oppression based on colour, race and ethnicity.

15.2. The Symbolism of Mediation Fostering Black Consciousness: Jane Taylor's Model

Jane Taylor's *Ubu and the Truth Commission* addresses national reconciliation between White and Black in a post-Apartheid context using symbols and images. The puppets in the play act like human beings who are themselves archetypes of parties in conflicts: the black and the white. Three puppet-types, — the vulture, the witnesses, and Brutus the dog and Niles crocodiles are symbols alluding to the treacherous people who act wickedly under the masks of disguised humans. The playwright uses symbolism for double purposes: first to unveil the hypocritical tendencies of some citizens who do evil without wanting to face the punishment of the law, hence covering up their true identity to be unveiled. Secondly symbolism is used as a thought provoking device. As artists, the playwrights prefer to have spectators or readers think out the meaning for themselves. Yet no matter the perspective from which one stands to gauge facts, mediation strategies stands out as the ultimate goal of Maisha Maponya and Jane Theylor. To better grasp the contextual meaning let's bind Sara Horowitz to our purpose. The word mediate according to Sara Horowitz means to act between two conflicting parties as a peace-maker (Horowitz, 2007: 51). Given this framework, he defines mediation in a dispute or negotiation as the intervention of third party unfamiliar to the conflict, trustable, unbiased and intending to be neutral:

> Being a mediator involves artful skills to assist the parties in reaching a mutually acceptable agreement on the issues in dispute. The task of a mediator is creating the conditions for an open dialogue and assuring the parties involved in the conflict freedom of speech and, above all, autonomy in decision making. The mediator is 'a facilitator, educator or communicator who helps to clarify issues, identify and manage emotions, and create options, thus making it possible to reach an agreement avoiding an adversarial battle in court' (Ibidem).

The goal of mediation as explained here is assisting the parties in conflict to solve their differences. Fisher and Ury (quoted by Sara Horowitz), and other Harvard scholars, speak of joint problem solving to reach a win-win settlement or integrative solution (Ibidem). In *Ubu and the Truth Commission,* Jane Taylor aesthetically represents the images of post-apartheid society in search for a true model of mediation and reconciliation. Characters, very often the epitomes of parties in conflict express their emotions and feelings after being witnesses of social injustice. Jane Taylor's play advocates that dates, deadlines, scarce resources, different needs, and especially emotional issues that raise feelings such as hate and resentment, makes mediation a hard task for the commissioner. Bloomfiel has reported that athough Landau et al. listed the following 'goals of a mediator' as typical of family mediation, Jane Taylor the playwright suggests through theatrical illustrations that they can be perfectly applied to mediation in other fields (Bloomfield, 2003: 151). To emphasize their comprehensive nature, the comments about aspects specific to family conflict have been omitted. From the first scene of the play through the last one, the steps of mediation seem to follow Sara Horowitz proposal scheme as credentials for a true post-conflict mediation:

- To develop trust and cooperation between the parties, so they can share relevant tasks and information.
- To improve communication between the parties, or, in other words, to understand the feelings of their counterpart, and share the decision making.

- To assure all the relevant parties their perspectives will be heard, and therefore, make them feel they are fairly treated.
- To reduce tension and conflict, so those who have a close relationship with both parties are not involved in a conflict of loyalties.
- To help the parties appreciate relevant information, in order to make decisions based on proper data, after having considered alternative proposals to solve the same issues.
- To favour confidentiality, while developing a voluntary resolution to the conflict.
- To reach a reasonable and fair agreement, unlike what usually happens in court. The mediator's role is crucial, but his skill must focus on granting the continuity and successful conclusion of the process rather than substituting the parties at the moment of proposing or deciding on a solution (Bloomfield, 2003: 40).

These are some important mediation and reconciliation tips that emerge from the reading of *Ubu and the Truth Commission*. It is crucial to underline that in every conflict, the impartiality of the mediation stands prime. The mediator's role becomes even greater when negotiations come to a standstill and are at risk of breaking of for reaching a stalemate. The mediator should guarantee a favourable environment for negotiation, allowing parties to listen and understand themselves and each other; acknowledge and appreciate their own interests and needs, and arrange them in order of importance; and build – together with the mediator – options that would let them reach a fair, feasible and long-lasting agreement, flexible enough to consider the possibility of future adjustments to its clauses. Jane Taylo's dramatic ideology points to the fact that when the mediator meets the parties at the beginning of the process, he finds them entrenched in their own personal views regarding their perspectives and demands, which they consider to be the best and fairest. Both parties are fixed in those positions, since they are unwilling to resign their values and views. Taylor's art further give hints to the fact that the mediator must build an atmosphere of trust in himself and the process, which will allow working towards the conflict resolution, each party leaving aside their fantasy of recreating life according to their own wishes. Where Taylor's philosophy of reconciliation mostly blends with the South African realism is that it starts by repositioning the debate on the aim of cultural struggle by hosting both South African theatre and literature as cultural media, to reinforce African culture and replace the imposed English traditions to South Africans as the standard cultural medium:

> This cultural struggle is not confined to South Africa but can be observed as well in other parts of the continent where the legacy of European theater conventions is being challenged, modified, or replaced with new forms of performance expression. Such replacements have not been based on mere cultural chauvinism. On the contrary, they are the benefits of research into indigenous African performance traditions in the effort to take theater down from the ivory towers to the grassroots of Africa's population (Amankulor, 1993: 166).

Adding to cultural denigration are physical violence translating into acts of kidnapping, killings, mutilation and rape. It is a sum total of criminal and barbaric assaults, that suppress peace and concords among the citizens of the same nations. In *Ubu and the Truth Commission*, some of the atrocities committed during political turmoil are reported by a Witness: "The police came to fetch me in my house. They said they had found the bodies of our children, they must take me to see them. When I saw them, they were without eyes" (*UTC, PP:* 37). Reading such a testimony about criminal infanticide and cruel manslaughter may arouse in the listener a feeling of disgust, hatred and contempt for the torturing faction. At the same time, intellectual judgment and moral probity call for a sense of self-examination and a critical propensity that considers peace perspectives as an exit door to stamp out violence, build social cohesion and a peaceful environment. For peace and national cohesion to prevail, forgiveness becomes an imperious necessity. This should be a free choice of the people who want to live together as a nation. It is not imposed on them: Pa Ubu asserts "we have opted for concealing rather than revealing (*UTC, PP:* 37). In other words, it means that, establishing the framework in which to implement peace education as praxis of post-conflicts reconciliation in the South African context can help design a sustainable reconciliation policy. Peace education may mean different things to different people and in different contexts. It is the context that can dictate the strategy to be adopted. The ethos of national reconciliation in South African context viewed through the specter of Jane Taylor's drama recommends a fostering of a culture of peace through a social integration that takes into account the interests of all ethnic groups, an equal treatment before the law. It should promote a sustainable economic, social and cultural development that targets the eradication of poverty among the black majority or minority groups.

According to Kofi Annan, the former UN secretary general,

> Prolonged armed conflicts don't only kills people: they destroy a country's physical infrastructure, divert scarce resources, and disrupt economic life, including food supplies. They radically undermine education and health services. A war of national liberation or self-defense may sometimes bind a nation together – albeit a crucial and unacceptable human cost. But almost all today's conflicts are civil wars, in which civilian populations are not incidental casualties but direct targets. These wars completely destroy trust between communities, breaking down normal social relations, and undermining the legitimacy of government – not to mention investor confidence (Annan, 2006: 49-50).

This critical assessment is decipherable through the dramatic art of Jane Taylor in *Ubu and the Truth Commission* through the dialogic discussion between Pa Ubu and Nile:

> PA UBU: I have heard of Truths, and know distortions, but what are these Proportions you talk about?
> NILES: An inquiry is to be conducted by great and blameless men who Measure what is done, and why, and how.
> PA UBU: And just what can these brilliant mathe munitions do?
> NILES: They can beyond all ambiguity indicate when a vile act had a political Purpose.
> PA UBU: And if they so resolve?
> NILE: Then they can and must absolve. The righteous have to forgive the Unrighteous. (*UTC, PP*: 33)

Nile is the character who espouses Taylor's authorial ideology that true reconciliation entails forgiveness, tolerance and the respect of inalienable human rights. We can say with Christof Heyns and Karen Stefiszyn that the African continent and South Africa in particular provide a clear reminder that human rights is a dynamic concept and that it cannot be seen in isolation from the context and environment in which it operates (Heyns and Stefiszyn, 2006: 1). Adherence to human rights norms could simultaneously be a response to conflict and one of the mechanisms that can be used in the pursuit of a lasting peace. As such conflict is the ever–present shadow, the permanent alternative to human rights, and much is to be learned of human rights by understanding the nature of conflict and methods to combat conflict. This critical stand is corroborated by Barbara Mbire-Barungi who asserts that politically, a niche for the harmonious coexistence for both traditional leaders and progressives will have been found (Mbire-Barungi, 2001: 96). Sound governance structures that combine the old and the new ways will be erected. There will also be greater awareness and recognition of our deep ethnic diversity and the need for universal democratic participation alongside preservation of the vast and diverse cultural heritage.

Maishe Maponya and Jane Taylor sustain the philosophy of empathy in mediation process. Empathy allows mediators not only to get trapped in the negative feelings that are part of the mediation process but to also identify themselves as human beings, seeking legitimate goals based on respect for human rights, especially those related to the fulfilment of basic needs. Every party to a conflict, over and above violent means or expressions, has valid and legitimate goals and demands on which nonviolent and creative solutions can be built.

Dehumanizing a party (the opposite to empathy) prevents the mediator from identifying the legitimate claims present in every dispute. The mediator needs to stimulate the search for a settlement which would not make parties feel rejected. We must remember that sometimes to understand is to forgive, and that the role of the mediator is assisting the parties to end a situation by nonviolent means, opening a dialogue between them. Generating empathy has to do with establishing a respectful and deep relationship with the different people. It may also be necessary, in order to build mutual trust and generate empathy, to allow parties to share their feelings, establish an open dialogue with each party and, after achieving a deep understanding of each one, foster communication between them. At another level of interpretation, the symbolic message in the plays *The Hungry Earth* and *Ubu and the Truth Commission* functions to work out the principles that attitudes should be softened, trying to reach the goals without violence, without the intention of hurting the other, and working with nonviolence at four levels:

1. In thought, meditating and promoting an inner, self-reflective dialogue.
2. In speech, avoiding labelling, blaming, demonizing the other while searching for common roots and sharing the future

responsibilities, calming anxieties and fears, helping the parties to visualize a future in which they could live.
3. In action, making use of different resources, meeting to negotiate, avoiding repressive answers and the use of weapons.
4. In creativity to overcome contradictions. Creativity implies that the solution transcends the conflict; it goes beyond saving the 'honour' or 'face' of the parties or the actual situation.

This is a possible reliable way of implementing creativity to prevent the parties from building defenses and opposing new ideas; it is considering the new situations as possibilities rather than statements, since the original ideas suggested by others tend to be rejected by those who have not considered or proposed them. In order to get people to transcend contradiction and become creative, it is necessary to enter a new perspective, a new dimension.

The basics of the mediator's profile, as Taylor's *Ubu and the Truth Commission* let them read though, are to be a trustworthy and honourable person, unfamiliar to the conflict or problem, who has the skills and the will to help in an empathic way, understand and assist in an unbiased way the parties to the dispute. In mediation, there are three central issues that all mediators should learn and consider:

- The communication, including the divergence of perceptions present in every conflict.
- The conflict process, since it has a predictable path, the mediator should recognize and predict escalation, stalemate and other variables that may arise during the conflict. His or her own negotiating style when facing a disagreement situation, as well as identifying the different negotiating styles of others. It is also important that the mediator should know how to ask, listen and recognize differences in a sensible way; consider each party as a human being; and be able to follow each party's speech without getting involved or imposing his personal values. The mediator should be a person who asks a lot and generates empathy in the response; who is external to the society or group he will try to assist. Mediation is a confidential process, embedded in the parties' values and wishes rather than the mediator's. In order to help solve a conflict, the mediator seeks to create an appropriate atmosphere; share the existing information on the parties'

interests; and help them suggest and reduce options, until they can make a rational decision, located in some point between the prospective agreement and what they claimed.

Dealing with traditional mediation, we must insist that the mediator's role is crucial, but his skill must focus on granting the continuity and successful conclusion of the process rather than substituting the parties at the moment of proposing or deciding on a solution. In the transcendent transformative mediation, when a mediator knows enough of the local culture, he should be recycled, go to another place and start the task once again, as diplomats do. Finally, a transcendent solution is oriented towards a legitimate, positive and constructive future. Sometimes this solution does not agree with the law or with the structural violence that may exist in a society in which there is enough food but the population is starving because they do not have the money to buy the food. Therefore, it can be legal – according to local laws – but not legitimate. Human rights and basic needs are non-negotiable, and so should be for the whole of humankind. If mediation implies opening the dialogue between two parties which see themselves as antagonist, maybe the education of future generations should be focused on the development of the virtues which, according to Comte-Sponville (2004), are applied values, instead of on teaching theoretical values which have fallen in disuse.

Modern South African drama and theater spearheaded by Jane Taylor and Maishe Maponya have been prominent and successful on the cultural front of the war against apartheid. Not only have these playwrights combated the unjust system of Apartheid with its white supremacy ideology, but they have actually sought to mediate conflicts, promote peace and peaceful coexistence to lay the foundations of true nation building. Contemporary Black South African plays reflect the material existence of Black people under the apartheid government. Theater is considered an effective method of portraying that existence.

Both Maponya and Taylor wrote plays that pitch out racial integration and tolerance as important decimals of a society's survival. In Taylor's *Ubu and the Truth Commission* an experimentation of the national reconciliation organ, the Truth Commission highlights the ideological stands of a creative writer in search for pragmatic solutions to conflicts through the advocacy of forgiveness. If in *The Hungry Earth*, Maponya foregrounds the ideological stand of colonial effects on the people during and after European colonization, the era of post-independence should see the renewing of the society in the concerted effort of forgiveness, tolerance and mutual concessions. The wounds and scares of civil strife are not easy to heal but volition and determination towards that end can initiate change. Maponya and Taylor have eschewed the intrusion of such personal problems by devoting their energies to raising the consciousness of their fellow Africans in the light of the historical and cultural contradictions inherent in apartheid.

The vibrancy and vitality of contemporary Black South African theatre couched in Maishe Maponya and Jane Taylor's plays are the result of an ideological commitment to promote the image and views of Black people in their struggle against apartheid. The creative vigor that has flourished in the 1970s and 1980s corresponds with the heightening of awareness of the role art must play in the fight for freedom and a distinct identity. This cultural struggle is not confined to South Africa but can be observed as well in other parts of the continent where the legacy of European theater conventions is being challenged, modified, or replaced with new forms of performance expression. Such replacements have not been based on mere cultural chauvinism. On the contrary, they are the benefits of research into indigenous African performance traditions in the effort to take theater down from the ivory towers to the grassroots of Africa's population. Playwrights like Maponya and Taylor have succeeded in converting the traditional African folktale convention into a contemporary dramatic form. It is not far-fetched to see their dramaturgy as being influenced by revolutionary theater techniques. Nonetheless, Maponya is simply using an indigenous African performance format that may have been lost to those Africans who seek cultural and artistic validation from outside the continent. Maponya has continued to experiment with storytelling and other dramatic forms rooted in indigenous South African traditions.

In his approach to Maishe Maponya's dramatic works, E.J. van Alphen has focused on *Letta,* an unpublished play to establish that Maponya's theatre "tends to stress the political and social urgency of the contemporary South African predicament" (Alphen, 2011: 143). The significance of Apartheid and post-apartheid events in South Africa is that it was the height of political activism, culminating in the Rivonia Trial that resulted in the sentencing of Nelson Mandela, Walter Sisulu and Govan Mbeki to life on Robben Island (Ibidem). This political drama was strongly reflected in the theatrical literature of many South African playwrights among whom Maishe Maponya, as the critic Alphen puts it:

> Maponya starts his play by recreating the atmosphere and scenery of life of ordinary people in the townships and villages of South

> Africa. There is heavy smoke hanging in the air from numerous fires whether in the form of stoves or open fires as people prepare their evening meals. He observes that often these fires are made by older children since parents leave early in the morning to go to work and return late in the evening. As a result, older children are left to take care of the domestic work. This makes things easier for their parents, on their arrival home, to finish off what the children had started while the children go and play (Alphen, 2011: 143).

The critical assertion that literature which operates in the form of drama here concurs to promoting authorial ideology about the contemporary South African reconciliation problem stands. Something what catches the eye with this exposition is a direct violation of the children's rights as can testify the child labour in mines. However, Maponya seems to argue that it is the way of life for many Africans and South Africans are no exception to have suffered blunt socio-economic injustice. The playwright uses child game as a symbolic device to convey the message about reconciliation. Through the frictions and reconciliation of the children, he releases the message that a national social cohesion and peaceful coexistence is possible. The first thing that Maponya engages is the rivalry between boys and girls before the courting stage. Letta and her friends listen to a group of boys as they sing. The girls pick up the same song as soon as the boys stop, but sing it better, which makes the boys jealous. In real life, the defeated boys often disrupt the girls' singing and chase them around, with each boy chasing after the girl he likes. Most of the time this ends with each couple hiding in their little secret place. In this scene Maponya captures the harmony and peace for which blacks strived, despite the oppressive system that governed their daily lives. But it is the artistic talent amongst young black South Africans and the need to identify and develop it that he pursues further. In the next scene one of Maponya's characters, James, mesmerized by the talent of the girls and especially Letta, takes the matter further.

There are two issues here Maponya attempts to instill in his audience, especially the youth and talent scouts. First, that youth should avoid engaging in activities without the approval of their parents, as has become the norm contemporarily. The possible reason is that youth are likely to be tricked and trapped in things without being aware that they are taken advantage. Second, according to African cultures, children are answerable to their parents and anything that concerns them should be dealt with through their parents.

The findings in this chapter are that Maponya and Taylor through *The Hungry Earth* and *Ubu and the Truth Commission* exposes conflicts in Apartheid and post-Apartheid contexts as challenges to take up in order to build social peace in cultural diversity on the one hand; and on the other, the possible ways in which conflicts can be transformed into peace seeking strategies. Two key ideas emerge: firstly, Black consciousness Movement was sustained by a spirit of reconciliation which was mandatory in the Truth and Justice Commission. At this point in history South African intelligentsia has to build a form of organic African discourse that puts the African subject at the centre of existence. Secondly, for a long time now Africa has been an object of outsiders' reflections. Time has come to reposition discourse within the ambit of African constructive mind through art.

References

Alphen, E. J. Van. *Political Shift and Black Theatre in South Africa*. South Africa: Francis L. Rangoajane, 2011.

Amankulor, J. Ndukaku. "English Language Drama and Theatre". In Oyekan Owomoyela, ed. *A History of Twentieth Century African Literatures*. Nebraska: University of Nebraska Press, 1993. 138-172.

Annan, Kofi. "Peace and Development – One Struggle, Two Fronts". In Christof Heyns and Karen Stefiszyn, eds. *Human Rights, Peace and Justice in Africa: A Reader*. Pretoria: Pretoria University Law Press, 2006. 149-154.

Barrios, Olga. *The Black Theatre Movement in the United States and in South Africa*. USA: PUV, 2008.

Bloomfield, David et al, *Reconciliation after a Violent Conflict: A Handbook*. Sweden: IDEA, 2003.

Etherton, Michael. *The Development of African Drama*. New York: Afrikana Publishing Company, 1982.

Gilbert, Helen, ed. *Post-colonial Plays: an Anthology*. New York: Routledge, 2008.

Gilbert, Helen and Joanne Tompkins, *Post-colonial Drama: Theory, Practice, Politics*. London and New York, 2001.

Heyns, Christof and Karen Stefiszyn, *Human Rights, Peace and Justice in Africa: a Reader*. South Africa: Pretoria University Law Press, 2006.

Horowitz, Sara. "Mediation". In Charles Webel and Johan Galtung, eds., *Handbook of Peace and Conflict Studies*. New York: Routledge, 2007. 51-63.

Maponya, Maishe. *The Hungry Earth*. In Gilbert, Helen. *Postcolonial Plays: an Anthology*. New York: Routledge, 2008.

Mbire-Barungi, Barbara. "The African Development Challenge: Living the Experience". In Olugbenga Adesida and ArunmaOteh, eds. *African Voices, African Visions*. Sweden: Elanders Gotab, 2001. 95- 109.

Nnolim, Charles E. "African Literature in the 21st Century: Challenges for Writers and Critics". In Ernest N. Emenyonu, ed., *New Directions in African Literature*. Nigeria: Heinemann Educational Books, 2006. 1-9.

Rivkin, Julie and Michael Ryan, eds. *Literary Theory: An Anthology*. USA: Blackwell Publishing, 2004.

Taylor, Jane. *Ubu and the Truth Commission*. In Gilbert, Helen. *Postcolonial Plays: an Anthology*. New York: Routledge, 2008.

PART FOUR

SOCIOCRITICISM

CULTURAL STUDIES

AFROPOLITANISM

ECOCRITICISM

16

A SOCIOCRITICAL APPROACH TO FRANCOPHONE DRAMA AND THEATER

This chapter examines the sociology of francophone drama. Aspects examined include the William Ponty drama, village drama, urban drama, and historical and political drama. The analyses relay the researches of French theatre scholar Alain Ricard who has done a seminal work on the functioning modes of theatre in West Africa in general and Francophoe west Africa in particular. His account shows how theatre in Francophone Africa has functioned as a medium for cultural expression and a tool for debating politics. I will give in extinso his findings as they appear in *A History of Twentieth African Literature*, an anthology published by Oyekan Owomoyela.

Bakary Traore's *Le théâtre négro-africain et ses fonctions sociales* (1958; *Negro-African Theater and Its Social Functions, 1972* translated by Dapo Adelugba) clearly shows the influence of missionaries and of the public-school system in French-speaking Africa (Ricard 1993). Unfortunately, Traore does not draw a strict line between the concepts of theater and drama. Drama is a constant in social life: dances, rituals, and burials all have an element of show and action that is indeed dramatic. But theater is something different: it originates in a desacralized society that is willing to play with its problems, even with its myths. The Bambara koteba—sketches acted out by youngsters—is no doubt one of the indigenous African theater forms; so are the Malinke puppets. Both deserve to be included in a history of theater in Africa. The same can be said of other, very different forms that also contain this element of narrative playacting. The Togolese *kantata* in Ewe—religious drama using biblical themes—dates as far back as the 1920s and is still being staged today. In other parts of what was considered French-speaking Africa, in Malagasy, one can cite the *mpilalao*—a kind of musical vaudeville—whose origins are traditional and which also persists today. Strictly speaking, these forms (*koteba, kantata, mpilalao*) do not belong to the history of theater in French, but they have had an influence on writers in French. They flourished throughout the colonial era and are still being maintained. To write the history of African theater in French is to write the history of texts staged by actors, that is, by people playing a role for fun or for money, but certainly not for ritual reasons. There are very few professional actors in Africa today, yet the existence of a professional society of actors is what would define, for the sociologist, the presence of theater. In the case of theater in French-speaking Africa, let us say that such a corporation exists in embryonic form and that the texts produced during the last two decades have helped shape it.

Actors attempt to create a work of art by presenting a story composed by somebody else. Their craft is a form of art, not a part of daily or ceremonial life. Theater is thus a way of telling stories using people and relying on a fixed scenario, which then allows the actors to improvise. A breakthrough transforms the traditional performances. Language, gestures, and music are suddenly presented in a new synthetic form, or rather should be. Language is now an imported one. What happens then to a medium—theater—that strives for a synthesis of the arts when the relationship between spoken language, music, and dance is no longer embedded within a tradition, and has to be totally re-created? The story and the future of theater as an art form in French speaking Africa is the record of several such attempts to re-create this relationship.

I concentrate in this study on those texts that can function as works of art, that can communicate a message beyond the boundaries of their original ethnic group, and that can exist independently of those who first composed them. The essay is divided into three parts: (1) a historical overview of the birth and development of theater in Francophone Africa; (2) an analysis of the plays, grouped into three categories; and (3) remarks on the new directions present writers are taking and an attempt to assess what this means for theater as an art form.

16.1. Historical Survey: The William-Ponty Formula

It can rightly be said that theater in French on a stage in Africa started at the Ecole William-Ponty, a teachers' training college established in 1930 in

Senegal by the French colonial administration. Here, schoolteachers from all over West Africa were trained. Dramatic activity within the school curriculum emphasized stories and dances from the different cultural groups to which the students belonged. As these stories were dramatized, a dialogue in French was added, and an annual theater show presented the results of this interesting pedagogical experiment. These shows became African theater: at the 1937 Colonial Exposition in Paris the students won critical acclaim. Their dramatic training would have numerous consequences throughout West Africa, since the students came from all the different French territories. They brought to their home countries a concept of theater that has had profound influence, until the 1980s, on dramatic productions in French-speaking Africa. The "Ponty formula"—if we judge by the texts published in the journal *Présence africaine, such as Sokame* (1948), a ten-page historical play about a Dahomean queen— consisted of spoken text in French with sung text in an African language. Text was interspersed with songs and dances, which probably attracted most of the audience response, at least during the European tour. The spoken text was, according to L. S. Senghor, "bland and stiff, without style" (*Liberté I* [*Liberty I*] 66), and could not pretend to the dignity of literature if it were not for the formula that invented this type of didactic folkloristic theater, so widespread until today and so well suited to the students' demands. The Ponty formula provided an outlet for the students' two basic and suddenly complementary desires: to speak French in a public situation, and to present publicly on a stage their native songs and dances.

In 1938 in the Ivory Coast, Ponty alumni Coffi Gadeau and Amon d'Aby created the *Théâtre indigène de Côte d'Ivoire*. Bernard Dadié, also a Ponty alumnus from the Ivory Coast, was to become the most famous dramatic writer in French in the late 1960s. And in 1958 another Ponty alumnus, Bakary Traore, published his book on African drama. Theater was in the hands not only of schoolteachers but also of missionaries. Missionary forms paid more attention to African languages and thus aimed at a better aesthetic synthesis, mediated by indigenous African music. The Togolese kantata, with its blend of music, songs, dances, and biblical evocations, is directly descended from that effort. But missionary theater, rarely being in French, does not fall within the scope of this study, even though it had a considerable influence on the concept of dramaturgy that was to preside over the efforts of many an aspiring writer. Theater in the Ponty vein, acted by students, was to experience a kind of revival (after the school changed emphasis during the overhaul of the colonial educational system in 1948) with the creation by the French colonial government of the Cultural Centers in French West Africa in 1953. These centers subsidized and controlled cultural life within the colonies. Buildings were provided that could be used as libraries and theaters under the aegis of the French colonial administration. The annual drama competition of the Cultural Centers rapidly became a feature of African dramatic life and created the competitive pattern so important even today in African theater.

Not enough attention has been given to the two most original dramatic texts of the end of the colonial era: from Senegal, Senghor's *Chaka* (1956), and from Guinea, Fodeba Keita's *Aube africaine* (1955; African dawn). Chaka is a poetic drama, a kind of oratorio, "a dramatic poem for several voices with a drum accompaniment." The text, included in the collection Ethiopiques, is dedicated to the "Bantu martyrs of South Africa." It is a meditation on power, a drama of the man of action sacrificing his love to the necessity of armed struggle: "Power is not obtained without sacrifice. Absolute power is obtained by giving the blood of the most cherished being." *Chaka* is a short play with a choir, an interesting experiment in marrying French text and African music. *Aube africaine* is a dance drama, marked by the hope for better days after the end of colonization. Both *Chaka* and *Aube africaine* try to reconcile the spoken text with music and with dance, because as selfi conscious artists, Senghor and Keita Fodeba know that theater is an art form that seeks a dynamic synthesis of image, words, and sounds, and not an educational medium, as was the fashion in the Ponty vein. Their example was not followed (was it understood?). Independence saw the flourishing of school drama to an extent that even the most enthusiastic Ponty zealots could not have envisaged.

16.2. The Dominant Genres: Village Drama, Urban Drama, and Historical and Political Drama

Jacques Scherer, head of the Institute for Theater Research at the Sorbonne, undertook a survey of African theater in 1965; in six months he read 136 plays and met with many authors. He found that the proclaimed goal of universal primary education and the correlated development of high schools in all countries had given the necessary manpower to theater in French. The output of plays has been large, but their quality has remained low, and no writer stands out, as for instance, Wole Soyinka does in the same period in Nigeria. Works can easily be grouped into three categories: the village drama, the urban drama, and the historical drama.

The paradigm of village drama is the Cameroonian playwright Guillaume Oyono-Mbia's *Trois prétendants, un mari* (1964; *Three Suitors, One Husband*, 1968). *The play has been a best-seller (fourteen editions to date) and the all-time favorite of school groups for over two decades, and rightly so. It deals with the cupidity of a father who wants to marry his daughter to a rich suitor in disregard of the girl's preference. In the best Molièresque style the play is written with a touch of lightness, a zest for social criticism. It has all the ingredients to ensure its success among students wishing to separate themselves from so-called backward village practices. Oyono-Mbia's achievement remains unchallenged. Unfortunately, the play uses only the resources of the classical comedy and does not show the theatrical inventiveness of a comparable work by Wole Soyinka: The Lion and the Jewel* (1963), which addresses the same kind of audience but, for instance, uses dance in a very creative way.

The Congolese playwright Guy Menga also produced a play, *L'oracle* (1969; *The oracle*), whose topic is the humorous condemnation of village practices, in this case, fetish priests. *L'oracle* is a great favorite of school groups and one of the repertory classics in French-speaking Africa. *L'os* (1973; *The bone*), by Birago Diop from Senegal, a poet and an accomplished writer of folktales, was first produced in Dakar in 1965. In the vein of the village comedy but with the bite of satire, *L'os* deals with human greed in a situation of extreme need such as prevails in many Sahelian villages. Just as village life is a great topic for the satirist, so is office life, but the urban dramas' achievements do not measure up to the standards of the village dramas. Corruption in high places, graft, and abuse of women are the topics of many plays, from *La secrétaire particulière* (1970; *The private secretary*) by the Republic of Benin's Jean Pliya and *Monsieur Thôgô-Gnini* (1970) and *Papa Sidi, maitre escroc* (1975; *Papa Sidi, master swindler*) by Senegal's Bernard Dadié to *Le club* (1984) by Togo's Senouvo Agbota Zinsou. Independence also saw the development of historical drama. It had been in the Ponty tradition to present the ways of the old African kingdoms, but no political discussion was included. After Independence, the new states tried to reflect upon their history, and drama was seen by the students and the new elite as a proper vehicle for such soul-searching. A long list of plays using the pageantry of traditional courts were written and presented. Among them we can cite, from Mali, Seydou Badian's *La mort de Chaka* (1961; *The death of Shaka*) and Djibril Tamsir Niane's *Sikasso, ou la dernière citadelle* (1971; *Sikasso; or, The last citadel*); from Senegal, Amadou Cissé Dia's *Les derniers jours de Lat Dior* (1965; *The last days of Lat Dior*) and

Cheik Ndao's *L'exil d'Albouri* (1968; *The Exile of Albouri*); from Benin, Jean Pliya's *Kondo le requin* (1966; *Kondo the shark*); from Niger, André Salifou's *Tanimoune* (1974); and from the Ivory Coast, Raphaël Atta-Koffi's *Le trone d'or* (1969; *The golden throne*).

Themes of death and exile are dominant; they can be confronted now that the new nations have been born. These plays have been widely presented in their respective countries of origin as well as in festivals, and they constitute another salient feature of the repertory of school companies. Unfortunately, their artistic achievement does not match the interest of their political content. No balance has been achieved between the spoken and the sung parts, and the result is often weak. Reflection on history should be combined with a reflection on artistic forms, as is the case in Soyinka's *A Dance of the Forests* or *Kongi's Harvest,* "where poetry becomes an instrument of power in itself and not a mere illustration of political theories and of historical knowledge. Some plays try to deal with the political theme in a more ambitious way, attempting an aesthetic as well as political debate of the dominant discourse on history. Such is the Ivorian playwright Charles Nokan's Les malheurs de Tchako" (1968; *The trials of Tchako*), which heralds the type of critical outlook that would become the norm in the next decade, although in a rather unaccomplished way.

The best work of the 1960s is probably *Béatrice du Congo* (1969 ; *Beatrice of the Congo*), written by the grand old man of African drama, the former Ponty student Bernard Dadié, who, along with Amon d'Aby and Coffi Gadeau, was a former leader of the Cercle culturel et folklorique de la Côte d'Ivoire. Beatrice is the daughter of the King of the Congo. She exhorts her father and her people not to submit to the people of Bitanda (i.e., Portugal), not to abandon their wealth and their culture for a mere mimetism of European ways. Her speeches and her personal commitment make her a kind of African Antigone. She is sentenced to death, her last scream a call for a grant of happiness and joy by the elemental forces of the continent. The play is written with mastery; dialogues are fast paced and the historical setting well constructed. *Béatrice du Congo* was the only African play to be produced at the Avignon Drama Festival (1971), one of the best-known drama festivals in Europe, under the direction of Jean-Marie Serreau, former director of many of Aimé Césaire's plays. One of the more original plays of the 1960s was *L'Europe inculpée* (1969, 1977; *Europe indicted*) by the Congolese writer Antoine Letembet-Ambilly, first produced in 1969 first produced in 1969. Here is the argument of the play as presented by the author:

This play uses the biblical episode of Noah with his three sons Sem, Cham and Japhet. In this five-act play, Japhet, father of Europe, upon learning that his daughter Europe is accused in front of judge Humanity, exhorts his father Noah, back on earth, to intervene and stop the trial. (Letembet-Ambilly 5-6) The schematism of the situation, as well as the coded rhetoric, has an interesting, operatic quality. It belongs to the universe of religious drama, of passion plays, often produced, but in an African language, by missionaries. This is the first example, and still a rare one, of the influence of this type of dramaturgy on theater in French. This survey of the first period of African theater in French would not be complete if we neglected Guinea and Zaire, where historical developments have been quite different from the other French-speaking countries. In Guinea, the promising debut of Fodeba Keita came to a halt with the dictatorship of Sekou Touré: writers and poets were killed (Keita, himself once a minister, disappeared) or went into exile. Theater was reduced to the competitive singing of praise for the so-called revolution. A Guinean play presented in Lagos in 1977, *L'aube sanglante* (*Bleeding dawn*), was an obvious sequel to Keita's *Aube africaine*. Its aesthetic treatment was "based on socialist realism using a fighting vanguard technique opposed to the contemplative theater" (d'Aby, Dadié, and Gadeau, *L'aube sanglante*; my translation). In its ethical proposal, it glorifies "all fighters who fell on the front of the anticolonial struggle." And true to this announcement, the play treats anticolonial struggle in a realistic and prosaic way, using all the techniques of the so-called bourgeois theater it claims to replace. It is supposed to be "a collective creation," which probably expresses the difficulty of finding a self-respecting writer in the nightmarish republic that Guinea had become at that time.

In Democratic Republic of Congo (ex Zaire), the theatrical movement has deep roots in missionary activities. Many groups existed in the 1950s and put on plays in African languages. There even existed a popular theater in broken French, which was often broadcast over the radio. Plays written by Albert Mongita enjoyed vast popularity. Theater was thus at the same time a popular and an educational medium to an extent unknown in other French-speaking countries. Plays by Justin Disasi were published in the journal *Présence congolaise* in 1957, while plays by Mongita appeared in *La voix du congolais* in the same year. It is fair to say that this theater, although active and popular, remained poor artistically. The schooling of the authors did not go far, since the intellectual promotion of an African elite was not high on the agenda of Belgian colonization. Still, granting the crudeness of the language and artistic devices, these plays had a strange revealing power, according to the Zairean scholar P. Ngandu Nkashama, who has written a profound and simulating study of theater in Zaire. It is because of the plays' very marginality "that they signify the relevant manner in which colonial reality was reflected in the frightened and troubled eyes of the elite of the Belgian Congo ... and of Rwanda Burundi. They [the elite] remained inhibited and panicked at the thought of a theatrical discourse that would investigate deeply and reflect upon their very conditions of existence" (Nkashama 65; my translation).

One could not better express the limitations of colonial drama. In a way, the lack of formal slickness, of that Ponty polish, makes Zairean theater more revealing, more in touch with the essential realities. It has a more direct relationship to truth, and this may be a better road to art.

In the mid- 1960s Zairean theater was very active inside the country: students in the big cities such as Kinshasa and Lubumbashi provided a large and receptive audience. Hardly anything was known of the outside world, although eager Zairean students would put on foreign plays. Nkashama has documented some of this activity: names such as D. Bolamba (*Geneviève, martyre d'Idiofa—Geneviève, martyr of Idiofa*) and Valerien Mutombo-Diba (*Le trône à trois—The throne for three*) were well-known among students (Nkashama 68). In 1967 a national theater group was created, and by the early 1970s it counted as many as four hundred people in its company.

16.3. New Perspectives

I would like, in this final section, to reflect upon the sociological conditions of theater production and to analyze in this light recent developments and essential trends.

16.3.1. Institutions

The creation of national theater companies was for a time a new element in the picture. Senegal built the Théâtre Daniel Sorano in 1965; the Ivory Coast had the *Institut national des arts* and later the Ecole nationale de théâtre. Zaire, as mentioned above, created a national company in 1967, as did the Congo in 1972 and Togo in 1973. Today (1985), few countries are without some kind of official support of or involvement in theater: in the Cameroons it was the university theater that, following the Nigerian example, was supposed to stimulate dramatic creativity. Official cultural polices were developed in the early 1970s and varied from a liberal and tolerant attitude, as in Senegal or even in the Congo, to the militant, verbose, and more or less totalitarian postures of Zaire and Guinea. These policies have direct bearing on dramatic writing and production. For instance, how can one speak of theater in what was the Central African Empire? Reality was far beyond anything that could be written, so writers went into silence or exile.

More beneficial to the long-term development of theater has probably been the gradual development of publishing. In the late 1960s only a few publishers— P. J. Oswald, who started the *Théâtre africain* series in 1967; *Présence africaine;* and CLE—included plays in their catalogues. The French radio network (ORTF) started its own series (Ricard, "The ORTF"). Then a new multinational company, Nouvelles Editions Africaines, created by Senegal and the Ivory Coast, built quite a sizable theater list, as did Hatier, which now publishes the prize-winning radio plays of the Concours Théâtral Inter-africain, sponsored by the ORTF, now Radio France Internationale (R.F.I.). The diffusion of drama through the radio is still a significant feature of cultural life in French-speaking Africa. The aforementioned competition is a major event, and the grand prize is usually won by writers who are either confirmed— Jean Pliya from Benin and Guy Menga from the Congo, for instance—or of great promise, like the Congo's Sony Lab'ou Tansi or Togo's Senouvo Agbota Zinsou.

A permanent hindrance for the development of theater is the lack of qualified professional actors. Guillaume Oyono-Mbia comments thus: It is unnecessary to recall, I believe, that there is still no professional theater troupe in the Cameroons. Many African countries are in the same situation. Consequently, there is nothing astonishing in the fact that dramatic authors are themselves not professionals....

> One of my dearest desires would be, as you might guess, the creation of one or several professional theater troupes in the Cameroons and elsewhere in Africa. This is so, on the one hand, for the reasons already enumerated above and, on the other hand, because authors who merit it should be able to earn a living with their work or at least be justly remunerated. (Oyono-Mbia, *Le train:* 8)

Where professional companies exist (Senegal and the Congo, for instance), they have become bureaucratized: administration and diplomacy take precedence over responsiveness to innovation and creativity. Where they do not exist, authors and actors have hopes that soon they will. A rather difficult balance must be achieved between a strictly administrative approach and an approach that would encourage only specific productions. If actors are unable to secure a means of livelihood, how can they improve their art? How can authors experiment and develop their skills? It is worth noting that some of the most creative groups of the last decade have been only marginally supported by cultural institutions. Such was the case of the Mwondo Theater from Lubumbashi, which experiments with dance drama. The same is true of Rocado Zulu from Brazzaville, which uses (in an independent way) actors from the national theater group to produce Sony Lab'ou Tansi's plays, and of Koteba, which borrows the name of the traditional genre from Abidjan and experiments with dance drama and popular French, trying thus to achieve a new synthesis of words, gestures, and music.

16.3.1.2. New Experiments

The key problem remains one of achieving this new synthesis of words, gestures, and music. Several playwrights have tried to respond to this challenge: Werewere Liking in the Cameroons with the ritual theater, and Porquet Niangouran in the Ivory Coast with *griotique*. *One grasps the intent, but unfortunately, few works exist, and the results are difficult to judge. Other experiments tackle the language problem and in the name of social realism try to reconcile the spoken French on the stage with the language spoken in the streets. One of the most successful such attempts is by the Congolese playwright Sylvain Bemba in Un foutu monde pour un blanchisseur trop honnête (1979; A wretched world for a too honest washerman).*

The quest for new means of expression, for a new dramatic form, goes along with the desire for a more direct political expression. Such at least is the case with Sony Lab'ou Tansi, especially in *Je soussigné cardiaque* (unpublished; I, the undersigned cardiac), and Chadian M. Naïndouba in *L'étudiant de Soweto* (1981; *The Soweto student*). The recent interest for the Soweto theme should also be put in perspective, since it has a strong element of parody in Zaire, but also elsewhere, as P. Ngandu Nkashama remarks:

> In denouncing apartheid ... in South Africa, by sublimating the unarmed struggle of students in the face of violence and weapons, in the search for a more just and freer society, the authors are in

fact superposing two distinct languages: the general revindication of all African countries and their personal revolt against a society that rejects them (74; my translation).

This perceptive quote helps us understand the frequent re-creation of the South African political scene in Francophone theater. It forces us to deal with an interpretative sociological criticism that cannot simply describe the contents of the play. The transition is from Shaka as emblem of the political ruler to Soweto as metaphor of political oppression, valid south as well as north of the Limpopo. For many writers caught in small countries that stifle freedom of expression, South Africa offers an easy and efficient way to parody their own situation. In many countries, what is not possible on a stage is the direct questioning of abusive political power, of what political scientists call the patrimonial character of many African regimes, especially in French-speaking Africano in Togo and Zaire, to name a few. The concept of patrimonialism is of direct relevance to the art of drama, since it is meant to describe the concentration of power in the hands of the head of state, leading to confusion between the private and public domains. The state tends to become the private property of the president, and accordingly, political criticism is taken personally and castigated directly. It is, then, quite understandable that political plays should be written by expatriate writers. Tchicaya U Tam'si, a well-known poet from the Congo, has taken to drama, and his play *Le zoulou* (1977; *The Zulu*) was produced in France Zulu) was produced in France. Aside from the resources of exile and parody, little room remains for directly political plays. The last and probably central problem of African theater in French has been, and still is, the lack of theoretical reflection, of confrontation between theory and practice. The conservatory tradition—by which I mean special technical schools of drama such as exist in Senegal, the Ivory Coast, and Zaire—by separating technical training from general university education in the humanities and social sciences, is probably responsible for this state of affairs. The situation is on the way to change. The work of P. Ngandu Nkashama on Zairean theater and of Senouvo Agbota Zinsou on Togolese theater, as well as their own plays, for instance Zinsou's *On joue la comédie* (1984; *We are doing comedy*), show a new direction, conscious of the necessity to combine social and historical information with an aesthetic awareness. Both writers are particularly concerned with the development of popular forms, either in French or in African languages, and try to adapt their writing to this grass-roots creativity. Neither writer theorizes his work in an ideological sense.

Zaire, for instance, is not a place for social criticism. But their example opens new avenues of freedom to dramatic writing.

From the analyses, it transpires that no writer of Soyinka's stature has emerged in African theater in French, and too few confirmed poets and novelists have tried their hand at dramatic writing. A strange phenomenon has occurred, though: creativity in representational arts seems to be concentrated in movies. This is where the good actors and the good directors are to be found. No dramatists equal cinematographers like Souleymane Cisse or Sembène Ousmane in the mastery of their art. The question arises, Why are there such good films and such poor plays in French-speaking Africa? One might suggest an answer by taking into account the development of the film industry as well as the history of theater. Filmmaking in French-speaking Africa was introduced at the time of the New Wave movement in France. African filmmakers had the best possible training in the late 1950s and were in the vanguard of film as an art form. On the contrary, theater was taught by schoolmasters who were not real artists. Training in the dramatic arts was continued in second-rate conservatories trying to emulate French institutions. Many African actors worked with Jean-Marie Serreau, one of the best French directors of the 1960s, but Serreau never worked in Africa, and many African actors lived in Paris. In English-speaking Africa, the reverse was true: in Nigeria, for instance, the film industry was started by second-rate Hollywood directors working with brilliant Nigerian actors and it failed, whereas a young Nigerian writer could work for several years with the Royal Court Theater, one of the leading centers of theater in the late 1950s. Theater, like film, is a specific art form, and its development cannot be confined to a mere didactic medium. African film in French was directly in tune with the New Wave. African theater in French was never really in tune with the development of the medium: the Living Theater or the Performance Group never went to Africa, and Peter Brook limited his stay to Nigeria. In the 1970s many repressive regimes came into power, hiding their cultural conservatism under the disguise of authenticity; but this authenticity is only folklore and not the adventurous search for a language that would create a new synthesis of word, music, and gesture, which would be real theater. The history of African theater in French has so far been the history of an artistic failure. Recent years have shown an awareness of this situation among young writers striving to confer autonomy on theater as an art form and to separate it from the schools. Only by cutting the umbilical cord that links it with the school can theater thrive as an art form.

References

Anonymous. *L'aube sanglante* [*Bleeding dawn*]. Conakry, Guinea: Imprimerie Patrice Lumumba, 1977. A play presented by the Republic of Guinea at the Second World Festival of African Arts and Culture, January 1977, Lagos.

Le Théâtre populaire en république de Côte d'Ivoire [*Popular theater in the Ivory Coast*]. Abidjan: Cercle culturel et folklorique de Côte d'Ivoire, 1965.

Atta-Koffi, Raphaël. *Le trône d'or* [*The golden throne*]. Paris: ORTF-DAEC, 1969.

Badian Seydou [Kouyaté]. *La mort de Chaka* [*The death of Shaka*]. Paris: Présence Africaine, 1962.

Bemba, Sylvain. *Un foutu monde pour un blanchisseur trop honnête* (*A wretched world for a too honest washerman*). Yaoundé: CLE, 1979.

Bonneau, Richard. *Ecrivains, cinéastes et artistes ivoiriens, aperçu bio-bibliographique* [*Writers, filmmakers, and artists of the Ivory Coast: a bio-bibliographical survey*]. Abidjan: NEA, 1973.

Chevrier, Jacques. *Littérature nègre* [*Black literature*]. Paris: Armand Colin, 1984.

Cornevin, Robert. *Le théâtre en Afrique noire et à Madagascar* (*Theater in Black Africa and Madagascar*) Paris: Le Livre Africain, 1970.

Culture française 3 and 4 (1982) and I (1983). Colloquium on theater in countries where French is the national, official, cultural, or popular language, 26 and 27 May 1982.

Dadié, Bernard B. *Assémien Déhylé roi du Sanwi, précédé de Mon pays et son théâtre* [*Assémien Déhylé, king of Sanwi, with My country and its theater*]. Abidjan: CEDA, 1979.

—. *Béatrice du Congo* [*Beatrice of the Congo*]. Paris: Présence Africaine, 1970.

—. *Monsieur Thôgô-Gnini. Paris: Présence Africaine, 1970.*

—. *Papa Sidi, maître escroc* [*Papa Sidi, master swindler*]. Dakar: NEA, 1975.

Dia, Amadou Cissé. *Les derniers jours de Lat Dior; La mort du Damel* [*The last days of Lat Dior; The death of Damel*]. Paris: Présence Africaine, 1965.

Diop, Birago. *L'os* [*The bone*]. Dakar: NEA, 1973.

Disasi, Justin. *Arrivé tardive* [*Late arrival*]. Présence Congolaise, 1957.

Ecole William-Ponty. «Sokame.» *Présence africaine* 3 (1948) : 627-41.

Huannou, Adrien. *La littérature béninoise de langue française des origines à nos jours* [*Beninois literature in French from its origins to the present*]. Paris: Karthala/ ACCT, 1984.

Keita, Fodeba. *Aube africaine* [*African dawn*]. In Frantz Fanon, *Les damnés de la terre* [*The Wretched of the Earth*], 157-62. Paris: F. Maspero, 1961.

Le théâtre indigène et la culture franco-africaine [«Indigenous theater and Franco-African culture»]. Special number of *L'education africaine* (Dakar, 1937).

Letembet-Ambilly, Antoine. *L'Europe inculpée* [*Europe indicted*]. Paris: 1969; Yaoundé: CLE, 1977.

Liking, Werewere. *Une nouvelle terre, suivi de Du sommeil d'injuste* [*A new land, with About the sleep of injustice*]. Abidjan: Nouvelles Éditions Africaines, 1980.
- Menga, Guy. *La marmite de Kola-Mbala* [*Kola-Mbala's cooking pot*]. Paris: ORTF, 1969.
- —. *L'oracle* [*The oracle*]. Paris: ORTF, 1969.
- Mongita, Albert. *La quinzaine: Cabaret Ya Botember* [*The fortnight: Cabaret Ya Botember*]. *La voix du congolais*, November- December 1957.
- Mouralis, Bernard. «L'Ecole William-Ponty et la politique culturelle.» In *Le théâtre négro-africain* [*Negro-African theater*]. Proceedings of the Abidjan Colloquium 1970; 31-36. Paris: Présence Africaine, 1971.
- Naïndouba, Maoundoé. *L'étudiant de Soweto* [*The Soweto student*]. Paris: Hatier, 1981.
-Ndao, Cheik Aliou. *L'exil d'Albouri, suivi de La décision* [*The Exile of Albouri, with The decision*]. Paris: P. J. Oswald, 1967.
- Niane, Djibril Tamsir. *Sikasso, ou la dernière citadelle* [*Sikasso; or, The last citadel*]. Paris: P. J. Oswald, 1971.
Niangoran, Porquet. *Soba, ou la grande Afrique* [*Soba; or, The great Africa*]. Abidjan: Nouvelles Editions Africaines, 1978.
Nokan, Charles. *Les malheurs de Tchako* [*The trials of Tchako*]. Paris: P. J. Oswald, 1968.
Nkashama, P. Ngandu, «*Le théâtre et la dramaturgie du masque au Zaïre*» [Theater and mask dramaturgy in Zaire]. *Culture française* 8(1982-83): 58-76.
Nzuji, Mukala Kadima. *La littérature zairoise de langue française* [*Zairean literature in French*]. Paris: Karthala/ACCT, 1984.
Oyono-Mbia, Guillaume. *Jusqu'à nouvel avis* [*Until further notice*]. Yaoundé: CLE, 1981.
—. *Le train spécial de son excellence/ His Excellency's Special Train*. Bilingual edition. Yaoundé: CLE, 1979.
—. *Trois prétendants, un mari*. Yaoundé: CLE, 1964. Three Suitors, One Husband. London: Methuen, 1968. *Three Suitors, One Husband and Until Further Notice*. London: Methuen, 1974.
Pliya, Jean. *Kondo le requin* [*Kondo the shark*]. Cotonou: Editions du Bénin, 1966; Yaoundé: CLE, 1981.
—. *Le secrétaire particulière* [*The private secretary*]. Cotonou, Benin: ABM, 1970; Yaoundé: CLE, 1973.-
Ricard, Alain. «*Francophonie et théâtre en Afrique de l'ouest: Situation et perspectives*» [Francophony and theater in West Africa: Situation and perspectives]. *Etudes littéraires* 71, no. 31 (December 1974): 449-76.
—. *L'invention du théâtre* (*The invention of the theater*). Paris: L'Age d'Homme, 1986.
—. " The ORTF and African Literature." *Research in African Literatures* 4, no. 2 (1974): 189-91.

—, ed. *Le théâtre en Afrique de l'ouest* [*Theater in West Africa*]. Special issue, *Revue d'histoire du théâtre* I (1975).

Salifou, André. *Tanimoune.* Paris: Présence Africaine, 1974. Scherer, Jacques. «Le théâtre en Afrique noire francophone» [*Theater in Francophone Black Africa*]. In *Le théâtre moderne*, vol. 2, edited by Jean Jacquot, 103-16. Paris: Editions du Centre national de la recherche scientifique, 1967.

Senghor, Léopold Sédar. *Chaka.* In *Poèmes.* Paris, 1956; Paris: Seuil, 1964.

—. *Liberté I: Négritude et humanisme* [*Liberty I: Negritude and humanism*]. Paris: Seuil, 1964.

Sokame. Présence africaine 4 (1948) : 627-41.

Soyinka, Wole. *A Dance of the Forest.* Oxford: Oxford University Press, 1964.

—. *Kongi's Harvest.* Oxford: Oxford University Press, 1964.

—. *The Lion and the Jewel.* Oxford: Oxford University Press, 1963.

Tansi, Sony Lab'ou. *La parenthèse de sang* (*Brackets of blood*). Paris: Hatier-Paris, 1981.

- Tchicaya, U Tam'si [Gérard Félix Tchicaya]. *Le zouluo, suivi de Uwene le fondateur* [*The Zulu, followed by Uwene the founder*]. Paris: Nubia, 1977.

- Traore, Bakary. *Le théâtre négro-africain et ses fonctions sociales.* Paris: Présence Africaine, 1958. *The Black African Theater and Its Social Functions.* Translated by Dapo Adelugba. Ibadan, Nigeria: Ibadan University Press, 1972.

- Waters, Harold A. *Black Theater in French: A Guide.* Sherbrooke, Quebec: Naaman, 1978.

- Zinsou, S. Agbota. *Le club.* Lomé, Togo: Haho, 1984.

—. "La naissance du théâtre togolais moderne" [*The birth of the modern Togolese theater*]. *Culture française* 3, no. 4 (1982): 49-57.

—. *On joue la comédie* [*We are doing comedy*]. Paris: ORTF, 1972; Lomé, Togo: Haho; Haarlem: In de Knipscheer, 1984.

17

ASPECTS OF TOGOLESE THEATRE: FROM CULTURAL PARLANCE TO POLITICAL INFLECTIONS

The study analyses the contributions of theatrical art to cultural development and sociopolitical surveys in Togo through the examination of aspects of indigenous popular theatre and the reflections of Senouvo Agbota Zinsou in *La tortue qui chante, La femme du blanchisseur, Yevi au pays des monstres* and Kangni Alemdjrodo in *Chemins de Croix, La saga des rois* and *Atterrissage*. The analysis takes into account the critical perspectives of their plays in Togolese literary thoughts that support development and highlight their ideological struggles for a freer, fairer and more fulfilled Togolese society. The main argument is that Togolese theatrical art, beside its cultural function as an ideological weapon of intellectual reflections, also functions as an instrument of sociopolitical education.

Critical receptions in Togolese literature have shown interest in theatre as a cultural product without highlighting its contributions to cultural and sociopolitical debates related to development. Discourses have limited themselves to conceptual frameworks about dramatic designations of festivals and rituals, the painful take-off of dramatic literature and the adjuncts of what Biodun Jeyifo calls "the phenomenon of interculturalism" (Jeyifo 2002: 458). Some authors admit that theater, despite the bottlenecks that have hampered its development, can today congratulate itself on its fundamental achievements in political debates which give it a place of choice in the Francophone literature of Africa; while other thinkers remain dissatisfied with the performance of this art. Martin Banham, Errol Hill and George Woodyard have expressed a negativist view on Togolese theatre by asserting: "Togo's triple heritage has had a direct influence on its modern culture, especially the theater. Literary theater declined in part as a result of an aggressive French policy that promoted literacy in French" (Benham, Hill and Woodyard 2004: 117). These three critics were joined by Simon A. Amegbleame who opines that "theater appears to be in the Ewe community [major community in the south of Togo] literature the most eclectic form (Amegbleame 1992: 192). This first group was criticized and counter-attacked by Alain Ricard and Kangni Alemdjrodo who redeployed critical thought in favor of Togolese dramatic art. Ricard points out that it would be a sad mistake to assert that theatre is a dying art in West African countries like Togo. "In Lome [Togolese capital town], I met actors emerging to become professional comedians" (Ricard 1986: 12). He is supported by Kangni Alemdjrodo who says:

> Togolese theater did not remain on the sidelines of the novel. Its beginnings date back to the late fifties with the publication in 1956 of *Fasi* by Anoumou Pedro Santos. But it was especially from the period after independence that playwrights became famous. The genre then enjoyed a great success with playwrights like Modeste d'Almeida, Senouvo Agbota Zinsou or Koffi Gomez and occulated for years the novel (Alemdjrodo 2016: 1). [My translation]

It results from the analysis of these critical tendencies that scholars do not agree on the status of theatre in Togo, failing thereby to show the contributions of drama to cultural development and the use of this art in the assessment of political life. In other words, criticism is stammering on the question of the merits of theatre in the advancement of cultural development and political analyses. That is why I propose to re-examine aspects of these issues where criticism failed to make explicit the merits of theatre in the cultural and political lives in Togo.

What I offer to do here is to examines the contributions of theatre to socio-cultural and political development, taking indigenous performances into account and the plays of two Togolese dramatists, Senouvo Agbota Zinsou and Kangni Alemdjrodo, as examples. Two points are developed. First, the contributions of indigenous popular theatre to cultural development and second, the political inflections in Zinsou and Alemdjrodo's plays : *On joue la comédie, La tortue qui chante, La femme du blanchisseur, Yevi au pays des monstres, Yevi, l'éléphant chanteur* by Agbota Zinsu, and *Chemins de croix, La saga des rois* and *Atterrissage* by Kangni Alemdjrodo. The methodological approach adopted is the postcolonial theoretical. This approach seeks to examine endogenous and exogenous forces that have shaped the literary relations between Togolese theatrical literary creativity, and socio-political and cultural developments.

17.1. The Aesthetics of Indigenous Popular Theatre and Its Contribution to Cultural Development

17.1.1. Festivals

Togo is home of cultural performances that are pivotal to the religious lives of respective communities. In every community, every ceremonial, be it secular or sacred gives rise to colorful and elaborate performances that sometimes last for days, or weeks, which showcase what John Conteh-Morgan refers to as "the finest of verbal, plastic and performing arts of the community" (Conteh-Morgan 2004: 88). Oral theatre developed in Togo in three forms: the concert-party, the *cantata* and the *albera*. The concert-party which was imported from Ghana is inspired by the English boulevard theater. It is a neighborhood theater that is being prepared and seen as a true community experience. The themes are drawn from everyday life, especially domestic problems and social conflicts. The decor does not matter. The emphasis is on the comic, the pathetic and the subtle play between identification and distancing. The performance is accompanied by songs and dances. Everything is done to constantly solicit the emotion and the implication of the audience that exchange with actors, who are part of the party. "Festive dramatization imposes on the creators of popular theater an aesthetics whose reception is easy in the decoding of symbols, metaphors and myths" (Adodo 2006: 22). Concert parties have much in common with festivals celebrated in every region of the country. For example, in January is celebrated *Kamaka* the traditional festival of the Tem of Assoli; In February *Tislim-Lifoni Oboudam* the harvest festival in Keran. In March the Tem celebrates *Gadao,* the festival of the harvests of Tem of Tchaoudjo. In April *Kurubi*, religious festival of the girls of the Oti is celebrated. In July the Moba community celabrate *Tingban-Pab,* their harvest festival; Mid-July *Evala*, the wrestling contest festival is celebrated by the Kabyè community. These religious festivals at varying degrees incorporate cantata aesthetics inside them. The cantata, a theater of religious inspiration originally from Ghana is performed through songs and dances with dominance of local music. These various festivals display theatrical spectacles with stage (usually the local public square), actors (the traditional priest or dancers dressed in masks and displaying acrobatic dances and movements), and the audience or spectators (composed by the native populations and the invited guests). The *albera* is a theater often played around the mosques on the occasion of the Muslim festivals. The performances are organized around secular subjects, dramas in the style of films that invaded the African screens in the sixties (Ricard 1986: 12). This is performed by Muslim communities during Ramadan and Tabaski.

There is another form of popular theater in Togo called Brotherhood Festival Theatre (*FESTHEF*). The Brotherhood Festival Theatre has become a major international event and a reference on the African cultural scene for some decades now. FESTHEF is a space for intellectual and artistic stimulation that encourages young African creators. The Brotherhood Festival Theatre (FESTHEF) conducts a policy of development of the live show that articulates training, creation, performance, sensitization on sociopolitical topics like civic rights, democracy, the necessity to work, artistic creativity, entrepreneurship, and dissemination of ideas about women's emancipation. Health and sanitation, housing, educational opportunities, farming cooperatives, women's economic organization and empowerment are also debated through these theatrical sessions. The festival is the key element, around which the various action plans are organized. It takes place, usually late August, in the small village of Asahoun, 45 km from Lomé, and gradually develops decentralized actions throughout the country (Lomé, Kpalimé, Atakpamé etc.). The artists are invited and welcome without distinction of origin and culture. They represent the diversity and richness of the artistic world. The FESTHEF usually includes more than one thousand people. It performs plays which are either adapted from African playwrights' works or spontaneously created to respond to the needs of the context. For instance:

- "We are among those who say no in the shade", an adaptation of Aimé Césaire's *Cahier d'un retour au pays natal*, co-produced with the French company Anopée Théâtre and the Malian Company Kouma Sô.
- "Nanou" a co-production with the French company Anopée Théâtre
- "Catharsis", a co-production with the municipality of Saint Etienne.

In addition to the festival, FESTHEF organizes shows and exhibitions, encourages mobility of national and international artists in Togo, offers the best creations to other broadcasters and participates in the design and organization of various actions such as translating Holy Scriptures or organizing Togolese drama contests. The association is also famous for the protection of the heritage, with the restoration of several cultural and artistic sites (Davié Cemetery, Sacred Forest of Asahoun and place of the purification ceremonies of Togoville) in the valley of Zio.

17.1.2. Theatrical Folktales

Theatrical folktales play an important role in the cultural education and development in Togo. Composed and performed by comedians and talented story tellers, this type of drama gathers large crowds especially on weekends and public holidays. Alain Ricard in his book *L'invention du theatre: le theatre et les comediens en Afrique noir [The Invention of the Theater: Theater and Comedians in Black Africa* (1990)] highlighted the important role played by comedians and storytellers in Togo. His demonstration applies to a category of individuals who are recognized by various names such as griots, storytellers, actors.

> The relevance of the tale, the talent of comedians ensure success, thus the professionalization. Such a research that focusses on the sociology of the actors and makes through their passage to the status of actors, the genuine birth of theatre can be retraced here through one Togolese example called in Togo and Ghana – concert-party; or as people are used to calling it in Lome, concert, this noun has integrated the standard spoken French in Lome. The comedians settle in front of a wall plan, stretch a canvas and lay out a bench. They have taken care to hang a light bulb or an oil lamp on a tree or a mat. The spectators sit on benign lines facing the actors. In front of the benches an area of two to three meter-wide is reserved for small children who wrap themselves in loincloths and lie down on the ground to watch the show (Ricard 1990: 27). [My translation]

He adds "Many concert actors made their debut in religious or school groups which played […]" (Ricard, 1990: 27). These observations point to the importance of theatrical tales and other forms of entertainment in rural, semi-urban and urban environments where people seek to entertain themselves after a day work. In Togo, tales are an integral part of social entertainment practiced by rural and sometimes urban communities. In each community, there are individuals, both men and women, who are endowed with narrative talents with which they galvanize their audiences. These storytellers and comedians have done so well that their names have been associated with this specific type of theatre. In Lome, south of Togo, for instance, the theatre of Gbadamassi and Gogoligo, the theatre of Lekponvi and Sanfou have become popular for their troop *Carre Jeune* has integrated public medias. Topics range from daily life struggles for survivals, bad marital experiences, educational challenges for parents and teachers, accommodation and housing difficulties in cities, joblessness and its consequences. The narratives of storytellers, comedians, or griots often take place either on weekend or in busy-days evenings in public places, or compounds which bring together an important and curious audience. In Lome, they are supported by many television channels including the national channel *TVT*, *TV2* channel and *LCF*. *TV Zion* channel is famous for playing and commenting the Nigerian Igbo movies. Among the Moba, a community of northern Togo, theatrical tales originally took place in rural areas, but soon integrated urban areas with the rapid transformation of peripheral villages into semi-urban areas. Story telling sessions have been integrated to local radio programs. Sometimes, if not very often, the sessions of theatrical tales can turn into a concert. This has been noted for several years with the rise of comedian singers performing their prowess in the public squares. I will consider some characteristics of these groups.

They are groups formed by the talented storytellers who often meet in the moonlight in the public square for performance and entertainment. The setting is organized by the youngsters themselves and are adapted to the shape of the theater in the round. The singer occupies the center of the stage and spectators sit on benches in semi-circle. The narratives are drawn from the African fables which always end in a moral lesson. Most of these fables have characters from well-known sub-Saharan African animals that have typical behaviors. In almost all the stories, the animals in question have become archetypes since they always have the same behaviors. For example, hare occupies the privileged place of cunning animal, and flatters its comrades, who never succeed in detecting the mystery of his tricks. Lion is associated with untamable physical power. Whether a story involves hare and lion for instance, they always happen to dribble these animals to get out of trouble. The narrator in such stories puts a special emphasis on what to remember about them. Some of these tales are accompanied by musical instruments such as *yelgue* [whistle], *lone* [talking drum] *natun* [blowing horn]. What gives a theatrical color to these narratives is the participative interaction between the storyteller / narrator and his audience. The audience actively participates with the clapping of hands or comments. Occasionally the storyteller sketches steps of dances, appeals to the audience and is joined by volunteers who also dance to make the atmosphere rather cheerful. He makes mimetic gestures that identify him with the characters of the fables he narrates. Mimes and gestural language are very strong in theatrical tales. Apart from the narrative, other games are also practiced. Riddles and proverbs are quoted in recitatives to create spectacles. The storyteller calls the audience each time by a signal interjection, *terrrrrrrrrr*. When the riddle or proverb is given, the audience is asked to give the answer without hesitation. The first who finds the right answer often nods the acclamations of the narrator and his companions. Here are few examples of these riddles and proverbs:

Proverbs and Riddles

Moba Riddle or Proverb	English Translation	Intended Meaning	Moral Lesson Taught
Riddle: *Ja jinjing guul bad*	A short man who subdued the king	Slippery ground, symbol of dangerous lusts like women, money, power	One should be wise not to be addicted to such tempting and corrupting values like women, money and power
Riddle: *Nna den u mani gui fan gluol*	My mother dried gombo and it disappeared the next morning	Moon or teeth, symbols of youth vigor always move with time	We must get old someday. We need to be wise and humble in life.
Riddle: *tag yin g bon gu kad u jium g muan*	The man who emptied his drinking water jar at the sight of clouds (assuming rain will fill it)	The fool	It is foolish to rely on promises and destroy or trample down the old garment or asset you have in hand
Proverb : *B'gini kpi luong*	By trying one can actually kill an elephant	It is by aiming high in life that one eventually gets a good social position	Dream big and dare to fail

Proverb : *Yenbua naag g fag*	Where there is a will, there is a way	Success comes when, one is determined to succeed	Let us be willing and determined for success
Proverb: *G bual kpaab ko lantuna*	Ill-will is the source of laziness	Laziness is the main cause of poverty or failure	One should run away from laziness
Proverb : *Nassanliig kan nu nungblaa*	The first to come is the best served	The best places are for those who are excellent	We must strive to be excellent and to deserve better positions
Proverb : *Ni monii cien waad*	The wise man knows how to get away from a fool	Wisdom is the best virtue through which one avoids all kinds of problems	Let us be wise to better solve our problems
Proverb: *Yami cua diuog*	Through wisdom, one can live in peace in his house	To build a household or to live a successful marriage requires a lot of wisdom	Let us be wise to build a good family
Proverb : *Tuoni tie niil*	Work makes man	Through hard work we become useful to ourselves and to our society	Let us be always industrious
Proverb : *Juun tie nalmani*	Patience/endurance is a great wealth	When we are patient we overcome a lot of troubles	Let us be patient
Proverb: *Nu yen kan fid gui bobinn tuolg*	One hand cannot tie a baobab tree	It takes two persons to achieve something good	Unity makes strength, let us be united

Proverbial performance takes place during story telling times in Moba land and follow a theatrical display. Story tellers gather crowds (the audience), the performance takes place in a public square, and the audience vividly participates with handclapping, drum beating, gong rattling, whistling and dances. It can be observed that these riddles and proverbs are in the main moralistic. They essentially aim at teaching moral values, good behavior and encouraging people to work, to be responsible and social. They are often dissected after the stories. Sometimes these proverbs-riddles may constitute in themselves a recreational evening. The atmosphere is often friendly, interspersed with laughter and explanatory comments either by the narrator or by the spectators. The interest for the theater is that even with modern written literature, these riddle proverbs have served and continue to serve by contemporary writers as a raw material to create African originality in plays. The recovery of the oral tradition serves as a bedrock for modern literature.

The second forms of theatrical expression are the very popular songs and dances of the girls commonly called *ampe* and *bimbaad*. In the case of *ampe*, the girls clap their hands and jump into the air before landing with agility on their feet. By executing these jumps, they count the goals they score. The *bimbaad* games are played in a circle or a semicircle where they sing, dance round and round, knocking their buttocks in sequential rhythms. Here also, a main singer takes the lead of the song and the others assist her by taking back the refrain. The atmosphere is very lax, lively and cheerful on hearing the melody produced by the singer. It is not uncommon to see drummers accompany this performance and a real theatrical atmosphere sets in. These forms of games are widespread and practiced in the majority of the meetings of women and girls. The second group is the griot singers. These often serve as companions to the chief or king. They are versed in the knowledge of oral tradition. Hache-Bissette highlights this description by saying:

> The traditional oral literature of Black Africa is mostly related to everyday life, so it is likely to be said, sung or tapped at all times of the day: women sing when they go to draw water and, In the hottest hours of the afternoon, the old men, seated in front of their huts, throw themselves into the narrative of great legends and proverbs while trying to impart to the children the teachings of their wisdom (Hache-Bissette 2005: 11). [My translation]

Traditionally, tales are narrated in the evening, at nightfall, once the labors and work of the day are completed. The moment is conducive to listening and all the population of the village (children, old people, men and women) is grouped in the village public arena. The recitation of the oral literature is a privileged moment which gives rise to exchanges between the villagers but also with the griot storyteller. While the latter often appears as a wise man and is respected for the knowledge and wisdom accumulated throughout life, he is not the only one to speak. In turn, the villagers themselves go into a narrative, share an anecdote, suggest a riddle, evoke a proverb, the word circulating in the audience. In some beliefs in Togo, telling in the evening also means helping the night to succeed the day and ensuring the good passage of the following day.

17.1.2. Political Inflections: Senouvo Agbota Zinsou and Kangni Alemdjrodo Speculating on Political Morality in Togo

The plays of Senouvo Agbota Zinsou and Kangni Alemdjrodo are part of the political and social satire of public and political life in Togo. Zinsou has adopted the theater of the absurd as a dramatic mode. The theater of the absurd that had appeared in the 20th century at the time of the Second World War, was characterized by a total break with the other genres of theater in vogue, namely comedy and tragedy. It is a genre dealing with the absurdity of man. Its movement was linked to the fall of humanism due to the effects of the First World War (Marvin Carlson 1993: 344-45). The goal that Zinsou aims at by opting for the theater of the absurd is very likely impacting audiences through distancing which consists in revealing to the spectator a truth by creating defamiliarization. *On joue la comedie* (1984) translates this ideology of the absurd approach by the playwright. Some critics assimilate his theater to that of the German playwright Bertholt Brecht. In his article "African Theater and Theater in Quebec: a Comparative Approach", Suzie Suriam gives the following testimony about Senouvo Agbota Zinsou:

> That is why he never forgets that the reader/spectator is witnessing the creation of a work; underlining, for example, the alternation of the 'read'/ 'speak' didascalies. Zinsou even pointed out that the goal of theater as he conceived it was to involve all the spectators personally, hence an indispensable recourse to distancing. One recognizes there the double movements of the epic theater of Bertolt Brecht which rests on the *verfremdungseffekt* effect of distancing. A distancing reproduction is a reproduction which, of course, makes the object recognizable but at the same time appears to be foreign (Suriam 2002: 21).

So Zinsou purposefully uses distancing or defamiliarization to show how far political leaders in Togo have gone from the norms. For instance, in *La tortue qui chante [The Singing Tortoise],* tortoise is used as a prophet and fortune teller, prophesying good future for the king and proclaiming that his rule is God-given. When audiences see this imagery, they feel a distance between actors and spectators. Here, unlike the European theatre of the absurd, he combines comedy and tragedy, but keeps the theme and dramatic techniques. The artist's commitment to a more just, democratic and transparent society is read through his theatrical art. Neither the king, nor Podogan, nor Agbo-Kpanzo are really motivated by a patriotic ambition for the nation. They are all at the service of their 'stomachs'. Moreover, once in power, no one wants to let go. It important to note that Zinsou uses magical realism as a narrative device. As evidenced by the use of the magical predictions of the tortoise to claim the divine origin of his leadership. Magical realism becomes a metaphor the meanings of which are the indestructibility of the throne, and the leader's office for life. Through this metaphor, Agbota Zinsou makes a satirical but realistic deciphering of his country which he knows so well, having been close to power, when he was appointed High Councilor of the Republic, Parliament of the Transition before his exile in Germany in 1993.

Setting plays a determinant role in the definition and shaping of Zinsou's creative ideology. It functions as regulator, having incidence on characters' behaviors. *La tortue qui chante* is set in a traditional setting and makes a satirical portrayal of the flagrant attitude of some Togolese officials who negotiate their services to the head of state for the only purpose of their bellies. The story is simple and the style easy to understand because the playwright wants to make the message accessible to the public: The king of a small village (the name of which is not mentioned) is in search of an assistant, to assist him in his duties; and it is Podogan (big belly in Ewe language) who jumps on the occasion to be a candidate. But he runs up against another rival Agbo-Kpanzo the hunter. In the language of the author, Ewe, this name means "the ram carries fire", symbol of danger). The author plays on the metaphor of the name he gives to the character to load the play with a satirical ideology: the confrontation of Podogan (the big belly) and Agbo-Kpanzo, the ram who carries fire) gives a profound meaning that brings the spectator or reader to reflect on the absurdity of certain men who confront one another with the mystical power, kill their rivals or make bloody sacrifices, initiatory rites through fire to occupy a privileged position next to the king. Agbo-Kpanzo meets the tortoise who sings his happiness and predicts that he will be the chosen king but on condition that he declines the current post offered by the king and that he waits patiently. To this end, he must work his character, his inner man, to forge a moral strength of endurance, courage and perseverance. In the symbolism of the play, the tortoise takes on the meaning of resistance, silent perseverance and hard work. The play ends on a note of satisfaction and contradictions as Agbo-Kpanzo did not comply with the request of the tortoise. Meanwhile, the king was seduced and interested in the mystical power of the tortoise to predict the future of the people he encounters. Here the king wants to keep the tortoise to hear the predictions he would like, that is to say, that the gods chose him to reign for life on the kingdom. Starting from the interpretation of the names of the characters, their actions and the plot of the story in *La tortue qui chante*, Zinsou's ideology emerges as a humorist and satirical attack on African political patronage of the great sycophants who bless the "yeses" of political leaders to fill their bellies. In an article entitled "The Return of Klatcha", Senouvo Agbota-Zinsou declares:

> [...] knowing that I attach particular importance to the symbolism of the tortoise, whose sense is quiet resistance, silent perseverance and ironic lucidity, facing the noisy agitations ... In their visions and actions, the public authorities are distinguished by their conception of the essential on the one hand and their aloofness on the other, this aloofness being the main characteristic of some. It is in this that the degree of human development and civilization of a country is measured, and not by some action of false brilliance, of trompe-l'oeil. When the vision is well thought out and clearly defined, and the actions taken after a thorough deliberation, especially after a good democratic debate, the risks for these powers to fall into aloofness, bathing in carefree attitude are less. Error is human, but persevere in error, that is to say, deliberately and deliberately in errors, with the same methods, the same men as far as possible, if not new ones which resemble perfectly the old ones who play the comedy of novation, is properly machiavelic (Agbota-Zinsou 2015: 1).

It transpires from this extract that the ideology of Agbota-Zinsou seeks to expose the political and social deviations for the purpose of rectifying deviant mores. It obtains that the writer becomes the conscience of his society and gives himself the duty to say what is going wrong in his society.

On joue la comedie [They Play Comedy] (1984) is an allegorical play, in the sense that the writer moves the local from Togolese premises to South African. At the heart of this play is an ideological projection of the frustrations and frictions experienced by the Togolese in the face of tribalism in the administration of the country, although in reading the author engages South Africa grappling with social injustices of the Apartheid regime. For a superficial reading, it is obvious that the framework of history takes place in South Africa under the Apartheid regime. The bone of contention between the whites and blacks is the color skin. But beyond the superficial, there are many similarities and reconciliations between the political experiences of Togo and those of South Africa. Though there is no color bar in Togo, ethnic frictions and regional disparities are dominant. The ethnic group of the president in power is accused of being privileged to the detriment of the others. History informs about political tensions between the military and civil society, culminating in many killings and property destruction to the extent that it became necessary to create Truth, Justice and Reconciliation Commission to mediate and pacify the victims. Such commission was copied on South African model. Here, Zinsou creates with great mastery of theatrical techniques a play-within-a play, where the actors perform inside the play. This technique of inserting a game into a game is used to highlight the method of distancing which is the preferred mode in Zinsou. For example, Chaka in place of the preaching of the old man, substituted imprecations to the god N'koulou N'koulou. *On joue la comedie [They Play Comedy]* is a play performed mainly by the Togolese national troupe in a staging led by the author Senouvo Agbota Zinsou.

The focus of *La femme du blanchisseur* [*The Wife of the Bleacher*] (1987), *Yevi au pays des monstres* [*Yevi in the Land of Monsters*], *Yevi et l'elephant chanteur* [*Yevi and the Singing Elephant*] (2000) and *Medicine* (2003), is the questioning of the political morality and leadership ambitions which most often animate Togolese leaders and their ruling circles. Adjunct themes include marital unfaithfulness and attendant consequences.

Adultery is treated with rigor in Zinsou; it is a vice and a headache in his hero characters as is read in *La femme du blanchisseur (The Wife of the Bleacher)*. Here, too, he reveals the social satire and the indignation he feels at the absence of morality and the poster of the hypocrisy of some African elites: "Our duty is to provide this little happiness to those who Without us would never know." We must treat the evil at the root. In his conception, therefore, the lack of morality in the individual when not taken seriously can become a collective evil. In *La femme du blanchisseur* [*The Wife of the Bleacher*], the setting is contemporary Togolese society, and the play depicts the ambitions of married men who cross their marital thresholds to seek other women who in most cases create more problems for them and jeopardize their homes. Afua is a man of about fifty years married to two women and father of numerous children. However, despite his age, his renown as an inveterate seducer ceased to spread in his society. He leaves his wives and endeavors to obtain the favor of the laundress's wife. But his inability to achieve his objectives, as the protective jealousy of the co-wives and the revenge of its former mistresses stand in his way. Here, as in the other plays, Zinsou emphasizes the moralization of the public by a theatrical lesson. In matrimonial matters, contentment is a source of great happiness. The insatiable craving for women is the source of all the devastating evils of marriage.

Sociopolitical satire is a privileged narrative mode for Zinsou because even when it changes literary genre, the technique and the thematic remains. For example, in *Yevi et l'éléphant chanteur*, he takes up satirical art to call for political morality. Yevi, who has already been made hero in several works, is a character dear to the author since he assigns him a special mission. Begun in an adventure of conquest of power in a foreign country called Cotes-des-Merveilles, he finds himself struck with troublesome experiments in the whirlwind of Machiavellian machinations orchestrated by the people he meets. These people are among others King Bodemakutu 1st, and his people. They act in a system that the writer calls *bodemakutism* characterized by the reign of violence and the cult of personality. The epic character of the book makes it easy for the author to intermingle humans with animals. Thus, one sees the elephant, leopards and guinea fowls easily having recognizable features. Given that symbolism has a prominent place in Zinsu's works, these animals at varying degrees of representation are distinguished by the abusive behavior, especially the leopard - known for its cunningness and its ability to catch its prey. The elephant is symbol of dictatorship and guinea fowl symbol of fragility and vulnerability. Social criticism and political denunciation are the imprint of his art. Zinsou states:

> Who is Togolese, or African conscious and capable of projecting himself into the future, whose country, like Germany, has known tragedies, bloody and nightmarish days throughout history, which, passing near this monument, would not think of the victims of his own country, who died for having resisted the totalitarian power …? In Togo one would surely write one day: «To the victims of the totalitarian dynasty of Gnassingbe, dead in torture places, dead in the street, dead drowned in the lagoon, shot at the Freau Garden, dead rejected on our beaches, dead in Agombio dead to the fauna of Mango … dead of hunger, beating, burned dead in carcasses of burnt vehicles, … all killed by a power that has always preferred macabre deals to the essentials (Agbota-Zinsou 2015: 1).

Here, the dramatist has removed the artist's mask to talk directly about the realities of his country. This formula underlies the logic that fiction needs to be endorsed with direct statements by the author. Zinsou addresses his criticism to the regime of the former head of state Gnassingbe Eyadema whose name he mentioned, to question the violence caused by the army who acted on its behalf. In this logic, the non-fiction position takes part in a dynamic of reinforcing the stream of ideas which seek to redress the political face of the country by a confrontational criticism in the writing. The writer unveils his critical ideology which is not limited only to fiction, but to the internet and social networks as well, to be heard. Perhaps there is a paradox between the past life and the ideological outlook of Zinsou who becomes declamatory and aggressive in his remarks when one remembers that he was one of the beloved of President Eyadema, with whom he first collaborated as the founding director of the Togolese national theater before taking up more senior positions.

Kangni Alemdjrodo is the second Togolese playwright whose work I will consider. His plays are noted on the international scene for his important ideological struggles for democracy, individual liberties and human fulfillment. Three plays will be examined: *La saga des rois* [*The Saga of Kings*, 1992], *Atterrissage* [*Landing*, 2002] and *Chemins de croix* [*The Ways of the Cross*, 2005]. The theater of Alemdjrodo focuses on three fundamental axes: the emancipation of the girl in a traditional environment, the situation of democracy and development in his country, and the problem of immigration. *La saga des rois* [*The Saga of the Kings*] illustrates the ideological struggle of the author for democracy and the rooting of human rights. The author tackles the oppression of young girls in a traditional environment where excision (a form of genital mutilation) and despotism of patriarchy reign supreme. *La saga des rois* can be rated a play of social education and political morality check-up. The story is set in the village of Sorgolo in the morning. He introduces us to a heated debate between the notables of the village about the excision of girls at marriageable age, a ritual that often takes place before marriage. Excision is the ritual that consists in ablating part of the clitoris of young girls. The debate divides the group of notables on the issue. While some think, it would be wise to ask for and obtain the consent of parents before submitting the girls to the ritual, others do not find this procedure necessary. Not having found common ground, this debate was postponed until the next day. At the appointed time, at the large gathering of parents and notables in the village chief's compound, the news falls like a heap of ice on the assembly, that the ritual of excision will indeed take place. At this precise point, a fierce opposition from a mother requires the assent of the others who take upon themselves to claim to the chief the revocation of the ceremony of excision. A serious conflict opposes the women, victims of this body mutilation on the one hand, and the council of notables on the other hand. But above all in the discussions, the fundamental question of the legitimacy of the political power of the village chief and his transition was raised: "We want the mouth that no longer eats for her alone. If one of you wants to be king, we do not oppose it but in the future, we demand that the people be associated with power" (*LSDR*: 41). Theater becomes a key instrument of political opinion. Here in this extract, it is the women who speak to the notables and the king. They demand a legitimate power that can govern them and the people's association in decision-making. Alemdjrodo has given his female characters the tenacity and intellectual courage to claim their rights. Also, important in the play is the fact that Alemdjrodo creates and stages a prodigal son as king. This person has neither intellectual nor political maturity to direct the village, and yet he is the head of this village, out of respect for tradition and not as a democratic choice of the villagers. What is shocking is that he does not want to accept the injunctions of his people in matters of democracy and human rights: The Child King: "Leave me alone. I do not care about democracy" (*LSDR*: 55).

The grumbling is great among the villagers, for the king continues: "... insulting whoever he wants (except me), kissing whoever he wants, shitting or wanting, I offered them real democracy and instead of applauding, this people detested me" (*LSDR*: 56). This episode evokes the symbolism of the clan and ethnic dynasty of political power in the African countries of which Togo can be pointed out as an example. Highly symbolic, the scene represents the satire of a people governed by a leader whose immaturity undermines the principles of political morality. Alemdjrodo wants to be realistic and pragmatic by challenging the collective consciousness through art. Between tradition and reason, what must prevail was to be determined by the political maturity of the people. The fact that women declamatorily claim for their rights to be associated to the decision-making process in a patriarchal society of the village denotes the writer's ambition to create the beginning of revolution so much desired by all the oppressed masses of the society.

A description of the traditional society in Togo can help us to better understand the magnitude of the problem Alemdjrodjo deals with in *La saga des rois*. Furthermore, it must be said that the phenomenon of excision is a very serious problem in Togo, especially in rural areas. The fact that Alemdjrodo chooses to inscribe this topic in his theater denotes his commitment to the improvement of the girl's living conditions. Practiced since the precolonial age, excision is a serious societal scourge in several villages in Togo till date.

The consequences range from bleeding and uncontrollable hemorrhage to the death of the victims. Mention should be made of genital infections and transmission through these wounds of lethal diseases such as AIDS, syphilis, to mention but a few. Sterility due to imputations of body organs have also been reported. Alemdjrodo has chosen popular theatre as communicative mode in order to gather the largest audience possible to convey sensitization message about the damages of excision so as people will change. Kangni Alemdjrodo has chosen to discuss this theme and its target, because the phenomenon of excision is serious in Togo. *La saga des rois* is usually performed as a popular theatre to gather the largest audience possible. According to a 2008 report of the Togolese Ministry of Social Action, Promotion of Women, Protection of Children and the Elderly

> The prevalence of female genital mutilation is a function of ethnicity. The ethnicities in which they are practiced are: Cotocoli / Tem (25.6%), Tchamba (25.5%), Yanga (25.0%), Peulh (21.2%) and Mossi , 8%). As for religion, 34.2% of Muslim women surveyed were circumcised, compared with 0.6% of Catholic women, 9.7% of women of traditional religion and 1.1% of women of other religions. Also, qualitative data confirm this trend. However, group discussions and interviews with religious leaders show that the practice of excision is not a recommendation of religion (MASPFPEPA 2008: 26). [my translation]

This report draws a sad picture of the situation of women subjected to genital mutilation in traditional areas in Togo and the score is high. In total, an average of 30 per cent of girls are victims of genital mutilation in traditional settings. Alemdjrodo is conscious of the extent of the phenomenon and has made it his project of theatrical combat. At the heart of the problem, as revealed in analysis of *La saga des rois* [*The Saga of the Kings*], is the absence of jurisdictions or institutions that are capable of listening to and handling cases of disputes related to genital mutilations. The playwright translates this reality through the claim of the villagers who demand that the power that will govern them will now be democratic, and participatory when it comes to decision-making: "Put foresight and power on the principles of democracy. This will be the case for centuries to come. The land will bear the signs of Democracy. Or it will be handed over to barbarism" (*LSDR*: 54). The sociopolitical vision emerging from the analysis of *La saga des rois* is a Togolese society freed from vicious practices and responsive to the solicitations of the development of its citizens. This vision calls for the emancipation of women, their autonomy in financial matters and their participation in political life.

The second play by Alemdjrodo under consideration is *Chemins de Croix, [The Ways of the Cross]*. Two students, Amouro and Amel Kanye, are in prison for distributing leaflets claiming for students a better distribution of scholarships and an improvement of their living conditions: "The creation of jobs, freedom of expression, the liberation of the students locked up in the prisons of the Empire" (*CDC*: 14). A tete-a-tete between the two students (interrupted by the intervention of the prison guard, the chaplain, Lucette, Amouro's girlfriend) offers them an opportunity to reflect on the chances of the revolutionary ideal in the face of an existential reality: "how can we dream of positively changing the country when, on all sides, material and emotional temptations arise above all? (*CDC: 11*)" Amouro embodies the ideal of the pure revolutionary, the one who does not ask questions about his commitment, who knows / wants to "speak only with his heart" (*CDC*: 10). Amel, Daddy's son and ethnic brother of the Emperor (and thus taking advantage of the ethnic patronage of the country) makes up much more with the material dimension of life and recognizes that it occurs in the life of every person « to feel in his flesh the fear, the suffering, the hunger, the cold and the thirst (*CDC*: 10-11)»

Through this skillful artifice Alemdjrodo reminds his audience that they are indeed in the theater, a discursive space of possibilities and dreams that can spur up intellectual reflection about ways of implementing change in society. Amouro is shot dead by the «valiant soldiers» of the Empire as the speaker announces. Yet, he does not betray his revolutionary ideal and his death does not go unnoticed as he feared. Here is a play which, in three sequences or acts, illustrates eloquently the difficulties of students' political engagement in an African country like Togo in the late 1980s stifling under dictatorship. *Chemins de croix* constructs revolutionary potential through creative literature.

Furthermore, one can contend that the artistic ideology of Alemdjrodo denotes a position-taking on the side of the oppressed, the weak and the most destitute of the community. It is in line with the statement of Aimé Césaire who said "My mouth will be the mouth of misfortunes that have no mouths. My voice is the freedom of those who sink into the dungeon of despair" (Césaire 1956) [my translation]. What makes the particularity of *Chemins de Croix [Way of the Cross]* is the creative genius of the dramatist in representing through theater the socio-political realities of his country of the 1980s. This play, which depicts the struggle of young academic elites for the improvement of their living conditions and above all the inaction of the authorities, marks a decisive turning point in Alemdjrodo's dramatic journey. The socio-political reflection role that theater played on the spectator and the reader is bound to provoke a germ of idea inclined towards the necessity of change. This denotes the direct correlation between the daily life and the artistic representation of this experience on the stage as the audience is invited to reflect to determine the course of action to be carried out. Between the dramatist, his text and his representation on the stage or his mise-en-scene there is a participative complicity. Spectators plunge their gaze into a discursive semiology that provokes thought and criticism either of oneself, of society or of political actors. It follows that no one leaves unaffected the live-theater. In this logic, Kagni Alemdjrodo is an artist engaged in literary, social and political discourse for a better future of man and his society. The positive impact of theater on the public remains his predilection. This writer is concerned with both the content of his art and the impact it produces on his audience and hence on his society. This, it seems to me, explains the author's growing enthusiasm for the theater to the detriment of other genres such as romance and poetry. In an interview with Susanne Gehrmann, he says:

> Ah, I believe that drama has all the advantages over the novel. The problem of the novel is that anyway, whatever you do, readership will always be limited, but theater allows you to reach a bigger audience. You write a piece of theater, you are sure that 10, 20, 30 years later, this piece will continue to be performed from time to time in several places of the world. I notice this with my play *Chemins de croix [Ways of the Cross]*, my very first piece of theater. From time to time I read on the internet that the play was performed in Kinshasa by a troop of amateurs. I see that it has been performed in the Central African Republic. Someone writes to me from the United States to tell me: «We will perform this play in translation in a small theater in New York.» Each time I am surprised that one has the impression that theater material is easily transposable from one place to another. As for the novel, once you have it published, it is there, freezing, waiting for a problematic adaptation (Alemdjrodo 2015: 120).

If theater as stipulated by Alemdjrodo has a vast and profound impactation force, it follows that society cannot remain indifferent to its message. Thus, staging plays, broadcasting radio and television programs are privileged means to strengthen educational system. Theatre becomes a weapon of reflection, propagation of ideas and transformation of mentalities from ignorance to knowledge. The well-being of citizens is the fundamental aim. This well-being can only be achieved if the right information is conveyed. Alemdjrodo responds to this call for art to revalorize the artistic and cultural heritage, and to participate in a revitalization of social ethics which tend to be weakened today with the invasion of the artistic products of moral degradation of Western countries. In a discursive logic that is concerned with education, training and information about being, with respect to duties, rights and responsibilities towards society, the writer endows himself with intellectual principles that transcend political or ethnic limitations and divisions, to bring together within the same family all the citizens who share the cherished values of the Togolese nation; respect for the other and participatory development in a nationalist ethic. Art is transported from fiction to realism to render a utilitarian service to the community. The cultural fact is an offshoot of the social fact from which it draws its umbilical cord and its force so that the imaginary can only realize its objective in a frame where the reflection aims at the renovation. Togolese theater is present on the international scene thanks to the ingenious creations of several artists of whom Alemdjrodo is part.

Then, the writer turns to a wider audience that shares the same development needs: Africa in its globality. Thus in 2002 Alemdjrodo published *Atterrissage, [Landing]* which deals with one of the most burning problems of the African society, that of the illegal immigration and the questions of insecurity facing the compatriots who engage in this adventure. We are introduced to two Guinean teenagers Yaguine Koita (14 years) and Fodé Tounkara (15 years), two stowaways of a Sabena flight from Guinea to Brussels. Their bodies were discovered on 2nd August 1999 in the landing gear of the aircraft at Brussels-National Airport. Alemdjrodo through these tragic episodes levels a severe criticism to European Union leaders who have not taken any preventive measures to curve the intractable phenomenon of clandestine immigration. African leaders too are to be blamed for not guaranteeing security to the youth in terms of education, employment, food, housing and health. In *Aterrissage*, the lack of hope in their country Guinee, pushes Yaguine and Fodé to flee to Europe from where they expect well-being and promising future. The smugglers who charge them very expensively use the chaotic situation of the country as incentive to persuade the two teenagers to embark on the journey: "Imagine only my efforts to help you leave this shit country, where young people have only one alternative: to take up arms or prostitute themselves" (*A*: 11). This brings Fodé to become worried with his future as he does not see a prospective promising outlet:

> We must leave here; things have become headless or tail-free, nothing works as expected. The school, to learn how to build, the hospital to cure diseases. Even rain is rare. Everything is closed. And Yaguine and I do not want to drag on the streets to dream that this war ... idiots stops, who knows when, and that the school resumes, that the hospital again opens its portal to take your meds. If at least we were going to school again, but no ... My Carnélia, in the streets, drags only dog-men, those who smoke and drink and say to you: «Hey, little, if you came to war With us, you would have everything, the villas of the wealthy merchants, the women want you here, since you would be given a big gun! (*A:* 13)

In this reply, Fodé gives two major reasons for his desire to immigrate to Europe: a dark future and a lack of security in his home country Guinee. This is the reality of many African countries whose populations live in destitution and insecurity engendered by «bad life» and conflict. Carnélia seeing Yaguine and Fodé preparing the clandestine trip to Europe expresses her fear for young people carried away but who never returned, leaving the village children, mothers and elderly women totally desperate:

> Ma Carnelia.
> Then I say to you: Go! Go but come back! Even if there is no one selling the car of my dreams, come back! Even empty pockets, come back! I need something to be buried. Of arms. To transport my body and dig the earth where I would go to rest my rheumatism. Others that you are gone, they have not returned.
> Fode
> Egoists!
> Ma Carnelia: No ! Fear lest they should fail. Going poor to adventure, return poor, as much die there, they say. Still glad that the earth welcomes poor and rich, indifferently. Only those who are successful pay in advance, and dearly return the corpse on the ground of departure. Just to show off, one last time. With their coffin coming from Europe, brand new as a coach (*A: 14*).

Alemdjrodo downgrades the rebuttals of clandestine immigration that offers no positive perspectives to the youth who engage in such deal. The enterprise that comes under attack here is the adventurism per se that leaves no good future to Yaguine and Fodé. The playwright has strategically constructed irony of situation by having the two characters meet death instead of life and happiness. Such irony builds up the tragedy of the play and functions as a technical device to convey the message that adventurism is a misguiding enterprise that pays evil when necessary precautions are not taken to guarantee travelling security.

Fodé and Yaguine, in *Atterrissage*, fell into the net of ruthless smugglers, having no sense of humanity and craving for interest, lust and profit. They imagine elsewhere different «from home», as land where wealth is within reach. Just bend over to pick it up: "We leave but we will return, like the desert locust at the harvest season. We'll come back rich, Mama. Very rich even. It is said that in the white man's country, even those who do not work have enough to eat and drink" (*A: 14*). Fodé and Yaguine are dreaming deep for this distant land where the snow falls. A land of abundance and happiness. This dream is undoubtedly the source of a blind fascination that drives African immigrants to the most tragic adventures. Alemdjrodo conveys the message that measures should be taken by authorities both in Africa, Europe and America to solve the problem of clandestine immigration. Conditions must be created to keep the youngsters at school until they are enough educated to get jobs. Unless the problem is solved at preventive levels, teenagers will continue venturing in misguided adventurism at the cost of their lives. This situation is the consequence of an alienation which turns to the tragic since the young candidates for exile, blinded by «the western mirage, have no other choice than exile in Europe to try to escape misery. In the clandestine immigration, the journey is already a slow descent into hell. The characters, Yaguine and Fode, endured hell in the landing gear before dying.

The study aimed at showing the contributions of theatre in the expression of cultural development and political analyses in Togo. The main results I came up with are three. Firstly, indigenous popular drama has actively participated in the cultural lives and identity affirmation of Togolese populations as they have used it to celebrate and express their religious convictions. Secondly, Senouvo Agbota Zinsou and Kangni Alemdjrodo have revitalized the theatrical literature and criticism through a politically committed play that criticize and expose the deviations of the political regimes in Togo. Thirdly, Togolese drama is characterized by a critical outlook that defines its priorities as art committed to social education, political analysis and cultural dynamization. From the intellectual viewpoint of scholarship, critical debates are open legacies aiming to redirect new orientations of critical studies of drama in Togo.

References

Adodo, Ketline. *Etude sur la poésie, la tradition orale et la littérature au Togo et programme d'initiation pour les élèves de l'école primaire.* Document written in preparation for the First World Conference on Arts Education held in Lisbon, Portugal in March 2006. 2001. Web. http://portal.unesco.org.

Alemdjrodo, Kangni. « Interview ». Susanne Gehrmann et Dotsé Yigbe, eds., *Créativité inter médiatique au Togo et dans la Diaspora togolaise.* Berlin : Verlag. 2015.

------------------- *Chemins de Croix.* Cameroun : Bertoua. 2005.

------------------- *La saga des rois.* Lome : Nouvelles Editions Africaines. 1992.

------------------- *Atterrissage.* Cameroun : Bertoua. 2002.

Amegbleame, Simon A. "Le théâtre dans la littérature Ewé. " *Peuple du Golfe du Benin : Aja-éwé : colloque de Cotonou.* Paris : Karthala. 1984.

Anne, Gaudin. *Les contes illustrés jeunesse d'Afrique noire dans le paysage éditorial et culturel français.* Mémoire. Paris : Institut Universitaire de Technologie René Descartes. Web. http://www.ricochet-jeunes.org. 2005.

Apedo-Amah, Ayayi Togoata. "Togo". In Don Rubin, Ousmane Diakhate and Hansel Ndumbe Eyoh. Eds. *The World Encyclopedia of Contemporary Theatre.* New York: Routledge Taylor and Francis Group. 316-320. 2001.

Benham, Martin, Errol Hill and George Woodyard. *The Cambridge Guide to African and Carribbean Theatre.* Cambridge: Cambridge University Press. 2004.

Benham, Martin, ed. *A History of Theatre in Africa.* Cambridge: Cambridge University Press. 2004.

Carlson, Marvin. *Theories of the Theatre: A Historical and Critical Survey, from the Greeks to the Present.* Ithaca: Cornell University Press. 1993.

Césaire, Aimé. 1956. *Cahier de retour au pays natal.* Paris : Présence Africaine.

----------------. *Et si les chiens se taisaient.* Présence Africaine. 1958/1997.

Chevrier, Jacques. *Littératures d'Afrique noire de langue française.* Paris : Nathan. 1999.

Ricard, Alain. *L'invention du théâtre : le théâtre et les comédiens en Afrique noire.* Lausanne: L'Age d'homme. 1986.

Lamko Koulsy. *Emergence difficile d'un théâtre de la participation en Afrique noire.* Thèse de Doctorat. France : Limoges Cedex. Web. *epublications.unilim.fr/thèses/2003/lamko-koulsy/lamko-koulsy.* 2003.

Ministère de l'Action Sociale, de la Promotion de la Femme, de la Protection de l'Enfant et des Personnes Agées. 2008. *Etudes sur les Mutilations Génitales Au Togo.* Lomé : UNICEF Togo. Web. https://www.unicef.org/wcaro/wcaro_togo

Suriam, Suzie. «Théâtre africain et théâtre québécois: un essai de rapprochement». In *L'Annuaire théâtral : revue québécoise d'études théâtrales.* 31. 12-32. 2002.

Zinsou, Senouvo-Agbota. «Le Retour de Klatcha» http://news.icilome.com. 2015.

------------- *La tortue qui chante. La femme du blanchisseur. Yevi au pays des monstres.* Paris. Karthala. 1980.

------------------- *Yevi et l'éléphant chanteur.* 2000.

18

AFROPOLITANISM IN ADE SOLANKE'S *PANDORA'S BOX*

This chapter examines postmodernist aesthetics and the articulation of Afropolitanism and cultural ambivalence in Ade Solanke's *Pandora's Box*. Taking as point of departure the experience of the African immigrants in England, it asserts that in a globalized changing world marked by rapid spatial migration of individuals and cultural interpenetration, literary discourses have shifted from Afrocentrism to focus on Afropolitanism as a theory of global citizenship, giving way to the building of a new African identity in hybrid modern world. The article maintains that identity, sometimes a controversial concept, is very flexible and can be reshaped to suit with the needs of times and circumstances. Taking the example of the African immigrants living in England in *Pandora's Box*, the article asserts that cultural homecoming is also essential for the survival of African values.

The concept of Afropolitanism has not received sufficient attention in African literary criticism. When examining African literary discourses, intellectual reflections on the Africans' displacement in the postcolonial space tried to explain the factors that compel citizens to leave the black continent without offering broader perspectives on the ambivalent view of these spatial and cultural dynamics. Emilia Ilieva and Lennox Odiemon-Munara posit that "Migrations of the displaced within, and from, violence-prone nations are thus opening up new debates and discourses on borders and spaces; as well as on the resultant identities that are being assumed and negotiated" (Ilieva and Odiemon-Munara 2011: 183) They do not specify the context in which Afropolitanism operates as important tentacle of migration that can offer both good opportunities and bad incidences in reshaping the individuals' identities in the context of contemporary globalization. Bill Ashcroft, Gareth Griffiths and Helen Tiffin take a different stand by affirming that "Diasporas, the voluntary or forcible movement of peoples from their homelands into new regions, is a central historical fact of colonization. Colonialism itself was a radically diasporic movement, involving the temporary or permanent dispersion and settlement of millions of Europeans over" (Ashcroft, Griffiths and Tiffin 2000: 61). These critics have also ignored Afropolitanism as a positive aspect of migration in which cultural exchange operates as enriching experience. Another critic Petronella Breinburg submits that when people migrate, cultures meet and there is the fusion of aspects of one culture by another culture group, the result of which is the domination of the stronger culture by the weaker (Petronella Breinburg 1996: 227). This interpretative view is also narrowed as it ignores the positive aspect of cultural confrontation. It is Simon Gikandi who has looked closely at the phenomenon of Afropolitanism in his foreword to Jennifer Wawrzinek and J. K. S. Makokha's *Negotiating Afropolitanism:* "the discourse of Afropolitanism goes far beyond the existential situations of Africans born across languages, nations and identities. Afropolitanism reflects a new attitude towards Africa and the wider world in which it is part" (Gikandi 2011: 26). Yet, Gikandi's formulation also does not describe in accurate manner the kind of Afropolitan experiences that the playwright Ade Solanke has her characters undergo in *Pandora's Box*. That is why I propose a critical examination of that play

In this chapter, my concern is to show the relevance of Afropolitanism as a postmodernist imperative, and the ambivalent aspect of migration which concomitantly offers a solution to the problem of unemployment and poverty, and yet creates another series of problems, for both the migrant parents and their offspring: the loss of African cultural identity, and the decline of moral values of the teenagers.

18.1. The Roots of Afropolitanism in the Postcolonial Space: The Search for Survival

Afropolitanism is the literary theory that identifies and analyses in literary texts the trans-bordering challenges of African descents engaged in the dynamics of migration, identity shift physical and cultural displacement and who struggle to reconnect with their roots either physically or through the medium of education, or the mass-media or other means of information. It is also the state of Africans from the diaspora who, having been outside the African continent redefine their identity as global citizens. In the postmodernist space controlled by globalization, migration has been a dynamic phenomenon. Globalization is the process whereby individual lives and local communities are affected by economic and cultural forces that operate world-wide. Lyotard's essay 'Answering the Question: What is Postmodernism?', first published in 1982, added in 1984 as an appendix to *The Postmodern Condition* and included in Brooker's *Modernism/Postmodernism* (1992), takes up this debate about the Enlightenment, mainly targeting Habermas, in a slightly oblique manner. Lyotard opens with a move which effectively turns the debate into a struggle to demonstrate that one's opponents are the real conservatives (a familiar 'bottom line' of polemical writing on culture). From every direction', he says, 'we are being urged to put an end to experimentation', and after citing several other instances he writes (obviously of Habermas): I have read a thinker of repute who defends modernity against those he calls the neo-conservatives. Under the banner of postmodernism, the latter would like, he believes, to get rid of the uncompleted project of modernism, that of the Enlightenment. (Brooker: 141) Habermas's is simply one voice in a chorus which is calling for an end to 'artistic experimentation' and for 'order ... unity, for identity, for security' (Brooker: 142). In a word, these voices want 'to liquidate the heritage of the avant-gardes'.

In fact, it is the process of the world becoming a single place. Afropolitanism was given some intellectual reflections in the critical book *Negotiating Afropolitanism, Essays on Borders and Spaces in Contemporary African Literature and Folklore* edited by Jennifer Wawrzinek and J. K. S. Mahokha. In this book, J. K. S. Makokha explains:

> There are two main descriptions and deployments of the term Afropolitanism currently acknowledged in cultural discourses. One of the interpretations is 'the newest generation of African migrants. They are Africans or children of Africans who moved to the west in the 1960s and 1970s for various reasons. Most of them are now embodiment of intercultural or interracial union between Africa and the rest of the world. African immigrants and citizens of African nations living in the West are automatically Afropolitans. Their dispersal across the world cities is an ongoing phenomenon powered by personal ambition, political strife, the dynamics of transnational capital and corporate culture as well as the quest for a better life away from an 'unpromising continent'. [The second interpretation]

identifies as Afropolitans the Africans at home and abroad who subscribe to anti-nativist and cosmopolitan interpretations of African identities and cultures (J. K. S. Makokha 2011: 16-17).

The literary reflections of the English born Nigerian female playwright Ade Solanke in *Pandora's Box* circumscribe the Afropolitan debate in the same logic as defined by J. K. S. Makokha, as she places at the center of her analysis the cultural and material conditions of her characters and herself within the epistemological orientation of Africans engaged in two worlds: African and European. At the core of her play are questions of cultural borders and spaces of new African identities of Nigerians migrated to London. The examination of how spaces and borders can be engaged anew within the parameters of criticism to bend the nexus of dialogic parlance between history, culture and identity between Africa and Europe is the ground on which Solanke deploys her discourse.

Homi K. Bhabha, one of the theoreticians of postcolonialism contends that the physical and cultural displacement in the postcolonial space has produced cultural ambivalence (Bhabha 1994: 311). Bhabha has produced a theory of cultural hybridity that goes beyond previous attempts in trying to understand connections between migration and globalism. Ade Solanke has used allegory to expose a series of interconnected phenomena that compel African citizens, namely Nigerians, to leave the African continent to seek living conditions in England. The informing rationale that accounts for migration in *Pandora's box* is in the main the economic precarity of Africa. That precarity is related to capitalism and colonization exploitation of the African continent. She shows that colonial did not only loot Africa's wealth and resources, but it impoverished the African's mind culturally. Thus, material and mental poverty from which Africans are running to migrate in Europe – London in the context of *Pandora's Box*, are caused by one fearful event, colonization. Many reasons inform the drift of African people to Western societies. The playwright lays emphasis on three: the search for education, economic relief and emancipatory jobs. Young students leave Nigeria for England to further their education and get higher degrees in Western universities. Others migrate in search for jobs and better living conditions. Thus, the youth is in majority the social class concerned with migration problem:

> BABA: Toyin, twelve million unemployed. Graduates wandering the streets. Students rioting. Social protest. Turmoil. (*PB*: 49)

Here, Ade Solanke is tracing the mass migration in England to the problem of unemployment and poverty in Africa. Many are educated and hold degrees without jobs. The youth in quest for jobs are dissatisfied with home country, and want to migrate to forge ahead abroad. "Today, there is a mini-exodus of young people leaving Nigeria in search of work" (*PB*: 15). Sometimes these young men and young ladies are well educated and don't see home as a fitting setting to develop their intellectual skills, since they cannot find employment. This constitutes a brain drain which Baba the character denounces (*PB*: 49). As a corollary of unemployment, the playwright points out extreme poverty of the masses, armed robbery, ransom kidnapping and ramshackle infrastructures, which all contribute to make heavy the burden of precarious social life for the population to endure:

> BABA: Armed robbers on the loose. Security is nowhere - instead, police who Should protect us are extorting money from motorists with impunity. Where is the rule of law? Ransom kidnapping so rife in some areas People are afraid to venture out. Ramshackle infrastructures in urban Areas, and rural areas are worse, like ... back in the stone age. People Are starving! I'll say it again: Nigeria is a tinderbox waiting to explode. (*PB*: 49-50)

It is not far fetched to say that poverty, hunger, insecurity, constitute the lynchpin in the motives driving the youth away from home; and that such precarious living conditions cannot guarantee a hopeful future to them. Once they migrate to England, they seek to settle there permanently and build their families. They manage to secure jobs and afterwards, they opt for permanent residence. Such permanent settlements impose some demands on the immigrants, namely the acquisition of residence permit, citizenship papers, and other formal requirements for permanent residents. To obtain such legal papers African immigrants do resort at times to wrong statements about their identity, their family background, their cultural background, their education and their marital status. For instance, a married person may declare himself/herself single and vice-versa. It is here that the playwright draws my reflection as a reader to the problematic of identity loss. Should one deny his identity for socio-economic considerations? I think it is not good from the stand point of an African to hide or mispronounce one's identity for economic gains. A long stay abroad can impact on one's cultural identity through education and cultural assimilation, especially when considering the offspring of the immigrant at the second or the third generation. It is in this context that Toyin, a Nigerian mother living in London, who was born from parents who had migrated to London more than thirty years ago to complete their studies and search for a job is no more able to speak her native Yoruba language. Ade Solanke presents her as a "London mother" because she has acquired the English citizenship (*PB: 21*).

18.1.3. Negotiating Identity in Diasporic Space: Afropolitanism and the Metaphor of Migration

In her thought line, Ade Solanke questions postcolonial identity by showing that it is a flexible concept. Under the pressure of life demands, characters in *Pandora's Box* are engaged in the dynamics of displacement, shifts, in and out travels between Lagos and England. Sis Ronke for instance is an English born Nigerian who, is shared between Africa and London, a mobility that inflects on her identity. Such a character for instance possesses double citizenship, therefore double identities: English and Nigerian. She finds it difficult to define herself. Understandably, the playwright relocates the postcolonial identity debate within the scope of cultural hybridity that functions to shape the mindset of that character who wants herself to be identified as an Afropolitan. Postcolonial critic Pal Ahluwalia adjoins that "the conception of citizenship is based upon the recognition that individuals have more than a single identity, that within a society, individuals occupy multiplicity of positons, depending on circumstances at a particular time" (Ahluwalia 2001: 107). This assertion is in line with Ade Solanke's characters and confirms their postcolonial inflection towards the global citizenship. But also, the negotiation of identity in a postcolonial diasporic context goes beyond physical identity, as migration may be metaphor.

By choosing as the play's title *Pandora's Box* Ade Solanke is writing a metaphor. She is referring to the interconnected evils of material poverty in Africa, migration (drain of manpower and brains), and the cultural alienation or the loss of African identity. Philosophically speaking, the image of *Pandora's Box* originates from the Greek myth in which Pandora was created by the god Zeus and sent to the earth with a box containing many evils. When she opened the box, the evils came out and infected the earth. Literally, Pandora's Box is a process that, if started, will cause many problems that cannot be solved (Hornby 2007: 1054). In Ade Solanke's *Pandora's Box*, the three evils concerned are poverty in Africa, migration to England and the loss of one's identity. Poverty, I maintain with Chinua Achebe, is caused by African leaders' mismanagement of resources, some cases of migration are related to that poverty and the loss of one's identity is due to poverty (Achebe 1984: 1). At a deeper level of interpretation, the evils of *Pandora's Box* are colonialism, capitalism, cultural and material poverty. The playwright by choosing title to her play is levelling a criticism at the chain of unhappy events the African continent has been subjected to, namely colonialism, its twin sister capitalism and their corollaries, material and mental deprivation. What Ade Solanke insists on in her play is mental poverty, the loss of one's cultural identity.

Then, migration to western societies for different reasons advocated can be akin to exile, because at times the migrants meet the opposite of their expectations abroad.

When people migrate to Western societies, they take away with them their brains and skills. As a result, they display these skills over there to develop European societies. In this respect, migration is perceived as a drain of both manpower and intellectual skills. Africa, one should recognize, is very rich in terms of manpower and brains. But, such rich potentials are not used in Africa due to the phenomenon of migration. Many are the Africans who excel in various domains of professions in England and other European countries as civil, mechanical, electrical engineers, medical doctors, architects, lawyers, technocrats, chattered accountants and economists. These highly competent brains are the riches from Africa who have contributed enormously to Europe's development. They constitute a loss for Africa, for since their services are not done in Africa, they are not totally useful to the continent. It is true that many immigrants from abroad send a lot of money to their countries and families, but Ade Solanke as a descendant of African immigrants in London is expressing what she feels as a writer. She sees herself in the profile of the writer depicted by Sam Ukala:

> But the creative writer also imbibed western education. His own mind was colonised and he could not effectively politick in the aesthetics he had lost. In trying to grapple with this problem […] the African creative writer necessarily passes through three phases: in the first he shows that he has assimilated the occupier's culture by imitating his artistic values and forms; in the second, he becomes uncertain and decides to go back to his past through remembering his early rural life and his people's tales, which, he however, dresses

in western aesthetics. This does not take away his alienation from his people with whom he cannot effectively communicate, using foreign aesthetics. So in the third phase, he seeks to reintegrate himself with his people by non-literate means, through mobilizing and joining them […] (Ukala 2001: 30).

This profile is about the African creative writer living for example in Europe. The writer encounters many problems because of the following reasons: he is imbibed with western culture; his mind that was colonized does not effectively allow him to effectively politic in the aesthetics he had lost. He is also alienated to his people and cannot effectively communicate with them. It is true that the creative writer's art can travel across the countries' boundaries, but here, the critic wants to lay emphasis on the fact that the migrated writer is culturally hybrid, sometimes, he is more European than African culturally speaking.

18.1.4. Cultural Ambivalence

Afropolitanism is inscribed in a context of postcolonial migration, cultural hybridity, and spatial movement. The drift of African populations towards Western societies generates new identities for migrants as they become endowed with new citizenship defined in the standard of the universal values. The fact that some Africans from the diaspora have difficulties to reconnect with their roots can inform their preference for Afropolitan identity. Some children born from African immigrants cannot speak their native language or mother tongue. This constitutes a serious cultural dereliction, that is, a situation where African languages and cultural values are totally neglected to the detriment of the English ones. As a result, African languages are dying in the white communities. The case in point in *Pandora's Box* is Toyin, a Nigerian woman born in London from Nigerian immigrants. When Sis Ronke speaks to her in Yoruba, she doesn't get the meaning:

> Sis Ronke: O ye ko so fun Timi nisiyi. K'o mo pe o nlo pelu Principal ati Tope k'o bale ni igba die ti o ma fi mo l'ara.
> Toyin: What did you say?
> Sis Ronke: Why don't you learn your language? A Yoruba girl who can't Speak Yoruba! It is a pity […] I will translate later.
> (*PB: 90*)

This excerpt shows that Toyin cannot understand what is said in Yoruba, her mother tongue except it is translated in English. She is African language acculturate since she cannot even understand something in her mother tongue and has to rely on English translation. What Solanke the playwright indicts to her immigrant characters is that they have abandoned their culture and civilization for the English ones, while they should keep theirs first, and add to them the foreign ones. For African cultures to survive in Europe, Africans of the diaspora have to speak African languages and perpetuate their cultures. Sometimes, the setting may not be appropriate for a full display of African cultural show, but the playwright Ade Solanke is making a plea to Africans to make an effort to perpetuate them. It is not appropriate to totally abandon one's cultural values to adopt foreign ones. Culture is the picture and reflection of one's identity. It defines our being, our image in the universal values. Just as a body cannot be separated from the soul and the human being will remain alive, we cannot be emptied of our culture and civilization and still keep our identity. So, when people from different cultural horizons come together, every individual or group should bring their values to make the cultural melting pot richer. But if unfortunately, some people are acculturated, they won't have anything to offer.

It is to re-evaluate that new identity as a world citizen that Ade Solanke has attracted international attention to that phenomenon of migration in a theatrical representation of Nigerian family engaged in a dynamics cultural and physical migration and homecoming from Lagos to London and from London to Lagos. *Pandora's Box* reads as Ade Solanke's contribution to the understanding of the causes, the effects and the implications of the phenomenon of migration, the exodus of African population to European megalopolis.

The phenomenon of migration is opted to solve the problem of unemployment and poverty in the context of *Pandora's Box*. Nevertheless, the African immigrants after finding better living conditions are confronted to two crucial problems: firstly, how to keep in touch with their African cultural roots in a white community? Secondly, how to ensure that their children do not become totally African-acculturates and wayward in a criminality prone and morally corrupt white community of English cities? Can the idea of having children spend some of the time of their education in Africa palliate to that problem of cultural loss?

Migration to Western societies puts the African in-between two cultures, the African culture and the European. One can talk of cultural ambivalence of diaspora Africans. In this context characters like Sis Ronke, and Mama Ronke are engaged in what Elliot P. Skinner describe as "the determination of the African peoples to end with the feeling of self-alienation and to restore their civilizations in an imperative for the twenty-first century" (Skinner 1999: 28). The playwright shows that migration in England and the choice of settlement in there have implications at cultural, economic, social and even political levels. Generally speaking, African immigrants have difficulties to get inserted in metropolitan London of rapid change. Eventually the adjustments that immigrants do to fit in the metropolitan society and the new identity they resume make them a kind of 'alien' people.

Culturally speaking, the mobility of individuals from one geo-linguistic setting to another implies a transplant or grafting from African culture to the English one. African immigrants have difficulties to adjust themselves with a rapidly changing cultural life of London. It is that transplantation that leads to alienation, cultural dereliction and loss of identity that Ade Solanke highlights in the play. They also face the problem of linguistic barriers and unevenness. Some migrate to London with elementary school education and find it extremely difficult to adjust themselves with the highly sophisticated linguistic command and accent of the native English speakers. So, this poses the problem of communication. To communicate efficiently, one needs to possess an acceptable knowledge of the English language, and this takes time to Africans to rehearse themselves to reach that level. At the end of the day some of the immigrants are so immersed in the English culture that they can no more express well their original cultural values like language, songs, dance, dressing, and eating habits even when they are back home. Thus they become culturally alien to their own people. At the level of religion, African immigrants of strong religious convictions are bewildered to see that the English society shows no concern in religious matters. Some strong believers' faith declines with the long run. Selections in sportive teams, musical competition and other artistic competitions are tough. English culture in London is oriented towards technological culture with sophisticated musical instruments, refined machinery and apparatus. Some characters forsake their religions and become alien. Eating habits also change because of the industrial food technology. In the introductory notes to the play, Ade Solanke, born in England, tells her experience when she came back home in Nigeria, at the age of eighteen:

> Nowadays, though I have not so much a feeling of sitting on a fence between two cultures [...] I consider myself an African

abroad. Sometimes, especially after the first time I visited Nigeria as an 18-year-old in 1982, I have felt more a part of 'there' than 'here'. The food, the clothes, the music, the customs, the sound of the Yoruba language, the ubiquitous muslim prayers (though I am not a muslim) and the sheer energy zapping around in places like Lagos; all signal "home" (*PB:15*)

Socially speaking migration is a factor of depopulation of African cities. It reduces manpower, source of economic development. Many African immigrants who have poor professional qualifications have difficulties to get socially inserted in European megalopolis like London and are either expatriated or made to live on the fringe of the society. Such Africans have precarious lives and definitely live in slums and resort to such jobs as prostitution, housemaids and barmaids. Some are prone to become drug addicts. They are at the mercy of criminals. At the same time, they feel ashamed to come back to Africa in a state of dire destitution. They become alien to their people.

18.1.5. Afropolitan View of Multiculturalism: A New Model of Identity

Ade Solanke as a playwright uses dramatic literature to call for multiculturalism, a new model of identity. Her cultural orientation falls in line with the postcolonial critical ideology that accommodates with a model of African identity based on multiculturalism and pluralism. For her, in order to overcome the tendency toward exclusionism, one needs to reconstruct a new model of identity resting on the fundamental values of cultural pluralism, exchange and dialogue. Homi Bhabha is of the same opinion when he says: "The postcolonial perspective forces us to rethink the profound limitations of a consebsual and collusive liberal sense of cultural community. It insists that cultural and political identity [sic] are constructed through a process of alterity" (Bhabha 1994: 251).

Immigration is a fact. In a 21st century globalized world, Africans cannot live in an ivory tower of cultural puritanism or geographical confinement. For economic, social, educational, political reasons, Africans will always migrate in Europe or elsewhere. The search for better living conditions informs migration, and migration stirs the wheel of cultural hybridism. Ngugi wa Thiong'o advocates the wealth of common global culture (Ngugi 1993: 12) and Paulin Manwelo sustains the idea of cultural pluralism, an antechamber for peaceful environment (Manwelo 2011:

105). They have argued in the favour cultural cross-fertilization, pointing out the idea that the coming together of diversity of cultures is a source of enrichment in that it provides occasion for learning from one another. True, the coming together of people from different civilizations and cultures provide a venue for clash in which people learn from one another when they exchange views, select values and better equip themselves. Culture contacts produce cultural diversity. Ade Solanke whose play is under study here also advocates cultural pluralism as a source of wealth. Yet, it is not superfluous to acknowledge that migration causes African cultures to remain fallow. In *Pandora's Box*, Ade Solanke has shown that migration is responsible for the loss of African cultural values. Living in a majority white community offers little opportunity to Africans to express their cultural values. The pressure of school education and the demand of professional orientation impose on African immigrants to give priority to English language and cultural practices, while still being open to the other cultural communities. Some African parents do not communicate with their children in their native languages.

Chinua Achebe highlights this idea as follows: "Let every people bring their gifts to the great festival of the world's cultural harvest and mankind will be all the richer for the variety and distinctiveness of the offsprings" (Achebe 1989: 89) Achebe through this statement is inviting communities around the world to come together in a cultural diversity, but each people should keep his identity and be holding his own culture. The great festival of cultural harvest of mankind he is talking about is an imagery to mean that, cultural melting pot is an enriching experience only if every people have his own values to give.

Another reason why children must come back to their source is that London is a big city. It is a cosmopolitan megalopolis and as such, it is criminality prone. The insecurity problems do not guarantee sound moral upbringing of the African teenage youth. Mama Ronke expresses this through the following remark:

> Mama-Ronke: [...] Timi is a good boy, but in London he is not safe. You saw What happened to Rio? Shot and killed on his doorstep. You Know what happened to Samuel? Stabbed for his phone. [...]
>
> Please, my dear, don't let what happened to your brothers Happen to him. My only grandson, don't let another generation Be lost in that land
> (*PB: 38-39*)

Here London is presented as a place of insecurity, both physical and cultural. As a highly populated city, physical insecurity is rife, and teenagers are vulnerable and easy preys to criminals. The London urban population is composed of different nationalities coming from different parts of the world, who migrated to the city in search for better living conditions. The life in that town is compared to that of a jungle where the inhabitants are subjected to the rule of the survival of the fittest. A watchful eye of the parents is indispensable for the security of the teens. Culturally speaking London is also a place of insecurity in that, African indigenous values are quickly stifled by the metropolitan cultural mixture. For the African teenagers, companionship and peer pressure are another factor informing their cultural dereliction.

With regard to social realities, in *Pandora's Box,* the society is a white society, different from the black society in Nigeria. The immigrant has to interact with white people, to weave relationships, make new acquaintances, and be introduced to new social organizations. The immigrant faces also new cultural realities: the languages change, the religion practice varies, and so do the music, the art, and the sports. The economic system also changes with new currency. There is also a change in the nature of business, business transactions. The immigrant changes his economic activities. Intellectually speaking, the immigrant must broaden his intellectual horizon. He must change his reflective capacity, that is broaden his world view and perception or at times narrow them. The real problem of Ade Solanke's characters is that, they come from Africa to live in London. African culture is abusively thought of by some Europeans to be inferior to their culture. These Europeans still have the colonial mind. They perceive Africans as culturally inferior people who still have to learn from them. This explains their discriminatory behaviour.

18.1.6. African Global Citizen: a Quest for New Identity and Self-redefinition

Identity is defined in *Oxford Advanced Learner's Dictionary* as "who or what somebody or something is". It is "the characteristics, feelings, or beliefs that distinguish people from others" (Horby 2007: 739). Identity is instable and flexible. It can change under the influences or strains of the social, economic, cultural, or political conditions surrounding the person. What determines one's identity is related to the external prevailing conditions which directly influence the consciousness of the person. Hans Bertens speaking as a postcolonial theorist confirms this idea by saying that "identity is inherently unstable […] Identity is constructed in interaction with 'others' and with the 'Other" (Bertens 2003: 207). In-between two cultures, Africans immigrants are looking for the kind of a new identity that will help them keep in touch with their origin and cultural roots, but at the same time forge ahead in the new residence of England without facing problems of racial segregation. As a result, they become culturally hybrid, with the two cultures overlapping each other. Two major problems prove sometimes difficult to solve: the choice of names for their children and the choice of school.

African immigrants in England are confronted with the difficulty of names choice for their children. First, they are aware of their being Africans, and as such, they show volition to keep in touch with their African origin by giving African names to their children. Toyin for example has named her son Rotimi, a Yoruba name. Africans give African names to their children to fill in the nostalgic vacuum created by the distant separation from their hometown. Calling children by typically African indigenous names, bring back home memories, create an atmosphere of familiar conviviality and helps quench the nostalgic thirst of going back home. Giving African names to children is also a way of trying to perpetuate one's family line and culture. The preservation of family name is only possible if children of the younger generation continue to bear it. Nevertheless, that choice has never been as easy one because, African parents also see in the African names their children bear, a potential and possible subject of rejection or discrimination on behalf of white people, which may occur at school or at the working place. A name is first of all a subject of identification. Through the names that people bear, one can identify their race, their socio-cultural or ethnic group and trace their origin. Therefore, in a selection for job, one may possibly be discriminated on the basis of his African origin. Racism is still rife in some parts of England, and the black community is sometimes victim of it. This is the point Bev raises when she tells Baba: "You're in Africa. You don't understand about racism. You can't (*PB*: 85). Racism is the unfair treatment of people who belong to a different race. It is also a belief that some races of people are better than others (Hornby 2007: 1195). When one is victim of racial segregation due to the name s/he bears, s/he'd rather change that name to avoid trouble. A person bearing an English name in such circumstances can be of great advantage, because, one can avoid being unjustly discriminated. Thus, it proves difficult for Africans to select names for their children. This poses the problem of identity and self-definition. On the one hand, Africans are proud to be themselves, but on the other hand, they are afraid that their identity revealed may cause them segregationist problems. Africans are in perpetual quest of their identity.

To solve that problem, immigrants choose their social identification and self-definition through actions. It is a process through which Africans display extraordinary skills and competence through the feats they accomplish. In areas of competitiveness like football, music, art, Africans have to excel in competence in order to outdo their English fellows and hold public attention. Soccer players for example are selected only on the basis of their competence and performance. As Baba, one of the characters in the play says, "the world is a market place... Everywhere you go, life is competition" (*PB*: 83). This highlights the idea that the African immigrants have to be very competent and performant. The quest of African identity is expressed also in the play through the choice of schools for children of African immigrants. As far as academic excellence is concerned, Principal Osun, a director of Wide Horizons Academy explains:

> PRIN OSUN: Here is the new science lab. Here is the new science theatre. As an institution, we believe in mixing excellence with innovation, discipline with creativity. That is why we attract the best. We are the best. From tomorrow your son will be mixing with the cream of Africa. At Wide Horizon Academy we have the sons of kings and queens, ambassadors, politicians, professors. He will be mixing with the leaders of tomorrow's world (*PB*: 69).

Through this excerpt, Ade Solanke shows that intellectual excellence, competence and performance are the leitmotiv of Africans at home and abroad. African training institutions like Wide Horizon Academy encourage academic excellence and performance. An example can be testified with the many students who excel in London, in science, technology, medicine, law, engineering, arts, sports to mention but a few disciplines, holding their educational background from Africa. These Africans sometimes outdo native English youth in areas of competition.

18.1.7 Cultural Homecoming: Ade Solanke's Perspective

Homecoming is literally speaking an arrival home after a long absence. In this study, I borrow the term homecoming from Ngugi wa Thiong'o to mean the consciousness awakening on the part of Africans about their values, language and culture especially (Ngugi 1972: 82). Today, we are not going back to militate in the Negritude movement but I think there is need to preserve our Identity as Africans. Ade Solanke is looking at the African world through literature and its politics, as the African world moves into the sixth decade after the independence. She has no illusion that true independence is yet to be achieved. The most significant rationale informing the necessity of cultural homecoming in Ade Solanke's *Pandora's Box* is the emergence of a distinctive consciousness on the part of Toyin of her belonging to a collective identity in the African continent, and this functions as a hose to strengthen her relationship to the rest of the world. As Abiole Irele has it,

> This consciousness derives from the character's experiences of the encounter with life in London and in an even more immediate way, represents the profound subjective response to the peculiar pressure of the cultural alienation situation – that is the political, socio-economic and moral state of dependence created by England. The sense of African identity and the impulse towards its explicit affirmation gives force to the expression of homecoming in Africa (Irele 1981: 89).

This awareness has become prolonged into an intellectual and ideological exploration of the avenues of endeavour which can give a meaning to the collective experience into a quest for positive orientation of African ideas and action in the contemporary world (Ibidem). One might say, then, that there is abroad inside the immigrants, governing their feelings and consequently their expression, a certain idea of Africa, a certain ideal vision of selves founded upon their awareness of their constitution as a people and race, and of their fundamental attachment to a distinctive culture and spiritual background (Ibidem). The consciousness of our singularity as Africans thus forms the live core of the intellectual idea we hold of Africa and by implication of our destiny.

Ade Solanke has used drama as a tool to call for a cultural homecoming. Cultural homecoming is the return to one's cultural roots. Many reasons are used to account for the necessity of that cultural homecoming. The been-toes have difficulties to adjust themselves in their original cultural milieus. The difficulties come from the fact that these been-toes have lost many of their cultural milieus' habits. Culture makes one's identity and enables people to be socially identifiable and identified. Culture is to identity what the body is for the soul. Without it (culture), it is difficult, even impossible to identify an individual's or a people's origin. What Ade Solanke indicts to her characters who have migrated in London is that they have been disconnected with their roots. This, Bessie Head has experienced and is recommending "a search as an African for a sense of historical continuity, a sense of roots" (Head 1986: 101). They have lost their African cultural potentials, once they have acquired the English citizenship. Here one can easily talk of cultural alienation. What has conspired to embolden the sense of alienation in the African immigrant is traceable to the ascendancy of Western civilization in the context of colonization, because, it did effect a distinct orientation of African minds away from indigenous culture (Ibidem). Even the prestige of the conqueror turned his way of life and system of values into the reference-culture for the African. Thus the African started copying blindly the European practices to the extent of totally loosing his own repair. Within the global process of acculturation, which as a result has affected the African society in its entirety, is situated a more intensified absorption into a western way of life of the new category of African immigrants.

The African Diaspora in *Pandora's Box* are seeing themselves as men on trial and their feelings of cultural insecurity is heightened by the fact that they form a fragile minority in relation to the tremendous mass of White people around them. It would not be far-fetched to observe with Abiola Irele that

> this sense of ambiguity attaching to their situation as Africans living a foreign culture on English soil, the incongruous disparity between their way of life and the imposing reality of their immediate environment, led the most sensitive among these Diaspora characters to an interrogation of their situation. The content of the playwright's writing indicates that the characters are inflicted with a profound *malaise* arising out of their situation as 'marginal people'. Their sense of cultural dependence on the west and the singular disparity between their borrowed culture and the African reality which surrounds them cannot but provoke within them a moral and spiritual discomfort which, neither the material benefits of western civilization nor the undisputed prestige which they enjoy in colonial society could altogether palliate (Irele 1989: 94).

This statement points to the fact that the characters in situation of immigrants acknowledge themselves to be people without any stable cultural links and consequently without a firm sense of identity, and tormented by an apprehension about themselves. There is already an intellectual recognition of

Africa as a possible reference for thought and action and indeed awareness.

But Ade Solanke is calling for a homecoming. Homecoming is a kind of consciousness awakening, to retrace one's roots and to get back in touch with them. Toyin has become aware of the danger of being disconnected with her roots and has brought back her son Timi to Lagos to attend an African school. She believes that, the stay in an African setting will equip him with some African values: the Yoruba language, the African home education, the moral values of respect and traditional wisdom, and even the African religion, that is the African way of worshiping God. Ade Solanke's perception of society is of a complex in which politics, economics and culture are inextricably tied up and no where on that spectrum can she see cultural dereliction offering any hope of progress. In a post-colonial society and in a European setting in which doctrine and practice run counter to the traditional communal values and works against the total involvement of the people in what is theirs (Ngugi 1972: xiv) the singular becomes the global and the global becomes singular. Ade Solanke's objective analysis lies in her realization that in the search for social well being, questions arising from "the experience of yesterday must lead to a consideration of here-and-now as a basis of hope for the yet-to-come. Not only where the rain began to beat us and how severely, but also how to save ourselves from perpetual exposure, and our houses from flood" (Ibidem). Cultural homecoming can be traced to the experience of Africans during slavery. In fact, this can help us grasp the meaning of what Africans of Diaspora feel. I owe much in this explanation to Abiola Irele who reaffirms that a sense of African belonging has always been a functional aspect of the black experience and consciousness in Europe (Irele 1989: 90). The early communities of Africans transported across the Atlantic had already began to perceive the mother continent as an entity due to their detachment under the pressure of slavery from their immediate primary bonds, on the one hand, and on the other, their differentiation in terms of race and social status from their oppressors.

Ade Solanke shows another aspect of the Africans' quest for identity through choice of school. School is the place of education and training. It is the setting where intellectual and sometimes moral competences are taught. School trains children for their future social insertion. As an educational centre, it heavily influences the trainees' mind and behaviour. Being such a place, the learners' future character and behaviour heavily depend on the kinds of teaching and training they receive. For an African immigrant in England, the choice of a school is sometimes problematic because of the future profile parents wants to confer on their children. Many parents dream of great future professional careers for children. As Toyin tells her son Timi "I want you to amount to something, Timi. To grow into a man. A good man. A decent man (*PB: 93*). They want them to graduate from the best renowned schools, institutes, and universities of England, but at the same time, they do not want them to be disconnected with their African roots or identity. As Professor Osita Okagbue remarks in his foreword to the play,

> Ade Solanke has written a very entertaining play, one which boldly takes on a very crucial issue of our time: the question of what it means to an African diasporic parent, living in the United Kingdom today and bringing up children, especially male children, in a society which, explicably, it seems, is constructed to make them fail. (*PB:16*)

Ade Solanke notes that

> The play explores the universal human subject of a parent's struggle to do what's best for his/her child [...] These challenges are happening to us for the first time. These dilemmas are upon us here and now, as we raise our kids and try to navigate them through life, and come of age as British-born children who are now parents ourselves. (*PB: 18*)

The two extracts express the dilemma African parents of diaspora in England are facing. The dilemma is between London and Lagos, an African setting and a European one, which one fits the best for their children's education. Toyin's major preoccupation as a parent of a 15 year-old student is to find an educational environment that will make Rotimi a wholesome citizen. She understands that, for a good social insertion, one needs to be educated intellectually and morally. As such, only an environment that can offer better chances to equip her son with moral and intellectual education and that can match her aspirations for a future brilliant professional career is her present concern. She complains about the loss of moral values in the London society. Such a society is morally and culturally depraved. Immorality, debauchery, pornography, cyber criminality, rape, drug addiction and trafficking, violence, "streetism" and waywardness are the common ills that dictate the order of the day. Teenagers are vulnerable to and victims of these moral deviations. Although the Nigerian society too is not exempt of some of these deviations, Toyin believes that with the help of Principal Osun, the Principal of Tope's school where she intends to enrol her son, the son will make it. Then for Toyin, the Nigerian setting shall help to reshape her son's identity. It will contribute to readjust his moral character and equip him with socially accepted moral values.

The focus of this study was to discuss the relevance of Afropolitanism as a postcolonial imperative and to highlight the ambivalent aspect of immigration. The findings are two: firstly, Ade Solanke defends the idea of Afropolitanism as an important ideological discursive tool in *Pandora's Box*. Her characters are driven by self-consciousness that is located within and outside Nigerian national boundaries. They wear both the capes of Africanness and universalism. Secondly, in *Pandora's Box* there is a relationship between migration, cultural hybridism and the quest for new identity. Migration causes culture contacts and clashes and this brings about the need to adapt to change and cultural hybridism. The key idea developed is that nowadays' world is engaged in a rapid globalization with intercultural penetration. No individual can afford to remain purely conservator. At the same time, one should not be totally disconnected with his/her cultural roots. The new socio-economic realities impose on people physical mobility, and socio-economic and cultural exchange with the outside world. The good citizen today is the one who is culturally rich and balanced.

References

Achebe, Chinua. *The Trouble with Nigeria.* London: Heinemann. 1984.
--------------------. "Colonialist Criticism". In *Hopes and Impediments, Selected Essays.* New York. London. Toronto: Doubleday. 1989.
Ahluwalia, Pal. *Politics and Postcolonial Theory: African Inflections.* New York: Routledge. 2001.
Ashcroft, Bill, Gareth Griffiths and Helen Tiffin. *Post-colonial Studies: the Key Concepts.* New York: Routledge. 2000.
Bertens, Hans. *Literary Theory, The Basics.* Routledge: Taylor & Francis Group. 2003.
Bhabha, K. Homi. *The Location of Culture.* New York: Routledge. 1996.
Breinburg, Petronella. "Culture, Fusion and Language: the Case of Surinam." In Peter O. Stummer and Christopher Balme, eds., *Fusion of Cultures, Cross/Cultures 26 ASNEL Papers 2.* Amsterdam, Rodopi. 1996. PP. 225-231.
Breitinger, Eckhard. "Bole Butake's Strategies as a Political Playwright." In Martin Banham, *African Theatre, Playwrights and Politics.* Oxford: James Currey. 2001. PP. 7-17.

Gikandi, Simon. "Foreword on Afropolitanism." In Jennifer Wawrzinek and J. K. S. Makokha, eds., *Negotiating Afropolitanism: Essays on Borders and Spaces in Contemporary African Literature and Folklore*. Amsterdam: Rodopi. 2011. PP. 9-11.

Head, Bessie. "Biographical Notes: A Search for Historical Continuity and Roots". In Ernest N. Emenyonu, *Literature and Society: Selected Essays on African Literature*. Nigeria: Zim Pan African Publishers. 1986. PP. 95-103.

Hornby, A S. *Oxford Advanced Learner's Dictionary*. Oxford: Oxford University Press. 2007.

Ilieva, Emilia and Lennox Odiemon-Munara. "Negotiating Dislocated Identities in the Space of Postcolial Chaos: Goretti Kyomuhendo's Waiting." In Jennifer Wawrzinek and J. K. S. Makokha, eds., *Negotiating Afropolitanism: Essays on Borders and Spaces in Contemporary African Literature and Folklore*. Amsterdam: Rodopi. 2011. PP. 183-203.

Irele, Abiola. *The African Experience in Literature and Ideology*. London: Heinemann Educational Books. 1981.

Manwelo, Paulin. "The Politics of Identity in Africa: Diversity and Inclusion" in Gerard Walmsley (ed) *African Philosophy and the Future of Africa*. USA: The Council for Research in Values and Philosophy. 2011. PP. 100-110.

Oko Akomaye. "Towards a Sociology of the Nigerian Playwright: the Playwright as an Intellectual in Society" In Ernest N. Emenyonu ed. *Literature and Society: Selected Essays on African Literature*. Nigeria: Zim Pan African Publishers. 1986.

Szondi, Peter. *Theory of the Modern Drama*. Cambridge: Polity Press. 1965.

Ukala, Sam. "Politics of Aesthetics" pp. 29-41 in Martin Banham, *African Theatre, Playwrights and Politics*. Oxford: James Currey. 2001.

Ngugi, wa Thiong'o. *Homecoming Essays on African and Caribbean Literature, Culture and Politics*. New York. Westport. 1972.

----------------------------------. *Moving the Centre: the Struggle for Cultural Freedoms*. London: James and Currey. 1993.

Skinner, P. Eliott. "The Restoration of African Identity for a New Millenium". In Isidore Okpewho, Carole Boyce Davies and Ali Mazrui, eds., *The African Diaspora: African Origins and New World Identities*. Bloomington: Indiana University Press. 1999. PP. 28-45.

Solanke, Ade. *Pandora's Box*. London: Oberon Books. 2012.

19

INTERROGATING POST-APARTHEID LEGACY FROM HUMAN RIGHTS PERSPECTIVE: A READING OF ATHOL FUGARD'S SELECTED PLAYS

This chapter studies the critical ideas of Athol Fugard in his questioning of post-apartheid legacy in *My Children! My Africa!* and *No Good Friday*. It asserts that the end of Apartheid in South Africa was supposed to bring a certain number of prerogatives to the black community, among which the erasure of colonial stereotypes, equal access to education and employment and stop to police vagaries and brutality, but unfortunately, these expectations were not met. The main question addressed is to what extent do the survival patterns of apartheid constitute human rights violation and a roadblock to peaceful coexistence in multiracial South Africa? How does Fugard's critical assessment of post-Apartheid violation of human rights read as a deconstructive strategy of white imperialist hegemony? Using postcolonial critical approach, the study brings out the interconnection between postcolonial theatre narrative strategy and the struggle for a human rights restoration in the context of South African postcolonial era.

Many critics have tried to construct a comprehensive approach of the political dimension of Athol Fugard's plays without however insisting on how he advocates human rights as development praxis. Alan Shelley asserts: "The core of Fugard's political drama is backgrounded by the reality of this hotbed of political activity…His plays after 1990 can be said to reflect the ethos of the TRC [Truth and Reconciliation Commission]" (Shelley 2009: 21-22). This statement doesn't take into account Fugard's preoccupation for human rights. Russel Vandenbroucke holds the view that "Because Athol Fugard speaks openly about the conditions in South Africa that he abhors, and because his plays are set in his homeland and confronts the inhumanity spawned by its laws and values, it is facilely assumed that he is a propagandist and that his plays are mere devices" (Vandenbroucke 2002: 529). These opinions do not reveal what Fugard looks as fundamental concern with regard to human right. J. Ndukaku Amankulor opines that Athol Fugard "attacks the evils of the Apartheid legislations" (Amankulor 2001: 138) without specifying the very legislation that problematizes Black Africans' human rights. It follows that criticism lingers on the aesthetics of human rights in Athol Fugard's plays especially *No Good Friday* and *My Children! My Africa!,* thereby inviting new approaches from this angle. My concern in this article is to show how Athol Fugard's human rights advocacy stands out as development praxis that engages theatrical craft. The specific question I am trying to answer is when do the violation of inalienable right impede social cohesion and development at socio-political level?

I will analyse in Athol Fugard's *No Good Friday* and *My Children! My Africa!* the playwright's aesthetic representation of human rights violation as a roadblock to development.

19.1. Discourse Against Marginality: Athol Fugard's Advocacy of Human Rights in *No Good Friday and My Children! My Africa!*

Postcolonial theory, to borrow Bill Ashcroft and Pal Ahluwalia's definition, "investigates, and develops propositions about, the cultural and political impact of European conquest upon colonised societies, and the nature of those societies' responses." (Ashcroft and Ahluwalia 2001: 15). By this submission, the two critics mean that postcolonial theory questions in literature the power relationships that has engaged Africa and Europe on the contested ground of dominated and dominating or otherwise of margin and center. One would say that postcolonialism is as much interested in the far- reaching consequences of colonialism, the very legacies of apartheid when looked at from the South African perspective. From this perspective, Athol Fugard has questioned the neocolonial impacts of European racism which, contextualized in South African setting reads as post-apartheid shattered dream. Apartheid is the racial discrimination practiced by the white community of South Africa against the Blacks. It translates into acts of injustice namely the refusal to Blacks to have access to the same education, employment and political office tenure opportunities like Whites. Under Apartheid, the police exercise violence on innocent black citizens and rape black women without being questioned by the law. The end of Apartheid was supposed to bring to the black community in South Africa lot of changes in terms of human rights restoration and the emergence of the blacks in the spheres of politics, but unfortunately, more than a decade after the abolition of apartheid system, racial discrimination persists in the social fabric of South Africa. Larger opportunities of education, employment, women's emancipation, the erasure of colonial stereotypes, the stopping of police vagaries and brutalities were some of the very much expected reforms that were on the agenda of the anti-apartheid struggles. But unfortunately, the end of apartheid did not bring the materialization of the expected changes in terms of human rights mentioned above. Athol Fugard has questioned the logic that sustains the survival of a system that is supposed to be erased in practice. His interrogations come in the form of 'wh-questions' namely "why" [does the system persist?] (*MCMA, AFP1:* 214), "When" [will the apartheid legacy end?] (*MCMA, AFP1:* 213), "who" [is able to stop this injustice?] (*MCMA, AFP1:* 214). These questions are addressed not to a specific person, but to the political actors and the intellectual community that need to think out ways of ending the survival patterns of racial discrimination. I am going to consider the three questions.

 Fugard's first question "why" [does apartheid legacy survive its abolition]? is philosophical and rhetorical in the sense that it is not addressed to one particular individual but it is put as a thought provoking question. Apartheid ideology is detrimental to social peace and harmony. Its discourse is divisive and revolting. Fugard by asking this question seeks to deconstruct its tenets through a criticism that locates the violation of human rights as the negation of the very essence of human existence. He has strategically written a theatrical discourse that looks at the opposition between black marginality and white hegemony on which the dichotomic stratified society of oppressed and oppressor emerged. He has also shown legitimate resistance as the main means of struggle against oppression and injustice. Edward Said has admitted the necessity to question "flexible *positional* superiority, which puts the Westerner in a whole series of possible relationships with the Orient without ever losing him the relative upper hand." (Said: 2003: 90).

He fictionalizes in *No Good Friday* and *My Children! My Africa!* the binary oppositions and contradictory living conditions between white south Africans and their black counterparts. When Apartheid regime fell in 1994, much was expected, but segregation and social injustice persisted in every fabric of the South African social sphere. Fugard questions the legacy of a system that was supposed to end but still looms in the cultural practices of the white minority groups. In other words, the playwright finds it abnormal that racial discrimination and its attendant injustice should outlive the abolition of apartheid. This needs to change. Marginality reads in the two plays as an exclusion of Blacks from employment, education, housing, land tenure, decent living, police brutality on Blacks, rape of black women. It is a discriminatory system that emerged in South Africa in the context of Apartheid and survived the fall of the regime. Imperialism in that society takes the form of racial segregation against black community, translating itself into a numerous cases of human right violation. Apartheid brought a bipolarization of the South African society into black and whites with antagonistic and unequal privileges regarding education, employment, health, food, housing. White population took the monopoly of these life facilities, marginalizing thereby Africans left to occupy lower social status. Not only did the marginal system pervade the social life of black South African community, but it actually negated the possibility of change for many decades.

The second question, "when" [will postapartheid legacy end?] complements the first question "why does it survive?". Two critical configurations read in the *My Children! My Africa!*: the advocacy of human rights and the resilience society. For Fugard, the duration of the, postapartheid legacy depends on the political leaders' initiative to stop the practice. In fact apartheid itself was protected by the law and one needs another law to bring it to the end. If such a law already exits, there is need to see to its very applicability by all citizens. Human rights in the play refers to fundamental rights namely the erasure of colonial stereotypes and restoration of rightful names to Africans, equal education opportunities for black and white children, decent jobs for black Africans, a stop of police vagaries and brutalities and the cessation of arbitrariness in courts and the law enforcement agencies. Above all the cessation of violence in its most vicious forms constitutes Fugard's premises with regard to human rights. Fugard perceives disparities in education and the results of this policy as serious roadblocks to true emancipation of black African communities of the post-Apartheid period. Athol Fugard's approach questions the political morality that guides the white community when they proclaimed the end of Apartheid in theory but continued its ideology in practice. Philip Pettit summarizes political morality as:

> the legacy of the analytical tradition for thinking about ... the political good... to consider the legacy of the tradition for thought about what is politically right. To have views about the politically good is to identify one or another property or set of properties as desirable in political institutions: in institutions that are susceptible to political shaping. It is to prize liberty or democracy or equality or whatever (Pettit 2007: 28).

Postcolonial theory also reads in literary texts the ethics that rate political actions in Africa as good or bad and inform the critical value of political actors. From this perspective, Fugard shows through the experience of Thami that marginality functions in the same way as social exclusion in the context of colonialism with the difference that Apartheid-based marginality discombobulates the victims and offers fewer options for protest. In fact, the state has instored police patrolling and secret information services that locate potential protesters, arrest them and sometimes kill them. Characters are living in a state of terrorism. Being on the margin, Thami feels the psychological effect of rejection as a wounding blow when he finds that no good professional qualification can guarantee him a decent job. He perceives the unjust social system of discrimination as prejudicial to the realization of his full potential as an intelligent citizen. He feels what can be described as double colonization: he is colonized as an African, but doubly colonized as a black south African with lower social condition. Bill Ashcroft, Gareth Griffith and Helen Tiffin have found out that:

> The perception and description of experience as 'marginal' is a consequence of the binaristic structure of various kinds of dominant discourses, such as patriarchy, imperialism and ethnocentrism, which imply that certain forms of experience are peripheral.... Structures of power that are described in terms of 'centre' and 'margin' operate, in reality, in a complex, diffuse and multifaceted way. The marginal therefore indicates a *positionality* that is best defined in terms of the limitations of a subject's access to power (Ashcroft, Griffith and Tiffin 2007: 121).

This assertion has implications in the understanding of the marginal conditions of characters like Thami. First, the confrontation of Thami with the hegemonic superstructures of the Apartheid regime obliterates his future chances for emancipation. Secondly, Thami belongs to a social group that has no recognized identity that can possibly initiate social actions with the intention to negotiate change with local authorities. Fugard's discourse against marginality institution stems from the very fact that white south African regime has erected superstructures and enacted laws that sustain the apartheid ideology, promotes black subalternity with the intention to perpetuate imperialism.

The third question, "who"[can bring an end to post-apartheid legacy?] points to the responsibility of both political leaders and the civil society in the working out of strategies that can reduce social injustices of the postapartheid era to the maximum. In *No Good Friday*, marginality is the doorway to resistance by its assumption that power is an instrument of oppression and centrality. One would say that the perversion of justice, the unequal education system and job opportunities between Whites and Blacks, and the smearing tendency of the establishment of intimidation and violence are predicated on the belief that black community should be maintained under subaltern status as long as possible to prevent potential resistance, or socio-political uprising from happening. Such resistance can become a process of replacing the centre rather than deconstructing the binary structure of centre and margin, which is a primary feature of post-colonial discourse. Marginality unintentionally reifies centrality because it is the centre that creates the condition of marginality. In other terms, one could ask 'what purpose serves the proclamation of the end of Apartheid in theory but continue in its very ideology in practice? The replies come spontaneously, 'Apartheid marginalizes through its very belief in the inequality of human races and the acceptance of the white hegemonic domination over the black community. Fugard objects to the post-Apartheid legacy its failure to implement egalitarian society whereby all South African society citizens share equal opportunities. Apartheid functions as a structure, a geometry of power that leaves the black on the margin. Marginalization is continuous, processual, working through individuals as well as upon them. It reproduces itself within the very idea of the subaltern. Therefore, due to its ubiquity as a social injustice, to indicate various forms of exclusion and oppression, the theatricalization of the social reality endorses the deconstruction of post-Apartheid legacy as a narrative strategy that seeks to demote the system that established the marginality of black South Africans.

Athol Fugard has established that one of the great challenges of South African revolution is the search for ways of thinking, ways of perception, that will help to break down the closed epistemological structures of South African oppression, structures which can severely compromise resistance by dominating thinking itself. The challenge is to free the entire social imagination of the oppressed from the laws of perception that have characterized apartheid society. For Fugard, this means freeing the creative process itself from those very laws.

In *No Good Friday,* Fugard has captured the daily frustrations of black Africans confronted with the legacy of post-Apartheid social injustice and the constraints of survival in a society where the white minority in power has concentrated all good and decent jobs, major social amenities, best schools and training institutions, leaving the black majority to menial jobs and fewer educational opportunities. The play is set in Sophiatown, a suburb of Johanesburg, South Africa. Sophiatown as setting reinforces the idea of human right violation. The city was a legendary black cultural hub, but it was destroyed under Apartheid, and rebuilt under the name of Triomf. Sophiatown is depicted as one of the oldest black areas in Johannesburg and its destruction represents some of the excesses of South Africa under apartheid. In spite of the violence and poverty, it was the epicentre of politics, jazz and blues during the 1940s and 1950s. It produced some of South Africa's most famous writers, musicians, politicians and artists. But Sophiatown was profoundly affected by the 1976 Soweto Revolt, a mass uprising organized to claim for the human rights of the black community. The vagaries and brutalities of the police constitute one of the violations of human rights, the case in point being the bloody repression that followed the revolt. The revolt was violently repressed by the police, causing hundreds of dead people and thousands of casualties. Fugard considered this as a serious violation of black communities' human rights and dignity, and used drama as a creative medium to denounce the unjust mass killing and the general social injustice prevailing in South Africa.

> Higgins. All right. Tobias was an innocent man. A simple and a good man. He came to me on Friday looking for a chance to work and live. He asked for nothing more. This afternoon, two days later, I buried him. You know what it was like… I've buried others like that, Willie. It wasn't my first time even if it might have been yours. I know life is cheap here; I have heard that sort of talk until I am sick of it (*NGF*: 33).

This extract is taken from the episode in scene three where Father Higgin a white priest is telling Willie the painful testimonies of the violent killings he witnesses as a clergyman. The right of life and freedom are the first to be acknowledged and mentioned in the Universal Declaration of Human Rights by the United Nations Organization. The murder of Tobias shows the extent to which the fundamental human rights of persons, the right of life is being violated by the White South Africans with the cover up of the police. Fugard by creating this episode is exposing murder as a social cancer that needs strategic remedy and cure. The strategy put in place in the play is legitimate resistance that consists in claiming for one's rights without resorting to violence. But this strategy starts from the understanding of the concept of human right and see the role that the state is expected to play in the protection of citizens against the violators of these rights. An-Na'im proposes that "The basic concept of human right as claims to which all people without restriction are entitled as of right by virtue of their humanity firmly locates these rights and their implementation in the social and political realm of human affairs" (An-Na'im 2004: 165). This idea suggests that whatever these rights are, their implementation will necessarily require the allocation of resources over extended periods of time. The realization of human rights also presupposes the existence of an authority that can mediate among rights in case of conflicts and adjudicate the competing demands of claimants of rights. Therefore, the basic concept can only be achieved through some form of wide-scale political organization that is capable and willing to undertake these functions. The state is the form of political organization that is universally established, indeed assumed by the present system of international human rights. This reality not only involves the apparent paradox of expecting the state to vindicate human rights against its own organs and officials, but also to be able to act affirmatively in the implementation of these rights.

Nadine Gordimer explains the rationales behind the social revolts leading to Fugard's writing *No Good Friday* as follows:

> … Johannesburg's black township of Soweto exploded in revolt. Ostensibly the cause was the enforced use of Afrikaans – 'the language of oppressors', as the black students were calling it – as the medium of instruction in certain subjects in the schools; but a whole range of issues accreted around this one. What was new was that this was primarily a revolt of school children… The cost however was tremendous: official (and probably underestimated)

figures put the toll at 575 dead – most of the school children shoot by the police – and 2,389 wounded. The Soweto revolt as it became known, was a concerted challenge to the state, and it set the tone for the decade to come. At the same time however, it was also a challenge to white sympathizers. The black consciousness movement had categorized white liberals and radicals as being integrally caught up in the structures of white supremacy (Gordimer 1988: 118).

The account of the social injustice as described here is illustrated in *No Good Friday* and Fugard uses the contextual events to critically assess the general malaise and call for the respect of fundamental human rights and dignity for the black community.

The social mood prevailing gives most inhabitants "melancholy, loneliness, despair" (*NGF: 10*) because society is ruled by arbitrariness. Not only is it difficult to find decent employment, but the lucky Africans who find jobs are very often subjected to arbitrary humiliating practices like unjustified sacking, arrest, police brutalities and street criminal assaults. As Higgins says, "Every time I leave a house here in Sophiatown, I can see the neighbours putting their heads together to discuss the troubles of the family". Willie confirms to this by saying "Sophiatown is a fertile acre for troubles" (*NGF:* 10-11). The play is set in Sophiatown, and opens with a contention that the black community is victim of violence and injustice shown in the white racism in work place, schools and other social structures. Alan Shelley asserts "The core of Fugard's dramas is backgrounded by the reality of this hotbed of political activity" (Shelley 2009: 20). This statement reinforce the artist's perception of Apartheid South Africa as a violence-prone society, a situation which needs urgent remedy.

Athol Fugard sees the respect of human rights as the fundamentals in the repair of the prejudices. This should start from implementing inclusive educational policies to enable all citizens to be fully educated. The next step should be to give equal job opportunities to all citizens regardless of race, sex or gender. It follows that educational policies that are discriminatory in practice are prejudicial to the future of the South African nation. Fugard locates human rights within the ambit of social justice that need full application both in schools and in public services. Denial of school opportunities and arbitrary sackings from employment that pervade the social atmosphere of *No Good Friday* impede social cohesion and give rise to strife and resentments. Advocating the right to education and employment is not just a literary propaganda but an ideological commitment of the playwright for the social change in South Africa.

In *No Good Friday,* Athol Fugard has established a link between human right and legitimate resistance. In the play, Fugard shows that legitimate resistance has strong root in the struggle against the legacies of racial discrimination, an adjunct of Apartheid. But to fully understand Fugard's critical ideology about the necessity to re-establish the respect of human rights to black Africans, it is necessary to contextualise the political events that led to the removal of such rights. One major historical event that created social injustice in South Africa was 1993 Natives'Land Act. The Natives'Land Act of 1993 was created to separate whites' territories from blacks'. It created the basis of a territorially segregated South Africa. Under that legislation, Africans were prohibited from buying and renting lands outside the native reserves or "scheduled areas". These areas accounted for less than 7.7 percent of the combined land in the country, and eventually expanded to about 13 percent. The act also prohibited African sharecropping. White farmers helped push the legislation through parliament. In doing so they were able to attack the economic livelihood of thousands of African sharecroppers and rent tenants who lived on lands owned by white farmers. Awakening on Friday morning, June 20, 1913, the South African native found himself, not actually a slave, but a pariah in the land of his birth. Athol Fugard choses the title of his play *No Good Friday* with reference to that particular painful historical political decision that made black South Africans sink in oppression and despair.

In *No Good Friday,* Athol Fugard highlights South African postcolonial predicament through the tragic vision and life experience of Willie. Willie is the main character and the scholar in the township. He has realized that although he is educated, he will be unable to advance socially and economically because of the colour of his skin. His dreams and hopes fade away as he realizes that they now mean nothing, it was a waste of time to dream in the first place. There is no social mobility and the blacks have no rights of job access, education, and speech freedom. He refuses to adopt this mentality and to accept fate. Fugard has created and used Willie as the epitome of the average black South African citizen. Willie is different from Tobias in temper and in social vision. While Willie is committed to his vision of change, he is conciliatory in his approach to that change. But Tobias is a quick-tempered character, reactionary and violent. He dies during a night protest meeting, shoot by the secret police. The critic Dennis Walder views Tobias as a tragic hero rather than a tragic figure

(Walder 2000: xix). A tragic hero may be defined as an honourable character with a fatal flaw that eventually leads to his ruin. Fugard uses Willie's tragic vision of South African society as a theatrical strategy to question the legacies of racism that survived the abolition of the apartheid. I advance this critical stance because, Willie's fatal flaw was his desire to live a fair life without restrictions. He resented that the whites were in control of socio-political life and wanted to be set high above blacks. He was admired by the people of Sophiatown for being educated. They looked up to him and held him in high esteem. Because he was educated he was able to view certain issues from a different perspective. Unlike the typical residents of Sophiatown who simply accepted their social conditions, he stood for change and equality.

Another point highlighting Fugard's questioning is that, from the beginning of the play it is noticed that Willie does not accept the status that the dominant whites have given to him. When Guy explains to Watson how he strived to get a job but failed, the latter encourages him and both decide to fight, to proceed through revolutionary protests:

> Watson: The time for sitting still and submitting to every latest injustice is past. 'We gotta do something about it.' But then, I remembered that this was a meeting of the organizing committees and they might not like that. Just now, I had another idea. 'We must weld ourselves into a sharp spearhead for the liberatory movement'(*NGF, TP*: 8).

Watson and Tobias are well educated and degree holders who cannot find jobs due to the fact that they are black. The government and other private companies offer jobs to the white applicants who are less educated and less qualified than Tobias and Watson. What is worse is that they can do little to change that situation. Here one can notice that this very social injustice creates in both black men feelings of anger, resentment and an awakening of their consciousness. Fugard has created two characters with different approaches to socio-political problems of racism and injustice. His strategy is to consider the South African post-apartheid situation from different angles and select the one that better fits in the context. Fugard adopts a pragmatic approach to a complex problem: racial discrimination. Drama being a visual art, the presentations of this pragmatic approach may certainly be useful in thinking out ways of coming to terms with post-apartheid legacy.

19.2. From Interrogating to Foreseeing Resilience: Reconstruction of Human Rights

Athol Fugard has gone beyond the fact of interrogating the legacy of post-apartheid injustice by projecting in *My Children! My Africa!* the image of South Africa as a unified society where the white and black races live in harmony and tolerance. He is optimistic about the South Africa's future. Fugard says that human existence itself advocates freedom as the necessary condition for that existence and living in hope for a better future is predicated on the construction of present conditions that guarantee the protection by law of the acquired human rights. Fugar's militancy for human rights is perceptible through his narrative style. He gives the oppressed characters voice to express their inner frustrations and formulate their future hopes beyond the dire social injustices that pervades the social system of the play. Thami says:

> In fact, we want all the peoples of South Africa to share in that future. … black, white, brown, yellow… the future! … our future, the country's future, a wonderful future of peace and prosperity… I look around me in the location at the men and women who went out into that 'wonderful future' before me. What do I see? Happy and contented shareholders in this exciting interprise called the Republic of South Africa? (*MCMA, AFP1*: 207)

Thami represents the average black African citizen who lives in the hope of seeing a new South Africa with reconciled white and black communities. Here, she expresses the wish to see a new South African society where racial barrier has collapsed, and black Africans are enjoying the same opportunities like whites at two levels: equal access to education and employment, change in status of women from sexual objects to independent and emancipated beings, and end of police vagaries and brutalities. The legitimate resistance struggles in the play inform the desire and determination of Africans to see the foregoing ideals be fulfilled. Legitimate resistance as Fugard has it happen points to black South African people's claim for freedom and equal access to education and employment as they were advocated in the Declaration of the 1945 Pan-African Congress: "[We] are determined to be free. We want education. We want the right to earn a decent living; the right to express thoughts and emotions, to adopt and create forms of beauty. We will fight in every way we can for freedom, democracy and social betterment" (Shepperson and Drake 2008: 3)

This means that large scale political resistance of the Black Africans in the play come as a questioning of the social inequalities established by the Apartheid regime and which have survived for years after the abolition of the regime. In *No Good Friday,* characters like Tobias, Guy and Moses use civil disobedience as an instrument to oppose racist policies aimed against people of African origin. They use the same strategy of protest as Thami and Isabel in *My Children! My Africa!* Fugard's approach is unique in that he has characters temper with the confrontation traditionally associated with defiance of the law by acting in a non-violent way. This makes defiance of the law a viable option for the masses who often are not willing to engage in an all-out confrontation. Fugard also establishes a third option for protesters, strikes. This last option, a legitimate right for workers is usually badly received by employers and company directors who are use economic exploitation to maintain employees in abject poverty and servility. Fugard uses non-violence in the play as a powerful instrument of mobilization of the masses that has as effect the total commitment of the population to the struggle for freedom. Had he resorted to violent uprising and riots, this would have resulted in violent repression, manslaughter and endless killings. Non-violent form of protest reads as peace seeking strategy created by Fugard, not only as a narrative device but also as an ideologically oriented means of communication. Even though some critics do not see the same logic, I opine that Fugard believes violence breeds violence and there is possibility to stamp out such violence by using pacific means of struggle. The South African post-Apartheid injustices is a serious problem to solve, and Fugard uses theatre, the best means to reach the largest audience possible in sensitization and information spreading to have the message conveyed.

With *My Children! My Africa!,* Fugard has used drama to envision a society beyond the fractures of Apartheid. The creative potential of artist looks beyond the social fragmentation of racial discrimination to seek a resilience that passes tabula raza on the years of racial discrimination and plots new social relations. *My Children! My Africa!* is narrated in an interpersonal dialogue between staff members: "Isabel: I discovered a new world!" (*MCMA, AFPI:* 172). This statement advocates an ideological construction of a new South Africa that emerges as the product of a rejuvenated society. Drama as a performing art form, enables the stage representation of a creative potential that points out to the innermost aspiration of the artist for social peace and cohesion. It integrates idealistic values into the artistic realm that purveys new ethos in the constructive outlook of the playwright. When the debate opens, "Mr M is at a table with Thami and Isabel on either side of him. A lively inter-school debate is in progress" (*MCMA, AFP1: A*155). The ideas that come out of the debate are to promote new South African society based on new perception of women, the fundamental respect of their rights. Based on the ideas that emerge from the debate, curricula would be designed to integrate emancipatory becoming ideas the objective of which is to create a new South African.

The new South Africa of Fugard's conceptual framework rests on the idea that the different ethnic and social groups who constitute South Africa should sit together around the table of dialogue, debate in fairness on issues related to their society's wellbeing, arrive at a consensus and implement rules and decisions for their freedom and liberation. Dialogue should include all socio-political issues that constituted bones of contention in the past, locate reasons of failure and redefine new strategies for solving them efficiently. It entails on the one hand the coming together of the different socio-political actors involved in the Apartheid conflicts with the desire to let bygones be bygones, and on the other hand a constructive synergetic ethos that adumbrates formal and informal actions towards appeasement and mutual understanding: Dialogue therefore, is more than a discursive concept in the literary sense of the word. It foregrounds the implementation of a social strategy that ignites purposeful peace target and seeks a new social departure in the constructive model of a society governed by tolerance and mutual understanding. As Mr M explains to Thami,

> 'The orderly regulated discussion of an issue with opposing viewpoints receiving equal time and consideration.' Shouting down the opposition so that they cannot be heard does not comply with that definition. Enthusiasm for your cause is most commendable but without personal discipline it is as useless as having a good donkey and a good cart but no harness (*MCMA, AFP1*: 156)

Fugard's imaginative craft and his socio-political realism are a foreshadowing of the meteoric role of the Truth and Reconciliation Commission, a pivotal organ in the post-conflict mediation in South Africa. In South Africa's context, the historical advent of European colonization that swept by African continent and attempted to erase its past and to trample down its civilization constitute a challenging enterprise for Fugard in that it makes the playwright ponder in depth the problem of black identity and cultural redefinition.

Fugard refutes the Eurocentric claim of cultural superiority that was used by Europeans to enslave and colonize Africa. His premises are that Africa was unjustly victimized and now is the right time to write back:

> They come from a culture, the so-called Western Civilization, that has meant only misery to Africa and its people. It is the same culture that shipped away thousands of our ancestors as slaves, the same culture that has exploited Africa with the greed of a vulture during the period of colonialism, and the same culture which continues to exploit us in the twentieth century, under the disguise of concern for our future (*MCMA, AFP1:* 157).

Several aspects of societal reconstruction hold Fugard's attention. At the cultural level, the redefinition of South African culture as the cement that binds citizens is speculated at the beginning of the play. The picture that emerges is that of a cosmopolitan culture of African descents that blossoms at the pinnacle of African ancient civilization, a culture that redirects African values at the center. Inside these values stand hospitality, unity, respect for people's lives and self-discipline. Stress is put on education, gender parity and political freedom. Special treatment should be given to women: "the nation is achieved when education of the little ladies takes these facts into consideration. Would it be right for a woman to go to war while man sits at the sewing machine?" (*MCMA, AFP1:* 157). This should highlight the erasure of sexist stereotypes that consider women as less intelligent than men or as endowed with fewer intellectual potentialities. Culture serves a good social purpose when it promotes social cohesion, encourages the respect of human rights and creates an atmosphere of mutual tolerance and understanding. One of the reasons why Fugard offshoots the Eurocentric claim of civilizing mission advertised by colonialism is their legacy of cultural superiority on the peoples they sought to dominate, oppress and conquer.

Not only European colonialism was responsible for Africa's political turmoil and economic delay but it actually militated against women's education, their social well-being. It is not an overstatement to say that the colonial enterprise was responsible for women's social predicament as it supported patriarchy and its ideology. Taking into account women's well-being is therefore an essential literary project in Fugard's drama. The theatricalization of scenes showing the liberation of women from neo-colonial yoke, the creation of dialogue that set women's emancipation on the agenda and the possible gender equality dialogue are within the premises of his theatrical art. In the intellectual debate that engages school leaders in critical dialogue about the implementation of new curricula for students in the introductory scenes of *My Children! My Africa!* is intended to instill in their minds ideas about women's rights and their protection against all forms of abuse. The debate also considers the possibility of erasing in texts stereotypes about Africans depicted as being primitive or lacking civilization. Fugard goes beyond artistic construction to launch a true sociopolitical lampoon against colonial Europe and it contemporary cultural legacy in African affairs:

> Maybe there was a time in the past when a woman's life consisted of bearing children and hoeing the fields while men sharpened their spears and sat around waiting for another war to start. But it is a silly image that relies on that old image of primitive Africa for its strength. It is an argument that insults your intelligence. Times have changed (*MCMA, AFP1:* 156).

Athol Fugard is believed to be not only a Panafricanist, but a devoted writer whose sympathy for Africa and African affairs goes beyond the claim of artistic invention. He chatters the legacy of committed drama in the Shakespearean sense of the term. He relates directly drama to African nebulous past, bereft of her prerogatives as a rich, hospitable and generous continent which laid the foundation of development to the other continents, especially Europe and America. It is expedient to read his art as a patriotic claim for the restoration of Africa's cultural and sociopolitical dignity. In bit to deconstruct the discombobulating literary propaganda of Euro-centric oriented writers, Fugard engages the spectators or the readers in a test of critical examination of what art can do in the awakening of self-consciousness and the redefinition of personal and collective identity. The ethos that redirects perceptual framework in the adjacent role of the playwright as the reformer of his society finds here a strong endorsement for what art can do in the politics of path-finding, showing thereby the importance of drama, not only as an ideological tool used to question mistakes past and present but to actually initiate a talk for actual change. In this perspective, the dramatist is seen in a new light as society is able to see fundamental reflections of its own rebuttals on the dramatization of day to day life experiences.

In this perspective, and in the context of women's liberation struggle, Fugard considers that African women are shelters of human potentials, intellectual abilities and creative ingenuity that match their American counterpart. More clearly, African women are viewed in a new light as intellectually productive, technologically industrious and socially committed for the development of the African continent and from this claim, have no complex of inferiority in front of their American counterparts:

> The American space programme now has women astronauts on board the space shuttles doing the same jobs as men. As for the difference in the emotional and intellectual qualities of men and women, remember that it is a question of difference and not inferiority and that with those differences go strengths which compensate for weakness in the opposite sex (*MCMA, AFP1:* 158).

Beyond the women's question, Fugard offers meditations on how drama can be taken to the public, dramatizing the day-to-day post-Apartheid life and the survival struggles of black communities. The playwright redeploys theatrical discourse in the direction of self-abnegation and the pursuit of general interest among the black African communities. By addressing aspects of violence in South African societies, Fugard seeks to elaborate an art form that peels out inter-ethnic conflicts and suggest in specific terms some ways these can be definitely dealt with. The presence in the play of a debate on Africa and subjects related to peace strategies in Africa is real. What obtains from these issues is not a critical appraisal of Fugard's plays, nor a literary discourse per se, but a committed evaluation of artistic intent, that goes in the sense of social reforms, political renaissance and intellectual commitment: "Forget the faces, remember the words" (*MCMA, AFP1:* 159). He strives to inform, educate and enlighten the audience on the basics of human rights. The most targeted are the right to freedom of speech and opinion, the right to education, the right to decent living, the right to fair trial before the law, the protection of the law. That is what Thami says when advancing that:

> There is no comparison between that and the total denial of our freedom by the white government. They have been forcing on us an inferior education in order to keep us permanently suppressed. When our struggle is successful, there will be no more need for the discipline the Comrades are demanding…. I have liberated your mind in spite of what the Bantu education was trying to do to it (*MCMA, AFP1:* 217).

What Fugard is saying through Thami's mouth is relevant from two perspectives: firstly it means that Fugard uses the technique of presenting a learning process directly to the audience. The crutial monologues are delivered across the footlights, as the stage directions says.

Maria Lizet Ocampo explains that

> The apartheid system created educational inequalities through overt racist policies. The Bantu Education Act of 1952 ensured that blacks [would] receive an education that would limit educational potential and remain in the working class. This policy directly affected the content of learning to further racial inequalities by preventing access to further education. In addition to content, apartheid legislation affected the educational potential of students. School was compulsory for whites from age seven to sixteen and for blacks from age seven to thirteen. Clearly, the less education students received, the fewer choices they had in the working world and in accessing more education. Since these policies ensured that the content and amount of education perpetuated social inequalities, changing these policies in a post-apartheid era was the logical step towards social equality (Maria Lizet Ocampo 2016: 15).

Maria's explanation captures attention when she says that educational inequality was also evident in funding. The Bantu Education Act created separate Departments of Education by race, and it gave less money to black schools while giving most to whites. Since funding determines the amount and quality of learning materials, facilities, and teachers, disproportionate funding clearly created disparities in learning environments. For instance, apartheid funding resulted in an average teacher pupil ratio of 1:18 in white schools .... and 1:39 in black schools (*US Library of Congress*). Furthermore, the apartheid system also affected the quality of teachers. White schools had 96% of teachers with teaching certificates, while only 15% of teachers in black schools were certified. In addition to affecting the quality of education, the Bantu Education Act also resulted in the closure of many learning institutions since it withdrew funding from schools affiliated with religion. Since many church schools provided education for a large number of blacks, the black students were the ones most profoundly impacted by the withdrawal of these funds.

In *No Good Friday*, Fugard project in the future the image of a society reconstructed for black Africans to enjoy their citizenship rights. It is a society where one should be treated according to his qualifications, not the colour of his skin. Towards the end of the play, Pinkie tells Willie: "Willie, I got a good job." Willie replies:

> The world I live in is the way it is not in spite of me but because of me…There is nothing that says we must surrender to what we don't like. There is no excuse like saying the world's a big place and I am just a small little man. My world is as big as I am. Just big enough for me to do something about it. I can't believe that there is no point in living (*NGF, TP:* 50-51).

Fugard has Willie say his future perspectives on South Africa's post-apartheid problem. First, he asserts that the existence of problems does not prevent people to live in hope of a better future. Secondly, he refuses to confine himself in the cocoon of prevailing social difficulties. He chooses to see life beyond the current circumstantial difficulties but to believe in the next generation society where things will be different. Projecting oneself in the future is a wise manner of coping with life and believing in its future change. Reading carefully the two plays, *No Good Friday* and *My Children! My Africa!*, Fugard has questioned with an intellectual mind the logic of post-apartheid legacy in a society that is supposed to be apartheid-free and respectful of human rights. Looking into that questioning, Fugard has gone beyond interrogative praxis, to foresee better perspectives of hope for the South African black communities. But to arrive there one needs to be strategic, by being perseverant in hope and patient in character.

This paper tried to read Athol Fugard's *My Children! My Africa!* and *No Good Friday* as deconstructive narratives of the post-Apartheid legacy by questioning how the system promotes inequalities in education, employment, women's oppression and stereotypes. Two key ideas emerged: postcolonial theatre ascribes to the critical efforts to question Eurocentric hegemony both in society and in literature and to advocate the necessity to respect the black community's rights to be respected, educated, employed and liberated from all forms of oppression. Secondly, Fugard's, selected plays go beyond interrogations to foresee ways of avoiding past mistakes by envisioning a resilient society where all races interact on equal ground. The implementation of the policy of inclusion, mutual tolerance and peaceful co-existence is possible.

References

Amankulor, Ndukaku J. "English-Language Drama and Theatre". In Oyeka Owomoyela, ed., *A History of the Twentieth Century African Literature*. Nebraska: Nebraska University Press. 2001. 137-171.

An-Na'im. "Possibilities and Constraints of the Legal Protection of Human Rights under the Constitution of African Countries". In Christof Heyns and Karen Stefiszyn, eds. *Human Rights, Peace and Justice in Africa: A Reader*. Pretoria: Pretoria University Law Press. 2004.

Ashcroft, Bill, Gareth Griffiths and Helen Tiffin, *Post-colonial Studies: The Key Concepts*. London: Routledge Taylor and Francis Group, 2007.

Ashcroft, Bill and Pal Ahluwalia, *Edward Said: Routledge Critical Thinkers*. New York: Routledge, 2001.

Fugard, Athol. *My Children! My Africa!* London: Faber and Faber Ltd. 1998.

- ------------------. *No Good Friday*. Oxford: Oxford University Press. 2000.

Gordimer, Nadine. *The Essential Gesture: Writing, Politics and Places*. New York: Alfred A. Knopf, 1988.

Ocampo, Maria Lizet. *My Children ! My Africa ! Study Guide* retrived from *parksquaretheatre.org/.../My-Children-My-Africa-Study-Guide-20*. Consulted April 23, 2017.

Pettit, Philip. "Analytical Philosophy". In Robert E. Goodin, Philip Pettit and Thomas Pogge, eds., *A Companion to Contemporary Political Philosophy*. Maryland: Blackwell Publishing. 2007. 5-35.

Said, Edward. "Orientalism" pp. 87-91 in *Bill Ashcroft, Gareth Griffiths and Helen Tiffin*. New York : Routledge. 2003.

Shelley, Alan. *Athol Fugard, His Plays, People and Politics*. London: Oberon Books, 2009.

Shepperson, George and St. Clare Drake. 2008. "The Fifth Pan-African Conference, 1945 and the All African Peoples Congress, 1958," *Contributions in Black Studies*: Vol. 8 , Article 5. Vol 1. 2008. 1-32.

http://scholarworks.umass.edu/cibs/vol8/iss1/5 Assessed 20th June, 2017.

Vandenbroucke, Russell. "Robert Zwelinzima Is Alive". In Biodun Jeyifo, ed. *Modern African Drama A Norton Critical Edition*. New York: W. W. Norton and Company, 2002. 528-535.

Walder, Dennis.. 2000. "Introduction" in *Athol Fugard's Township Plays*. Oxford: Oxford University Plays.

20

ECOCRITICISM AND ENVIRONMENTAL ETHICS IN WOLE SOYINKA'S *THE BEATIFICATION OF AREA BOY*

This chapter conducts a literary reflection on the necessity of environmental ethics and the preservation of the natural ecosystem, through the struggle against pollution in Wole Soyinka's *The Beatification of Area Boy*. The reflection asserts that environmental ethics being the prior condition for a wholesome and decent environment, deforestation, pollution and other unbecoming degradations of the nature are to proscribe from human behavior, if life is to continue. From a literary perspective, this study purports to make explicit Wole Soyinka's critical concern for the preservation of the natural environment and bioethics through a literary approach.

The preservation of the environment has been a serious concern for many writers across the time. But a look at African literature reveals that few writers give enough space in their works to raise public awareness on environment. Chinua Achebe ironically remarks that "There is nothing wrong with the Nigerian land or climate or water or air or anything else" (Chinua Achebe 1988: 1) implying that they don't deserve special literary attention. Scott Russell Sanders in his article "Speaking a Word for Nature" complains about the fact that "a deep awareness of nature has been largely excluded from mainstream fiction" (Scott Russell Sanders 1996: 192). Helga Kuhse and Peter Singer assert that bioethics and the concern for environment "have gripped the public consciousness in unprecedented ways" (Helga Kushe and Peter Singer 2009: 3). Ian Thompson makes the point that "the failings that have led to environmental destruction have been human chauvinism and narrowness of sympathy" (Ian Thompson 2013: 452). These critical views prove that little attention is given to environmental ethics in African landscape and ecology in African literature; hence the necessity to conduct a study that focuses on the African setting. Pollution, its causes and consequences on the environment in Lagos city have fuelled theme and subject matter for the Nigerian playwright Wole Soyinka in the writing of *The Beatification of Area Boy* (Wole Soyinka: 1992). He seeks to attract the public's attention to the degradation of the environment by man. His play echoes that we live in an historic transitional period of bourgeoning awareness of the conflict between human activities and environmental constraints. On these grounds I purport to complement to the debate on the alert of global changes and attendant consequences as introduced by Wole Soyinka in *The Beatification of Area Boy*. In my critical analysis I will examine Soyinka's perception of the environment through the lenses of ecocriticism, paying attention to his call for new attitudes towards the environment.

20.1. Man as the Pathogenic Agent of Climate Change

20.1.1. Human Activities on the Ecosystem

Soyinka is of the view that human being is an active agent of global change. Adding his voice to that of experts on environment protection, he has been raising public awareness on the continual degradation of our environment due essentially to human activities on the resources of the earth. The warning echoes that if necessary measures are not taken to reduce to the maximum the degradation of our environment, life will be made difficult, even intolerable for future generations in the coming years. The stagecraft is the panel proposed by Soyinka, a writer of dramatic expression to continue the debate and let out the alert cry for social actors on the environment to reconsider the importance of our ecosystem and promote protection of fauna and flora (*TBOAB*, P2: 229). Desertification of Africa's forests and green spaces, has done harm to our natural environment and it is high time Africans give serious thought and take responsibility to preserve them if we want to enjoy the more a peaceful environment. In his lectures given on the occasion of the W. E. B. DuBois for Pan African Culture in 1990 in Accra, Wole Soyinka complained about:

> The little known geographical hiatus created by the desertification of once fertile lands of the Northern half of Africa, calculated to have taken place some twelve thousand years ago, appears to have been complemented, in an age closer and more relevant to our present, by the far too understated hiatus in African history [..]
> (Wole Soyinka 1993: 17)

What the critic's statement underscores here is the awareness that desertification has done much harm to African natural environment and threatens to make human life unbearable. Soyinka is an ecology sensitive writer. Apart from his literary commitment for peace, social justice, democracy and human rights in general, the playwright also identifies himself as a defender of the ecosystem, for, in his philosophy, one must live in a decent ecological environment to better produce material and intellectual wealth. Literary ecocriticism is the study of the relationship between literature and the physical environment. According to Cheryll Glotfelty, ecocritics and theorists share the fundamental premise that human culture is connected to the physical world, affecting it and affected by it (Cheryll Glotfelty 1996: xviii-xix). Ecocriticism takes as its subject the interconnections between nature and culture, specifically the cultural artifacts of language and literature. As a critical stance, it has one foot in literature and the other on land; as a theoretical discourse, it negotiate between the human and the nonhuman (Cheryll Glotfelty 1996: xviii). Ecocriticism can be further characterized by distinguishing it from other critical approaches. For instance, literary theory, in general, examines the relations between writers, texts and the world (Cheryll Glotfelty 1996: xix). In most literary theory, the world is synonymous with society – the social sphere. Ecocriticism expands the notion of "the world" to include the entire ecosphere.

Two things are to bear in mind, the preservation of African ecosystem and the bioethics. Soyinka's is the growing concern for ecologically informed criticism which signals the necessity to develop an ecological or environmental politics in African societies at large and the profession of humanities in particular; as well as to bring ecological consciousness to the practice of literary criticism (Serpil Oppermann: 2014: 2). Soyinka is responding to the global environmental crisis by turning to the field of literary ecology (*TBOAB, P2*: 243). The ecological investigations and interpretations of the relationship between nature and culture toward formulating ecologically informed critical principles in literary criticism and theory, inevitably leads him to an ecological oriented approach. As a result, Soyinka's ecocriticism seems to arrive with the promise to raise awareness on the crucial need to revalue our environment, to reshape agendas for more constructive environmental politics. Soyinka seems to say that "if we are not part of the solution, we are part of the problem (Cheryll Glotfelty 1996: xviii-xxi)". Therefore, his question is akin to Cheryll Glotfelty's "how then can we contribute to environmental restoration from within our capacity as teachers of literature? (Cheryll Glotfelty 1996: xviii-xxi) It is here that Soyinka's concern for bioethics finds full expression. Much of his literary output is directed against the cannibalistic attitude of eliminating human life through chemical weapons:

> [...] Nor does Iraq, which supplied the new Sudanese regime with chemical weapons to be used on black Africans even as Iraq itself had utilized it against the troublesome and "inferior" Kurds. I similarly avoid the massive, mutual depradation of Rwanda-Burundi over the past decade and half in which, yet again, the intervening voice at those critical times could be guaranteed not to be from the Black family. (Wole Soyinka 1993: 8)

Side by side with environmental ethics Soyinka is mostly concerned with bioethics, the preservation of human life, the bedrock and mainstay of human society. He evokes armed conflicts on the African continent which are the tunnel through which the elimination of human lives with chemical weapons is attained. The Nigerian civil war, Iraquian conflicts, the war in Sudan, Rwanda and Burundi are some few examples in which chemical weapons are said to have been used on human population, which is abnormal and needs to change (*TBOAB, P2:* 243). To echo the message, Soyinka thinks that stagecraft can better suit as a medium to speak to larger public, hence the writing of the theme of environmental ethics and ecocriticism in *The Beatification of Area Boy.*

In *The Beatification of Area Boy*, a play published in 1995, Wole Soyinka the Nobel Prize for Literature Laureate exposes some of the human activities that are damaging the environment. Deforestation, tear gaze spray, bombing, dynamite explosion, unleashing smoke through industries and overused cars, anarchic deposition of rubbish and waste material in the heart of cities, overconcentration of shanty buildings with poor sanitation conditions are among many other activities those that threaten the ecosystem and destroy our environment (*TBOAB, P2:* 259). Adding to these, the smoking and trafficking of cocaine affect not only the environment but also people's health in a way that causes prejudice to all efforts of development. At the center of these activities stands man, the perpetrator and the sufferer of environment degradation activities, and the question of responsibility leaks behind, for man is not ready to face the consequences of his activities on the environment. Glen A. Love taking inspiration from Arnold Toynbee remarks that,

> the present biosphere is the only habitable space we have, or are likely to have, that mankind now has the power to 'make the biosphere uninhabitable, and that it will, in fact produce this suicidal result within a foreseeable period of time if human population of the globe does not take prompt and vigorous concerted action to check the pollution and the spoliation that are being inflicted upon the biosphere by short-sighted human greed. (Glen A. Love 1996: 225

Adding to the foregoing, the critic postulates that "In the intervening decade-plus since Toynbee's statement, we have seen little in the way of the prompt and vigorous concerted action which he calls for, and we must consider ourselves further along the road to an uninhabitable earth. (Glen A. Love 1996: 225)"

These critical analyses highlight Soyinka's premises that man is the destroyer of the natural environment, but hardly thinks of replenishing what has been destroyed. In other words, human beings destroy the forests; pollute the soil, air and water, without replacing what has been destroyed. As Glen A. Love points it out, the catalogue of actual and potential horrors are rampant: the threat of nuclear holocaust, or of slower radiation poisoning, of chemical or germ warfare, mounting evidence of global warming, destruction of the planet's protective ozone layer (Glen A. Love 1996: 225). It also includes the increasingly harmful effects of acid rain, overcutting of the world's last remaining great forests, the critical loss of topsoil and groundwater, overfishing and toxic poisoning of the oceans, inundation in garbage, an increasing rate of extinction of plant and animal species. The doomsday potentialities are so real and so profoundly important that a ritual chanting of them ought to be replaced by concrete actions to renew the biosphere in which man lives. But rather than confronting these ecological issues man prefers to think about other issues. The mechanism which David Ehrenfeld calls "the avoidance of unpleasant reality (David Ehrenfeld in Glen A. Love: 1996: 226)" remains firmly in place. When the milieu becomes unsuitable for life due to cruel activities on the nature, man furtively leaves the place only to continue his destructive activities elsewhere, leaving to mother nature the task to replenish what he has destroyed. Soyinka has pleaded in the favour of environment preservation when he deplores "the destruction of villages and farmlands", with machine-gunning, the spraying of teargas. (Soyinka 1996: 150-151)

Soyinka's major concern lies with land and water pollution. Due to man's action on the environment, like deforestation, the nature has turned wild with shortage of rains, the disappearance of vegetation, the vanishing of species. This is illustrated in the conversation between Sanda and Mama Put:

> The clouds have vanished from the sky but, where are they? (*Jabs the tip of the bayonet against her breast.*) In the hearts of those below. In the raftyers. Over the hearth. Blighting the vegetable patch. Slinking through the orange grove. Rustling the plantain leaves and withering them – oh I heard them again last night – and poisoning the fish- pond. When the gods mean to be kind to us, they draw up the gloom to themselves – yes, a cloud is a good sign, only, not many people know that. Even a wisp, a mere shred of cloud over my roof would bring me comfort, but not this stark, cruel brightness. It is not natural (*BAB: 246-247*).

The alert against pollution and destruction of the nature is perceptible in this extract. Soldiers have sprayed toxic gas and it has affected plants, animals and fish, threatening their lives. What Soyinka indicts to the society is the fact that man undertakes actions susceptible to cause his own ruination without self-criticism. Scientists have established that although there may be questions about the causes of a specific drought or flood, there is no controversy about some basic facts about our atmosphere (Cheryl Simon Silver 1991: 64). Trace gases such as water vapour, carbon dioxide, methane, chlorofluorocarbons, tropospheric ozone, and nitrous oxide create a greenhouse effect by trapping heat near the earth's surface, and the concentrations of many of these gases are increasing in the atmosphere (Chery Simon Silver 1991: 64). Because of these increases, the gases are expected to trap more energy at the earth's surface and in the lower atmosphere, in turn causing increases in temperature, change in precipitation patterns, and other as yet unpredictable changes in the global climate. Soyinka's message is important: humans do not tread softly on the earth. In just a small fraction of the time of our brief presence on earth, humans have become powerful agents of change in the global environment.

20.1.2. The Spectrum of Pollution

One such destructive activity that causes spoilage and ruination to environment in Soyinka's outlook is pollution. When something is added to the environment which is very harmful, poisonous or fatal to the animal, people surrounding it and other living things, such a contamination can be called pollution. In simple terms pollution is a contamination by a chemical or other pollutant that renders part of the environment unfit for intended or desired use. It is triggered by industrial and commercial waste, agriculture practices, day to day human activities and most notably, modes of transportation and many the other sources. Pollution has many forms; it may be chemical substances or energy, such as noise, heat or light. Pollution is a very voluminous term; here we present some of the common pollutions.

Among the different types of pollution which are decried by the playwright Soyinka, one can point out:

20.1.2.1. *Water pollution*

Water pollution constitutes one of the causes of diseases and sporadic endemics and epidemics that sometimes plague African societies. For Soyinka the lack of good city planning policy, especially waste disposal infrastructures, haphazard garbage dispersal, brief absence of sanitation conditions can cause drastic health degradation. The criticism of this type of pollution is highlighted in *The Beatification of Area Boy* through a song that Soyinka has Minstrel sing with a box guitar:

> Maroko o. What a ruckus
> Over a wretched shanty town.
> It was stinking
> It was sinking
> We were rescued or we would drown.
> The lagoon breeze was pestilence
> A miasma hung over the horizon.
> We were banished
> Or we we'd be finished
> By sheer atmospheric poison
> No electricity or piped water
> No sewage or garbage disposal.

Was it decent
To be indifferent?
(*TBOAB, P2:* 312)

In this song Soyinka's indictment to the city of Lagos is the "ruckus" or excessive noise, "shanty town" insalubrities which stink, the lagoon polluted water that brings pestilence, the "miasma" which is a thick poisonous mist, and the total lack of "sewage or garbage disposal" dumps. It is then clear that for Soyinka, a polluted environment can but generate unhealthy medical conditions for the inhabitants of that environment. Therefore, it urges that the government of African countries put in place sustainable sanitation infrastructures to improve the living conditions of the overpopulated towns, in order to avoid health calamities.

Soyinka also denounces water pollution in *King Baabu* where Basha Bash undutifully spreads fertilizers and other chemicals along the roads without foreseeing the risks that such chemicals will eventually be carried by rain waters into rivers and wells where the population fetches drinkable water. Water pollution causes due to the introduction of chemical, biological and all sort of physical matter into large bodies of water that degrade the quality of life that lives in it and consumes it. We can blame fertilizers, pesticides, or petroleum derivatives for water pollution (Timothy Clark 2011: 88). In addition to that the other contributors towards water pollution are waste treatment facilities, mining, pesticides, herbicides and fertilizers, oil spills, refiners, failing septic systems, factories, oil and antifreeze leaking from cars, animal waste, Soap from washing your car, house hold chemicals and many more to count.

20.1.2.2. Noise and Air Pollution

Noise pollution is amply exposed and criticized in plays like *The Road, The Beatification of the Area Boy,* and *Opera Wonyosi.* It is the excessive noise that may disrupt the activity or balance of human or animal life. The main causes of noise pollution in *The Road* are machines, transportation systems, motor vehicles, aircrafts, and trains which come along with modern technology and industrialization. The release of smoke and cacophonic noise by overused cars contributes to endanger the human health. Characters like Professor, Salubi and Samson are active agents in the trading of overused lorries' spare parts in defiance to all environmental degradation and the impacts on human health the use of these cars can cause. The playwright highlights the fact that in addition to that the other causes of noise pollution are poor urban planning, the indoor noise caused by machines, building activities, music performances, and in some workplaces also.

Air pollution comes into picture due to the accumulation of hazardous substances into the atmosphere that endanger human life and other living matter. The most dominant player responsible for pollution is automobiles, the product of man's modern technology. Man then is the torturer and the suffer head of his own invention and actions (Timothy Clark 2011: 121). For Soyinka, man must revisit his actions. Apart from that the other causes are combustion of coal, acid rain, manufacturing buildings, tobacco smoke, paint fumes, aerosol sprays, nuclear weapons and wild fires. As far as effect of air pollution is concerned, respiratory diseases tops the chart of health problems. The second one is heart diseases caused by increased level of carbon monoxide in the air. We human beings could avoid some risks of asthma, eye irritation and a range of bronchial diseases due to air pollution if attention were paid to environmental ethical rules, for instance keeping the environment from pollution. If statistics is to be believed, every year air pollution segment will count for 80% of premature deaths. Soyinka highlights this idea through the statement of Barber, a character in the play:

> BARBER: The city's gone to pieces if this can really happen
> They are trying to pull us back to some prehistoric
> age Evil is on the loose; we've got our wits to sharpen
> Supernatural forces are out to dent our image Not even
> children ride a bike to school – it's indecent It shames
> the home, embarrasses the status-conscious parent Even
> a messenger would go on strike for an official vehicle
> Than be caught dead delivering letters on a bicycle. Even
> a messenger etc. (*BAB*: 258)

Soyinka's character is complaining about the fact that in Lagos, everybody wants to use a car, without predicting the damage that such cars bring on the environment through the emission of smoke. What is being underscored here is the fact that the careless manipulation of modern technology has created more problems to man than solved. The automobile, one of the most pervasive symbols of modern culture, serves as an apt metaphor for the ways in which humans charge the global environment. Automobiles emit carbon dioxide that adds to the buildup of greenhouse gases in the atmosphere, nitrogen oxide that reacts in the atmosphere and rain down as acid deposition, and other gases and particles that contribute to smog and local air pollution in urban areas. Soyinka's character has a point by indicting that it is abnormal for everybody in Lagos to be willing to drive a car.

20.1.2.3. Solid Waste

Solid wastes have a lion's share among total pollution. Such wastes are found in the cities environments of plays like *The Beatification of Area Boy* and *The Road*. Mainly it is composed of municipal solid waste (MSW), hazardous waste, plastic waste and E-waste. MSW also called trash or garbage is mainly composed of everyday items that are discarded by the public. Again MSW is of two types, biodegradable or recyclable and non biodegradable. The non biodegradable is more harmful in nature as it can't be degraded. Hazardous wastes always pose a great threat to an environment. Under RCRA in 40 CFR 261, hazardous wastes are classified into 4 categories: ignitability, reactivity, corrosives and toxicity (Cheryl Simon Silver 1991: 40). Plastic wastes always pose a great threat to the environment. Due to its non degradable nature it always tops the chart in pollution. E-Waste otherwise called as electronic waste, waste electrical and electronic equipment. E-Waste comprises of office electronic equipment, television sets and refrigerators, discarded computers, entertainment device electronics and mobile phones. All E-Waste poses lead, cadmium, beryllium, or brominated flame retardants, which trigger the pollution. Now E-Waste has been a global concern and all effort is being made to minimize it.

20.1.2.4. Grassroots Effects of Pollution on Environment

In his approach to the environment, Soyinka has taken into account the fact that pollution always causes harm to humans, pets, plants, trees, and aquatic life. Acid rain, eutrophication, ozone depletion, haze, global climate change, crop and forest damage are the major effects of pollution on environment. Pollution always takes away the balance of the fragile ecosystems of earth. Hence we should make all our efforts to incinerate waste and not to throw it into the ocean or on the land. To illustrate this, Soyinka has the prisoners sing:

> The forest depths are nothing, the savanna holds no surprise
> Does the bridge not leap over the gorge?
> [...] Be it the river, be it the ocean

> The wind leaps over them both
> The railway merely boasts; there is nothing new to the eye
> The sanitary inspector is a liar
> The dungheap is ever a dungheap.
> Mosquito larvae still inhabit the waterpot
> [...] soldier political, incorrigible robber
> Father of mayhem, you no longer bear arms
> You fight no wars but chase contracts all over the place.
> (*TBOAB*, P2: 321)

Through this song, Soyinka is concerned with both urban planning and rural landscape usage. He questions man's destructive actions on "the savanna", "the river", "the ocean", as through deforestation, excessive digging of sand, uncontrolled throwing of garbage and chemical deposition he turns the natural environment into a reservoir for dangerous parasites like mosquitoes, tsetse flies, the vectors of malaria and sleeping sickness. Soyinka also indicts "the sanitary inspector" and the political leaders for neglecting their job of "modernist urban planning" to borrow the expression from Peggy Tully (Peggy Tully 2013: 43). As Soyinka's *The Beatification of Area Boy* essentially bears on city, he thinks it is necessary to privilege urban planning, for a healthy post-industrial urbanity (Peggy Tully 2013: 43).

Ecologists argue that today there are 500 million registered automobiles throughout the world, each of which burns an average of nearly two gallons of fuel a day (Cheryl Simon Silver 1991: 49). Automobiles consume one third of the world's production of oil. As the population grows, so will the number of automobiles. In addition, the average number of automobiles per person is growing up, and the number of automobiles is increasing faster than the population, particularly in developing countries. Some estimate that if current trends continue, by 2025, there will be four times as many automobiles as there are today. Soyinka's alert then is that if one cannot forsake the purchasing of the automobile due to vital reasons, it behooves to the producers of automobiles to make automobiles that do not pollute the environment. If pollution reaches its apex degree, greenhouse will increase and as a result, climate may change, affecting rain falls. The situation to scare is that droughts may occurs. Thus, pollution can indirectly lead to climate change and to drought. In the play Soyinka says this through Sanda:

> SANDA: Some countries have it every year - Ethiopia for one.
> Such sights are common enough where droughts ravage

> the land and Governments do not care. The whole world predicts the drought But, it is always news to those in charge (*TBOAB, P:2: 302*)

It transpires from Sanda's statement that man's action on the ecosystem especially through deforestation and pollution is the major cause of drought. Soyinka has the character say this because drought itself is a human tragedy, considering how animals and human beings are decimated in areas where drought occurs. In the Sahel countries of Africa where drought is a recurrent phenomenon, animal decimation is a rampant phenomenon. In line with this stance, John P. Holdren, an expert on energy and resources is reported to have said that the damage that humans cause to the environment is a product of three factors: the total number of people, how much each person consumes to maintain his/her standard of living, and how much environmental damage is incurred in producing the goods consumed (John P. Holden in Cheryl Simon Silver 1991: 50). In that logic, to pursue the automobile metaphor a moment longer, the same can be said of the environmental damage caused by automobiles or, for that matter, factories and other manifestations of society. Literature and science having relation, Soyinka for instance, lets us perceive that the future environmental damage from the automobile will depend not only on the total number of people owning them, and the rate at which the number of automobiles per person increases but also on how much pollution each automobile emits. The synthesis of the analysis therefore postulates that our ability to change the global environment increases along with our numbers, our quest for, and achievement of affluence, and our technological capabilities. That is why in the play, Barber warns Sanda against "those overnight millionaires" who get quickly rich (*TBOAB, P2*: 240) and later reiterates that "The affluent are about to take over" (*TBOAB, P2*: 287). These intertwining factors, as products of decisions made by individuals and societies around the world are the main forces driving negative change in the global environment.

An environmentally informed reading of *The Beatification of Area Boy* suggests that Soyinka is preoccupied with the fact that in the context of widespread disciplinary evaluation, African literary criticism seems to have remained unwilling to address questions which are at the forefront of public concern - environmental ethics (Glen A. Love 1996: 229). Beside African writers' tendency to postpone or to relegate to lesser priorities ecological considerations, it urges also to recognize a general failure to consider the narrow anthropocentric view of nature. The extension of human morality to the non human world suggests that time is past due for a redefinition of what is significant on earth: human, animal and vegetation lives (Glen A. Love 1996: 229). In other words Soyinka is advocating the necessity to maintain biodiversity. A discussion of the human causes of global environmental change would not be complete if one does not mention the pressures that the numbers of people inhabiting the earth place on the environment. It is in this logic that at the beginning of the play, Sanda, a character uses the "incident of genitals removal - in which a magic maker makes a man's genitals disappear-"to draw attention of the fact that the Nigerian government "has been preaching population control" and "the tactics they would think off" to reach the goal (*TBOAB, P2: 279*). This incident of genital removal is caused by a suspect magic maker who is believed to have touched a man's genitals to cause their disappearance. This incident has caused a bewilderment and vivid commotion in the market and a big crowd gathered to see what really happened. Soyinka's worry is understandable because Nigeria is to the best of my humble knowledge the most populous country of Africa, at least of West Africa.

At the world scale, the explosion in the numbers of people inhabiting the earth is significant because, at the very least, each of these people requires food, clothing and shelter. Growing numbers of people cut forest for land to grow food and graze cattle, with global consequences for the hydrologic cycle, the ability of the land to sustain agricultural productivity, and the earth's genetic resources as millions of plant and animal species are driven to extension. Soyinka's writings amply highlight pollution in its diversities as active agent of the degradation of the environment.

20.1.2.5. Literary Perception of Soyinka's Bioethical Pragmatism

Soyinka advocates in his writings the imperial necessity to defend and protect the ecosystem and the natural resources of fauna and flora. He is pragmatic, for, he says, as all living beings draw livelihood and subsistence from the nature, it urges for individuals to develop environmental and biomedical ethics for the preservation of the common earth. Godfrey B. Tangwa in his reflections on biomedical and environmental ethics has amply highlighted what Soyinka also considers the negative impacts of Western technology on the global climatic change, and laid emphasis on global warming,

> The process of globalization, which today has turned the world into a veritable global village is increasingly bringing both the benefits and hazards of Western technology and especially, biotechnology to all parts of the globe. Some of the most urgent hazards involve human health and the global physical environment (Godfrey B. Tangwa 2004: 394).

This view takes into account the multi-facets changes that the Western technology that sprang in Europe from the Industrial Revolution era brought with it all over the world, as machinery in industries replaced human labour. Thus, in the domain of military technology, the creation of the nuclear arms occasioned the proliferation of massive destructions of human lives, animals' and plants'; the anarchic implantation of industries engendered the various pollutions of water, land and air with the continual depletion of ozone layers. The ensuing global warming and the climatic changes with the continual advancing of sea waters on human habitation areas have caused the public alert of imminent danger by scientists and environment experts. At practical level, there has been the phenomenon of new technology accompanying the globalization process. The concept of globalization, Godfrey B Tangwa writes, can be considered as referring to both a descriptive and a prescriptive levels (Godfrey B. Tangwa 2004: 394). As a descriptive process, globalization has been made possible and inevitable by advances in Western science and technology, especially in locomotion and communication technologies. This has led to the increased contact between the various peoples and cultures of the earth. At prescriptive level, globalization arises from increasing awareness of both the diversity (ecological, biological, cultural, linguistic, anthropological), and interdependence of the various parts of the world. It arises also, from the simple deduction from this last consideration that the dangers facing the world as a whole, even if emanating largely from only a small part of it can best be tackled only from a global perspective (Kwasi Wiredu: 2004: 394). That every discipline seeks to give a considerable place in the research on and study of environmental with the sole objective of stopping the advancing rapid degradation of our planet earth. Disciplines such as eco-philosophy, environmentalism, eco-criticism, eco-feminism, bioethics, tele-detection, all aim at finding ways and means to stop the rapid degradation of our environment and possibly find alternative renewable energies (solar energy for instance) to palliate and remedy to the shortage of natural energetic resources of our globe which are running out slowly but surely. At international scientific conferences topics on the agenda include global warming, climatic changes, and their impacts on human lives, animals' and plants' are frequent to stimulate reflections and conduct researches for finding out lasting solutions to these problems. This may be the philosophy behind which James Rachels argues that the human endeavors in contemporary time should strive to orient researches towards a utilitarian goals. According to James Rachels,

> Utilitarianism is the leading example of an ethical theory that might be thought to solve bioethical problems by the straightforward application of its ideas. Utilitarianism says that in any situation we should do what will have the best overall consequences for everyone concerned. If this is our theory, and we want to decide what should be done in a particular case, we simply calculate the likely effects of various actions and choose the one that produces the greatest benefit for the greatest number of people (James Rachels 2009: 15).

The cogency of this remark lies in what I will call Soyinka's political perspective, that is, his efforts to persuade his audience to develop a new set of attitudes towards the environment. Soyinka is a nature writer in whose drama one can see a growing concern for the preservation of the environment, the safeguarding of the ecosystem and the encouragement of biodiversity. The fauna and flora need particular attention from humans, if we are to maintain the equilibrium of our ecosystem. These ideas are dear to him because all living beings draw their subsistence from the ecosystem. Trees, plants, soil and rain are the natural resources that supply us with food, water, shade, oxygen when needed. Therefore, practices like deforestation, nature intoxication, and pollution of all kinds should be avoided.

It is a fact that biotechnology holds a certain justified fascination for human beings, because of its potential in such domains as preventive and therapeutic medicine and in agriculture. In the face of these developments, human ethical sensibilities and responsibilities are urgently called for. As human beings, we carry the whole weight of moral responsibility and obligations for the world on our shoulders. I agree with Godfrey B. Tangwa who posits that, the claim that humankind is the apex of biological existence, as it is known, has sometimes been dismissed as an arrogant spiciest claim and contested by some human militants for the rights of animals and/or plants (Godfrey B. Tangwa 2004: 388). However, one has to admit the fact that, while human beings have putative moral responsibilities towards animals, plants and inanimate objects, the latter cannot be considered without absurdity, as having reciprocal moral obligations towards humans (Godfrey B. Tangwa 2004: 388).

In the same perspective Soyinka thinks with Ph. Bourdeau that "our behavior and policies with regard to nature and the environment should be guided by a code of ethics, which is to be derived from basic principles and from a pragmatic consideration of the issues at stake (Ph Bourdeau 2014: 3)." The man-nature relationship has always been ambiguous, nature being seen as both a provider and an enemy, in the sense that man has to conquer, tame and subdue it to feel his needs. Now, as nature is threatened by man who has become detached from it, it is high time he became aware of the threatening danger of man-provoked environment degradation, a step towards natural calamities (Ph Bourdeau 2014: 3). Nature can be seen as beautiful and harmonious, but it also inspires fear if man has had to fight in order to survive. Technology has endowed humans with the power of a major geographical agency, which may act on a continental or even planetary scale. Examples include acid rain, photochemical smog, radioactive contamination, stratospheric ozone depletion, climate change and global warming.

Soyinka's writing is geared towards what I can term the defense of post-colonial ecojustice. An environmentally informed reading of Soyinka can both enhance and question the common interest between defending the natural world and defending the cultures of indigenous people (Timothy Clark 2011: 123). We can see in *The Beatification of Area Boy* and possibly *The Lion and the Jewel* a disruption to old traditions rooted in the local or regional where identity is based on communal values rather than on possessive individualism, and on aspects of the natural world as opposed to capitalistic exploitation (Timothy Clark 2011: 123). The various characters' responses to environmental injustice as Lagos city and the village of Ilujinle turn into destination for mass tourism and are damaged through various industrial pollutions, energy, military and infrastructure projects, reveal a preoccupation for a redemption of the nature, for land must survive for man to survive. Soyinka's art offers itself as both post-colonial and environmentalist at the same time. *The Beatification of Area Boy* reveals how resistance against the destruction of the environment means resistance against capitalism of dominant cultural groups, social and political marginalization, especially for Lagos suburb poverty-ridden masses. This is so because it is their shanty towns that serve as humping dumps for the industrial waste material and garbage of the manufacturing industries. Localism and resistance to national and international capitalism are taken to be green, that is a simple identification of this kind informs most criticism striving to unify post-colonial and ecocritical stances.

Ecological or environmental language also acts in Soyinka as a middle ground for him in most of his post-colonial writings. For instance in *The Open Sore of a Continent a Personal Narrative of the Nigerian Crisis,* Soyinka relates human lives destruction to two factors, misruling of the nation by corrupt leaders and the misuse of modern military technology:

> Millions have drowned into those storms, however, let us never forget that. Millions of that humanity have been swept away, millions have perished, never really understanding why, never really understanding to what gods they were sacrificed other than the state or the aspiring state had ordered it, that some programme in the cause of a mere concept of nationhood demanded they be uprooted from their homes, turned into the stateless non persons […] (Wole Soyinka 1996: 115)

This is a critical appraisal of the consequences of modern technology misuse by a power-drunk military dictatorship, who takes to arms and chemical weapons at the least dissident uprising to massacre the innocent populations. Soyinka's stance here is anthropocentric, a criticism pleading for the preservation of human life, bioethics. For the contemporary African nature writer like Wole Soyinka, the process through which he can verbalize personal experience, demand the cessation of nature degradation and contribute to raise human awareness of self and non-self, to name nature is the approach of dramatic art. As a playwright, his use of writing and stagecraft aims to restore if not wholly, at least partially the nostalgic environment of Eden garden, the purity of nature. His is a kind of pastoral ideology that aims at the restoring of the nature.

In this chapter, the main results achieved evolve around three key ideas. First, Soyinka has a deep ecological concern about the preservation of the environment, a sine qua non condition for human and non human lives. This concern shows up in *The Beatification of Area Boy* through the denunciation of pollution (air, land and water), global warming, ozone depletion, waste disposal, animal farming, endangered species and his call for energy and ecosystem preservation. Second, present human actions on the natural environment seem to be more destructive than constructive. Third, African writers should also incorporate ecological concerns in their works. Soyinka's philosophy is 'human centered' and provides reasons why human interests should be given priority.

References

Achebe, Ch. *There Was Once a Country. A Personal Narrative of Biafra.* London: Penguin Group. 2012.

---------------. *The Trouble with Nigeria.* London: Heinemann Educational Books. 1988.

Clark, T. *The Cambridge Introduction to Literature and the Environment.* Cambridge: Cambridge University Press. 2011.

Glotfelty, C. and Harold F. eds. *The Ecocriticism Reader Landmarks in Literary Ecology.* Georgia: The University of Georgia Press. 1996.

Harris, M., Martin N. and Bronwyn C. The Politics of Identity: Emerging Idigeneity. Sydney: UTSePress. 2013.

Inness, C. L. *The Cambridge Introduction to Podtcolonial Literatures in English.* Cambridge: Cambridge University Press. 2007.

Kachru, Y. and Larry E. S. *Cultures. Contexts and World Englishes.* London and New York: Routledge. 2008.

Kuhse, H. and Peter S. *A Companion to Bioethics, Second Edition.* USA: Blackwell Publishing. 2009.

Rachels, J. "Ethical Theory and Bioethics", in Helga Kuhse and Peter Singer (eds.) *A Companion to Bioethics.* UK: Wiley-Blackwell A John Wiley & Sons, Ltd., Publication. 2009. 15-23.

Rivkin, J. and Michael R. *Literary Theory: an Anthology.* USA: Blackwell Publishing. 1998/2004.

Sanders, S. R. "Speaking a Word for Nature" in Cheryll Glotfelty and Harold Fromm (eds), *The Ecocriticism Reader: Landmark in Literary Ecology.* London: The University of Georgia Press. 1996. 182-195.

Silver, C. S. *One Earth, One Future Our Changing Global Environment.* New Delhi: National Academy Press. 1991.

Soyinka, W. *The Open Sore of a Continent a Personal Narrative of the Nigerian Crisis.* New York. Oxford: Oxford University Press. 1996.

--------------------- . *The Beatification of Area Boy.* London: Methuen Publishing Ltd. 1995/1999.

------------------. *The Blackman and the Veil Beyond the Berlin Wall.* Accra: Sedco Publishing. 1993.

Tangwa, G. B. "Some African Reflexions on Biomedical and Environmental Ethics" in Kwasi Wiredu ed. *A Companion to African Philosophy.* USA: Blackwell Publishing. 2004. 387-395.

Thompson, I. "Landscape and Environmental Ethics" in Peter Howard, Ian Thompson and Emma Waterton (eds) *The Routledge Companion to Landscape Studies.* London and New York: Routledge. 2013. 450-460.

Tully, P. "On Landscape Urbanism" in Peter Howar, Ian Thompson and Emmanuel Waterton (eds) *The Routledge Companion to Landscape Studies*. London and New York: Routledge. 2013. 438-449.

Tyson, L. *Critical Theory Today A User Friendly Guide Second Edition*. London and New York: Routledge. 2006.

Ngugi, w. T. *Moving the Center The Struggle for Cultural Freedoms*. London: James and Currey. 1993.

Web sites

Bourdeau. "The Man-Nature Relationship and Environmental Ethics" in *Journal of Environmental Radioactivity*" http://www.sciencedirect.com. 2014.

Oppermann, S. 2010). " Ecocriticism: Natural World in the Literary Viwfinder". 2010.

CONCLUSION

The contour of the literary theories and the critical approaches offered in this book have taken into account symbolism naturalism, nativism, the quest for indigenous aesthetics, oral narratives, narratology, Marxism, cultural materialism, structuralism and poststructuralism, postmodernism, psycho-analytic criticism, new historicism, ecocriticism, feminism, postcolonialism, intertextuality Afropolitanism and black consciousness aesthetics. Modern African drama is read with the lenses of these theories. The findings are as follows. To begin with, my argument has been counteracting the stereotypic argument that African drama cannot be theoretically interpreted. African drama and theatre cannot be theory-free. African indigenous traditional drama is grounded on the cultural performances namely ritual, festival, rites. The nativist movement are pioneered by African nationalist dramatists who turned to indigenous material for inspiration and creativity. Indigenous aesthetics are fused into drama by paywrights as strong cultural material that hamper the nostalgic evocation of African originality, genuineness and authenticity. It has been advanced that the domestication of literary genres like drama respond to the necessity to create an African version and variant of performative arts adapted to African cultural parlances, local aesthetics and indigenous prints. Domestication is felt at different levels: the setting, the plot, the use of language, characters' delineation, the themes discussed, and the authorial ideologies conveyed. At language level, indigenous words are coined, borrowed and typical African ideas are translated or transliterated. Greetings, conversation techniques, day-to-day stock exchanges unveiling the African oral and oratorical skills are displayed. Proverbs, riddles, puns, wise popular sayings are exhibited to fit in the African conversational arts and widom lore.

It has been argued that some African plays have been adapted from European plays. For instance, Ola Rotimi' s *The Gods Are Not to Blame* is adapted from Sophocle' s *Oedipeus Rex*. Soyinka' s *Opera Wonyosi* is an adaptation of John Gay' s *The Beggars' Opera*. Bamgbose, Gabriel Sunday in his article "Reading with an Eagle-Eye: The Theory and Practice of African New Criticism" has observed that:

> The assertions that the appraisal of African literature lacks theoretical rigour are not valid. The reading of literature cannot be theory-free. Every discourse written or spoken about literature is grounded in theory(ies)… If the reading of literature cannot be divorced from theoretical rigour, then the appraisal of African literature cannot be an exception" (Gabriel 2013: 1).

By this submission he means that the reading of African literature namely drama has been enriched by the application of methods drawn from contemporary literary theories. The appraisal of African drama, borrowing the words of Bill Ashcroft, Gareth Griffiths and Helen Tiffin (1989:155), "intersect in several ways" with contemporary literary theories such as postmodernism, Marxism, feminism, psychoanalysis, ecocriticism and so on. Even though African literature is "utilitarian" (Tanure Ojaide, 1995:4), scholars and critics of African drama have attempted to apply intrinsic or texts-based theories such as formalism, New-Criticism, structuralism and post-structuralism to the study of African literature for proper elucidation. Prominent is the effort of the African critic, Sunday Anozie, to apply the structuralist poetics to African literature. Amaechi Akwanya (2000:68) posits that "there are no theories which apply exclusively to African literature." This implies that the study of African literature is placed on the pedestal of contemporary critical traditions. The "appropriation" of contemporary literary theories "offer perspectives which illuminate some critical issues addressed" by African literary texts, although African literary discourse "itself is constituted in texts prior to and independent of" these theories (Ashcroft, Griffiths & Tiffin, 155). Contemporary theories of literature are "viable for the discussion of African literature but they need constantly to be interrogated and rethought" (Akwanya, 68).

The practicability of African New Criticism, to borrow words from Sunday, a sort of hybrid of the textual and the contextual as opposed to the Anglo-American New Criticism, which is extremely textual; is a formalistic explication of text with focus on the intrinsic. However, it strives to resist the temptation of ignoring the extrinsic since both are modes of signification of meaning. Attempts is made to examine how New Critical theory is "interrogated" and "rethought" in African context. The New Critics, just like the Russian formalists "pay close and careful attention to the language, form and structure of the literary texts while regarding individual texts as the principal object of critical investigation" (Ogunpitan, 127). New Criticism is a reaction to the traditional approaches to the study of literature, which subject a work of art to extrinsic details such as history, biography, socio-economic conditions, etc. The New Critics simply ignore the life outside the text. At first, it is associated with the "Fugitives", an informal group that engages in the discussion of literature.

The structuralist and poststruralist reading of African drama hold that the anti-colonial ideology of African drama reveals an Afrocentric philosophy and critical thought. And it is seemingly redundant in a 21st century drive towards cultural globalization and multi-racism. Thus, any rejection of hybridity is restrictive and ironic on the grounds that the variety of European languages used in expressing African literatures is sometimes not the type acceptable to or even intelligible to the average scholar of African drama. Rather, the language is domesticated, and African indigenous thoughts are violently forced or imposed on the foreign language in for more translation or transliteration to make it bear the burden of ritual aesthetics and speech idioms of the race. Thus, even though a large chunk of African drama bears the burden of European language, much of them are however conveyed in special hybrid variety that is not spoken anywhere in European literature, except perhaps amongst the new African arrivals in the West. Therefore, neither the Euro-American nor the Africana conservative concept of African literature is appropriate for being used as yardstick for the definition and canonization of reading theories for African dramatic literature. African theatre is very wide and varied. Such diversities are caused by linguistic and cultural heterogeneity as historical consequences of foreign domination and control under colonial rule which gave rise to new languages and invariably new and variegated patterns of cognition, thinking and living along such cultural divisions such as Anglophone, Francophone, Iusophone countries. This lays validity to Achebe's time-tested assertion that "No man can understand another whose language he does not speak" (1962:62). Here Achebe does not just mean language in the sense of syntactic, lexico-semantic or phonological properties of human speech alone. Rather he means language as it subsumes all aspects of the totality of human history, culture and entire world-view. Thus, Bernth

Lindfors warns that "foreign critics should heed this warning and not attempt to tresspass brazenly on territory that belongs to others who acquired the indigenous grammar while young and thus know how to decode and interpret the deep structures underlying their own semantic universe." (2002:7).

The anti-colonial ideology of African drama reveals an Afrocentric philosophy and critical thought.

Staying in the streamlight of critical theories, I focused on feminist African playwrights which I divided in three waves. The pioneers or first wave feminists include Nawal Al Sadawi, Flora Nwapa, Zulu Sofola, Tess Onwueme, Efua T. Sutherland, Ama Ata Aidoo. The second wave comprises Chinyere Grace Okafor with her *The New Toy Toy* (2007) and Irene Isoken Oronsaye-Salami's *Sweet Revenge* (2007). The third wave of African drama feminists are Ade Solanke an Zeynab Jallo.

Julien made a valid observation about the shifts, changes and evolution of African literature in certain perspectives: understanding of African literature has changed tremendously in the last twenty years, because of several important developments the ever increasing number of women writers, greater awareness of written and oral production in national languages (such as Yoruba, Poula and Zulu), and greater critical attention to factors such as the politics of publishing and African literature's multiple audiences. These developments coincide with and have, in fact, helped produce a general shift in literary sensibility away from literature as pure text, the dominant paradigm for many years, to literature as an act between parties located within historical, socioeconomic and other contexts (295-6).Julien's critical observation is another valid site for the consideration of the various transformations which have taken place in the nature and characteristics of African literature – all of which should add up to the criteria for developing a theory for the reading of African literature. But, beyond critical recognition of this problem and intricacy for defining and developing a theory of African literature is a very compelling need to explore the context sensitive nature of the problem and to configure their epistemological implications for the theory, criticism and meaning of African literature.

The contextual and cultural crisis in African drama is partly predicated on its 'post-colonial status' leading to inevitable modal transition from oral to written. And this is largely informed by its linguistic, cultural and artistic hybridity – all of which conspire to underline its elusive definition. Thus, invariably, European concept of drama/ theatre or literature is being foisted on the African forms of verbal performance and ritual aesthetics. In the early sixties, the application of European idea of literature to African literature was being hastily done with the view, perhaps, to disproving the then canonized intellectual error in European idea that pre-colonial Africa never had literature or it genres and aesthetic sensibility. Indeed, the early European historianswho wrote about Africa had ignorantly misrepresented Africa as a dark continentwhose people basked in primitive customs of animism and religious fetish. This was an unscholarly view which smacked of parochialism anchored on the disgust of colonial missionaries for any 'Other' but Judeo-Christian forms of worship. In order to counter this insulting claim and cultural denigration of Africa, some early'Africana' scholars were desperately poised to establish that pre-colonial Africa hada form of dramatic art which was either embryonic or fully mature and comparableto the European forms of drama and theatre. This claim again appeared whimsical. And it was meted with resistance in the works of Oyin Ogunba, Isidore Okpewho, Ngugi wa Thiong' o, Ama Ata Aidoo, Athol Fugard, Biodun Jeyifo, Abiola Irele and Karin Barber to mention a few. The early Africana scholars argued that such comparisons are often not cautious to compare African forms of literature - especially the dramatic poetic and the narrative - with its western type only at comparable periods of history. After all, there is marked difference between pre-colonial African drama and colonial or modern African drama. The question is: with what sense of propriety could onedescribe the African festivals, rituals and ceremonies as 'drama' or 'theatre'? This poses a problem of identity for African verbal art and performance because thecultural context that informs the European drama is different from that of the African verbal performance. Thus, African drama is in dilemma of universal literary statusand invariably, the problem of evolving a zero-European critical theory is createdsince the cultural instruments for decoding its meanings are neither resident inwestern literary establishment nor even in European trained African scholars butin the very indigenous active bearers of the tradition. By tradition here is meantthe totality of the anachronistic values, customs, culture, religion, and the timeless, eternal, cosmological four-dimension space of the living (present) the dead ancestors (past), the unborn (future) and the interlocking cosmic space between history and cryptic future. However, there are African scholars and literary critics, especially those whose scholarships are obtained in indigenous African cultures and languages, whose study of the signifying timbers of African verbal and literary idioms have enabled the distillation of African–centered methods of interpretation. This effort is, however, still embryonic; but there is hope of striking the water level in this quest since there is, nowadays, more interest in oral research especially in African language literatures and cultures than European studies, in spite of the seeming terror of globalization whose questionable method, at times, is towards the eclipse of post-colonial, third world, values by the so called 'universal' western cultures. The half-a-century old search for an African literary identity on the geo-literary global map seems over now that the world speaks with one voice in acknowledging 'the significance' of African drama to global literary scholarship.

Biodun Jeyifo (1990) and Dan Izevbaye (2008: 8) have both agreed that African drama enjoys profound theoretical wealth since 1986 when Wole Soyinka became the first African writer to win the prestigious Nobel prize for literature) provides evidence that African literature needs no further theoretical justification in aid of its status as a standard variety of world or commonwealth literature. Thus, the immediate next task for African literary scholarship is to look within and look around the context and culture of its episteme and verbalization in order to evolve poetics of readings and interpretations that would excavate its own unique indigenous technology and theory of existence.

Re-configuring the relative status of rituals in developing an African theory amounts to integrate oral performances and traditional festivals into the intellectual fabric of drama. Apart from the problem of nomenclature, several scholars of African drama have always locked horns on the labeling of African ritual performances and festivals, which have certain propensity for mimesis and dramatic or theatrical echoes, as drama or theatre. Kerr (1981:131) observes that the English words "theatre" and "drama" are loaded with certain "dramaturgical and aesthetic expectations arising from the long history of western theatre". In the Western theatre or drama, these "dramaturgical and aesthetic expectations" would include the formalized dramatic and theatrical elements such as character, dialogue, diction, mimesis, dance, audience, costume, plot complication, suspense, concealment and disclosure, reversals, causal relationship between happenings, conflict generation, conflict resolution, proscenium effects of lighting, formalized stage, curtain, scenery and spectacle. Although some of these aesthetic elements are also, in varying degrees, present in pre-colonial African dramatic forms, they are, however, not backed up by sophisticated canonized theories. Enekwe (1981) opines that what constitutes drama is functionally determined by the conceptual framework of this aesthetic medium. Dramatic art, as aesthetic communication, is based on the appetite for art, celebration, creativity and didacticism in 'culture-specific' and variable ways, as observed in each cultural space across the world. Enekwe (1981:152) suggests that: Function determines the nature of drama in every culture. In the 5th century B.C. Greece, for instance, poetry was central to drama because for the Greeks it was the most desirable and perfect art form. In Asia and Africa, on the other hand, dance mime and music are the essence in the theatre. While the mainstream European theatre is syllogistic in form, the Asian and African theatres are ritualistic. In Greek tragedy moral order must be redirected by the order of events.

I have considered ritual drama, festival drama and symbolism due to the profound and complex symbolic dimension of African worldview. According to Echeruo (1973:25), the rituals do not pass for drama because they are, functionally spiritual, sacred and transcendental occasions. He posits that "the dramatic content of the ritual is buried in its ritual purity". In his own study, Okafor (1991) deconstructs the likes of Echeruo's perception of African rituals with a European critical lens. Okafor argues that "Misunderstanding… arises when it is evaluated on the basis of Western critical criteria" (39).

Obviously, Echeruo's view of drama is grounded on the very lack of symmetrical correspondence of African ritual performances and the Greek and Western concepts and practices of drama. Bill Ashcroft et al (*The Empire Writes Back*, 1989) have observed that the failure of the so called universal western literary hegemony "to deal adequately with the complexities and varied cultural provenance of post-colonial writing" (12) provided "unprecedented" opportunity for the 'marginal' post-colonial discourse to attain "creative energy" of resistance and to challenge the center.

Equally important has been the chapter devoted to ecocriticism and environmental ethics basing on Soyinka's *The Beatification of Area Boy*. Nature and environment are directly connected with human life and their treatment cannot elude dramatic literature; nor their approach be theory free. It becomes necessary to conclude that dramatic literature is rich and profound when it comes to the deployment of critical theory to analyse its contours. It is, perhaps, appropriate that some theory and poetics of African drama should be allowed to evolve naturally from the long history of aesthetic and mimetic experience of verbal art in the African world. Consequently, African literary theories should emerge from the various dynamics of cultural and aesthetic transformation influencing African drama within time and space. Gates Jr. (1986:20) has expressed the necessity to explore the possibility of devising a distinct critical theory for black and African indigenous arts: I once thought it our most important gesture to master the canon of criticism, to imitate and apply it. But now, I believe that we must turn to the African indigenous tradition itself to develop theories of criticism indigenous to our literatures. The need to distil a critical aesthetic poetics for African drama is an imperious necessity owing to the textual richness of the indigenous verbal arts, which were the enabling texts, and the written form. An indigenous theory could, however, be evolved for the African primordial features because, except in some modern versions, these primordial forms suffer from the eroding influence of Western theatrical tradition. The adoption of the written mode of artistic expression in Africa has led to the textual enslavement of the oral text-mode. Thus, the aesthetic principles of the Western writing culture have not only silenced, but have also disabled and marginalized the unique oral aesthetic values of African texts. Despite the above, the social, psychological and thematic contents of some African scripted plays bear a heavy burden of classical and Elizabethan traditions of the theatre.

INDEX

A Critique of the Postcolonial Reason   126
A Dance of the Forest   11, 33, 42, 43, 45, 49, 55, 65, 94, 161, 223, 426, 435
A Play of Giants   13, 19, 43, 45, 136, 192, 204, 223, 396,
Abolition   485, 486, 493, 495
Achebe, Chinua   29, 178, 332, 351, 480
Adichie (Chimamanda Ngozi)   254, 285, 286
Aesthetics   ix, x, xiv, xv, xvi, xvii, 1, 10, 11, 24, 26, 28, 31, 33, 45, 46, 60, 61, 62, 94, 126, 128, 154, 162, 163, 177, 189, 199, 200, 231, 233, 290, 291, 295, 309, 353, 357, 371, 397, 398, 399, 400, 401, 439, 461, 467, 468, 481, 484, 523, 525, 526, 527, 539
Africa (contemporary)   14, 19, 50, 56, 64, 96, 115, 161, 173, 221, 222, 223, 247, 279, 291, 315, 463, 481, 519
Africa (modern)   51, 55, 56, 63, 64, 65, 66, 67, 68, 69, 93, 96, 130, 136, 159, 173, 179, 180, 183, 185, 192, 196, 197, 200, 202, 204, 222, 280, 326, 327, 336, 502, 523, 528, 539
Africa (traditional)   x, xi, 11, 18, 20, 49, 51, 56, 57, 79, 83, 84, 97, 189, 228, 264, 275, 415
Africa (East)   103, 118, 148, 234, 236
Africa (West)   19, 28, 70, 71, 72, 73, 85, 108, 120, 164, 178, 189, 192, 194, 229, 253, 319, 333, 421, 423, 424, 434, 435, 438, 515
Africa (South)   xvi, 11, 19, 23, 28, 29, 39, 71, 73, 150, 151, 152, 153, 161, 201, 202, 216, 217, 226, 375, 399, 400, 401, 402, 403, 404, 406, 407, 409, 410, 411, 414, 415, 416, 417, 424, 430, 431, 448, 449, 483-499, 501,
African feminism   vii, xiii, 256, 257, 259, 283, 541
African-American   8
African drama   400, 414, 417, 423, 424, 426, 427, 502, 523, 524, 525, 526, 527, 528, 530
African Performance Conventions   20
African theatre   xi, xii, 3, 7, 10, 15, 16, 25, 42, 46, 47, 55, 56, 69, 84, 86, 87, 90, 94-96, 125, 136, 156, 157, 159, 160-162, 165, 166, 168, 169, 174, 175, 180, 183, 185-188, 199, 203, 205, 210, 211, 215, 217, 218, 220, 226, 229, 252, 278
Afropolitanism   xvii, xviii, 22-24, 28, 29, 285, 419, 461, 462, 463, 466, 468, 480, 481, 523
Ahluwalia, Pal   338, 352, 466, 484, 502
Aidoo (Ama Ata)   xiv, 7, 11, 26, 39, 42, 45, 49, 55, 71, 167, 192, 193, 204, 251, 253, 259, 277, 279, 352, 387, 526, 528
Ambivalence   xi, xviii, 25, 28, 127, 128, 129, 131, 154, 461, 464, 468, 469

Annan (Kofi)   411
Anowa   11, 19, 39, 42, 45, 49, 55, 192, 193, 204, 259, 278, 286, 387, 397
Anthropology   6, 7, 24, 77, 128, 156, 168, 169, 170, 179, 335
Anthropology (Cultural)   7, 77, 179
Apartheid   xviii, 19, 20, 28, 29, 45, 71, 151, 201, 202, 226, 399, 400-408, 414, 415, 417, 430, 448, 483-489, 491-496, 499-501
Argument   xi, 3, 4, 8, 10, 11, 24, 25, 26, 50, 55, 79, 84, 86, 89, 97, 103, 156, 158, 159, 160, 164, 169, 170, 174, 177, 185, 196, 211, 228, 253, 254, 255, 258, 289, 330, 343, 344, 426, 437, 498, 523
Art, Dialogue and Outrage   10, 136, 167, 180, 205, 228
Asante (Molefi Kete)   8
Ashcroft, Bill   11, 125, 126, 178, 308, 338, 462, 484, 487, 502, 524, 530
Asian   127, 133, 142, 529
Athol (Fugard)   xviii, 7, 16, 19, 29, 39, 44, 45, 151, 167, 171, 179, 198, 201, 483-486, 489, 491, 492, 494, 498, 501, 502, 528
Bhabha (Homi K.)   127, 128, 464
Biko (Steve)   16, 20
Birth of a Dream Weaver   147, 176
Black community   19, 29, 405, 406, 474, 483, 485, 486, 488, 489, 491, 501
Black consciousness   xv, xvi, xvii, 20, 309, 399, 400, 401, 402, 404, 405, 407, 417, 491, 523
Black identity   174, 194, 496
Bloomfield (David)   349, 403, 405
Bye-Bye, Babar   22, 285
Césaire, Aimé   143, 174, 426, 440, 454
Chinweizu   18
Clark (John Pepper)   19, 86, 161
Colonialism   8, 11-13, 15, 19, 21, 22, 25, 69, 126, 128, 132, 134, 142, 144, 145, 147, 155, 167, 174-176, 183, 186, 189, 193, 197, 199, 202, 203, 219, 223, 234, 235, 245, 279, 293, 302, 315-317, 331, 338, 365, 462, 464, 467, 484, 487, 497, 523
Colonization   x, xv, 6, 9, 10-12, 17, 18, 44, 46, 92-94, 126, 132, 142, 143, 157, 169, 216, 279, 302, 317, 331, 339, 414, 424, 427, 462, 464, 477, 487, 496
Commonwealth   150, 272, 529
Conciliatory   402, 492
Conflicts   xv, xvi, 27, 28, 33, 42, 120, 172, 173, 203, 239, 258, 267, 269, 300, 309, 311, 312, 320, 324, 327, 330, 331, 335-339, 344, 345, 348-351, 358, 367, 373, 399-403, 407, 410, 411, 414, 417, 439, 490, 496, 499, 506
Criticism (literary)   vii, ix, 3-6, 30, 126, 175, 179, 204, 210, 232, 307, 311, 316, 461, 505, 514
Cultural struggle   338, 409, 410, 415
Cultural materialism   126, 317, 333, 375
Culture and Imperialism   126, 317, 333, 375
DeGraft, J. C.   217
Deconstruction   5, 20, 36, 47, 155, 171, 199, 488
Derrida (Jacques)   20, 35, 36
Decolonization   x, 11, 12, 17, 18, 132, 142, 143
Discrimination   127, 151, 239, 247, 350, 405, 474, 485, 486, 487, 492, 493, 495
Displacement   9, 129, 143, 176, 279, 314, 395, 396, 461, 462, 464, 466
Domestication   x, 24, 38, 41, 47, 48, 64, 65, 129, 523
ecocriticism   xvii, xix, 419, 503, 505, 506, 520, 521, 523, 524, 530, 539

Education   10, 14, 15, 28, 29, 42, 55, 68, 69, 84, 93, 95, 117, 128, 164, 165, 170, 197, 215, 221, 222, 224, 235, 254, 255, 257, 258, 260, 263, 266, 269, 275-278, 282, 283, 286, 293, 307, 308, 315, 325, 338, 350, 352, 367, 368, 375, 387, 398, 405, 410, 411, 414, 424, 431, 433, 437, 440-442, 451, 456, 458, 459, 462, 464, 465, 467, 469, 470-472, 475, 478, 479, 481, 483, 485, 486, 488, 489, 491, 492, 494, 497, 499-501

Edufa   xiv, 11, 19, 49, 65, 273, 274, 276, 277, 287

Emancipation   57, 136, 145, 162, 256, 258, 267, 273, 282, 440, 451, 454, 485, 486, 488, 497

Empire   84, 121, 159, 167, 178, 180, 308, 331, 429, 454, 530

Employment   29, 42, 166, 192, 219, 357, 358, 360, 361, 362, 366, 368, 405, 456, 462, 465, 469, 483, 485, 486, 491, 494, 501

Enlightenment   10, 218, 273, 353, 354, 355, 463

Environmental ethics   xix, 29, 503, 504, 506, 514, 515, 520, 521, 530

Epic Performance   xi, 119

Etherton (Michael)   10, 155, 185, 187, 203, 210, 217, 228, 236, 320, 322, 400

Eurocentrism   18, 19, 132, 315

Eurocentric Discourses   126, 316

European colonialism   145, 147, 174, 189, 197, 199, 234, 497

Experience   5, 8, 9, 11, 22, 23, 25, 28, 31, 33, 50, 51, 53, 54, 57, 58, 61, 67-71, 80, 92, 96, 105, 117, 118, 125, 129, 138, 145, 147, 161, 164, 165, 169, 183, 185, 190, 193, 194, 196, 198, 199, 233, 234, 256, 278, 279, 285, 292, 301, 312, 324, 336, 346, 365, 379, 381, 383, 385, 387, 390, 393, 396, 399, 403, 418, 423, 439, 442, 448, 449, 455, 461, 462, 470, 472, 476-478, 481, 487, 492, 498, 519, 530

Fanon, Frantz   16, 30, 132, 143, 164, 219, 223, 317, 404, 433

Feminism   vii, xii-xiv, 5, 26, 153, 155, 181, 204, 253-257, 259, 261, 263, 264, 268, 278, 282, 283, 285, 516, 523, 524, 539, 541

Feminist-Marxist   153

Festival drama   94, 95, 194, 228, 529

Fiebach, Joachim   167, 169

Finnegan, Ruth   103, 157-159, 221

First World Women   149

Folktale   106, 107, 273, 316, 415

Forgiveness   136, 176, 337, 349, 351, 402, 410, 411, 414

Foriwa   xiv, 11, 19, 39, 42, 49, 65, 273-276, 287

Foucault (Michael)   76

Freedom   xiii, 14, 15, 20, 23, 25, 26, 45, 64, 130, 145, 146, 167, 168, 179, 199, 210, 211, 213-227, 229, 231, 233-238, 240-245, 247-249, 257, 260, 264, 267-269, 272, 277, 279, 281, 282, 285, 292, 295, 297, 307, 333, 338, 344, 346-348, 396, 405, 407, 408, 415, 431, 432, 454, 481, 490, 492, 494-497, 499, 521

Freud (Sigmund)   192, 312, 361

Fugard, Athol   xviii, 7, 16, 19, 29, 39, 44, 45, 151, 167, 171, 179, 198, 201, 483-486, 489, 491, 492, 494, 498, 501, 502, 528

Gender   vii, 5, 26, 41-44, 49, 63, 78, 96, 107, 125, 133, 141, 142, 147, 149, 153, 154, 175, 203, 204, 253, 255-257, 260, 262, 266-268, 271, 272, 279, 283, 335, 340, 350, 361, 368, 457, 491, 497, 516, 541

Gilbert (Helen)   226, 290-292, 357, 387, 388, 396, 400, 402, 404
Griffith, Gareth   11, 30, 125, 126, 178, 308, 333, 462, 480, 487, 502, 524
Hello and Goodbye   19, 45
Historical context   17, 207, 242, 313
Historicism (new)   5, 16, 75-79, 96, 97, 178, 400, 523, 539
History   xiii, 5, 8, 14-16, 18, 24, 25, 38, 40, 56, 58, 68, 69, 70, 75-77, 82, 85, 88, 90, 95-97, 106, 107, 114, 118-122, 125, 127, 129, 132, 134, 143, 147-149, 162, 172, 176, 178, 183, 186, 193, 195-198, 201-204, 208, 212, 216, 221-223, 227, 232, 234-236, 243, 250, 254, 290, 302, 303, 306, 308, 312, 331, 333, 335, 336, 338, 339, 340, 346, 351-355, 361, 379, 393, 398, 401, 403, 404, 417, 421, 422, 425, 426, 432, 449, 450, 459, 464, 502, 505, 525, 526, 528-530
Homecoming   xviii, 29, 96, 145, 252, 461, 469, 475, 476, 478, 481
Human rights   xviii, 20, 29, 141, 200, 201, 225, 296, 307, 345, 350, 375, 411, 412, 414, 417, 451, 452, 483-486, 489-492, 494, 497, 499, 501, 502, 505,
Hybridity   xi, 25, 127, 128, 130, 135, 464, 466, 468, 525, 526, 527
I Will Marry When I Want   11, 13, 14, 33, 43, 49, 65, 145, 192, 201, 204, 222, 228, 396
Imperialism   8, 10, 13, 15, 126, 132-134, 136, 142, 144, 145, 147, 151, 163, 180, 200, 203, 234, 242, 246, 247, 250, 256, 278, 291, 293, 297, 302, 317, 333, 375, 395, 396, 400, 404, 486-488
Indigenous Aesthetics   ix, x, 1, 11, 24, 31, 523, 539

Injustice   12, 42, 172, 225, 233, 238, 254, 255, 258, 260, 263, 265, 272, 283, 291, 296, 299, 324, 328, 330, 349, 357, 360-362, 372, 405, 408, 416, 434, 448, 485, 486, 488, 489, 491-495, 518
Inter-racial   406
Jemie   18
Jeyifo, Biodun   157, 159, 179, 180, 185, 204, 317, 437, 502, 528
Justice   112, 172, 199, 224, 225, 233, 238, 239, 243, 254, 255, 258, 260, 263, 265, 272, 283, 291, 292, 293, 296, 299, 302, 324, 328, 330, 349, 350, 354, 357, 375, 417, 449, 488, 491, 502, 505
Kerr, David   167, 170, 197, 210, 217
Kongi's Harvest   33, 49, 55, 136, 167, 191, 194, 223, 396, 426, 435
Lacan (Jacques)   6, 7, 313, 323
Ladipo, Duro   93, 160, 178, 217
Language   x, xiv, xvi, 5, 7-9, 14, 15, 19, 21, 24, 26, 27, 32-34, 36, 47-50, 52, 57, 60-63, 67-70, 72, 101, 108, 110, 115, 126, 129, 144, 145, 149, 150, 154, 157, 167, 179, 187, 189, 190, 196, 199, 203, 222, 227, 242, 247, 270, 278, 291-294, 296-300, 305, 307, 308, 311, 314-316, 321, 324-326, 333, 336, 338, 352, 369-371, 373, 375, 382, 388, 398, 417, 422, 423, 427, 430-433, 443, 447, 462, 466, 468-473, 478, 480, 490, 502, 505, 519, 523, 525-528
Latin America   7, 142
Legend   24, 38, 45, 46, 51, 55, 57, 58, 65, 84, 85, 99, 100, 102, 105, 107, 108, 109, 119, 187, 189, 236, 245, 247, 251, 306, 308, 319, 445, 489
Levi-Strauss (Claude)   6, 7, 31, 34, 313
Liberation   xiii, 8, 10, 19, 62, 145, 167,

168, 210, 215-217, 222-224, 226, 229, 235-237, 244-246, 250, 254, 255, 260, 262, 265, 273, 280, 282, 283, 317, 318, 332, 401, 404, 405, 411, 448, 454, 496, 497, 498

Linguistic (s)   6, 7, 24, 34, 125, 333

Lyotard (Jean François)   20, 354

Madmen and Specialists   136, 202, 396

Madubuike   18

Maponya (Maishe)   xvi, 19, 28, 399, 400, 401, 403-406, 412, 414, 415

Marginality   xviii, 8, 9, 78, 428, 484-488

Marxism   x, xii, xiii, xvi, 6, 12, 13, 14, 16, 17, 75, 181, 201, 231, 232, 353, 354, 359, 523, 524, 539

Marx (Karl)   231

Mediation   xvii, 27, 28, 42, 77, 323, 335-337, 339, 350, 377, 385, 386, 390, 399, 401, 407, 408, 409, 412, 413, 414, 417, 496

Memmi Albert   132

Mime   14, 46, 50, 64, 69, 71, 85, 119, 370, 387, 388, 529

Mimicry   xi, 25, 47, 58, 127, 130, 131, 135, 154, 397

Minority groups   159, 411, 486

Modernity   xii, 25, 38, 44, 128, 133, 134, 135, 141, 144, 353-355, 361, 463

Moving the Center   145, 179, 333, 521

My Children! My Africa!   xviii, 19, 29, 44, 198, 483, 484, 486, 494, 495, 498, 501, 502

Myth   10, 24, 34, 35, 38, 45-47, 51, 55-58, 60, 65, 69, 70, 80, 82, 84, 85, 89, 95, 96, 99, 100, 102, 107, 108, 112, 115, 119, 120, 123, 128, 130, 158-161, 167, 187, 189, 190, 195, 196, 199, 211, 213-215, 218, 221, 223, 224, 248, 252, 261, 265, 291, 292, 299, 304-306, 316, 318, 319, 354, 356, 396, 404, 421, 439, 466

Narratives (Oral)   xi, 1, 24, 99, 100, 102, 104, 109, 167, 523, 539

Narratology   ix, xi, 1, 24, 99, 100, 104, 123, 379, 386, 397, 398, 523, 539

Narratologists   99, 101

Nativism   ix, x, 1, 11, 12, 19, 24, 31, 38, 150, 326, 523, 539

Naturalism   xii, 25, 183-186, 188, 196, 197-203, 523, 539

Ngugi (wa Thiong'o)   xiii, xvi, 7, 11, 13-16, 26, 27, 30, 49, 96, 144, 146, 148, 155, 166-168, 171, 176, 179, 180, 192, 198, 201, 204, 217, 222, 228, 231, 233-235, 243, 250, 252, 317, 325, 333, 377, 379, 381, 396, 398, 471, 475, 481

No Good Friday   xviii, 16, 19, 29, 39, 483, 484, 486, 488-492, 495, 500-502

No More the Wasted Breed   xiv, 26, 55, 94, 196, 289, 290, 292, 294, 296, 297, 305, 308

Nwahunanya, Chinyere   3, 175

Nwapa (Flora)   xiv, 26, 253, 259, 268, 269, 287, 526

Ogbeche (Frank Ogodo)   16, 19, 42, 180, 199, 280

Ogunde, Hubert   93, 160, 161, 178, 217

Ogunmola, E. K.   160, 217

Once Upon Four Robbers   xvi, 13, 19, 27, 42, 65, 224, 228, 353, 357, 358, 359, 361, 365, 371, 373, 375

Oppression   16, 42, 45, 132, 143, 148, 174, 175, 201, 208, 221, 223, 226, 233, 235-237, 239-244, 246, 250, 254-256, 260, 272, 279, 281, 283, 290-292, 294, 297, 307, 317, 358, 361, 362, 363, 372, 400, 405, 406, 407, 431, 451, 485, 488, 489, 492, 501

Oral Narratives   xi, 1, 24, 99, 100, 102, 104, 109, 167, 523, 539

Orientalism   126, 127, 132, 133, 150, 155, 180, 502

Osofisan (Femi)   xiv-xvi, 10, 13, 21, 26, 27, 42, 43, 55, 64, 65, 70, 72, 94, 95, 113, 171, 173, 178, 196, 202, 224, 225, 229, 251, 252, 289-299, 301, 303-308, 335-340, 343-349,

Our Husband Has Gone Mad Again   33, 40, 41, 44, 45, 65, 133, 173, 287

Pan-Africanism   7, 193, 204

Performance (dramatic)   24, 46, 58, 59, 61-63, 72, 84, 87, 156, 158, 393, 398, 406

Performance (oral)   58, 59, 61, 73, 84, 94, 96, 113-117, 159, 529

Performance (poetry)   38, 46, 60, 401

Phenomenology   9

Polygamy   44, 258, 259

Post-apartheid   xviii, 19, 28, 29, 399, 400, 401, 407, 408, 415, 417, 483, 484, 486, 488, 489, 493-495, 499-501

Postcolonialism   xii, 22, 25, 30, 126, 127, 132, 134, 137, 141, 151, 175, 185, 464, 484, 523, 539

Postmodernism   x, xv, xvi, 20-22, 30, 309, 353-360, 368, 375, 463, 523, 524

Poststructuralism   ix, x, 6, 35, 36, 37, 72, 75, 76, 378, 523, 539

Proverbs   24, 33, 38, 48-55, 57, 65-66, 69, 73, 100, 102, 115, 118, 187, 189-191, 300, 306, 369, 370, 371, 443-445, 523

Racial Typology   130

Racism   7, 151, 153, 167, 174, 226, 400, 474, 484, 491, 493, 525, 526

Realism   xi, xii, 19, 25, 60, 68, 106, 183-185, 194-202, 204, 243, 409, 427, 430, 447, 456, 496

Reconciliation   28, 349, 352, 399, 400, 402, 403, 406-411, 414, 416, 417, 449, 484, 496

Renaissance (African)   130, 171, 176, 179

Representations of the Intellectual   126, 180

Resistance (postcolonial)   xiv, 289, 300, 304

Ricard, Alain   28, 221, 421, 438, 441

Rights   xviii, 13, 28, 29, 141, 147, 176, 200, 201, 214, 225, 254, 257. 260, 261, 265, 270, 279, 285, 286, 289, 296, 305, 307, 329, 336, 337, 345, 350, 366, 367, 375, 400, 403, 405, 411, 412, 414, 416, 417, 440, 451, 452, 456, 483, 484, 485, 486, 489-492, 494, 496, 497, 498, 499, 501, 502, 505, 517

Ritual (s)   11, 25, 33, 38, 39, 45, 55, 56, 69, 75, 79, 80, 81, 83-87, 89-94, 99, 157-159, 161, 167, 170, 187, 189, 190, 196, 292, 319, 421, 437, 528-530

Ritual drama   25, 79, 94, 95, 194, 529

Rubin, Don   167, 168, 179, 459

Romance   185, 455

Rotimi (Ola)   xv, 7, 10, 11, 21, 26, 27, 33, 40-44, 49, 51, 55, 65, 73, 113, 129, 133, 171, 172, 191, 194, 196, 201, 205, 224, 257, 311, 315-322, 324, 325, 327-329, 331-333, 524

Saussure (Ferdinand de)   x, 6, 32, 313, 316

Self-affirmation   13, 127, 401, 407

Selasi, Taiye   22, 285

Slave-trade (Atlantic)   7, 192, 193, 216

Social cohesion   27, 28, 262, 335, 399, 402, 406, 410, 416, 484, 491, 497

Sociology   6, 24, 28, 103, 169, 170, 335, 421, 441, 481

Something Torn and New   130, 171, 179

Songhay   121, 122

Sophiatown   489, 491, 493

South Africa   xvi, 11, 19, 23, 28, 29, 39, 71, 73, 150-153, 161, 201, 202, 216, 217, 226, 375, 399, 400, 401, 402, 403, 404, 406, 407, 409, 410, 411, 414, 415, 416, 417, 424, 430, 431, 448, 449, 483-497, 499, 501

Soyinka (Wole)   vii, xiii, xix, 7, 10, 11, 16, 20, 26, 27, 29, 33, 38, 42, 45, 55, 65, 70, 79, 83, 85, 91, 94, 115, 133, 136, 157, 160, 161, 163, 167, 171, 175, 178, 191, 192, 195, 196, 198, 201, 202, 217, 221, 223, 224, 227, 228, 231, 233, 234, 240, 250, 251, 258, 290, 342, 357, 358, 359, 363, 371, 373, 374, 394, 396, 424, 425, 503-506, 519, 528, 541

Space (cultural)   529

Space (postcolonial)   xviii, 25, 128, 172, 461, 462, 464

Space (Third)   xi, 25, 127, 130, 131

Spivak (Gayatri)   132

Stereotypes   29, 44, 130, 154, 221, 404, 483, 485, 486, 497, 498, 501

Story   xi, 27, 38, 39, 40, 46, 47, 49, 58, 60, 63, 69, 76, 82, 85, 89, 90, 95, 101, 102, 104-113, 119-121, 134, 148, 171, 191-193, 201, 238, 240, 244, 273, 278, 317, 318, 323, 328, 346, 356, 371, 377, 378, 380, 382-387, 389-392, 422, 441, 442, 444, 447, 448, 451

Storyteller   57, 67, 101, 104-108, 109, 113, 116, 117, 159, 162, 167, 441, 442, 443, 445

Sutherland (Efua T.)   xiv, 7, 11, 26, 39, 42, 49, 55, 65, 94, 217, 253, 255, 259, 273, 274, 279, 526

Symbolism   xii, xiv, xvii, 25, 181, 183, 184-192, 194-196, 203, 242, 243, 247, 248, 252, 273, 304, 306, 316, 369, 373, 407, 447, 448, 450, 452, 523, 529, 539

Taylor (Jane)   xvi, xvii, 11, 19, 28, 42, 151, 151, 399, 400-403, 407, 408, 410-412, 414, 415

Textual analysis   17, 75, 76, 203, 207, 208, 210, 388

The Afropolitan Magazine   23

The Black Hermit   13, 16, 44, 49, 53, 65, 145, 396

The Empire Writes Back   126, 530

The Hungry Earth   xvi, 19, 28, 226, 399, 400, 401, 403, 405, 412, 414, 417

The Lion and the Jewel   33, 38, 43, 44, 49, 129, 133, 136, 223, 229, 258, 425, 435, 518,

The Midnight Hotel   13

The Marriage of Anansewa   11, 42, 43, 49, 55, 65, 94, 161, 273, 287

The Nostalgic Drum   171, 180, 196

The Novelist as a Teacher   18

The Oriki of the Grasshopper   13, 21, 65, 113

Theory (critical)   ix, 3-7, 16, 24, 30, 72, 73, 95-97, 125, 126, 143, 145, 156, 157, 159, 169, 171, 175, 178, 179, 185, 187, 197, 199, 204, 255, 307, 308, 332, 333, 521, 525, 528, 530

Theory (literary)   4, 5, 15, 36, 73, 96, 136, 156, 163, 196, 233, 251, 255, 313, 338, 375, 418, 462, 480, 505, 520

Third Space   xi, 25, 127, 130, 131

Third World Women   255

This Time Tomorrow   145

Tiffin (Helen)   11, 30, 125, 126, 178, 308, 333, 462, 480, 487, 502, 524

Time   xi, xvi, 5, 27-29, 33, 35-39, 40, 43, 44, 47, 48, 50, 54, 56, 59, 60-62, 65, 68, 73, 79, 80, 82, 83, 85-91, 93, 101-106, 108, 110-112, 114, 116-122, 126, 128, 131-134, 139, 140, 144-146, 150-154, 156, 159, 162, 164, 165, 173, 184, 188, 191, 193, 197, 201, 207-210, 212, 213, 217, 219, 221, 223, 224, 233, 236, 238, 241, 245-248, 254, 255, 257, 258, 261, 264, 266, 268, 271, 274, 276, 278, 281, 282, 284, 295, 302, 305, 313, 316, 328, 329, 332, 335, 339, 340, 342, 345, 348, 349, 353, 356, 368, 370, 371, 377-385, 387-391, 393-397, 401, 402, 404, 405, 410, 416, 417, 425, 427, 428, 432, 443-

446, 451, 455, 457, 465-467, 469-471, 473, 474, 479, 480, 489-493, 496-498, 503, 504, 506-508, 513, 515, 517, 518, 525, 526, 528, 530

Township   20, 39, 71, 415, 490, 492, 502

The Burden of Memory,
   The Muse of Forgiveness   136, 176

Truth and reconciliation commission   28, 399, 402, 484, 496

Ubu and the Truth Commission   xvi, 11, 19, 28, 42, 399, 400, 401, 402, 407, 408, 409, 410, 411, 412, 413, 414, 417, 418

Universalism   xii, 21, 25, 134, 135, 155, 211, 463, 480

Voice   xvi, 8, 9, 12, 26, 27, 28, 32, 46, 48, 50, 51, 52, 61, 62, 65, 106, 114, 136, 166, 168, 179, 196, 217, 224, 243, 245, 253, 255, 259, 260, 262, 267, 269, 270, 271, 273, 277, 290, 301, 302, 313, 337, 354, 377, 378, 379, 380, 382, 383, 384, 385, 386, 388, 389, 391, 392, 398, 418, 424, 454, 463

White community   403, 406, 469, 472, 485, 487

William Ponty   xvii, 28, 166, 421, 422, 433, 434

Wolof   121, 122

Womanism   287

Women of Owu   xv, 27, 335, 337, 338, 339, 340, 343, 344, 346, 348, 349, 351, 352